Modern Australian Usage

Modern Australian Usage

NICHOLAS HUDSON

Melbourne

OXFORD UNIVERSITY PRESS

Oxford   Auckland   New York

OXFORD UNIVERSITY PRESS AUSTRALIA

Oxford   New York   Toronto
Delhi   Bombay   Calcutta   Madras   Karachi
Kuala Lumpur   Singapore   Hong Kong   Tokyo
Nairobi   Dar es Salaam   Cape Town
Melbourne   Auckland   Madrid

and associated companies in
Berlin   Ibadan

OXFORD is a trade mark of Oxford University Press

National Library of Australia
Cataloguing-in-Publication data:

Hudson, Nicholas, 1933 –   .
   Modern Australian usage.

   ISBN 0 19 554860 4.

   1. English language — Australia — Usage. I. Title.

428.00994

Cover illustration by Rob Hall
Typeset by N. S. Hudson Publishing Services Pty Ltd, Melbourne
Printed by Impact Printing Victoria Pty Ltd
Published by Oxford University Press,
253 Normanby Road, South Melbourne, Australia

PREFACE

This is a book about Australian English. That sounds like a simple enough statement, but Australian English is, for some curious historical reasons, not a clearly defined entity. Many people think of it as a collection of colourful slang expressions, the names of native flora and fauna and a few Aboriginal words. The implication is that when we use other words or expressions we are not talking Australian. As this is not the definition used in the book, I had better start by saying what I mean by Australian English.

Australian English is *the language Australians talk and write*, just as American English is the language Americans talk and write. It is thus one of many regional variations of English, all of which have a common core. The common core enables us to talk to one another and exchange books without any great difficulty. Australian English consists of a great many shared elements plus those usages which are peculiar to Australia.

Next, the book is about formal communication, which I define as communication in which the form is important as well as the content. Most writing is formal in this sense, because most of us, even when writing a note on the door saying 'Back in ten minutes', want to get it right. We feel that we leave ourselves exposed if our spelling or grammar is wrong; and with good reason: many of us would make assumptions (often very unfair) about an unknown person who wrote 'Bake in 10 minnits'. And we don't want this to happen to us.

The book is the outcome of a long career as an editor and publisher, dealing with the problems of Australian writing and writers. The issues it discusses are not invented: they are the issues which most often arise. The questions are the questions most often asked. The mistakes are the mistakes most often made. There are in addition a few entries which reflect personal enthusiasms or prejudices, but the general aim has been to cover the real issues. Since many writers are as deeply concerned with copyright and defamation as with gerunds and subjunctives, the book includes articles on these practical topics.

Many of the grammar and usage questions would be equally relevant to British or American speakers and writers, and the answers would often be the same, too, as one would expect from the definition of Australian English given above. However, the book lays special emphasis on the issues which are peculiar to Australian English, not so much because Australians need to be taught their own language, but because we need to be aware of the differences when speaking or writing for overseas consumption. Similarly, the legal and practical questions are the same the world over, but the advice given is based on Australian law and practice.

Some of the questions are related to straightforward common errors, which can be dealt with by giving a simple and dogmatic answer.

Most of the troublesome problems, however, are less cut-and-dried. They are related to issues on which writers and authorities differ, so that there may be no single correct answer.

Those who want decisive answers to such questions should get themselves a style manual, and several good ones are available. I like the ones produced by our newspapers, because they are designed solely to ensure a coherent style within the newspaper, and do this by giving clear and concise decisions on the knotty problems. But they do it by cutting the knots. We can defer to their decisions, and will then avoid being wrong, but we must remember that there is a difference between not being wrong and being right. We cannot use the decrees of a style manual as evidence that a different view is wrong.

This book is for people who want to make up their own minds. It reports variance, and attempts to give the readers the information they need in order to discuss the issue and find the solution which best suits their own situation.

One critical problem for many younger writers is that they came through the schools in an era when the teaching of formal grammar was frowned upon. Pedagogically, this made sense – teaching grammar is an ineffective way of teaching good writing; but the technical terms of formal grammar disappeared in the process, and this removed a set of useful tools for discussing the reason why one construction may sound better than another. So this book says a fair amount about the vocabulary of formal grammar, and uses it in the discussions.

Finally, it is a book written by an amateur, in both senses of that abused word. Firstly, it is by an unashamed lover of words in general, and of the Australian idiom in particular. Secondly, it is by one who is not a professional scholar. On the good side, this means that the book can speculate intuitively on issues on which, in the absence of proper research, a respectable scholar would remain silent; I have no academic reputation to lose. But intuition can be wrong. The late Professor Manning Clark once said to me, 'Who needs facts, if he has intuition?'. Manning had the good fortune to have a great deal of both. I hope that I have enough of them to make my love affair with words respectable.

ACKNOWLEDGEMENTS

This book is the outcome of a meeting with Louise Sweetland, then the Publisher of Oxford University Press. We were talking about Australian usage, and she suggested that my thoughts could be the basis of a book. If the result is appreciated by its readers, she deserves their thanks. She certainly has mine.

Next, I would like to thank Peter Rose, her successor at OUP, who caught her enthusiasm for the project and kept it warm through the rest of a five-year writing period. He organised several critical readings of the first complete draft: because of this, I can thank Dr Bill Ramson (and his monumental *Australian National Dictionary*) for suggestions about my handling of some Australianisms, and Edmund Weiner, editor of the *Oxford English Dictionary*, for a very close and careful reading of the whole text. Edmund Weiner identified a largish number of errors in the first draft, but also drew little smiling faces in the margin from time to time, indicating that he thought some point particularly apposite. This showed a very sensitive awareness of the need to maintain an author's morale; which it did.

Other readers who made valuable comments include (in alphabetical order) Richard Coleman, Max Margison and Jenny Walker. Finally, Shirley Purchase, Kerry Herbstreit and Fiona McDonald undertook the mammoth task of copy-editing. It is easier to preach than to practice, and some vagaries are deliberate: see LICENCE/LICENSE.

The major inspiration of the book was Fowler's *Modern English Usage*, as will be obvious (but I hope not objectionably so) to lovers of Fowler. However, a secondary inspiration was Dupré's *Encyclopédie du Bon Français*, an admirable work representing a totally different approach to lexicography from either the British or the American tradition. I particularly like Dupré's use of the one-word sentence *Soit!* From him I learnt the secret of ebullient confidence.

In some respects, the book has taken thirty-five years to write; but the first thirty were spent in gathering the experience which underpins it. For this I must thank the many authors whose work I edited, and hundreds of others whose work I read and rejected. It was all experience.

It is not easy to write a book like this as a self-employed publisher. I had to rely on my wife and business partner, Sandra, and our sole employee, Carol Hosking, to keep us afloat. To them, therefore, I owe a debt in several literal, as well as innumerable figurative, ways.

NICHOLAS HUDSON
Melbourne, September 1992

CONVENTIONS AND ABBREVIATIONS

As far as possible, this book is written in plain language. One practical point I have learnt in my years as a publisher (not mentioned elsewhere in this book) is that nobody reads the introductions and explanatory notes – except, perhaps, reviewers, who may read them as an alternative to reading the book.

The only conventions which are not self-evident are the use of SMALL CAPITALS to indicate cross-references and the use of the /solidus/ to enclose pronunciation guides. The guides themselves are pragmatic rather than systematic: my experience is that this approach is more likely to be helpful than any other. Relatively few of us are so fluent in IPA (*International Phonetic Alphabet*), for example, that we can instantly interpret guides written in IPA, particularly if the word represented is one which is new to us and not in English. Furthermore, the more people need help, the less likely they are to know IPA. But I apologise to those who know and love IPA, who will find my approach crude.

From time to time I refer to other books. Sometimes this is an act of deference: if I have no view on an issue which nevertheless seems important, I simply report the one which makes the best sense. More often, however, I quote them to show that they are in dispute, or that they make dubious assertions and judgements. But I do not list the hundreds of other occasions on which they provide clear, consistent answers to our questions. Thus the citations give an unbalanced view both of the books in question and of my view of them, which is one of profound respect.

The works cited are:

ACOD	*The Australian Concise Oxford Dictionary*
AND	*The Australian National Dictionary*
AWEG	*The Australian Writers' and Editors' Guide*
CAPED	*The Collins Australian Pocket English Dictionary*
Mac	*The Macquarie English Dictionary*
OED	*The Oxford English Dictionary*
RW	*Right Words*, by Stephen Murray-Smith
SOED	*The Shorter Oxford English Dictionary*

In all cases, references are to the editions of these works which were current in the early 1990s, partly because these are the editions most likely to be on readers' shelves, but also because they were the ones which were on my own shelves. Where other editions are known to be significantly different, the edition is indicated by an inferior figure after the citation: $ACOD_2$.

References to Fowler are to the book, *Modern English Usage,* rather than the man. I do not distinguish original Fowlerisms from the contributions of Sir Ernest Gowers except where the distinction is significant to an argument.

A

a, an When the authors of *The Book of Common Prayer* wrote that marriage was 'an holy estate', they were not breaking the rules about *a* and *an*, nor were their rules essentially different from those of today. The difference was that they were expecting the words to be read 'an 'oly estate'.

The rule is simple: *a* before consonant sounds, *an* before vowel sounds. This is the same as saying 'before consonants' and 'before vowels' except for a few cross-overs:

(a) There are some combinations in which vowels are consonantal: *a European, a one-track mind, a U-turn, a union.*

(b) Similarly, the names of some consonants sound vowelish, i.e. *an F sharp, an H-bomb, an L-plate, an MP, an NCO, an R-rated movie, an S-bend, an X-ray.*

(c) *Y* is normally a consonant (*a yacht*) but is a vowel in *an ytterbium atom, an Yves St Laurent T-shirt.*

(d) Words starting with *h* constitute a special problem, but it concerns whether or not to sound the *h*. For a discussion of this, covering the cases of *heir, honour, hotel, hour, humour* and the strange case of *herbs*, see SOCIAL ASPIRATIONS. For *aitch/haitch*, see H, and for *historian*, see HISTORIAN.

Some abbreviations cause anxiety: is it *a MS* or *an MS*? The problem exists only because of the ambiguity of the written form; if spoken, it would be unequivocally *a manuscript* or *an em-ess*.

Sentences should be written as they are intended to be read. Just as we write *a $10m loan* but *an $80m loan*, so we write *an MA student* but *a Mrs Beeton cookbook*. If there is any doubt, the word should be written out in full: *a millimetre ruler* rather than *a(n) mm ruler*.

For notes on the grammatical status of *a, an*, see ARTICLE.

a-, an- See NEGATIVE PREFIXES.

abbreviation Two questions: (1) Should we put full stops after abbreviations? (2) What else should we watch out for?

(1) The current fashion is to omit full points from abbreviations.

Provided the abbreviation is unambiguous and the result aesthetically pleasing, there is nothing wrong with omitting the points. However, this is not a general *instruction* to omit all such full points. The first criterion must be that of clarity.

(a) Points must not be used after the abbreviations for SI units (mm, kg, etc.). The forms of these are prescribed by international agreement – see SI UNITS.

(b) Points should be omitted from acronyms which have an existence independent of their origins (*radar, laser*), and may be

1

omitted from letter sequences which cannot possibly be mistaken for other words (UNESCO, PhD, NSW). See ACRONYMS.

(c) Points should be retained in abbreviations which are identical to complete words: thus we write *in.* rather than *in* for inch. The sad case of 'aids' should be seen as a caution rather than a model. For A.D. and B.C., see DATES, WRITING OF.

(d) Courtesy demands *A. A. Milne*, and clarity demands *i.e.* and *e.g.* (Using *ie* and *eg*, though unlikely to generate an ambiguity, can stop readers momentarily in their tracks, which is precisely what our writing conventions are designed to avoid. The halfway houses *ie.* and *eg.* are inelegant.)

Between these extremes, there are thousands of cases which can fall either way. Indeed, some publishers allow *A A Milne* (or even *AAMilne*) and *ie*. However, this does not make them any the more graceful. I like a point on *etc.*, but there are not many of me.

In sum, the omission of full points is a general fashion; but it is sensible to leave points in if any ambiguity, discourtesy or oddity would otherwise arise, particularly in instructional writing.

Finally, we should note that there is a convention which distinguishes between *abbreviations* (words which have lost their tails) and *contractions* (words which have lost their middles), and requires a point after the former but not the latter. However, this produces some anomalies: we get *Dr* but *Prof.*, *paras* but *para.*, and so on. The convention continues to appear in some style manuals but is not recommended.

(2) Some general points about the use of abbreviations:

(a) If there is any doubt about the meaning of an abbreviation (even with its full stops) it should be spelt out in full when first used. The International Reading Association knows all about this problem. However, there are some entities which are best known by their initials (e.g. KGB and QANTAS) where the full versions are of importance only in quizzes.

(b) The use of an ad hoc abbreviation to make a trivial remark sound important is a modern disease discussed under OBSCURANTISM (8).

(c) Texts should be written as they are supposed to be read, so that we have *an MS* or *a manuscript*, but not *a MS*. The only exception is with units attached to numerals: for example, 'Cut off 25 cm of string' is naturally read as '…twenty-five centimetres…', and it would be silly to write it out in full. But this is not so of the unit on its own. 'Cut off a few cm of string' is not recommended.

-able, -ible, -uble (e.g. *amiable, possible, soluble*)   There are few subjects on which so much conflicting advice has been given as on the *-able/-ible* question.

The words with these endings can be divided into two groups, which we can call *English* and *Latinate*.

English: In English, we can take any verb, e.g. 'to boot' (of computers), and coin an adjective, *bootable*. Everyone who understands 'boot' will understand 'bootable', and there will be no dispute about its meaning. We will here define as *English* all the words which are built on recognisable modern English words.

Latinate: Latin used *-able* and *-ible* (and, very occasionally, *-uble*) according to the form of the verb to which the suffix *-bilis* was attached. We adopted a large number of these: *probable, possible, voluble*. They are called Latinate rather than Latin because in a few cases words have been built according to Latin rules though the words never occurred in ancient Latin.

For practical purposes, all those which are not built on a recognisable English word can be assumed to be Latinate.

(1) Choice: -able or -ible? If in doubt between *-ible* and *-able*, the *-able* form is to be preferred. It is the English form.

There are no merits in the *-ible* spellings except those of etymological purity and established usage. Etymological purity is based on distinctions whose significance was lost with the passing of Latin, but established usage demands respect.

(a) *English formations*: the preferred spelling is almost always *-able*. One of the few exceptions is *gullible*, for which *gullable* was an early and desirable but, for some reason, short-lived alternative.

(b) *Latinate formations:* here, the accepted form is likely to be *-ible*, since in Latin *-ibles* outnumbered *-ables* by twenty to one. Furthermore, these include some very common words, where the traditional spelling is likely to resist change: e.g. *audible, credible, edible, eligible, fallible, feasible, indelible, irascible, legible, plausible, possible, susceptible, tangible, visible*. (Note that in all these cases the root is not a recognisable English word.)

(c) There are words which could be either (e.g. *compress*). Here, *compressible* is the currently accepted spelling, coming to us from Latin; but *compress* is an English word in its own right, so that the form *compressable* will pass today, and probably be the accepted form within a few years.

(d) The form *-uble* is not common (*soluble, voluble*) and its sound is so distinct that spelling is rarely a problem; for the same reason, the chances of its drifting into oblivion are small.

(2) Blending The main spelling problem (once the *-ible/-able* choice has been made) is to make an appropriate junction between an *-able* suffix and whatever goes before it.

(a) If the root word ends in *e*, the *e* can be removed, e.g. *inflate, inflatable*. However, if the last consonant is a soft *c* or *g*, the *e* is needed to retain the soft sound, e.g. *change, changeable* (compare *singable* with *singeable*). The same goes for *-ee*: *agree, agreeable*.

The Americans tend to leave the *e* out in all other cases, but this leads to some strange-looking words: *ratable, salable*. If there is any doubt, it is never wrong to leave the *e* in: *rateable, saleable.* (For discussion of a converse confusion, see ASTABLE.)

(b) A lone final vowel *y* becomes *i*: *justifiable*; but after another vowel the *y* stays put: *payable.* The *y* should also be preserved on short words where the meaning might otherwise be confused or lost: *fryable* (of fish) to distinguish it from *friable*; and *flyable* (of aircraft) where *fliable* would look strange.

(c) Final consonants may need to be doubled to preserve short vowels, e.g. *stoppable.* Note, however, that the converse is not true. Many words, especially Latinate ones, have a short vowel despite the spelling, e.g. most of the items listed in (1(b)); and we have even shortened some of them: for example, we no longer pronounce *improbable* as *improbe-able.*

(3) Negatives   The negatives of the English forms tend to be *un-* and of Latinate ones *in-*: thus we write *unsolvable* but *insoluble.* Exceptions include *un-* for words whose positive form begins with *in-* (*unintelligible*), and *in-* for some English coinage, perhaps to add lustre to some dud coins: *insurmountable.* For the modification of *in-* to *im-* (e.g. *imperishable*) see PREFIXES.

(4) Meanings   The basic meaning is 'able to be somethinged', where 'something' is a verb, but there are exceptions. Many Latin originals have meanings whose connection with *ability* is obscure (e.g. *affable, plausible, vegetable*). Tracing the semantic history of such words is a good game, but of limited practical value.

There are some cases where a Latinate form exists alongside an English one, often with a different cluster of meanings. For an example of this, see SOLUBLE....

(5) Coinage   When coining new words, the *-able* form should always be used, and the negative should be *un-*. (See NEGATIVE PREFIXES and IN-.)

The suffix should be added to a verb. As most English nouns can double as verbs, this does not inhibit us greatly: thus although *action* is the noun from *act*, we can have both *actable* and *actionable*, meaning *able to be acted* and *able to be actioned (e.g. at law)* respectively. The word *clubbable* broke this rule, which may in part explain its awkwardness. However, for a successful coinage which appears to break this rule, see DUTIABLE....

Aboriginal words   Two questions arise: (1) What do they *really* mean? (2) How are they *really* spelt?

(1) Meanings   The old story goes that *kangaroo* is not the name of an animal, but was the answer to a question and *really* meant 'What is this idiot talking about?' or some such. Whether this story is true or not, it is highly plausible. Almost every Aboriginal place name, for example, comes to us complete with an alleged meaning, but given the circumstances in which they were first assigned it would be astonishing if there were *not* many gross misunderstandings.

Should we worry? There are two good reasons for saying 'No'. The first is that, if we have blundered, the joke is on us: we are not insulting anybody by getting it wrong, we are merely showing our ignorance. The second is that, whatever *kangaroo* meant to the people from whose language it was taken, it is now in our language as the name of certain animals, and that's that. But we should be very careful not to blunder with any new adoptions.

(2) Spellings   The answer to the spelling question is similar. Individual words were transliterated piecemeal long before standard spellings for the various languages were adopted, so that early writings inevitably contained different spellings of the same words: *Aranda* and *Arunta*, for example. Neither of these was 'wrong' in the sense of being non-standard, as no standard existed.

Since then, however, decisions have been taken on many of these. A useful reference is Dickson, Ramson and Thomas, *Australian Aboriginal Words in English: their origin and meaning* (OUP, 1990).

Aborigines, Aboriginals   The word *aborigines* is very old, having been coined by the Romans to describe people whose ancestors inhabited a country *ab origine*, that is, from the beginning. It was applied both generally to the earliest known inhabitants of any country, and specifically to the original inhabitants of their own country, Italy.

In Latin, it had no singular or adjectival form. The Latinate adjectival form *aboriginal* came later, and was applied in English, as in Latin, to original inhabitants in general; but the singular back-formation *aborigine*, coined c. 1850, was applied particularly to the original inhabitants of Australia.

The words present two problems: (1) Are they written with capital letters? (2) What is the preferred singular noun form?

(1) When applied to the original inhabitants of Australia, they should always be capitalised, since they are the official designations of these people, as in *British*, *American*, etc.: *The Aboriginals have occupied Australia for some 40,000 years.*

When applied to original inhabitants in general, they should not have capital letters: *Every country has, by definition, an aboriginal population, though in Europe they have lost their identity over the centuries of conquest, migration and intermarriage.*

(2) There is no clear consensus on the form of the noun. The preference of the Australian Institute of Aboriginal and Torres Strait Islander Studies is to use *Aborigine(s)*. However, I prefer *Aboriginal(s)*, and this is the preference of many, and perhaps most, Aboriginal communities. The lack of consensus reflects the fact that neither term is likely to cause any offence.

For alternative names for the original inhabitants of Australia, see KOORI; for a discussion of some words which can cause offence, see TABOO WORDS.

absolute This word is used in the labels for four phenomena in our language: (1) the *absolute usage* of a word; (2) the *absolute possessive*; (3) the *absolute adjectives*; and (4) the *absolute construction*. In all cases, *absolute* means *removed* or *on its own*.

(1) The absolute usage of a word Consider the sentence *The execution took place at dawn*. This was originally a short way of saying *the execution of the sentence took place at dawn*, and 'the sentence' could in theory have been three hours of community work; but *execution* has come to be applied *absolutely* to the execution of a sentence of death. By a further transference, we now execute the prisoner rather than the sentence, and make a distinction between an *executor*, an *executive* and an *executioner*.

Thus absolute usage is *the use of a common language word in a specific sense*, where that sense theoretically demands the presence of additional words of explanation. Absolute usage is very common in private language and technical jargon. Private language (family jokes, school slang) need not concern us, but the absolute use of common language words in technical jargon can cause real troubles. *The pill* is readily understood to mean *the contraceptive pill*, and is unlikely to be ambiguous, but *the bar* can be misunderstood. One solution is to use capitals to indicate an absolute use (*the Bar*), but for this see CAPITAL LOSSES.

For an example of another class of absolute usages, see EMPOWER.

(2) Absolute possessives In the sentence *These books are hers*, the word *hers* is called an *absolute possessive*, whereas *her*, as in *These are her books*, is an adjective. Note that *hers* does not have an apostrophe (any more than the others do: *mine, ours, yours, his, its* and *theirs*).

The absolute possessive is a survival from the days when there was *case inflection* in English (see CASE). To use *of* and a possessive form, as we do when we say '…that book of hers', seems to us like overkill, but it was simply the case demanded by the word *of*.

(3) Absolute adjectives are those which cannot logically have comparative and superlative forms (e.g. *unique*). See COMPARATIVE CHAOS (1).

(4) The absolute construction In the sentence *Work being over, fun could begin*, the element *Work being over* is called an *absolute construction*. It is a phrase consisting of a noun and a participle, having no structural relationship to the principal clause. Semantically, it is clearly an adverbial phrase, perhaps of time (= *later*, or *when work was over*) or cause (= *because work was over*).

Some will recognise this as the English equivalent of Latin's *ablative absolute* construction, and may be distressed that in English the construction is in the subjective case; thus:

> *He having left the party, the conversation deteriorated.*

If the writer is insecure about subjectives and the like, it is best to avoid the absolute construction and write *When he had left the party*.... In any case, excessive use of the absolute construction gives a jerky effect which is best avoided.

abstract nouns   For a discussion of the dangers of over-use of abstract nouns, see OBSCURANTISM (4).

academe   Fowler pointed out that, while we might talk (with Milton) of *the grove of Academe*, we should not follow Shakespeare (e.g. *Love's Labours Lost*, IV. iii. 352) in treating Academe as a place, since Academe is a male person. Australians bravely follow Shakespeare, and are even known to *enter Academe*.

   In our defence (if we need any) we might argue that we are not talking about Academus the person, but are using an alternative transliteration of the Greek *academeia*, the place, normally anglicised as *academy*.

academic   The word *academic* is used as an adjective and a noun, and both should be used with care:
   (1) The **adjective** is used neutrally in such phrases as *academic discipline* and *academic staff*, but is mildly pejorative in the sentence *That is an academic question* (= *a question which has little or no relevance to real life*).
   (2) As a **noun**, it can be a neutral term meaning *a member of the academic staff of a university* or a strongly pejorative term meaning *a person who presents opinions which are opposed to our own, supported by arguments which we do not understand*, as in the sentence *They are just a lot of academics and greenies*.

   Between these two extremes lies a spectrum: if we say *There is only one academic in cabinet*, we imply that cabinet has only one member of high intellectual calibre, and could do with more; if we say *Cabinet is full of academics*, we imply that it has many members who are out of touch with the realities of government, and could do with fewer.

accent   For a discussion of accent in the sense 'a mark on a vowel which modifies its sound', see SORTS. The rest of this article is about accent in the sense *manner of pronunciation*.

   We are all well aware of racism, sexism, ageism and so on, but we have no commonly agreed name for prejudice based on accent. It is, however, deeply ingrained in speakers of all nationalities. It is not new, nor is it confined to English. We have clear evidence that a Megarian accent was always good for a laugh in fifth century Athens.

   It is important to distinguish accent from *dialect, register* and *pronunciation*. A change of *dialect* will generally involve translation of words and grammatical constructions into those of the new dialect; a change of *register* means adapting our message to a new readership (assumed to be either better or less well informed than the present audience or readership) without changing the dialect;

and *pronunciation* concerns the approved way(s) of saying words. *Accent* cuts right across these distinctions: this text could be read with an American or Scottish *accent* without changing any of the words.

While we may not all have the keen ear of Professor Higgins, most of us can immediately identify many accents, including several from the British Isles, at least two from America and one from South Africa, and a number, including sundry second-language accents, within our own community. There is nothing wrong with this. An accent can be like a national flag sewn on the rucksack of a hitchhiker – a good starting point for conversation.

What is wrong is the stereotype which may then be attached to the person. The Ocker accent of Australia, Britain's Cockney and America's Brooklyn are examples of accents which identify their speakers as uneducated, and those who speak with these accents start behind scratch in the race up some social ladders. One can argue that it is deplorable that this should be so; or one can argue that, as with Groucho Marx's comment that he wouldn't join any club which would let him in, the ladders in question are not worth climbing. But one cannot argue that accent prejudice doesn't exist.

This is, of course, only one example of an accent prejudice. Stand-up comedians can always rely on jokes about the accent of New Zealanders, or of Greek greengrocers. Positive stereotypes are almost equally dangerous, even if not so offensive – we tend to give the benefit of the doubt to a person who speaks as we do, a phenomenon which appears to underlie the word in New Guinea Pidgin for a particularly close and trusted associate: *wontok* (one-talk).

Australian comes in a range of accents, commonly labelled *broad*, *general* and *cultivated*. This is now taken for granted, but for many years it was not so: then, Australian speakers used to be judged against British standards. An 'Australian accent' meant broad Australian, which was perceived as a disease infecting Australian speakers to varying extents.

There are still vestiges of this attitude. Some people find it hard to believe that an Australian pronunciation can be both different from a British one *and* acceptable. Indeed, some linguists have recognised a fourth Australian accent, termed *modified*, which was a deliberate aping of a British accent. In Melbourne, it was known as *SE2* (a reference to *Toorak, SE2*), but the term did not survive the conversion to postcodes, which suggests that it had even then become obsolete. The accent is heard, however, on archival recordings and the soundtracks of some old Australian movies.

It is sometimes suggested that the prejudice arises from the fact that the accents in question are ugly. This view, however, does not bear very close examination. The old joke 'Did you come here to die?' 'No, yesterdie' works because the sounds are *the same*, so either they are both ugly or neither is. Similarly, the Queen is noted for calling our country */Or-stralia/*, the */or/* being part of a lah-di-dah accent. But the identical sound in */Or-strylia/* is characteristic of the broadest of broad Australian. It seems, then, that we have to look elsewhere for the source of the prejudice.

The most likely candidate is experience: empirical evidence. So long as it is true (statistically) that particular speech patterns tend to march with particular educational and social attainments, speech patterns will be taken as indicators. We will then continue to make gross mistakes in specific cases, underrating or overrating people on first acquaintance as a result of the way they speak.

Examples of this occur in job interviews and court appearances. Every employment agency and barrister knows the importance of looking and sounding respectable when we need to get jobs or justice. We should try to put these prejudices aside when we find ourselves in the position of employer or judge. In the meantime, it behoves the plaintiff to beware.

accessory/ary   There was once a distinction between these two spellings, the first being the term in law for *an accomplice*, the second being used for *accompaniments* (handbags, tools, etc.). This distinction was always arbitrary and is now on its way out, *accessory* being an accepted spelling for all senses.

accident   See INCIDENT....

achieve   When Fowler described the phrase *officers achieving redundancy* as 'absurd', on the grounds that *achieve* implies *successful effort*, he was not reckoning on the Australian experience, summed up so well by Joseph Furphy in the opening words of *Such is Life*: 'Unemployed at last!'.

acquaint with   See PLODDERY.

acronyms   An *acronym* is a word formed from the initial letters (or parts) of other words. Thus *RADAR* is *RAdio Direction And Ranging*, and *ANZAAS* is the *Australian and New Zealand Association for the Advancement of Science*. The essential difference between an acronym and a string of initials is that the acronym is pronounced as if it were a word.

It is sometimes alleged that *ANZAC* was the first acronym. Alas, it was not. It would be dangerous to say what was, but the early Christian use of the fish as a symbol must be a contender: the Greek word for fish was *ichthus*, the words represented being *Iesus Christos Theou Uios Soter* (= Jesus Christ, God's Son, Saviour). Maybe *ANZAC* was the one which popularised the acronym in modern English, but if so, I am not sure that it is an achievement of which we should be too proud.

The problem with acronyms is to decide whether they should be treated as:

(1) common nouns, written in lower case, without an initial capital, as in *radar, flak, laser*;

(2) proper nouns, written in lower case but with an initial capital, as in *Anzac, Benelux and Gestapo*;

(3) strings of initials, written in capitals, as in *ASIO, NIDA, SEATO*, but pronounced as words and hence qualifying as acronyms; or

(4) strings of initials which are not sounded as words, and hence are not yet acronyms, but could change: for example, *FOI* (freedom of information).

There is a general tendency for movement up this ladder from (4) towards (1). Only the writer can decide where on its progress up the chart a given word is at this moment. For example, in ten years people may be talking about *FOI* as /foy/; the original *Gestapo* retains its capital letter, but we have *gestapo-style* operations; and *Quango* (*QUasi-Autonomous Non-Government Organisation*) never had any real existence other than as an acronym.

Acronyms need not exactly reflect the initials on which they are based: thus *Wrens* (in the naval context) arose from *W.R.N.S.*, and *Jeep* from GP (General Purposes). If these are not admitted as acronyms, we have to invent a new word to describe them.

The rules about initial capitals are the same as for any other nouns: specific labels have capitals and generic terms do not; see CAPITALS, USE OF and CAPITAL LOSSES.

An all-capital spelling should be retained if it helps to avoid an ambiguity. Thus *AIDS (Acquired Immune Deficiency Syndrome)* is generally sounded as /aids/, but is best written in capitals, and should certainly be *Aids* rather than *aids*. (This advice is given despite the fact that it is probably too late.)

For an option available in typography if capitals seem too straggly, see SMALL CAPITALS, and for a discussion of some other problems with acronyms, including ambiguity and tautology, see SALT.

The considerate author remains a step behind the leaders, which means continuing to use capitals until an acronym is fully established in the language.

activate, actuate　　Fowler asked us not to allow *activate* – a word deemed obsolete in 1888, but revived in our century as a term of science (*activated charcoal*) – to displace *actuate* as the normal word for *making a machine or person active*. The plea came too late, or was ignored: we *activate, re-activate* and *de-activate* machinery, social welfare organisations, nuclear installations and ourselves.

Meanwhile, *actuate* survives, but as a conveniently woolly word to use if the relationship between two events is not clear: 'The depression was actuated, though not caused, by the Wall Street collapse'.

active (grammar)   See VERB (2(c)).

acute, chronic   In medical parlance, *acute* means *sudden*, and its antonym is *chronic*, which means *long-term*. Thus a sneeze may be called
an *acute* event, while AIDS is a *chronic* condition. It is, in short, all
about time-span, not about seriousness.

In common language, it is the other way round. We associate
acute with urgency, and hence with seriousness, and associate
chronic with conditions with which one has to learn to live, and
which are thus less serious.

The two meet because some acute conditions, like *acute appendi-
citis*, are extremely serious and demand immediate attention, but
strictly *acute* refers only to the time-span. By contrast, in the following pattern

The prolonged drought led to $\left(\begin{array}{l} \textit{an acute} \\ \textit{a chronic} \end{array}\right)$ *shortage of fodder*

the word *acute* will generally imply a more serious, and not necessarily more temporary, event than *chronic*.

Are we wrong? No: if anyone is wrong, it is the doctors, who took
the word *acute* (which had meant *sharp*, as of the points of needles)
and applied it to points in time. In any case, the use of *acute* to mean
serious is now well entrenched in the usage (and in our dictionaries).
The only reason to mention the topic at all is to remind ourselves
that, in the mouth of a doctor, an *acute dermatitis* (for example)
means one which has arisen suddenly, and may well be gone by the
morning.

A.D. (*anno domini*)   See DATES, WRITING OF.

address   We no longer try to solve our problems; we *address* them. It
implies action but makes no commitment, and is therefore a useful
political euphemism.

Maybe the clear-thinking writer should avoid such woolly words.
If what is meant is *debate* or *discussion*, the action words are *debate* or
discuss; if you will not rest until the problem is solved, the word is
solve. But most of us like to be non-committal at times, and *address* is
unquestionably useful on those occasions.

-ade, -ado   The problem is one of pronunciation: /aid/ or /ahd/?
/aidoe/ or /ahdoe/? There is no logic to the present conventions.
   (1) Say /aid/ for all common *-ade* words except *facade*. (*Charade* and
       promenade are still often pronounced /ahd/, but are clearly in
       transition. In square dancing, the pronunciation /promenaid/ is
       obligatory.)
   (2) Say /ahdoe/ for all common *-ado* words except *tornado*. (*Desperado*
       may be in transition to the /aidoe/ pronunciation.)

adhere, adhesion, adherence   Fowler spoke of 'the established phrase
give one's adhesion to a policy, party leader, etc.' To Australian ears, this

sounds like a disastrous experiment with Superglue™, and we give our *adherence* to such things.

Note that *giving one's adherence* to a policy is a matter of the moment, with implications of instant change should circumstances alter; *adhering* to a policy means maintaining support for it over time, despite moves to change it.

ad hoc This Latin term is not necessarily pejorative.

(1) An *ad hoc* committee is one established to deal with a specific issue, and an *ad hoc* decision is one which applies only to the present case and need not be a precedent for future similar cases. (Latin *ad hoc* = to this (i.e. for this purpose).) This meaning is precise and useful.

(2) Because such committees tend to be set up in haste and come to ill-considered conclusions, the term has come to be associated with bad management practices, and we have the pejorative term *adhockery* to describe temporary solutions which fail to get to the roots of a problem. This meaning is also useful.

The two meanings can co-exist happily provided readers and writers are clear about which one is being used; but it will be assumed to be (2) unless otherwise stated. Compare BAND-AID.

adjective For the meaning of the term, see GRAMMAR (3(a)).

(1) The purpose of adjectives is to add precision or colour to our meaning.

(a) All too often, adjectives are merely tautologous. Picture Captain Flinders looking at the line of hills on their horizon: 'How would you describe those mountains, Bo'sun?' 'With your permission Sir, I'd call them lofty.' 'Very good, Bo'sun. Lofty they shall be.' And we have had to live with Mount Lofty ever since, as we live with *true facts* and *grateful thanks.*

(b) Similarly, there are the hackneyed phrases: do we ever fight to an *end* which is not *bitter*? or make a *swoop* which is not *fell*? (The answer in the latter case is 'Yes', but only by mistake – see FELL.) It is very difficult to avoid hackneyed phrases, but well worth trying.

(c) There appears to be a deep human need to fill out otherwise bald sentences, and in the absence of anything better we use fillers, i.e. expletives. Thus, instead of *I hit my thumb with the hammer*, we say *I hit my — thumb with the — hammer*, where the — represents a word which adds nothing to the sense, and may, if taken literally, even be inappropriate. Adjectives should refine the meaning, or provide further detail which enhances the sense.

In sum, well-chosen adjectives can add greatly to the colour and precision of writing, but the writer should ask whether a given adjective does either of these things. If the answer is *no*, omit it.

(2) Adjectives always precede the noun in English except in one or two French-derived expressions, notably those of heraldry (lion *rampant*, bend *sinister*) and the monarchy (crown *imperial*, poet *laureate*, battle *royal*), plus some odd legal terms (e.g. body *corporate*, court *martial*) and *proper* as in *Ultimo is not part of the city proper*. See also GENERAL.

Adjectival clauses and phrases, however, normally come after the noun, e.g. we say 'The man *who has plenty of good peanuts...*' and 'a man *with one leg*'; and they come as close to it as possible, so that the adjective is assumed to refer to the last noun mentioned. This is the source of the old problem of the 'table for a lady with carved legs': we have two adjectival phrases, both referring to the table, but the second is taken to refer to the noun immediately before it, *lady*. It is solved by changing the order in which the two adjectival clauses appear. See ANTECEDENT and WORD ORDER (4).

(3) If a noun phrase is used as an adjective, it is often a good idea to hyphenate it, even if it is not hyphenated as a noun: thus we write *post office* but *post-office box*. The same goes for other phrases, e.g. *a never-to-be-repeated offer*, and if this looks like too many hyphens, change the phrase, not the hyphens; see HYPHENATION (2).

admit   This word has three senses: (1) the *open the door to* sense: *the host admitted the guests*, which presents no problems; (2) the sense related to *sins*, where we have to decide whether to *admit* them or *admit to* them; and (3) the sense related to *replies*, where we must decide whether our arguments *admit* no reply or *admit of* no reply.

Usage is changing rapidly. Fowler would not allow us to *admit to* anything, but approved *admit of* in certain contexts, quoting *a hypothesis admits by its nature of being disputed*.

It appears to depend on the sentence structure:

(1) If the *sin* or *reply* is close to the verb *admit*, no *to* or *of* is needed: we *admit our sins* rather than *admit to our sins*, and say (if we use the rather dated idiom at all) *This hypothesis admits no reply*.

(2) If there is an intervening phrase, as in Fowler's example, the *of* is helpful, and the same is true for *to*: *The defendant admitted, after some close cross-questioning, to having forged his father's signature*.

The logic seems to be that the word *admit*, being semantically weak, needs some sort of amplifier if its message is to be heard over more than a short distance.

advance(ment)   *The advancement of science leads to its advance*. This is not a profound statement, but is not tautologous. *Advancement* is a process and *advance* is a product. Thus the whole phrase means *scientific research leads to new scientific knowledge*.

In grammatical terms, we can say that the verb *advance* can be used either transitively or intransitively, and has two related nouns, *advancement* representing the transitive and *advance* the intransitive.

adverb   For a discussion of the meaning of the term, see GRAMMAR (3(b)), and the discussion of the over-use of ADJECTIVES applies also to adverbs.

The problem with adverbs is largely a matter of position, and is both the defining quality of good writing and the biggest single source of ambiguity and clumsiness if writers get it wrong.

(1) When all the shouting dies down (and there is a lot of it) there are just two rules:

(a) When attached to adjectives and other adverbs, adverbs act to intensify or clarify that word, and they come immediately before the word they modify:

I have a surprisingly heavy cold.	(adverb on adjective)
The answer was mathematically correct.	(adverb on adjective)
He took it very badly.	(adverb on adverb)

(b) The traditional statement is that all other adverbs, and all adverbial phrases and clauses, are attached to verbs, and define how, when or why the action of the verb took place, and they are assumed to refer to the last verb mentioned. Compare the sense of these two:

He landed   heavily   as if he had been drinking.
He landed   as if he had been drinking   heavily.

The value of these two rules is not that they cover all cases, nor that they are always followed, but that they illustrate (and hence help to explain) how positioning can be the source of many problems.

(2) The first major class of exception is a set of modifiers, notably *always, never, almost, nearly, hardly,* which come before the verb to which they apply:

He never goes out.

Many strong adverbs can be used this way:

He finished off the bottle quietly.	(strong sense)
He quietly finished off the bottle.	(as modifier)

The first one is a simple case of (b). The second is more akin to (a), and as with (a) is effectively restricted to single-word adverbs. Adverbial phrases and clauses can be used, but there is an awkwardness, generally resolved by placing them at the beginning of the sentence:

He in the end finished off the bottle.
In the end, he finished off the bottle.

(3) The second class of exception is the parenthetic adverb, which provides a comment on the word which comes before, whatever its grammatical status. Compare these sentences:

He caught a surprisingly bad cold.	(modifying *bad*)
He surprisingly caught a bad cold.	(modifying *caught*)
He, surprisingly, caught a bad cold.	(parenthetic).

See HOWEVER for a further example of this usage.

(4) Ambiguity can arise from doubt about the status of a phrase. Thus if we write

He painted the boat on the beach

the phrase *on the beach* is either adverbial, saying where the action took place:

He painted   the boat   on the beach

or adjectival, referring only to the boat:

He painted   the boat [which was] *on the beach.*

(5) The discussion here has, I hope, highlighted the ultimate source of the problem. It is not that the patterns are themselves particularly complex; most of us use them all correctly without having to think about it. The problem is that the patterns overlap, and our hearers and readers may not pick the one we had in mind. Avoiding the problem demands awareness of possible ambiguity rather than advanced grammatical understanding.

advocate (that)   Strictly, the verb *advocate* is synonymous with *speak in favour of.* Thus we can say *The Prime Minister advocated caution* but not *The Prime Minister advocated that caution was needed.* However, there are arguments against this narrow view. Firstly, *that caution was needed* is a noun phrase; if it was the label on a motion in parliament, it would be legitimate to advocate it. Secondly, the use of *advocate that* is so widespread that only a linguistic King Canute would try to stem the tide. The second argument is the more persuasive, though Fowler uncharacteristically asked us to play Canute.

Æ-, Ae-/-æ-, -ae-   See DIGRAPH....

-ae, -as   See PLURAL DILEMMAS (3).

affect(ive/ed), effect(ive/ed)   One problem with these pairings is that, in speech, they are more or less indistinguishable; the other is that, although they have significantly different meanings and usages, they interlock. The following sentences all carry essentially the same meaning:

The war had an effect *on my attitude*

(*effect*, noun = influence)

The war affected *my attitude*

(*affect*, verb = to have an effect on)

The war effected *a change in my attitude*

(*effect*, verb = to bring about)

The war was effective *in changing my attitude*

(*effective*, adjective = having an effect)

In practice, the problems within this set are not as great as they appear. In most cases, the intended meaning is clear, so that a mistake will not be noticed in speech, while in writing it will damage credibility but not communication.

The problems all arise from the other meaning of the verb *to affect*, i.e. *to put on* or *display*, of feeling or emotions. Its range of meaning can be seen by looking at the nouns it has spawned:

affection and its adjective, *affectionate* (= love, loving)

affectation and its adjective, *affected* (= a pose, artificial)

affect and its adjective, *affective*

(*in psychology* = emotion, emotional)

The third pair carry ill-defined meanings and, in speech, are liable to be mistaken for *effect* and *effective*. They arrived from Germany in the baggage of the psychologists. In German, *Affekt* was a jargon word of psychology standing largely on its own, so it caused no trouble. However, instead of being translated, it was merely transliterated, as if the existing English word carried the same meaning.

This kind of translation error is noticed if it produces nonsense (e.g. the jokes in which the German *bekommen* (= receive) is anglicised as *become*: 'When do I become a sausage?'). However, the psychologists saw nothing funny about saying *the affective domain*.

Although blessed by the dictionaries, it is not a word which is used by people who wish to make their meaning clear. If it has to be used in speech (e.g. in quoting people who use it) the /aff/ sound should be stressed.

a fortiori See LOGIC (5).

afternoon tea See MEALS.

again, against *Again* and *against* have common ancestry, but today have totally discrete meanings, so both words are necessary. (1) So what? (2) How did they drift apart?

(1) Most other words which have grown up in the same way are synonyms: *amid/amidst*, *among/amongst* and *while/whilst*. *Amid* and *amidst* are no problem, since both are obsolescent, occurring only in poetry and the NAUTICAL FOLLY *amidships*. *Among/amongst* seem both to have a role to fill: if in doubt, say *among*, but if you feel that *amongst* sounds more euphonious, no one will mark you wrong. By contrast, *whilst* always sounds like a bit of PLODDERY, and is best avoided.

(2) The origins of *again/st* are an interesting exercise in semantics.

The *gain* part is akin to the German *gegen*, and meant *back*. This original sense can best be seen in the obsolescent word to *gainsay* (= to speak back, deny). It has nothing to do with *gain* = win, which is related to the French *gagner*.

The *a-* is *on*, *in* or *to*, as in *ahead* (= *to the head*).

In earlier times, *again* was both a preposition and an adverb, normally of place. In the antique tag *Turn again, Dick Whittington*, it meant *turn back*, but we can see how the connotation of place can drift into the connotation of time (*turn one more time*).

Over the years, the usage of *again* became restricted to that of an adverb of time, while the usage as a preposition of place was taken up by its inflected form, *against*.

Meanwhile, the original use of *again* in this sense survives in some North British dialects in the form *agin*. (This is often written *agin'* by standard English speakers in the mistaken view that it is a shortened form of *against*.) This form has then re-entered the language with a flavour of revolutionary politics, as in the phrase *agin the Government*.

agenda   *is* or *are*? See SINGULARITIES (i(c)), where it will be found that the answer is *is*, despite the fact that *agenda* is a plural form.

agree   Can we say, as the Americans do, *The President agreed the transfer of arms*, or is this intransitive use a nasty Americanism? RW is in no doubt, asserting that we should not use it this way, and many people share this feeling. But it is not as simple as RW suggests. The Americans believe that it is a British usage, and they have the record on their side. Indeed, at least one well-established British transitive usage is found in Australia: in accountancy, *to agree the figures* is a jargon phrase meaning 'to check that two versions of the same figures agree with one another'. (*Reconcile* is a closely related term.) The phrase *to agree the price* is a related idiom, and comes dangerously close to the American usage RW deplores.

However, the question raises two general points.

Firstly, does it make any difference if keen-eyed lexicographers have located a similar usage in an antique document? It is certainly interesting, but it adds only a footnote to the argument about contemporary practice. If today's usage is in conflict with that of the past, today's usage must win.

Secondly, this is only one case of a widespread phenomenon, the coming and going of prepositions in noun phrases, which for some reason is a constant source of distress to those who like to be distressed by such things. Do we *appeal/protest* a decision, or should we *appeal/protest against* it? Do we *meet*, *meet with* or *meet up with* people? There is no pattern to the answers: the Americans tend to omit the prepositions in the former and add them in the latter; but almost all these 'Americanisms' prove on investigation to have a good British pedigree, so the historical record is less than helpful, while appeal to aesthetics is perhaps the most dangerously subjective of the lot. We are thrown back on arguments from clarity and practicalities. For relevant conclusions, see APPEAL, PROTEST and MEET (WITH).

In the case of *agree*, there is a good practical argument for RW's view. The transitive usage obscures a very useful distinction which is currently available to us: we can agree *to* a proposal or agree *with* a proposal, where *agree with* implies that we are positive about it, whereas *agree to* implies only that we are not opposed to it. This appears to be a distinction many Australian writers make, and presumably would like to go on making.

agriculture   This word has two meanings: in the phrase *The Ministry of Agriculture*, it is a general term covering both the growing of crops and the raising of stock; but it is often used in Australia to distinguish the growing of crops from the raising of stock: *Not fields for agriculture, but pastures for cattle*. A similar distinction is made between *farm* and *station*. This distinction is rarely made in British usage, where a farmer may well get his living from cattle living in fields, but is well understood in America (*Oh, the farmer and the cowman should be friends*, as the chorus sang in *Oklahoma!*).

aide   OED₁ was able to dismiss this word as a short form for *aide-de-camp*, which it defined as an exclusively military term, yet included a citation which might have caused its editors to pause. Dated 1876, and cited from *North American Review*, it reads: *...was picked out by Washington to serve as his confidential aide*.

   Aides is today the normal American word for *assistants* in general and for *members of staff of politicians* in particular. But what is its status in Australia?

   The dictionaries all list *aide* with two meanings: as a short form for *aide-de-camp* and as an assistant in general, and they quote *teacher's aide* and *nursing aide* as examples of the latter usage.

   But are there really any more? Australian politicians have *staff*, not *aides*. It seems that the word exists in Australian English only in the two specific job designations mentioned above, plus, of course, in the text of American news releases where *White House aide* can be treated as an untranslated quotation of an American usage.

   However, because the word occurs so frequently in our news media, it can only be a matter of time, say tomorrow, before we can talk about *Parliament House aides*.

AIDS   Never write this as *aids*. See ACRONYMS.

aitch, haitch   Which? See H.

à la   *Moussaka à la King* looks like a bastard phrase, but is really quite respectable. Certainly it has elements from three languages, but the assemblage is good English and not bad French. The key point is that *à la* does not demand a female noun, nor should it be changed to *au*, because it is short for *à la mode....*

algorithm   SOED dismissed this word as an 'erroneous refashioning' of *algorism* under the mistaken impression that it was related to arithmetic, and so do I. But alas, all the Australian dictionaries now admit it, implying that the refashioning, whether erroneous or not, is now established. They may well be right. The rule is, apparently, that *algorism* retains the historical connotations while *algorithm* carries the modern meanings, e.g. in computer jargon (where it means an analytic process by which a computer reaches 'decisions') and the one which has made the word so beloved of primary school teachers, namely, the way you lay out sums.

alliteration   Alliteration is the deliberate choice of words containing (and especially starting with) the same letter, with a view to a special effect. The classic mechanical exercise in alliteration starts

> *An Austrian army awfully arrayed*
> *Boldly by battery besieged Belgrade...*

while a more poetic one starts

> *I have seen old ships sail like swans asleep*

The effect is more striking with consonants than with vowels, if only because repeating the same initial vowel does not necessarily produce a repetitious effect.

allotment   The use of this word to mean *a grant of a piece of Crown land*, and hence by transfer *the piece of land so granted*, is Australian. In British English, a related usage generally refers to land distributed through the Allotment System, a scheme under which householders can get access to small pieces of public land (often less than 50 square metres) for growing vegetables.

The crucial difference between the two usages are (a) that the British use involves no transfer of title, whereas Australian allotments could, and generally did, become freeholds, and (b) that the Australian usage was very much broader, covering not only grants of small urban building sites for community services (e.g. churches) and grants of small agricultural blocks to settlers to encourage rural development, but also grants of very large tracts of pastoral land to those whom the authorities wished to reward for services rendered. Compare SELECTION....

all right, alright   People get very upset about *alright*, but why this is so is not clear. If the *all* were a separate component of the sense (as it is in *all-embracing*) the objection might be logical, but *all right* has become two words for a single thought – much more so than *altogether* and *almighty*, which we happily allow.

Furthermore, *alright* is in common use, and is sensible. It can be used to distinguish the sentence *The sums are all right* (= each line is correct) from *The sums are alright* (= they are collectively under control).

As it happens, I find it hard to write 'alright', but that is my problem.

allusion   An *allusion* is a reference to some character or event, real or fictional.

A major category of allusion is the use of the names of such characters as generics, e.g. *Edna Everage* has become the generic for a suburban housewife, so that we can say 'The room was full of

Edna Everages'. But quotations and parodies are also allusions, inasmuch as their full force and meaning depends on the reader recognising where they come from.

(1) In theory, then, all allusions depend for their success on a common culture. If you haven't read Shakespeare, how can you pick allusions to his work? In practice, it doesn't always work like this. Many allusions acquire an autonomous meaning, so that we can use them correctly without knowing much of their origins, e.g. Shylock and Falstaff, Houdini and Sarah Bernhardt. Some generics (especially TRADEMARKS) lose their capital letters and enter the common language; and see EPONYM(OUS) for the common ground shared by *Brisbane, furphy and pavlova*.

(2) What do we know of Macchiavelli except that he was a devious schemer? What do we know of Frankenstein except that he was a monster? The answer is, of course, that neither of these pieces of knowledge is correct. We have here, in fact, the exact opposite of case (1): everybody will know what we mean, although we have actually got the facts wrong.

(3) Allusions may be or become ambiguous: thus 'a Ned Kelly' would generally be understood as a rogue with a heart of gold; but some might use him as a generic for a larrikin. Similarly, the legend of Robin Hood has taken a beating recently, so that his name could become a generic for a fallen idol.

Other allusions are to historical events: people *meet their Waterloos, cross their Rubicons*, and have their *Dunkirks* and *Pyrrhic victories*. Again, the sense can be clear even if the origins are scarcely understood. We do not need to know all about the campaigns of Fabius Cunctator to know that the Fabian Society is not like the WOBBLIES.

All Australians (and almost no one else) will respond to the name *Phar Lap*. This is a characteristic of a private language: references to shared experience and knowledge which enrich communication with friends. Indeed, communication with strangers often starts with an attempt to discover shared experience, so as to set up a framework of allusion.

There are only two dangers in the use of allusions.

Firstly, if shared allusions can bring people together, allusions which are not understood can drive them apart. It is foolish to avoid allusion on the grounds that this may happen, but it is very bad manners, as well as ineffective, to make the sense of what we say or write depend on an obscure allusion. If, for example, you did not know who the WOBBLIES were, the reference to them above would be meaningless, and you might have been alienated by it.

Secondly, if there is one thing more dangerous than assuming that everybody else is as clever as we are, it is assuming that everybody else is as dumb. Being caught misusing an allusion is an unpardonable offence.

When saying the word *allusion* it is helpful to put a slight stress on the /a/ sound. This is to prevent the hearer thinking (albeit only for a moment) that you are using the rather more common word, *illusion*.

alternative, alternate   The words are full of traps for those who wish to fall into them.

(1) How many alternatives can there be?   Some writers (including me) cannot utter the phrase *a third alternative*, suffering as we do from the Latinist fetish that there can be only two alternatives – if there are more than two, we say *choices* or *options*. Happily, most people suffer no such disabilities.

We are in better company in objecting to *no other alternative*. The *minimum* number of alternatives is two. If fewer than two, then we have *no alternative*, not *no other alternative*.

Alternatives should be linked with *and*, not *or*: *the alternatives are filet mignon and sausages*. This is a matter of logic rather than usage, and, like many logical imperatives, is widely ignored in the New Age.

(2) alternative(ly), alternate(ly)   *Alternate* is mathematically precise, meaning *every other*:

> *The club meets on alternate Thursdays;*
> *Elizabeth and Joan take the chair alternately.*

By contrast, *alternatively* is imprecise and implies arbitrary choice:

> *The club meets on Thursdays, or alternatively Fridays;*
> *Elizabeth takes the chair, or alternatively Joan.*

(3) alternative (culture)   In this 1960s expression, *alternative* means *alternative to the established order*, with the particular reference to simplicity, natural process, conservation of the environment and the avoidance of the evils of technology. Thus although the Governor-General lives differently from the average Australian, his is not an *alternative lifestyle*.

The word is used slightly differently in the phrase *alternative medicine*, where it tends to mean *all medical practices which do not have the blessing of the Australian Medical Association*.

ambiguity   The following examples illustrate some of the main sources of ambiguity:

(1) *The house needs painting badly*. Careless positioning of adverbs and adverbial phrases is among the most common sources of ambiguity – see ADVERB and WORD ORDER. This problem is particularly common when negatives are involved – see (7).

(2) There is a similar problem with adjectives: *The architect sited the house on the edge of the cliff, overlooking the encroaching sea*. The structure of this sentence is very common, involving a delayed adjectival clause, but the delay generates an *ambiguous antecedent*. (It would not be ambiguous in practice but for the double meaning of *overlooking*.) The celebrated *table for a lady with carved legs* is similar. The problem is again WORD ORDER, and see ADJECTIVE and ANTECEDENT.

(3) *More help needed for my expanding contracting business.* For this excellent example I must thank Richard Coleman. Theoretically, any word which has more than one meaning is potentially ambiguous, but in practice the ones which cause real problems are few. Fowler's delightful example, *Miss Pickhill grasped the pince-nez, which hung from a kind of button on her spare bosom*, is not going to cause trouble very often.

The biggest danger is with words whose sense is weak, and for a discussion of some insidious ambiguities, see AS (3), LIKE, AND/OR and OR. For some more obvious problems see BREAKDOWN, CASE (2), CERTAIN, COMMON..., CONCERN, CRITICAL, INTELLIGENCE, INTEREST, MATERIAL, MEAN and PROPER. Among proper nouns, *Indian* is ambiguous, particularly in America, and for an ambiguity with *English* which has been surprisingly neglected, see BRITISH(ISM) (2).

Jargon is a rich source of ambiguity, both by preserving old meanings and applying new strong senses to common-language words. However, the stronger the senses in which a word is used, the more likely it is that the ambiguity will be so obvious that it will not cause misunderstanding.

(4) *Gladly my cross I'd bear.* While not an ambiguity if written down, this homophone (same sound, different written forms and meanings) was heard by at least one child as, *Gladly, my cross-eyed bear.* Most puns depend on homophones. Homophones which have caused trouble include *red/read, gilt/guilt, right/rite,* and a host of cases with plurals and possessives (*buses/ bus's/ buses'*).

Near-homophones can be worse. A trivial mishearing produced

> They climb'd the steep ascent of heav'n
> Through peril, toil and pain;
> O God, to us may grace be given
> To follow in the train.

For a discussion of some risky near-homophones, see ENSURE/INSURE, COMPLEMENT/COMPLIMENT, AFFECT/EFFECT, DEFUSE/DIFFUSE and the separate articles on ALLUSION, ILLUSION and DELUSION. When saying these words, we should be careful to avoid confusion by giving a careful or even exaggerated pronunciation to the key syllables. See also TRANSCRIPTION...(3).

(5) *Unionised* is the converse of (4) – ambiguous if written but generally unambiguous if spoken: *un-ionised* or *union-ised.* Such pairs of *homonyms* (two words with the same written form, often different pronunciations, and different meanings) are generally distinguished by the context, but this one must be watched for wrong hyphenation if it occurs at the end of a line – as does *man-slaughter/mans-laughter.*

Homonyms which cause real trouble include *lead* (compare *a lead singer* with *a lead balloon*) and *windy* (*twisty* or *blowy*?). Note that these are different from the ones mentioned in (3), being separate words with the same written form, not divergent meanings of the same word; but the effect can be similar.

(6) *50% off, with 10% discount for cash.* Is the net price 40% or 45% of the original? The ambiguity here may well be deliberate – see PERCENTAGES. For a similar problem of ambiguity of reference, see CONTEMPORARY.

(7) *He didn't speak because he was a coward.* Did he speak for some other reason, or fail to speak because he was a coward? This is a member of a class of *structural ambiguities*, many of which are associated with negatives. How does one reply to the question *Do you want no part in it?* Logically, the answer has to be 'Yes' (= *I want no part in it*) or 'No' (= *I want a part in it*), but in practice the answer is often given as if the question was in the positive, making *yes* and *no* interchangeable and hence ambiguous.

(8) When the first Voyager spaceship was approaching Jupiter, Australian radio listeners were surprised to learn that it was 'close to Jupiter's satellites, and had photographed ten'. In a later broadcast, this was corrected to 'had photographed Io'. There are not many cases when such a confusion could arise; apart from anything else, it could happen with a text written in capitals. But it illustrates the operation of Murphy's Law of Ambiguities: if an ambiguity can arise, sooner or later it will.

(9) Conclusion The problem with ambiguity is that the misunderstanding is in the mind of the hearer/reader, not of the original speaker/writer. We know precisely what we meant to say, and may not be aware of potential misunderstandings until it is too late. However, the problems in (1) and (2) can be avoided if we school ourselves to take great care with the positioning of adverbs, adjectives and their related phrases; for the rest, we can only watch out for the problem words and constructions, and avoid them.

ambiguous, ambivalent   An *ambiguous statement* is one which can be interpreted two or more ways, through internal inconsistency or the use of vague terms. An *ambivalent attitude* is one which is indecisive. Politicians can conceal their *ambivalence* by resort to *ambiguity*, as in the sentence *Appropriate attention will be paid to the problems of the rich.*

The rest of us should avoid ambivalent attitudes and ambiguous utterances – see AMBIGUITY.

Ambivalent is such a common word today that it is hard to believe that it entered the language only in 1916, and then as a technical term of Freudian psychology, but such is the OED's report. But maybe the Freudians stole it from the chemists, who used *ambivalenz* half a century earlier in the context of valency.

American English   Australian writers need to understand American English for two main reasons: firstly, to understand messages from America; secondly, to make sure that our own messages are understood by Americans.

The first problem is relatively trivial. We hear and read so much American that we understand hundreds of American words and phrases which we never use, to say nothing of the ones we adopt.

Indeed, the puzzles are more often cultural than semantic. Thus, for example, in the common American road sign NO RIGHT ON RED, all the words are used in normal senses, yet the whole sentence is meaningful only in the context of American traffic law. However, we know when we are not understanding, so we know when to stop and check. At the very worst, we may be a bit surprised to be invited to *wash up* before dinner, but the perils are not great.

The reverse problem, however, is more profound. We can of course assert that our American readers *should* come to grips with Australian in the same way as we come to grips with American, but the reality is that they will not. There is no problem with Australian idiomatic expressions, most of which are self-evident when seen in context. The problem is with content words. If we want to be understood, we had better talk American (which is why Paul Hogan puts a *shrimp* on the barbie in his American commercials, which we would never dream of doing) or at the very least to know which words will need explanation or should be avoided. Worse than the danger of not being understood at all by Americans is the danger of being *mis*understood, as can happen if we say we would like to *help them to wash up*.

For the academic writer, the problem is not great, as such writing tends to be in formal international English, and the writer is likely to be aware of all problem words. For the general popular writer, however, it is best to have the work gone through by (effectively) a translator, who will identify the words and expressions which are for any reason strange. We will not necessarily change anything, but we should at least be aware of the problem.

If, of course, the writer is bilingual in Australian and American, the work can be written in an interlingua from the outset. Indeed, the writers of children's books designed for distribution in the USA and Australia are sometimes given lists of forbidden words, so that John and Conchita can run and jump, but they cannot then get a drink from either a *tap* or a *faucet*, an item for which there is no internationally understood term. If no such list is available, it is better to write a complete text first and deal with the translation problems as a separate issue.

Writing for the American educational market also requires some special attention to offensive material, and the rules go a long way beyond what might be identified by common sense. They have resulted in strange creations like a version of *Bluebeard* entirely cleansed of sex and violence, producing a somewhat thin and pointless story. As with translation, the writer is advised to produce a complete text first and deal with the rules on offensive material as a separate editorial exercise.

Americanisms The fact that we use the same word as the Americans for something for which the British have another word does not make our usage an *Americanism*. The general principle is that, when we find a gap in our language, we can fill it from whatever source we like, either coining for ourselves or borrowing from outside. If we borrow, British English and American English are simply banks on which we have unrestricted drawing rights. Thus, when we speak of *kerosene*, this is no more (and no less) an Americanism than our use of *petrol* is a Britishism or *kindergarten* is a Germanism. They are all now Australian words.

By contrast, if we have a perfectly good word (from whatever source) in our language, but for some reason use the American word, this is an Americanism. For example, cattle *rustling* is an American term for what we call cattle *duffing*, and a *mustang* is an American term for what we call a *brumby*. Such terms would be inappropriate Americanisms if used in an Australian context.

Are Americanisms to be avoided? The answer is yes, just as Britishisms are to be avoided: clarity and courtesy demand that we speak our own language, whether this happens to coincide with British usage, with American or with neither. See BRITISH(ISM).

Note that *to Americanise* means *to translate a word of text from another dialect of English into American*. It should not be used to describe the change which may occur when a non-English word or phrase is adopted into the English of America. *Anglicise* is the correct word for this process wherever it occurs. See ANGLICISE.

amok, amuck The best thing about this word is that it is one of the very few words we have acquired from the Malays, and hence should be cherished. The spelling *amuck* probably arose from its pronunciation /a muck/ and the resultant association with *muck*, while the more peculiar spelling, *amok*, is likely to remind us of its origins, and our special friendship with the Malays. But it was pilloried by Fowler as a didacticism, so perhaps we should adopt some other Malay word, like *teksi*.

amphisbena This useful word is not current in Australian English, though it appears in the admirable ACOD. It means *a snake with a head at both ends, and therefore capable of changing direction without turning round*. It can usefully be applied not only to ferries, trams and XPTs, but also to many politicians. Those who like digraphs can spell it *amphisbaena* or even *amphisbæna*; its adjective is *amphisbenic*.

anabranch   This word can be dated to 1834, when, as reported in AND, a writer in the *Journal of the Royal Geographical Society* coined it. The reference was to Australia, and its currency is virtually restricted to Australia. It means an anastomosing branch of a river, i.e. one which rejoins the main stream lower down, a phenomenon common in Australian rivers but rare elsewhere. With the passage of time, an anabranch may become landlocked and turn into a *billabong*, but this term is also applied to stagnant pools left behind after the main stream of a river dries up, an event which is rare on the Thames or the Mississippi.

anacoluthon   An anacoluthon is a sentence which changes its grammatical structure in mid-flight. 'I tell you that if the people of Queensland want me to be Premier, what is wrong with that?' As with a medical diagnosis, putting a label on the disease does not effect a cure.

analogous   Should the *g* be sounded *g* or *j*? RW plumps unhesitatingly for *g*, supported by logic and ACOD; Mac offers both without expressing preference.

The merits of the soft sound are considerable. Mac is right in reporting its use: many Australians say it this way, perhaps to stress the connection with *analogy*.

This has become particularly important since the resurrection of the word *analogue* by the computer industry. It is quite possible that we will shortly have two adjectives, one with a soft sound related to *analogy*, the other with a hard sound related to *analogue*; and if we want to preserve the phonic conventions, we will spell them differently, *analogeous* and *analogous*. This would unfortunately encourage those who already pronounce the former /anna-**low**-jus/, and if we want to avoid this, we are wiser to leave the spelling alone.

Cutting through the ambivalence of this argument, we should at the very least not call a soft *g* sound in *analogous* incorrect.

analogy   There are three separate issues:
(1) Analogy/simile/metaphor   *Analogy* is primarily a logical device, where *simile* and *metaphor* are rhetorical devices designed to add colour to an otherwise drab statement.
(a) The Treasurer who explains the national accounts in terms of a family budget is drawing an *analogy*, explaining the unknown in terms of the known, or the complex in terms of the simple.
(b) The Opposition spokesman who says that this explanation is like the nutrition notes on a cornflakes packet is offering a *simile*: it does not explain anything, but presents a point of view in graphic terms.
(c) The backbencher who then says that the acid test is to whet the economy on the anvil of expediency is using a *metaphor*, and a mixed one at that.

Although they can be distinguished, the three have something in common: they all presuppose that the hearer can make the transfer between what is being said and the real topic.

Since *analogy* is a process of explaining the unknown in terms of the known, it is (though often in veiled form) the most common device by which we teach, learn and discover. This leads to its greatest danger – the *plausible analogy*, which appears to work well, but is then extended to reach an unproven or untrue conclusion.

Simile and metaphor are less pretentious, since they do not pretend to prove anything, and are therefore less dangerous. But well-turned similes or metaphors can be very effective in argument, not so much for what they say as for their connotations. They are therefore among the most insidious features of demagogic rhetoric – as well as providing some of the greatest joys of poetry and poetic prose.

(2) Analogy in language development   When we are searching for a word, we may sometimes coin one which makes sense to our hearers. Once we have a new word, say *nork*, we can immediately coin a range of other words, *norkless*, *norklike*, etc., by analogy.

This process is not limited to new words. The child who says *She's eating she's hair-ribbon* has constructed this sentence on the analogy of *It's chewing its bone* (which she used successfully a few minutes earlier); the outcome is wrong because she took the analogy too far. The sentence I am now writing is new, in the sense that this particular string of words has never before appeared in print, and its success as communication depends on writer and reader having a common store of analogous patterns of grammar and meaning, and picking the right ones.

Poor communication occurs when these analogies break down, either because the writer uses words in senses which are unconventional, or assembles them in structures which do not match the set of structures available to the reader. The considerate writer has the reader's comfort in mind at all times, and avoids writing sentences as long (and hence as novel, in structural terms) as those in this paragraph.

(3) False analogy in language development   False analogy is not confined to children's language. Many of the most common errors in adult language stem from false analogies. Thus, having been told that *John and me are going out* is wrong, and should be *John and I are going out*, we change the perfectly correct sentence *Can you give John and me a lift?* to the incorrect *Can you give John and I a lift?* For a further discussion of this particular problem, see CASE (2).

What we learn from this is that analogy in language development is just like analogy in any other sphere: it provides the patterns which make greater understanding possible, but in doing so provides a plentiful source of misunderstanding.

analyse   Even those who prefer *-ize* to *-ise* (e.g. *realize* to *realise*) should not spell *analyse* with a *z*. It is a back-formation from the noun *analysis*, so that the etymological argument for the *z* does not apply. However, the Americans insist on spelling it with a *z*, and there are an awful lot of them, even if they are all wrong. See -ISE/-IZE/-ICE.

and   This word has a strong sense in certain sentences: *Come* and *get it*. *Wait* and *see*. *Try* and *do it*. It is not just linking two separate actions, but implying a purposeful relationship between one and the other, so much so that some people have seen *Try and...* as an error for *Try to...* (just as *I could of danced all night* is an error for *...could have...*).

It is certainly idiomatic (in the sense that, if translated into another language, the grammar would almost always have to be different). But it is a perfectly respectable idiom, moving happily in all but the most formal situations.

and/or   Fowler objected to the use of *and/or* except in certain legal and commercial documents, in which he recognised its value. If it is valuable in such documents, why is it not equally valuable elsewhere? And, if it is valuable, why not permit it?

There are occasions when there is no equally neat alternative. The reason for this is that *and* is an ambiguous term:

We eat our food with knives and forks [simultaneously]

We travel around in cars and buses [but only one at a time]

If this distinction is important, *and/or* is a convenient shorthand for the latter. We should, however, continue to object to *and/or* when it is used purely to save the trouble of deciding which is appropriate. Compare OR (which is also ambiguous).

anglicise   This word refers to the adaptation of a *foreign* word into English. For example, the pronunciation of 'Paris' is *anglicised*, while the spelling remains French. In the case of 'Dunkirk', the spelling is anglicised and the pronunciation remains (roughly) as in French.

The term is used even if the word is being imported into a regional dialect of English. Thus the word *godown* is an anglicised version of a Malay word meaning 'warehouse', used widely in the business English of south and east Asia. We can say it is 'anglicised' although the word has no real currency in the English of Britain, America or Australia.

It should not be used for the process of adapting an Australian text for British readers. We are not often tempted to do this, but we should recognise that the British do it all the time. Effectively, they are confusing the country with the language, but they are bemused by the proposition that there is any difference: see BRITISH(ISM) (2).

'Anglicise' is best written, as Mac does, without a capital letter, to stress that we are talking about the language, not the country.

anglicism   This word has two meanings:
  (1) When speaking of French, an *anglicism* is a word imported from English (whether British, American or Australian), just as a *gallicism* is a word imported into English from French.
  (2) When speaking of the English language, *anglicism* can be both the process and the product of adapting a foreign word or phrase into English; as with *anglicise*, the reference should be to the language, not to the country, so that it should not be used for transfers between dialects of English.

  This is a recommendation, not a description of current usage. The word *anglicism* is often used in Australia for a word imported from Britain, and in Britain (where it tends to be given a capital letter) it may refer either to the English language equivalent of a foreign word or to the British equivalent of an English but non-British word. Compare ANGLICISE, and see BRITISH(ISM) (2).

anon(ymous)   For a word of warning about this seemingly innocent attribution, see MORAL RIGHTS.

antagonist   See PROTAGONIST.

ante-, anti-   These are etymologically quite distinct words, *ante-* being Latin and meaning *before*, *anti-* being Greek and meaning *against*. The common antonym of *ante* is *post*, as in *a.m./p.m.*, *anterior/posterior*, and *antedate/postdate*. The common antonym of *anti-* is *syn-*, as in *antonym/synonym*, *anticline/syncline*, but more often the antonym has no prefix (*climax/anticlimax, cyclone/anticyclone*).

  In theory, there could be confusion between *ante-* and *anti-* with the elision of the distinctive final letter before a vowel, but this does not happen in practice:
  (1) All the words based on *ante-* retain the *e* (e.g. *antediluvian*).
  (2) All the elided words (e.g. *antagonise, antonym*) are elided forms of *anti-*, and *anti-* is never elided into an *e*.
There are, of course, many words beginning with *ant-* which belong to neither camp, e.g. *antelope*, while *antique* and its derivatives have a kinship to *ante-*; but there is no ambiguity when *ante-* and *anti-* are used as prefixes.

  In new coinage, *anti-* is common (*the anti-smoking lobby*) and *ante-* almost unknown, the most recent *ante-* coinage in common use being *antenatal* (first noted by OED in 1817). It would be unwise to coin new *ante-* words, as they would tend to be mistaken for *anti-*, and *pre-* offers a generally satisfactory alternative.

antecedent   This is a useful term meaning *what has gone before*, and is used in grammar to mean the word or words which a pronoun stands for, or to which an adjectival clause refers:

  Ann Boleyn had the misfortune to lose *her* head.

  (*Ann Boleyn* is the antecedent of *her*)

We can get in trouble with an *ambiguous antecedent*:
Paul was sitting on a horse *like a big teddy bear*.
We do not know whether it was *Paul* or *the horse* which was *like a big teddy bear*. Other things being equal, the assumption is that it is the nearer; but the sense tells us otherwise.

For a further discussion of this, see ADJECTIVE, ADVERB and WORD ORDER.

antenna   Despite what some dictionaries say, the *aerial* sense of this word is no longer a jargon word of electronics (which it was when it entered common language with the arrival of television). It is the normal term for the technologically advanced device on the roof of a house to pick up TV signals.

The bent clothes hanger jammed into a severed stump on a car, however, is better called an *aerial* – to call it an *antenna* sounds slightly pretentious. The rabbit's ears on top of the TV set are an *antenna* to the TV technician, and an *indoor aerial* (an interesting modern example of OXYMORON) to its owner.

The plural is *antennas*. *Antennae* is the plural of the biological term for an insect's feelers.

anthropo-   This word part is generally translated *man*, but it is inclusive, the Greeks having the good fortune to have *anthropos* as an inclusive term in contrast to *aner* (*andr-* in derivatives) meaning male, as did the Romans with *homo* and *vir*. It occurs in this sense in such words as *anthropology*, *anthropoid* and *misanthrope*, and if we want an inclusive term for the human race, therefore, we might talk about *anthropes*.

How does 'The proper study of anthropekind is anthropes' appeal?

anthropomorphism   This word means the attribution of human forms or characteristics to inanimate objects or lower animals, as when we speak of a computer having a 'memory', or depict animals talking or displaying human emotions. It is a logical nightmare. See NATURALISTIC FALLACY.

anticipate   This is a favourite word of purists, who assert that the sentence *he anticipated my arrival* can only mean *he got there first*, and should not be used to mean *he expected me to come*. If so, a very large number of excellent writers have been wrong for a very long time – the error is at least two centuries older than Australian English, for example. Hence we might expect this dead duck to lie down. However, as Disraeli said, *What we anticipate seldom occurs; what we least expect generally happens*, and the argument rages on.

antipodes   The best use for this word is discussion of the possible plurals of platypus: *platypodes* for purists (see PLATYPUS), *platypi* for ignorami, and *platypuses* for us as speak proper.

Antipodes means *with the feet opposite*, and has been used since ancient times to indicate people living on the backside of the Earth, who had day when the people on top were having night. (The Romans had an excellent joke in which people who held lamp-lit night revels were called *antipodes*.)

We should not use the word at all. To us, it can only mean the North Atlantic, but it has been established as a label for Australia, as has *Down Under*, and using it the other way will simply get glassy stares. But we are used to this sort of thing. We all know that the Wild West is in the far east, and the Far East is in the near north, but these are just the labels on the cans. Indeed, the name of our continent, *Australia*, means the South Land, whereas we know very well it is plumb in the middle. See MENTAL MAPS.

antique   In Britain, a serious attempt is made to restrict the application of this word to items which are at least one hundred years old. No such attempt is made in Australia, where it means (in the words of the Fodor *Guide to Australia*) domestic bric à brac.

any   The usage of this simple little word is very subtle. If we are asked *Have you any apples?* we can reply *No, I haven't any apples* but not *Yes, I have any apples*. Meanwhile, *Have you some apples?* is unusual, and the reply *No, I haven't some apples* even more so, while *Yes, I have some apples* is good English.

Fowler explained it by saying that *any* requires an actually or possibly negative context, which makes as much sense as any.

For *any...their*, see EACH (ONE)....

apartment   See FLAT.

apology   The original sense of this word, as a legal term meaning *a statement for the defence*, survives only in the title of Plato's masterpiece, *The Apology of Socrates*. This doesn't matter a jot, provided we remember that Socrates was not *apologising* in the modern sense.

a posteriori   See LOGIC (2).

apostrophe   The apostrophe is used in English in two ways: (a) To indicate the dropping out of some letter(s), as in *can't*; (b) To flag a possessive form, as in *the dog's dinner*. We will see, however, that (b) originated as a version of (a).

There are four usages of the apostrophe:

(1) those which are logical and 'correct';

(2) those which are illogical but 'correct';

(3) exceptions to (2);

(4) those which are logical but 'incorrect' (of which, as we will see, a small subset may be all right after all).

Section (5) covers use in proper names, where the rules cut across those in (1) to (4).

(1) Omissions   The original use of the apostrophe, to show that some letters have been omitted from a word, is illustrated by *can't* and *we're*. Only slightly less simple are formations like *won't* for *will not* and *I'd* for both *I had* and *I would*, where the elided letters cause no problems for native speakers, though those learning English as a second language may find them puzzling.

There is a leap into obscurity with NAUTICAL FOLLIES like *bo'sun* for *boatswain*, and when one sees how many letters have disappeared from other words, as when *God be with you* becomes *goodbye*, one wonders why one should put an apostrophe in *bosun* at all. It is therefore good to see that AWEG says we can leave it out.

(2) Possessives   The possessive apostrophe, as in *the hen's nest*, originated as an example of (1). In early English, they would have written *the hennes nest*, the *-es* indicating the possessive case. Pronunciation then changed, and the second *e* became mute. They showed this by replacing it with an apostrophe: *hen's*.

Such apostrophes were used to represent mute vowels in plurals and *-ed* forms as well as possessives, so they would have written *I sav'd the egg's from the hen's nest*.

With the passage of time, the convention changed. We now apply it only to possessives, but we apply it whether or not an *e* has disappeared. Thus it has changed from an indicator of pronunciation into an indicator of possession. In the case of plurals ending in *s*, the apostrophe is placed at the end:

	Two-syllable	One-syllable
Plurals	places	phones
-ed forms	ragged	tapped
Possessives	boss's	phone's
Possessive plurals	bosses'	phones'

It has lost all significance to pronunciation. Thus in *I tapped the boss's phones*, the word *boss's* contains only one vowel but makes two syllables, while *tapped* and *phones* contain two vowels each but are monsyllables.

So much for the illogical but 'correct' set.

(3) Absolute possessives   It would follow from the rules in (2) that we should use an apostrophe in words like *hers, theirs, ours* and *whose*; but here the possessive form is written without the apostrophe. This leaves the form *it's* free to be used for the contraction of *it is* and *it has*. See ABSOLUTE (2) and CASE (2).

(4) Plurals   Meanwhile, putting an apostrophe before the plural *s* is commonly regarded as an error made, for example, by illiterate milk bar proprietors (*sandwich's*); but, as noted above, this could be a deliberate archaism by a highly literate milk bar proprietor wishing to promote a two-syllable pronunciation of the word.

A more real dilemma occurs in such phrases as *In the 1920's…, A bevy of VIP's…* and *Dot your i's and cross your t's*. All the apostrophes here are, according to current usage, incorrect, and in the first two cases their omission is recommended:

> *In the 1920s...*   *A bevy of VIPs...*

But *Dot your is...* looks very odd, and, unless you can think of a better alternative, I recommend the incorrect and illogical form *Dot your i's....*

(5) Proper names For a variety of reasons, not least being the lunacy of the rules and the insecurity of those who have to apply them, apostrophes are generally omitted altogether from *Perishers Creek Boys High School*. (Since it is a school for boys, not just one boy, it would be *Boys'*; but who knows how many Perishers there were?)

Possessive apostrophes are dropped from virtually all Australian place names (*Crows Nest*). The only apostrophes to survive are those indicating an elision, e.g. *O'Connor*. In Britain, apostrophes tend to survive in both cases (*Land's End, John O'Groats*).

Unless apostrophes are in the official titles of institutions (as in *Mentone Girls' Grammar School*), we should leave them out. They are generally on the way out, especially if there is a double possessive, but there are unexpected exceptions: the *Builders' Labourers' Federation* retains its full array.

appeal We appeal *against* a decision, but do not (as the Americans do) appeal *a case*. We can, however, *take a case to appeal*. Compare AGREE.

appendix The things at the end of books are generally *appendices*; while the things removed by surgeons are *appendixes*. Despite this, the operation is an *appendicectomy*. Compare INDEX.

a priori See LOGIC (1).

apropos This little French tag is used in English with much less imagination than in its native French. Consider the following:

> He spoke briefly and *à propos* (= relevantly, adverb)
>
> After dinner, we had an *à propos* speaker (= relevant, adjective)
>
> His speech had the merit of the *à propos* (= relevance, noun)
>
> He spoke *à propos of* the merger (= concerning, preposition)

These are literal representations of good French usage – as adverb, adjective, noun and preposition. So much for those who believe that English is the only language in which words can wander from one part of speech to another. If we regard the word *apropos* as French (although we make it one word), all these usages should be good in English, too.

Note that, if we want to reflect the French, we should say *apropos of* when using it in the 'concerning' sense, since the French is *à propos de*. This is not a compelling reason to do so, but it does call into question the views of those who tell us that inserting *of* is wrong.

Finally, the French phrase *à propos de bottes* has precisely the opposite sense, signalling that what is about to be said is *not* relevant to what has gone before, and the word can be used on its own with the same sense. Thus Ionesco: 'À propos, la cantatrice chauve'. This could be used as an alternative to a cringing *excuse me* when one has to break in on a conversation; thus

> *Apropos*, the house is on fire.

If we are to have the word at all, let us use it as much as possible, and the above are some attractive possibilities.

It is pronounced /*appra-poh*/.

apt Very short words *are apt to* lose their power. *Apt*, meaning suitable, relevant, fitted to a purpose (*she proved an apt pupil; the choice of hymn was apt*) has become a word of faint praise. By contrast, its longer derivatives (*aptitude, adept, inept, ineptitude*) retain strong meanings.

Apt has lost all sense of occasion in its most common usage, the phrase *is apt to*, where it means *has the habit of* or *tends to*, with connotations of unwanted outcome; of ineptitude rather than aptitude:

> *The milk is apt to curdle when the lemon is added.*
> *The chairman is apt to fall asleep during his own speeches.*

aquatic For pronunciation, see QUAGMIRE.

archaism If we label a usage as archaic, we are liable to find it restored and flourishing next day. Similarly, there is nothing so archaic-sounding as yesterday's cult words (see NONCE WORDS). Fowler was well aware of this when he spoke of the threatened revival of such words as *anent, howbeit, perchance* and *surcease*. If these particular words are not on everybody's lips, consider the others which he put in the same category, only fifty years ago: *albeit, chide, confidant* (noun), *parlous* and *save* (as a preposition = *except*).

Nevertheless, the wise writer leaves the restoration of derelict words to others, if only because of the risk of ignorant blunder.

arguable, debatable The phrases *It is arguable that...* and *It is debatable whether...* can both be used to introduce an assertion, but the speaker is assumed to be in favour of the motion in the first case and against it in the second. Both are used by insecure writers to ensure that whatever opinion follows is deniable if prudence or the wisdom of hindsight demands denial. See OBSCURANTISM.

It is debatable whether the preferred model is that of deceasal or ongoing vitality. It is arguable that it is more conducive to holistic positive perception by third parties if the actor endures an attitudinal trauma engendered by the incidence of adverse happenstance, rather than institutes palliative remedial procedures to mediate what Klott (1977) termed 'incremental betterness' within the situational environment, and, through the medium of pluralistic countermeasures in the affective domain, subject them to termination.

Shakespeare put it more simply, yet we are reliably informed that Shakespeare is hard to understand.

artefact/artifact Both these spellings are reported in our dictionaries. I prefer *artifact*, if only because it is consistent with *artificial* (which is always so spelt).

article *Article* is the name given by grammarians to the words *the* and *a/an* (called respectively the *definite* and *indefinite* article). In the simplest terms, if we are describing a unique, defined item, it is *the*; if it is any one of several, or undefined, we say *a* or *an*. 'First pot *a* red ball, then pot *the* black.' And, of course, there are many constructions in which we use neither.

The rules are astonishingly complex, but native speakers of English have very little difficulty with them, and sometimes find it hard to imagine why second language speakers get the articles wrong.

One reason is that many languages have no articles as we know them. Indeed, languages which have them are, on a worldwide basis, the exception. Japanese, for example, has none, and makes the distinction between a general statement ('This is *a* book') and a specific one ('This is *the* book') by the use of *particles*, a class of word which does not exist in English, though some of our affixes have a similar effect: e.g. *-ish, -ship, -let*.

Modern European languages tend to have articles, but the precise way they are used varies. The French, for example, generally put the definite article on the names of countries – *La France, L'Australie*; and they use them on abstract nouns much more often than we do: the proverbial *Noblesse oblige* is French, but old French: in modern French it would be *La noblesse oblige*. They go shopping and buy *un peu de lait, du lait* or *le lait*, but never just *lait*.

As a result, English as spoken by the French tends to have too many articles; English as spoken by the Japanese tends to have too few.

For discussion of some problems with articles, see THE and A/AN.

art union This phrase is not understood outside Australia and New Zealand. It referred originally to a raffle with a work of art as a prize, but it acquired two wider meanings:
  (1) A work of art was not necessarily of any value, and it was understood that the real prizes were in cash; that is, an *art union* was a device to get round the laws governing lotteries.
  (2) The phrase was also applied to raffles in general, irrespective of the prize.
As a common language expression, the phrase is now obsolete. It survives only in the official titles of a few raffles and lotteries, e.g. *The Stradbroke Art Union*.

as *She was a good cook as cooks go, and as good cooks go she went.*

(1) Many of the phrases containing the word *as* are odd. Should they be treated as idioms, that is, strings of words which cannot sensibly be taken apart, or should the meanings of the component words be borne in mind?

(a) **As well as** The sentence *The hat suited her as well as me* preserves the original sense of *well* (i.e. *the hat suited both of us equally well*), and shows how the phrase *as well as* became virtually synonymous with *and*. Do we therefore object to *The crash hurt me as well as you*, on the grounds that the sense demands *as badly as*?

(b) **As far as** Do we object to *as far as Ayers Rock is concerned…* or *as far as Ayers Rock goes…*, on the grounds that Ayers Rock is unlikely to be concerned, still less to go anywhere?

The simple answer is that these little idioms have acquired meanings which are well understood despite any illogicality. At the same time, it is worth watching for them, and avoiding them if their literal meanings could be noticed and raise an unwanted smile.

(2) There are usages which can cause grammatical problems:

(a) **As if** and **As though** The problem here concerns the form of the finite verb which follows them. If we say *It happened as if by accident*, there is no verb and no problem, but note the following:

The cat looks as if it *has eaten/had eaten* the canary.

If what follows *as if* is likely to be the case, the *indicative* form (*has eaten*) is appropriate; if what follows *as if* is hypothetical, the subjunctive form (*had eaten*) is needed. Since *as if…* is generally followed by a hypothetical, the subjunctive is in practice the most common.

For a discussion of the subjunctive forms, including the vexed question of *was* versus *were* for the present subjunctive, see SUBJUNCTIVE.

(b) **As from** In the sentence *The new rate should apply as from last July*, the *as* is tantamount to *as if*, and is included to show that a special retrospective adjustment must be made. If the date of application is in the future, the word *as* is redundant: *the new rate should apply from next July*.

(c) **As to** is in most cases an insecure substitute for *of, concerning* or *about*. At the beginning of a sentence: *As to your third point…* (= *turning to your third point…*) is concise and clear, but in *He asked as to his name* the phrase is redundant, and is an example of PLODDERY. Likewise, in the phrase *the question as to*, the phrase *as to* is either redundant or better replaced by *of* or *about*.

(3) The most serious problems are those which create ambiguities. For example, the causal *as* (= because) should be used with care, since it can be confused with the temporal *as* (= when), and vice versa. *As he was leaving, he put on his coat* could be either, and the use of the more specific *because* or *when* is preferred.

The moral of all these varied points is that the word *as* is perilous: writers and speakers know what they mean and assume that it is equally unambiguous to their hearers and readers. They are advised to use more specific constructions wherever possible.

assets   It is of purely academic interest that *assets* was once singular, deriving from the Latin *ad satis* (= to sufficiency) via the French *assez*. If *riches* (from *richesse*) is now plural, *assets* is more so, since it has a singular form, *asset*, in circulation.

We might also remember that, in accountancy, *assets* refers to capital items, not income or benefits, and when we use the term metaphorically in descriptions of people and places, we should make the same distinction. Thus, in the sentence

Albury has many assets for the tourist, including a picturesque town hall and boating on the Hume Weir

the *town hall* and the *Hume Weir* are perhaps assets, but *boating* is a benefit derived from the asset, not an asset in its own right.

assurance   There was until the 1960s a distinction between *life assurance* and *life insurance*. Life assurance was an arrangement under which you (or your successors if you died in the interim) were 'assured' of getting an agreed sum on an agreed date; life insurance was an arrangement by which your successors received an agreed sum if you died before an agreed date, no money being payable if you didn't.

There may be some documents in circulation in Australia which assume that this distinction is understood. In new documents, however, the word *assurance* is no longer used. One word, *insurance*, covers all such arrangements, the distinction being between various classes of life insurance policy; the 'assurance' approach is similar to what is now called an *endowment policy*.

astable   This absurd but important word (meaning *having no stable state*, and applied to elements in transistorised circuits) is encountered by every electronics student in our schools. As it is an antonym of *stable*, it must be pronounced to rhyme with *hay-stable*.

The word is interesting because it illustrates the value of the rules for new coinage: that the pronunciation of the new word should be unambiguous and that its sense should be as self-evident as possible. The word breaks both.

astronomical   See BILLION.

at, in   A great deal of learned ink has been spilt on the subject of the difference between *We will meet in Fredsville* and *We will meet at Fredsville*. The distinction is fairly clear: we meet *in* Fredsville unless Fredsville is so small that it can be considered as a single space.

If we say *We will meet at Adelaide*, we are not talking about Adelaide in the general sense at all, but to a specific time and place which will be unequivocally understood by the people we are talking to. Thus, if we are talking to people who are travelling to Adelaide on the same plane, we mean that we will see them again at Adelaide *airport* in an hour or so. If we are at an artistic gathering, it would probably mean that we will meet again at the next Adelaide *Festival*. If we are Grand Prix drivers, it will be the next Adelaide *Grand Prix*, and so on. Grand Prix drivers even meet *at Japan*.

atom   The language of atomic science has given us many new words and specific technical meanings to existing words. These occur so frequently, even in non-technical writing, that a brief discussion seems appropriate. The following entry attempts to use the vocabulary in context. It starts from *elements*, moving first downwards in size, then upwards.

An **atom** is defined as *the smallest quantity of an element which has the properties of that element*. (Etymologically, it means *indivisible*, and the name survived the discovery that this was not the case.)

An atom is a bundle of **subatomic** or **elementary particles**:

(1) The **proton**, which has mass and charge (positive).
(2) The **neutron**, which has mass but no charge.
(3) The **electron**, which has charge (negative) but relatively little mass.

The protons and neutrons cluster in the **nucleus**. The electrons orbit the nucleus, moving so fast that they are said to form an *electron cloud*.

The neutral atom has equal numbers of protons and electrons, giving it a net charge of zero.

The atom of each element is characterised by its **atomic number**, which is the number of protons in its nucleus. The list is full from 1 (hydrogen) to around 107, with man-made (and increasingly unstable) elements filling all places above 92 (uranium). It is thus highly unlikely that any further stable atom will be discovered.

Each atom also has a **mass number**, which is the total number of protons and neutrons in its nucleus. These contribute almost all the mass of the atom, so mass number is effectively an indication of mass.

(1) If an atom gains or loses a *proton*, it becomes a different sort of atom, i.e. an atom of a different element.
(2) If an atom gains or loses an *electron*, it becomes an *ion* of that atom.
(3) If an atom gains or loses a *neutron*, it become an *isotope* of that atom.

An **ion** is an electrically-charged atom or molecule. The gain or loss of an electron upsets the balance and *ionises* the atom.

An **isotope** of an element is identified by its mass number (e.g. Carbon-14, or ^{14}C), and may be stable or unstable. An unstable isotope **decays** (that is, splits into two or more stable isotopes, and/or emits **radiation**, notably α-(alpha)particles (which are bundles of 2 protons and 2 neutrons, i.e. helium nuclei), β-(beta)particles (which are actually electrons), and γ-(gamma)rays (bursts of energy). The rate of decay is quoted in terms of the **half life**, this being the time taken for half the unstable species to decay.

If an element has no stable isotope, it is known as a **radioactive element**, and its ultimate decay products will be atoms of another element or elements.

A reaction involving a change to the nucleus is termed a **nuclear reaction** (as distinct from a *chemical reaction*, which involves only the electron clouds). In **nuclear fission** a large atom is split into two or more smaller atoms. In **nuclear fusion** two smaller atoms are fused into one larger one. The key fusion reaction occurs when hydrogen nuclei fuse to form helium – the reaction which powers the sun.

Moving up the scale from the atom:
An **element** is a substance composed entirely of atoms with the same atomic number. There are thus as many different known elements as there are different known types of atom, currently 107.

A **molecule** is a structure formed of atoms bonded together in specified proportions by *covalent bonds* formed by the sharing of electrons between two or more atoms. A moelcule is the smallest amount of a molecular substance which has the properties of that substance.

An **ionic substance** is one formed from ions bonded by equal and opposite electrostatic charges.

Australian   See COMMONWEALTH.

Australianisms   Until recently, Australian was popularly seen as a vernacular with its own colloquialisms and slang, not as a form of English with its own vocabulary and idioms. The assumption was that any departure from British English was an uneducated aberration. See BRITISH(ISM), and compare ACCENT.

The hundreds of technical terms for specifically Australian objects and phenomena (flora, fauna and Aboriginal artifacts) can indeed be regarded as Australia's contribution to international English, and many have taken their place in British and American usage. However, it is hard to describe as *slang* the very large range of words and usages which are simply the Australian way of talking about quite ordinary things.

The following illustrates some *classes* of word which may puzzle non-Australian readers, either because the word does not exist in their versions of English, or because it has different connotations:

(1) *History*: Many words have to us unequivocal meanings and connotations, but need explanation to overseas readers: *squatter, selector, allotment, trooper, diggings, bark/slab hut*.

(2) *Politics*: Apart from our special experience of some labels (*Liberal (Party), Commonwealth*) we make a distinction between *Premier* and *Prime Minister*, and the words *nexus, caucus* and *faction* are among many which have special connotations.

(3) *Household*: Most of our usage is British, and hence may puzzle Americans; but we depart from British usage in some of our recent adoptions (e.g. *zucchini* for *courgettes, doona* for *duvet, spa* for *jacuzzi*); we go our own way with some foods (*lamb's fry*), clothes (*bathers*), and parts of a house (*lounge room*).

(4) *Transport*: Most of our road transport vocabulary is British, though we have *semis (semi-trailers)* rather than *articulated lorries* or *juggernauts, mufflers* rather than *silencers* and drive on *bitumen* rather than *tarmac* roads.

(5) *Americanisms adapted:* We use the word *interstate* much more broadly than the Americans. In both countries, an *interstate* bus is one which travels between States, but in Australia we can talk about a car with *interstate* plates (= from another State) and of a person being *interstate* (= in another State) where the Americans would say (more logically) *out of State.*

These examples (several of which are further discussed, along with many others, elsewhere in this book) are chosen purely to illustrate the point (if it still needs to be made) that slang, while perhaps the most obvious feature of Australian or any other dialect of English, is not the end of the story.

authority   This word has several separate meanings:

(1) Originally, it meant something akin to what we now call *leadership qualities*, as distinct from *power*. This is its meaning in such phrases as *she speaks with authority*, i.e. *she gives the impression that she knows what she is talking about*. This sort of authority may, in fact, reflect the manner rather than the matter. A good debater can speak with authority on any topic under the sun.

(2) Its second meaning describes an institution. As William McGonagall wrote:

> *The Municipal Authorities considered it no sin*
> *To decorate with crepe the beautiful city of Berlin*

(3) The third is more or less synonymous with *permission*: *You have authority to spend up to $1000.00 without further approval.*

(4) The fourth is illustrated by the sentence *He is an authority on snails,* where *authority* simply means *expert*. Expertise does not automatically bestow power or leadership quality, nor imply infallibility. What it does mean is that, if the question is about snails, the answer given by this 'authority' will carry special weight.

When we speak of the *authority* of a dictionary, it is in the first instance expertise we are talking about. Dictionaries are essentially reports on the way language is used, and their authority is measured by the extent to which they are accurate reports. Some, indeed, make a fetish of being purely descriptive, reporting misprints and ignorant mistakes alongside neologisms and unusual metaphors. This is not as silly as it might sound, since our language is full of meanings and spellings which started life as mistakes of one sort or another. But it does mean that the existence of a citation in a dictionary does not necessarily imply that the usage in question is, or ever was, good English.

However, most dictionaries are based on value judgements. They report what their compilers believe to be the best versions of the language, the ones used by the best speakers and writers. This starts their slide into becoming prescribers, the creators of rules which ordinary mortals should obey.

At this point, a dictionary may acquire authority in the first sense, that of leadership quality; the status of arbiter. Even so, the authority falls far short of power. A word doesn't change meaning because a dictionary, however authoritative, says it is so; it changes only if people in general accept the dictionary's judgement and act accordingly.

Nevertheless, most people are more interested in the answers than the questions. We want good clean solutions to doubts and disputes. We don't like the idea that language is a sort of alphabet soup, seething and rearranging itself at whim. So we are happy to give greater authority to the dictionaries and their writers than those writers would claim for themselves.

auxiliary verb   See MODAL AUXILIARIES.

average   See MEAN....

awake (up) to   There are three clear-cut usages and one questionable one:

(1) *be awake to* a problem (= be aware of);
(2) *wake up to* a problem (= become aware of);
(3) *be a wake-up* (= be a lively person; possibly a reference to *a wake-up*, a person whose job it was, in the days before alarm clocks became common, to go round town in the early morning banging on bedroom windows).

All these usages are well attested, with the third having a particularly Australian flavour (e.g. Cyril Pearl: *Be warned, or, as we Ordinary Australians say, be a wake-up*).

But then there is:

(4) *be awake-up to* (= be aware of, as (1)).

It unquestionably exists: *I'm awake-up to that kind* (Dymphna Cusack). But it seems likely that this started with a mis-hearing of (3), *a wake-up*.

There is no way this can be proved either way, but the point is interesting because it illustrates one of the ways in which change can occur: an authentic idiom or usage is mis-heard and then written down wrongly by a reputable writer; this usage is then reported by the dictionaries, and becomes 'right'.

axes   If this is the plural of *axe*, it is pronounced */axiz/*; if it is the plural of *axis* it is pronounced */axeez/*.

B

bacillus   The word is pronounced /b'sill's/, and has the plural *bacilli*.

back blocks   In the subdivision of land, a *back block* was originally one with no access to the road or (more often) watercourse. However, the term is also used to indicate remoteness from an urban area, in such phrases as 'in the back blocks'. See BUSH and BLOCK.

back-formation   'The Boy Scouts caterpilled through the hedge'. In this sentence, the verb *caterpilled* has been back-formed from caterpillar, and this, curiously, is the way many of our words have arisen. For example, the noun *burglar* was derived from a medieval Latin legal word, *burgulator*, and the verb *to burgle* was back-formed five hundred years later. If we object to back-formations, we should prefer the American *burglarise*, and *burgulate* would be better still.

Recent successful back-formations include, in ascending order of acceptability, *liaise, escalate, enthuse, diagnose* and *scavenge*. Their success is based on the fact that each of them represents a useful cluster of meaning and connotation for which no other word exists.

Should we object to back-formations? Given that the invention of new derivatives by adding bits on is an accepted part of language development, and results in ever longer words, back-formation (which fulfils the same need, but results in shorter words) should be encouraged. But, for some reason, some people find taking bits off more shocking than adding bits on, as if it were some literary strip-tease, and write anxious letters to the press suggesting imminent collapse of civilisation-as-we-know-it whenever a new one comes in view.

backlog   See METAPHOR.

back of   The Australian usage, as in the phrase *back of Bourke*, is not like the American, where *It is back of the house* simply means *behind*. It is better seen as a special idiom, analogous to the British *back of beyond*.

backward(s)   Fowler said that either form can be used as an adverb, while the only adjectival form is *backward*. RW says either word is correct, though *backward* is now more common. Perhaps so; but *backward* and *backwards* are not synonymous. There are many sentences in which only one can be used:

> *He is a backward reader.*
> *He knows it backwards.*
> *He was backward in coming forward.*

All these illustrate, however, special senses of the word. In its normal sense, Fowler's advice holds, with the possible rider that 'he walked backward' implies a direction of movement away from the observer, while 'he walked backwards' implies the direction relative to the way he was facing.

Compare UPWARD....

back-yard   See YARD.

bail, bale   *Bale* is unquestionably the correct spelling in the *bale of hay* sense (and its related verb, *I baled up the hay*) and in the unrelated word *baleful*.

There is an argument that all the other senses should be *bail*, since they are derived from a variety of old French words in roughly this form:

(1) *baille* = an enclosure, gave us *the Old Bailey*, a *bailiff*, the recently-revived archaism *bailiwick*, cricket *bails* and *bail*, a form of cattle crush, which in turn gave us the Australian expression *to bail up* as in *The bushranger bailed up the banker*.

(2) The same French original, passing through a different chain of modifications of meaning, gave us the legal term *bail* and the verb *to bail out* as in *The bushranger was bailed out by the banker*.

(3) A separate French word, *baille* = a bucket, gave us the transitive verb *to bail out* as in *They bailed out the boat*. However, the spelling *bale* has been widely adopted for this sense, and it is certainly no longer wrong.

(4) The intransitive verb *to bail out*, as in *The pilot bailed out of the crippled aircraft*, dates from the 1914–18 war, and we will probably never know whether its first users had in mind (2) or (3), neither of which is used intransitively.

Our dictionaries are divided on the issue, and AND shows clearly that both spellings have good provenance. I always use the spelling *bail* in all the above senses, but this is more likely to be laziness than a subconscious respect for etymology.

balance   The equal-arm balance is a device which, since its invention some four thousand years ago, has stimulated the popular imagination. It is the only man-made object in the Zodiac, the first truly scientific instrument, the physical embodiment of algebra and the symbol of justice. Small wonder, then, that it has produced a large crop of metaphorical usage, and that this crop harbours some weeds.

For the worst of the weeds, we have the accountants to blame. The word was first applied to the process of balancing incomes and expenditures, balance being achieved when the income and expenditure columns were equal. However, it rarely worked out like that – there was always something left over on one side or the other, which was carried over to the next page in the accounts. This *balancing item* was illogically called the *balance*, so that the term became associated with an amount carried forward: effectively, a remainder, an extra or *unbalanced* amount. Similarly 'an unfavour-able balance of payments' should logically be an unfavourable *imbalance* of payments. But the usage, though illogical, is too en-trenched to be changed.

Strangely, the use of the word in the sentence 'the balance of the day is given to amusement', to which Fowler objected on the grounds that no balance is involved, is actually closer to the original concept. There are twenty-four hours available, of which we spend eight sleeping, eight working and the account is balanced with the eight we spend in amusement.

banal   ACOD offers us three acceptable pronunciations for this word, */bay-n'l/, /b'nahl/* and */b'nal/* and the other authorities are even more tolerant. Fowler listed *and recommended* the fully anglicised */ban'l/*, which is not heard in Australia (or in Britain, for that matter). I prefer the pronunciation *b'nahl*, as it makes an attractively appro-priate sound, like a yawn.

band-aid   It is the dream of every adperson to get a trademark into the language (though there are then fresh troubles – see TRADE-MARKS), and *Band-Aid™* must be regarded as a triumph, even though its connotations are pejorative.

The word is used in conjunction with such words as *solution* to describe a temporary, patch up job. But we should remember that this is precisely what *Band-Aids™* are supposed to do, and they work because nature heals most ills if given the chance. *Band-Aids™* were never intended for major surgical problems like decapitation, but neither is major surgery recommended for a scratch.

If we want to be fair to the *Band-Aid™* folk, therefore, we should perhaps talk of *appropriate* and *inappropriate* use of *band-aid* solu-tions.

barbarians   The word comes from the original Greek meaning of the word *barbarian*, which did not mean 'wild' or 'brutal', but 'saying *bar bar* instead of talking proper Greek'.

The related adjective is **barbarous**, which implies contempt.

(1) Barbaric is an alternative adjective which is both stronger and weaker: stronger through being associated with **barbarity** (a very nasty phenomenon) and weaker, almost indulgent, if applied to taste. When applied to customs, however, it has a strange ambigu-ity. We say that public executions are *barbaric*, while being reluctant to recognise that this particular barbarity was brought to Australia by the First Fleeters, whom we would hesitate to describe as bar-baric.

(2) Barbarian, both a noun and adjective, is best retained only as a historical label for the sundry folk who invaded Europe from the north-east in the first millenium A.D., though it is used of later destructive invaders by some writers.

(3) Barbarism (in grammar) is an error of grammar or usage arising from lack of specialist information, particularly of formal grammar and etymology, which the critic has the good fortune to possess.

An example is the phrase *bona fide*. This is an adverbial phrase meaning *in good faith*, and hence fits happily in the phrase 'a *bona fide* traveller', one who travels in good faith. But if we want to say *We question your good faith*, we need a noun, not an adverbial phrase, and should say (so the story goes) 'We question your *bona fides*'. Thus 'We question your *bona fide*' is a barbarism.

In this particular case, there is something to be said for the purist position, not because it is better Latin, but because it is better English (i.e. educated speakers of English make the distinction). Other Latin tags have lost their original grammatical status, but for some reason this one hasn't. (As it happens *bona fides* is questionable too, being in the subjective case where it should be the objective case; but this does not seem to worry the purists.)

Many of our words and grammatical usages were at one stage barbarisms. Let one example illustrate the point: the word *exit* originally occurred as a Latin tag in stage directions for plays, where it meant *he/she goes out*. Used this way, the plural is *exeunt*, they go out. It then became a noun with theatrical connotations (*They have their exits and their entrances*); it was applied, as a jargon joke, to the doors in theatres, which were marked *Exit*. Finally, it became an English verb, *to exit*, with such forms as *he exits, they exit*. These are barbarisms of high order – but they were all generated before the time of Shakespeare and perpetuated by him; so today's barbar-hunters do not worry about them. (Compare INTEREST.)

barbecue   It comes as a bit of a shock to find that OED cites usages starting in 1697 (as a wooden framework for sleeping or cooking on, derived from a Haitian corruption of the Spanish word *barbacua*). It was used to describe an animal roasted whole on such a contraption in 1764. Thus, though the first usage as an outdoor meal is not reported by OED until 1809, it is perfectly possible that the 'orgy' with which the First Fleet celebrated its arrival in Oz included a barbecue.

The alleged origin in a cattle ranch with the brand *Bar-B-Q* is an attractively plausible falsehood.

bark   The word *bark* has a much wider significance in Australia than in Britain or America. Many Australian trees, including the paperbarks and stringybarks, have barks which can be stripped off to produce large flexible sheets of watertight material. This was very well understood by the Aboriginals, who used these barks for making shelters (*gunyahs, humpies*), shields, containers, canoes and, of course, as a surface on which to paint. The earliest surviving Aboriginal paintings (on cave walls) suggest a high level of sophis-tication at a period when European cave painting was very primitive, and it is possible that this skill was developed in bark paintings centuries before the Egyptians discovered the use of papyrus for a similar purpose.

The making of canoes left its mark with the survival of so-called *canoe trees* (trees bearing a large oblong scar where the bark has been stripped to make a canoe).

The European settlers quickly learnt the potential value of the barks, and the result was the *bark hut* (see BUILDING TERMS). Less happily, the settlers also learnt that a labour-saving way of clearing land for pasture was *ring barking* (killing trees by cutting a ring from their bark). Bark also had a value as a source of tannin for curing leather, and *bark-cutting* gave a livelihood of sorts to those without the skill or ambition to do anything else.

bar mitzvah   A *bar mitzvah* is a cultural rather than religious occasion and therefore does not need to be capitalised.

barrack   The verb *to barrack* was once claimed to be home grown, and was even assigned an Aboriginal etymology, the word *borak*. This is now generally discounted, and the word seems to be Irish. Nevertheless, it has acquired a distinctly Australian flavour.

The original meaning is *to make an uproar*, and the earliest use in Australia reported in AND is in this sense. In British English, it retains this sense, with the particular connotation of politics: noisy interruptions during political speeches. A *barracker* is thus assumed to be against whatever is being said. But in Australia (where the word is much more common), it has connotations of sport, and we *barrack for* the team of our choice. A barracker is thus a *supporter*, assumed to be shouting words of encouragement.

barrage   Most usages are older than one thinks, but a *barrage* in the context of *artillery* dates only from the First World War. The French, who gave us the word, associated it with its earlier meaning, a *barrier* or *dam*, and it was used by them only as a *defensive* tactic. Hence they might speak of *a barrage of ministerial answers* but not, as we do, *a barrage of questions*. Despite this, we pronounce the word in an Anglo-French way, /ba-rahj/.

barrier   It all started with breaking the *sound barrier*, a feat first performed by a Bell X-1 rocket-powered aircraft in 1947. This was fair enough – the sound barrier represented a real physical phenomenon, and no one was absolutely sure what effect the shock wave would have on the plane.

The *sound barrier* was for a short time the talk of the town; and, since then, hardly a day has passed without report of the breaking of a barrier of some sort.

There is nothing wrong with this provided that there is some sort of barrier to break: thus, for example, the public at first objected to paying over a dollar for a newspaper, so that in this context the *dollar barrier* represented a genuine point of resistance; but to talk about the population of Australia *breaking the 15 million barrier* was absurd – the arrival of the fifteen-millionth presented no peculiar difficulties or hazards.

If the metaphor is not to be discredited, becoming another weak synonym for *level* or *rate*, it should be used only in cases where an obstacle of some sort can be shown to exist.

base, basic, basis   These words have a strange history. We start with the Greek word *basis*, meaning a *step* (in both the 'pace' and 'step-ladder' senses), hence a pedestal, and hence the foundations of a building, and finally the foundation of a logical argument.

In English, this word appears in two forms, *base* and *basis*, whose plurals are both written the same – *bases* – but pronounced differently (respectively, */bay-siz/* and */bay-seez/*).

In the nineteenth century, the word *base* was adopted in chemistry to describe a class of ionic compounds which release hydroxyl ions when in solution, the choice of name reflecting the state of chemical understanding at the time; and the adjective *basic* was coined to describe them.

Thus though *basic* looks like any other anglicised version of a Greek adjective ending in *-ikos*, *basikos* never existed in Classical Greek, and was first recorded by the OED in 1842 in the context of chemistry. But it was a very successful coinage. Today, it is a common language word with no chemical connotations whatsoever, and is used as an adjectival form of *basis* as well as *base*.

This is relevant to Australia because without it we would not have our greatest innovation in social justice, the *basic wage*. Alas, the basic wage is no more; indeed, the spokespeople of Treasury are even trying to change its pronunciation, rhyming basic with *classic*, when those who knew and loved it said */bay-sick/*.

bas-relief   ACOD wisely advises us to rhyme *bas* with *lass*. Mac and RW prefer to rhyme it with *tar*, in memory of its French origins. If it is to be regarded as French, the whole phrase should be gallicised – */burrelly-eff/* or some such, with a nicely trilled */r/* in the middle. Those whose trilling is not up to much should anglicise the word entirely.

bastard   This word has a wider range of connotation in Australian idiom than in the idioms of Britain and America. While it certainly carries strong senses (*You bastard!* will generally be a powerful response to unpleasant behaviour), it can also be used quite affectionately, as in *He's a likeable bastard*, with the possible implication that the person is involved in slightly shady practices which, however, do not harm the speaker; and even *You bastard!* may be an admiring response to some clever stratagem of which the speaker would like to have been the author.

Bastardry, on the other hand, is a strong term, little known outside Australia, indicating iniquitous behaviour, with a strong hint of malicious harm to the speaker, and is quite separate from the technical term of genealogy, **bastardy**.

Bavarian   Say /B'varian/, not /Bar-varian/.

B.C. (*before Christ*)   See DATES, WRITING OF.

be   The verb *to be* does not have a subject and object, but a subject and COMPLEMENT. In the following sentence pattern, the verb *to be* agrees with its subject (the one which comes first):

> You   *are*   the problem
>
> The problem   *is*   you.

This is always the case. In the sentence *A hundred dollars was the cost of the meal*, we use the singular verb not because of the singularity of the complement, *cost*, but because we want to depict *a hundred dollars* as a singular entity, a fistful of money.

Similarly, the sentence *The wages of sin is death* is an antique curio, originally written *The wagis of synne is deth*, and at the time *wagis* was a singular noun which happened to end in *s* (compare *riches*). The sentence is now a proverb and hence past scrutiny.

Nor is the rule broken when we say *There is one answer* but *There are two answers*. Here, the sentences are inverted, the word *there* not being a pronoun but a flag signalling the inversion; see IMPERSONAL.

There are of course doubtful cases, but they occur not because of any doubt about the rules, but because we have not decided whether the subject of the sentence is singular or plural. These and other problems are discussed in SINGULARITIES.

be-   This common prefix rarely has anything to do with the verb *to be*. It has various effects, but the only one which is alive today is to turn a noun into a verb. Words in this class include *befriend*, *bejewel* and *behead* – a curious trio, within which a single meaning for the *be-* is hard to discern. But in new coinage, its effect is always like that of *bejewel*, i.e. to *equip with....* We can already be *bespectacled*, and we could be *bethonged* and *bejeaned* if we wished to be.

If *be-* is added to an existing verb, it has a different effect. It is supposed to be related to *by-*, and it spreads the effect around: thus we get wet if we are *sprinkled* with water, but wetter if we are *besprinkled*. A similar effect is seen in *deck – bedeck, smear – besmear*. These words sound quaint to our ears, and we would not be readily understood if we coined a new word along these lines.

because   We say *the reason is that...*, not *the reason is because....* For the dangers of *not ... because*, see AMBIGUITY (7).

behalf   Do not confuse *on behalf of* (= in favour of, *or* representing) with *on the part of* (= by) in such sentences as *This was a mistake on* *behalf of Mr Keating.* Maybe it has never occurred to you to make this mistake, but many do. Compare SAKE.

belles-lettres   Fowler wanted us to abandon this word, saying that it existed only in publishers' catalogues, etc., its place having been taken elsewhere by the terms *literature* or *pure literature*. It is certainly not a happy phrase, being ill-defined and hard to pronounce – the voiced yet vowelless /-tr'/ doesn't go well with an untrilled *r*. But amputation is not a complete solution.

Belles-lettres is not synonymous with *literature*. *Pure literature* sounds well suited to the job, but has failed to catch on (unlike *pure science*, which is well understood). Interestingly, the adjective *literary* (as in *literary novel*) has the required connotations; it is the noun alone which is missing.

The word is needed to cover prose writing whose principal attraction is its form rather than its content. One possibility is to use the established distinction between *poetry* and *verse*, and popularise the term *poetic prose* (and the equally useful term, *prosaic poetry*).

But delicious prose is not necessarily poetic, and until some genius (a *belletrist*, perhaps) invents a better term, *belles-lettres* might as well survive … at least in publishers' catalogues.

benign, malignant   A useful subtlety is dying here. Until recently, *benign/malign* described the state or effect of a thing (as in *a benign law*), and *benignant/malignant* described the intention of a person (as in *a malignant lawyer*).

Medical jargon adopted *benign/malignant* to describe cancers, and this pairing seems to have overridden the older one, so that *benignant* and *malign* are now obsolescent as adjectives except perhaps in the context of superstition, where deities and spirits may still be *benignant* and an influence *malign*.

Meanwhile, *malign* survives as a verb meaning *to speak ill of (somebody)*.

bereaved, bereft   These two past participles (and the derived noun *bereavement*) are all that is left of the verb *to bereave*. The root verb is alive and well in our dictionaries, but not in our language.

The two participles are now best treated as two quite distinct adjectives, *bereaved* referring to those who have lost their relatives and *bereft* to those who have lost their minds, senses or feelings.

between   The phrase is *between you and me*, not *between you and I*. If you want to know why, see CASE (2).

beware   This word is an outstanding current example of a DEFECTIVE VERB, existing as it does only in the imperative (*Beware the Dog!*), and the infinitive (*You ought to beware…*).

The other inflections have died; but Milton, for example, wrote 'I had bewared if I had foreseen…'.

bi-   Two questions: (1) When can we omit the hyphen? (2) What does bi-weekly mean?

(1) Hyphenation   The only purpose of hyphenating prefixes is to preserve sense and pronunciation (see HYPHENATION(1)).

(a) *Sense.* Failing to hyphenate *bicycle* has led to the tautologous expression *two-wheeler bicycle*, but it is used by recent graduates from *three-wheeler bicycles*, so this is a lost cause. *Bicarbonate* is a label on a can. If we want to stress that there is a numerical prefix lurking there, we can hyphenate it: *bi-carbonate*; but as it happens it does not help with the chemistry of it.

Bi- retains its identity better than its Greek cousin, *di-*. Where both are available (as in *bivalent* and *divalent*) *bi-* is the preferable term, and is the better choice for use when coining new words. If internal consistency is a good idea, this means using *univalent* rather than *monovalent*. See NUMERICAL PREFIXES. If the sense is *both*, *ambi-* is better still.

(b) *Pronunciation.* If there is no ambiguity in pronunciation (which we test by listening for misreadings) no purpose is served by hyphenation. Words which do not pass the reading test include *bistable*, which should therefore be hyphenated. I recently heard the word *biplane* read on the radio (with some puzzlement on the part of the young reader) as *bip-lane*. This word caused no trouble fifty years ago, when it (and *monoplane*) were everyday terms, but is so rarely seen today that it may need to be re-hyphenated to stress both its pronunciation and sense.

(2) Meanings   There is endless trouble with the words *bi-weekly*, *bi-monthly* and their more upmarket relations, *biannual* and *biennial*. Do they mean *twice a week/month/year* or *every two weeks/months/years*?

In the case of *biannual* and *biennial*, there are established conventions: *biannual* means twice a year, while *biennial* means every two years. Thanks to *The Biennale*, citizens of Sydney have no difficulty remembering this (or its Italianate pronunciation, */The beer narly/*).

But there are no such rules for *bi-weekly* and *bi-monthly*. Our dictionaries simply tell us that they can mean either one or the other, which is true but unhelpful. ACOD goes on to say that, given this ambiguity, we should not use the terms at all, using instead *twice weekly* or *two-weekly*, and *twice monthly* or *two-monthly*, which makes good sense. (Those who favour the word *fortnightly* should remember that Americans do not know about *fortnights*.)

bibliographies   Writers of PhD theses, which are as much prizes for neatness and adherence to convention as for academic excellence, are well aware that there are approved rules for bibliographies. Other writers should make sure that the reference gives the information that the reader needs.

The basic PhD rules are illustrated in the following:

Llewellyn, K., *The Waterlily*, Hawthorn, Vic., 1987.

Thus a bibliographical reference comprises:

(1) *Author, surname followed by initials.*

If there is more than one author, the names should be listed in the same order as they appear on the title page. Alternatively, the first one can be followed by *'et al.'* (*et alii* = and others), but this should not be done if the details of the authorship of the work are important, as in scientific papers.

Foreign names in which the surname comes first (e.g. Chinese) should be written out in full unless an established short form is available: *Mao Zedong*.

If the book is attributed primarily to an editor, the editor is treated as the author, but with the addition of '(ed.)' after the name. The plural *eds*. is taking over from *edd*.

In the case of pseudonyms, the author's true name may be given in brackets after the pseudonym:

Culotta, Nino [John O'Grady], *They're a weird mob…*

The square brackets indicate that this is not how the name appears in the book, but is an interpolation by the author. The same device can be used to bring a pseudonymous work into alphabetical order alongside the author's other works.

[O'Grady, John] Nino Culotta…

Note that the inversion of surname and given name serves only to establish alphabetical position, so that inversion of names other than the first is otiose.

(2) *Title of work, in italics.*

The title of a book or periodical is written in italics (or underscored). It is permitted (but not necessary) to use lower case letters for all words in the title of a book except the first and those which demand capitals (e.g. *The prisoner of Zenda*).

The title of an article in a journal or a collection of papers is written in roman in single quotes, followed by the title and full bibliographical details of the larger work. In any case of ambiguity, the word 'in' should appear between the title of the article and the description of its location.

(3) *Place of publication and year of publication.*

Note that the rules allow quotation of the place and date of the edition used by the author, and do not require the name of the publisher. This is sensible for periodicals, but results in some strange sources of academic wisdom, e.g. Ringwood, Vic.

If the work is unpublished, this should be stated, followed by reference to the collection where the MS is held and was made available.

If the publisher's name is included (and in the case of books this is often more helpful to the reader than the place of publication), it should appear before the place of publication.

(4) *Chapter and page references.*

Although not necessarily required, it is often helpful to quote specific chapter or page references. These should occur right at the end.

> Several of the variations listed above are used in the following:
> Nurks, F. *et al.*, 'An interior view' in E. Rackham (ed.), *Prison life*, unpublished, collection of the University of Knox, 1975, page 59.

To make citations concise, some special abbreviations may be used:

ib. or *ibid.*	(*ibidem*) the same work as the last note.
id.	(*idem*) the same author as in the last note.
	The combination *id. ib.* is sometimes used to stress that both author and work are the same.
op. cit.	(*opus citatum*) the cited work (used to avoid repeating the full detail when a work has been cited earlier: 'Nurks, F. *et al.*, *op. cit.*, p. 60.').
p., pp.	page(s) and f., ff. = following: 'pp. 95f.' means pages 95 and 96; 'pp. 95ff.' means page 95 and several following pages.
passim	here and there (used when a matter is referred to intermittently throughout a work or chapter) as in '*ibid.* Chap. 14, *passim*.'

Some people would like to discourage use of the Latin terms. If they could supply equally concise and clear alternatives, they would probably carry the day. In the meantime, the terms are widely understood and harmless, particularly if the Latin ones are distinguished from the plain text by being italicised, as here.

Strangely, most style guides discourage italicisation of any of them, and even remove their full stops. Without these clues that they are special terms, they are indeed liable to cause trouble. But PhDs are not withheld on this account.

Citations in literature destined for publication

The above notes summarise the academic rules. While it is never wrong to follow them, they should not be taken as compulsory for normal published work, where common sense, aesthetics and the convenience of the reader are much more important.

For example, it is sensible to quote authors' names in the form in which they are best known (e.g. *Conan Doyle* or *Doyle, Conan* rather than *Doyle, C.*).

If the bibliographical details are being collected with a view to copyright clearance and acknowledgement, the citation should include place and date of *first* publication, together with the name of the original publisher. See QUOTATIONS (3).

billabong   See ANABRANCH.

billion   An Australian *billion* is, as RW points out, *a thousand million*. The old British and German usage, which made it *a million million*, is obsolescent in those countries and incorrect elsewhere. It made its final Australian appearance in ACOD₁.

The *million million* sense was rarely used since (as Fowler pointed out) it was useful only in astronomy, though hyper-inflation caused it to appear briefly on German banknotes in 1923, when the *milliard* (their word for *one thousand million*) became small change.

Nowadays, when any self-respecting government can lose a thousand million in the wash, we need an agreed set of terms, and the world is standardising on the US/French convention, which is to use a series of numbers which increase by a factor of 1000: *million, billion, trillion, quadrillion, quintillion*. These match the SI prefixes *mega-, giga-* and *tera-* to indicate large quantities; see SI UNITS.

However, in deference to the old folk, we should be a whisker careful about using *billion* in mixed company without making sure that everybody is on our wavelength.

biological nomenclature   See TAXONOMY.

bi-stable   See ASTABLE and BI-.

bitumen, tar, asphalt   *Bitumen* is the normal Australian word for the surface of a sealed road. In the UK, the term *tarmac* (short for *tar-Macadam*, *Macadam* referring to the inventor of a way of building a road from crushed rock, and *tar* to the material used to seal it) is used in the same way, as is *asphalt* in America. These are generic terms for sealed roads, irrespective of the material actually used.

The term *tarmac* occurs in Australia only to describe the apron beside an airport building on which aircraft stand when loading, and *asphalt* to describe a sealed surface in a school playground, again irrespective of the material actually used.

Historically, the word *tar* was generally applied to materials derived artificially from wood and coal, bitumen and asphalt being naturally-occurring materials now known to be oil derivatives. *Asphalt* was a little used term until it was applied to a lake of such material found in Trinidad.

Today their chemical similarity is understood, and the distinction between them has changed. Australian usage is as follows:
(1) *Bitumen* is the generic term for liquid and solid hydrocarbons, some of which are known elsewhere as *tar*. Thus we say *bitumenised felt* (or use the trade name, *Malthoid*) for the material known elsewhere as *tar paper*.
(2) *Asphalt* is bitumenised concrete, an adopted American usage.
(3) *Tar* is rarely used in Australia in the context of road surfacing, most examples being quotations of overseas usage; but it is used for the same material when it is used in shearing sheds as an antiseptic dressing for wounded sheep.

(4) The 'tarmac' at our airports is most likely to be asphalt, and the 'asphalt' playground to be a bitumen-bonded material akin to tarmac.

The phrase *run out of bitumen* can have two meanings. The sentence *the road ran out of bitumen* means that a sealed road turned into a *gravel road* (see ROAD). The sentence *I ran out of bitumen* means that the car I was driving left the road, an alternative phrase being *I took to the bush*. All these usages will be more or less strange to UK and US listeners and readers.

Purists may object to the normal Australian pronunciation, /bitch-m'n /, but any other sounds alien. On the other hand, *asphalt* should start with /ass/, not /ash/, if only because the latter encourages spelling errors.

black, Black   There was a time when *black* was a racist term for which the non-racist equivalent was *coloured*. Today, *black* is a term of pride, and *coloured*, if used at all in Australia, is used in the South African sense, i.e. for people of South Asian origin.

As with the distinction between *aboriginal* and *Aboriginal*, so *Blacks* should be capitalised when used as a noun.

See also ABORIGINES… and KOORI.

block   Australians buy *blocks* of land for building our houses, where the British buy *plots*, the Americans buy *lots* and the New Zealanders buy *sections*.

This is not to say that the other words do not exist in the language of real estate. The word *plot* is used for very small pieces of real estate in cemeteries, and some people use the American-inspired phrases *parking lot* and *vacant lot*. *Lot* is also the legal term for a parcel of land on a plan of subdivision, and *lot numbers* are sometimes used for addresses in the absence of street numbers.

The precise hierarchy of names which define a given block of land varies from State to State, but the key sequence is as follows:

> *Lot number …*
> *Plan of subdivision number …*
> *Parish of …*
> *County of …*

In some States (e.g. New South Wales) a given title will carry a sequence of 'Plan of subdivision' numbers which shows the historical progression from the first subdivision; in others (e.g. Victoria) a title carries a single subdivision number, the latest one, numbers being assigned consecutively as they are registered, irrespective of location. For all practical purposes, the counties and parishes exist in Australia only in the records of the Registrar of Titles.

The phrase *real estate* is perceived in Britain as an Americanism. The term *realtor* for estate agent is perceived as an Americanism in both Britain and Australia.

blond(e)   There are two words concealed here. The first, *blond*, is a perfectly normal English adjective meaning *fair*, which can be masculine or feminine. The second, *blonde*, is an imported French noun, meaning *a blond female*. Those who use the word *blond* as a noun, meaning a fair male, should consider the situation with *brunette*. Its French male form, *brunet*, exists in ACOD but not in the language, i.e. the imported words apply only to females.

Incidentally, the word *brunette* is properly a diminutive (*une petite brune*). The French, who are suffering from the re-importation of the word, are reminded by Dupré that in English it has connotations of youth and beauty but not size, whereas in French it has connotations of size but neither youth nor beauty.

blossom, bloom   Plants which are *in blossom* will, we hope, shortly produce cherries, apples, etc., whereas we cherish plants which are *in bloom* for their own sake. However, while *pick some flowers* sounds fine, *pick some blooms* smacks of Dame Edna Everage.

bludger   RW warns us to remember that this excellent Australian word originally meant *a pimp*, and should be used with care since, to anyone who knows this fact, it may be unpardonably offensive.

Despite this, a *bludger* was until the 1980s a person who avoided work (a reasonable aim in life), and the term could be used quite safely to describe people who were, for example, failing to help with the washing up. In the 1980s it was applied pejoratively to the unemployed, as in the phrase *dole bludgers*, where the implication is that their unemployment is voluntary.

boats, boatswain   For comments on the language of the seas, see NAUTICAL FOLLIES.

bogy, bogey, bogie   Write *bogy man*, *bogie* on a railway vehicle, and *bogey* at the ninth hole.

ACOD accepts all three as possible spellings for the usage as *a place for swimming*, but in this context AND suggests that *bogey* has the numbers. (The usage is virtually unknown outside New South Wales.)

bona fide   See BARBARIANS (3) and compare LATIN TAGS.

book   It is unlikely that any reader of this work would be so ignorant as to offer a literary manuscript to a *bookmaker*, or call a magazine a *book*. It remains only to remark that, until a century or so ago, it would have been perfectly normal to do both.

boot   An argument for the reduction in the range of meanings of this word will be found under TRUNK, and for the extension of its range under COMPUTER TERMS.

born(e)   If the word is used in any sense other than that of birth, the spelling is always *borne*:

He has borne our griefs and carried our sorrows.
The theory was borne out by the experiments.

In the context of birth, the mother's role is also represented as *borne:*
she has *borne* a child (= carried). The child's role, however, is to be
born: a born fool, born on the Fourth of July.

The *bourne from which no traveller returns* is a totally separate
word, meaning boundary, and survives only in this one quotation.

both   *Both* is a useful flag to warn that what follows is the first item of
two. Two points should be watched:

(1) The words *both* and *and* should be followed by equivalent
words or phrases: *I both drink coffee and tea* should be *I drink both
coffee and tea.* If the sentence starts *I both drink coffee…* the *and* must
be followed by another verb, e.g. *…and clean my teeth in it.*

(2) *Both* is normally used to stress the presence of two items where
only one was expected: *He wore both belt and braces.* The word *both* is
not only superfluous but also misleading in the sentence *There was
a meeting between both the Prime Minister and the Treasurer in Canberra
yesterday,* since *between* demands two parties. In such a sentence,
both can only link two items against a third, e.g. *There was a meeting
between the Archbishop and both the Prime Minister and the Treasurer…,*
implying a meeting between two sides, church and state.

bottleneck   *Bottleneck* is a word which appears to have acquired a
metaphorical usage without having ever been used literally. We
never try, and have never tried, to *get the cork into the bottleneck*; we
get it *into the bottle.* However, *bottleneck* presented a vivid and
attractive image, and has been widely used as a metaphor for *a point
at which flow is restricted.* See METAPHOR.

bourgeois(ie)   In France, the *bourgeoisie* is best translated as *the business community* or, if the speaker is working class, *the bosses.* Karl
Marx, who popularised the terms in English, had both of these
meanings in mind; yet the connotations that have come through to
our language have little to do with business or employer/employee
relations, but are of cultural philistinism, moral orthodoxy, intoler-
ance and intellectual mediocrity.

It does not matter what a word 'really' means provided we all
agree about it, and that is the case with these words: none of us is
bourgeois, but many have bourgeois people living next door.

B.P. (*before the present*)   See DATES, WRITING OF.

brackets   See PUNCTUATION (9).

breakdown, broken down   The problem of *The population of America,
broken down by age and sex* has been widely canvassed without,
unfortunately, teaching us the lesson it contains: that sensible writers and speakers do not use *broken down* as a synonym for *divided,
analysed, listed, sorted, distributed* or *classified.* It is far easier to school

oneself to avoid using *broken down* in these senses than it is to work out in each case whether an ambiguity may arise. A similar list can provide nouns to replace *breakdown* in the statistical sense.

British(ism) Lacking a better term for an important category of word, I use *British* for the version of English spoken in Britain, and *Britishism* (rather than the awkwardly-formed *Briticism*) for a word or expression used by the British in situations where we would use other words or expressions. Thus *lorry* is a Britishism for what we call a *truck*.

(1) Britishisms in Australian English The use of Britishisms should be regarded in just the same way as is the use of AMERICANISMS. We are guilty of using an Americanism if we use an American word when we have a perfectly good one of our own, and the same is so with Britishisms. This may seem obvious, but for the better part of our two centuries of English-speaking history, it has not been the received view. Instead, British English was regarded as the standard, so that there were *Americanisms* (which were substandard) but there could be no such thing as a *Britishism*.

While this attitude is not as prevalent as it was, it remains true that many people who are very critical of what they term Americanisms are not aware of Britishisms as a similar class. The fact that there is no accepted name for them is both a symptom and a cause of the disease.

So long as Britain remained the fountain of English-language culture and development, this was understandable. Today, however, the British comprise less than one fifth of the world's English speakers, and we need a name to describe the variant they speak.

(2) British vs. English *English* is an ambiguous term:

(a) *I am singing a folk song in English* (i.e. not in French or Russian);

(b) *I am singing an English folk song* (i.e. not Scottish or Welsh).

It seems simple enough, two quite separate usages of the same word; but problems arise at the frontier between them. Our university departments of English offer courses in American and Australian Literature, but not in British Literature. And if we wanted unambiguously to exclude Scottish, Welsh and Irish, we would have to say *the Literature of England*.

The British find it hard to appreciate that the problem exists. Fowler, for example, said 'there is no alternative to *British* English if we want to distinguish our idiom from the American', but then proceeded to have a long article on American usage in which the word *British* never occurred, the columns of equivalent terms being headed *American* and *English*. Then, seeking a term to distinguish between words 'adopted in England and Scotland respectively' he came up with *Scotch* and, yet again, *English*. His own great work would more appropriately have been entitled *Modern British Usage*, but that is not a thought he would have seriously entertained.

To him, it was simple: English was the language of England, which some other people – Welsh, American and Nigerian – had the good fortune and good sense to speak. Our perception of English, i.e. as the name of an international language within which American, British and Australian are three major variants, is recognised in theory but not in practice.

The confusion shows not only in the ambiguous use of the word *English*, but also in the definition of *anglicise*. Australians *anglicise* the pronunciation of a foreign word or expression but *Australianise* the pronunciation of an American or British one. American usage is similar. But the British use *anglicise* in both senses. Fowler did not discuss the word, and British dictionaries define anglicise as 'to make English' without apparently recognising that this covers two quite distinct concepts.

More surprisingly, ACOD and Mac do the same.

Briton   Despite an appearance in the chorus of *Rule Britannia* and in the phrase *Ancient Britons*, the word *Briton* does not really exist. As Fowler pointed out, a person cannot call him or herself a Briton 'without a sneaking sense of the ludicrous'. The lack of a word for a British person, an inhabitant of Britain, is the main reason why people make the mistake of using *English* in this sense, much to the distress of the Welsh, the Scots and the Irish.

The word *Britisher* is an obsolete American term, and the other words (*Pom*, *Limey*) tend to be pejorative and are at best informal, if not slang. The word *Brit* (heard in both America and Australia) is less pejorative, but scarcely more formal. It is even used occasionally (and slightly self-consciously) by the British themselves, particularly when they are abroad. However, the only phrase that really works is Mrs Thatcher's: 'We in Great Britain…'.

brunette   See BLOND(E).

bugger   The word is derived from *Bulgarian*, though, just as the citizens of Sodom were not all sodomites, neither are all Bulgarians buggers. The reference is only to the members of a heretical Bulgarian sect, alleged in the Middle Ages to have practiced buggery.

The word came to us through France, where its original sense is almost entirely lost. Thus *Pauvre bougre!* is not the language of the salons, but is well above the gutter. The French even have a female version, *bougresse*, though the intensifier *bougrement* (*C'est bougrement terrible*, cf. it's bloody awful) is now obsolete.

Our similar non-technical use of *bugger* (*Poor bugger!*) can thus be treated as an equivalent of a weak French idiom rather than a weakening of a strong English legal term. But the French have no equivalents for our splendid verbs, *bugger up* and *bugger off*.

building terms   Australian building terminology is rich, reflecting the great resourcefulness shown in the building of early houses. The great distances and lack of roads meant that settlers had to be self-reliant. Even simple items like nails presented a problem, and the use of them was kept to the minimum.

One important material was bark (see BARK). The simplest *bark hut* was effectively a tent formed from a light frame of saplings with sheets of bark leaning against it, in imitation of Aboriginal humpies. At its most sophisticated, it was a framed building with the bark used as a cladding. The bark was lashed to the frame with thongs.

An early alternative to a bark hut was the *slab hut*. The timber was fissile and straight-grained, and slabs of remarkable regularity could be cut with an axe and wedges, and tapered to fit into axe-formed grooves. The slabs of timber were cut to the height of the wall, and slotted vertically into grooved horizontal *soleplates* (or into the ground itself) and held at the top by grooved *roofplates*. In short, there was no need for sawing. If a truer surface was required, the slabs could be smoothed with an *adze*.

Lighter walls were built with *wattle and daub*. A wattle was a mat of saplings, woven into one another like a wicker basket. The trees whose saplings were found most suitable for this were called *wattle trees*, and the name stuck, giving us our popular name for a wide range of acacias.

The daub was generally called *pug*, a word used in Britain for clay prepared for brick making. If good clay was not available, the pug was made from dirt bonded with cow dung. Pug was used not only in wattle and daub construction, but also to caulk the cracks between the timbers in slab huts and as a crude mortar in masonry.

Another primitive wall-building material was the mallee, whose knobbly tuber-like roots were stacked like the boulders of a dry stone wall, and caulked with pug.

Although American log-cabin style construction was sometimes used for chimneys (see below), Australian timber is too heavy and hard to work to be used in the American way. When the phrase *log cabin* is used in Australia, it is either a misnomer or a modern building built of pine logs in imitation of the American style.

Until the arrival of corrugated iron, bark remained the preferred roofing for simple buildings, being easier to apply, and more widely available, than straw or reeds. Purlins were laid along the length of the roof, and the bark placed loosely over them, with the grain running down the slope. Battens were then placed on top of the bark, coinciding with the purlins, and lashed to the purlins through the bark with thongs. Thus a workable roof could be constructed without nails.

Corrugated iron killed the bark roof, and competed successfully with slate as a roofing for urban dwellings and even public buildings, like the splendid dome on the Melbourne Public Library. It was not until the twentieth century (and then only in urban areas) that it was challenged by clay tiles, giving rise to Prime Minister John Grey Gorton's memorable couplet (allegedly produced as his plane approached Mascot airport):

> *What a lotta*
> *Terra cotta.*

Interior walls and ceilings of early houses were often lined with hessian, and newspaper was stuck on with flour-and-water paste to make a smooth, dust-free surface.

Building chimneys was the biggest problem in isolated settlements. In some cases stone was available, which was bonded with pug. In others, mud bricks or even fired bricks were made on the spot. But in many cases chimneys were made of thin logs laid log-cabin style, bonded (and theoretically fireproofed) with pug. Not surprisingly, few of these survive. The arrival of corrugated iron solved this problem: chimneys were made from two sheets of corrugated iron snibbed together down the long sides and then pulled apart down the middle to form a thin, eye-shaped flue. One of the sheets was then cut at the bottom to make the fireplace, the cut-out part being bent up to form the chimney breast.

With improving transport facilities, the need to improvise from local material receded, and Australian rural architecture became a debased replica of urban styles and techniques, which in turn reflected overseas fashions and techniques. Most building timber was imported, giving rise to the terms *baltic* and *oregon* as generics for softwoods from Europe and America respectively. (Use of the term *oregon* puzzles Americans, and distresses lumber dealers who do not hail from Oregon.) Other Australian terms include *k.d.* (for kiln-dried), used as a generic for native hardwood joinery timber, and the words *stump*, *spouting* and *stink pole*. The term *brick veneer* is also indigenous, though the claim that the technique itself was invented here is disputed by the Americans.

The 1950s saw a return to nature and innovation, with great interest in *pisé* (rammed earth) and mud brick. It is a happy thought that Australia leads the world in the rainproofing of unbaked mud brick walls.

bull   In *The Australian Language*, Sidney J. Baker lists *bull, bullo, bulldust* and *bullshit* as all meaning 'nonsense'. But *bull* is not just any old nonsense. It is a particular sort of nonsense talked by the enthusiastic salesmen of used cars and political utopias. If the OED is to be believed, this sense is very old, and the addition of *-shit* relatively recent.

The word can be traced back to at least two possible origins:
First, there is the cock-and-bull story. As W.S. Gilbert put it:

> *What a tale of cock and bull*
> *Of convincing detail full...*

a cock-and-bull story being abbreviated both to *cock* and to *bull*.

Second, there is the stock exchange usage. Today, a *bull* is a respectable individual who places forward orders at current prices on the expectation that prices will rise. But the term arrived two centuries ago to describe a somewhat less respectable person who helped the rise on its way by spreading stories purporting to be inside knowledge, and the story, as well as the storyteller, was known as a *bull*.

Either way, *bull* had originally no direct connection with male cattle (whose erratic behaviour may stem from the fact that they are perpetually drunk on the alcohols produced in their ruminant stomachs), still less with their excrement.

Nevertheless, *bull* is today out of place in polite conversation, being heard as short for *bullshit*. Interestingly, this is less so of the phrase *bull artist*, which is an almost respectable term used in Australia and New Zealand to describe a purveyor of *bull*.

Bulldust, of course, has a perfectly respectable technical usage as the powdery dust which makes driving on some outback roads hazardous, as well as being a more polite variant of *bullshit*.

bungalow   Our dictionaries all report the British sense of this word – as a single-storey house. The Australian usage is, however, different. In Britain, a house is assumed to be of two or more storeys unless otherwise specified, and 'bungalow' is a generic term applicable to all but the most grand single-storey houses. In Australia, a house is assumed to be of one storey unless otherwise specified. Hence there is no need for the generic term. When English visitors say that most Australians live in bungalows, it sounds odd.

It sounds particularly odd in Victoria, where bungalows are habitable sheds in back-yards (alternatively called *sleep-outs* or *granny flats*). In South Australia, the term is used for a particular style of small semi-detached house of the Federation period. There is also the technical use in the term *California bungalow*, which is applied to a popular architectural style of the 1920s, many of which had attic bedrooms and were thus not even single-storey.

burgle, burglarise   See BACK-FORMATION.

burgundy   There is no such wine in France as *burgundy*. The French name, *Bourgogne*, applies to a royal province, and covers a full range of wines and brandies, including the dry white wines of *Chablis*. The region is, however, particularly noted for its red wines, and in Australia the term *burgundy* has come to mean a full-bodied red wine, as distinct from *claret*, a lighter red wine.

In addition, Australian sparkling red wines tend to be known as *sparkling burgundy*, and a class of full-bodied dry white wines as *white burgundy*. See WINE NAMES.

bush   It is best to regard *bush* as two words with the same form. They have a common etymological ancestry, but have reached us by separate routes: the one which means 'a small woody plant' came straight from Britain, while the one associated with the non-urban landscape is a South African anglicisation of the Dutch term *bosch*, meaning heathland.

Australians have made the latter their own. Abroad, it is widely perceived as an Australianism, and for all practical purposes this is now the case. Yet it causes no translation problems: the Australian usage is immediately understood and rapidly adopted by English-speaking visitors. (Compare COUNTRY.)

The word *bush* occurs in many Australian colloquialisms, with a wide variety of connotations: in *bush lawyer*, it implies a degree of homemade wisdom without a degree in law; *bush tucker* means food derived from indigenous flora and fauna, of which white Australians were until recently suspicious or ignorant; *to go bush* means disappear (of people and things); *to take to the bush* used to apply to escaped convicts, but today refers most frequently to car drivers leaving country roads at speed. None of these has, however, entered formal language except as reflections of the popular idiom.

The term *bush band*, however, is the only name for Australia's unique contribution to the world of music, whose instruments include the *bush bass* (a single-stringed instrument with a tea-chest as a resonator) and a *lagerphone* (consisting of beer-bottle tops nailed to a board, which produce a congenial cacophony when the instrument is thumped on the ground).

but, however   In normal usage, *but* is a conjunction linking (but stressing the contrast between) two elements in a single sentence, whereas *however* introduces a new sentence.

(1) *I wanted to go out, but it was raining.*
(2) *I wanted to go out. However, it was raining.*
    Both these usages are fine.
(3) *I wanted to go out, however, it was raining.*
    This is called a *run-on sentence* (see HOWEVER), and loses its writer several brownie points. (There is no problem in speech, as (2) and (3) are virtually indistinguishable.)

Some people assert that we should not start sentences with *but*, the same people arguing that we should not start them with *and*. They are wrong in both cases. The use of a conjunction at the beginning of a sentence is a useful device to stress the sense of the conjunction. Just as

   I had three beers for lunch. And a couple of whiskies...
is a stronger statement than
   I had three beers for lunch and a couple of whiskies...
so it is with *but*:
   He promised not to do it. But he lied.

by and large   See NAUTICAL FOLLIES.

C

C See K.

cab Despite the *Yellow Cab Company, Cabcharge* and sundry other corporate imports from America, the most common Australian word for a car plying for hire is *taxi*. For a discussion of the recent history of the words *cab* and *taxi*, see TAXI.

cable It is not so long since we used to debate whether *cable* (short for *cablegram*) was a nasty Americanism or the preferred Australian word for what the British called a *telegram* or *wire*. (The general consensus was a compromise: that a *cable* came from overseas and a *telegram* was domestic.) Today, thanks to the already obsolete *telex* and the likely-to-survive *fax* (short for *facsimile transmission)*, the cable and its surrounding arguments are now forgotten.

cadre The word is today applied almost exclusively to the key members of left-wing political groups. (It was originally military, meaning the nucleus of permanent officers round whom a regiment would be assembled if the need arose, and is derived from a word meaning *framework*.) It should be pronounced /kah-der/, plural /kah-derz/.

calorie, Calorie One of the great joys of the adoption of SI UNITS was to have been the death of the *calorie* and the *Calorie*, as confusing a pair of units as any: 1 Calorie = 1000 calories. Furthermore, these units had acquired quite unwarranted pejorative connotations in popular writing on nutrition.

Alas, some scientists are still talking about *calories*, though the big-C Calorie has become the *kilocalorie* in scientific circles. They say that they like calories because they are more convenient than joules, though whether the convenience is felt by anyone but themselves is dubious. Meanwhile, the food-faddists have transferred many of the pejorative connotations of the Calorie to the luckless *kilojoule*.

We should remember that a *high-energy food* (a phrase which is often used approvingly, as if it made you spring up like a jack-in-the-box) and a *high-calorie* or *high-kilojoule food* (a phrase which is invariably used pejoratively, meaning the things that make you fat) refer to exactly the same nosh. See RESPIRATION.

candid This word has suffered a terrible decline in its fortunes: it started life as a Latin adjective meaning *gleaming white*, applied to gods and clean clothes. It was a colour beloved of aspiring politicians – hence *candidati*, those dressed in purest white. *Candid* entered English meaning truthful, kindly and compassionate. But then, in the middle of the nineteenth century, it started going downhill. From truthful it became frank, and from frank it became outspoken, so that today a *candid remark* can be assumed to be unpleasant and malicious, and, in diplomacy at least, a *candid discussion* is a euphemism for an exchange of insults. More recently, the *candid camera*, whose truth stemmed from its subjects being *unawares*, has changed to one whose truth stems from its subjects being *unclothed*.

Meanwhile, our *candidates*, like the Roman ones, continue to be whiter than white.

capital losses There is a powerful lobby in Australia which would have us reduce the use of capital letters. For a short time in the early seventies, an extremist section of this lobby, led by Richard Walsh, gained control of a national newspaper, *Nation Review*, and for a time we could read about *the australian government*. This extremism failed to catch on, but a slightly less extreme position is winning some support.

(1) The first argument of the de-capitalists involves the capitalisation in such sentences as *The federal government is in conflict with the states over the law as it applies to the courts and the bar*. The rules are chaotic, and unquestionably time may be wasted trying to decide which words to capitalise. Since the meaning of this sentence is unequivocal, the argument runs, why have any capitals at all?

The lower-case lobby also argues that the capitals do not distinguish themselves in spoken English, and since few problems arise from this fact, few problems would arise if the distinctions were removed from written language.

These arguments are more plausible than practical. The advantages are real and the difficulties can easily be exaggerated. The basic guidelines are clear enough – see CAPITALS, USE OF. It is foolish to throw away such advantages just because they are not available in spoken language, where stress and intonation can replace them.

If a confident and competent writer is in doubt about whether to capitalise a word, it generally means that it does not matter. Time-wasting doubt more often reflects a deeper malaise – a fundamental insecurity about the purpose of the convention; and it is sad to abolish a convention which readers find useful merely because some writers find it difficult. (See SIMPLICITY.)

(2) The National Library of Australia would have us remove the capitals (except the first one) from titles of books, paintings, etc. This advice is designed to help librarians and bibliographers, who can now generate uniform references without the tedium of thought or investigation, which is doubtless a worthy aim. This does not mean, however, that capitalising titles is wrong. If you feel that *Great expectations* looks silly, or that *1066 and all that* is a travesty of the authors' intentions, or that *She's got it* is different from *She's got It*, you cannot be wrong in leaving the capitals in. See CONSISTENCY.

capitals, use of   There are really only two uses for capital letters, plus one freak. The freak is the first person pronoun *I*, where the sole purpose of the capital is to give dignity to an otherwise truncated and miserable little word. It is not capitalised in German (where it is a dialect variant of *ich*) and does indeed looks truncated and miserable: *Muss i' denn, muss i' denn, zum städtele hinaus....*

(1) The first major use of capitals is to indicate **the start of a sentence**. It is also used at the start of direct speech, in quotation marks, even if the speech is part of a larger sentence:

    He smiled and said 'Good morning'.

(2) The second major use is on **labels**. Proper nouns and titles, the names of geographical locations and institutions, the days of the week, the months of the year and trade names must be capitalised: *Mr John Smith, General Pershing, Wagga Wagga, the Faculty of Medicine, Monday, January, Omo. Aboriginals* is a proper noun when applied to Australian Aboriginals (see ABORIGINES...).

    Words formed from proper nouns are also capitalised:

    Australia → Australian, Australianised.

An exception is made, however, in the case of words which have lost (or never had) any connection with their apparent proper-noun origins, as in *french polish, frankfurters, teddy bears, sandwiches, chauvinism* and *boycott*. The conventions here are far from clear, and the variation between and within our dictionaries suggests that it depends on the perception of the writer. Thus Mac capitalises *Americanise* but not *anglicise*, whereas ACOD capitalises both; almost all our lexicographers eat *peach Melba* but *strawberry pavlova*, a distinction which might indicate culinary nationalism but is probably just healthy inconsistency.

(a) Capitals are useful when a title is used to distinguish a specific application from a generic. Thus they may be used to distinguish a monotheistic *God* from a *god* who is a member of a pantheon, or to distinguish His Word from words in general.

    This process can be extended. The sentence

        As I entered the Department I was met by the Professor

    implies that the department is in a university and that the professor is in charge of it; whereas the sentence

        As I entered the department I was met by the professor

    could refer to the Myer shoe department, and the professor could be a fellow customer.

    There is no rule here; it is just a widely understood and useful convention that a capital letter identifies a specific entity which is particularly relevant to the context.

(b) There are certain common nouns which acquire very specific meanings which exist alongside their generic meaning. The term for this is *absolute usage* (see ABSOLUTE (1), which instances the cases of *the pill* and *the bar*). It is often useful to distinguish these with capital letters, and this is customary in many cases: *the Great Powers, the Resistance (movement)*, and so on.

The process is similar to (a) above, but rather than refining a general term into a specific example (as in (a) above), it may actually modify the meaning of a word. Thus, for many writers

I entered the Church

means something quite different from

I entered the church.

I like to use this convention to distinguish *the State of Tasmania* (the political entity) from *the state of Tasmania* (its current condition). This is a convention which can often be useful, especially if two senses of the same word are used in the same passage.

(c) The abbreviations for the points of the compass are always capitalised (e.g. *a SW wind*) though the words north, south, east and west are capitalised only if they are part of a name. So we might write *He lived in the north of South Australia.*

There are in addition abbreviations in SI whose meaning changes with capitalisation: thus mg = milligram, 0.001 gram, while Mg = megagram, 1 000 000 gram; see SI UNITS.

(d) The 'label' convention may be extended to achieve special effects of sense or style. AND cites a splendid example from Anthony Hill's *Bunburyists*: 'Suburban householders may own property. Graziers, however, have Properties.'

These conventions are useful and should be retained. Those who want to abolish them should consider the argument raised in the entry on SIMPLICITY.

car This word, which in the eighteenth century became restricted to poetry (*Phoebus' car*) and the small wagons used in mines, was resurrected in the nineteenth in America as a rail vehicle (see RAILWAYS). However, the most important application of the word belongs to the twentieth century, with the arrival of the *motor car*.

Motor car was first abbreviated to *motor* (a usage which survives in the phrases *motor racing* and *the motor industry* and in the Cockney dialect). The term *autocar* was not a popular success, though it survived for many years as the title of a magazine. The Americans tried *gas buggy* for a time, but that, too, bit the dust. A much more successful term was *automobile*, with its adjective *automotive* and proposed abbreviation *mobile*. An optimistic oil company even thought automobile fuel might be called *mobile-gas*, and promptly registered a variant on this, *Mobilgas*, as a trademark. As it was, the more common abbreviation of automobile turned out to be *auto*. However, *car* was the term which really caught on, despite its obvious ambiguity.

In Britain, the term *car* appears in railway language only in American-inspired items: *dining car, sleeping car* and *saloon car*, and in sundry imitations, e.g. *buffet car*. It is never used for rail freight vehicles, and *tramcar* was abbreviated to *tram*. Thus, if used without qualification, a *car* will be an automobile, and the word *automobile* is a museum piece surviving only in proper names: *Automobile Association*, etc.

In America, where the word *car* is used for rail vehicles of many types (e.g. *freight cars, passenger cars, streetcars*) and is therefore highly ambiguous, *automobile* retains more of its early currency. The motor industry is known as the *automotive industry*, but *motor* survives in the names of the automobile producers: *General Motors*, etc.

In Australia, usage of *car* on rails is in general like the British, but with two odd exceptions:

(1) The first Melbourne trams were American 'cable cars', and they came complete with a vocabulary which included signs saying CARS STOP HERE. This traditional wording survived well into the 1980s, but the signs now say TRAMS STOP HERE.

(2) Although the normal words for rail passenger vehicles are *carriages* and *coaches*, as in Britain, the vehicles become *cars* for the purposes of numbering on tickets; and the vehicles for passengers' impedimenta, in Britain called *luggage vans* or (improperly) *guard's vans*, tend to be, as in America, *baggage cars*.

When it comes to road vehicles, the term *car* is as dominant in Australia as it is in Britain. Nevertheless, we clearly associate the word *motor* very strongly with the car. We do not need to explain that the *Motor Registration Branch* does not register electric motors. Indeed, the Yellow Page entries about car-related topics are all under *M* for *Motor* except *Carports*. There is even the relatively recent coinage, *Motorail*. In most usages (including the phrase *motor vehicles*) trucks and buses are included, but *motorists* is restricted to the drivers of cars.

Automobile survives in Australia, as in Britain, largely in fossilised form, e.g. in such names as the *Automobile Chamber of Commerce* and the various *Automobile Clubs*. But the words *auto* and *automotive* appear in the names of many companies supplying parts and service for cars. It seems that a *car* becomes a *motor* or an *auto* when it needs attention.

See MOTORING TERMS.

carillon   Despite Fowler's recommendation that the word be fully anglicised, /karrill-on/, Australians call the gadget in the middle of Lake Burley Griffin a /k'rill-y'n/. ACOD gives Fowler's pronunciation a mention, but agrees with Mac in giving /k'rill-y'n/ top billing.

case   The word *case* has a dozen strong senses and dozens of weak ones, a recipe for ambiguity and misunderstanding. The result is a medico-legal nightmare of ambiguity, which is discussed in (1). The use as a technical term of grammar is then dealt with in section (2).

(1) Meaning   The problems arise when two or more of the strong senses collide, and is made worse if there are some weak senses scattered among them. (See STRONG....) The following is not a quotation, but our newspapers frequently contain passages which are only fractionally less absurd:

> *In many cases* (= often) the police find that a murder *case* (= investigation) becomes manslaughter if the judge hearing the *case* (= trial) thinks that the police have no *case* (= valid legal argument). *In any case* (= whether this is so or not)), if the defendant proves to be a mental *case* (= patient), the doctor in charge of his *case* (= the medical condition of the patient) should be called to give evidence, *in case of* (= to avoid) subsequent appeal for mistrial.

The careful writer avoids using idioms containing a weak usage of the word *case* in any passage likely to involve a strong usage of the word. This presents few problems. The passage above gives clues to other phrases with equal effect.

(2) Grammar   When Dame Edna Everage says 'Scuse I', her error is one of *case*. She has used the *subjective case*, *I*, where she should have used the *objective case*, *me*.

The problem with understanding case is that there is precious little of it left in English. Thus, in the sentence

> *The cat bit the dog because the canaries bit the cat*

we know which animals did the biting and which got bitten only by their *position* in the sentence. In an inflected language, subject and objects are distinguishable by the form of the words themselves (see INFLECTION). In English, case inflection is really only evident in our pronouns:

> *She bit him because they bit her.*

Here, *she* and *they* are in the subjective case, and *him* and *her* in the objective case.

We start with a section on the nomenclature, and then deal with five problems related to case.

(a) The names   The cases have been given names which are supposed to show how they are used. Alternative names, derived from names assigned to them in Latin, are used by some writers, and are given in brackets in the list below:

(1) The *subjective (nominative)* is used for the subjects of main verbs: '*He* came in'.

(2) The *objective (accusative)* is used for direct objects: 'She shot *him*.'

(3) The *possessive (genitive)* case survives in the absolute possessive forms, e.g. *hers* as in 'This book is hers' (see ABSOLUTE (2)) and in the possessive *s* which causes us so much apostrophe trouble: see APOSTROPHE (2) and (3). (The words *my, your, our, her*, etc., are not nouns in the possessive case but are adjectives which happen to imply possession.)

(4) In addition, other languages may have a *dative*, which implies *(given) to*, an *ablative*, which implies *from* or *by*, a *vocative*, used in addressing people, and a *locative*, denoting position; and see (e).

English uses the objective form for all these except the vocative, for which it uses the subjective form, e.g.: *O thou of little faith.*

(b) Does English have a dative case? If we examine sentence patterns with the verb *to give*, we can see two different ways of distinguishing the thing which is given (called the *direct object*) from the recipient of the gift (the *indirect object)*:

(1) *Give*	*the dog*	*a bone*
(2) *Give*	*a bone*	*the dog*
(3) *Give*	*a bone*	*to the dog*

In pattern (1), we know from the word order who gets what, and this is why we know immediately that there is something wrong in (2). In the language of formal grammar, the indirect object must come directly after the verb. Example (3) shows that, if the indirect object is separated from the verb, we have to reinforce the 'dative' sense with the word dative preposition, 'to'.

(c) I/me People who would never say *Me should try again* may say *You and me should try again*, and likewise (perhaps through having been corrected for this 'mistake') people who would never say *He gave it to I* will say *He gave it to you and I.*

This example demonstrates a quick way to decide whether it should be *I* or *me* (and the similar problems: *he* or *him, she* or *her, we* or *us, they* or *them*). You simply ask yourself what you would say if there were just one pronoun; then put the other back in. Thus, if we would say *It is too difficult for me*, we also say *It is too difficult for you and me.*

Similarly, if you are in doubt about

> We /us *Australians must try harder, or it will be difficult for* we/us *Australians to survive*

remove the word *Australians* and the solution becomes clear:

> *We must try harder, or it will be difficult for us to survive.*

If, of course, you cannot hear anything wrong with *...it will be difficult for we to survive*, then you have a problem. The best answer is to use the accusative forms, *me/him/her/us/them*, in both cases. The reason is that while saying *You and me should try again* is not good usage, it is less offensive than *It is too difficult for Fred and I*. But it is better still to get it right.

For what it is worth, in Afrikaans, a derivative of Dutch, a similar problem has been solved as suggested above, but in their case the equivalent of *we* has disappeared. Thus they say:

> *Ons moet harder probeer* (literally, *Us must try harder*).

(d) Who/whom The substitution test has to be rather more sophisticated in the case of *who/whom*, and *whom* is on the way out, so that to say, or even write, Who *are you talking about?* is no longer the unforgivable crime it once was. Note that here it is the *objective* form that is on the way out.

(e) It's me/It is I   Some people, including Fowler, assert that *it is me* is incorrect, arguing that, being the complement rather than the object of the verb *to be*, the subjective case is required. But *It's me* has a perfectly sound pedigree, being the English equivalent of the French *C'est moi*, where *moi* is described as being an *emphatic* or *demonstrative* case. This explanation has the great merit of giving respectability to what we are going to say anyway.

caste   Despite a number of examples from writers who should be respected, the spelling *caste* is best used only for the Indian social orders. In all other senses, *cast* is preferred.

casual(ty)   The story of these words is very similar to that of accident/al and incident/al – see INCIDENT…. Etymologically, they are closely related (though that is an irrelevancy which need not distract us).

   Casual originally meant 'chance'. We use it this way in the sentence *He was chosen to fill a casual vacancy in the Senate.* More often, however, it is used with the connotation 'not serious', as in *a casual remark* and *a casual acquaintance*, or 'informal' as in *casual clothes.*

   Meanwhile, in hospitals, the word *casual* was used to describe the business which came in unexpectedly off the street, as opposed to patients who were admitted to the wards. The patients themselves were *casualties*, and the section of the hospital dealing with them called the *casualty department*. As most were the injured, the word came to mean *a person who had been injured*, and this led to its use in warfare to mean people who had been wounded. From there, it was a small step to talk of *casualties of the recession*, etc. Meanwhile, however, the term has been abandoned by our hospitals: see HOSPI-TAL.

catalog(ue)   The vestigial tail is on its way out, the omission being encouraged by RW. The dictionaries still call the shorter form an Americanism, and we certainly think of it as one, but OED cites a use of it in sixteenth century England.

   It is normal in the context of computers (as in *analog*) and cannot be wrong elsewhere. Other words, e.g. *epilogue* and *monologue*, are resisting amputation.

Catch 22   This is such an antique form of sophistry that it is surprising that it had no name until Joseph Heller gave it one. Readers will probably be aware of his version: an airman must fly bombing missions unless he has a certificate of insanity; but you have to be insane to fly, so anyone who does not wish to fly is evidently sane, and therefore cannot get a certificate of insanity.

   Older versions of the same concept occur in conundrums: in a village where the barber shaves everyone who does not shave himself, who shaves the barber? when did you stop beating your grandmother? if God created everything, who created God?

Wittgenstein provided the basis for an answer: if a question can be put, he said, an answer can be found. Thus an unanswerable question will on analysis be found to contain undefined or self-contradictory terms; but this, of course, makes his solution the ultimate Catch 22.

caterpillar   See TRADEMARKS.

catholic, Catholic   The original sense, *universal*, more or less survives in our phrase *he has catholic tastes*. If he has *Catholic* tastes, this is a very different matter.

The word is not, however, the peculiar property of a single Christian denomination. The Anglican communion is among several which call themselves *catholic* in their creeds, and whose adherents may resent the use of the term *Catholic* as if it were peculiar to the church of Rome.

However, the *Roman Church* and the *Church of Rome* are often used (and heard) as offensive titles. The body's official title is *The Catholic Church*, and in any official reference this should be used, just as the correct registered name of any business concern should be used, even if it seems inappropriate.

If there is any doubt, the compromise title *The Roman Catholic Church* and the initials *RC* are recommended as terms which are precise and rarely cause offence. The adherents can be called Roman Catholics rather than just Catholics.

caveat   See LEGAL LATIN.

Celtic   Do we spell it thus, or Keltic? And do we pronounce it /keltic/ or /seltic/?

If we adopt the *K* spelling (offered as a second option by Mac), we must adopt the *K* pronunciation. But the K spelling is rare, perhaps because, as Fowler said, it 'serves no useful purpose' (an argument which might, however, be used of a great many variations in spelling).

If we are to believe the Celtic Club (and what better authority could we ask for?), we should also use the *K* pronunciation except in the context of football clubs. Perhaps because the name crops up most commonly in the context of football, non-Celts tend to say /seltic/ rather than /keltic/.

centi-   See SI UNITS.

centrifugal, centripetal   Fowler told us to put the stress on the second syllable, but most of us give the words double stress, on the first and third syllables, as reported by ACOD. For a comment on Fowler's general argument, see STRESS.

certain   There is a potential ambiguity with this word.
(1) In the phrase *I am certain that…*, *certain* can only mean 'sure', and this is the only sense of the adverb, *certainly*.
(2) In the sentence *Certain procedures have to be followed in registering a car*, it means 'fixed' or 'specified', implying that the specification is important.
(3) In the sentence *There may be certain people who disagree*, it is virtually synonymous with *some*, i.e. it implies that the specification is unimportant.

The problem arises from (2) and (3). The sentence *Sausages must contain a certain amount of meat* can either indicate sense (2) – that the amount is specified, or sense (3) – that the amount is unspecified. It will generally be taken to be vague, so writers who wish to convey sense (2) should choose another word.

chablis   In France, this name is restricted to wines produced in the environs of Chablis, in the province of Burgundy. In Australia, it is a generic name, less used than it once was, for dry white wine in French-style bottles. See WINE NAMES.

chairperson   See SEXIST LANGUAGE (2(a)).

chameleon   The *ch* is pronounced *k* as in *Christ*, not *sh* as in *champagne* or *ch* as in *church*.

champagne   In France, the name *champagne* can be applied only to the products of Champagne, an old royal province centred on the city of Troyes. These include a full range of wines and brandies. However, the name is for all practical purposes synonymous with the district's most famous product, a sparkling white or pink wine whose sparkle is generated spontaneously in the bottle. Wines produced in other regions of France by the same process are labelled *méthode Champenoise*.

In Australia and America, the name is not protected, and it is commonly (though decreasingly) applied as a generic to all wines produced by this method. As a result, Australians and Americans tend to call the genuine article *French Champagne*.

This is not so in Britain, where champagne is assumed to be French unless otherwise stated. Thus they speak of *Spanish* and *Russian champagne*, but to speak of *French champagne* in Britain would be a tautology.

In the UK, champagne remains synonymous with the good life; in Australia, it has become somewhat déclassé. See CHARDONNAY SOCIALIST.

chaperon   Although a chaperon is always female, and although the word is pronounced to rhyme with *bone*, it does not have an *e* on the end.

chardonnay socialist   This phrase is David Williamson's, and is the exact equivalent of UK author John Mortimer's *champagne socialist*. This is not, as John Mortimer believed, through the absence of good champagne in Australia, but through the fact, accurately observed and reported by Williamson, that the socialists in question take their wine seriously, and would not consider drinking anything so frivolous as champagne, French or otherwise.

charisma   The word entered our language through the New Testament, where it refers to the divine gift which enables *evangelists* (= bringers of good news) to inspire and convince their hearers. It was a specialist term of theology until taken into the language of sociology by Max Weber, to describe the power of politicians to spellbind their followers. It entered the common language in this sense in the 1960 US presidential campaign, when it was applied to the popular appeal of John F. Kennedy. The adjectival form *charismatic* achieved popular currency at the same time.

   The original theological meaning of the words has recently been revived by the *Charismatic Churches*, which believe in the direct divine inspiration of their members, and particularly of their leaders.

Chauvinism/Chauvinist   Properly, we should write these words with a capital letter (cf. *Marxism*) and use them only in the context of *extreme patriotism*. They were used only thus until the adoption by the feminist movement of the 1960s of the term *male chauvinists* (without a capital) to describe males who obstructed the advancement and recognition of women. So closely is the term now associated with feminism that *chauvinist* is as likely as not to mean *misogynist*, even if the word *male* is not used.

check, cheque, checkers, chess   All these words have a common origin. A board game arrived in medieval Europe complete with Arabic vocabulary, its key piece being the Arabic *Shah* = king. This, through various corruptions, gave the name of the game (*chess*), the warning given by players when the king is under attack (*check*), and the pattern of squares on the board (a *checker*).

   The 'warning' sense then became used in wide contexts, giving us our family of words in which *check* connotes obstruction.

   Meanwhile, medieval accountants used a huge checker as a form of spreadsheet, piling money and account books on the squares. In English, this arrived with a modified spelling, giving us *exchequer* and, much later, *cheque*. It is thus not derived from the French *chèque*, which is a borrowing from English.

   The Americans spell the word *check*, and etymologically this cannot be faulted. Nevertheless, the British spellings have merit: they distinguish the two now quite separate senses. More importantly, this is the established convention in Australia.

The most curious development is the American use of *checkers* as their name for the game we know as *draughts*. What is curious is not the name – *checkers* is more picturesque than *draughts* – but that any change occurred. The vocabulary of games is generally unchanging, transmitted as it is through that most conservative of media, the language of children. But *checkers* supplanted *draughts* within fifty years of the War of Independence.

chemical   This word should not be used as a synonym for *poison* or *additive*. All matter is composed of chemicals.

In the context of food, a *poison* is a substance which, in sufficient concentration, is toxic, i.e. will cause damage to a living organism. Small quantities of many of these substances are essential for the maintenance of life. Conversely, a very large number of highly desirable substances are toxic if taken in sufficient doses.

An *additive* is a very hazy concept. Substances which are present in the ingredients of one food may be additives in another, e.g. salt. The term is particularly applied, however, to artificial flavourings, colourings and preservatives. Writers should decide (and make clear) whether they are using the term in reference to all non-basic ingredients or only the ones which they consider offensive.

chemical nomenclature   The following notes, together with those found under ATOM and ORGANIC CHEMISTRY, are designed for writers whose use of chemical names is casual, but who want to get them right, and does no more than pose the questions. Writers needing all the answers should consult the relevant guides to nomenclature issued by IUPAC (the International Union of Physics and Chemistry).

The major problem arises from the fact that many substances are known by several names, and the question is one of choice between these options:

Non-systematic name(s)	Systematic name	Notes
salt, common salt	sodium chloride	1,2
ferric oxide	iron(III) oxide	3,4
chloroform	trichloromethane	1,2
oil of vitriol, sulphuric acid	sulfuric(VI) acid	3,4
marsh gas, natural gas	methane	2,4,5
olefine	alkene	4
(ethyl) alcohol	ethanol	1,2
alcohol (as a generic)	alkanol	2

(1) If the substance is being used as a reagent in a chemical experiment, the systematic name should be used.

(2) It is perverse to use the systematic name if a substance is not being used as a reagent and is readily and unequivocally identified by a non-systematic name, whether that name is a common-language one or a survivor from an earlier technical vocabularly. Thus, if the context is human diet, there can be no objection to talking about *salt*. The term *common salt* should be avoided: if *salt* is ambiguous in the context, *sodium chloride* should be used.

Similarly, *alcohol* can be used for *ethanol* if the topic is clearly intoxicating drinks, although it is also a generic term covering a range of substances of which ethanol is one. The term *alkanol*, which might have resolved this ambiguity, has not caught on.

The name used should match the name most likely to be found on the labels: thus, in contexts other than chemical reactions and analyses, *baking powder, Vitamin C* and *Epsom salts* may be more appropriate than any chemical name, systematic or otherwise.

(3) The use of the suffixes *-ic* and *-ous* to distinguish oxidation states is frowned on by IUPAC. They recommend *iron* for both *ferric* and *ferrous*, the oxidation state (if relevant) being indicated in roman numerals: *iron (III) oxide*. Similarly, they recommend *tin* for *stannic/stannous* and *copper* for *cupric/cuprous*. The spelling *sulfur* is recommended for *sulphur*, and *sulfuric* for both radicals.

(4) Writers should remember that the name which is familiar and friendly to them is not necessarily the one which will be most familiar and friendly to their readers. They would not be tempted to speak of *oil of vitriol*, as this was already obsolete when they were at school, but they feel that *olefine* and *ferric oxide* are somehow more friendly then *alkene* and *iron oxide*, and certainly more so than *iron (III) oxide*. This view may be shared by middle-aged academics and industrial chemists, but will not necessarily be shared by younger readers – at least until they get to university and have to humour their middle-aged mentors.

(5) If translating from one register to another, equivalence will depend on context. For example, marsh gas, fire damp and natural gas are all largely composed of methane, but the names are in no sense interchangeable.

chimera   Say /*kye-meera*/ rather than /*tchimmera*/.

chlor(o)-   The original pronunciation, /*clawr*/, survives in names for chemical substances, e.g. *chloro-benzene* and *chlorine*. In general vocabulary, the *o* can be short: *chlorophyll* (/*klorra-fill*/), *chloroform* (/*klorra-form*/) and even *chlorinated* (/*klorry-naytid*/, though ACOD reports /*klawry-naytid*/).

choir   *In quires and places where they sing, here followeth the anthem.* Thus *The Book of Common Prayer*, and thus was the word always spelt until two hundred years ago, when the spelling *choir* was introduced and swept all before it. They even spell it *Choir* in the Mormon Tabernacle. The reason for the change is said to have been a mistaken impression that it was related to *chorus*.

chord, cord   This is a bit of a mix-up. The Greek word *chordé*, a string, gave us the geometric *chord*, and the *h* would be etymologically correct in the common language word *cord*, but is today omitted: so we write *vocal cords* and *spinal cord*.

Meanwhile, the words *accord*, *concord* and *discord*, based on the Latin *cor* = heart (see HEART), gave us the musical *chord*, where the *h* is thus etymologically wrong but is always inserted.

Christian name   See GIVEN NAME.

Christmas   The plural is *Christmases*, despite the fact that the word is derived from *Christ Mass*.

chronic   See MEDICAL MIST.

cine-, kine-   These two prefixes are versions of the same Greek root, which connotes *motion*, but have established separate identities, *cine-* being preferred in the 'motion picture' context (*cinema*) and *kine-* in physics (*kinetics*). Thus the spelling *kinema* looks quaint and *cinetics* is unknown.

For a discussion of the origin of this curiosity, see K.

citation   A citation is a reference to a document. A citation may be merely to draw the work to the reader's attention or to indicate the source from which the author has derived some information. The rules of the PhD thesis require that authors quote the source of all facts.

A citation may be given entirely within the text, but more often comprises a mark in the text referring the reader to a footnote or endnote giving details of the work cited. There are two acceptable conventions for referencing citations: (1) by author-and-date, and (2) by sequential reference numbers.

(1) Author-and-date   The convention looks like this:
        As was noted by Nurks (1988), the price of fish rose steeply.
There will then be a bibliography with a listing of the relevant works, alphabetically by author and then numerically by date. If Nurks publishes more than one work in the year, they will be distinguished with letters:
        The matter is discussed in Nurks (1988B).
This procedure saves space where a limited number of references are cited many times, as the details of each work need be given only once. However, if page references are required, they have to be given in text: *Nurks (1988, p.15).*

It also looks rather pompous when the work cited is one of the author's own works, though few academic writers seem to be afraid of a spot of pomposity.

(2) Sequential references   These may be given by numbers on the line in brackets (7) or by superiors[7]. The citations may appear as footnotes or as endnotes – see FOOTNOTES (2).

Unlike the author-and-date scheme, where several references to the same work will all point to the same line in a bibliography, sequential references will normally be specific to the single reference point, so that page numbers can be included in the citation.

For the way in which a cited work should be described, see BIBLIOGRAPHIES.

city Australia follows Britain in having two meanings for this word: (a) a large town, and (b) a local government region (municipality or shire) which has been proclaimed a City. Capital letters can be used to distinguish the technical sense from the general one. Thus *There are seven Cities, one of which is the City of Sydney, within the city of Sydney.*

In practice, the risk of serious ambiguity is negligible. Within our larger cities the word CITY on a signboard, and in the sentence *I work in the city*, will be understood unequivocally as meaning the CBD, the central business district.

claret This word is the corruption of the French *clairet*, a little-used term for a light red wine. It is pure chance that it was this word which became adopted in Britain as the generic term for such wines, and in particular for the red wines of Bordeaux.

In Australia, it reverted to meaning a light red wine, a sense in which it is still used. This is not as objectionable as the use of terms with European *regional* connotations (e.g. BURGUNDY, CHABLIS and MOSELLE), but most Australian winemakers now identify their light red wines in other ways, e.g. by the variety of grape from which they are made. (See WINE NAMES.)

classic(al) The word *classic* originally meant *of the highest class* and was applied in particular to the best writers and their work. Thus our uses of the term in such phrases as *a classic wine* and, when describing a book, *an Australian classic* are both respectable, referring to quality, not style or antiquity.

Classical, by contrast, refers to antiquity and style but not quality, and has almost as many meanings as it has applications:

(1) *Classical history* and *Classical studies* can be assumed to refer to the affairs of the sundry Mediterranean states from c. 600 B.C. to A.D. 400, and particularly those of Athens in the fifth century B.C. and of Rome in the first century B.C.

(2) In architecture *classical* is a term indicating the use of features of Greek and Roman architecture, particularly columns and colonnades, pediments and arches. In this sense, classical features can be seen in Australia in buildings of all periods. More specifically, it refers to an architecture which sought perfection of symmetry and proportion, which flourished in Europe in the late eighteenth century.

(3) In music, *classical* properly applies to the music of the late eighteenth and early nineteenth centuries, of which the supreme exponent was Beethoven. The music was noted for discipline and the adherence to conventions of form and structure. In this sense it is in contrast to the Baroque period which preceded it and the Romantic movement which followed it. However, the term is also used very broadly for the kind of music played by orchestras, as opposed to that which is played by bands.

(4) In such labels as *classical physics* and *classical dynamics*, the term refers largely to the world view of Sir Isaac Newton, before the publication of Einstein's theory of relativity and its subsequent development in quantum theory.

Note that classical physics is in no way outdated. It is merely a special case of relativistic physics in which the velocities involved are infinitesimally small compared with the velocity of light. Since almost all our daily activities go on at a modest pace, classical physics remains the relevant version for all practical purposes, even for civil and mechanical engineers.

clause   The term has two relevant applications:

(1) Legal   In a legal contract, a *clause* is simply a term of the agreement, which may be of any length and complexity, though it is usual to apply it to a paragraph dealing with a specific topic, together with any riders to it. Typically, the clauses are numbered in arabic numerals and will include riders numbered alphabetically. The same goes for the *clauses* in laws.

(2) Grammar   In grammar, a clause may be defined as *a string of words containing a subject and predicate*, which may be either a *main* (= *principal clause)* or a *subordinate clause*. Thus

> *I open the door and the flies swarm in*

is a sentence containing two principal clauses linked by the conjunction *and*. The sentence

> *The dog which lives under the house eats what we put out for the cat if it gets the chance*

can be analysed as

> *The* (specified) *dog eats* (something) (somehow)

the brackets identifying three *subordinate clauses* acting as an adjective, a noun and an adverb respectively.

Clauses can thus be identified by the presence of finite verbs. If there is no finite verb, it is called a *phrase*. They are generally linked to the sentence by conjunctions, but these may be omitted, as in the sentence *The dog I love ate my porridge.*

Some people prefer other definitions. Fowler made it narrower, eschewing the phase *main clause* and using the term only for subordinate clauses, and RW makes it broader, making it include strings of words containing a participle rather than a finite verb. No one will go to gaol either way, but the definition requiring a finite verb appears to be useful. What it is useful *for* is another question.

The following are examples of the main types of subordinate clause recognised in formal English grammar:

(a) Adverbial clauses	Name
I went *because I was told to.*	A *causal clause.*
I went *although I was told not to.*	A *concessional clause.*
I will go *if I am told to.*	A *conditional clause.* See IF… CLAUSES.
I was *so* tired *that I couldn't go.*	A *consecutive clause.* See THAT (CONJUNCTION).
I went *so that I might see for myself.*	A *final clause* or *clause of purpose.* See THAT (CONJUNCTION).
I went *when I was told.*	A *temporal clause* or *clause of time.*
I went *where I was told.*	A *locative clause* or *clause of place.*
(b) Adjectival clauses	
Here is the book *which you wanted.*	A *relative clause.* See THAT, WHICH.
(c) Noun clauses	
I said *that I would go.*	This is called *indirect speech.* See SPEECH….
I asked *whether I should go.*	This is called an *indirect question.* See QUESTIONS….

Clayton's   This advertising triumph (see TRADEMARKS) arose from the slogan *Clayton's – the drink you have when you are not having a drink.* It entered our language immediately, in such phrases as *a Clayton's budget* (a budget presented with all the usual mystique, but having no significant content). This was such a useful expression that it seemed destined to survive, but it is less often heard than it once was.

cliché   I once heard two non-Anglophone publishers at the Frankfurt Book Fair discussing a deal in the thick guttural English which is the idiolect of the Fair. The conversation concluded: 'So, it is agreed. Ve vill haf our own text, but use your clichés.'

This usage recalls the original French meaning: a printing plate, and in particular the etched metal block used in the days of letterpress printing to reproduce pictures, and hence (at least in Frankfurter English) the colour separations which perform the same function today.

In normal English, a *cliché* is an expression or idea which was once upon a time novel and exciting, but has since been repeated so many times that it has lost impact. Thus, for the committed clichémonger, every end is *bitter*, every swoop is *fell*, every relationship is *meaningful*, and every situation is *ongoing*. They are both for and against farmers, being happy that it is raining, since rain is *good for the crops*, but unhappy about the slaughter of animals, since *they*

are only human, aren't they? Proverbs are the quintessential clichés:
Waste not want not, as I always say.

The above list includes examples of the main classes of cliché.
They have in common the fact that they are reflex responses, and
therein lies the problem. Talking is itself a set of acquired reflexes –
we are not generally aware of the mental processes which turn our
thoughts into words, still less the ones which arrange the words
according to the rules of grammar. The difference is that in original
speech the reflex response reproduces what the speaker is thinking
at that moment, while in cliché the reflex response reproduces what
the speaker has thought or heard on previous occasions. In particular, one word may trigger another as surely as lightning follows
thunder.

Happily, clichés are only used by people other than ourselves.
Our own thoughts and expressions are invariably novel and vivid –
though we have been known to repeat some of our more pleasing
ones.

climate, weather   The difference between the two is well known: the
weather is what is happening today, and the *climate* is a general
statement about the permanent weather patterns in any given area.

It is thus odd that we talk about the *economic climate*, etc. If a
meteorological cliché is wanted, it would better to call it the *economic weather*.

clique   A *clique*, like a CLICHÉ, is about them rather than us. In theory,
it just means an informal closed group in society. In practice, it is
pejorative: nobody admits to belonging to a clique, but we are all
aware of cliques to which we do not belong.

co(-)   To hyphenate or not to hyphenate? That is the question.
  (1) The more common the word, the less the need for a hyphen,
      particularly if the pronunciation is unequivocal. Hyphenation
      looks odd in *coalition, coerce, cohabit, cohere* and *coincide.*
  (2) The more rare the word, the greater the need for the hyphen,
      particularly if its absence causes pronunciation problems or
      confuses meanings. Thus for my money the following are better
      with hyphens: *co-religionist, co-pilot*, and especially *co-worker.*
      Cooperate is acceptable without a hyphen, but its abbreviated
      form, *co-op*, needs one. *Co-respondent* must have one, if only to
      stress that the writer does not mean *correspondent.*
  (3) There is a tendency (associated with the general move against
      hyphenation) to omit hyphens in doubtful cases. This is regret-
      table. The presence of a hyphen, even in common words like *co-
      operate*, cannot hurt anybody, and many people who would be
      stopped in their tracks by, for example, *coheir* have no trouble
      with *co-heir.* Swim with me against the tide, therefore, and insert
      hyphens in any doubtful cases. See HYPHENATION (1).

coccyx   Those who use this word say /*cock-six*/. It means the bone at the bottom end of the spine, the last vestige of our ancestors' tails.

cockatoo   The use of this word in reference to SELECTORS goes back to the 1850s, but precisely which characteristics of the cockatoo they were supposed to share was in doubt even then. AND quotes two good stories, both from the 1850s: one was that they, like cockatoos, 'scrape the outsides of the trees for grub', the other was that cockatoos settled on their newly-sown paddocks in such abundance that the selectors appeared to be growing cockatoos rather than grain. Whatever the truth, the usage of the term is well established: today it is invariably abbreviated to *cocky*, and it can be a noun or an adjective (i.e. a cocky = a cocky farmer); it no longer has any connection with *selectors*, but it is generally a contemptuous term, with connotations of poverty and backwardness.

AND also reports a use of the term *cockatoo* meaning a *desperado*, the term being derived from Cockatoo Island, in Sydney Harbour, which (before the naval gentlemen moved in to mend their boats) was home to the most intractable convicts. This usage is obsolete.

cohesion   *Cohesion* is a useful word applied to a concept otherwise known more laboriously as *contextual implication*. It is applied to the process by which each word in a sentence may have its meaning clarified by the presence of the others. Jonathan Anderson offered a particularly good example in the incomplete sentence
    … but he also did one of a street in Sydney.
Although the words in this fragment do not tell us what it is about, almost every reader correctly identifies it as referring to an artist who did not generally paint urban landscapes.

Cohesion is thus the process by which we sort out which of many possible meanings of a word is applicable in a given sentence, which pronunciation to apply when we read words which have more than one (e.g. *lead*), and which word is being said when we hear one which has several spellings (e.g. *hear/here*).

It is also the process by which we may understand speakers' intentions even if they have used the wrong words or left a sentence incomplete; many types of verbal joke (e.g. the pun and the *double entendre*) depend on it; a cliché is a phrase which is so cohesive that it can be predicted before it is uttered; and, conversely, much of the pleasure we get from great writing stems from its use of words which are not obviously cohesive, and therefore surprise us.

One of the principal problems in developing mechanical translation devices is to replicate the power of the human brain in this respect. When the first supercomputer laughs at a new joke, but groans if it has heard it before, the human race will be doomed.

collaboration, collusion, conspiracy   These three words have related meanings, and are distinguished by the extent of the criminality involved. *Collaboration* will normally be legal and moral, but was used pejoratively of the citizens of German-occupied countries who worked with the Germans in the Second World War, and has been used since in similar circumstances. *Collusion* is occasionally respectable, but generally means that two people who are overtly in competition agree not to compete with one another. *Conspiracy* is always pejorative, and is the legal term for collaboration in an evil enterprise.

collective nouns   See PLURAL DILEMMAS (9).

colloquialisms   See IDIOM....

collusion   See COLLABORATION....

colon   The colon (:) is the punctuation mark used to express the thought 'as follows'. See PUNCTUATION (4).

comma   The comma (,) is the lightest, most used and most abused of the punctuation marks. See PUNCTUATION (6).

commence   It is hard to explain why the word *commence* is so unacceptable. Saxonists will say that it is because it is a redundant non-Saxon synonym for *start* or *begin*, but, if so, why do we not object to *finish* as an equally redundant synonym for *end*?

Whatever the cause, however, the effect is clear: *commence* is a word which in Australia is used by policepersons giving evidence in court. See PLODDERY.

common, vulgar   The ancestors of these words had overlapping meanings in Latin, which survive in our words as *communicate* and *divulge*, both of which mean, in some sense, 'to share with the public'. The *Vulgate* is the name for the Latin translation of the New Testament, produced for the proletariat of the time.

Common has two meanings in mathematics, one of which it shares with *vulgar*: it means 'shared' in *common denominator* and 'ordinary' as in *common* or *vulgar fraction*.

The words have quite distinct meanings in linguistics, *common language* meaning either *ordinary* or *shared* language, and *vulgar language* implying *obscenity*.

In everyday use, they describe standards of taste or behaviour which the speaker dislikes or despises. In traditional British usage, *common* was essentially about breeding and *vulgar* was about ostentation. In Australia, breeding is not an issue (we are all happy to be tolerably ill-bred); *common* is about ostentation and *vulgar* is about chatter, i.e. risqué.

Commonwealth, Australian, Federal   These words must be used with care.

In Australia, *Commonwealth* is most likely to mean *Australian*, as in the phrase *Commonwealth Government*. The phrase *Australian*

Government was briefly used during the Whitlam administration, but became associated with moves towards centralism, and the incoming Fraser administration reverted to the term *Commonwealth Government* as a political gesture to the States. Meanwhile, the phrase *Federal Government* has no official status, but is useful if one is wanting to stress the distinction between State and Commonwealth governments.

The moment one leaves the country, however, the only term which will be understood is *Australian Government*.

In Britain, *Commonwealth* refers either to the administration of Oliver Cromwell or to the present *British Commonwealth*. The British take little pride in either. In America, *Commonwealth* is a neutral archaic term associated with Massachusetts.

The word *Federal* is used in the USA almost exactly as we use it, and is associated with the same range of issues, e.g. the division of powers. However, this usage is not understood in Britain, where Australian States are widely assumed to have a status comparable to that of the British counties. Thus, if the topic is one in which the powers of Canberra and Westminster are similar, as in the sentence *Federal cabinet last night agreed to declare war on New Zealand*, all is well; but a sentence like *The Federal Government's new Companies Act is not applicable in the States* is likely to cause puzzlement.

compact   In normal usage, the verb (= *to squash*) and the verb-adjective (= *squashed*) have stress on the second syllable, while stress on the first syllable is used for the noun meaning *an agreement* or *a container for face powder*. However, the times are changing, and the adjective is increasingly being stressed on the first syllable. This might be believed to be an American influence (*compact cars*, *compact disks*) but it seems that the *Compact Edition of the Oxford English Dictionary* has gone the same way.

comparative chaos   Let us first define the topic and the issues. Most adjectives can exist in *comparative* and *superlative* forms, the following being examples of the three most common ways in which they are constructed:
    (a) by adding *-er* and *-est* to the end of the adjective;
    (b) by adding *more* and *most* before the adjective;
    (c) by using special formations.
Here are examples of these three:

	Example	*Comparative*	*Superlative*
(a)	tall	taller	tallest
(b)	objectionable	more objectionable	most objectionable
(c)	good	better	best

Multiple forms may have different connotations:

out	outer *or* utter	outermost *or* uttermost
late	later *or* latter	latest, last *or* lattermost

The points that arise are: (1) Can something be *more unique*? That is, are there *absolute adjectives* which cannot have comparative and superlative forms? (2) If there are only two people, can one be *the tallest*? (3) How do we decide how to form comparatives and superlatives? (4) What about double superlatives?

(1) Absolutes   Since *unique* means 'the only one of its kind', how many would there be if something were more unique? Other words to which similar arguments are applied include mathematical absolutes like *perfect, complete, infinite, minimum, adjacent, square* and *circular*, and a large number of common language terms which are either applicable or not, as *bankrupt, pregnant, dead* (of living things) and *bad* (of eggs). Words to which the argument could be applied, but is not, include *empty* and *full*.

So much for logic. In practice, however, these terms often carry a less-than-absolute meaning. Thus *unique* is used to mean 'hitherto unknown' or even 'very rare'. Thus the *predicament of Gough Whitlam in 1975 was unique in Australian history*. However: *Whitlam's predicament was unique, but less unique than some people thought. While he was the only Australian Prime Minister to be removed from office by the monarch's representative, a similar situation had occurred in State politics....* If this sentence is admitted, then one could say *Whitlam's predicament would have been more unique had it not been for the Lang precedent*. In short, we are arguing that the uniqueness depended on a number of factors, and the greater the number of unique factors the *more unique* the total experience.

The superlative in such cases will often represent a retreat. If we say *Anne's drawing was perfect*, the sense is clear. If we say *Anne's drawing was the most perfect*, the implication is that it fell *short* of perfection, but was more *nearly* perfect than Tom's, Dick's and Harry's.

In sum: while the comparatives and superlatives of absolute adjectives are strictly meaningless and hence should be avoided, they are in practice commonly used. They may, however, have unexpected connotations, and should be used with care.

(2) The best of two...?   It is often claimed that, if we are talking about (say) the heights of several people, one can be the *tallest*, but if there are only two, we must say *taller* rather than *tallest*.

If we know that there are only two, use of the word *taller* has the elegance of giving this extra information, and there are times when this elegance has value, as in the Bible, where we read of *the greater light to rule the day, and the lesser light to rule the night*, excluding the possibility of a third light. However, to make a fetish of this distinction is today (and probably always was) an absurd pedantry. If asked for the biggest apple we can find, we do not come back empty handed if we only find two apples, on the grounds that there was no biggest one.

However, while we may sometimes talk about *the biggest of two*, we cannot talk about *the bigger of three*. This problem rarely arises except in the case of the comparatives *former* and *latter*. These terms cannot be used when more than two options are being discussed.

(3) Choice of forms   In general, the longer and less common the word, the more likely it is to form its comparative and superlative with *more* and *most*. In particular, the adjectival suffixes *-al, -able, -tive, -ous*, and *-ic* resist the addition of *-er* and *-est*, and participles even more so: *more sinned against than sinning*. The suffix *-er* is an odd one: while *eagerer* sounds wrong (so that we might think that *-erer* is resisted) we do say *cleverer*. *Well-intentioned* can accept *better-intentioned* and *best-intentioned*, but most compound adjectives take *more* and *most*.

(4) Double comparatives (e.g. *more better*) are said to be characteristic of childish and uneducated speech, and the same goes for double superlatives, despite Shakespeare's *this was the most unkindest cut of all*. He would not have got away with it with today's critics. There is also a good argument that there is an implied comparative in *preferable*, so that *more preferable* is a double comparative, too.

For a note on baseless comparisons, see COMPARATIVELY… below.

comparatively/relatively   These words are often used by the insecure to avoid commitment (compare ARGUABLE…). There are so many already ruined words available for this task that it seems like vandalism to destroy useful words in such a cause.

The words should be used only when a comparison or relativity is being presented. *The Ford is a comparatively/relatively common make of car in Australia* implies that the comparison is with other makes, and states that the comparison is based on Australia. Thus it is a sound use of the words. But what of *It is comparatively easy to pluck chooks*? Is the comparison with doing something else to chooks, or with plucking some other birds, or what?

The same argument applies to all comparatives. To say that a product is cheaper, cleaner, and stronger is a useful refuge for advertising copywriters, because in the absence of a specified basis for the comparison it is meaningless and hence cannot be proved false. (See PERCENTAGES for other examples of *baseless comparison*.)

complement(ary)/compliment(ary)   Those who confuse these two words may find the mnemonic 'I get the complIments' useful. Alternatively, remember that the senses of complEment are all related in some way to complEteness.

When saying the words in an ambiguous context, a light stress on the middle syllable can help to ensure that the listener identifies which word you are saying.

Complement (grammar)   In the sentence 'She is *a solicitor*', the phrase in italics is called the *complement* of the verb *to be*. It *completes* the pattern following a *copulative verb*. The complement can also be an adjective: 'The people's flag is *deepest red*'. See CASE (2), COPULA-TIVE VERBS and BE.

computer terms   As with any jargon, the jargon of personal computers produces some strange sentences. Do you reboot when a stack collides with a heap? Can you mount the finder when running under windows?

Popular computer jargon offers us surprisingly few totally new words. The words in the above sentences are all (with the possible exception of *reboot*) simple enough; it is the specialist sense of them that is obscure. Up to a point this is inevitable: new ideas need new words. It is the non-technical statements which need to be watched. Editors should remember that the awfulness of much computer writing, like that of legal writing, stems from the incompetence of the writers, not from the demands of the subject matter.

Computer jargon has many acronyms: *RAM* (Random Access Memory), *ROM* (Read Only Memory) and *Modem* (Modulator–Demodulator). There are also joke acronyms like *Wysiwyg* (What You See Is What You Get). But even these are made up from largely non-technical components. One of the very few totally new words is *bit*, which is nothing to do with its common-language homonym, but was coined from *bi*nary dig*it*.

Computer jargon is also unusual in the extent to which metaphors it drew from the outside world are rapidly moving back out again with their connotations refreshed. Thus the computer *bug* and *viruses* are metaphors from public health, but are now going back into circulation as double metaphors: when people say they have a bug in their TV set, it is a metaphor from computers, not from public health. The same goes for *down-time* and *up-time*, *networks* and *interfaces*, even *programs*, *hardware* and *software*. None of these words and phrases was a creation of the world of computers, but all of them have been changed significantly by it.

Perhaps the most useful one is *real time*. It is the computer equivalent of While-U-Wait shoe repairs. Early computers took a long time to process data, so the programs separated the input and processing functions, like the repair shop where they take your shoes and tell you to come back in a week. Modern computers process data so fast that they can be programmed to update all records in *real time*, that is, while the new information is being entered. At least, that is the theory. Such delay as occurs is termed *response time*, the equivalent of the time spent standing on one leg while the While-U-Wait man battles with your broken shoe.

concern   *Concern* has a double meaning: *I am concerned about the project* (= worried) and *I am concerned in the project* (= involved).   Careful writers will make sure that their usage is not ambiguous, as it might be in *The crowd was shouting for blood, but I was not concerned*.

conjunction   For a discussion of the meaning of the term and its basic uses, see GRAMMAR (3(g)). For more about clauses and phrases introduced by conjunctions (e.g. *if, because, that, although*) see CLAUSE (2) and PHRASE, and for the specific types of clause, see IF… CLAUSES (3) and THAT (CONJUNCTION).

conjuror   The normal pronunciation starts /*kun*/, but /*kon*/ is frequently heard and appears to be gaining ground. This is an example of say-as-you-write.

connotation/denotation   David Cunningham tells me that the students of hotel management at Dandenong TAFE are not allowed to utter the word *gravy*. There is no ban on the substance which the word *denotes*; but the word is felt to carry the wrong *connotations*. So they serve the bangers and mash with *jus* (except that *bangers* and *mash* are also unlikely to be on the menu).

Connotation often has to do with stereotype. When the headline reads 'Mother and stepmother in court brawl' we know whose side we are on. It is all very unfair, but mothers have been getting a better press than stepmothers for at least 2000 years. Mothers turn apples into delicious home-made pies. Stepmothers poison them.

A third class of connotation is closely related to ALLUSION. A classic example was the change that came over the word *appeasement* when it was used to describe the attempts to reach an understanding with Hitler in the late 1930s. Until that time, it had been a perfectly respectable word with connotations of reconciliation. From that moment on, its connotations were of giving in to a bully. (Ultimately, of course, such connotations become the denotations of the word.)

Connotation is also evident in some sets of near-synonyms. The novelist, for example, has access to a number of near-synonyms for 'shouted' in the sentence *'Come here,' he shouted*. They include *yelled, screamed, roared, shrieked, screeched, bawled*. Each of these only *denotes* different noises (e.g. *roared* implies high volume, *shrieked* implies high pitch) but also may *connote* different states of mind (*yell* and *scream* imply rudeness, *roar* implies anger, etc.). This is discussed under SYNONYM….

Connotation can be indicated in very subtle ways, an example being given in the entry under ACADEMIC. Here there are two possible connotations, but the sentence patterns will resolve any resulting ambiguity.

As all the above examples show, connotation can be an economical way of getting over a rich message, and is therefore one of the resources of great writers. But, as with ALLUSION, it depends on a common culture. Dictionaries have difficulty dealing with connotation, and foreigners who have learnt English from books can often produce very strange expressions, like the sign on the huge water clock in Beijing's Palace Museum, which reads DO NOT SCALE. No dictionary could predict this (and every other) unidiomatic usage, or explain why they sound so peculiar. See MEANING.

conservative, conservation   In common language, the phrase *conservation of energy* denotes measures to reduce the demand for and waste of fuel energy; in the physical sciences, it means the natural law which states that, in physical and chemical reactions, energy can be transformed but not destroyed: the *Law of Conservation of Energy*.

This can result in ambiguity, as both senses can be used within a single piece of writing. Generally, it is the physicists' usage which causes the problems; if readers may not be aware of it, the distinction should be explained (or some other phrases used).

Cutting across this is the political sense of the word, a *conservative* being an adherent of an ideology concerned with the preservation of the political and economic status quo, *conservatism*, whose antonym was *radicalism*. This usage is never likely to collide with the physicists' usage, but can cause some awkwardness in writing about social issues, in which political *conservatives* may be in conflict with *conservationists*. Those who use both terms a great deal distinguish them without difficulty; but the general reading public may not.

consistency   The craving for consistency is a modern disease. We are told that Shakespeare spelt his own name in different ways according to his mood; but we require that our authors and editors be consistent, and chastise them if they are not.

There is nothing wrong with consistency. Indeed, it is in many respects admirable that a book should be at least internally consistent.

However, remembering the fates of the businesses which go to the wall with their account books in perfect order, one must always remember that literary consistency is a means to an end – clarity – not an end in itself. The most disastrous writers and editors are those who are so concerned with ensuring the *consistency* of the composition that they fail to recognise that its content is nonsense.

See EDITOR (1).

conspiracy   See COLLABORATION....

construction   In grammar, a *construction* is like the plans of a building. The plans show how the various rooms will fit together, but do not say how each room will be furnished and decorated. Just as we cannot install a bath in a room where the plans do not allow for plumbing, so we cannot put a noun in a position in a construction which calls for an adverb.

By the same analogy, a false construction in grammar is like a set of plans in which a room is left with no door to it, or the position of the lift-well changes from floor to floor.

contemporary   There is a nasty ambiguity in this word. If we say *the book contains a contemporary analysis of the federation debate*, it could mean *contemporary with the book* or *contemporary with the debate*. There is no magic way of avoiding this ambiguity: both senses are correct and useful. But writers and speakers should make sure that their meaning is clear.

Contemporary was also adopted as a label for sundry popular artistic styles (especially in architecture and decor) of the 1950s and 1960s. If used in this sense, it is best given a capital letter, as should the word *modern* when used as a label for styles of the 1920s and 1930s. See MODERN.

continu(al/ous)   By one of those happy conventions which make English so subtle, *continuous* is today agreed to mean 'all the time' while *continual* means 'repeatedly'. Thus if you are interrupted *continually*, you get little work done; if *continuously*, none at all.

It is useful and has the blessing of Fowler, so let us preserve it, and not mention that *continual* has also been used as a synonym of *continuous* by great writers of all periods.

contone   This is printers' jargon for *continuous tone*, e.g. an ordinary photograph or bromide print, as opposed to a *halftone*, in which the same image is reduced to an array of dots of varying size. See HALFTONE.

controversial   When applied to books, films, etc., this word should be used only to indicate that controversy has actually arisen. It should not be used as a synonym for 'containing taboo material'.

convict   Too much has been written in Australia about *convicts*, and perhaps too little about the word *convict*. We start with the common language word *convince*. If a barrister convinces a jury of something, they *come to a conviction* about the truth of the case. The conviction is then handed, via the judge, to the defendant, who *gets the conviction*, is *convicted* and becomes a *convict*. But for this, Australian history might have been very different.

co(-)op(erate)   See CO(-).

copulative verbs   This phrase describes verbs which are followed by *complements* rather than *objects*, the term indicating that the verb does little more than link subject and complement:

I   *am/grow/become*   older but no wiser.

Of these, the only one which is always copulative is *to be*. The others may or may not be. The verb *to grow*, for example, can be:

(a) *transitive*   I am growing mushrooms.

(b) *intransitive*   The mushrooms are growing in my cellar.

or (c) *copulative*   The mushrooms are growing bigger.

copy preparation   See KEYBOARDING.

copyright   This is not the right place to offer comprehensive guidance on the law of copyright. However, the following points are designed to cover the key questions which are most often asked about literary copyright, 'literary' simply meaning words rather than music or pictures.

(1) Questions asked by authors:

(a) How is copyright established? Copyrights (unlike patent rights and trademarks) do not have to be registered. They come into existence automatically when a literary work is compiled. This protection continues until the work is published; after that, protection is claimed by the insertion of a copyright note in the form

> © *Fred Nurks 1988*

The copyright note does not itself give protection, nor does its absence automatically invalidate a claim to copyright. However, in the event of dispute, it shifts the burden of proof in the author's favour, and may be of considerable importance in establishing copyright overseas.

The law also requires that copies of a published work be lodged with the National Library of Australia and the State Library in the State in which the work is published (the latter being the sole relic of the pre-Federation copyright laws), but failure to do this does not prejudice copyright; you just get fined.

(b) Who owns copyright? The simple answer to this question is 'the author'. The only major exception is works compiled by an employee as part of his or her conditions of employment, in which case the employer owns it.

The exception to this exception is that, in the case of the employees of newspapers and magazines, the employer will own only the newspaper, magazine and broadcasting rights. In the case of free-lance writers, the 'employer' is presumed to have bought only the rights nominated in the contract (or, if there is no contract, only the first publication rights).

Copyright, like any other property, can be given away, bequeathed, sold, licensed or leased.

(c) What about co-authors? A co-authored book is defined in law as one in which the authorship is fully collaborative, so that no individual contributions can be identified, and the work is then covered by a single copyright jointly owned by those authors. If there is no agreement to this effect, however, authors may be able to claim copyright on their own contibutions even if the division of responsibility is not indicated in the published edition. It is therefore vital that authors who believe they are working collaboratively should have an agreement with their colleagues to that effect.

Conversely, if it is intended that the various components belong to specific authors, the split should be clearly indicated in the contract and in the printed edition.

(d) What constitutes publication? Publication is generally understood to occur when copies are made available to members of the general public, and in most cases this still holds. In particular, it covers all routine cases where a work by an Australian author is first published in Australia. Having said that, however, the definition varies according to the purpose; see PUBLISH....

Under the 1991 revisions to the *Copyright Act* (see below, (j) on territorial copyright), the establishment of Australian *territorial* copyright on books published overseas depends on their being published in Australia within thirty days of publication overseas. This made a more rigorous definition of 'publication' necessary.

In the new law, publication is defined as having occurred when 'reproductions of the work ... have been supplied (whether by sale or otherwise) to the public', but it then goes on to say that publication in a quantity which is 'colourable and is not intended to satisfy the reasonable requirement of the public shall be disregarded'. The full practical implications of the second clause, designed to inhibit the access of foreign authors to Australian territorial copyright, are not yet clear. In particular, the word 'colourable' sounds like the subject for a toast at a legal banquet.

(e) What is a work? The key point is that a literary work is a string of words long enough to eliminate any reasonable chance that someone else would spontaneously write the same string of words. This leads to the next question:

(f) Can a title be copyright? The simple answer is 'No', because it is so short that there is every chance that someone else could write the same string of words spontaneously. An unusual title may be registerable as a trademark, but the best legal protection of a title is in the common law rules about 'passing off' and the sections of the *Trade Practices Act* dealing with deceptive conduct, both of which could be successfully invoked if a book were published with the same title as an existing book *with the object of deceiving the public.*

(g) Can facts be copyright? Again, the simple answer is 'No'; but their literary form can be. However, the borderline is sometimes ill-defined. It is said that the compilers of four-figure maths tables always used to insert a deliberate error to provide immediate evidence of plagiarism, the intriguing implication being that while the truth is not protected, falsehoods are.

(h) How long does copyright last? The duration of author's copyright under current Australian law is fifty years from the death of the author, or, in the case of posthumously published works, from the date of publication.

(i) What action should I take to protect my copyright once the book is published? In general, copyright in this country is respected, so that commercial printing and distribution of pirate editions is virtually unknown. This is fortunate, as an individual author can do very little against poachers operating in places where copyright is regarded as fair game.

The best action an author can take, therefore, is to do everything to promote public respect for copyright. This is one of the aims of the Australian Copyright Council, and support for the Council through membership of the Australian Society of Authors is thus strongly recommended.

(j) What is Territorial Copyright? Copyright can be split into parts in many ways, one of which is *by territory*. The normal territorial copyright agreement gives a publisher an exclusive right to publish the book within a specified area, and may also grant non-exclusive rights to other areas. Conversely, the publisher is not permitted to sell in any area which is not mentioned, this being the subject of another territorial copyright agreement.

The issue has acquired special relevance because of the recent changes in the Australian law. The important change is that Australian territorial copyright is no longer recognised in law unless the work is published in Australia either before or within thirty days of publication elsewhere.

This need not concern Australian authors who are first published in Australia provided that other countries do not retaliate, which seems unlikely. However, those who are first published abroad should make sure that the book is published in Australia within the prescribed time limit. If this is not done, the Australian territorial copyright is permanently extinguished and it may be difficult to get anybody to promote the book here, since they have no way of ensuring that they reap the benefit if the promotion is successful.

(2) Questions from authors wishing to quote from copyright works:

(a) How can one tell if a work is copyright? Just as a car would be assumed to belong to somebody unless it were clearly derelict, literary work should be assumed to be copyright unless there is clear evidence to the contrary.

The work of authors who died more than fifty years ago, however, can be assumed to be out of copyright unless it was first published posthumously.

(b) What about folk works? 'Folk' works are commonly believed to be different from literary works, having sprung spontaneously from the soil. This view is patently absurd. Words simply do not come together in sensible ways without intervention by specific human beings, called authors, and people using recent 'folk' work should take particular care to ensure that no injustice is occurring. For some interesting examples, see MORAL RIGHTS.

(c) What about 'copyright in the edition'? If the published edition is less than twenty-five years old, there may also be a copyright in the typographical arrangement on the page, known as the *copyright in the edition,* and owned by the publisher. Thus, for example, although Shakespeare's works are out of copyright, the publisher of a newly-reset edition is protected for twenty-five years against another publisher or author reproducing the typeset image without permission. The most important relevance of copyright in the edition is in the matter of photocopying.

(d) What about unpublished work? It is worth remembering that, because unpublished works belong automatically to their authors, writers who quote from diaries and letters should be certain that they have the permission of the writers. This advice is particularly relevant to educational writers quoting from student work.

(e) How do I make sure that the quotations are accurate and correctly attributed? This important practical issue is covered in the entry under QUOTATIONS (2). The reason for it is discussed under MORAL RIGHTS.

(f) What is fair dealing? The fair dealing provisions of the *Copyright Act* are designed to allow you to quote a small part of somebody else's work in a work of your own. It is designed for academic and research works and news reports, but may also be relevant for quotations in novels. A simple test is the following: if you quote a passage instead of writing one of your own (e.g. to save time, or because the other author has done it better than you can) this is likely to be a breach of copyright unless you have the written permission of the copyright owner.

Quoting in reviews is slightly different. A reviewer may quote short passages from the work under review without permission, since the whole purpose of the exercise would be defeated if permission had to be sought. But they must be 'fair', i.e. be relevant to the specific point you are making.

(g) What about letters? The copyright in a letter belongs to the author, but the letter itself belongs to the recipient. The recipient cannot prevent publication, but may be able to control access to the original document.

(h) What about pictures, etc.? Copyright covers a wide range of non-literary forms, including music, pictures and computer programs, and the copyright belongs to the artist *unless* a specific arrangement to the contrary has been made. The sale of the work itself does not normally imply any transfer of copyright. However, the current owner of the work may, as in the case of letters, control access to it.

Authors asking galleries for permission to reproduce pictures should therefore be careful to distinguish between copyright clearance and the service fees charged for access and for supplying photographs. If an author enters into an agreement with the gallery to pay such fees, then the normal law of contract requires that the fees be paid; but payment of such fees may not discharge the author's liabilities under copyright law. Authors should be careful about paying large sums without a written confirmation of what they are buying.

Similarly, in the case of items like newspaper cartoons, the newspaper may have bought only first publication or syndication rights. Again, enquiries are essential. The point made under QUOTATIONS (3) may be useful.

(i) What about material published in a form other than print-on-paper? There are complex questions here. The rules are constantly changing to keep up with the development of new technologies, and the current Australian law contains a badly formulated clause which has muddied the waters. The intention of the law, however, is clear: to give intellectual property the same copyright protection irrespective of the means of storing and displaying it.

(3) Questions from the copyright user – the reader who would like to take a photocopy of a work:
(a) How can one tell if a work is copyright? In general the advice is as given in (2(a)) , but the question of *copyright in the edition* (2(c)) is obviously more pressing, since all photocopies are potentially breaches of it.

(b) What are the rules about copying for private study? The general principle underlying the law is that if the copying is done as an alternative to buying the book, it is a breach of copyright. However, it is understood that a researcher may need to copy a few pages from a book in the library so that work can continue at home. Various amounts, e.g. 10% of any given work, are specified in the Act.

If the general principle underlying the law is borne in mind, it is unlikely that the user will get into trouble.

(c) What about the special provisions for copying by educational institutions? The statutory licence provisions of the *Copyright Act* were designed to permit teachers to make multiple copies of small bodies of copyright material required *immediately for a special purpose*. The previous law required teachers to negotiate permissions and fees with each copyright owner, which effectively made it impossible for teachers to respond to the needs of the moment.

As with copying for private study, statutory licence is not intended to provide an alternative to buying books. If the making of the photocopies reduces the demand for authorised editions, whether of the books copied or of other books, the spirit of the law is certainly being flouted and the letter of the law may well be. Furthermore, copyright owners no longer feel reluctant to sue, as they did under the old draconian law, and tend to win every case they fight. Full details of the rules can be obtained from Copyright Agency Limited, the body which acts as an agent for copyright owners in this matter.

In addition, statutory licences do not affect the authors' 'moral rights' of *integrity* (that the quoted matter should not be edited so as to distort their message) and of *attribution* (that all copies should carry their name and the title of the work from which the extract is taken). See MORAL RIGHTS.

correctness   Correctness in speech and written language is elusive. It changes over time, as can be seen in consecutive editions of the same dictionary; and it changes as one travels from place to place, as can be seen by comparing British, American and Australian dictionaries. It also depends on the perception of the lexicographers, as can be seen by comparing any two dictionaries which purport to cover the language at the same point in time and space.

This gives rise to the widely-held view that correctness does not really exist, and hence that the chase for it is futile. In extreme cases, people assert that there is no such thing as a grammatical or spelling *error*, and that the items which are called *errors* are merely variant usages, which are just as respectable as any other. They point out that grammars and dictionaries only *describe* what is the case; they cannot *prescribe* what *should* be the case.

At the other end of the scale, there are those who believe implicitly in the existence of correctness. They often assert that they once saw it, when they were at school, learning the rules of English grammar and the Grade 5 speller, or that it lives in the pages of their favourite dictionary.

There are problems with both these extreme positions.

Those who adopt the permissive approach are forgetting the prime purpose of language, which is communication. Communication is at its best when we all use the same conventions of spelling, pronunciation, grammar, punctuation and meaning. We can object to labelling these conventions as 'correct' without denying that it is sensible and desirable to follow them. In particular, they are very useful to those who are learning English as a second language.

However, those who believe in absolute standards of correctness have a logical problem. Whatever the truth is today, they will have to make some agonising decisions tomorrow. They will get reports of the day's crop of rebellious new words, new usages and new connotations. By definition these are all 'incorrect', since they were not in accordance with the standards when they were uttered. If purists refuse to accept the new material, the standard is on its way to becoming a fossil, a description of a language no one speaks any more. But if they accept the new material, they are challenging the standards, requiring retrospective blessing for 'incorrect' usages. This is the denial of authority. (See AUTHORITY.)

Most people recognise that, while there is no such thing as absolute correctness, there are absolute errors. If I type *hte* for *the*, it is simply bad typing. I am not claiming it as a legitimate variation, and however often it is repeated it will not become one. And if I type *medecine*, for example, I might think that this was the normal spelling, but change my mind when somebody showed me how it was spelt in the dictionary; in which case, once again, my spelling would be regarded as a simple mistake.

But what if I insisted that this is how I want to spell the word, despite the dictionary? If I was an eight-year-old in primary school, I would be regarded as naughty. But if I was an internationally acclaimed novelist, my spelling might well find its way into the dictionaries as a MUTANT SPELLING, and this could start a fashion which might well take over. The Australian spelling of the word might then become *medecine*, in contrast to the spelling in Britain and America.

Indeed, the main differences between British and American spelling arose in an even cruder way. They can be traced to the first edition of Webster's Dictionary, in which Noah Webster set out to popularise some spelling reforms which he liked. If nobody had followed his lead, the dictionary would have become a curiosity, a doomed attempt by a lunatic to change people's habits overnight, a futile challenge to the irresistible authority of Samuel Johnson. But as it happened it worked.

Where does this leave us?

Provided we are a bit careful, there is no problem in talking about 'correctness'.

(1) If we are talking about spelling, 'correct' can be taken to mean 'in accordance with the dictionaries'. It is then not a value judgement but a verifiable statement of fact. If two dictionaries differ (as they often will), we can take our pick.

(2) If we are talking about grammar and pronunciation, 'correct' can be taken to mean 'in accordance with the grammar and pronunciation of the people we know whose speech we ad-mire'. This may sound a trivial definition, but in fact it removes the biggest obstacle to the hunt for correct speech, which is a feeling that it exists a long way away, among people one has never met and is never likely to meet. So long as this is the case, it hardly seems worth trying to attain correctness; but if one fastens on some specific accessible people, correctness itself becomes accessible.

(3) If we are talking about meaning, 'correct' can be taken to mean 'in accordance with the sense which the readers/hearers will extract from what I write/say'. Again, this may sound trivial, but it stresses the point that the purpose of correctness is communi-cation. Of course there will be occasions, many of them, when we use words which other people do not understand. Some-times we explain them, or they become self-explanatory through the context, which is how people expand their vocabulary. But

essentially the content of whatever we say or write is what other people can get out of it, not what we have put in, and writing that is incomprehensible has failed. If it has failed its essential purpose, how can it possibly be 'correct'? Conversely, if everybody has understood us, how can we have been 'incorrect'?

(4) In some specific contexts (notably the rules for air traffic controllers and SI, the international system of scientific units) the term 'correct' has added force and meaning: safety may depend on strict adherence to the rules.

So much for an analysis of correctness; yet it explains only part of what we mean when we speak of correct English. Most of us would say that we recognise correct English when we hear it, and we do not need to check with a dictionary, a pronunciation guide or a grammarian to assure ourselves that this is the case. We know right from wrong, in English usage as in personal morality.

The process is rather like recognising familiar faces in a crowd: we know we can do it, even if we are not at all sure how we do it. Sometimes we see people who seem familiar yet are not quite as we remembered them, and we have to check to see whether they are friends or not. But most of the time we simply recognise the familiar faces quickly and accurately; and we do the same with correct English.

correspondent/co-respondent   The latter should always be hyphenated, and pronounced /*koe-respondent*/, to avoid confusion with the former. See CO, CO-.

councillors/counsellors   The French may be blamed for this disaster. It all started with two Latin words, *concilium* and *consilium*, with quite separate etymologies and sounds. The French took these two words, and converted them into *councile* and *counseil*, both pronounced with an /s/ sound. They handed them over to the English in this form.

In French, the *u* dropped out again, and while *conseil* is still a common word in French, *concile* has become restricted to a very limited role, as a technical term for a meeting of bishops to discuss theological questions, though it survives in the derived verb *concilier*.

In English, by contrast, both words survived, as *council* and *counsel*, as well as the derived verb *conciliate*.

The distinction can be summarised:

> *Councillors* sit on *councils* and *conciliate*
> *Counsellors* give *counsel* (= advice)

It remains only to add that, in America, courtroom lawyers are sometimes known (and addressed) as *counsellors*. In Australia, like Britain, they are known as *barristers*, referred to in Court as *Counsel* (both singular and collective plural), addressed by colleagues as *My Learned Friend* and addressed by judges as *Mister So-and-So*. In embassies, counsellors are what used to be called *attachés*. The possibilities of misunderstanding are considerable.

country It is not that the British word *country* does not exist in Australian English, but the contexts in which it exists are specific: we have *country towns* and *country roads*, and a doctor may have a *country practice*, but we rarely use *country* as a general term for non-urban areas as the British do. The word for that is BUSH. So far from being non-urban, *country* is used in Australia for urbanised aspects of the bush environment.

It is also used in mines to describe a region which is being worked. Thus if a miner runs into *dangerous country*, it implies gas pockets and unstable geological structures, not crocodiles.

court *See you in Court* implies legal action; *See you at Court* implies a royal levée; *See you on court* implies tennis.

cray(fish)/lobster The zoological distinctions are complex enough, but the gastronomic almost as difficult. The French, whose language is the most helpful on this sort of question, distinguish four: the *homard*, a big red one with outsize front claws, caught in the north Atlantic; the *langouste*, a similar but more prickly animal without claws, caught in southern hemisphere waters; the *écrevisse*, a freshwater animal otherwise similar to (but much smaller than) the *langouste*; and the *crévette*, a miniature *langouste*.

In English:

Homard is unequivocally *lobster*. There are no *homards* in Australian waters.

Langouste is variously known as *spiny lobster, rock lobster, sea crayfish* and, in Australia, *crayfish, cray* or *lobster*. It is best called a *cray*, to stress that it is not pretending to be a lobster and is not a fish. Happily, this is also the name by which it is best known. (*Crawfish* is an Americanism.)

Écrevisse is *freshwater crayfish*; in Australia, *yabby*. The word *crayfish* is a phonetic rendering of this word – hence its fishy ending.

Crévette covers a multitude of small crustaceans. In Australia, the variety of these is great, and the names we give them connote size: *shrimp* for the smallest, then *prawn* and *king prawn*, and (*Balmain/ Moreton Bay*) *bug* for the largest.

The distinction between *shrimp* and *prawn* is less clear in Britain, where *potted shrimps* and *prawn cocktail* are likely to be created from the same very small animals, and prawns are shrimps in America: hence Paul Hogan's un-Australian 'throw a shrimp on the barbie' – see AMERICAN ENGLISH.

credible, credulous, credit *Credible* means *believable*. It can be applied either to people or to what they say and do, and they are then said *to have credibility* and *to be given credence*.

Credulous applies only to people, and denotes that they will believe anything.

Credit has lost much of its original connection with belief. In the world of commerce, where a *creditor* grants *credit* to someone who is *credit-worthy*, the word originally meant *trust in a borrower to repay a loan*, but has come to mean the loan itself. When a bank gives you credit, what you get is *debt*.

Credit Foncier　This rather quaint French term was at one stage used for its exact equivalent in Australia, namely, an institution lending money on real estate, either a department of a bank or a building society. The pronunciation was fully anglicised: /*Credit Fon-seer*/.

Equally quaint was the adoption of *Mont de Piete* by upmarket pawnbrokers. Again, it was fully anglicised: /*mont d'peet*/, though Mac gives it accents (… *Piété*) and a gallic pronunciation.

The term *Credit Foncier* is defunct, and *Mont de Piete* survives only in the names of some pawnbrokers. But both were earlier used as generic terms (without capital letters) for the businesses involved: *He took the watch to the mont de piete*.

criterion/criteria　If you are the kind of person who uses the word *criteria*, you ought to be the kind of person who knows that the word is plural, the singular being *criterion*.

critical, criticism, critic, critique　The word *critical* has many meanings, and can therefore be ambiguous.

The original sense was all about *judgement*, in the legal sense. It then became broadened to covering other judgements, aesthetic and so on. But it was still neutral: being *critical* of something did not mean that you thought it was bad.

In the literary world, it still has this meaning, as in the phrase 'a critical analysis', and in the related words *criticism* (as in *literary criticism*) and *critic*. Meanwhile, the word *critique* was for years a rare or obsolete one meaning an intellectual discourse, more or less confined to the title of Kant's turgid work, *A Critique of Pure Reason*, but occasionally used as a synonym for a book review, as when Byron said that Keats was 'killed off by one critique', the sense being clear from the context:

> *'Tis strange the mind, that very fiery particle*
> *Should let itself be snuff'd out by an article.*

In general language, *critical* has acquired two additional senses, *adversely critical* (as in *She is critical of the government's policy*) and *crucial* (as in *Negotiations are at a critical stage*, and *The alibi is critical to the defendant's case*). The words *critic* and *criticism* are often used in the 'adversely critical' sense.

Recently, there has been a revival of the use of *critique* as a synonym for review, as in *I have just published a critique of the new book*. The word implies a full-length review – we would not use it for a three-liner in the *New Paperbacks* column – and a serious one, a contribution in its own right as well as a discussion of the book. If reviewers produce reviews, critics produce critiques.

The word *criticism* was not available for this purpose because it had become synonymous with *adverse* criticism. It is therefore sad that *critique* is going the same way. We hear *What are your critiques of modern science?* when the meaning is *What do you think is wrong with modern science?* This usage appears to be a product of ignorance, and is worth resisting.

cross-section It is worth remembering that a cross-section is a cut across something to show internal structures, especially trees and other biological specimens. What you see depends on the location of the cross-section. If a cross-section of the population is taken low down, you will find nothing but feet. In short, the phrase should not be used as a synonym for *random sample*.

Crown, the We should remember that *the Crown* in Australia is different from *the Crown* in England, since it refers, not to a gracious lady or her headgear, but to *the Government*.

This advice may appear obvious, but the point is sufficiently obscure to have confused Her Majesty's Attorney General in and for the United Kingdom when preparing the *Spycatcher* case, and it might therefore confuse an equally ill-informed Australian, if such exists.

cult The word *cult* refers (a) to a *group* formed round a charismatic leader, a hero, a god or an ideology, or (b) to the set of *practices* which identify the group. It is mildly pejorative, so that we ourselves do not belong to cults: we find the practices of cults strange and threatening, and their members *gullible* and *superstitious*. Our own irrational beliefs are, by contrast, reasonable and enlightened, and our fellow members *sincere* and *devout*.

In the phrase *the book has developed a cult following*, the connotations of strange practices are missing, the implication being that the book, while not appealing to the public at large, captivates a select group within society.

cultural cringe The phrase *the cultural cringe* was coined by Arthur Phillips for use in an essay published in *Meanjin* in 1950. It was used to describe our insecurity about Australian artistic standards, which showed itself in a reluctance to recognise local talent until it had been recognised abroad. The phrase immediately entered the language, clear evidence that it covered a phenomenon of which many Australians were aware.

However, the Gospel writers were aware of it, too (*A prophet is not without honour, save in his own country, and in his own house*). Indeed, there is nowhere in the world where overseas accolades are not valued more highly than the home-grown variety.

What was different was that, in Australia, it *mattered*. If today the cultural cringe is less evident, it is not because of any general improvement in our standards, but because, thanks to improved communications, we realise that our standards are not at all bad.

What remains strange is that the concept of the cringe was restricted to matters cultural. Arthur Phillips might have noted that the economic, industrial and political cringes were far more profound. What is more, in the period since, during which the cultural cringe has largely been overcome, the economic, industrial and political cringes have become deeper and deeper.

cyclone, hurricane, typhoon All these words refer to the same phenomenon. Spectacularly high winds were first observed in specific parts of the world, and given different names in each; but modern meteorology shows that they are all essentially the same.

Cyclone is the latest of these names, dating from the nineteenth century, when meteorological studies showed that these winds moved along circular paths. A *cyclone* is strictly the whole system, comprising a region of still air at very low pressure and its surrounding wind system. Although *cyclone* is the normal word for the phenomenon in Australia, it is known only as a technical term of meteorology in Britain and America. However, its antonym, *anticyclone*, is used more widely there, perhaps because until the arrival of detailed barometric and wind-direction records, the phenomenon was not recognised, so there was no pre-existing term.

Today, thanks to constant exposure to satellite photographs and weather maps, it is hardly necessary to add that cyclonic winds are most likely to occur between latitudes 15° and 30° north and south of the equator, and that they rotate clockwise in the southern and anti-clockwise in the northern hemisphere. If you want to know why, follow the index reference to *Coriolis force* in a physics or meteorology text.

D

dactyl(lic)   See FOOT.

dam   In British usage, the word *dam* normally refers to the wall, not to the water behind it. Thus the British may fall off, but not into, a dam.

In Australia, a dam can mean

(1) the wall, as above; but more often refers to

(2) the body of water, as in the sentence *He fell into the Warragamba Dam*; or (most often of all) to

(3) a small artificial depression on a farm property, scooped out with a bulldozer, and designed to catch run-off after rain.

Dam is a generic term for water storages, irrespective of the purpose. More specific terms are *reservoir* as a holding basin for water supply purposes, *pondage* for a pumped storage for hydro-electricity, and *weir* for a flood-control dam on a river.

In Britain, the word *weir* most commonly means a spillway built alongside a lock in a navigable river, to maintain the water level above the lock at a constant level, whereas in Australia it more often refers to the body of water behind a wall. Thus British boats are *accidentally carried over the weir*, while we *go sailing on the Hume Weir*.

Australian dictionaries tend to reflect the British usage.

dash, hyphen   Dashes are among the devices available in a typographical text but not in a typewriter text. The typewriter has only a hyphen, whereas the typesetter has in addition the *en-dash* and the *em-dash*. The following examples show the effects:

	hyphen	*en-dash*	*em-dash*
unspaced	This-that	This–that	This—that
spaced	This - that	This – that	This — that

In typography, the hyphen is used in two ways: the true hyphen (as in *semi-literate*) and the forced hyphen (i.e. where a word is broken between two lines). It is never spaced.

The *en-dash* (so called because it is – or at least was – as wide as the capital N in the relevant font) is used unspaced to represent *to*, as in *1914–18* and *Melbourne–Sydney*. Spaced, it is used as a minus sign in mathematical setting as well as being one of the options for presenting a *true dash*.

The true dash is a punctuation mark – see PUNCTUATION (8). The choice between en- and em-dashes, and the decision whether to space them, is up to the typographer. Until recently, unspaced em-dashes were generally used, but spaced en-dashes are today more common – as in this text.

In typing, dashes may be represented by a pair of hyphens with space before and after. See KEYBOARDING.

data   See SINGULARITIES (1(e)).

dates, writing of   The current fashion is to write dates in the form *1 March 1999* (as opposed to *1st March, 1999*), though many readers would, if called upon to read this aloud, say *the first of March, 1999*. Despite this anomaly, the fashion is good, being simple and neat.

Writing *1 March 1999* is better than writing *1.3.99*, if only because it is unambiguous. To an American, *1.3.99* means *3 January 1999*, and this format is starting to appear in Australia, thanks to being used for the automatic dating on some imported American computer programs. As this ambiguity is potentially very dangerous, and as the day-month-year is the established (and more logical) convention, use of the month-day-year format is strongly discouraged.

The letters B.C. (*before Christ*) appear after the number: *404 B.C.* The letters A.D. (*anno domini*) should appear before the number: *A.D. 404*, though they appear after the number in phrases like *the fifth century A.D.* The term B.P. (*before the present*) must appear after the number. It can only be used to represent very distant and approximate dates, e.g. those in geology, since the datum point changes every year. Historians, dealing in exact dates, must use a fixed scale.

All these are best written in small capitals (as here).

AWEG (like most current Australian style manuals) recommends omitting the points in all cases. I feel that the points are helpful to readers, particularly in phrases such as *the fifth century AD*, but I have few friends on this trivial issue. In any case, AD is the only one which causes trouble, and it is, as *The Age* guide points out, rarely used, since all dates are assumed to be AD (or A.D.) unless otherwise stated.

de-   This prefix, which orginally had a variety of connotations (notably *down* or *away*, as in *decline* and *deduct*, and *concerning*, as in *debate* and *declare*) has only one possible sense in new coinage, and that is as a special type of negative prefix: *defrost, decontaminate*. In this sense it should always be pronounced /*dee-*/, if only to avoid confusion with similar words starting with *de-* or *di-*. See DEFUSE for an example of the problem and NEGATIVE PREFIXES for the usage.

deadline   See METAPHOR.

debate   Do we debate issues or people?
> *Mr Ambrose debated animal rights with Prof Thomas.*
> *Mr Ambrose debated Prof Thomas on the subject of animal rights.*

Until recently, the former was the only acceptable usage, the latter being an Americanism. Indeed, the noun *debate* was applied only to a particular form of disputation in which a specified *motion* is proposed and opposed according to strict procedural rules.

However, we have now imported from America the 'television debate', in which 'debate' means a battle of wits between two

unarmed combatants, and the latter usage seems to have arrived at
the same time. At the very least, the 'American' usage is now well
known and understood. It is used by the ABC, for a start. But I still
wish they wouldn't. Proper people debate *issues*.

decimal   This Latin-looking word did not exist in classical Latin: the
roots of it existed (*decimus* = ten + *-al(is)*, an adjectival suffix), but the
two halves were not put together until medieval times, and the most
important current meaning, as in the phrase *decimal system*, is of
seventeenth-century origin. This is perhaps strange, given that the
Romans used a decimal system for counting. A possible explanation is that although their names for the numbers were based on
multiples of ten, their way of writing them down had no place
value, and 5 (V), 50 (L) and 500 (D) were almost as important staging
points as 10 (X), 100 (C) and 1000 (M).

The choice of ten as the base is biological rather than mathematical. Its sole merit is that we are all born with decimal calculators
attached to the ends of our arms; twelve would have been better for
almost all purposes, being exactly divisible by two, three, four and
six. Non-decimal bases were adopted centuries ago for a number of
applications: thus the day was divided into twelve hours, and the
circle into 360 degrees, and both hours and degrees were divided
into 60 minutes each of 60 seconds; feet were divided into 12 inches,
shillings into 12 pence, pounds weight into 16 ounces. While the
origins of these are lost in the mists of time, it seems likely that these
numbers were chosen precisely because they were so conveniently
subdivisible into equal portions, e.g. a pound could be divided into
exact ounces using only an equal arm balance.

decimate   See ORPHANS.

de facto   This little chunk of legal Latin is an adverbial phrase,
meaning *in fact*, and is contrasted with *de jure* (= *in law*). The tags are
pronounced */day fac-toe/* and */day jooray/*. The most common use is in
the context of *de facto* (or *common law*) wives and husbands.

How should this state be described? Not so long ago, it was a
major issue. There were people who were married, and people who
were not married, and people who, though supposedly husband
and wife, were in fact 'living in sin'. This phrase has moved from
being commonplace into being a quaint archaism in a matter of just
thirty years, and its first replacement, 'co-habiting', is on the skids.
The normal term now is 'living together'. The difference between
the general usage and the absolute usage is shown by stress: 'living
together' for shared accommodation and '*living* together' for a de
facto marriage. A one-time major issue has disappeared from the
social agenda.

The most common term for people who are living together is
'partners', and although (like 'living together') this is an absolute

usage which could cause misunderstanding, it rarely does. Where a misunderstanding seems possible, the nature of the relationship is generally specified, e.g. 'We are business partners'.

Meanwhile there remains a minor issue: the children of a *de facto* relationship are simply *grandchildren* to their *grandparents*, and vice versa, but we have no specific word for the *de facto* equivalents of *mother-in-law, father-in-law, son-in-law* and *daughter-in-law*.

The problem is not with terms of address; the *in-law* terms were never used as terms of address except as a mild joke. But there is a need for an unequivocal mode of introduction, to replace 'This is my father-in-law', etc. Circumlocutions like 'This is my partner's father' are not the happiest of solutions, and to say that the question rarely arises because such relationships are generally irrelevant is not true in a significant number of contexts, not least being those of the law.

defamation   Defamation is a big, complicated, expensive subject. Writing a short, non-technical summary like this is therefore risky. Reading it and believing it can be riskier still; if you are in any doubt, take proper legal advice.

With that proviso, the following general points may be helpful:

(1) Definitions

(a) A *defamatory statement* is one which is likely to bring a person into hatred, ridicule and contempt.

    An evil thought becomes a defamation when it is transmitted to a third party (i.e. any person other than the defamer and the defamee).

(b) A *slander* is a defamatory statement uttered in non-permanent form, which normally means *spoken* as opposed to *written*.

(c) A *libel* is a defamation in permanent form, generally written words, but it can be a cartoon or other non-verbal statement.

(2) The purpose of the law   The alleged purpose of the law is the protection of people's reputations. Up to a point, it achieves this: the existence of the law may deter people from defaming one another. However, once a case has gone to Court, the law offers little protection; a court action is likely to give further publicity to the defamatory allegations, and winning a case (especially under Australian law) can rarely be said to 'set the record straight'. It is different in America, as we shall see.

There is a basic conflict between freedom of speech and the law of defamation, and the law reflects this conflict.

In America, freedom of speech tends to win. In particular, exposure to hatred, ridicule and contempt is regarded as an occupational hazard of public figures, so that (for example) a politician would be unlikely to win an action over a defamatory statement made by an opponent during an election campaign. Furthermore, defamation actions in America can succeed only if the plaintiffs can show that the defamatory statement was untrue, or win damages unless they can show that they have suffered damage, i.e. have become less rich and famous. This is tough on the plaintiff. The other side of the coin is that winning such an action really means something: it is a vindication of the plaintiff's case.

In Australia, as in Britain, freedom of speech is taken less seriously, and the law of defamation takes scant account either of the harm which the plaintiff has really suffered or the truth of the allegations. Hence public figures can (and do) take action over statements which are palpably true and clearly have not disadvantaged them, since they are still in their positions of leadership. This is sad for those who are genuinely defamed: there is no procedure under Australian law for setting the record straight.

(3) How to avoid getting a writ The first point to note is that *the purpose of most defamation actions is to get money*. If you have none, people will not sue you. Thus the best defence against actions for defamation is *poverty*.

If you have the misfortune to be rich (or, more likely, are writing for publication by a rich publisher), there are two things which you should watch out for, and these are *malice* and *accidental libel*.

Malice should be easy to identify. If, as you dip your quill in the vitriol, you imagine your enemy squirming with pain, you are almost certainly being malicious. If you want to cause somebody trouble, it is best not to do it in writing. In theory, our very technical laws (which allow a well-advised plaintiff to get damages without being damaged) also allow a well-advised defamer to do a lot of damage without paying damages. But you have to be a *very* well-advised writer. Evidence of careful wording can show evil intent.

Many books are, of course, intrinsically defamatory. As a leading Sydney lawyer once said of the story of an industrial dispute 'This book is highly defamatory: it would be boring and pointless if it were not'. In such cases, it is vital that authors inform their publishers of what they are doing. If you have not told your publisher that your work contains a deliberate attack on specific individuals, the publisher may have a case against you for breach of contract: see PUBLISHING CONTRACTS (3(c)).

Accidental libel is almost impossible to guard against. For example, a well-known Australian author wrote a novel containing a character who was depicted as a society artist. Unknown to the author, there was a society artist with the same name and other remarkable similarities to the fictional character, who threatened to sue. The case was deemed indefensible, and the edition was pulped, although there was no suggestion of intention to defame. Happily, such cases are very rare, and are normally settled with less radical action.

(4) Defences Defending an action for defamation can be arduous and expensive; this is why almost all cases are settled out of Court.

Defamation is a State matter, and the rules vary from State to State. Almost everybody agrees that the variations are absurd, but all attempts to establish uniform legislation have failed. Last time a uniform law was mooted, a quite reasonable first draft was produced by the Commonwealth, but the States then proceeded to write all their most obnoxious clauses back in, so that the final draft had the worst features of all the individual State codes.

In general, New South Wales is a good place to be a plaintiff, and Victoria is a good place for a defendant. This does not help Victorian defendants, however, as it is the plaintiffs who decide where to take action, and (given that most major libels are published in all States) they can choose the jurisdiction in which they are most likely to win. Hence it is best to assume that you will be sued under the law which is best for the plaintiff, under which the defence must prove *truth, fair comment and public interest.*

Truth has to be proved with hard evidence. Circumstantial evidence, received opinion and common sense are none of them proofs that a defamatory statement was true.

Fair comment is generally interpreted as *relevance.* Thus the allegation that a person was sexually promiscuous might be held defamatory despite copious evidence of its truth if it appeared in a discussion of the person's financial reliability.

Public interest does not mean proving that the public was fascinated by the revelations. It means proving that it was to the benefit of the public to be told.

In all cases, the burden of proof is on the defendant, a reversal of the normal presumption of innocence.

The trouble is that litigious individuals are almost by definition the ones we feel impelled to attack, and the actionable phrases are almost inevitably the ones which go to the heart of the matter. We may be distressed to have palpable lies told about us, but most of us are even more distressed by an allegation we know to be true.

Things will not improve until some jury tells a rich and famous litigant that his continuing wealth and fame is *prima facie* evidence that he has suffered no real damage and hence can receive no damages.

(5) Critics and defamation Critical and analytical writing tends to be intrinsically defamatory, inasmuch as the author's intention is to evaluate people and their actions, and to make a comparative assessment of alternatives: if one alternative is preferred, another has to be demoted.

Until recently, the limits of critical licence, though unstated, were reasonably well understood. We thought we knew the difference between fair comment and actionable statements. Recently, however, the rules have changed. There have been spectacular cases in which an author sued a book reviewer and a restaurateur sued a food critic, winning punitive damages for statements which might have been thought to be legitimate expressions of opinion.

These decisions have unquestionably caused worry to critics and their publishers. We can only hope that new decisions (or a new law) will clarify the position.

(6) Privilege and limited privilege Parliamentary privilege was designed to ensure that the proceedings could be frank and open, and (amongst other things) gives immunity from actions for defamation to politicians speaking in our parliaments. Statements made in Court are similar. Verbatim press reports of remarks made under privilege are themselves subject to limited privilege, and this will generally extend to books quoting these same remarks. However, it must be made clear that the writer is quoting a privileged statement. Limited privilege might apply, for example, to the headline 'Premier guilty of corruption – QC' but not to a far more cautious statement which represented the writer's own view.

Limited privilege also applies to defamatory remarks made about one another by members of closed groups, provided the remarks are not then disseminated to wider audiences. Hence it is of little use to authors of books designed for a general readership.

defective, deficient We have here two words which were once interchangeable, but which are now commonly recognised as having separate meanings: a car may be said to be *defective* if the doors won't open, but *deficient* if it has no doors at all.

defective verb In grammar, the word *defective* retains the *lacking parts* sense, e.g. the verb *can* is described as a *defective verb*, having only two forms, *can* and *could*, the infinitive, participle and other forms being supplied by *to be able, being able*, etc. Compare BEWARE.

defuse/diffuse When we hear that *a dispute has been d'fused*, as we do almost daily on the radio, we may well wonder how the *diffusion* (= spreading out) of a dispute is going to help resolve it. The answer, of course, is that the word being attempted is *defuse*. The metaphor is drawn from bomb disposal, and the word should be pronounced /*dee-fuse*/ to make this clear. See STRESS.

de jure See DE FACTO.

delusion/illusion A *delusion* is a false belief, existing in the mind only of the believer, though other people may become aware of it, e.g. *delusions of grandeur*. An *illusion* is a false visual image, the term covering many natural optical effects, including mirages and apparent distortions of geometry, tricks involving perspective used by artists and architects and the special effects produced by magicians. However, you may be *deluded* (= tricked) by an *illusion* devised by somebody else, particularly as *illusion* is used to describe, for example, the way politicians manipulate statistics, so there is a huge overlap of the terms.

If speaking in a context which involves both of these words (and/or *allusion*) it is helpful to enunciate the first syllable very clearly to indicate which one you are using.

demonstratives   This is a small class of adjectives, notably *this* and *that*. Normally, *this* implies here and *that* implies there, but Americans who have missed your name on the phone ask 'Who is this?', which sounds to us like the wrong question.

dialect   A *dialect* is best defined as a way of using a language which is different from the standard form of that language, but has remained close enough to it to allow the users to understand one another. The differences will include non-standard words and grammatical constructions. (The standard form will itself be the product of evolution, being simply the most successful of a collection of derivatives from a lost source language, so that 'dominant dialect' is a better phrase than 'standard form'.)

Most dialects are also strongly associated with specific *accents*, but strictly speaking a regional accent and a regional dialect are separate phenomena. A useful, if simplistic, definition is that accent shows in the way people speak while dialect shows in the way people write. This text could be read with a Scottish accent, but this would not translate it into the Scottish dialect.

The evolution of a dialect into a separate language is gradual. First, the various dialects of a language can be in communication with the dominant dialect yet be mutually incomprehensible to one another; see ENGLISH (3). Then the words and grammatical structures change so much that the link to the dominant dialect breaks down. At that point, a dialect becomes a language in its own right.

However, the dividing line is not clearcut. The Scandinavian languages (Danish, Swedish and Norwegian) are separate, but the impetus for separation was as much political as linguistic, and some of the differences were contrived. Afrikaans separated from Dutch following a long period of relative isolation. At this moment, Swiss German is moving towards independent status. Much of the language of the street is already incomprehensible to standard German speakers, fulfilling the requirement for status as a separate language. (Tourist buses already offer the option of a German or Swiss commentary.) But a more-or-less standard German remains the language of commerce and even literature. If there is a parting of the ways, it may, as with the Scandinavian languages, finally come as a political statement rather than as the recognition of an evolutionary process.

For a discussion of the evolution of dialect in English, see ENGLISH.

dialogue   For notes on punctuating dialogue, see PUNCTUATION (7).

dictionary, choice of   Every writer needs a dictionary, and since we are Australian, it seems sensible to make it an Australian one; but which is the best? There is no one answer, because there are many quite different requirements.

(1) What do we mean by 'Australian'?   Whenever a new dictionary is released, popular commentators tend to discuss its coverage of *barramundi, beaut* and *boomerang* (to quote examples of the three classes of word which are generally seen to distinguish Australian English from the rest: flora and fauna, slang and Aboriginal words).

They are in good company. Sidney Baker (in *The Australian Language*) has some good words to say about the topics referred to under AUSTRALIANISMS in the present book, but concentrates on flora and fauna, Aboriginal words and slang. The overall impression given by the book is that we lapse into Australian only when English fails. Bill Ramson's *The Australian National Dictionary* specifically restricts itself to 'Australian words and phrases', by which it means those which are peculiar to Australia.

This is not to criticise these works, which are both excellent within their own self-defined limits. But in both cases these limits stop short of any exhaustive coverage of Australian usage, or even of usage which would be labelled 'Australian' in a comprehensive dictionary of international English. Noah Webster took a broader view when he was inventing American English.

If we are choosing an Australian dictionary, *Australian* has to be taken to mean 'English as used by Australians'; all of it, not just the bits which diverge from the mainstream of international English.

(2) English–Australian or Australian–English?   We can easily see the difference between a French–English and an English–French dictionary, but what do we mean by an Australian dictionary?

An English–Australian dictionary would draw its headword list from the corpus of international English, but would explain the words and usages in Australian, i.e. in terms which would make sense to Australian readers.

An Australian–English dictionary would draw its headwords from the full range of Australian usage and explain them in international English.

None of our major desk dictionaries (*The Concise Macquarie Dictionary, The Australian Concise Oxford Dictionary* and *Collins Concise Australian Dictionary*) is truly one or the other. All are based on overseas originals. This is a sensible way of proceeding – re-inventing the wheel is tedious – but the result is that unless their editors make changes, the overseas text stands. This means that many words are defined in a language which is not ours (i.e. they are not English–Australian dictionaries) and their coverage of Australian usage is haphazard (i.e. they are not Australian–English).

Their language base shows in subtle ways. They often label as 'Australian' words and definitions which are exclusively Australian, but only in exceptional cases label as 'British' words and definitions which are exclusively British. The best that can be said for this is that British dictionaries are worse in this regard, rarely labelling a usage as British, perhaps because they regard English (the shared language) as synonymous with British (the version they speak), so that any such labelling would be meaningless.

It is likely that the next generation of Australian dictionaries, based on computer analysis of millions of words of ordinary Australian text, will record a great number of subtleties of connotation and usage which at the moment have not been noticed. We will find many words which are never used in Australia at all, and others which are most commonly used in senses which are not in our current dictionaries. In short, we will discover that the Australian language is not just distinguished by our flora and fauna and outlandish slang, but by a whole host of variations in frequency, connotation and usage which have never been recorded.

If none of the existing dictionaries is perfect, each has its merits, and the choice will depend on personal capacities and needs. The best test is to pick some of the queries you are most likely to ask, and see how well the dictionary answers them.

(3) What do we expect of our dictionaries?

(a) *Headword list*   It may seem self-evident that what you want is the Australian words, but many of us are more often worried about what a *rutabaga* or a *bloater* is than what is meant by *larrikin* or *brumby*; that is, we know all about Australian words, and need the non-Australian words which are encountered in literature. Scrabble players may go for quantity at all costs, and relish *Chambers' Twentieth Century Dictionary*, with its wealth of high-scoring Scottish dialect words. For the same reason, it is preferred by many compilers and solvers of cryptic crosswords.

(b) *Spelling*   You may only want to know how Australians spell things, or to be warned if others spell differently. It may be important to have easy access to the spelling of derivatives, e.g. is it *refering* or *referring* (and is the answer different in America)? Define your needs, and see how well they are catered for, since the conventions for giving this information vary greatly.

(c) *Pronunciation*   It is worth checking that the pronunciation guides work. Look up some for which there are several acceptable pronunciations (e.g. *banal, grimace*) and see whether the guides seem reliable and comprehensible.

(d) *Meanings*   We normally just want to find out what a word means, but we may also want to be warned if others would not understand the Australian usage. Alternatively, our main interest may be in technical usage, in which case the standard dictionaries may be of no help at all: *Chambers' Dictionary of Science and Technology* has two volumes packed with words and usages which are largely absent from any normal dictionary. But it doesn't have anything about *snifter valves*, those vital devices on which the superheaters of steam locomotives depend. But the gargantuan OED doesn't mention them either. This should not surprise us: there is no such thing as a comprehensive dictionary.

Some dictionaries (e.g. the first edition of ACOD) are 'based on historical principles', and list the meanings in order of antiquity, so that the reader can trace the way in which the meaning has changed over the years. This is often fascinating, but may mean that the most common usage appears well down the list. Others (e.g. Mac and the second edition of ACOD) are based on frequency, which brings the most common meaning to the beginning. This is best if what you are wanting is a guide to frequency, but may obscure the history of the word. Which is more important to you? I am more likely to be wanting to check the history than the current meaning, so I regret the change in ACOD. But that's just me.

(e) *Grammar and etymology* If you expect grammatical or etymological advice from a dictionary, think of some sample questions and see whether you can get the answer.

It is a case of horses for courses, and only you know the course that your horse will be required to run.

dieresis Some would prefer to spell this word *diaeresis* or *diëresis*, the merit of the latter being that it illustrates its own meaning: a dieresis is a pair of dots over a vowel to indicate that it is sounded separately from the one before. This should not be taken as advice to pepper our words with such dots. They are rarely helpful and never necessary. See LIGATURE (1).

The same mark is used in some languages, notably German, to modify a vowel sound, and is then known as an *umlaut*. See SORTS.

differ(ent/ently) from/than/to This is another favourite amongst purists, who say that *differ* and *different* should be followed by *from* rather than *to* or *than*:

Your new flat $\left(\begin{array}{l} \textit{differed from} \\ \textit{was different from} \end{array}\right)\left(\begin{array}{l} \textit{mine.} \\ \textit{your first one.} \end{array}\right)$

However, the use of *to* in such sentences is of such long standing, and occurs in such distinguished authors, that, while many of us will continue to use *from* ourselves, we will not take to the barricades in its defence or shoot those who do otherwise.

The same may be said for the use of *than* in this construction (i.e. where *from* is followed by an adjective or noun). Furthermore, *than* provides a very useful way of linking *different* directly to a verb, as in *The weather was different than I expected*. If we compel ourselves to use *from*, we get involved in circumlocutions, and it is hard to see why *than* should not be accepted, particularly as it, too, is widely used, and not only by Americans. I find it hard to use, as the word *from* always comes popping out the moment I say *different*. But I admire those who have overcome this reflex.

diffuse   See DEFUSE / DIFFUSE.

digraph, diphthong   First, let us decide on the terminology:

Digraphs are 2-letter combinations (vowels or consonants) representing a single sound, as in r**ai**n, m**ea**t, **ph**one.

Diphthongs are vowels made up of two distinct *sounds*, whether represented by two letters (the *ia* in *dial* and the *ue* in *fuel*) or the very similar sounds made by just one letter (the *i* in *mile* and the *u* in *mule*).

(1) From the above definitions, *digraph* and *diphthong* are mutually exclusive terms.

These definitions are strongly recommended, but they are not universally agreed upon. Many writers use the term *diphthong* in reference to ligatures (e.g. referring to the *œ* in *œuvre* as 'O-E diphthong'). Likewise, some writers use the term *digraph* for any two adjacent vowels, even if they are sounded as a diphthong. I regret this, since it destroys the useful precision of the terms.

(2) We can agree on the definitions without agreeing on their application. Mac and ACOD₂ for example, make the vowel sound in *dial* a diphthong but in *mile* a single sound, whereas I hear them both as diphthongs; conversely, they make the *ai* sounds in *mail* and *main* identical single sounds, whereas I hear *mail* as a diphthong.

(3) A more practical problem concerns the use of *ae* to represent the Greek *ai* and Latin *ae*, and *oe* to represent the Greek *oi*.

Americans are often said to have abolished both, replacing them by a simple *e* (*medieval, esophagus*). This is not strictly true: they achieved cultural independence before these forms were popularised in Britain in the classical revival of the late eighteenth century and continue to use *ae* and *oe* (as pairs of separate letters, not as ligatures) in words which were established in this form before Independence. Thus spelling differences arise only in words which have come into the language since Independence, or whose spelling has changed *in Britain*. As so often happens, the ex-colonial version is more loyal to tradition than that of the mother country.

Two questions arise: (a) Should we follow the Americans in preferring *e* to *ae* and *oe*? (b) How do we pronounce the words?

(a) *Spelling: aesthetics or esthetics? anaemia or anemia? paean or pean?* Total consistency either way would fly in the face of usage, for American contains numerous examples of *oe* and *ae* forms, while

British and Australian writers use many *e* forms. This can even happen within the same word part: thus our dictionaries suggest *paediatrics* but *pederast*, although the *paed-* and *ped-* represent the same Greek root word (originally *paid-*).

In general, the following rules seem best:

(1) If in doubt, prefer the simpler form, which is generally *e*. Thus write *diarrhea, encyclopedia* and *medieval*, but do not chastise those who write *diarrhoea, encyclopaedia* and *mediaeval*, particularly since they include the authors of ACOD. For a special case of unusual perversity, see FETUS....

(2) Do not attempt to change a spelling which is universally agreed (*poem, Oedipus*) in a vain chase for consistency.

(3) Do not use spellings about which you feel self-conscious. This is most likely to happen with spellings which affect the initial letters, since they are very obtrusive, and influence indexing. Thus I have no worries about *encyclopedia* but feel awkward about *esthetic*. But I have to remember that *aesthetic* may look as quaint to an American reader as *oeconomic* looks to me, and must learn not to be shocked by the *e*. (For a similar problem, see -OR/-OUR.)

(b) *Pronunciation*

RW warns that the *e* spelling may cause us to forget that these words should always be pronounced /*ee*/. The argument is that otherwise the *ped-* in *pediatrician* (Greek = *child*) may be confused with the *ped-* in *pedal* (Latin = *foot*).

The trouble is that the battle has already been lost. The Australian dictionaries generally recommend the /*-ee*/ sound where they adopt the *ae* spelling, and the short /*e*/ sound for the *e* spellings: *paediatrician* /*-ee-*/ but *pederast* /*-e-*/. ACOD offers /*peed*/ as an acceptable variant in some cases, including *pederast*, but the short *e* is the only pronunciation offered in others. Likewise, the short sound is the only one offered in *economy*, and is an optional alternative in *economic*.

For the moment, then, well-established usage flies in the face of consistency; but if consistency is ever achieved, it is far more likely to be in a short *e* than in a long one. Thus, as with spelling, say whichever you are comfortable with, but (despite RW) prefer /*-e-*/ in all doubtful cases.

dilemma   This word is a technical term of logic, the *di-* part meaning 'two' and *lemma* meaning 'a proposition'. It is properly used only for the choice between two options, the 'horns' of the dilemma, not just as a synonym for 'problem'.

diminutive   In common language, the word implies a smaller size than is natural and proper. A *diminutive* person is neither a child nor a dwarf, but just a very small normal person.

In grammar, it is used to describe a word part which implies small size: *-let* as in *wave, wavelet*; or *-ling* as in *goose, gosling* are termed *diminutive suffixes*.

Graham Pizzey tells a story that the Melbourne *Herald* once had a passionate objection to the phrase *wristlet watch*, then current for a dainty female version of a wrist watch, on the dubious grounds that it was the watch which was small, not the wrist. The reporters then vied with one another to be first to get the phrase *wrist watchlet* past the vigilant sub-editors.

dinner   See MEALS.

diploma   The plural is *diplomas*, not *diplomata* or (worse) *diplomae*. The word means *a sheet of paper folded in two*, the traditional form for a letter of recommendation. A person carrying such a letter is called a *diplomate* if the letter is from an educational institution and a *diplomat* if it is from a Head of State.

direct questions/speech   See QUESTIONS... and SPEECH....

disc, disk   There is no reason for having two spellings. RW identifies *disk* as American and associates it only with computers. This information is questionable on both counts: OED described *disk* as the better spelling and *disc* as a scientific interloper, the science being medicine, and says nothing about the Americans.

However, RW may well be right in saying that *disc* is the more common spelling in Australia.

What is the answer? It doesn't matter either way, but if we want to standardise, *disk* (which is entrenched in computers, the field in which the word is most commonly used) looks like a better bet. We need not correct medical publications which talk about *slipped discs*, but we should be abrupt with anyone who attempts to correct *disk*.

discography   This term can been coined as the equivalent of *bibliography* when applied to recorded music. It is a useful term on which to hang a brief discussion of the contribution of the recording industry to common language.

The first words for devices to reproduce sound came from the trademarks of the most popular examples: *phonograph* in America and *gramophone* in Britain and Australia. These were acoustic machines with clockwork motors, and played *records*. The advent of electric recording was quickly followed by that of electric reproduction, and the devices were built into large cabinets, *radiograms*, housing the radio and the record-playing equipment. Records were sometimes marketed in large book-like containers with separate pockets for each record, called *record albums* (on the analogy of stamp albums).

The 1950s saw rapid changes. *Full frequency range recording* (*FFRR*), then *high fidelity (Hi-Fi), long playing (LP)* and *extended play (EP) microgroove* records in the 1950s led to the popularity of *record players*, devices which played through the radio set or, for the enthusiast, through a separate amplifier and multiple loudspeakers, *woofers* for the low frequencies and *tweeters* for the high. As several old records ('seventy-eights', from the fact that they ran at 78 rpm) might be included on a single new one running at 33 rpm, the word *record* became ambiguous, and its senses were divided in three: the process became a *recording*, the physical object a *disk*, and the separate items *tracks* on the disk.

The word *album* was adopted from the earlier technology to describe a single LP disk containing tracks of several separate recordings, and the word *discotheque* was coined on the analogy of the French *bibliothèque* (= library).

Meanwhile the integrated radiograms and record players were totally rejected in favour of *sound systems*, with separate *turntables*, *cassette decks* and *amplifiers*, a process accelerated by the introduction of *stereo* recording. The term *stereo(phonic)* was coined on the analogy of the much earlier word *stereoscopic*, while *digital recording* uses computer technology, in which a contrast is made between continuous (*analog*) data and discrete (*digital*) data.

Much of this vocabulary is ephemeral, as is the equipment. *CD* (= *compact disk*) *players* have caused the great collections of LPs we prized so recently to be dismissed contemptuously as *vinyl*.

discovery, invention   *Discover* means to remove the cover from something. It must be there, under the cover, before it can be dis-covered. Hence scientists discover fossils, comets, new elements and facts about the structure of molecules, but not pacemakers, lasers, microwave ovens and sticky tape. These are *invented*.

Can the same thing be discovered more than once? In common language, the answer is patently 'yes', since I can, following exploration, *discover* my spectacles afresh every morning. We say that a baby *discovers* its toes, and we have the 'discovery method' of teaching science, in which students are given, for example, some lengths of wire, batteries and globes, and told to discover Ohm's Law.

However, in the case of scientific and geographic discovery, we attach particular kudos to *first* discovery. The assumption here is that, once the covered fact has been dis-covered, it cannot be dis-covered again.

All this is important to the debate on the discovery of Australia. One argument has it that William Dampier, Abel Tasman, Captain James Cook and the rest discovered nothing, since Australia and Tasmania had long since been discovered and thoroughly explored by countless generations of Aboriginals. This is undeniably true.

However, it is contrary to normal practice in the scientific community, where the kudos of discovery goes to the first person to *publish*, and many great scientists and explorers have missed out through failing to put notice of their discoveries in the mails. All this presupposes a community of knowledge, disseminated by printing. By this argument, the Aboriginals missed out because they never advised the European authorities of their discoveries.

Alternatively, it can be argued that, just as each baby finds its toes as a fresh act of discovery, so Australia represented a very fresh discovery to every explorer who bumped into it, which they did frequently until it was properly enshrined on the European maps.

This reduces the issue to a semantic quibble, depending on the definition of 'discovery'. Unfortunately, it is more than that, since it has major social and legal consequences, in tragically different ways, for today's black and white Australians, discussion of which is beyond the scope of the present book or the wisdom of its author.

discreet, discrete   These two words have very different meanings, but are etymologically identical (Latin, *discretus* = separate). It is only recently that the present convention became established: *-ete* for the sense 'separate', *-eet* for the sense 'confidential'. To remember which is which, remember that *discrete* (= separate) is the opposite of *concrete* (= lumped together).

discrimination   Discrimination means *discernment*, the exercise of judgement. Until recently, it was a neutral term, implying logic and impartiality, the qualities expected of a judge; if anything, it was positive, a sense that survives in such phrases as *the discriminating customer*, implying not only the capacity to *distinguish* good from bad and right from wrong, but (unless otherwise stated) to *choose* the good and the right.

However, the word has beco`me closely associated with irrationality and prejudice, and especially racial and sexual prejudice. Thus *the decision showed evidence of discrimination* is likely to refer (or be understood as referring) not to a careful weighing of the pros and cons, but to the prejudiced rejection of some options. *Positive discrimination* is then the prejudiced acceptance of these same options.

It is futile to argue that discrimination should not be used in this way. This is how it is likely to be used and understood, and those who use it in the original sense should take care to make this clear.

disinterested   This word means *not standing to gain or lose by the outcome* of the matter being observed, discussed, etc. The word for *not giving a damn either way* is *uninterested*. This useful distinction is threatened, and is worth fighting for. See INTEREST.

disjunctions   See GRAMMAR (3(g)).

disk   This spelling has greater antiquity and respectability than *disc*, and should be used in all senses. See DISC....

dissoluble, dissolvable   See SOLUBLE/SOLVABLE.

dittography, haplography   These are the technical terms for two forms of transcription error which can easily occur in copy typing and typesetting. (The terms are taken from a harmless academic sport known as *textual criticism*, which attempts to reconstruct, on the evidence of unreliable manuscript copies produced by tired, bored and often semi-literate medieval monks, what ancient authors originally wrote.)

Dittography is accidentally writing the same letter(s) or word(s) twice. It is so common that many word processing programs contain routines to query any repeated words.

Haplography is writing only once a repeated sequence. It often occurs when the same word appears in the same position in consecutive lines of a manuscript. The copyist ends one bout of copying on the first appearance of the word, and picks up again after the second, so that the words between the two identical words are omitted.

There is a related error which can occur in new writing. Fowler called it *cannibalism*, defining it as *the tendency of words to devour their own kind*. It occurs most frequently with the word *that*, as in the sentence *There is no question that that is my jacket.* In spoken language, the problem hardly exists: the two *that*s are stressed differently, and a *speaker* perceives no problem. But the *writer* is liable to feel that the juxtaposition looks wrong, and omits one of the *that*s: *There is no question that is my jacket.*

A similar problem can occur with *as*: *Paterson is known not so much as a short story writer as a balladist.* This construction requires that the sentence should end *as as a balladist*, but any writer who noticed this would reframe the sentence rather than put both of them in.

do   Shakespeare would happily have written *Like you sausages?* Today, however, we would say *Do you like sausages?* What is the status of *do* in this sentence?

Modern English does not like interrogative inversions except with auxiliary and very weak verbs (*Are you…? Have you…? Will you…? Can you…? Must you…? Ought you…?* etc.). Where none of these will fit, we use an equivalent inflection of the verb *to do* (*Do you…?*). (See QUESTIONS….)

A similar situation arises with negative statements. We do not like attaching *not* to verbs other than these same weak and auxiliary verbs, and again use *to do* as a fill-in. The patterns can be summarised:

Positive statement   Question   Negative statement
He likes sausages.   *Does he like sausages? He doesn't like sausages.*
Strong (i.e. not-auxiliary) uses of *have* and *do* cannot be inverted and are treated in the same way:

He has a cold.   *Does he have a cold?   He doesn't have a cold.*
He does physics.   *Does he do physics?   He doesn't do physics.*

The idiom has been extended in two further ways:

(1) In forming emphatic tenses of verbs:

> *I do like sausages.* (present)
> *I did put the cat out.* (past)
> *Do come and stay with us.* (imperative)

(2) In acting as a general-purpose repeater for whatever verb has gone before:

> *I like sausages, and so does she.*

Once again, these patterns cannot be used with weak or auxiliary verbs, the original verb being in such cases stressed or repeated. This leads to problems in long sentences, where the pattern can get lost in the verbiage:

> *Cabinet may consider the option of tariff protection for the industry, but, like its predecessors, may find it inexpedient to do so.*

The sentence as it stands can only mean that earlier cabinets found it inexpedient to *consider* the matter, whereas the writer intended it to mean that earlier cabinets had found it inexpedient *to grant tariff protection*. The careful writer makes sure that the structure of the *do* clause echoes the structure of the clause it is supposed to echo.

See MODAL AUXILIARIES.

dramaturge ACOD defines this word as 'dramatist'; Mac does not mention it at all, while recognising *dramaturgy* as 'the dramatic art'. These entries have sadly been overtaken by events.

The term dramaturge is used in many Australian theatres and theatre schools to describe a person with stage experience who acts as an adviser to playwrights. If our specialist world needs such people, it also needs a word to describe them.

due to The sentence

> *Due to the rush-hour traffic, I was late*

causes the grammarians endless trouble, because (they say) *due* is an adjective, and hence needs an antecedent. It is also one of those usages which offends people who like to be offended. So we must either justify it or join in the condemnation.

The first point to note is that it is a common usage. There is something seriously wrong with a grammatical system which cannot accommodate proven usages.

Fowler regarded it as a fledgling preposition. If we replace *due to* with *because of*, there is no problem. He pointed out (as do ACOD and Mac) that *owing to* is now a preposition, and predicted that *due to* would shortly follow. His prediction has now been fulfilled.

For more about this, see PREPOSITIONAL PHRASE.

dunny ACOD tells us that *dunny* originates in an English dialect word *dunnekin*, becoming *dunny* as a Scottish dialect word meaning *a cellar under a tenement*. RW tells us that it started off as 'the old

British word *dunnaken* or *dunnakin*, meaning *a place of dung'* and Mac says much the same. AND has a single citation from 1843 for *dunnekin*, and then a flood of citations for *dunny* from 1933 on.

The ACOD story looks after the form of the word, but not the sense – use of a cellar as a privy is improbable, even in Glasgow. But none of the other stories is very clear on the most important question: what is the evidence that those who first used the Australian word *dunny* actually had the others in mind? AND provides evidence of a use of *dunnekin* in Australia, but what happened to it from 1843 to 1933? The story implies that the first modern users of the words had an astonishing access to obscure or forgotten usage – usage which then disappeared without trace, leaving only the abbreviated version.

Anyway, *dunny* is a perfectly delightful word, which has moved from being a coarse term, nearly as bad as *shithouse*, to being (a) a jocular, inoffensive general term, as in the phrase 'go to the dunny', and (b) a nearly-respectable nearly-technical term for a back-yard privy of the pre-WC era, and its still-operational counterparts in the bush.

Durex™   This word should be used with care. In Australia, it was a brand name for cellulose tape, and became widely adopted as a generic. 'Such parcels must not be sealed with durex' said a post office regulation of the 1950s. In Britain, it is likewise a brand name which became adopted as a generic, but it means a *condom*.

The original Australian usage has lapsed, and inasmuch as the word is still used in Australia it is understood in its British sense. But of course references to the former sense survive in the literature.

The word is not found in our dictionaries in either sense.

dutiable, taxable   These words mean *currently subject to duty/tax*, not, as their form suggests, *able to be subject to duty/tax*. They are thus political euphemisms. This does not result in any ambiguity, because there is no need for a word meaning *able to be subject to duty/tax*, there being nothing on which ingenious governments are *unable* to levy duties or taxes if they have a mind to do so. *Dutiable* was first noted (spelled *dutyable*) by OED in 1774, just after that great tax-revolt we know as the *American War of Independence*.

Dutiable has the additional shortcoming that the *-able* suffix has been added to a noun (see -ABLE… (5)).

E

e-/oe-   Those who are shocked by the spelling *esophagus* should ask themselves how they feel about *oecology* and *oeconomy*. That's how Americans feel about *oesophagus*. For more about this, see DIGRAPH....

each (one), every/some/any(one/body)   All these are logically singular, so they cause trouble in inclusive language. We can say *Each child must help itself*, but this crude solution doesn't work when we start talking about grown-ups. Even *Each parliamentarian must help itself* is not acceptable. In the past, we might have used *his* as inclusive, but this is now regarded as SEXIST LANGUAGE.

There are some contexts in which *them/their* is (and has long been) acceptable, particularly if the tone of the sentence is plural: thus the objection to

> *Everybody must help themselves*

is pedantic and recent. At the other end of the scale, there are structures which are powerfully singular, so that

> *Somebody has to be the first to help themselves*

sounds odd even to non-pedants.

There are four possibilities:

(1) We can opt out by rewriting the sentences in the plural, or using a different construction;

(2) We can use *him or herself* every time, at the risk of tedium;

(3) We can assert that *himself* includes *herself*, which has the support of history but incurs the risk of appearing sexist, and in any case does not solve all the problems;

(4) We can persuade ourselves that *themselves* can be used as singulars.

Those whose ears are still at the formative stage are strongly recommended to adopt option (4). The rest of us will probably never be able to hear it without feeling pain, still less use it ourselves, and should adopt, in order of preference, (1), then (2), then (3). But we must learn not to *show* our pain when we hear option (4).

The problem is not confined to the missing third person singular. Well over a century ago, the hymnster Rev. Edward Caswall wrote the ambiguous lines

> *Soon will you and I be lying*
> *Each within our narrow bed.*

This is an awkward construction in English, requiring a single possessive pronoun meaning 'of each of us' which also does not exist. The problem could be solved by saying 'each within our respective narrow beds', but it doesn't sound very hymn-like.

economy   The word *economy* has two separate clusters of meanings, the one related to private housekeeping (the original sense of the

122

word) and the other to national housekeeping, originally called *domestic economy* and *political economy* respectively, with an adjective for each, *economical* and *economic*. The distinction is arbitrary but has become well-defined:

(1) *Economical* means *related to the saving of money*: An economical (= *careful with money*) person chooses economical (= *cheap*) goods as a matter of economy (= *to make the money go further*).

   The noun *economy* was first established as an adjective in this context in the Second World War in Britain: *economy labels* (= sticky labels enabling re-use of envelopes). It is now common: *economy pack/size* (= a pack that is *good value for money*). (It was not unknown before this: OED cites a lonely 1821 reference to *œconomy Leghorn hats*, but one cannot imagine Jane Austen speaking of one, still less wearing it.)

(2) *Economic* means *related to financial aspects of trade and commerce*. *Economics* (the current name for *Political Economy*) deals with *economic* issues and is practiced by *economists*.

   The term *the economy* is used to describe the current state of trade and commerce, and implies 'national': *the economy is in recession*. It can also refer to specified parts of the economy, as in the phrase *the rural economy*.

The adjective *economic* is also used in one sense which cuts across the division: in the sentence *Councils should charge an economic rent for public housing*, the word *economic* means *one which covers costs*.

Pronunciation: economy and *economist* have stress on the second syllable and a very light first syllable: /ick-onomy/. The main stress shifts back in the others and the first syllable retains its *e* sound, either short or long: /ecka-nomics/ or /eeka-nomics/, etc. There is nothing to choose between the last two, except perhaps that economists seem to use the short sound, so those who do not wish to be mistaken for economists should use the long one.

edition, impression, reprint, reissue   When does a reprint becomes a new edition, and what is an impression?

   An *impression* is a print run. Strictly, a *reprint* is an exact repetition of the previous impression, whereas a *new edition* is in some respects different. In practice, the following rules are used by most publishers:

(1) The new impression is called a reprint not only if it is unchanged, but also if the changes are restricted to correction of *typographical* errors.

(2) If the changes include correction of minor *author* errors (simple slips which do not alter the thrust of any argument), it is said to be *reprinted with corrections*.

(3) If there is *new matter* (e.g. extension of statistical tables to include more recent information) or *changes to the thrust of an argument*, then it is a *new edition*.

Another criterion is that of pagination: if the changes are so minor that old and new copies are effectively identical for the purposes of page references, then it is a reprint. If the pagination changes for any reason, then it is a new edition, even if there are no changes to the text. This may be an important distinction in books which are frequently referred to, e.g. school textbooks. If relevant, the reason for the change is specified: *large print edition, illustrated edition*, etc.

Counting *impressions* has the advantage that the count is continuous, the first *reprint* being the second *impression*. However, the term rarely appears on the imprint pages of Australian books.

Re-issue is a trade term for a reprint produced some time after the earlier edition went out of print, in the hope of reviving demand, and hence promoted afresh. *Cheap edition* is an obsolete Australian trade term for a *remainder*.

The above definitions of *edition* apply to trade descriptions. In law, an *edition* is 'a number of books put on the market at the same time', so that every new impression is a new edition. It has even been held that if copies of an impression are deliberately held in store for later release, the later release constitutes a new edition.

editor   For a discussion of the relationship between publishers and editors in periodical and book publishing, see PUBLISH…(2). The present article will discuss the prerogatives and responsibilities of (1) the book publisher's editor; (2) the book editor as a re-writer; (3) the general editor of a collection of papers by different authors, or an anthology; (4) the author in dealing with publishers' editors.

(1) The publisher's editor   Book editing is like a Chinese meal – it can theoretically continue indefinitely. The first essential is to know where to start; the second is to know when to stop.

An editor's main responsibility is to satisfy the reader. This is not an act of treachery to the author and publisher, but the way in which the editor can best serve both author and publisher: by giving them prior warning if the reader is likely to find the text unsatisfactory, and suggesting practical ways in which it can be made more satisfactory.

In a well-run publishing office, the editor's brief will be spelt out by the person responsible for allocating editorial jobs, who will have read enough of the manuscript to know what sort of attention it needs. The editor then works to a closed brief, and need not feel responsible for dealing with shortcomings not mentioned in the brief.

Most book publishers, however, do not work this way. Manuscripts come to editors (even freelance editors) with no clear brief, and it is left to the editor to decide what to do.

Samuel Johnson showed that he would have made a good editor when he wrote: *There are two things I am confident I can do very well. One is an introduction to any literary work, stating what it is to contain, and how it is to be executed in the most perfect manner; the other is a conclusion, showing from various causes why the execution has not been the equal of what the author promised to himself and the public.*

The editor's first task is to compile (at least in the mind) an 'introduction' and 'conclusion', as Johnson described them. The difference between the two is the editorial brief.

The brief should answer a number of more specific questions:

(a) Is the material presented in a manner suited to the readership at which it is aimed (reading level, clarity of presentation, breadth and depth of coverage)?

(b) Is the writing competent (spelling, punctuation) and consistent?

(c) Given that almost every book has a factual element, are the facts correct?

(d) If there are quotations and references, are they accurate? And has permission been obtained for any quotation of copyright material?

(e) Does the book contain anything actionable or offensive – evidence of defamation, blasphemy, racial and sexual prejudice, etc.? (See DEFAMATION, PREJUDICE.)

A first, quick reading of the whole manuscript should yield simple yes or no answers to all these questions. It is important to remember that first impressions, though not always right, are more likely to mirror the impressions of readers and reviewers than any subsequent reading, and that first impressions only happen once. Notes taken during this reading may be of great value in sorting out vital from peripheral issues when the second, more detailed reading is undertaken.

The first reading will identify any areas which require specialist attention. It may be good to have a manuscript read for libel, fact, or appropriateness to the readership by an expert – and the expert may in the case of 'appropriateness' be a typical target reader. No editor can be expected to be an expert in all these fields, but likewise every editor should be able to recognise the points on which expert advice is needed.

The relative importance of the five points listed above will vary greatly from book to book. In many cases, a check on competence (essentially, copy editing) is all that will be needed. In other cases, technical or structural editing may be needed if the job is to be properly done.

Technical editing does not, of course, mean that the editor should check every fact, every quotation and every reference. The editor should have a nose for error, and check at least enough dubious items to be able to say whether a more complete check is necessary. If the problem is appropriateness to the anticipated readers, rewriting may be necessary, a topic discussed in (2) below.

Perhaps the biggest bane of an editor's life is the quest for consistency. In certain classes of academic book, the style must be consistent with established conventions – for bibliographical references, SI units, etc. This is generally more simple (since it is the systematic application of objective rules) than the maintenance of internal consistency. Consistency can be particularly elusive in books with a complex structure of headings and subheadings, or whose material is drawn from a range of sources and is hence in different styles.

During the first reading, the editor of such books should make notes on all the classes of problem likely to arise. Decisions can then be made, and applied during the second reading. There is nothing so time-wasting as going through a manuscript and deciding that a spelling which appears on the last page should be adopted throughout, so that the whole MS must be worked through again to apply it at all previous appearances, and this remains true despite the availability of helpful routines on word processors.

At the same time, there are many books in which consistency is of less importance, and the editor who tries, for example, to tidy up the punctuation of a poet with idiosyncratic ideas on the subject is unlikely to be thanked by anyone.

What of the editor's rights and responsibilities in matters of law and ideology? If an editor runs into potentially libellous or offensive material, the author should be informed. Usually, authors will agree to make the necessary changes; failing agreement, the publisher must be notified. Much the same goes for offensive phrases, e.g. evidence of racism, sexism, etc. The wise editor starts by informing the author. In most cases, the offence will be accidental, and the author will be pleased to have been warned, giving the editor the go-ahead to make appropriate changes.

However, if the matters in dispute seem to be critical and the author is adamant, the editor must refer the matter back to the publisher (who presumably accepted the book for publication in its original state). On no account should an editor attempt to make the changes by stealth or deceit.

Who wins if editor and author disagree? The answer is quite simple – the author. Any editorial changes are technically breaches of the moral right of authors to the integrity of their work. Most authors appreciate the help of good editors – indeed, the professionalism of authors can often be measured by the extent to which they recognise the help that a competent editor can give. However, just as the author should recognise that the editor can offer a preview of the reaction of future readers and reviewers, and hence should be listened to, so the editor should realise that the text is the author's child, and it is quite wrong for an editor to perform surgery on it without the consent of its parent.

(2) The editor as a re-writer   Many so-called 'editors' are for all practical purposes ghost writers. This is particularly true within institutions which prepare material for public consumption which has been drafted by people who make no claims to expertise as writers. In this case, the editor has less need to respect the words in the original draft, the main responsibility being to produce a text which presents the author's facts and ideas in a form suited to the potential reader.

The editors employed by publishers of educational and instructional books will often fulfil a similar role. Indeed, few such books are published in which the editor has not contributed sentences, paragraphs or a lot more.

The wise editor will make sure at the outset that the author understands this. Some very incompetent writers can prove unexpectedly protective of their turgid product. Tact and sensitivity are thus two important attributes of a good editor.

This is particularly important when rewriting technical drafts. Nothing will upset an author more than a rewrite which distorts facts or concepts. This does not mean that the editor must have an expertise matching that of the writer, but the editor should have an expertise matching that of the anticipated *reader*. If such an editor misinterprets the author's draft, that is then *prima facie* evidence that the draft was unclear. Even if the proposed clarification is wrong, what is needed is a fresh clarification, not a return to the draft text.

For the more extreme case, see GHOST WRITER.

(3) The general editor   A general editor fills a role between that of the author and that of a publisher's editor. If a book is a collection of papers by different authors, the general editor ensures that the contributions are consistent and cover the ground without too many overlaps or gaps. Often, the job is given to one of the contributing authors. In the case of an anthology, the general editor will choose the contributions.

In some respects, then, the general editor fulfils the role of author, taking overall responsibility for the coherence, scope and depth of the book. In order to do this, the general editor must have some of the rights of the author: to choose what material is included, and to cut and even change it if it doesn't fit the grand design.

In the case of an anthology of previously published work, each text will usually be sacrosanct, so that the editor's only decision is whether or not to include it.

In the case of a symposium (e.g. a set of conference papers), the extent of the editor's prerogatives should be agreed in advance with the contributors, and ideally should be as broad as possible, as authors need to understand that a published collection must have a coherence which separately written papers will rarely have. In the absence of any such agreement, the original authors retain their right to the integrity of their texts, and every change must be approved by them.

Even if general approval for editorial changes has been given, it is a courtesy to submit the final text to the original authors for their approval, but problems are minimised if they have understood from the start that their work may be subject to editorial change.

If extensive quotation of copyright material is involved, as often happens in such work, the points made under COPYRIGHT (2) are particularly relevant.

(4) Authors and editors   Most authors, particularly the more professional ones, get on very well with their editors. The more professional the author (and, of course, editor) the more likely this is to be true, because the value of a good editor is recognised.

The most common source of problems is the belief of some authors that the relationship between author and editor is that of an adversarial court, where each side is trying to preserve its position and changes are negotiated by tit-for-tat concessions. Authors should remember that good editors do not suggest changes simply for the self-gratification of stamping their own idiosyncrasies on the MS, but because they believe the changes will improve the book. The interests of the author and editor should largely coincide: to make the book as acceptable as possible to the readers.

Authors have the ultimate right to say what is published under their names. This means that, in the last resort, the author has all the trump cards. But if authors insist on rejecting the editor's suggestions, they are liable to find that the same suggestions turn up in adverse reviews, when it is too late to do anything about it.

If, therefore, authors feel that their editors have misunderstood their intentions, it is as well to ask why. An editor may indeed have misunderstood the text, so the specific suggestions may be wrong. However, if an editor (who will read the text more carefully than most readers) has misunderstood it, this implies that the text needs clarification.

-ee, -ée   *Fiancée, entrée, matinee, licensee, settee.* Words with these endings present three problems:

(1) Which of them must, which of them can and which of them must not have accents?

(2) Which ones are feminine, so that the final *e* should be dropped if the subject is male?

(3) How are they pronounced?

(1) Accent   The accent should be retained if the word is perceived as French or if it helps remind people of the pronunciation (both of which apply to *entrée*). *Fiancée* often gets one, but would not suffer from losing it, and *matinee* can have one but generally doesn't. Accenting *licensee* and *settee* would be wrong. A word which looks pretty silly without one is *née*; but it also looks rather silly with one, and we can be grateful that it is rarely seen these days (and never in the masculine form).

General rule: if in doubt, leave the accents out.

(2) Second *e*   The second *e* in *fiancée* is a feminine inflection. The masculine form is *fiancé*. Other similar words are rarely seen in the feminine form: *émigré, roué*. Indeed, some words never take a feminine *e* even though they are palpably French and feminine: *She was blasé about the whole affair*. The other words listed above are nouns in which the second *e* is an integral part of the word, not a gender inflection.

(3) Pronunciation   A fractured Gallic pronunciation is retained for many imported French words, including *matinee*, long after they have become effectively naturalised. For advice on pronunciation, see the long list under FOREIGN WORDS.

Licensee has lost any French connection it ever possessed. Although getting its form from that of a French past participle, it should under no circumstances be pronounced Frenchwise. It is a representative of a largish group of words, many of which are legal terms and have antonyms ending in *-or* (e.g. *licensor*): *lessee, mortgagee, referee*; but there are many in other fields: *debauchee, trainee, employee, escapee, evacuee, examinee, interviewee, refugee*. Indeed, the suffix is strong enough to be used in new officialese; i.e. if there was a verb *to squabulate*, a *squabulatee* would be understood as 'one who is being (or has been) squabulated'.

Settee has no French connection at all. It is a member of a small group of words which for various reasons have acquired this ending, but have no connection with French past participles: *bargee, bootee, goatee, grandee*.

effect(uate)   For the relationship between *effect* and *affect*, both as nouns and as verbs, see AFFECT....

Effect, in such phrases as 'effected an entry' (for 'broke in') is an example of PLODDERY. In this case, the source is some long dead legal draftsman, but it keeps turning up in new laws. Why it sounds so silly is not clear. It is not that there is anything wrong with *effect* or *entry*; one might suggest that it was an unnecessary circumlocution, but it is really no worse than hundreds of others. Its great crime, I suspect, is just that it consorts with known policemen.

Effectuate commits an even greater crime: it consorts with known behavioural scientists.

e.g., i.e.   These initials mean *for example* (Latin: *exempli gratia*) and *that is* (Latin: *id est*) respectively. Thus *e.g.* introduces a *selection* from a range of possible examples, whereas *i.e.* is either an *explanation* or an *exhaustive list* of what has gone before.

The retention of the twin full points is recommended, since *eg* and *ie* look like fragmented misprints, and *ie.* and *eg.* are uncouth.

-ei- For a discussion of the *-ei-*/*-ie-* problem in spelling, see SPELLING PROBLEMS (3).

elder, eldest These archaic forms of *old, oldest* survive in two usages:
  (1) In family relationships, where an *elder sister* is the normal phrase for a sister who is older than the person being discussed. *I have/he has an elder sister.* (*He has an older sister* would imply 'older than the sister currently being discussed'.)
  (2) Senior members of some social groups, including the Society of Friends and most Aboriginal communities, are called *elders*. This concept also survives in such phrases as ' …our elders and betters' and 'elder statesman'.
  Yet another spelling of *older* survives in *Alderman*.

electr(on)ic The distinction between *electronic* and *electric* is arbitrary but now well established. The sequence of coinage of the words is as follows:
  (1) The ancient Greeks called amber *electron*. It was known that an amber rod when rubbed produced various mysterious phenomena, sparks and the like, which came to be known as *electric* effects, and when similar effects were found to arise from other processes, the name stuck, the phenomenon being known as *electricity*.
  (2) At the turn of the century, the particle whose movements cause electric effects was identified, and called the *electron*.
  (3) The word *electronic* was coined as an adjective meaning *related to the electron*. This might have made *electronic* synonymous with *electric*, but *electronic* was used when the movement of the electron was the object of interest, particularly cathode rays (which were identified as streams of electrons), whereas *electric* referred to the effects of this movement (heat, light and motion).
  The word moved from science to common language in the Second World War in relation to radar, whose screens were cathode ray tubes. The post-war developers of semi-conductors, transistors and computers then adopted the word.
  The phrase *electronic media* means 'radio and TV'. See MEDIA. For the distinction between *electric* and *electrical*, see -IC(AL).

ellipsis The word means *omission*.
  (1) In grammar, an *ellipsis* is the omission of a word needed to complete the construction or sense, and is very common in both speech and writing. For example, we say *I think you are right*, where the full clause structure demands *I think* that *you are right*. We say that the missing word is *understood*.
  A very common form of ellipsis occurs when a word or words in a later clause or phrase are understood from an earlier one. The word(s) understood can be a repetition or a modification of what has gone before. Consider the following:

The lunch was over, and the table bare.   (*was* understood)
The lunch was over, and the bottles empty.   (*were* understood)
The guests had drunk more bottles than the hosts.
                                    (*had drunk* understood)

In each case, the sense is clear.

Sometimes, we can debate whether a pattern involves an ellipsis or not. For example:

He was wearing a clean though ragged shirt.

This construction is sometimes called an *abbreviated* concessional clause, implying that it is an ellipsis for 'though *it was* ragged'. However, we could not say

He was wearing a clean though it was ragged shirt

so there is no true ellipsis. Indeed, it is very similar to

He was wearing a clean but ragged shirt

where *but* is simply a conjunction between two adjectives, and there is no ellipsis. This construction is discussed in the entry on PHRASE as a *concessional phrase*.

(2) In writing, an ellipsis is the name for the three dots ... used to mark:

(a) a section omitted from a quotation:

The Constitution says 'The President shall ... be elected by the members.'

(b) an invitation to the reader to construct outcomes, particularly in comic or melodramatic situations:

All eyes were on the judge. Slowly, he placed on his head a black cap...

(c) an interrupted line of dialogue, also known as an *aposiopesis*:

'But I think...,' said Philomena.

'Don't think. It's dangerous,' said Lucy quickly.

Typographers are in disarray on the correct form and spacing of the ellipsis. The current recommended rules have been followed in the samples shown above.

(d) If the ellipsis represents an omission from a quotation as in example (a), the dots represent the words removed, so that a space should appear before and after the dots. In other cases the dots should follow straight on from the last word of the text.

(e) For punctuation purposes, the ellipsis is treated exactly as if it were a word, so that any inverted commas, question and exclamation marks and full stops should appear unspaced immediately after the ellipsis. However, in example (b) the intention is *not* to close off the thought, so the ellipsis can itself be regarded as the terminal punctuation.

When keyboarding, use the single-keystroke ellipsis offered by most keyboarding systems rather than three points. This has the immense merit that it cannot then be accidentally broken during text justification. It also ensures that the ellipsis is in the currently recommended form, i.e. three dots, unspaced. (The earlier preference for spaced dots is now rarely seen.)

eloquence   Considering the respect we give those who have the gift of the gab, it is very strange that we have so few positive words to use about them. We can say all sorts of nasty things about them, calling them *bombastic, garrulous, grandiloquent* and *loquacious*, but the nearest to a positive word is *eloquent*, and even this has a flavour of barristers' talk, a voice for hire. *Fluent*? This is all about flow, and has connotations of second-language skill. *Well-spoken*? It is spoilt by being used as a term of snobbery, the language equivalent of *well-born*.

So, how do we describe the eloquence of the person who is, quite simply, a pleasure to listen to? It is the gift of some of the great broadcasters. It is a subtle mix of medium and message, good sense delivered with apparently effortless grace.

The absence of a word for it is a pity.

This is no place to include a manual on public speaking, but there is a point about one aspect of it which is relevant to this book. This is that the essence of most good speaking, as of most good writing, is the search for what is simple, direct and clear.

There are some speakers, as there are writers, who impress us with the scope of their vocabularies: Shakespeare, for example, is believed to have used more different words than any other writer. But this does not mean that we can all become Shakespeares by buying a thesaurus and replacing the commonplace words with exotic ones. In practice, the outcome of this is at best PLODDERY and at worst nonsense: there is no quicker way of losing credibility than to use long words, but use them wrongly.

Similarly, there are speakers and writers who impress us with their power to control a very long sentence, but this does not mean that we become eloquent merely by lengthening our sentences and using more subordinate clauses.

A large vocabulary and an ability to keep complex sentences under control are both very admirable attainments, but for most of us a better path lies in using another class of eloquence, which depends on absolute clarity of thought and simplicity of expression. Here is an example of eloquence:

> *Two boys were playing with a frog, and it died. To the boys this was just part of the game, but to the frog it was reality.*

This is not from any of the great orators or raconteurs; it is from Plato.

emotive language   KILLER DOG MAULS OLD AGE PENSIONER, says the headline, and we shudder. PUPPY NIPS TRAFFIC WARDEN, says another, and we giggle. Yet the two stories are the same.

This kind of thing is common in newspaper headlines, and is fair enough. Both headlines are true. And both are more likely to make us read on than DOG BITES MAN (and making us want to read on is what a headline is supposed to do).

Emotive words are a very important part of our language. The richness of English lies in part in the connotations which surround so many words, and force most translators either to use many more words or to lose nuances.

The first danger is that abuse by newspaper headline writers, politicians, real-estate agents and advertising copywriters dulls the edges of these words; but most of us still know the difference between a woman and a mother, between a house and a home or (at the other extreme) wild animals and vermin. We each have our own ineradicable experiences of the emotive words; this is what makes them emotive.

The second danger is much more real, and it is that we may ourselves abuse them, and do a lot of damage in the process. It is easy to rephrase almost any proposition in a way which will win the support of people who do not know the issues – at least until they hear another equally powerful statement. This has been recognised by demagogues and their speech writers from the dawn of recorded time. If we think we have written particularly persuasively, it is worthwhile to look again and see if we are not confusing argument with emotion. If we only want to win a debate, or get our readers' momentary attention, the use of emotive words is fine; but if we want to resolve a conflict, we are only deceiving ourselves if we think we have won before the cheering has died down.

emphasis   One test of good prose is to read it aloud and see whether the rhythms of the sentence match the sense. If the reader stumbles, either losing track of the structure of a sentence or needing to go back and re-read a sentence with a different stress, something is wrong. Of course, good anticipation is part of the skill of the reader, and the writer cannot be blamed if the reader fails to notice the flags; but, other things being equal, good prose will flow more naturally than bad.

In speech, we have all sorts of devices to help us, including pace (we slow down on the important statements) and intonation (we can emphasise individual words, or say them sarcastically). The writer often tries to replicate all these in prose, and in manuscripts the most common way of doing this is by using capitals and underlining. In typography, we have in addition italic and bold characters.

Each of these has a place, and the following may help to sort them out:

(1) Underlining   Underlining (also known as *underscoring*) is the normal way of showing stress in manuscripts and typescripts, but it should not be used for this purpose in typeset text. Typographers sometimes claim that this is an aesthetic choice, but in fact it is a convention born of technology. In the old days of handset type, underlining was tedious and upset alignments. The first solution was to use letter spacing, a device which survives in German books set in black letter (Fraktur). For the last three hundred years, however, underlining in manuscripts has been interpreted by typesetters as italic unless otherwise stated.

(2) Capitals We are talking here about writing words ENTIRELY IN CAPITALS. This is another common way of showing stress in typescripts, one which is for some reason particularly popular with school teachers.

Capitals should not be used in this way in a typeset text. Initial capitals can be used to draw attention to the fact that a word is being used as a specific label rather than a generic term (e.g. *he would be doing a public service if he left the Public Service*). They can also be used in headings and subheadings (see SUBHEADINGS), and for special effects. (In this book, for example, full capitals are used for quoting newspaper headlines and public signs, and small capitals are used for cross-references – see SMALL CAPITALS.)

(3) Bold type Bold type should never be used for emphasis, though it can be useful for making **flags**. In this book, it is used to flag the main headwords and major subsections within long entries. In some cases, the best place for the flag may be the first occurrence of a word, which may be in the middle of a paragraph. Apart from this, however, bold type, like capitals, should never occur in text.

(4) Italics *Italics* are the normal way of representing special items in text. This includes titles of books, foreign words, new coinage and words used in unusual ways, as well as words which are being emphasised. It is the normal way of showing emphasis in print, and generally works well.

Italics are used for foreign words to indicate (1) that the words are perhaps unfamiliar, and (2) that they are essential to the sense of the passage. Hence italics should not be used for foreign words which are already integrated into the language (e.g. *de facto*). If unfamiliar foreign words are used, you should ask yourself whether you should be using them at all. (This is not a rhetorical question: there are often good reasons why you should.)

The following potential hazards should also be noted:

(a) Ambiguities can arise through using italics for a range of purposes (stress, foreign phrases, quotations, titles of books, etc.).

(b) Less-experienced readers may not recognise the convention.

Both these problems are particularly evident when a word which should be in italics occurs within a passage which is already in italics. The normal rule is to make it roman, but this can be tricky; see ITALIC.

empirical   This word is a term of logic: an empirical argument is one which is based on practical experience: see LOGIC (3). *Empirical* has nothing to do with the word *empire*. The adjective based on empire is *imperial*.

empower   The normal use of this word requires us to specify the scope of the power: thus we might say that authors *empower* agents *to* negotiate on their behalf. The word now has in addition an ABSOLUTE use: 'Our intention is to *empower* those who are currently oppressed'. Here it means *give power to*, without defining the nature or purpose of the power, though it is assumed to be political and social. This sense is not yet in the dictionaries, but it fills an apparent need and is readily understood, so it is likely to flourish.

endnotes   See FOOTNOTES.

English   This article is in three sections: English past, English present and English future.
(1) **English past**   The history of the English language is fascinating and complex. The present article has a very limited aim: to summarise those components and influences which are important to an understanding of the English we speak today.

Modern English is essentially an amalgam of two languages, its components being Anglo-Saxon and Norman French.

Anglo-Saxon is the general name for the languages brought to Britain by the Angles, Saxons and Jutes, who started arriving from northern Germany and Denmark c. A.D. 450. The language was not of course uniform: Kent was dominated by Jutes, East Anglia, Mercia (covering the Midlands) and Northumbria by Angles, and other areas by Saxons (Essex, Middlesex, Sussex and Wessex for the east, middle, south and west Saxons); and there were resultant dialects within Anglo-Saxon. But they adopted virtually nothing from the earlier British languages, e.g. Celtic, apart from a few place names. They simply drove the Celts out, calling them foreigners, *wealas*; hence 'Welsh'.

When, therefore, the first Norsemen arrived, around A.D. 800, they found a country in which a single language had been dominant for some 300 years; and although Norse had some impact on the language of northern England, Anglo-Saxon survived intact for another 200 years. When linguists talk of **Old English**, they are referring to the Anglo-Saxon of this period, and in particular to the dialect of the Kingdom of Wessex.

A second wave of Norsemen had a far greater effect. They did not come direct from Scandinavia, but were the descendants of Scandinavians who had settled in northern France, adopting the French language for almost everything except their own name. Thus *Norsemen* became *Normans*, and the region in which they had settled *Normandie*.

It was these French-speaking Norsemen who conquered Britain in A.D. 1066. They had at first all the power, wealth and influence, but Anglo-Saxon survived as the people's language. As the two languages were woven into the new cloth we now call **Middle English**, it was Anglo-Saxon which provided the grand design: the grammar, sentence structure and rhythms. Thus, while a modern English speaker cannot understand more than an occasional word or phrase from an Anglo-Saxon text, it feels familiar in a way which a truly foreign language text does not; and when we come to Middle English, the problem is overwhelmingly with the vocabulary and idiom.

The transformation from Old English to Middle English was not sudden. It was marked by a number of changes, of which the most spectacular was the arrival of French words. Middle English is generally defined as the English of the period 1150–1500. Its greatest exponent was Chaucer who wrote in a rich, subtle language, still fundamentally Anglo-Saxon in character but containing a large number of French words.

The adoption of this language (rather than French) as the language of government and commerce led to official efforts to rationalise dialect differences, and these efforts received a great impetus from the invention of printing. The first English printer, William Caxton, not only had to decide how to spell words (decisions which would disclose which accent he had in mind); in the case of translations, he also had to decide which of several alternative dialect words should be chosen to ensure that the translation was understood as widely as possible. Not surprisingly, he chose vocabulary and spellings reflecting the dialect of London.

His decisions did not, of course, immediately change speech patterns in other parts of the country, but they did have an impact on other printers. Caxton's spellings were widely adopted, even by printers who spoke dialects which made quite different noises. This influence extended to vocabulary: if there were two words with identical meaning, the one Caxton adopted was more likely to prevail. He thus invented the first printer's house style and the first Standard English. In tidying up Middle English, he was in effect inventing **Modern English** itself, the language of the period from 1500 to the present day.

Needless to say, Caxton's style influenced the style taught in schools and, ultimately, the style used in letters and private documents; but the process was slow. Many factors inhibited the move to uniformity. In the case of spelling, for example, people did not perceive consistency and uniformity as particularly desirable. Some regarded their spelling as an expression of their personality, varying it, like their clothes, according to the mood of the moment. (Shakespeare even varied the spelling of his own name.) Others used different spellings for different meanings of the same word, and some of these survived – see CHECK.... Most important of all, there was no general authority to defer to.

In the eighteenth century, all this changed. The Age of Reason brought with it a passion for order, symmetry, and consistency. It was a great period for seeking and discovering natural laws and rules and compiling lists, and there can be few better examples of this than the dictionaries of the period, notably Samuel Johnson's dictionary, published in 1755. It provided the authority.

How far this was his intention is another question. Today, we distinguish between descriptive and prescriptive lexicography, between the reporters who tell us how our language *is* used and the evangelists who tell us how it *ought to be* used. However, the distinction, even today, is not clear-cut. (See AUTHORITY and CORRECTNESS.) Johnson made many statements which suggest that he saw himself as a reporter, but he often behaved as an evangelist, bringing the good news that there was a right way of doing things. As so often happens when people are told the ultimate truth, the effect of his work was largely conservative: for all practical purposes, his spelling of English became a standard which has remained unchanged ever since.

Johnson's dictionary appeared halfway through the period from Caxton to the present day. Looking at it, this is hard to believe. Even allowing that Caxton was in many cases printing texts which had been written a century or more earlier, the gap between Caxton's English and Johnson's is altogether wider than the gap between Johnson's and our own. Furthermore, this is true whether we catch our sample of contemporary English in Britain, America or Australia. Johnson would not understand our English, with its overburden of neologisms and strange jargon; but his English is almost totally clear to us.

(2) English present English is currently spoken as a first language by an astonishingly diverse group of people scattered all over the globe. It is also the most widely used second language, the dominant international language of diplomacy, trade and culture, the language in which the Russians talk to the Chinese (bizarre though this notion may be).

Most interesting of all, however, is the use of English as the language of cultural exchange for people who speak minority languages. When a Nigerian scientist writes an academic paper in English, it is not just because it has to be in English if it is to be widely understood (though this helps); it is because the language of scientific research in Nigeria is English. Anglophones have the privilege of being able to enter almost any academic discipline and study it in their own language. For most of the people of the world, access to higher education involves working in a language other than their own, and for many this involves not merely translation but actually talking, writing and *thinking* in English.

It is worth remembering this when we are discussing the issue of 'cultural imperialism'. It is certainly true that language can be used as a weapon of domination. The suppression of minority languages, spectacularly illustrated in the history of the United Kingdom, is one of the ways the majority culture imposes itself. However, this can work both ways. The inventors of apartheid recognised this in framing a *Bantu Education Act* in which only such English would be taught as would allow the students to 'understand simple commands'. The implication was clear: teach them more than this, and they will start getting uppity.

We may have the best of intentions in encouraging language maintenance among minority groups, and there is no reason to believe that this is incompatible with learning fluent English; but we must not expect the children to thank us if, in the name of respect for the minority culture, we cause them to grow up with inferior English language skills, and hence denied access to the benefits of membership of the majority culture.

(3) English future   When it is suggested that English is dissolving into a series of mutually incomprehensible dialects which will in time become separate languages, it should not come as a shock or surprise: this has been the normal pattern in the past. We should be more surprised if it were suggested that things might not go that way.

The patterns formed by the relationship of dialects to one another are rather like a spoked wheel. The dominant dialects are located on the hub, and the others are on the spokes. In general, each dialect is in communication with the hub and with its immediate neighbours on the spokes, but not with dialects on other spokes.

Nobody chose which varieties were to be on the hub. They got there because they were the dialects spoken by people of influence, the varieties associated with government, the courts, commerce, education, the press and (later) broadcasting.

In the case of Latin, regional variants moved further and further apart along different spokes until they turned into Italian, French, Spanish, etc., and became mutually incomprehensible. At first, each of them still remained in touch with the hub language, Latin, but eventually this link broke and Latin itself survived only as a living fossil, a language of international diplomacy and scholarship which only the elite attempted to understand, and which nobody spoke at home. Eventually, it survived only for communication with God.

Will English inevitably go the same way? There are certainly dialects of English which are mutually incomprehensible, but there are still dialects on the hub which are understood very widely. Will this continue to be the case?

English has a penetration out of all proportion to the penetration of Latin in the medieval world. This is not just a matter of population numbers and geographical spread; it is a matter of the depth of the impact.

(a) *Broadcasting* penetrates not just to an elite, but to everybody. This can result in a babel of voices telling the story in every dialect; more often, however, it means a few voices telling it in dialects which are widely understood. Thus broadcasting provides a centripetal force, tending to maintain communication between the major dialect and the local variations.

(b) *The press* is another centripetal force: the readers of the Calcutta *Statesman* and the *Gleaner* of Kingston, Jamaica, can largely understand one another's newspapers, even if they cannot understand one another. And the hub dialects are constantly reinforced by the stories from the international news agencies.

(c) *Education* tends to promote Standard English, partly because of the massive problems of providing educational materials in local dialects and vernaculars.

In sum: there will always be the two conflicting forces, centrifugal and centripetal; local centrifugal forces make the dialects drift further and further from one another, while international communication provides centripetal forces tending to keep at least the major hub dialects in contact.

History teaches us that, in the end, the centrifugal forces win, but most of the relevant history happened before the invention of radio. It would be a reversal of all previous experience if the centripetal forces survived; but who knows?

enquire, inquire We are told (e.g. in AWEG) that *enquire* is the normal spelling of this word when used as a synonym for *ask*, while *inquire* is what Royal Commissions do. This is almost certainly a true report of Australian usage.

However, unlike *ensure/insure* (see below) where the distinction between the two meanings is clear-cut and the alignment of the spellings with the meanings is well established, the alleged distinction between *inquire* and *enquire* is neither clear nor well established, and seems pointless. Many writers, especially Americans, use *inquire* in all senses, and if *enquire* were allowed to die, few would notice, still less mourn.

ensure, insure Unlike *enquire/inquire* (see above) the two spellings of this word have marched off with different packages on their backs, and are best now treated as quite separate words.

Ensure means to make sure, as in *Let us in ensure that the house does not burn down, which we will do by installing sprinklers.*

Insure is all about insurance, as in *Let us insure the house, so that if the sprinklers don't work we can collect the insurance.*

-ent, -ant *Dependent* or *dependant*? We have here two problems: an unhelpful rule and an illogical exception.

The rule is that these words follow the form of the present participle of the Latin verb from which they are derived. This makes -*ent* the most common form, and would support *dependent* as the only correct form (as it is in American spelling).

The exception is that some such words are derived from the French present participle, and this is always -*ant*. *Pendant* is one such, and *dependant* another. This is the form for the noun (but not the adjective) in British and Australian spelling.

The rule is no help unless you have a fair amount of Latin, and very little help if you do. The good news is that the -*ant* words form a fairly tight set, most of which are very well known (e.g. *important, constant*, etc.) plus some legal ones (e.g. *litigant, defendant, dependant, pursuant*). Hence we will not go far wrong if we write -*ent* in all doubtful cases.

enthuse   If we object to this word, we ought to be able to say why. See BACK-FORMATION.

environment/ecosystem/ecology   The word *environment* has been around for a long time, but was a rare biological term meaning *the living space of a single species* (much rarer than its general language cousin *environs*) until it was popularised by ecologists in the 1950s. Ecologists considered species in mutually-dependent groups, *ecosystems*, within which equilibrium was maintained, and applied the term *environment* to the living space of an ecosystem, complete with living and non-living elements. Thus they spoke of *coastal environments*, etc. The study of ecosystems was termed *ecology*.

The word *environment* was then taken up by sociologists who saw parallels between biological ecosystems and the relations between people and their physical surroundings. They started talking about *the urban environment*.

Next, it reached business efficiency experts and the writers of manuals for computers, who talked about *the office environment*, meaning the physical conditions under which people and computers worked.

Finally, it became a pleonasm, similar to *situation*, so that things which previously went on *in the classroom* started to go on *in the classroom environment*.

The word has connotations of health and happiness (*environmental protection*) and this is admirable. Let us therefore try to use it in this context only, and not use it where the sense would scarcely be altered by its omission.

ephemeral   *Ephermeral* means, literally, belonging to the day. It does not mean trivial. Thus *Hansard* is an ephemeral publication, whereas this book is not. The word has acquired the connotation of triviality simply because ephemeral phenomena are more likely to be trivial than long-lasting ones: compare AD HOC.

The word *ephemera* started life as a Greek neuter plural (cf. *criteria*) whose singular was *ephemeron*. Naturalists used *ephemera* as a generic for certain very short-lived animals (e.g. mayflies) and it then it became a Latin-style singular, complete with a bogus plural, *ephemerae*. All this is accurately reported by Mac. Other naturalists are said to use *ephemera* as both singular and plural. Nobody seems to use *ephemeron*.

epidemic, endemic   In medical parlance, an *epidemic* disease is one which strikes a population suddenly and spreads rapidly, generally by contagion. The antonym is *endemic*, referring to a disease which is around all the time. The terms are in some respects the equivalents in community medicine to the terms *acute* and *chronic* when talking of an individual's state of health (see ACUTE...).

If we are tempted to say that *tax evasion has reached epidemic proportions*, however, we must take care. It is unlikely to be sweeping through the corridors of the People's Palace, since it is a disease of the rich, and hence by definition not *epidemic* – nor *endemic*, for that matter. If the point being made is that it spreads like a contagion, fair enough. But if the intention is merely to indicate the size of the problem, which *proportions* suggests, some other word should be used.

epithet   An *epithet* is a word or phrase which gets attached to a person's name, e.g. 'Diamond' Jim McClelland, 'Pig Iron' Bob Menzies. Unlike nicknames, which are names by which people are addressed, epithets are words by which they are distinguished but generally not addressed.

Epithets were very important in the days before surnames, as they were the normal way of distinguishing between the various Jeans and Johns and Janes. When the use of surnames became general, epithets (as well as nicknames) were often adopted for that purpose.

More recently, the word was threatened with losing its original meaning. As many epithets were derogatory and some were obscene, *epithet* became synonymous with *profanity*. (See EXPLETIVE for another word which nearly suffered the same fate.) The threat (which worried Fowler) seems to have subsided.

eponym(ous)   An *eponym* is the name of a person who gives his or her name to something; the adjective *eponymous* is more common. Thus *Sir Thomas Makdougall Brisbane* was the *eponym* or *eponymous hero* of Brisbane. If you wish to be remembered, this is how to do it: Sir Thomas left few other monuments to his four years as Governor of New South Wales, but his name lives on.

To call Brisbane an *eponymous city* is strictly wrong: the adjective meaning *named after somebody* is *eponymic*. However, Fowler spoke of *eponymous words* (meaning words derived from somebody's name), and so do our dictionaries, so we can take it that this distinction is dead.

When we put on *wellingtons* and eat *sandwiches* while organising a *boycott*, we are using three eponymous words remembering characters in British history. You can look them up if you wish. Nearer to home, when we sit with our *Lady Blameys* in our hands, telling one another *furphies* and eating *pavlova* among the *banksias*, we are using four more. For a similar phenomenon involving trade names, see TRADEMARKS, and for the underlying principle, see ALLUSION.

-er, -est   (as in *nearer, nearest*) See COMPARATIVE CHAOS.

-er, -or   The distinction between these two suffixes is blurred. Both are added to a verb stem to produce the name of a person or thing who/which performs the act: collector, planter.

One proposition is that, especially in cases where both forms exist on otherwise identical stems, the *-or* form applies to a thing and the *-er* form to a person, as in the case of *resistor* and *resister*. Another proposition is that if the root word is English the suffix is *-er*, and *-or* if it is not, thus *receiver* but *receptor*.

Both these propositions are worth remembering, as they have a better than 50–50 chance of giving the right answer. But they are a long way from being 'rules'. They are not even used in new applications: we have *computers* but *word processors*. It would save a great deal of unnecessary heartache if we could persuade the *-or* to crawl away and die. However, this is unlikely to happen while we are still fighting the -OR/-OUR battle.

There are, in any case, some common *-or* words which are likely to survive:

(a) Those whose connections with verbs are so remote that the spellings stand in their own right (*scissor, motor, factor*).

(b) Those which are familiar in the *-or* form (and not used in any other) so that no one seems tempted to spell them otherwise (*actor*).

(c) Sundry terms where the *-or* suffix is pronounced /aw/ in speech (*cantor*).

(d) Those which occur in LEGAL LANGUAGE (abettor, licensor) where tradition ensures that *-or* will survive.

People who believe that there is a simple solution are deluding themselves, but there is one reassuring point. In the majority of cases which cause headache, both forms are acceptable. *Conclusion:* if you are not sure that it is *-or*, write *-er*.

There is a third related ending, the French-style *-eur* (as in *amateur*, one who loves something or does it for love), sometimes with significant difference in meaning from *-er* equivalents (*poseur, poser*). These words generally have strong meanings, and are likely to survive in their alien forms.

Esquire   Fowler observed that the British males, all of whom used to
be *gentlemen* with a select few *Esquires*, were now all *Esquires* with
few *gentlemen*.

Esquire is a title which once identified the lowest order of chiv-
alry, below a knight, and which still has some vestigial existence in
the honours system. However, it then came to mean any male born
into an upper class family but lacking a title.

Its great moment came with the rise of letter-writing in the
nineteenth century, when it was adopted for use on envelopes
addressed to a male for whom no other mode of address (higher or
lower) was known to be more appropriate: *John Smith, Esq.* It was
thus what computer programmers might call a *default title*.

In Australia, use of Esquire died out in the 1950s, and the default
title is *Mr* (see MR... and LETTER WRITING); but everywhere (including
Britain) the rising fashion is to omit all titles, simply addressing
letters to *John Smith*.

ethnic   George Papaellinas has said that he doesn't mind whether he
is called a Greek or an Australian writer, but he does object to being
called an *ethnic* or *multicultural* writer. The complaint is totally
reasonable.

Ethnic is a rough equivalent of *national*, but with strong connotations of sharing a language and a culture rather than a homeland
and a race. All of us have by definition an ethnic attachment. It
therefore makes sense to talk of *ethnic minorities*; but the use of *ethnic*
as a synonym for 'not belonging to the ethnic majority' is an
offensive innovation which should be strongly resisted.

Multicultural is in this context even more absurd. *Multicultural*
makes sense in the phrase *multicultural education* if it is used to
describe an education based on a broad range of cultural awareness,
in which the dominant culture is seen as one among many. It should
not be used to mean 'concerned with the cultures of minority
groups'; but it is not appropriate to use it as a collective adjective for
the *members* of those minority groups. Using it as a noun is even
worse.

But what term should we use as a generic for immigrants? The
best term ever devised was *New Australians*, with its strong implication that they already belonged here; yet within months of its
introduction, it had become pejorative. What was wrong, of course,
was our attitude, not the term. So long as we fear people who are
strange to us, whatever general term is used to describe such people
will become pejorative.

The most promising model is supplied by the Blacks. They
deliberately took a simple word that was pejorative, *black*, and
systematically set about making it respectable – in the true sense, an
object of pride and respect. The word *wog*, formerly about the most
offensive of all the xenophobic words, may be in process of a similar

transformation following its use by, amongst others, the theatrical group *Wogs out of Work*.

For a general discussion of this vexed topic, see PREJUDICE.

etymology Etymology – the study of the origins of words – is fascinating and occasionally useful, but can be dangerous.

(1) Sources of words Etymology tells us that *mother* is a word whose origins can be traced to the very dawn of language; that *tobacco* is an American Indian word; and that *nimby* is a very recent acronym for *not in my back yard*. We can learn something of the history of our culture and attitudes by seeing when new words arrived and where they came from.

(2) Spelling Etymology tell us that *handkerchief* is a *kerchief* for the *hand*, which may help by reminding us that it contains a *d*. It tells us that *Nullarbor* was coined from Latin, *nulla arbor* = no tree, which reminds us that it is not *Nullabor*.

Morphology is the specialist study of the forms of words, and tells us what patterns of change can be expected, giving a clear trail between (say) *enchantment* and *incantation*.

False etymology, however, gave us *choir* (believed to be from *chorus*) as a 'correction' of *quire,* and *rhyme* (on the analogy of *rhythm*) for *rime*. *Foetus*-fanciers often claim etymological support.

(3) Pronunciation Etymology tells us that *apartheid* is an Afrikaans word, literally *apart-hood*, and hence that the *t* and the *h* should be pronounced separately, just as with *sweetheart* and *goatherd*.

(4) Relationships The etymological trail shows us how the various senses of a word evolved from one another. Examples explored in this book include HUMOUR and CHECK. It also shows us how the words *act, agent* and *agenda* are almost intact members of a single Latin word family which have now gone their separate ways.

(5) Meanings Etymology tells us that *australis* was the Latin for *south*, and the name *Australia,* meaning *the land in the south,* existed before it was applied to any particular bit of land. Many modern technical terms have been coined by taking classical word parts and stringing them together, so that, for example, *tox-* is used in many new words to mean *poison*. Many botanical names are coined this way: if you recognise the word parts, you can sometimes guess what the coiner had in mind.

It is dangerous, however, to use etymology as if it gave us direct access to a truth more real than the evidence of our ears. Many people find *a three-wheeler bicycle* rather odd, but few are worried by having three or even four *semesters* (= periods of six months) in one year, and no one (except me, perhaps) regards *dry humour* as an oxymoron. If etymology tells us that a word means *x* but everybody is using it to mean *y*, it is perverse nonsense to stand by etymology.

The dangers of etymology are not restricted to popular misconceptions. Linguists hate to admit defeat, and will grab at any plausible antique source rather then write 'deriv. uncert.'. Thus our dictionaries relate *flat* (in the 'apartment' sense) to the Anglo-Saxon *flet*, a floor, which seems to me to be unlikely (see FLAT). Similarly, Mac suggests a connection between *loo* and the Old English *hleow*, a shelter. Words do not simply disappear for centuries and suddenly re-emerge. 'Loo' could also come from *gardyloo* (*gardez l'eau*), an expression used by Edinburgh housewives before throwing their slops out of the window on the heads of passers-by, or it might be a contraction of 'ablutions', or (most likely of all) it could recall a play on the words *water-closet* and *Waterloo*.

When we are wondering about an etymology, we look it up, and unless the dictionaries differ, or say something totally absurd, we must accept what they say. But if they all say something absurd, it can be that are all copying the same dubious source.

euphemism   Some people have been known to *go to the euphemism*, which sums up our present perception of the topic fairly well.

A *euphemism* is a word or phrase used to speak about something to which we are for some reason reluctant to give its proper name.

There is one sensible use of a euphemism, and this is as a code. Thus antiquarian booksellers have used a variety of euphemisms over the years to identify *Erotica*, including *Curiosities* and *Facetiae*, the intention being to identify these books for those in the know without attracting the attention of those who are not. For another example, see RETARDED READERS.

More often, however, the euphemism is used on the assumption that the real meaning is universally understood, so it seems that the taboo is attached to the word, not the thought. This makes it seem rather a stupid exercise, and it is worthwhile asking how it ever arose.

The first class was probably the religious euphemism, arising from various injunctions against taking the name of the deity in vain. In some religions the name itself is taboo, so that the deity is addressed by a pseudonym, though 'a name which cannot be uttered' seems like a contradiction in terms. In other cases the name cannot be used in secular contexts, so that a replacement is required. We do this, whether we realise it or not, when we say 'Goodness knows...'. But in general religious taboos survive in our language not so much in euphemisms as in that other great repository of taboos, our swear words (see EXPLETIVE and OATHS...).

The second class is the euphemism of wishful thinking or super-stition, of which a classic example is the renaming of the *Cape of Storms* as the *Cape of Good Hope*. An astonishing survivor into our sceptical world is the use of 12A as a euphemism for 13 in the floor numbering systems in high-rise buildings.

The third class arises from a whole topic being taboo. Excretion and sex are today the great taboo subjects, and it is no surprise that these supply not only a lot of euphemisms but some key swear words. The range of these is as wide as Roget's coverage of it is narrow.

It is sometimes difficult to distinguish the well-established euphemism from straight speech, but a fair rule is that any word or phrase which could mean something else either is or was a euphemism. Thus *comfort station* is a recent and deplorable member of a chain of euphemisms stretching back over the centuries, a list so large that there is probably no non-euphemistic word which has ever been widely used.

We are hard put to decide what the emancipated speaker should say. *Toilet, Ladies* or *Gents, convenience, cloakroom, powder room, smallest room, privy, ablutions* and *WC* are all euphemisms, and the *rest room* on an interstate coach is a positive misnomer. The Americans go to the *bathroom* (with the added anomaly that, if there is a bath in it, the bath will be called a *tub*). *Shithouse*? It has at least the merit that it cannot mean and never meant anything else, but even the most emancipated speakers would not ask for one at Government House. *Dunny* is attractive, but has unfortunate connotations. What about *loo*? Whatever its origins (see ETYMOLOGY) it is now an unambiguous term, used very happily at almost all levels of society and in semi-official, if not yet official, parlance. Thus it appears on architects' plans, but not yet on public facilities (though its commercial derivative, the Portaloo™, does). In public places, the most popular identification is silhouetted male and female figures, the euphemistic element being that they are simply standing there, not doing anything.

Sex is another fertile field for euphemism, but far less so than it was. For years, *interfered with* was the police euphemism for *raped,* but this is so no more. The Victorian taboos, which led to trousers becoming *unmentionables* and the legs of tables being shrouded in heavy cloth, have also gone. In any case, it is worth noting that Thomas Bowdler, that great embodiment of what we call Victorian prudery, had completed his work of cleaning up ('bowdlerising') Shakespeare and gone to his grave twelve years before the young Queen ascended the throne, and the great period of euphemisms for trousers was pre-Victorian, too. But 'William IV prudery' doesn't have the same ring about it.

In a class by itself is death, a taboo subject which, unlike religion and sex, appears to become more intractable as society becomes more sophisticated. Its abundance of euphemisms is well represented in Roget.

The fifth and biggest class of euphemism today, however, is that of bureaucracy. Much of this language is PLODDERY rather than euphemism, that is, pompous phrases designed to give dignity to trivial activities, but there are plenty of euphemisms. Unlike ploddery, bureaucratic euphemism is designed to make questionable activities seem benign, and to conceal unpopular activities and, above all, mistakes. Thus we have *negative growth* for decline, *industrial action* for strike, *retrenchment* for dismissal of staff, etc.

(Incidentally, the self-conscious use of florid language, the literary equivalent of ploddery, is called *euphuism* – a word occasionally confused with *euphemism* by literary plods. Happily, most of us are not tempted to make this mistake, since we never use the word. Nor should we.)

every(one/body)   For the use of plural pronouns with *every*, see EACH (ONE)....

exclamation mark   See PUNCTUATION (1).

expletive   An *expletive* is a grammatical term for a word which *fills out* a sentence without adding to its meaning. It is not necessarily a profanity. The speaker feels that an exclamation, adjective or adverb is needed to emphasise a particular word; but, not being able to muster an appropriate word for the job, uses an all-purpose filler. Thus we can delete expletives without interfering with the sense of the sentence. Intensifiers like *very*, *extremely* and *terribly* are often used as little more than expletives.

The word moved from the pages of the grammar books into the common language in 1974, in relation to tapes of the US President, Richard Nixon, chatting in his office. The transcripts of the tapes contained the constantly recurring phrase 'expletive deleted'. As Mr Nixon's expletives tended to be profanities, common language made the word virtually synonymous with profanity.

Note that *expletive* does not mean 'all-purpose'. The words *whatsisname, whaddyacallit, gismo, thingamybob/jig*, are not expletives, since they cannot be removed from their contexts without disturbing the sense.

See also OATHS....

exponential   This word strayed from mathematics into general usage via the language of environmentalism.

Scientists noticed that the uncontrolled growth of animal populations was *exponential* ($y = a \times b^n$), whereas the growth of food supply was at best *arithmetic* ($y = a + bn$), where y is the outcome, n the timespan and a and b are constants. As any exponential series will sooner or later overtake any arithmetic series, *exponential growth* was seen as a recipe for disaster.

The word *exponential* was immediately seized upon, and has since been used as a synonym for *rapid* or *disastrous*, being extended to growth rates which may indeed be rapid and disastrous but are not exponential. It is a very precise mathematical term and should remain so.

F

face   For the use of this term in typography, see FONT.

faction   Two points of usage are worth mentioning:

(1) Outside Australia, the word *faction* is pejorative. It carries strong connotations of mischief, and is applied to sinister, secret groups – but only by their opponents: no one would normally admit to membership of a faction, any more than they admit to membership of a CLIQUE.

In Australia, this usage exists, but the most common application of the term is to the formally-constituted groups within the Australian Labor Party. Here it is not pejorative: it is the name by which the members identify their own groups.

(2) The word *faction* was recently adopted as the term for *a novel based on fact*. It was immediately accepted into the language, partly because there was a need for such a word, and partly because it was, with its suggestion of fact and fiction, so easy to understand and remember.

Far East   See MENTAL MAPS.

farther   See FURTHER....

fascism   Australia's right-wing extremists are attacked as being *fascist* but identify themselves as *Nazis*. Technically, they are correct. Racism, which is the core of their activities, was an integral feature of Nazism (Hitler's *National Socialism*) but not of fascism.

Fascism got its name from the term *fasci* (= bundles), which was applied to small groups of political dissidents (largely ex-soldiers) formed to oppose Communist activists in Italy immediately after the First World War. These groups provided the name, and the original core membership, of a right-wing authoritarian party led by Benito Mussolini, the *Fascisti*, which seized power in Italy in 1922.

The word *fasci* is also the modern Italian form of the Latin word *fasces*, used for the bundles of rods with an axe in the middle which were carried by the *lictors* of ancient Rome as insignia of power. A representation of the *fasces* was adopted as the emblem of the new party, giving rise to the inaccurate belief that this was the origin of their name.

feasible   *Feasible* does not mean the same as *possible.* Happenings which depend on the whims of nature, like hailstorms, are always *possible* but never *feasible*, and feasibility is generally about *desired* events. An event is *feasible* if no man-made obstacles (especially financial) stand in its way.

featurism   This word was coined by Australian architect Robin Boyd to describe the habit of adding 'features' (that is, superficial adornments) to otherwise nondescript buildings, as a substitute for genuine individuality and innovation. Thus a *feature wall* was a wall painted a different colour from the rest.

Strangely, the existence of the word *featurism* is not generally recognised by our dictionaries, though the habit lives on and, there being no better name for it, the word lives on as well.

Federal   See COMMONWEALTH.

fell   The cliché is *at one fell swoop*, not ...*foul swoop*. *Fell* means destructive, and the metaphor is from falconry. The sole merit of the phrase is that, without it, the menacing adjective *fell* would be extinct.

female, feminine   See GENDER, SEXIST LANGUAGE.

fence   In Australia, a *fence* can be made of almost anything: timber, wire, corrugated iron, brick or stone. In Britain, a fence can be made of timber, wire or corrugated iron, but not brick or stone. Such a fence, even if it is a low one surrounding a garden, is called a *wall*.

fetus/foetus   Unlike other words with an *oe/e* dispute, *fetus* is not Greek but Latin. (For a discussion of the Greek examples, see DIGRAPH....) *Fetus* is a member of a small group of words, mostly starting with *f*, whose spelling in Latin varied between the two forms. It was then largely forgotten until the nineteenth century, when it was revived as a medical term. In accordance with their current fashion for so-called classical spellings, the British adopted *foetus*, and we followed, while the Americans adopted *fetus*.

If we are serious about the classical purity of *foetus*, we should be arguing for having a foederal government making laws about foeminine foecundity, since in all these cases the *oe* form had greater currency in Latin. The etymological superiority of *fetus* is recognised by every dictionary.

However, that does not mean it will go away. As OED said (after a paragraph extolling the merits of *fetus*) '...in actual use [it] is almost unknown'. And those words, written well over half a century ago, remain true today. That is the only, but considerable, argument for *foetus*.

few/little; fewer/less   *Few* refers to the number of items; *little* refers to the amount of stuff, and their opposites are *many* and *much*. These words present no problem. But we do have trouble with their comparatives, *fewer* and *less*, perhaps in part because the opposite of both of them is *more*. The usage is illustrated in the following:

If you have $\begin{pmatrix} \textit{few} \\ \textit{fewer} \\ \textit{the fewest} \end{pmatrix}$ dollars, you have $\begin{pmatrix} \textit{little} \\ \textit{less} \\ \textit{the least} \end{pmatrix}$ money.

In simplest terms, *fewer* is used with plurals, *less* with singulars.

But what if changing *less* to *fewer* changes the sense? When people say 'We want less taxes', they generally mean that they want the total amount collected to be less, not that there should be fewer channels of collection. It breaks the rule, but it cannot simply be changed to 'We want fewer taxes'.

One option is to re-write the sentence, perhaps to read 'We want less taxation'. Another is to say that we are thinking of *taxes* as a plural noun that represents a single entity. There are many such words (though they have arisen for a variety of reasons): we can say that we want *less measles*, *less politics* and *less wages*.

However, such cases are rare. In most cases, *fewer* will not change the sense, and is the word to use with plural nouns.

Note also the curious double comparative, *lesser*. This is used instead of *smaller* in some legal documents and in such phrases as *the lesser of two evils*.

fiancée For spelling and pronunciation see FOREIGN WORDS…(4), and for comment on its form, see -EE, -ÉE.

field See PADDOCK.

financial The question *Are you financial?* meaning *Have you any money at the moment?* is one which may puzzle non-Australian hearers, but they will soon learn. It is colloquial. The technical term is *liquid*; see LIQUIDITY….

In the context of membership of an organisation, a *financial member* is one whose subscription is up to date, and the question *Are you financial?* can also refer to this. This, too, is an Australian usage.

finite In grammar, the word *finite* is used to describe verbs whose meaning is closed off by having a defined number (singular or plural) and person (first, second or third). Thus the verb *goes* is singular and third person. The contrast is with the infinitive (*to go*), participle (*going*) and gerund (*going*). Finite verbs can be indicative, imperative or subjunctive.

This definition is crystal clear in Latin, the language for which the word was designed, because each person and number has a separate inflection of the verb. It is less so in English, where inflections are minimal, and we normally identify a finite verb through its power to complete a statement. Thus 'He goes up the hill' and the imperative 'Go up the hill!' are complete statements, whereas 'going up the hill' or 'to go up the hill' are incomplete.

fission See ATOM.

flat, apartment *Apartment* is the oldest term in English for a self-contained set of rooms within a larger building. Robinson Crusoe had 'an apartment in the tree'.

In America, such things have been called *apartments* ever since, irrespective of the social standing of the inhabitants and the nature of the building (i.e. whether it was built as a single large house and subdivided, or designed as an apartment block). The post-war word *condominium* strictly refers to a block in which the occupants own their apartments on strata titles, but is often applied to a single apartment within such a block.

In Britain, *apartment* was used only for a superior type of accommodation, more modest ones being *tenements*. (In England, each domicile was a tenement, and the building was often called *The Buildings*, e.g. *Peabody Buildings*; in Scotland, the tenement was the whole building, in which each resident had a *house*.)

At the top end of the social scale, vast buildings arose in the late nineteenth century, whose names generally contained the word 'mansions', within which the new-fangled hydraulic lifts gave access to units which were called *flats*.

In Australia, the British usage was adopted, even down to the name 'Mansions'. Subsequently, however, Australian usage has become broader than British, being extended to cover almost any dwelling unit which does not sit on its own grounds. Thus the word *flat* is often applied to a free-standing building in the garden of the main house. This usage has been extended to the term *granny flat*, which in its native Britain will be part of the main house.

The word *apartment* is also used in Australia, but it has a somewhat pretentious ring, and is used more by real estate agents than by the occupants of the premises. In the phrase *holiday apartments*, however, it should raise more modest expectations.

Our dictionaries all follow OED in telling a highly improbable tale about the etymology of *flat*, namely, that it started as a variant on an Old English word *flet*, meaning house. We have no access to the mind of the person who first used the word in the modern sense, but it seems infinitely unlikely that anyone would choose an ancient word *and then modify its spelling*. It is far more likely that a London property dealer advertised *a 'flat' apartment* (in contrast to the ordinary British assumption that bedrooms are upstairs), and that this caught on. Maybe a diligent researcher will some day find the advertisement.

flying terms   French dominance of the early history of flying resulted in a number of strange French words entering our language, including *fuselage, aileron, longeron, nacelle* and *aeroplane*. Of these, only *fuselage* retains a remotely Gallic pronunciation.

Aileron is the normal French word for the steering feathers on the wings of birds, and is also applied to the fins of fishes which do the same job.

Nacelle originally meant basket, and was applied particularly to the gondola hanging under a balloon. It was then applied to the basket at the front of an aeroplane in which, in more sophisticated machines, the pilot could sit, rather than being suspended among the open framework. In English, it is used in this sense in gliders, but the more common application is to the pod in which an engine is enclosed.

The whole device was called an *aéroplane* until this 'gracious term' (as Dupré calls it) was conquered in French by *avion*, a word coined from the Latin *avis* and the tail end of *ballon*. But before this could happen, it had been adopted by the British, who hung on to it. The Americans, meanwhile, anglicised it as *airplane*.

The OED$_1$ entry for *aeroplane* is particularly fine. It reads (in full): 'a plane placed in the air for aerostatical experiments' – one of the best entries in the whole huge work. The entry in OED$_2$ is much less succinct.

folio   The word has two jargon meanings: see PAPER (4).

follow(er)   The sentences *I follow the football* and *I follow Richmond* illustrate two slightly different usages of *follow*, both of which are Australian. The noun *follower* also occurs in the language of Australian Rules, but is a position on the football field, not a synonym for *supporter*. The term *fan*, as in *I am a football fan* and *I am a Richmond fan*, is the normal term in Britain but rare in Australia. See BARRACK.

font   In the language of books and printers, a *font* means a complete set of type carrying a given *typeface,* comprising *upper and lower case characters*, *numerals*, *punctuation marks* and a range of *special sorts* (e.g. ∞, ©, ¥, ≥). Its alternative spelling, *fount*, stresses its origins: it is the product of a type *foundry*.

Originally, there was a distinction between the *face* (which was the design of the image) and the *font* (which was the realisation of that design in type metal) but today's technology has clouded this distinction. In the language of computers, *font* has reverted to something more like its original meaning, so that the medium, bold, italic and bold italic of the same typeface are counted as four fonts.

Body faces are designed for use in the run of text, and tend to be plain; *display faces* are often more striking and idiosyncratic, and are designed for headlines.

A type specification might read:

10/12pt	*Helvetica*	*u&lc*	*condensed*	*bold*	*italic,*	*set 24 ems.*
(a)	(b)	(c)	(d)	(e)	(f)	(g)

What does all this mean?

(a) *10/12pt* (say '10 on 12pt') defines the type size and the distance from the top of one line to the top of the next. Here, *pt* stands for *point*, a printers' measure equal to ½₂ of an inch (approximately 0.3 mm). The terminology derives from the days of metal type.

'10pt' defines the height of the *body* of the type, measuring from the top of the highest *ascender* to the foot of the lowest *descender*, plus a *beard*, a small overhang of the body to provide space between each line of characters and the next.

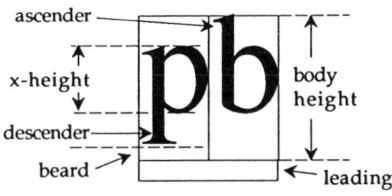

If the designer felt that the type would look better with extra space between the lines, *leading* could be added, the name coming from the strips of lead which were inserted between the lines. The specification would have been '10pt, 2pt leaded'. With the coming of machine setting, the extra depth was added to the body, so the same specification became '10 on 12pt' or 10/12 pt: a 10pt type on a 12pt body. Today, of course, most type is set electronically, but the terminology of metal type survives.

(b) *Helvetica* is the name of a *face* (= design). There are two basic classes of face, serif and sans serif, serifs being the crossbars at the end of strokes. There are hundreds of different faces within each class, a few of which appear in the table below. This text is set in the serif face Palatino, 9/10pt.

(c) *u&lc* means upper and lower case. The names come from hand setting, where the type was kept in trays called *cases* which came in pairs, with the capitals in the UPPER CASE and small characters in the lower case. A third option is SMALL CAPITALS (s.c.) which are supposed to be capitals of approximately the same height and weight as the lower case characters, though in this electronic setting they are simply scaled-down version of full-size capitals.

(d) *Condensed* indicates a variant on the normal design which squeezes the type horizontally. A third option is called *extended*. If not specified, the type is assumed to be the normal width.

(e) *Bold* indicates a variant which increases the **weight.**

(f) *Italic* indicates a variant which *slopes*, the alternative being roman, which is upright. This results in the potential oxymoron *Italic Roman numerals*. Call the upright type roman, not Roman.

(g) *Set 24 ems* means that the line length is 24 ems, where an em is 1/6 inch. This em is the nominal width of a 12pt capital M. As every type size has a different-sized M, the full specification was a *pica em*, where *pica* was a name for the 12pt size. This was variously abbreviated to *pica* and *em*.

Today, most people specify line lengths in millimetres, but *ems* and *picas* are still used by some traditionalists.

Class	Face	Variants		
Serif	Garamond	*italic*	roman	
Sans serif	Helvetica	condensed	normal	extended
Sans serif	Futura	light	medium	**bold**

For some other aspects of type, see KEYBOARDING, ITALIC, SORTS and TYPOGRAPHY.

foot   The story goes that someone once asserted that *dactyllic tetra–meters* could not be used for serious poems in English, so Tennyson marched off and wrote

> *Half a league, half a league, half a league onward…*

Dactyllic refers to one of the rhythmic structures of a metrical foot. The most important ones are:

dactyl	ǀ¯ ˇ ˇǀ dum-di-di	e.g. *traveller*, adjective *dactyllic*
iambus	ǀˇ ¯ǀ di-dum	e.g. *enchant*, adjective *iambic*
trochee	ǀ¯ ˇǀ dum-di	e.g. *running*, adjective *trochaic*

Others include *spondees* ǀ¯ ¯ǀ and *anapaests* ǀˇ ˇ ¯ǀ.

Tetrameter refers to the number of feet in the line, in this case four. Others are *trimeters* (3), *pentameters* (5) and *hexameters* (6).

A *foot* is a set of syllables containing a single stressed syllable, which represent a metrical unit. An incomplete foot (like *onward* in the first line quoted) is called *catalectic*.

This language, like the language of formal grammar, is very ancient, and was designed to describe poetry very different from our own, in which the *length* of syllables was important rather than *stress*, as in ours. Nevertheless, the terms are often used (and sometimes useful) in analysing the rhythmic structure of English poetry.

Thus we could describe the metre of

> *The lonely swagman through the dark*
> *Must hump his swag to Chandos Park…*

as an iambic tetrameter: *The lone-ly swag-man through the dark*

footnotes   In this article, the term *footnotes* is used to encompass three very different creatures:

(1) True footnotes, i.e. parenthetical observations which the author feels to be too important to be omitted but not important enough to be in the body of the text;

(2) Citations, the identifications of the author's sources for facts or quotations;

(3) Explanatory comments added by editors.

In each case, we will also discuss the options for placement of these notes: at the foot of the page, at the end of the chapter or at the end of the book.

(1) The true footnote   Aristotle managed to write a library-worth of books without requiring any footnotes, which leads us to ask whether we should use them at all. One good reason to avoid footnotes is that they are a hazard for typesetters; but the convenience of typesetters should not be a primary aim of writers. A better reason to avoid them is that they are a hazard for readers, who must either ignore them or get distracted by them.

One thing is certain: if a work has no footnotes, so much the better.

However, if a book has to contain *obiter dicta*, the footnote convention is very attractive. Its advantage is that the detour is visually distinguished from the main narrative. If an aside is inserted in the text, it looks like any other paragraph and the reader may have difficulty in seeing its relationship to the main narrative; the footnote convention enables the reader to return to the main narrative at the point of departure.

The success of the device depends absolutely on the footnote appearing on the same page as the reference to it. If the reader has to turn to the back of the book to find out whether the note is a major essay or a couple of words of explanation, the continuity is unnecessarily disturbed.

(2) Citations   Aristotle would never have got a PhD, as he provided no citations. We cannot believe that all his information about the number of teeth of rabbits, etc., was his own, and he might have spared himself some embarrassment had he cited his sources.

The PhD examiner insists on the citation of sources as it helps check that the work is academically respectable. The reader of the published version assumes that the work is academically respectable, and will only check citations when they are potentially interesting, e.g. when the name of the source may warn of a bias in the information given.

Since no reader is likely to want to check more than one in ten of citations in the average book, the citations need not be on the page. There is a lot to be said for gathering them all at the back.

For the form of citations and other options for referencing them, see CITATION.

(3) Editorial comments   Since these are presumably points that the editor felt quite strongly and urgently about, they should be accessible to the reader with minimum fuss, i.e. at the foot of the page. It is good manners to distinguish them from the original author's notes by adding '– Ed.' at the end of each. (This is not, of course, necessary in an annotated edition, where it is assumed that all the annotations are editorial.)

forceps   Outside the medical profession, *a forceps* is generally known as *a pair of forceps*, on the analogy of *a pair of scissors*, etc. (See PAIR.) This is well entrenched; *a pair of forceps* is now included in some dictionaries (e.g. ACOD).

Should we be concerned? Economy would disapprove of the use of two entirely unnecessary extra words, but English is full of entirely unnecessary extra words. The great merit of the usage is that it gives the etymology enthusiast the opportunity to point out why it is wrong, namely, that it is a direct borrowing of a Latin singular noun, *forceps*, whose Latin plural is *forcipes*.

foreign words, use of   The question here is largely of etiquette and practicality rather than style. If, as should be the case, you speak in order to communicate a message, the purpose requires that you do not use words or phrases which your hearers do not understand. For the general principles involved, see REGISTER.

(1) Meanings   Given the large number of words which have been imported into English, we should not be surprised that we sometimes get them wrong. A classic case is *nom de plume*, a phrase which does not exist in French, where a pen name is a *nom de guerre*.

Those who believe such problems with foreign imports have no parallel elsewhere may be relieved to know that the French are equally bemused to learn that their English imports *le smoking* and le *five o'clock* are unknown in English, being a *dinner jacket* and *afternoon tea* respectively:

Indeed, Jean Cunningham tells me that, on ferries operating between France and Britain, the British announcer says 'The buffet is open' whereupon the French one says 'le snack-bar est ouvert'.

Does it matter? If we agree about a word's meaning, then that is its meaning for us, irrespective of the views of its original owners. (See MEANING.) Of course it is nice to keep its original meaning, just as it is nice to keep etymological connections alive; but if they die, so be it.

(2) Pronunciation of foreign names in introducing people   If you are introduced to a foreigner, it is a courtesy to try to pronounce the name as it was given to you. Conversely, if you are introducing a foreigner, it is vital to get it as right as possible, as others will follow your lead. (For a relevant example, see the notes on the pronunciation of VAN GOGH.) If in doubt, it is quite appropriate to ask people how they like their names to be pronounced.

(a) Foreigners who come to Australia may well adopt anglicised or semi-anglicised versions of their names, particularly if they have had trouble with them: thus a Dutch *Jan* and a French *Jean* may adopt *John* if they keep getting called *Ms*.

(b) Likewise, many Australians have non-English names which were anglicised generations ago. The only crime worse than anglicising a foreign name is to foreignise an Australian one.

(3) Pronunciation of foreign names in talking about people and places   Consider the sentence

Jean Rothschild delivered lectures on Confucius and Don Juan in The Hague, Oude Tonge and Amsterdam.

This happily improbable utterance illustrates the problem of consistency.

(a) *Confucius* is the well-established Latinised and then anglicised form of the Chinese name whose Pin Yin form is *Kong Fuze*, and it would be perverse either to attempt an old Chinese sound or to pronounce *Confucius* in some imagined rendering of Marco Polo's Latin.

The Hague is a well-established English name for *Den Haag*, and English speakers should be grateful that it exists.

Amsterdam is slightly different, inasmuch as, although having an established English pronunciation, it is spelt as the Dutch original, tempting the unwary to try to pronounce it as the Dutch do. All these, however, should follow the rule that, if an established anglicised pronunciation exists, it should be used.

(b) *Oude Tonge* has no established English pronunciation, and the speaker should not lightly or inadvisedly attempt Dutch sounds in public. If the pronunciation is by consenting adults in the privacy of their own homes, anything goes.

However, those making public utterances, e.g. radio announcers, have a peculiar responsibility, since they are determining what their listeners will say. They should regard it as part of their normal professional responsibility to consult experts in advance if they are in doubt. The ABC has become astonishingly adept at getting very plausible, and probably 'correct', pronunciations of the names of Azerbaijani politicians, etc.

This has led, however, to the problem mentioned in 2(b): the ABC once gave Bernard Rechter a full set of gutturals in a news bulletin.

(c) If *Jean Rothschild* is an English lady, we have no problems. But if it turns out to be a French gentleman, we have a problem. We know we mustn't say *Jeen*, but if we make this French, we feel that we should gallicise *Rothschild*. But how do the French say Rothschild? Again, expert advice may be needed.

In the meantime, remember that the final *s* in the French *Jacques* is silent, and *Dietrich* is /Dee-trich/ (*ch* as in the Scottish *loch*), not /Dear-trich/.

(d) If the *Don Juan* in question is the hero of a Spanish work, then it is appropriate to say *Don Hwahn* or some such. But the hero of Byron's epic must be pronounced *Don Jew'n*, since this was what Byron intended. (See the general comment at the end of this article.)

Sentences of the sort discussed above rarely occur in ordinary conversation, but individual words crop up constantly, and mispronunciation can damage the speaker's credibility. This is particularly so if the words in question are French, since to the crime of mispronouncing they add the ignominy of being caught doing so. Mispronunciation of other languages is less likely to be detected, and hence less heinous, the heinousness diminishing with the increasing obscurity of the language.

A related issue arises from the habit of some countries and cities of changing their names. Our attitude should depend on context. If we are visiting a country or talking about its current affairs, we must use its current name, just as we should with a person who has changed his or her name. Thus we will talk of *Ho Chi Minh City* and *Sri Lanka*. However, if we are talking historically, the historical name should be used; it would be quite wrong to say that the French set up Emperor Bao Dai in Ho Chi Minh City. For more on this important topic, see HISTORICAL WRITING.

For the special problems associated with the adoption of Pin-Yin transliterations of Chinese names, see PIN-YIN.

(4) Common language words   By the time they are absorbed into our language, most imported words have acquired a received pronunciation and spelling, and the spelling will be a good guide to the pronunciation:

(a) If the word comes from a language which is not written in our alphabet, it will generally have been transliterated according to our phonetic rules (e.g. *safari*), and once it has arrived in this form it is idle to ask what the 'correct' (in this case Arabic) pronunciation was.

(b) The same will happen to words which come to us from a language which uses our alphabet but which reached us through an oral tradition (as did many Dutch nautical terms). The version we have is likely to be an attempted transcription of the foreign noise, using English phonetics, and the foreign origin can, for pronunciation purposes, be forgotten.

(c) If a foreign spelling has a plausible phonetic rendering in English, this will often be adopted.

   If the phonetic system of the original language is similar to ours, as in the case of German (*kindergarten, blitzkrieg, delicatessen*) there will be little trouble. Likewise, we say *smorgasbord* without worrying much about how the Swedes pronounce it, or even what it means. (It is the Swedish for what we call a *Danish sandwich*.)

   Anglicising Italian words (*peccadillo, fresco*) gives rise to very un-Italian noises. Many French imports are in the same category (*clairvoyance, guillotine, coupon*). Should we worry? No. The words are ours now.

At the other end of the scale, we will sometimes use foreign words which have not been assimilated and for which no agreed anglicisation exists. Here, the same cautions apply as for names in category (2): it is dangerous for common mortals to invent an anglicisation, but we can also lose a lot of points for a bad shot at the original pronunciation of French or German. If in doubt, we should check with an expert. This applies in particular to the vast territory of restaurant menu items. If in doubt, ask the waiter.

Between these two extremes come the words which make more trouble than all the rest put together. These are the words and phrases which can occur in quite ordinary language but whose spelling and pronunciation preserve some flavour of the original, so that they follow the rules neither of the source language nor of English. The received English pronunciation may be anything from a near perfect replica of the original to a near total anglicisation.

Plurals present problems: (1) *châteaux* or *chateaus*? Answer: as with some accents (see *château* below), the French plural should be used in French contexts and the English in English ones, and the *x* will be silent but the *s* sounded. (2) *Coups d'état* or *coup d'états*? Unless the context is French, we ignore the French rules and say, for example, 'There were two *coup d'états* (/*coo day-tahz*/) in quick succession'. But this is only because any alternative sounds pretentious or silly. On the write-as-you-speak principle, this means that we must write *coup d'états*. However, in formal writing, not designed for reading aloud, this might seem shocking, and *coups d'état* will then be preferred. The more a phrase is absorbed into the language the less likely this pedantry will be desirable, so that only an extremist would object to *cul-de-sacs*.

The following pages contain suggestions about a pronunciation and spelling which will generally be acceptable.

The first set are all French. The hardest sound is the nasalised *n* in *en*, *bon*, etc., here represented by *(n)*, but in many cases an anglicised *n* is acceptable and in a few cases preferred. The accents are shown, but in practice they are generally written without them. Where there is a clear preference for retaining or dropping the accent, this is shown (and the rule is: if in doubt, leave it out).

There is no suggestion that these pronunciations would be acceptable in Gay Paree; we are talking about acceptability in the salons of Balmain:

agent provocateur, /*azhaw(n) provocka-terr*/.

aide-mémoire, /*aid mem-wah*/, written without accent.

amour propre, /*ammore propr'*/.

appliqué, /*appli-kay*/, written with accent.

après ski, /*appray ski*/.

au fait, /*oh fay*/.

au pair, /*oh pair*/.

avant-garde, /*avvaw(n) gard*/.

bain marie, /*ba(n) m'rree*/.

barrage, /*b'rahj*/ or /*ba-rahj*/.

bas-relief, fully anglicised; see BAS-RELIEF.

béret, /*berray*/, written without accent.

bête noire, /*bate nwah*/, written with circumflex. Note that *noire* always has a final *e*, the gender of the word *bête* being feminine, even if the person referred to is male.

bon mot, /*baw(n) moe*/, but /*bon moe*/ is common and not a capital offence.

bon vivant, /*baw(n) veevaw(n)*/ rather than /*bon veevon*/.

boudoir, /*bood-wah*/.

bouquet, /*boo-kay*/.

brassière, /*brazzie-air*/, written without accent.

buffet, /*boofay*/, with /*oo*/ as in *woof-woof*.

cachet, /*kashay*/.

café, /*kaffay*/, though both /*kayf*/ and /*kaff*/ will be interpreted as jokes, not errors; written with accent only if the context is French, e.g. *Café de Paris* but *Star Cafe*.

cause célèbre, /*koze sellebr'*/.

chassis, /*shassie*/ plual chassis, /*shassies*/.

château, /*shat-oh*/; written with circumflex only if the context is French, e.g. *Château d'Yquem* but *chateau bottled*.

cliché, /*kleeshay*/, written with accent.

clientèle, /*klee'n-tell*/ or /*kly'n-tell*/, not /*kly'n-teel*/; written without accent.

comme il faut, /*kommeel foe*/.

communiqué, /*k'munikay*/, written without accent.

compère, /*kom-pair*/, written without accent.

corps, /*kor*/.

coup, /*koo*/.

coup d'état, /*koo day-tah*/, written with accent.

coup de grâce, /*kooda gruss*/, not /*kooda-grah*/; written with accent.

coupé, /*koo-pay*/, but /*koop*/ is no longer the Americanism which it once was.

crème de la crème, /*krame d'lah krame*/, written with accents.

crêpe, /*krape*/, written with accent. Those who attempt to encase it in French surroundings should remember that it is *la crêpe* if it is eaten and *le crêpe* if it is worn.

cri de cœur, /*kreeda kur*/.

crime passionel, /*kreem passeo-nell*/. Note that *crime* is masculine, so the second word is not *passionelle*.

crochet, /*crow-shay*/ crocheted, /*crow-shade*/ crocheting, /*crow-shaying*/.

cuisine, /*kwizzeen*/, not /*koozeen*/.

cul-de-sac, rhyme *cul* with *pull*. Rhyming it with *dull*, however, is generally acceptable.

de luxe, /*d'lux*/.

de rigueur, /*de ree-gerr*/.

débâcle, /*day-barkl'*/ or /*day-bark'l*/, written without accents.

débris, /*day-bree*/, written without accent.

début, /*day-biew*/ or /*day-boo*/, written without accent.

dénouement, /*day-noo-maw(n)*/, written without accent.

dépot, /*deppoe*/ or /*deepoe*/, written without accent.

détente, /*day-taunt*/, written without accent.

discothèque, /*disco-teck*/, written without accent.

distrait, /*distray*/.

élite, /*ay-leet*/, written without accent.

émigré, /*emmi-gray*/, written either with no accent or the second accent only.

ennui, /*on-wee*/.

entente, /*on-taunt*/.

fait accompli, /*fayta complee*/ – note that the *t* is *not* mute.

fête, /*fate*/.

fiancé(e), /*fee-onsay*/, and see -EE, -ÉE.

foyer, /*foy-er*/.

fuselage, /*fewz'lahj*/.

garage, /*ga-rahj*/ or /*g'rahj*/.

genre, /*zhonr'*/.

gourmand, /*gore-maw(nd)*/.

gourmet, /*gore-may*/.

Grand Prix, /*graw(n) pree*/; the plural is pronounced the same or /*graw(n) prees*/.

hors d'oeuvres, /*ore-derves*/. To attempt anything more Gallic is fraught with peril. We should not, however, back-form the singular, /*ore-derve*/.

laissez-faire, /*lessay fair*/ or /*lay-say fair*/.

lingerie, /*lahnjery*/, not /*lonjeray*/.

matinée, /*mattinay*/, written without accent.

meringue, /*m'rang*/.

métier, /*maytee-ay*/, written without accent.

milieu, /*mealier*/ rather than /*meel-you*/.

mirage, /*mirr-ahj*/.

morale, /*m'rahl*/.

né(e), /nay/. See -EE, -ÉE.

niche, /neesh/, but /nitch/ is increasingly acceptable.

penchant, /paw(n)-shaw(n)/.

piquant, /pee-kaw(n)/.

première, /premmy-air/, written without accent.

raison d'être, /rayson-detr'/, written with accent.

rapport, /rappore/ rather than /rapport/.

rapprochement, /raprosh-maw(n)/.

régime, /ray-zheem/, written without accent.

rendezvous, /rawnday-voo/, and

note that it is not used as a noun by the French.

ricochet, /ricko-shay/; for derivatives, see *crochet* above.

soirée, /swurray/.

soupçon: (a) /soups-aw(n)/, written with cedilla, in the phrase *soupçon de je ne sais quoi*; (b) on its own, /soups-on/.

trait, /tray/ (but /trait/ is winning favour).

venue, /venn-you/ rather than /veen-you/.

voilà, /vwullah/ (-*ull* as in *dull*), not /wullah/.

The Spanish have given us many words, almost all of which are happily anglicised. However, we have trouble with the Spanish *j*:

jojoba, /ho-hoba/

junta, /hoonta/ or /junter/

marijuana, /marry-hwahna/

/hohoba/ and /marihuana/ are fair enough, since they have not yet made up their minds whether they are exotic or acclimatised species. However, /hoonta/ for *junta* may sound precious. It is defensible if used of a regime in Latin America, but if used for a regime anywhere else, or as a general term for military oligarchies, it is best fully anglicised, starting with a /j/ sound, and rhymed with *hunter*.

Most Italian words are fully anglicised, partial exceptions being:

capuccino, /cappa-cheeno/, plural /cappa-cheenoze/ or /cappa-cheeny/

concerto, /con-chairtoe/, plural /con-chairty/ or /c'n-chairtoze/

crescendo, /cr'shendoe/, plural /cr'shendoze/

gelati, /jell-ahty/; this is plural but commonly used as singular; compare GRAFFITI.

minestrone, /minni-stroney/

scherzo, /skairt-soe/, plural /skairt-soze/

German words are anglicised with few difficulties except for a chronic problem with *ie* and *ei*. This makes for confusion between *Wien* (= Vienna, pronounced /Veen/) and *Wein* (= wine, pronounced /vine/). *Edelweiss* is /aidel-vice/, not /idle-vice/ (a common but strange mistake). News readers who know that a German *st* is generally pronounced *sht*, but little more, may pronounce *bundestag* /boonda-shtahg/. The word splits as *bundes-tag*, and is hence pronounced /boondas-tahg/.

The Dutch can fairly be blamed for a number of irregular spellings and pronunciations – *buoy, yacht*, etc. – but there is no body of Dutch words with characteristic spellings. Afrikaans gives us a lot more, many of them NONCE WORDS of the Boer War like *kopje*, but including also the *aardvark*, beloved of lexicographers, and of course *apartheid* (which should be /apart-hate/, not /a-path-ide/).

Inasmuch as many of these break our phonetic rules, what should we do about them? The answer is 'nothing'. We must live with them. To attempt to cleanse the language of them, as Hitler tried with German, is alien to our whole tradition of linguistic tolerance, which has been one of the sources of the richness of our language. For this richness, a few spelling and pronunciation problems is a low price.

(5) General comment English speakers show a great enthusiasm for maintaining the integrity of foreign forms and pronunciations. At one time, foreign names were commonly anglicised: Joan of Arc, Mark Antony, Christopher Columbus, Naples and so on. Since the sixteenth century, however, new anglicisations have been restricted to names without received spellings in roman characters. These apart, the set of anglicised proper names we have today is more or less as it was in Shakespeare's time. Indeed, it has if anything slipped back, with French kings called *Lewis* reverting to *Louis*.

This enthusiasm for maintaining at least enough of the original pronunciation to make the spelling non-phonetic is a habit few other language groups share. The Italians, for example, either preserve the foreign sound by re-spelling according to Italian rules, producing words like *sciovinismo* for *chauvinism* (which obscures the link to M. Chauvin), or they preserve the spelling and massacre the pronunciation. This is rather like ordering Gorgonzola cheese and throwing away the bad bits. You miss all the fun.

for ever, forever Charles Stuart Calverly was in no doubt about it:
> *Forever! Tis a single word!*
> *Our rude forefathers deemed it two:*
> > *Can you imagine so absurd*
> > *A view*

And Mac is equally self-assured, dismissing *for ever* as 'U.S.'.

Despite this, we have the un-American and post-Calverly lines:
> *If I should die, think only this of me:*
> *That there's some corner of a foreign field*
> *That is for ever England.*

What is the answer? Quite clearly both exist. The title of the notorious novel was and remains *Forever Amber*, and the phrase must be so written in combinations like *forever-remembered*. Conversely, the logic of the phrase *for ever and a day* would be distorted by writing *forever and a day*. Between these two extremes lie a range of more doubtful usages, in which there can be no unequivocal answer. There is, however, a good argument for using two words if the phrase is important to the sense and structure (e.g. *a candle lasts for an hour or two, but the candlestick lasts for ever*), but one word if the phrase is unstressed and hidden in the middle of the sentence.

former, latter   It is best to be pedantic here, and to apply these terms only to the first and second of *two*. If there are more than two, use *first* and *last*.

fortuitous, fortunate   *Fortuitous* means accidental, without any suggestion of benefit or otherwise. *Fortunate* implies good luck. The use of *fortuitous* for *fortunate* is worse than a malapropism: it is a ploddish malapropism.

forward(s)   See BACKWARD(S).

fount   See FONT.

fractions   See MATHEMATICAL WRITING.

frock   This word does not have as much currency in Australia as it does in Britain, so that it is seen as a Britishism.

Its original application as a male outer garment survives only in the word *unfrocked* (of dismissed priests) and the *frock coat*. However, in nineteenth-century England it was applied first to the short dresses of female children and then, perhaps as part of the general habit of the British upper class to carry the usage of the nursery into adult life, to dresses in general.

Its application in these senses has occurred since American and Australian English went their own ways, so the three are different. In British English, the first connotation remains that of garments worn by little girls, and as adult wear the connotations are of shortness and frivolity, though a *cotton frock* is a simple light garment for all ages and classes. The Americans do not use the word at all, using *dress* for everyday wear and *gown* (a word which sounds pretentious to Australian ears) for formal wear.

The word is effectively unknown to the younger generation of Australian women. If they are not wearing jeans, they wear *dresses* or *skirts*. Their mothers, however, may have happy memories of the *frocks* of their youth.

full stop   See PUNCTUATION (3).

function   See MATHEMATICAL WRITING.

further, farther   If we want to eliminate one, it has to be *farther*. *Further* can be used in all senses, whereas *farther* cannot be used in the sense *additional*: *The police are seeking further information; Technical and Further Education.*

fusion   See ATOM.

G

gainsay Curiously, this word (meaning *deny*) is used only with a negative. We are never told to *gainsay* anything; we are told that *it cannot be gainsaid*. The 'gain' part is as in *against*: see AGAIN....

Gallicisms For a discussion of French words in English, see FOREIGN WORDS...(4).

gambit This word comes to us from chess, where it means *the sacrifice of a piece to gain a positional advantage*. It is used metaphorically for any strategy which involves a short-term loss to win a long-term gain, and is thus a useful and precise term. We should be careful not to use it for clever strategies of other sorts, or (worse) in phrases like *run the whole gambit...* where *gamut* is the word we were searching for.

gamut The origins of this word are irrelevant but perhaps help us to preserve its special connotations. It comes to us from music. *Ut* is an alternative name for *doh*, the first note of the *tonic solfa*, and G (gamma) was the Greek character used to indicate bottom G. Put the two together and you have *gamma+ut = gamut*, meaning the lowest note on the scale. This came to be used for *the whole scale from bottom up* and was then applied metaphorically to other fields.

It is appropriate to use *gamut* for any *comprehensive* range of options.

Compare GAMBIT.

gaol, jail There is something very odd about this word. OED had the main entry under *J*. It reported that everybody *said* jail, that in America it was also the official spelling, and that it was the preferred form in all the then recent dictionaries, while *gaol* survived only as the *written* form in official documents. Goodbye *gaol*.

Fowler was less convinced. He was strangely silent about his own opinion, quoting OED without comment; but he placed the entry under G.

The Australian dictionaries also put the main entry under *G*, and call *jail* an Americanism, despite the evidence of OED – and of AND, which shows that it was used by James Hardy Vaux in 1819.

I suspect that we have here an example of wishful thinking. The arguments for *jail* are indeed very powerful: it is phonetically regular (unlike *gaol*, which has the unusual *ao* = /ai/ and soft *g* before *a*), and it has a considerable etymological pedigree. The only argument against it (apart from knee-jerk Americanophobia) is that, nearly a century after OED tried to get us to write *jail*, most of us still write *gaol*. This is, however, a pretty formidable argument.

164

garden See YARD....

gay This word has, sadly, ceased to be available in any sense other than *homosexual*. This statement is uttered as a warning, not a prescription. It is not that the word now *means* 'homosexual', but the connotations are there, and may interfere with the message we are trying to transmit. Meanwhile we have not lost *gaily, gayer* and *gayest*, or the stock phrase *gay abandon*, but this makes the word rather like a headless chook.

gender Fowler, in a brief entry, said that gender was 'a grammatical term only' and that its use as a synonym for *sex* was 'either a jocularity... or a blunder.' This is no longer true. Today, its use in this sense is widespread and no joke.

Initially, it was used by feminists to distinguish socially-derived distinctions from biologically-derived ones. This distinction was an important one (discussed in this book under the heading SEXIST LANGUAGE), so the need for such a word was clear. But it was unfortunate that they chose a word which was already in use in a related but different sense.

The result is that *gender* cannot any more be used in its original sense without the risk of misunderstanding. Those who wish to use it in the original sense are advised to say *grammatical gender* or supply a definition.

It would be plain defeatism to admit, in a book on usage, that this valuable grammatical term has gone down the gurgler, particularly as no one has yet come up with a replacement for it. So the rest of this article is designed to explain what *gender* means as a grammatical term, and hence incidentally to show why some of us regret its descent into ambiguity.

(1) Gender *versus* sex *Gender* as a grammatical term is attached to words, and describes whether they are *masculine, feminine* or *neuter*.

In English, gender generally marches with sex: males are masculine (*he*), females are feminine (*she*), and everything else is neuter (*it*). There are only a few exceptions, and they hardly seem worth noticing:

> *She* ... can include such non-female items as a ship (*She struck an iceberg*), a Great Power (*She declared war on Germany*) or (colloquially) a piece of clapped-out machinery (*She's only got 100,000 on the clock*) and in such phrases as *She'll be right* and *She's apples.*

> *It* ... can include sexual creatures (*The male is distinguished by its soft roe/The female cannot fruit unless it has been pollinated*), and even anonymous babies (*I heard a baby crying for its bottle*).

Cutting across the gender structure are words which are defined as *gender-inclusive* (e.g. *they*, which covers all three genders) or *common* (e.g. *doctor*, which can be a *he* or *she* depending on the sex of the practitioner), but the term *inclusive* is now often used in this latter sense.

The distinction between sex and gender is thus so trivial in English that many English speakers find it hard to imagine a language in which it is done differently. However, it is English which is the exception.

German and French are two languages with strong (yet very different) gender structures.

(a) In German, there are three genders, as in English. Every noun has a gender, and articles and adjectives are modified to show it: the word for *the*, for example, is *der* for masculines, *die* for feminines and *das* for neuters.

However, the sex/gender relationship is not clearcut:

Er (= he) could be referring to a hammer (*der Hammer*).
Sie (= she) could be referring to some butter (*die Butter*).
Es (= it) could be referring to a girl (*das Mädchen*).
Sie (= they) is inclusive, as in English.

(b) In French, there are just two genders, masculine and feminine. All the words which are neuter in English have to be either masculine or feminine in French and, as in German, articles and adjectives are modified to match the gender of the noun. The words for *the* are *le* (masculine) and *la* (feminine):

Il (= he) could be referring to bread (*le pain*).
Elle (= she) could be about jam (*la confiture*).
Ils ⎱ (= they) work just like the singulars. There is no inclu-
Elles ⎰ sive pronoun, though an assortment is *ils*.

Strictly speaking, then, *er* and *il* do not mean *he*. They are simply the pronouns used with masculine nouns, just as *she* is the pronoun we use with ships. If the word for something is masculine, French and German speakers cannot simply attach a feminine article to indicate that the particular example they are talking about is female.

Thus in French a doctor is always *un médecin*. To indicate a lady doctor by saying *une médecin* would 'solve it all but would seem shocking' (as French linguist Vendryes puts it); but the French are able to say *madame le médecin*… or, even more curiously, *la femme médecin*; and a lady who has been introduced as *le médecin* becomes *elle* if she reappears as a pronoun, just as in English.

Such is the grammatical phenomenon which had for centuries been called *gender*. Now we have no unambiguous term for it.

(2) The future of the term *gender* The discussion above is designed to show only one thing: that there is a topic which we used to call *gender*, and that it had fascinating ramifications and implications for our patterns of thought and writing, which are now harder to write about because the key word has changed its meaning.

We cannot complain about change as such: words are being put to new uses all the time, and it is impossible as well as undesirable to stop this happening. Furthermore, so long as it was only used in such phrases as *gender role,* in which the *gender role* (a social stereotype) was distinguished from *sex role* (a biological fact), the new sense had a subtle precision which demanded a new word.

The problems arose when people started to treat *gender* as a synonym for *sex,* as when offices started providing *facilities for both genders.* This destroyed not only the original grammatical use, but also the precision of the new sociological one.

Anyway, the fact is that we have lost *gender* as an unambiguous term of grammar. This may not matter to some, but to others it is like the loss of an old friend. We need a word to use instead of *gender* in the following sentence:

'*She struck an iceberg' illustrates the difference between gender and sex.*

As a minuscule protest (and despite the advice given above) the word *gender* will in this book always carry its grammatical sense except where another sense is specified by the context.

genealogy   Listening to talk-back radio, one might suspect that the battle to defend *genealogy* against *geneology* has been lost. The problem stems from the fact that the suffix is wrongly perceived as *-ology,* and *genealogy,* though correct, therefore sounds like a mistake. (A reverse fate has overtaken *ideogram,* which, perhaps because of its association with *ideas,* is often misspelt as *ideagram.*)

However, none of the dictionaries yet reports *geneology* as a legitimate variant, so let us nail our colours to this mast.

general   In military parlance, *general* started life as an adjective (derived from *genus* – compare GENERIC) attached to the titles of officers to indicate that their authority was *general* over a whole army rather than limited to a part of it. However, it soon became a rank in its own right. The main significance of this is in the plural forms: we speak of *major-generals* rather than the more historically correct *majors-general.*

This has not yet happened with *governors-general,* but the phrase *governor-generals* is used informally. The argument, however, is not that the governor-general is a special sort of general, but that the whole phrase represents a single thought. See PLURAL DILEMMAS (6).

The phrase *caviar to the general* has nothing to do with senior military officers, but enshrines an ode use of *the general* as a short form for *the general public,* and in particular the lower orders thereof.

generic   *Generic* is an adjectival form of *genus,* and *generic name* is thus a term of biology for the name of a genus – see TAXONOMY. However, the term *generic* is also used in several other contexts, one of which can give trouble:

(1) Certain common nouns can be used as *generic terms* to cover a host of specific examples: thus *utensil* and *tool* are generic terms which are almost identical in meaning except that *utensil* has the connotation of 'kitchen' and *tool* of 'workshop'. These are very useful words and cause no problems.

(2) *Generic products* are unbranded versions of products also available under brand names.

(3) Certain proper names from history and literature are associated with specific activities or characteristics. Thus we can call somebody 'a Martha' or 'a Judas', or say that an event is somebody's 'Waterloo' or 'Rubicon'. These are also known as *generic names*, names which identify a class of person or event. For a related phenomenon, see EPONYM(OUS).

Those who use generics of this sort need to be very sure (a) that the people they are addressing will pick the allusion, (b) that the people they are addressing will get the same message from the allusion, and (c) that they themselves have got it right. See ALLUSION.

Germanic, Romance   In the jargon of English etymology, *Germanic* is generally used in contrast to *Romance*: most English words are either Germanic (including the original Anglo-Saxon component) or Romance (including the Norman French component). The word *Romance* refers to the Latin-based languages of the Roman Empire.

How far the terms are extended then varies from writer to writer. Most would include Dutch and the Scandinavian languages as Germanic. All the Latin-based languages (from Portuguese to Romanian) are Romance, and many would also include classical Greek in Romance, on the grounds that most of our Greek words came through Latin or in Latinate form.

These two groups cover over 98% of the words in English, the exceptions being a few Slav words and a scattering from other Indo-European languages (e.g. Hindi and Arabic), plus a very few from languages which are not Indo-European (Chinese and Japanese, American-Indian, Australian Aboriginal, etc.).

gerrymander   The term *gerrymander* describes a method of rigging an election without running foul of a rule requiring equal numbers of voters in all electorates. This is done by drawing the boundaries in such a way that one side wins a few seats by massive margins, while the other wins more seats by narrow margins.

The term *gerrymander* should not be applied to other ways of loading the value of votes, of which the most common is a system permitting electorates to contain different numbers of voters. This is capable of producing far greater distortions than a gerrymander, and is the procedure which has caused trouble when used in drawing the electorate boundaries for the unicameral Queensland Parliament, but it is also used (with less public outcry) for the upper houses of other legislatures, notably the Australian Senate. Strictly, therefore, none of these is a gerrymander.

Nevertheless, the term 'Queensland gerrymander' is so well established that it is probably best to declare that, in Australian English, the word means 'any procedure designed to change the result of an election by manipulating electorate boundaries'.

gerund, gerundive   These two words mean, respectively, a verb-noun and a verb-adjective, and if that information is less than helpful, it will be good news that the latter does not exist in English.

The only reason why we ever need the word *gerund* is to label one of the two senses of the *-ing* form, the *present participle* and the *gerund* (= verb-noun). In the phrase *Seeing is believing*, we have two gerunds. See VERB (3(C)) and -ING FORMS.

The Latin gerundive forms survive intact in English in nouns like *memorandum* (literally, a thing to be remembered), *Amanda* (a lady to be loved), and in more assimilated form in the adjectives *horrendous* (fit to be horrified at) and *tremendous* (fit to be trembled at). *Agenda* is strictly a plural gerundive (things to be done) but this is best forgotten. So is the word *gerundive*.

ghost writer   The reader of this book is more likely to be acting as a ghost writer than to be employing one, but the following notes are designed to cover both.

There are many people who have a tale to tell but are not very good at telling it. Typically, they are business tycoons, politicians and film stars, but many quite literate people have the wit to realise the chasm of frustration that yawns between their first draft and the book they would like to write. Similarly, a ghost may be needed to turn, say, a highly literate research paper by an agricultural scientist into an article designed to be read and understood by the farmer.

What is the difference between heavy editing and ghosting? The editor is normally briefed to respect the integrity of the text, i.e. to retain as much of the shape, texture, style and substance of the original text as is consistent with making it readable; the ghost may start without a text at all, and, even if there is a text, is expected to go back to plain paper and create the literary version of the story from scratch.

Essentially, then, the editor will generally be making the best of what is already there, and is paid by fee-for-service; the ghost is a co-author, sharing in the creative process and therefore appropriately paid by royalties with a substantial advance payment (see below).

The skill of a ghost writer is in creating a style which is both readable and consistent with the personality of the nominal author. The ghost also has the moral responsibility to reflect the opinions and attitudes of the nominal author, but to a much lesser extent than the editor.

Both editor and ghost writer have one aim in common: to produce a work which will satisfy the reader. This is the way they can best serve their clients.

The greatest danger faced by a ghost writer is a falling out with the nominal author in the middle of the project. Although the ghost is a co-author, the partnership is not equal: the nominal author will normally be the main source of information, of permission to use documents, and above all of permission to use his or her famous name on the finished book. It is therefore unusually important (more so than in ordinary author/publisher contracts) to have clear statements of the rights and obligations of both parties, and simple mechanisms for resolving disputes. There should also be advance payment arrangements which ensure that the ghost earns wages for the time spent on the project even if an irreconcilable dispute arises and the book is never completed.

Finally, if a ghost is anonymous, there should be watertight arrangements to ensure that (s)he receives an agreed share of any payments which are made only to those whose names appear on the title page, e.g. public lending right.

From all this it will be seen that the normal publisher's contract is inappropriate or at least insufficient. There must be an agreement between the ghost and the nominal author, laying down the rights and obligations of each. One option is a partnership agreement, the partnership then becoming 'the author' for the purposes of the contract with the publisher. In the case of a major project, it may even be best for the partnership to be incorporated, but this will depend on advice on legal and taxation implications.

given name   We are told that, since we are not all Christians, we should not speak of *Christian names*, but of *first* or *given* names, or *forenames*. So be it – the terms are all perfectly acceptable, and the compilers of questionnaires should follow the advice. But the reality is that, in this context, the word *christian* (particularly if written thus, without the capital letter) has no more religious implication than the *holy* in *holiday*, the *Wodin* in *Wednesday* or the *Jove* in *joviality*. The term *first name* or *forename* has different significance for the Chinese, and *given name* will be ambiguous for foundlings. You can't win.

graduate   Americans *graduate from high school* as well as *graduating from college*. Hence they have to use the term *college graduate* in contexts where Australians (and the British) can simply say *graduate*. However, the use of the term *graduate* to cover school leavers is infiltrating Australia, so we will possibly need to be more specific in future.

Americans rarely use the term *university graduate*. In fact, the term *university*, while part of the official title of many institutions, is rarely used. See UNIVERSITY.

graffiti   The word started life as an Italian plural, but has become naturalised as a singular noun. Some of us still find it hard to say 'the graffiti is...', but we are a fuddy-duddy minority, struggling on.

It is one of the very few words which entered our language through the jargon of archaeology, having been first applied (in English, that is) to the antique scrawls on the walls of Pompeii, and in particular to the obscene ones. It was then applied to similar obscenities on our present-day walls, and finally to informal inscriptions and decorations in general.

grammar   Grammar can be defined as *the rules governing the way in which words are put together so that they make sense*. Grammatical sense must, however, be distinguished from logical and semantic sense. Thus

> *Banana the sat man fat on ripe*

is a string of words with individual meaning but no sense at all.

> *The fat banana sat on the ripe man*

makes grammatical sense but is logically and semantically improbable.

We are talking here only about *grammatical soundness*. If a sentence sounds wrong, grammar may give us the vocabulary and insight to explain what is wrong and what to do about it. This entry is largely about the vocabulary.

(1) Approaches to grammar   Approaches to English grammar can be broadly divided into two classes, formal and descriptive.

(a) **Formal grammar** offers us a set of rules governing the composition of an English sentence. Its merit is that it is *prescriptive*, i.e. it always comes up with an answer. Its shortcoming is that the answer is often wrong. This is because it was based on the analysis of Latin grammar, in which words clearly indicated their grammatical status by their form, and it does not always provide a helpful analysis of a language like ours, in which words indicate their grammatical status largely by their position. But its technical terms are very useful.

(b) **Descriptive grammar** starts from the way we speak and write, and tries to identify patterns within it. The status of each word is determined by the place it occupies within the pattern. Descriptive grammarians assert that children, for example, observe and absorb such patterns, and that this is how they can create, from quite an early age, 'new' sentences – sentences consisting of words they already know but in sequences they have never heard.

What follows, then, is an attempt to define the *terms* of formal grammar (which are the ones most widely used) using the *processes* of descriptive grammar (which are generally more helpful). In many cases, more extended discussion of the same points is included elsewhere in the book, covering specific problems. In particular, there is a special section on WORD ORDER, the key to English grammar.

(2) Words, phrases, clauses and sentences   It is best to start with the bricks and build up the edifice. The notes below are not definitions – the terms are effectively undefinable – but are more like Identikit pictures, to give some idea of the features of typical members of each class:

(a) A **word** is a string of letters enclosed at both ends with spaces or punctuation marks.

(b) A **phrase** is a group of words which together form a single part of speech: thus we have *noun phrases, adjectival phrases, adverbial phrases,* and so on..

> *He is   one of the men   setting fire to Sydney   in the rain.*
>   noun phrase   adjectival phrase   adverbial phrase

A phrase can be contained within another phrase. Thus *to set fire to Sydney* is an infinitive verb phrase which is part of an adjectival phrase. But it could be further subdivided. How you split a sentence up will depend on what you are trying to show.

A phrase will not contain a finite verb, though it can be one, i.e. a *verb phrase* is string of words which together make up a single verb (see (3(b)) adverbs, below).

(c) A **clause** is a string of words and phrases containing at least two elements (phrases or words) including a finite verb. If it is a complete grammatical structure on its own, it is a *principal clause*. If it is not, it is a *dependent clause*, which can then act as a noun, adjective or adverb:

> *He is one of the men   who set fire to Sydney when it was raining*
>   principal clause   adjectival clause   adverbial clause

(d) A **sentence** is a logically and grammatically self-supporting string of words containing at least one principal clause.

> *He is one of the men who tried to set fire to Sydney with damp matches.*

Some further expansion (and modification) of these bald statements will be found under CLAUSE (2), PHRASE and SENTENCE.

(3) Parts of speech   Formal grammar recognises eight *parts of speech*: adjectives, adverbs, nouns, pronouns, verbs, prepositions, conjunctions and interjections. (For a discussion of the problems associated with this, see PARTS OF SPEECH.)

Each part of speech is here defined by means of a model sentence, and words which can occupy the same position are assumed to be the same part of speech. For a discussion of the reason why this approach is adopted, see WORD ORDER.

(a) The term **adjective** is one of the more clear-cut of the terms from formal grammar. The term describes a form of grammatical lean-to, where the word it leans against is a noun. Thus, in the sentence

The *fat* man sat on the *ripe* banana

the words *fat* and *ripe* are adjectives, leaning against *man* and *banana* respectively.

This pattern can be transformed by replacing the adjectives by other words. If the proposed word fits, the new word is probably also an adjective.

The $\left(\begin{array}{l} \textit{bald} \\ \textit{emaciated} \\ \textit{Queensland} \end{array}\right)$ man sat on the $\left(\begin{array}{l} \textit{green} \\ \textit{above} \\ \textit{ripening} \end{array}\right)$ banana

Note that, in the last line, *Queensland* (a noun) and *ripening* (a participle) are shown by the pattern to be in use as adjectives.

In these examples the adjectives are used *attributively*, that is, they define the existing attributes of the item against which they lean. Adjectives can also be used *predicatively*, i.e. to *predicate* some new knowledge. This happens in particular when they are used as the COMPLEMENTS of the verb *to be* and other COPULATIVE VERBS:

> The mouse is   *afraid*   of the cat.
> He grew *old and bitter.*

Most adjectives can be used both attributively and predicatively, but *afraid* is an example of a small set of adjectives which can only be used predicatively (i.e. we cannot say 'The cat chased the *afraid* mouse').

Most adjectives have a set of *comparative* and *superlative* forms: *fat – fatter – fattest*. See COMPARATIVE CHAOS (1).

Two important subsets of adjectives are known as the *demonstrative* adjectives, e.g. *this* and *that*: see DEMONSTRATIVES, and the *articles*, *a* and *the*: see A / AN, THE and ARTICLE.

(b) The term **adverb** is used for a similar grammatical lean-to, where the word leaned against is a verb. Many (but not all) adverbs end in *-ly*, and most (but not all) words ending in *-ly* are adverbs:

He walked $\left(\begin{array}{l} \textit{slowly} \\ \textit{sadly} \\ \textit{away} \end{array}\right)$ up the hill.

Here, the adverb explains how, when or why he walked up the hill.

In the expression *Carry on!*, the word *on* is best regarded as an adverb, though it merges with the verb to give a new meaning which is not just *carry + on*. English has a host of *verb phrases* formed in this way.

Some adverbs can lean against adjectives rather than verbs. These include *modifiers* and *intensifiers*:

She carried a $\left(\begin{array}{l} \textit{very} \text{ deep} \\ \textit{scarcely} \text{ visible} \end{array}\right)$ scar

(c) A **noun** is generally defined as a naming word.

$$\left. \begin{array}{r} \textit{Annabelle} \\ \textit{He} \\ \textit{The dog} \end{array} \right\} \text{likes} \left\{ \begin{array}{l} \textit{Bali} \\ \textit{sausages} \\ \textit{extravagance} \end{array} \right.$$

Annabelle and *Bali* are **proper nouns**, nouns which name particular people and places (*proper* being used in the sense of *property*, the name being a property of the person or place) and are generally capitalised.

Sausages and *extravagance* are **common nouns**. *Common* indicates that they are applied *in common* to all members of a class of objects – it is not a comment on their vulgarity or frequency of occurrence.

Within common nouns, a distinction is made between **concrete nouns** (labelling things you can touch, see or smell, like *dogs* and *sausages*) and **abstract nouns** (labelling emotions, qualities, etc. like *extravagance*).

(d) A **pronoun** is a word which stands in for a noun. The most important pronouns are the **personal pronouns:** first person (I, we); second person (you); and third person (he, she, it and they).

However, there are several others. For example, in the sentences:

Who is Sylvia?	*who* is an **interrogative pronoun**
This is Sylvia	*this* is a **demonstrative pronoun**
This is Jim *who* likes sausages	*who* is a **relative pronoun**, introducing a *relative* clause.

(e) A **verb** is generally defined as a *doing* word.

$$\text{The parrots} \left\{ \begin{array}{l} \textit{ate} \\ \textit{chatted} \text{ (with)} \\ \textit{hated} \\ \textit{flew} \text{ (towards)} \end{array} \right\} \text{the budgerigars}$$

For further discussion of this most complicated subject, see VERB.

(f) A **preposition** is a word which fits the italic slot in the following pattern:

$$\text{I saw Fred} \left\{ \begin{array}{ll} \textit{in} & \text{the mirror} \\ \textit{with} & \text{my own eyes} \\ \textit{from} & \text{a bus} \\ \textit{by} & \text{accident} \end{array} \right.$$

In these cases, the preposition is placed before a noun or noun phrase, turning it into an adverbial phrase (explaining how, when or where the action of the verb took place).

A preposition may also introduce an adjectival phrase (adding information about one of the other nouns):

The dog *on the tucker box* is five miles from Gundagai.

(g) **Conjunctions** are joining-words. The simplest applications are illustrated in the following patterns:

John *and* Betty can jump   (*linking two nouns*)
The answer is right *or* wrong   (*linking two adjectives*)
She walked quickly *but* quietly   (*linking two adverbs*)

When they join two sentences, the range of possible conjunctions is greatly increased. In the sentence

I will go to Wagga   [?]   my name isn't Charlie

and, *or* and *but* would fit, but so would *if, because, for, when*, etc. The second half then becomes an adverbial clause, *subordinate* to the first (see CLAUSE (2)).

Or and *but* form a special class sometimes known as **disjunctions**, since they keep apart the items they link. This is important when considering the *number* of a following verb: 'Tom *and* Jerry *are* coming', but 'Tom *or* Jerry *is* coming'.

(h) **Interjections** are words which fit in the pattern:

Alas,
Hurrah, } the King is dead
Ouch,

Many adverbs could fit in this pattern (*sadly, surprisingly*), the significant point about interjections being that they can stand on their own. When they do so, they are often (but not necessarily) followed by an exclamation mark.

How far do all the parts of speech really exist in English? If almost every noun can be used as an adjective, why do we use a classification which labels words as one or the other? Similarly, the word *yes* is generally classified by dictionaries as an adverb. The argument for this classification is that its nearest synonyms (*certainly, with pleasure*) are adverbs. But it fits in precious few adverbial patterns, while fitting happily in the pattern for *interjections*.

This is not an argument for reclassifying *yes* as an interjection; it is, however, a strong argument against using 'parts of speech' analysis to prove that a given usage, although common and clear, is wrong. If a construction is *not* clear, analysis can sometimes be very useful in explaining why this is so; but if our normal, clear usage seems to defy formal classification, the fault is in the classification, not in the usage.

gram(me) If there is any surviving argument about *program(me)*, there should certainly be none about *gram(me)*. The form *gram* should be used in all senses. Compare PROGRAM(ME).

grimace The word is best pronounced /gr'mace/, though a lot of respectable people say /grimmus/.

gross Despite being heard from time to time in Parliament, the pronunciation of *gross* so that it rhymes with *moss* is not in any Australian dictionary. Nor should it be.

The source of the mutation is mysterious. Stranger still, several other words are suffering the same fate, *basic* being pronounced to rhyme with *classic* (see BASE), and *leverage* as if it was about */levvers/*. This last is an Americanism with possibly good antecedents, but is at best unhelpful: unless we decide to say */levvers/* for *levers*, we should preserve */leeverij/*.

The common factor in all these pronunciations is that they are emanating from the Treasury. Perhaps there is a linguistic mole there, acting for a foreign power with an interest in shortening our vowels along with our credit.

guernsey For the use of this word to label an article of clothing and a cow, see JERSEY....

H

H Australians believe (with some statistical justification) that we can tell people who were educated by the Christian Brothers or the Sisters of Mercy because they call this letter *haitch* rather than *aitch*, after the Irish fashion.

Why this should be a matter of reproach is less certain. The pronunciation (and spelling) 'aitch' merely enshrines the dropping of the aspirate, a matter of which we are not normally proud. When the Romans still sounded their aitches, they called it *ha*. When they started dropping them, the name changed to *acha*; hence the French *ache* and our *aitch*. The Germans, who sound their aitches, retain the name *ha*.

However, saying *haitch* is matter of reproach in Australia, so the upwardly mobile must learn, *in this one instance*, to drop their aitches. See SOCIAL ASPIRATIONS.

had For a modest discussion of this word as a subjunctive, see IF… CLAUSES (2).

hair-do This word is a good example of an occasion when a hyphen is useful, because both sense and pronunciation demand that its elements be perceived as separate. Fowler suggested that we should remove it, making *hairdo*, and our dictionaries recklessly follow suit, but AWEG retains the hyphen.

half For a discussion of such sentences as *Half the fish was/were bad*, see SINGULARITIES. For *seven and a half million(s)* versus *seven million(s) and a half*, see NUMBER PHRASES.

halftone This term is used in printing to describe the process by which a continuous tone (*contone*) original, e.g. a photograph or painting, is broken up into an array of dots of varying sizes so that a single colour of ink can be made to give the appearance of a range of tones. In commercial colour printing, a close approximation to original colour is produced by the *four-colour process*, in which the tones of the original are analysed for their content of the four *process colours*, black, yellow, magenta and cyan.

The dots were originally produced by inserting a grid, known as a *screen*, into the process camera. Although most halftones are now scanned rather than being produced in a camera, the term *screen* survives: a *150 screen halftone* is one which has 150 dots to the inch, a typical figure for average quality reproduction.

The term *screened bromide* is applied to images deposited on paper, which are generally positive, and *screened negatives* to images on film. However, computer technology is overtaking all these photographic processes, and the terms are likely to become obsolete in the near future.

happening, happenstance, eventuate   Once upon a time, *events happened by chance*. Today, *happenings eventuate by happenstance*. Fowler attributed *happening* to the battles of the Saxonists and anti-Saxonists, and had the good fortune to die before *happenstance* hit the streets.

Happening is an antique but rare word revived by social scientists in the 1960s just in time for it to be adopted as a technical term for a gathering of the alternative culture – see ALTERNATIVE (3).

Happenstance was coined by social scientists from *happening* and *circumstance* to describe *an event outside our control, whether arising from the circumstances or from chance.* There was a need for such a word, and it was sad that this admirably precise meaning was promptly corrupted, so that it is now used as a pretentious synonym for *chance*.

Eventuate is simply a redundant synonym for *happen*, blamed by the OED on the Americans, as is customary.

hautboy   See OBOE.

have   The elided form of this word, as in *I've* and (more dangerously) *could've* has caused trouble. *Could've* becomes *could of*, and *I've done it* becomes *I done it*.

Could of is a straightforward error, though it is so common that it may well become an accepted idiom at some time in the future.

I done it is often explained as a mistake for *I did it*. This may occasionally be so, but in most cases a lost *have* is a better explanation.

he, him   See CASE (2).

heart   We take phrases like *affair of the heart* so much for granted that we may forget that it is a survivor from the ancient belief that the heart was the seat of the emotions. For other similar survivals, compare HUMOUR.

hectic   This word was until recently very rare, being a medical term meaning 'arising from the condition of the patient'. In particular, the phrase *hectic flush* was used for the complexion of a tuberculosis patient, the disease being itself sometimes known as *hectic fever*. At this stage, it indicated solely that the flush was a symptom of an internal disorder, not (for example) sitting too close to an open fire.

Because the flush looked like the one we get from some strenuous exercise, *hectic* then acquired the meaning *sudden, rapid and wild*. Whatever it once was, this is not now an erroneous usage. ACOD$_1$, listing meanings historically, reported this as its second meaning (after the medical one), and colloquial to boot. Mac correctly reports it as the most common meaning. It is particularly used for excessive activity: *I had a hectic week-end*.

Some editions of *Roget's Thesaurus* list *hectic* as a synonym for *red*. This remains a mistake (similar to that which causes some people to think that *desiccated* means *grated*, as in *desiccated coconut*).

hect(o)- See SI UNITS.

help Fowler proved conclusively that the phrase *Don't sneeze more than you can help* is logically indefensible. He was of course right. The phrase *I couldn't help sneezing* is odd enough, but *Don't sneeze more than you can help* is worse. It would be more logical to say *Don't sneeze more than you cannot help*.

Gritting his teeth, however, Fowler went on to call it a *sturdy indefensible*, one of those idioms which would not stand scrutiny but survive because people in their right minds do not scrutinise idioms. He was right again.

herbs A common American pronunciation of this word is /erbs/, the only word which regularly loses its aspirate in American English but not in standard Australian. See SOCIAL ASPIRATIONS.

heredity, hereditary *Heredity* provides the noun, and *hereditary* the adjective. If I study *hereditary diseases*, I am interested in the topic of *heredity* (= the mechanism by which things, including diseases, pass down a family from generation to generation), and in particular the *heredity* (= family history) of people who have the disease.

hex The word *hexadecimal*, shortened to *hex*, is used in computer jargon to describe a system based on 16-bit bytes. The word is a bastard child with a Greek prefix and Latin ending. Why this is used, rather than the perfectly good Latin formation *sex(a)decimal*, is anyone's guess.

high(ly) Curiously, the normal adverb for *high* is not *highly* but *high*, as in *The house was perched high on the cliff-top*. The main use for *highly* is as an intensifier, as in *highly probable, highly entertaining, highly dangerous*, etc.

It should not be used as an intensifier when we are talking of things which are not normally categorised as *high* or *low*. It is this that makes *highly probable* and *highly dangerous* more acceptable than *highly entertaining*.

historian We can say either /an 'istorian/ or /a historian/, but not the belt-and-braces /an historian/. This does not solve the problem in writing, since we cannot predict the preferences of the unknown people who may read the work aloud. (The convention of writing *an historian* arose because in the past the *h* was generally not sounded, but today the convention is often believed to be a special rule applying to these particular words.)

Perhaps the best solution is to use *an* before *historian, historic* and *historical*, as most people can suppress the aitches in these unstressed syllables, but not before *history*, where the first syllable is stressed and the *h* is normally sounded. But we must recognise that in so doing we may be encouraging the belt-and-braces pronunciation. For more about this, see SOCIAL ASPIRATIONS.

Note that an *historical* event is one which happened in history; an *historic* event is one which made history.

historical writing   This article concerns itself with two specific problems frequently encountered by authors and editors of historical works: (1) how far to preserve the original names of geographical locations, and (2) how to deal with old units of length, money, etc.

(1) Location names   The general rule is quite simple: places must be assigned the names they had at the time. This is the best way to avoid anachronisms, since many changes in place names are related to specific events. To say that the British once ruled Israel is nonsense: there was no Israel to rule until its existence became official, which was at the moment of the end of the British mandate over Palestine.

Early Australian history presents particular difficulties. Consider the following:

> *The Aboriginal communities of Tasmania appear to have migrated from mainland Australia before rising sea levels created Bass Strait.*

This piece is a string of gross anachronisms, but there is nothing we can do about it. It is not just that we do not know the names. By the time of the first European settlement, it would seem that the Tasmanian Aboriginals had no memory of or name for Australia, and did not distinguish Bass Strait as a strait, still less as the site of a lost land bridge. So, by default, current names have to be used. But we should make it clear that we are speaking of labels on geographical areas. By contrast, if we were telling the story of the first European settlement, we should use the political name it had at the time, *Van Diemen's Land*.

Simply using the names of the period, however, is not sufficient. The choice of name can itself be a partisan statement. We talk of Gallipoli, while the Turks talk of Yarimadasi. Both were current at the time, but the choice depended on whom you asked, and our map-makers had asked the Greeks. This is particularly true when discussing current affairs. To call Israel *Palestine,* or suggest that there is a country called *Kurdestan*, is to take sides in a bitter conflict, however innocent the intention. Nor is this just an abstract problem. A Russian spy sentenced by an American court to be deported to the Soviet Union languished in jail because, before the sentence could be executed, the Soviet Union ceased to exist.

There is no simple solution to these problems, and the more contemporary the history the more dangerous a wrong choice may be. We can at least achieve consistency, however, if we adopt the names used at the time by the people whose story we are writing, and, in the absence of any such alignment, the ones which well-informed Australian readers are most likely to recognise and use.

(2) Money and units   Special problems arise in quoting original pre-metric units. When we read that land in South Australia was available in 1840 for '£1 per acre', we should not make the multiple mistake of 'converting' this to '$2.00 per 0.405 hectares'.

Firstly, the fact that pounds were changed to dollars in 1966 at two dollars to the pound is absolutely irrelevant except in the context of statistics spanning the change-over. Our sole purpose in quoting sums of money in historical writing is to give some idea of *value*, and a far better solution is to leave all sums in the original currency (as we would with Venetian ducats) and provide a note on their value at the time. For this purpose, figures for typical artisan wage rates provide the ideal standard of comparison. They gives a real sense of value, and one which never has to be corrected to allow for inflation.

The acre–hectare conversion makes better sense: it is at least true that an acre was, and is, roughly 0.405 ha. But '£1 per acre' was a convenient round figure, more a label than a price. Had they used hectares in 1840, they would have fixed a round price for a round number of hectares. Hence to say '0.405 hectares' is to put a totally unwarranted emphasis on the precision of the measurement. The issue of Implied precision is further discussed under MATHEMATICAL WRITING.

In the body of the text, of course, we should use metric units. Writers who are under forty will find it hard to understand why this point needs to be made. Older writers, however, may still feel that yards, feet and inches are 'simpler'. They should realise that this feeling is unlikely to be shared by their younger readers. It may help if they may recall their own discomfort with archaic units like *rods, poles, perches, links* and *chains*.

The remaining problem is that, when old units are used, explanation of conventional ways of writing them may be needed. Those who were at school in the sixties or earlier will take for granted that 4' 1" is a length and that 2/6 is a sum of money, and know how to read them aloud, but this cannot be assumed of younger readers. I heard a sophisticated radio voice read *It cost 4d* as 'It cost four dee', and younger readers of this book may wonder why this is wrong, or worthy of comment.

Conversely, the older generation will read *4d* as 'fourpence' (and *2/6* as 'two and six' or even 'half a crown') without realising the leap into the backblocks of memory that this has involved, and hence without realising how obscure it may be to others. In our own texts, we should avoid conventions of this sort, and we should watch for them in quoted matter, providing appropriate explanation if the sound and meaning are important.

hither   Fowler said that the word *hither* was defunct apart from the phrase *hither and thither*. Since he wrote, this has been unexpectedly joined by *hither and yon*, an archaism one might not have expected to be a candidate for resurrection.

hock   There is no such wine in Germany as hock. It is pure chance that an abbreviation of *Hochheimer* should have become our generic term for Rhine wines, the more inappropriate since Hochheim is on the Main, not the Rhine. The term still appears on some wine lists in Australia to indicate a class of German-style dry white wines, but they are now more commonly and appropriately called *(Rhine) rieslings*. Compare MOSELLE, and see WINE NAMES.

hoi polloi   This phrase, meaning (literally) *the many* in classical Greek, is among countless contemptuous phrases to describe those members of the community who are unlikely to read this book. It says something for our insecurity that we have so many words to describe them: *the lower orders, the rank and file, the common herd, the lumpenproletariat, the great unwashed, the masses, peasants, yahoos, punters…*. The list is so long that another word seems unnecessary. And we in Australia have our own *yobbos* and *lumpenbourgeoisie*.

  If *hoi polloi* filled an otherwise empty niche, it might be useful. As it is, the phrase has no special flavour, so let us not use it at all.

  Mac mutters darkly that it is 'sometimes prec. pleonastically by *the*'. This is a rare case of two truths making a falsehood. (1) It *is* often preceded by *the*. (2) Given that *hoi* means *the*, it is indeed pleonastic. But the phrase cannot be used comfortably without *the*.

Holland, Dutch   The best that can be said of these two words is that they reflect the antiquity of our association with *The Netherlands*.

  Dutch is an anglicisation of an old dialect version of *Deutsch* = German, and *Holland* is the name of a smallish province of The Netherlands. How would you feel if they called us all *Tasmanians*?

  Happily, the Dutch are tolerant folk, and do not march up and down with flags demanding to be called by their proper name, so the issue is not life-threatening. However, if we can school ourselves to talk about *The Netherlands*, and (possibly more tricky) *the Netherlanders*, it would show that people can have their rights recognised without marching up and down.

home   This noble and evocative word has been under attack for several hundreds of years, but has survived. Although real estate agents, journalists and politicians all use the word *home* when they mean *house*, the difference is still recognised.

  It has even survived its appearance in the phrase *home unit*, a term invented to permit a lowering of minimum building standards without changing the regulations covering houses.

  In Australia, *Home* (usually, but not always, capitalised) had until quite recently the additional sentimental sense of *Britain*. AND cites a 1942 statement that the sentence 'I have never been home' was a 'common paradox'. It also quotes an 1888 reference to an Aboriginal saying 'Bin home too, and along France.' This usage is now dead.

The phrase *stay home* was described by Fowler as an American-ism, but, whatever its provenance, it is also common usage in Australia.

The sports terms *home* and *away* are a delightful example of wandering grammatical status, being respectively a noun and an adverb used as complementary adjectives.

For a note on its pronunciation, see SOCIAL ASPIRATIONS.

homo-   In such words as *homosexual*, the *homo-* part has nothing to do with the Latin *homo* = a man, but comes from the Greek *homos* = same. The misunderstanding is not helped by the fact that the *-sexual* part is Latin, making the word a bastard, or by derivatives like *homophobia*, which ought to mean *fear of things which are similar to one another*. But etymologising rarely yields practical wisdom.

The prefix *homo-* occurs in a large number of English words, largely technical and scientific but including some we encounter every day, like *homogenise* (= to make uniform). By contrast, the only derivatives from the Latin for *man* are *homicide*, *hominid* and *hominoid*. Quentin Crisp's self-description as *one of the stately homos of England* is so packed with allusion as to be untranslatable.

homonym   A homonym is a word with the same spelling as another word but a different meaning (and often a different pronunciation), e.g. *lead* (= guide)/*lead* (=metal). See AMBIGUITY (5).

homophone   A homophone is a word which sounds the same as another word, e.g. *whether*/*weather*/*wether*. See AMBIGUITY (4).

honorifics   For a discussion of *Mr*, *Mrs*, *Miss*, *Ms*, etc., see MR....

hopefully   *We will arrive hopefully around noon*. Americans saying this would mean that they hoped to arrive around noon. Australian speakers might mean that they were arriving around noon and would be hoping for something: lunch, perhaps; but the American usage is understood and increasingly used.

This example is an artifact; a more natural word order would dispose of any possible ambiguity. However, we still have to decide which of these usages is/are acceptable, and the answer must be 'both'. But the American version is one of those usages which some people get very angry about, so those who like a quiet life should not use it.

hospital   The language of Australian hospitals has changed radically over the past few years. Leaving aside the new technology, which is beyond the scope of this book, we have (1) the breaking down of sexism and the replacement of the old nursing hierarchy with names reflecting the 'career structure'; (2) less obvious changes in the medical hierarchy; and (3) a move against the word *casualty*.

(1) In the old days, the nursing hierarchy presupposed an all-female cast, and people were addressed by their titles. Today, the titles are non-sexist, and people are addressed by their personal names, not titles:

Matron (recalling the mother superior in a convent) has become *Director of Nursing*.

Sister (again a reminder of convent hospitals), indicating a position in charge of a ward, has become *Clinical Nurse* (with the variant *Clinical Nurse Consultant* for those in charge of wards providing nursing education).

    Sister was used in many hospitals to indicate a fully qualified nurse whether or not in charge of a ward. Other terms were *Staff Nurse* or *Registered Nurse*. In this case, the person in charge was called a *Charge Nurse*, a term applied in particular to males.

    This distinction is no longer necessary: all those with the title *Nurse* are so qualified.

Nurse was applied to trainee and probationary nurses, the difference being that a trainee might have started nursing only that day, whereas a probationer had completed formal training and had to complete a further time on the wards before qualifying.

    Today, training consists of a pre-clinical period plus ward experience in a teaching hospital. Hence the 'probationary' category has ceased to exist, and trainees are found only in teaching hospitals.

Other categories, outside the 'career structure', are *nursing aides* ('Enrolled Nurses', one-year trained) and *nurse attendants* (untrained).

    All nursing staff are addressed by name rather than by title, as in a bank. Addressing people as *matron* and *sister* is an anachronism, and *nurse* is generally discouraged. However, the form of the name (e.g. on badges) varies: some hospitals encourage the use of given names only, particularly for those below the level of clinical nurse; at the other extreme are those which use the full name with honorifics: *Mr Alan Smith*.

    And, of course, there are plenty of hospitals where nothing has changed, and Matron still rules.

(2) The medical staff have been less quick to abandon protocols and sexism. The person in charge was generally termed the *Medical Superintendent* and is now the *Medical Director*, but otherwise there is little change. Male consultants still prefer to be called *Mr* —, to distinguish themselves from general practitioners, who continue to be addressed as *Dr* — (or just *Doctor*) to distinguish themselves from the laity. Female consultants, however, are likely to prefer to be called *Dr* —.

(3) The ambiguous word *casualty* is rapidly disappearing from the hospitals. Most casualty departments are now *Emergency* and/or *Accident* and/or *Road Trauma Departments*. See CASUAL(TY).

hotel   This word has two sets of connotations in Australia.

(1) In the phrase *I will be staying at a hotel*, the meaning is internationally understood, and indicates an establishment whose prime purpose is providing accommodation of a superior sort, as opposed to (in descending order of magnificence) a motel, a guest house, a boarding house, a rooming house or a hostel. (In country towns, the hotel may well be socially lower than the motel.)

(2) In the phrase *I am going round to the hotel*, the word *hotel* is likely to be the equivalent of the British *pub*. The word *pub* is also universally understood, but middle Australia still drinks at *hotels*.

For a note on its pronunciation, see SOCIAL ASPIRATIONS.

house style   House style is the set of rules adopted by a printer or publisher for the resolution of the curly questions which arise when a manuscript is being committed to type. This includes rules for capitalisation, punctuation (especially of abbreviations), spelling of words which exist in more than one form, and so on.

The purpose of house style is to ensure consistency. This is particularly important for newspapers and magazines, which like to ensure that the same curly question is dealt with in the same way throughout the paper. They do this by making lists of curlies and assigning a solution to each. The solution may be the result of deep intellectual debate or the spin of a coin; the essential point is that, either way, it is binding.

Typesetting houses also have house styles. A manuscript may be divided between several operators, and if the style of setting is to be consistent, it is essential that all of them are using the same rules. However, there is nothing to stop a composition house from offering a range of styles, or from following a style laid down by the author or publisher, or 'following copy', i.e. reproducing the MS, warts and all.

The key point about a house style is not that it is 'correct' in any absolute sense, but that it gives an unequivocal answer to every question which arises, so that all who use it will act identically. It is about *the style for doing something*, not about *doing it with style* (and for more on this distinction, see STYLE).

House style cannot (and makes no claim to) cover all the subtleties of stylish prose, still less those of poetry. It should not be a surprise, therefore, that while house style manuals are very useful to editors, providing simple answers to tricky questions, they can be a menace to authors. Authors who are told that they are wrong, and then shown a style manual to prove it, should rapidly compile their own style manuals to prove that they are right.

however   Two issues: (1) *However* and the run-on sentence; (2) The position of *however* and emphasis.

(1) A run-on sentence   This is a sentence with two main verbs and no conjunction to link them. If we write

I tried to get out, but I couldn't open the door

all is well, as we simply have two sentences linked by a conjunction, but replace *but* with *however* and you get a run-on sentence:

I tried to get out, however I couldn't open the door.

Why does it sound wrong? It is because *however* is not a true conjunction at all, but an adverb, a truncated form of an adverbial clause, perhaps *however hard I tried.* The following is a clear case of a run-on sentence:

I tried to get out, however hard I tried, I couldn't open the door.

To tidy it up, we must restart the sentence and comma off the *however*, as we would with any other adverb:

I tried to get out. (*However,* / *Unfortunately,*) *I couldn't open the door.*

(2) Position   The explanation given above helps in discussing the other difference between *but* and *however*: that whereas *but* has to be at the beginning of the words it introduces, *however* can appear almost anywhere in the sentence, and rarely appears at the beginning.

Why? Like any other adverb, *however* can attach itself to particular words in a sentence. *However* attaches itself to the the word immediately before it, and put stress on it. If there is no word before it, as in the first sentence below, it attaches to the whole sentence and implies no special stress pattern:

They were coming on Saturday by plane.
However, they arrived on Friday by train.
He *arrived on Saturday by plane.*
She, *however, arrived on Friday by train.*
She planned *to come on Saturday by plane.*
She arrived, *however, on Friday by train.*
She planned to come on Saturday *by plane.*
She arrived on Friday, *however, by train.*
She planned to come on Saturday by plane.
She arrived on Friday by train, *however.*

The careful positioning of *however* can be a useful way of showing stress if the use of italics is inappropriate. The dangerous converse is that careless positioning of *however* can damage the sense.

human(e), humanit(y/ies)   We all know what *human* and *humane* mean, but *humanity* is the noun for both. This has caused a curious misunderstanding.

We all know and admire the quality we call *humanity*, which we associate with *being humane*. We therefore associate the academic subjects we term the *humanities* with the finer things of life, in contrast to the *inhumanity* of the sciences.

This is not at all what was originally intended. The academic sense of the word *humanities* dates back to the European renaissance. The opposite of humanity was not inhumanity, but theology: it was human studies against religious studies, studies of profane literature against studies of holy writ. The gentle saints belonged with theology; the Borgias belonged in the humanities.

Renaissance scholars would find it hard to understand our current distinction between humanities and sciences, which causes us to include theology in the humanities but to exclude that most human topic, biology.

humour   A brief look at the semantic history of this word may help to relate the various meanings that it has today.

It started as *humor*, a Latin word meaning *moisture*, whose related adjective survives as *humid*.

This word was adopted as the name for bodily fluids, a sense which survives in the *vitreous* and *aqueous humours* of the eye. However, the principal reference was to the *four humours* which were believed to control human behaviour: blood (Latin *sanguis*), phlegm, choler (bile) and melancholy (black bile). Our understanding of human behaviour has changed, but the old explanation survives in our words *sanguine, phlegmatic, choleric* and *melancholic*.

The word *humour* was then transferred from the cause (the fluids) to the effect (the moods) so that we find in *As You Like It* 'I am in a holiday humour'. Although a person could be said to be *in a bad humour*, the word had a positive tone, so that the adjective, *humorous*, came to be associated with being in a good mood.

It then transferred back from effect to cause, this time finding the cause outside, so that *humorous* people or their *humorous* activities were ones which *put us in good humour*, and finally we have *humour* as the jokes and *a sense of humour* as the capacity to appreciate jokes.

A long way from moisture, but the path is clear.

hurt   The verb *to hurt* is normally transitive; that is, it must have an actual or implied object. The normal construction is as in the sentence *Inflation is hurting the poor*, and if we say *Inflation is hurting*, it is understood that it is hurting *someone*. If we wish to make the poor the subject of the verb, we have to make the verb passive: *The poor are being hurt by inflation*. Similarly, if we say *My arm is hurting*, the implication is that it is hurting *me*.

If we hear somebody say *The poor are hurting*, meaning *The poor are suffering*, they are using the verb intransitively. Is this usage acceptable?

There is nothing unusual about transitive verbs acquiring intransitive senses, so that if the usage survives it will not be seen as an oddity. Nor is it ambiguous: we all know what the politicians mean, even if we wince at the way they say it. But the strongest argument for it is that it expresses very succinctly an idea which we need to express. It implies a specific and recent wound (unlike *The poor are suffering*, which implies a chronic state of wretchedness). Hence it is likely to survive.

hyper-, hypo-   These two prefixes have opposite meanings but can sometimes have very similar sounds. Thus *hyperthermia* and *hypothermia* are the medical terms for (respectively) an *above average* and a *below average* temperature, an ambiguity which appeals greatly to the medical profession (see MEDICAL MIST.). Those whose business is communication rather than obscurity should enunciate them very clearly or, better still, use simpler words.

hyphenation   If you are frequently in doubt about whether to hyphenate a given word or phrase, you are in good company. Our authorities not only differ among themselves (e.g. *postcode* (Mac), *post-code* (ACOD) and *post code* (CAPED)), but exhibit some internal inconsistency (e.g. *post-box*, *post office* and *post-office box* (all in Mac)).

In this last example, Mac is right on all counts, but particularly in being inconsistent. It illustrates how the hyphen can be used to provide shape to phrases which might otherwise start to straggle.

The issue is, as ever, politeness to our readers. Before we decide between *postcode*, *post-code* and *post code*, we should ask which is the most helpful, given that hyphenation can help to clarify origins, meaning and pronunciation.

(1) One word *versus* hyphenation
Rule: Make one unhyphenated word (i.e. *postcode*) if the word is or has become a single thought, so that its origins are irrelevant. This has happened with *cupboard* and *handkerchief*. Hyphenation of these words would not only look silly, but would actually distract the reader, as their origins are in conflict with their present meaning and pronunciation.
Exceptions:
(a) A hyphen may help to resolve ambiguities with prefixes:
    She bought the coop from the coop   (co-op)
    Claridge resigned from North last week, but has now resigned
                                                        (re-signed)
    A useful rule of thumb is that whenever there are two words with the same spelling but different senses and pronunciation, we should hyphenate the one in which there is double stress: see RE-.
(b) A hyphen may also help with pronunciation. For example, the following scientific terms unquestionably represent single thoughts, but are made significantly more friendly by writing them with hyphens: *bistable, monounsaturated, bromomethane.*

The same may go for *biplane, hairdo, layby, reuse* and even *misled;*
and see CO-.

Quick test: read aloud the words *goatherd* and *potsherd.* If you
were stopped in your tracks just for a moment, it shows that at
least one of these is a candidate for hyphenation.

(2) Two words *versus* hyphenation

Rule: Leave the words separate (i.e. *post code*), if they still have a
separate meaning.

Exceptions:

(a) Even if you prefer (say) *post code* when it is a free-standing noun
phrase, hyphenation gives shape to the sentence when the noun
phrase becomes an adjective: *post-code book.* This is a very common pattern. (See TOOTH COMB for a word which has entered the
dictionaries following the loss of a hyphen.)

   The same goes when adjectives are formed from participles
with attached prepositions: the verb *to pass out* makes *a passing-
out parade,* for example. (Conversely, however, the hyphen
should be omitted when some hyphenated noun phrases become verbs: *The set-up was simple, and quickly set up.*)

(b) A hyphen is very useful when a modifier is added to an adjective: *a light-brown loaf, a very common-sense view.* This is particularly important if a line break occurs between the modifier and
the adjective. A careless editor might 'correct' *less careful readers*
to *fewer careful readers,* a danger which could be removed by
writing *less-careful readers* (or, if this looks peculiar, by reword-
ing the sentence).

(3) The prefixes *ex-, post-, neo -, non-, self-* etc., should always have
a hyphen in ad hoc and newly-formed words. Fowler commented
that *the ex-Prime Minister* suggested a Minister who was past his
prime, but the objection is to *ex* trather than the hyphen. Although
it looks odd, it is today commonplace and seems not to cause
genuine confusion. If confusion is feared, the only way round this
problem is to write *former* rather than *ex-.*

The hanging hyphen in the *four- and six-cylinder models* is a useful
device; ugly, perhaps, but acceptable in technical writing.

(4) Hyphenation at line-ends is a topic on which whole books have
been written. The key battle is between those believe that hyphenation should reflect etymology and those who believe in splitting the
word into phonetic components, and only occurs when these two
approaches give differing outcomes.

Computer word processing programs have automatic hyphenation routines which are now quite sophisticated, being based on
complete dictionaries in which the possible break-points are specified individually for each word. (The early programs only had fairly
primitive algorisms, which produced some disastrous results (e.g.
mans-laughter), and were particularly bad at proper names. The

modern ones refuse to hyphenate a word which is not in their dictionaries, and allow users to enter such words, complete with a hierarchy of possible break points.)

The only class of problem with which these programs cannot deal is the very few words which are spelt the same but have different hyphenation patterns according to sense. The classic example is *unionised* (*un-ionised* or *union-ised)* which looks peculiarly silly if the wrong one is chosen.

hypotheticals   See IF… CLAUSES (2).

I

I/me See CASE (2).

iambic See FOOT.

-ic (al) Some people object to the addition of a second adjectival suffix in *-al* to words which already carry the adjectival suffix *-ic*, like geographic(al). If economy were the only determinant, many of these duplications (along with much of the English language) would be scrapped. The trouble is, who is going to scrap them, and which ones are going to be scrapped?

(1) Let us clear away first the ones which do not require attention:

(a) There are words whose *-ic* form has become a noun: *cynic, fanatic, heretic, logic, music, tropic, topic, arithmetic*; the plural-like nouns, *physics, optics, politics* and *mathematics*; and those which have nouns in both forms, as with *mechanic* (the person) and *mechanics* (the topic). In all these cases, *-ical* forms are the normal forms for the related adjectives, with occasional *-ic* forms used only in very specific contexts (*arithmetic* series, *optic* nerve, *politic* behaviour).

(b) There are words on which mute inglorious pruners have already been at work, as with *hypothetical*, where *hypothetic* is obsolete, and *chemical, cylindrical* and *identical*, where *chemic, cylindric* and *identic* never existed in my vocabulary (though Fowler said *identic* existed in diplomacy).

(c) Conversely, in the case of *metabolic* and *anabolic*, the *-ical* forms do not exist. In the case of *cubic*, the extended form *cubical* is rare, *cubic* being applied to volume measurement and *cuboid* being used for 'cube-shaped' in all contexts except crystallography.

(d) In the case of *periodic(al)*, the *-ical* form has been adopted as a noun and *-ic* can only be an adjective.

(2) Having removed all these, we are left with a very large number of words which exist in both forms.

There are words whose *-ic* and *-ical* forms both exist, but have acquired well-defined differences: thus we talk about *electrical engineers* but *electric trains,*: *-ic* for 'driven by' and *-ical* for 'concerned with'. For *historic(al)*, see HISTORIAN. *Magic* appears to describe a process and *magical* a product. Slightly less clear-cut examples are *classic* (= very good) wines against *classical* (= very old) vases, *politic* (= tactful) procedures against *political* actions, and *economic* theories against *economical* recipes.

It is very hard to discern any pattern in all this, so it does not help with the choice between two apparently interchangeable forms, as with *geographic* and *geographical*.

Three arguments point, however, towards -*al*:

(a) Adverbs are always formed from the -*ical* forms (*electrically*), even if the -*ical* form is not an adjective (*periodically*). (The only exception to this is *politicly* = tactfully, which co-exists with *politically*.)

(b) In some cases (e.g. *botanic*(*al*)) the longer form can be used in all senses, whereas the shorter is restricted: we say *botanical* rather than *botanic* specimens.

(c) In the cases in which the -*ic* and -*ical* forms are not interchangeable, -*ical* is used far more often than -*ic*.

If in doubt, then, you will rarely be wrong using -*ical*.

For a detailed discussion of one case, including some etymological points, see MECHANIC.

ideographs   When writing was first developed, it took two quite separate courses: one was to draw sounds (phonetic writing) and the other was to draw meanings (ideographic writing). A Chinese character is an example of an ideograph (though I am told that originally some elements had phonetic significance). Nearer to home, each of our mathematical symbols is an ideograph.

The great merit of ideographs is that they enable a written message to cross language frontiers. The fact that they do not give any clues about the sound they make is seen as a small price to pay for the convenience of transfer. Thus the sentence

$$1 + 1 = 2$$

consists of five ideographs. We can vocalise it as 'One and one makes two' or 'One plus one equals two' or the same message in any language under the sun.

The Chinese script has been a potent weapon in maintaining the unity and integrity of China, whose population is in many respects more diverse than the population of Europe. Like our mathematical characters, the characters are sounded differently in the various languages and dialects of China, but the written form is common to all.

Learning to read Chinese is a totally different problem from learning to read a phonetic language. The Chinese accumulate characters, so that readers' skill can be measured by the number of characters they can recognise and reproduce. Most people get by with around 3000 characters, and a scholar will know over 20,000.

The Look-Say method of teaching reading treats words as if they were ideographs, and it seems that all readers of English develop a sight vocabulary based on the shapes of words when written in lower case characters. IF A SENTENCE IS WRITTEN ENTIRELY IN CAPITALS, IT IS MORE TEDIOUS TO READ, PARTLY BECAUSE MANY CLUES FROM THE OVERALL SHAPE OF THE WORDS ARE LOST.

When we come across a word we rarely see, like *pterogopalato-quadrate*, we may agree about how to sound it, but do not know what it means (though biologists will recognise it as meaning the rod of cartilage forming the upper jaw in fishes). The Chinese would (if it was a properly constructed ideogram or set of ideograms) agree on its meaning without agreeing on its sound.

idiolect This useful word means a *private language*. Strictly, it means the slightly different way in which each of us uses language, but it can reasonably be extended to professional jargon and the private language of very small, close-knit groups like families.

idiom, colloquialism, slang A few definitions:
  (1) An **idiom** is a string of words which may defy explanation in terms of normal grammar or semantics, but is clearly understood by native speakers of a language, and is acceptable in formal as well as informal writing and speech. Unless otherwise specified, idioms can be assumed to be part of the corpus of international English. Thus *How do you do?* is an idiom.
  (2) A **colloquialism** is a word or phrase which may or may not obey the rules of grammar and semantics, but is understood to be out of place in formal writing or speech. While some colloquialisms are very widespread, colloquial forms are often peculiar to the region whose language is being described. Thus *Hi* is a colloquial variant of *How do you do?* used as a greeting in America and increasingly elsewhere, though *Hi* in Britain was until recently what a young gentleman said if being eaten by a lion, as Belloc recorded:

> *No wonder that he shouted 'Hi'.*
> *The honest keeper heard his cry*
> *Though very fat, he almost ran*
> *To help the little gentleman.*

  (3) **Slang** is a private language, and may be restricted to a region (as in *Cockney rhyming slang*), an occupational group (*nautical slang*), or a social group (*the slang of a particular school*). Occupational slang is closely akin to JARGON.

Idioms and colloquialisms are essentially conservative and traditional, often preserving relics of antique forms; slang is ephemeral. Thus *Goodbye*, a corruption of *God be with ye*, is an idiomatic expression acceptable at all levels of discourse; *Farewell* is an archaism, *Cheerio* is colloquial, and *Ciao* a passing fancy (apart, of course, from its use by Italian speakers).

idiosyncrasy Please spell it thus, not *-cracy*, not only because this is the normal spelling, but also because *-cracy* suggests that it is related to *demo-cracy*, etc., which it is not. Etymologically, it means *a private mixture*, the metaphor being ultimately from mixing food or drink in a bowl.

i.e.   See E.G.....

if... clauses and phrases
  (1) Conditional clauses   English offers an array of subtly different ways of expressing conditions. The following is offered not so
much to explain the variety as to point out why *if...* clauses are such
a nightmare for second language speakers, to provide a possible
vocabulary for talking about the matter, and to discuss a few of the
problems of native speakers.

  Any conditional consists of a *protasis* (the *if...* clause) and an
apodosis (the outcome). As these words are not widely understood,
it is bad manners to use them in ordinary speech, but they are
appropriate for use in technical discussion.
  (a) The simplest conditional sentences are those which represent
    empirical truths:
      If you went out yesterday, you will have got wet.
      If you go out tomorrow, you will get wet.
    Here we have both verbs in the indicative mood.
  (b) We can mix the tenses almost at will to produce appropriate
    combinations:
      If you missed breakfast this morning, you will be hungry this
      afternoon.
      If you are hungry now, you must have missed breakfast.
    In each case, we have a cut-and-dried statement whose truth
    either has been or can be tested.
  (2) Hypotheticals   Each of the examples in (1) can be converted
into a less cut-and-dried form to produce an equally vast range of
hypothetical conditionals:
      If you had gone out yesterday, you would have got wet.
      If you were to go out tomorrow, you would get wet.
  Here we have both verbs in a SUBJUNCTIVE or subjunctive-like
MODAL AUXILIARY form (*would, should,* etc.) to indicate the uncertainty. For the simplest example, compare
      I will if I can   with   *I would if I could.*
  (a) Some hypotheticals take uncertainty still further. Compare
      If I were the Prime Minister...   with   *If I were you....*
    It is improbable but not logically impossible that I could become
    the Prime Minister, so it has an indicative equivalent:
      If I become the Prime Minister...
    But there is no indicative equivalent for *If I were you.* It can never
    be literally true, and the verb must be subjunctive. If we say
      If I was you...
    this is still a subjunctive. What has happened is a change in the
    form of the subjunctive, not (as is sometimes asserted) a change
    to the past indicative. (For more about this, see WERE (TO)....)

(b) We are tending to replace simple subjunctives by modal circumlocutions, perhaps because the subjunctive forms are not as clear-cut in English as in other languages. For example, Shakespeare might have written

If I had gone out, I had got wet.

Today we write

If I had gone out, I would have got wet.

We may soon be writing

If I would have gone out, I would have got wet.

In written English, the last example remains an unacceptable usage, but it is less shocking in its elided spoken form:

If I'd've gone out, I'd've got wet.

This is heard almost as often in informal speech as *If I'd gone out....* Note that *I would* and *I had* are both elided to *I'd*, and sound identical, so that speakers may be unable to say which of the elided forms they are using.

(c) The inverted form of protasis without *if...*, as in

O had I the wings of a turtledove, I'd fly on my pinions so high...

was available to Shakespeare as an alternative in almost any conditional clause, but is available now only with the verbs *had* and *were*.

(d) Insecurity about hypothetical usage has led to the popularity of evasive techniques, e.g. *but for...*, as in:

I would have come but for the rain (= *had it not rained*)

(e) Everything that has been said of *if...* applies equally to other conditional conjunctions, e.g. *unless* (= *if ... not*) and *whether ... or not.*

I will come unless it rains.

I will come whether it rains or not.

Also, the suffix *-ever* attached to an interrogative pronoun makes it behave like a conditional conjunction:

I will come whatever you say.

(3) *If...* in indirect questions   In the sentence

He asked if I was the boss

the word *if* is an *interrogative*, not a conditional. To make the verb a subjunctive, e.g.

He asked if I were the boss

is not a pedantry; it is a blunder.

(4) *If...* phrases   In the sentence

I will if possible get there by noon

the phrase *if possible* is best seen as a truncated conditional clause, the complete version being *if it is possible.*

By contrast, in the sentence

He was wearing a clean, if tattered, shirt

the phrase *if tattered* is not a truncated clause (no verb has dropped out) nor is it conditional. It is a phrase, and it is concessional (we could replace *if* with *though*). Fowler wanted to abolish this construction, but didn't say how he would set about it. Heavy fines for using it, perhaps. I like it.

if and when   Is there ever a good reason to use this phrase? 'If it happens…' and 'When it happens…' certainly mean different things, but can 'If and when…' mean more? The answer is 'Yes'. In the sentence 'Dial this number if and when the alarm sounds', the word *if* indicates that the alarm may not go off, and the phrase *and when* adds that, in the event of the alarm going off, action should be immediate.

  Most often, however, it is used by lazy speakers to avoid the necessity of deciding whether they mean *if* or *when*. The contrast between the two is not always as clear as might be imagined, but generally the decision is simple: use *when* for events which are sure to happen, *if* for events which may never happen.

  The argument about *unless and until* is similar, but it leads to a different conclusion: that the phrase *unless and until* does not have any sense beyond that in *unless* or *until*, each of which implies the other.

ilk   Whether we like it or not, the phrase *of that ilk* is in our language and has come to mean *of that kind*, used especially of people and carrying vaguely derogatory connotations.

  The original sense is *same*, so that *McRae of that ilk* meant *McRae of McRae*. But it occurs only in the titles of Scottish lairds, who do not figure in daily discourse in Australia.

illusion   Make sure the pronunciation of this word is clear. It is discussed under DELUSION….

imperative   See VERB (2(D)).

impersonal   In grammar, an *impersonal verb* is one whose subject is a disembodied *it*, e.g. *it is raining*; see VERB (2) and SUBJECT.
  Impersonal writing, such as was once demanded in scientific papers, takes the process a stage further and removes all traces of personal involvement, so that *I saw that…* becomes *It was observed that…* and *I was startled by a loud bang* becomes *A report was heard*. The idea was to concentrate the attention on objective truth, a laudable enough aim. But the result was to generate a lot of very turgid writing, and the best scientific journals now accept and encourage a more subjective style.

  For a discussion of the way impersonal writing can reduce clarity, see OBSCURANTISM (1) and (2).

  If impersonal writing is to be effectively personalised, we need to use *I, we, you* and *one* effectively and precisely:

(a) The word *I* is the only word to use in anecdotes and personal observations and opinions. To say *When one had one's fourth birthday...* is not self-effacing (the main argument for avoiding *I*); it is perverse.

(b) The word *we* is appropriate for statements made on behalf of a group and with their full approval. It is also appropriate for subjective statements with which the author has reason to believe all readers would like to be associated: *We no longer believe in burning witches*. For more about this, see WE.

(c) The word *you* is appropriate for subjective statements addressed to everybody *except* the author or the team, e.g. words of advice arising from the author's experience or wisdom. *If you are in doubt, take the day off.*

(d) The word *one* is appropriate for objective statements, i.e. those which could be made by and are applicable to everybody. *One can't eat ice cream and play the bagpipes at the same time.*

imply, infer   The confusion of these two words is one of the most common errors in educated Australian speech.

We *imply* things when we speak, but *infer* things when we listen.

Thus if I say that I have parked my Rolls Royce in the street, my statement *implies* that I am rich, and you can *infer* that I am liar.

Note that it takes a person, complete with brain, to make an *inference*, since it is an active logical process. But an *implication* can be carried by an inanimate object: *the presence of sedimentary layers* implies *that the mountain was once a sea-bed*.

in-   The main problem with *in-* is that it has two totally separate meanings: inward direction (as in *income, inlet*) and negative (as in *ineffective*). This does not cause many real ambiguities, but it does cause puzzles: *inflammable* and *flammable* are synonyms. The moral is that *in-* should not be used as a negative prefix when coining new words: see NEGATIVE PREFIXES.

Further puzzles can arise from confusion with the prefix *inter-*. Thus *interminable* is made up of *in + terminable*, but *intermingle* is *inter + mingle*. These are words whose hyphenation should follow etymology. Hyphenating them as *in-termingle* and *inter-minable* destroys important clues to meaning and pronunciation.

For a discussion of the way in which the prefix *in-* becomes *im-* before *b* and *p*, etc., see PREFIXES.

incident, accident   In the Second World War, *incident* was the word chosen in Britain to describe the result of an air raid, and in particular an isolated bomb site, away from the main target – an obsolete usage which survives in the title of C. Day Lewis's book, *The Otterbury Incident*.

This fragment of trivial information gives an example of one of the puzzles of semantics: that as fast as strong words (those whose etymology implies precise meaning) become weakened and generalised, weak words step into the breach by acquiring precise connotations.

Let us compare *incident* and *accident*. Etymologically, both are derived from the Latin *cado* = I fall, and the prefixes *in-* and *ad-* are virtually interchangeable, suggesting that they are weak words, and that any difference in meaning is arbitrary.

The adjectives *accidental* and *incidental* (and the adverbs *accidentally* and *incidentally*) both indicate lack of intent, *accidentally* implying an unwanted outcome and *incidentally* a neutral one (or introducing an irrelevant aside).

In music, however, both refer to intentional acts, and have strong, precise meanings: an *accidental* note is one which does not belong to the key signature of the piece, and *incidental music* is music to accompany an otherwise non-musical performance. Likewise, we have in optics the adjective *incident* with a very strong meaning in the phrase *incident ray*: the ray *falling on* a body.

The nouns *incident* and *accident* both have strong unpleasant connotations, the police using them to refer respectively to acts of Man and acts of God respectively, so that an *incident* can occur *accidentally*. The alternative noun *incidence* remains a weak word, synonymous with *occurrence*, while *accidence* has evolved by a devious path into a particularly strong word, meaning *the grammatical study of the various forms of a word* – what we are talking about at the moment, in fact.

Knowing the meaning of the prefixes would not help one iota in guessing the sense of the word. This is in fact the principal message of this laborious piece: that etymology rarely helps when it is most needed.

inclusive language This term is most often used to refer to 'non-discriminatory' language: thus *person* is an inclusive term for *woman* and *man*. For a discussion of the issues surrounding inclusive language, see GENDER and SEXIST LANGUAGE.

incremental If an employment contract insists on speaking of salary increases as *salary increments*, it is fair enough that the adjective meaning 'of or related to such increments' should be *incremental*. However, that should be the only use of the word. It should not be used as a general synonym for 'increased' or 'increasing' as in the sentence *Inflation is the result of incremental prices.*

independent When used in the context of schools, the term *independent* is used with two different meanings: (1) a school not run by the State; (2) a school run neither by the State nor by the Catholic Church. Since precious few schools in Australia are either financially or doctrinally independent, the term needs to be carefully defined whenever it is used.

For another phrase with ambiguous connotations in the field of education, see PUBLIC SCHOOL.

index   The only problem is the plural forms of this word. The convention is that the things at the back of books are *indexes*, while mathematical powers are *indices*.

The phrase 'the Index' could once be used absolutely to mean 'the list of books banned by the Catholic Church', but this would not be widely understood today.

indirect questions, indirect speech   In these phrases, 'indirect' means 'reported'.

	Direct	*Indirect*
Speech	'I like fish,' he said.	He said that he liked fish.
Question	'Do you like fish?' they asked.	They asked me whether I liked fish.

For a discussion of some of the problems, see QUESTIONS..., SPEECH... and SEQUENCE OF TENSES.

individual   Fowler did not like us to use the word *individual* as a synonym for *person*. He asked that we should use it only if we were contrasting a single person with society at large, as in the title of Bertrand Russell's Reith Lectures, *Authority and the Individual*.

Need we be so particular? It would indeed be a pity if this sense were lost (as has happened to the almost identical original meaning of *idiot*); but it does not appear to be at risk. Meanwhile, the colloquial use is a rich one. It would be hard to find a replacement for it in the favourite quotation of the late Stephen Murray-Smith, who was always hoping that someone would ask him whether he was related to the *great* Stephen Murray-Smith, so that he could reply, with Charles Ebden: 'I am myself that happy individual'.

induction, deduction   A logical induction is an argument based on experience. It states that if one event has always been followed by another in the past, it is likely that the one will always be followed by the other in the future. The more often this has happened, the stronger the argument is held to be.

The induction becomes particularly persuasive if we can find some cause and effect relationship between the two events. The relationship may then be stated as an empirical truth or natural law.

Once this is established, further statements can be *deduced* from it, *deduction* being the drawing out of specific conclusions or predictions from empirical observations and natural laws.

For example: in 1929, the astronomer Edwin Hubble observed that all galaxies he studied were moving away from us. Further checking showed that the further away they were, the faster they were receding. This led to an inductive conclusion, Hubble's Law, linking the *distance* and the *velocity of recession* of galaxies.

It was then pointed out that the only other phenomenon which behaved like this was the debris from an explosion. If you were sitting on one bit of debris, all the other bits would be moving away, and the further away they were, the faster they would be receding. At this stage, the logic moved from induction to deduction, the deductions being (a) that all future observations of galaxies would be found to obey the law; (b) that the origin of the universe was a gigantic explosion, and (c) that the explosion must have happened some 20,000 million years ago.

From all this it can be seen that an *inductive* argument is destroyed by finding a single case in which the alleged relationship does not hold. A *deductive* argument can be destroyed by a demonstration *either* that it has given a faulty prediction *or* that the propositions on which it was based are faulty (even if it has never produced a wrong prediction).

-ine   How do we pronounce the names of the halogens: *chlorine, fluorine, bromine, iodine* and *astatine*? Our dictionaries make them all rhyme with *mean*, but report a pronunciation rhyming with *mine* as an alternative for *iodine* (ACOD) and for *iodine* and *bromine* (Mac). Mac does not have an opinion about *astatine*.

Mac's is an accurate report of Australian usage: *bromine* as well as *iodine* is often heard rhyming with *mine*, and few people talk about *astatine* at all. However, there is a good case for schooling ourselves to be consistent within this set, and try to avoid rhyming any of them with *mine*. (We have no doubts with most other chemical words in *-ine*, e.g. *glycerine, benzine* and, of course, *margarine*, but the *amines* occasionally get the long *i*.)

infinitive   The *infinitive* is one of the two ways in which a verb can become a verb-noun, the other being the *-ing* form known as a GERUND:

> *Infinitives:* To see *is* to believe
> *Gerunds:*   Seeing *is* believing

There is a misdemeanour known as a *split infinitive*, a crime so minor that many writers do not know they have committed it.

First, let us define the crime: a split infinitive is a phrase consisting of an infinitive verb with a word (generally an adverb) down the middle, e.g. *...to never obey..., ...to exactly measure....* We are told that we should say *...never to obey...*, etc. Fowler devoted almost three pages to this one topic, and what he says is as witty as it is inconclusive, and as inconclusive as it is correct. It can be summed up in three generalisations:

(1) Split infinitives are often ugly, and *other things being equal* are best avoided. A writer who finds that a sentence is clumsy may find that there is a split infinitive in it, and that it can be greatly improved by removing the cleavage.

(2) If a writer has split an infinitive, and the result is not clumsy, there is no reason to remove it. There are many occasions when the adverb does not sit happily anywhere else. Split infinitives abound in our literature, sometimes as the lesser of evils, but sometimes deliberately, to achieve special effects.

(3) The only unforgivable crime is to remove a word which was splitting an infinitive, and then to plonk it down somewhere else where it is just as intrusive and no longer does the job it was intended to do.

inflation   Inflation is the rate (generally expressed as a percentage) by which prices have increased over a period. Hence the statement *Inflation has gone up by 5%* can carry a number of meanings, but cannot mean that *prices* have gone up by 5% unless the rate of inflation was previously zero. See PERCENTAGES.

inflection (grammar)   *Inflection* is the name given to the variation in form of a word to show something of its grammatical status. Spell it thus (rather than *inflexion*).

In English, the use of inflection is minimal.

(1) In nouns, it appears only in showing plurals and possessives

	Singular	Plural
All cases except possessive	spade	spades
Possessive	spade's	spades'

Some suffixes, both female (princ*ess*, suffrag*ette*, etc.) and diminutive (book*let*), are inflections of a sort. The French-style female suffix *e* as in fiancé*e* is more clearly an inflection, at least in French.

(2) The pronouns are the richest source of variation, but most of the variations are different words rather than inflections of the same word.

	Singular			Plural		
	1ST	2ND	3RD	1ST	2ND	3RD
Nominative	I	you	he she it	we	you	they
Objective	me	you	him her it	us	you	them
Possessive	mine	yours	his hers its	ours	yours	theirs

(3) Verbs show (by comparison with other major languages) astonishingly little inflection. There are four patterns, of which only the first (as in *to give*) has the full range of five variants. The most common is the second:

3rd person singular, present tense	gives	shouts	sets	comes
past tense	gave	shouted	set	came
past participle	given	shouted	set	come
present participle and verb-noun	giving	shouting	setting	coming
infinitive and all other forms	give	shout	set	come

(The verb *to be* has additional inflections: see VERB (2).)

(4) Adjectives are not inflected for number or gender, apart from the odd French words in which the French gender inflections are preserved: *fiancé(e)*, *né(e)*. However, many receive the inflection-like suffixes which supply comparative and superlative forms, and make many of them into **adverbs:**

adjective	comparative	superlative	adverb
fine	finer	finest	finely
old	older	oldest	
	elder	eldest	
(out)	outer	outermost	
	utter	uttermost	utterly

Elder is included in this list only to comment that its adverb-like inflection, *elderly* is simply another adjective, meaning *old*. This is a relic from a once-numerous set of adjectives formed by adding *-ly* to a noun, in this case the noun *elder*. Other examples include *cowardly*, *painterly* and *hourly*.

-ing **forms**   This phrase is commonly used to describe the inflections of verbs which end in *-ing*. There is no harm in using this phrase provided that it is remembered that the *-ing* form covers two quite different phenomena, the *present participle* and the *verb-noun*, also known as the GERUND:

I am walking   participle used in a verb phrase

I like walking   gerund, a noun = *the act of walking*

I have a walking *doll* participle used as adjective = *which can walk*

I have a walking *stick* gerund used as adjective = *for walking*

The distinction is useful in considering the alleged error called the *fused participle*. Consider these three sentences:

They, being tall, were a problem   *being tall* is here an adjectival phrase

Their being tall was a problem   *being tall* is here a noun phrase

They being tall was a problem   ?

The first two are grammatical, but have different shades of meaning. The third is an example of a fused participle. Seen in this simple example, the error is obvious enough, but what about this one:

General Eisenhower being appointed Supreme Commander of all allied forces in Normandy proved to be an excellent decision.

The sense demands that it was the *appointment* that was an excellent decision, not *General Eisenhower*, and *being appointed* is thus a gerund. The sentence should thus start *General Eisenhower's being appointed....*

The rule to avoid this problem is to check what the subject of the main verb is, the *-ing* word or its antecedent. The same holds if the *-ing* is part of the object:

The bomber pilot saw the city lying defenceless beneath him.
(not *city's*)

> *The Court deplored the Cabinet Secretary's perjuring himself.*
> (not *Secretary*)

It is particularly important if both would make sense, e.g.

> *The Party supported* Sinclair/Sinclair's *being the Parliamentary leader.*

Is the intended meaning *The Party supported Sinclair's appointment as Party leader*, or *The Party supported Sinclair because he was the Party leader*?

We are rarely tempted to put in an inappropriate possessive, but we are tempted to leave out an appropriate one, particularly where the possessive is to be attached to a lengthy phrase:

> *I deplore a Bill related to religious freedom being the subject of partisan debate.*

This is a clumsy sentence, but would scarcely be improved by saying *freedom's*, though it is 'correct'. In fact, the sentences about which there is doubt are almost invariably clumsy, and the best solution is to re-phrase with a less tortuous construction:

> *I deplore having a partisan debate on a Bill related to religious freedom.*

inspiration   For the survival of the original meaning of this word (= breathing in) see RESPIRATION.

intelligence   *Intelligence* has three meanings, which have very little in common.

(1) *Intelligence* is the phenomenon we observe in people we call *bright*; a capacity which goes beyond common sense; *uncommon sense*, perhaps. It is manifested in a capacity to find quick solutions to novel problems and to grasp new ideas.

(2) In the phrase *Australian Security Intelligence Organization, intelligence* has nothing to do with being bright, and is effectively synonymous with *information gathering*. Thus *American Intelligence, whose satellite surveillance of the former USSR was said to be capable of reading the registration plates on cars entering the Kremlin, missed the nuclear explosion at Chernobyl.*

(3) In the phrases *I.Q.* (*Intelligence Quotient*) and *intelligence test*, the original concept was that *intelligence* in the first sense was to be measured. Unfortunately, it has so far proved impossible to devise tests whose results are not influenced by lifestyle and experience, and cannot be improved by coaching. This means that intelligence in this context is not an innate capacity, but rather *the capacity to do well at intelligence tests*, a circular definition.

As a result of the ambiguity of the word, writers who use it should be very careful to make it clear which sort of intelligence they are talking about.

intensifiers   Now that we have computers with clever routines for identifying words and calculating their frequency of occurrence, we have a tool to diagnose one of the most common diseases of language – the over-use and hence devaluation of intensifiers. For the most dangerous one, see LITERALLY.

Intensifiers come and go. Thus Fowler identified *vastly* as a jocular archaism, but political speeches today are full of it. *The situation is* vastly *different from....* Other popular intensifiers are *spectacularly* (*The project was* spectacularly *successful*), *infinitely* (*The scenario today is* infinitely *better than it was under the previous administration*) and *abysmally* (*The situation is* abysmally *bad*).

The objection is not to the words, which have precise and often useful meanings, but to their use in contexts where their precision is not exploited. They become mere expletives, and may ultimately lose their original meaning. How many people still associate *abysmal* with the gloomy depths of an abyss, for example?

Shakespeare understood this danger, and attributed the disease to the lower orders. His working-class characters pepper their speeches with inappropriate intensifiers (*I'll speak in a* monstrous *little voice*). In our society, our rulers who do most of the peppering.

interest   Let us first deal (1) with the form of the word, and then (2) with the difference between *uninterested* and *disinterest*.

(1)   *Interest* is a good example of a barbarism which has become respectable with the passage of time.

It started life as the third person singular Latin verb *inter-est*, meaning literally *it is among*, and idiomatically *it is of interest*. When for the first time someone said 'It interests me', it would have made purists wince and write angry letters to the newspapers, had there been any purists or newspapers around at the time. But there weren't, and nobody objects to it any more.

(2) The word *interest* has two related but separate senses. The negatives, *uninterested* and *disinterested*, make the distinction clearly, and we should use them with appropriate care.

USAGE	OPPOSITE
1 *I have an interest in mining* (= Mining intrigues me)	*I am uninterested in mining* (= Mining bores me)
2 *I have an interest in mining* (= I have shares in a mine)	*I am disinterested in mining* (= I am not involved in mining)

In Court, *an interested party* is one who has a stake in the proceedings (as in sense 2 above), but *interested members of the public* will normally mean those who follow court cases as a form of sport (as in sense 1). This can be dangerously ambiguous if you are sued for libel and plead *public interest*: see DEFAMATION. But at least the opposites are unambiguous: the judge and jury are required to be *disinterested* but should not be *uninterested*.

Those who say they are *disinterested* when they mean that they find a topic boring are damaging this important distinction.

Meanwhile, we should be careful about the phrase 'public interest'. When media barons speak of 'public interest', they are generally thinking in terms of the ratings. But when the law of defamation asks defendants for proof of 'public interest', it is not enough to show that the public was enthralled by the sight of the dirty linen hanging out for all to see: the defendant must prove that the public had a stake in the issue. This is a common and quite dangerous ambiguity.

There is then a third use of the term *interest*, which does not cause trouble: *interest* on loans. This sense is an extension of the second, the abstract noun having been applied (as often happens) to the concrete manifestation. Those who loaned money were said to be *taking an interest* in a venture, and the word was attached to the rent they were paid for the use of their money. Doubtless the purists also winced the first time this usage appeared.

interstate   The Australian usage is broader than the American; see AUSTRALIANISMS.

intransitive   This is a term of grammar applied to verbs. An *intransitive verb* is one which, like *to sleep*, cannot have a direct object. See VERB (1).

irregardless of   This phrase does not exist in any of our dictionaries; nor should it. It seems to have arisen from a confusion between *regardless of...* and *irrespective of...*, and is a simple error.

irrespective(ly)   In the sentence *I pressed on irrespective of my instructions*, the sense is clear but the grammatical status of the word *irrespective* is not.

Fowler said 'The modern idiom is to use the adjective as a quasi-adverb (cf. *regardless*)'. The Australian idiom would seem to be better explained by treating *irrespective of* as a PREPOSITIONAL PHRASE.

is, are   There is really only one problem, though it has many manifestations: it is to decide whether the verb should be *is* or *are* when a singular and a plural face one another across the verb *to be*.

What we need is/are fourteen cakes	is...
The wages of sin is/are death	is...
Two sevens is/are fourteen	are...
There is/are fourteen cakes	are...
Twice seven is/are fourteen	*See below*
Two times seven is/are fourteen	*See below*
Fourteen is/are needed	*See below*

The rule is that the form of the verb *to be* is determined by what goes before. Hence it will be *What we need is...* irrespective of what happens next.

This rule is not broken by *The wages of sin is death*, because at the time when it was written, *wages* was a singular noun. Likewise, it is *two sevens are fourteen* even if seven and fourteen are regarded as single entities. The apparent exception is *There are fourteen cakes,* but *there* is a weak adverb heralding an inverted sentence. The subject is *fourteen cakes.*

The next three are doubtful cases, not because of any doubt about the rules, but because we have not decided whether the subject of the sentence is singular or plural.

Twice seven is ambiguous. It can be seen as a single entity, like *a pair of scissors,* and followed by *is,* or as a circumlocution for fourteen (as in Coleridge's *Twice five miles of fertile ground*) in which case it is plural. *Two times seven* is similar. Indeed the problem is seen at its clearest in *Fourteen is/are needed.* If you were talking about scores on a darts board, it would be *is.* If you were talking about chairs for a meeting, it would be *are.*

Other related problems are discussed in SINGULARITIES and PRONOUN (2).

-ise/-ize/-ice   These are just three of many ways of writing a series of phonemes, including /*-iss*/ as in *promise,* /*-eece*/ as in *police,* /*-ice*/ as in *device* and /*-ize*/ as in *rise.* The possibilities for confusion and error are endless, but there are two particular problems which afflict even good spellers, which are illustrated by (1) *realize/realise* and (2) *practice/practise.*

(1) -ise/-ize   It seems odd that the battle between *-ise* and *-ize* has been going on so long without resolution. Many people have produced good reasons for resolving it in favour of *-ise*; but the opposition is formidable: when Fowler and the leading academic presses of Britain join forces with the Americans against us, what are we to do?

ACOD$_1$ persisted with *-ize,* but ACOD$_2$ (like Mac and AWEG) plumps for *-ise.*

They are right, whether they are reporting what we (collectively) do or advising what we should do. There are four good reasons for this:

(a) While *-ise* may sometimes raise eyebrows, it is only wrong in a very few cases which rarely cause trouble, e.g. *prize,* whereas there is a long list of words where, for a variety of reasons, *-ize* is wrong in all but the most *-ize*-loving circles.

(b) The distinction between *-ize* and *-ise* is based on appeal to Classical Greek. We are told to use *-ize* for formations derived from Greek verbs in *-izo* and modern imitations thereof, whereas *-ise* must be used in the case of words like *supervise* which never had a z (some of which have the additional complication discussed in (2) below) and in words which have lost the z, e.g. in transmission through French. This argument would be more compelling if everybody knew Classical Greek, and if it really helped if they did. Neither is the case.

The normally sensible Fowler, commenting on the list of exceptions, said '...the difficulty of remembering which these -*ise* verbs are is in fact the only reason for making -*ise* universal, and the sacrifice of significance to ease does not seem justified.' This is a value judgement, and sensible Australians sacrifice the significance without noticing they have done so, coming down the other way.

(c) The passion for -*ize* has lead to the barbarism of spelling *analyse* with a z, for which there is no justification whatsoever except that the Americans do it. See ANALYSE.

(2) -ice/-ise There is a tendency for certain verbs and their related nouns to part company on this one: we *advise* some *advice*, and *devise* a *device*. Here we see a spelling variation reflecting a pronunciation difference, and this causes no problems.

However, there are some apparently similar words where the same spelling difference is asserted even though no pronunciation difference survives: the British *practise* a *practice*. (In other times, the words were spelt *practize* and *practise* respectively, a point on which the z fanciers are understandably silent.)

The Americans solve this problem by using *practice* in both senses. This is sensible, if only because the noun, *practice*, is much more common, and hence the common 'error' is to spell the verb with a c rather than the noun with an s. I follow the Americans on this; but see LICENCE....

It is probable that pedants will continue to delight in the subtlety of the British convention, but this is a plea for tolerance of those who, like me, do not.

Islam(ic) The word *Islam* means 'submission', and the main question concerns the use of three adjectives: *Islamic*, *Muslim* and *Muhammadan*. For the spelling of the last two, see the entries MUHAMMAD... and MUSLIM....

Adherents call themselves *Muslims*. They avoid the term *Muhammadans* (however spelt) because it implies that Muhammad occupies the same position in Islam as Christ does in Christianity. However, non-believers use both words, and perceive a subtle distinction between the two: an Australian convert may be said to have *become a Muhammadan* rather than *become a Muslim*, *Muslim* having the connotation of exotic origin.

The adjective *Islamic* means 'of or related to the faith of Islam' whereas Muslim means 'of or related to a follower of Islam'. Thus when we say a *Muslim* country we mean one whose population is largely Muslim, irrespective of its government, whereas when we say an *Islamic country* we imply also that it is governed according to Islamic law. This distinction is recent and may prove temporary.

How far should non-Muslims adopt Islamic rules in our own choice of words?

(a) They are proper nouns, and other things being equal, we should always use them the way their owners say. See PROPER (1).

(b) We should avoid using the word *Muhammadan*, however spelt.

-ist/-alist The problem here is to decide how to form job descriptions from certain abstract nouns: *education(al)ist, constitution(al)ist, agricultur(al)ist, natur(al)ist.*

There is no problem with words which have no relevant *-al* forms, and hence have no *-alist* forms either: *abolitionist, abortionist* and *extortionist.* Conversely, there are words which have no relevant short forms, and hence have to be formed from the *-al* version: *rationalist, specialist.*

When both forms are possible, there is rarely any one correct form, but one form will be more used than the other and one may make better sense than the other. Thus we use *constitutionalist* rather more than *constitutionist*, and this is explained by saying that the person is concerned with *things constitutional* rather than the constitution as such.

However, there is always the suspicion that such explanations run along behind usage, trying to supply rational justification for decisions which have already been made by chance. We use *naturalist* and *naturist*, for example, in separate well-defined senses, but their meanings are the reverse of what logic might suggest.

The *conservationist* saves trees by avoiding the more long-winded title *conservationalist*, but in general the longer versions tend to win: *conversationalist, traditionalist* and *nationalist.*

italic The word comes from the 'sweet Italic hand', the elegant slightly sloped lettering of Italian medieval manuscripts, which inspired typefaces designed by Aldus Manutius of Venice, perhaps the greatest of all typographers. Today italic is not so much a font as a style variant available within most fonts.

Italic can be used as a body type, particularly for poetry, to which it gives a lyrical look, and, if Swift is to be believed, increased satirical force:

> *To Statesman wou'd you give a wipe*
> *You print it in Italick Type.*
> *When letters are in vulgar shapes,*
> *Tis ten to one the Wit escapes.*

The more common use of italic, however, is to stress or otherwise distinguish specific words within a text.

(1) The only hard rules are those which apply to scientific nomenclature. Biological names given in the Linnean system must be italicised (see TAXONOMY) as must the symbols for physical quantities (see SI UNITS).

(2) There is a convention that foreign words are put in italics. The convention is now obsolescent: few people italicise *de facto,*

detour or *etc.*, and *per se, raison d'être* and *op. cit.* are moving that way. However, the convention remains useful on the odd occasion when an unknown foreign term has to be used: as a flavouring in dialogue, or because no existing word fits. It may look very odd if presented without some sort of warning flag. The decision on which words to italicise must depend on the intended readership as much as the words themselves.

(3) There is a current convention that the titles of literary works should be in italics (see BIBLIOGRAPHIES). A similar but less clearly codified convention italicises the names of ships and houses. It is useful if the name might otherwise get mixed up with text, though capitalisation will generally be enough.

(4) There is a convention that uses italics to supply the need for an exclamation mark in the middle of a sentence, telling the reader that the word is important or surprising. This is the typographical equivalent of underlining in a manuscript, and has the same dangers: a good writer does not need to show emphasis, as it should be clear from the sentence structure, and the presence of a great deal of underlining in a manuscript (like excessive use of exclamation marks) is generally a sign of an insecure or amateur author.

(5) The fifth use is similar but less objectionable: italics are used to show logical emphasis. Thus the sentence 'I hope you can help me' could be read in six different ways simply by shifting the emphasis word-by-word down the sentence, and one simple way of showing the writer's intentions is to use italics, e.g. 'I hope that *you* can help me.'

(6) The sixth use is like a flag, to draw attention to a word. This can be because it is the key word of the passage, or that it is being used in an odd way, or that it is in some sense a quotation. In the present work, italics are used in preference to quotation marks on usage examples.

These various conventions lead to the problem of italics within italics, i.e. how to italicise a word if the surrounding text is already in italics. The convention is to use roman:

I read Gone with the Wind *last night. It was a* ghastly *experience.*

This is not a wholly satisfactory convention: it may not be recognised by some readers, and it looks very odd if, as in the sample above, the convention is used twice in different ways within the same line. It would be better to indicate one or the other in some other way, e.g.

I read 'Gone with the Wind' last night. It was a ghastly *experience.*

This decision, of course, makes a nonsense of consistency; but if consistency and clarity are in conflict, clarity should win.

See EMPHASIS, and note the special rules given in the entry on SI UNITS.

its, it's   Everybody agrees that the approved form is:

> *it's = it is*, as in '*It's* a boy' or (at a pinch) *it has*, as in '*It's* got to go'.
> *its = of it*, as in 'The cat's eating *its* own tail'.

Why is this such a problem? It clearly is one: according to at least one analysis, it is the most common single mistake in children's compositions.

It is hard to prove, but perhaps it is because we have here an exception to an exception to a rule. The rule is that the apostrophe represents a missing letter, as in *it'(i)s*. The exception to this is the possessive apostrophe, which is used whether a letter has dropped out or not, as in *face's*. The exception to the exception is that the apostrophe is not used on the possessive *its* (or *hers, ours, yours* or *theirs*), this being the sole survivor of a true possessive case in English. This is discussed under APOSTROPHE (3).

We spend a lot of our time telling children not to put apostrophes on plurals, since they are used on possessives, and this is the price we pay.

When we say that it is the most frequent error, we mean that it is the most frequently *detected* error. It is detected because the writer's meaning remains absolutely clear to the reader. Thus it loses the writer marks in the school of hard knocks, but does not interfere with communication.

This seems to me to be a clinching argument for abolishing the possessive apostrophe. But I am not quite brave enough to do it in this book.

-ize   See -ISE....

J

J This letter has only emerged as a distinct entity in the last four hundred years. Until then, it was generally written as an *I*, which could be either a consonant or a vowel. In Roman times *I* had very much the same set of values as *Y* in modern English.

The consonantal use was occasionally distinguished by a lengthening of the downstroke, and this was the origin of the modern form: it even retains the dot in the lower case version: *j*.

It was rapidly adopted in almost all European languages, but its sound value depended on local conditions. This can be illustrated by the development of the name *John*. In ancient Greek, it was *Ioannos*, Latinised as *Ioannus*. The original Latin value is, curiously, best preserved in Germanic languages, where the *J* in *Johann* (German) and in *Jan* (Dutch) is sounded as *Y*. (The *I* spelling survives in the Scottish form, *Ian*.) In Spanish, *Juan* starts with an *H* sound. In French, *Jean* starts with a sound similar to the *s* in *measure*, while in English it is similar to the soft *g* in *magic*.

We can see the result of this variety in other words. For example, our words *mayor* and *major* are etymologically identical; *Jugoslavia* and *Yugoslavia* are merely alternative spellings (both pronounced with the *Y* sound).

Jacuzzi This trade name has triumphed in Britain as the term for the bath with underwater jets which Australians (and Americans) know as a *spa*.

jail See GAOL....

jargon Other people talk jargon; we, however, just use some technical terms of our callings. Similarly, other people use their jargon to obstruct communication and make us feel ignorant, whereas we use our technical terms to aid communication, because the common language terms do not mean precisely what we have in mind.

In short, talking jargon is rather like being a member of a CLIQUE: you can be genuinely taken aback to realise that you are doing it. Just as cliques are most easily observable when viewed from the outside, so the presence of jargon is best recognised by people who do not understand it.

These commonplace observations enshrine complete advice on the correct attitude to jargon. If we are talking to outsiders about our own professional or specialist interests, we should be careful to avoid jargon. If we are talking to professional colleagues, the use of jargon is not only acceptable but also makes good sense.

Real problems arise only when there is conflict between the common language sense and the jargon sense of a word, and it produces a misunderstanding or ambiguity. For examples, see MEDICAL MIST. and NAUTICAL FOLLIES.

jersey   The Channel Islands – Jersey and Guernsey – have given us cattle and clothing. However, whereas most Australian footballers wear guernseys, British footballers wear jerseys. Conversely, the Australian phrase 'to give someone a guernsey', meaning to give praise, promotion or a prize, is not understood in Britain (or would be taken literally, as a gift of a cow).

jingoism   *Jingoism* is one of the very few words whose origins can be fully documented. In 1878, the British politician Benjamin Disraeli was campaigning for the sending of a British fleet into the Black Sea, and was supported by a music hall song whose refrain went:
> *We don't want to fight, but by jingo if we do,*
> *We've got the ships, we've got the men, we've got the money too.*
> *We've fought the Bear before, and while Britons shall be true,*
>   *The Russians shall not have Constantinople.*

Disraeli and his supporters were immediately dubbed *jingoists*, and their campaign *jingoism*. The popular response to it can be judged from the success of the parody which appeared later the same year, and is perhaps better remembered today than the original:
> *We don't want to fight, but by jingo if we do,*
> *We won't go to the front ourselves, we'll send the mild Hindoo.*

Curiously, Disraeli's campaign was at the time more effective in Australia, where it stimulated a renewed outburst of building of defence works against Russian attack at strategic points along the coast.

Unlike CHAUVINISM, *jingoism* has retained its original sense: an enthusiasm for military adventure, masquerading as patriotism.

jojoba   Say /ho-hoba/. For a discussion of the logic of this, see FOREIGN WORDS… (4).

journalist   The current usage of this word is a form of euphemism. The first journalists were people who kept *journals*, and the words were synonymous with *diarist* and *diaries* (all being associated with words for 'day'). The word *journal* retains this sense in English (alongside its sense in bookkeeping). In French, however, the word for newspaper was *journal*, and the business of writing for them was *journalisme*. In 1833, the word *journalism* was adopted from French in this sense, and next moment all the reporters were calling themselves *journalists*. Today, it extends to people working for television and radio as well as for the press.

It remains a professional label rather than a job title. The jobs carry titles like court *reporter*, foreign *correspondent*, city *editor*, gardening *columnist* and so on, but the people who get these titles are all labelled journalists, belong to journalists clubs, and are perhaps graduates of a school of journalism.

Despite its connection with 'day' we should have no worries about applying it to other-than-daily periodicals. The French, for whom the connection with day is much stronger, do not worry, so why should we?

judgement/judgment   The authorities and the citations are so divided that it is clearly impossible to declare either of these wrong, so it is equally unwise to declare either of them correct.

It was suggested by Fowler that *judgment* was the better spelling in legal works and *judgement* in all others. No purpose is served by such a distinction (the alleged argument for it being that it saves space in legal works, which is not normally a prime consideration of legal writers). ACOD and Mac both quote both spellings, but (if the order of appearance means anything) ACOD prefers *judgement* in all senses, while Mac prefers *judgment* in all senses.

The same argument applies with other similar words, e.g. *abridgement, acknowledgement*. The spelling with the *e* has the merit that *-ment* should be no different from other suffixes starting with consonants. Some of them would look very silly without an *e*: *ridgpole, edgways*. None of them looks silly with one.

junta   For a discussion of the pronunciation (ending in the inconsistent advice that the South American manifestations may be */hoontas/* but that those elsewhere rhyme with *hunters*), see FOREIGN WORDS…(4). I see no merit in the halfway house, making the *u* as in *pull*.

K

K The /k/ sound has had a checkered career in the languages from which English is derived, and this is the source of some peculiarities in our spelling.

The letter K was rarely used in Latin or French, and the /k/ sound was represented by C for the Greek κ (*kappa*) and CH for χ (*chi*). Curiously, one of the very few words in which the Romans used a K was *kalendae*, which has come to us with a C in our word *calendar*.

However, in Germanic languages, K was the normal letter for the /k/ sound, and the letter C was the stranger, appearing in home-grown words only in combination with H and K.

English generally followed the leader: French imports followed the French (*catholic*) and Germanic imports followed the Germanic (*kindergarten*).

In the eighteenth century, K was revived in French for bizarre imports (e.g. *kangourou*) and Greek-inspired neologisms (including *kilometre*, which ought etymologically to have been *chilio-*) – another good example of the merits of ignorance. Again, English followed the leader.

Even this recent process has not been systematic. Thus, from the same Greek stem *kine-* we get both *kinetics* and *cinema*, modifying the sound on the *speak-as-you-spell* principle.

kern Thanks to typographical word processors, this word has entered the common language, so a word about its origins is perhaps apposite.

In the days of metal type, one of the problems was to fit characters snugly together. The problem can be seen best with the italic *f* and the capital V and A, though it affected many characters.

If the body (the solid metal on which the type was cast) was the full width of the character, the characters were too far apart from one another. The solution was to cast the characters so that the ends overhung the body, and they then fitted together closely:

unkerned   *kerned*   *unkerned*   *kerned*

The overhang was known as a *kern*, and the characters with overhangs were known as *kerning* characters.

In modern electronic typesetting, the word *kerning* is applied to the same effect, which is achieved by reducing the space between the images: *ff*   *ff*   AA AV AV

The equipment allows the operator to nominate the extent of the kerning between any pair of characters.

kerosene   Spell it thus (rather than *-ine*, the suffix *-ene* being recommended for double-bonded hydrocarbons of this sort), and remember that the British call it *paraffin*.

keyboarding   This is the new word for *typing*. Typing is one of the very few *skills* which might find a place in the compulsory core to a school curriculum, but became badly discredited in the years when educationists sought to remove from the schools anything vocational or sexist, since typing was seen as both.

The arrival of the computer caused a complete change. The keyboard became the gateway to the new technology, and typing, under the new name *keyboarding*, made a triumphant return. The main novelty is that today's word processors bridge the gap which used to exist between typing and typesetting, so that today's keyboarders have to know the differences between the two.

(1) Copy preparation – typewriting style   Typewriting style is the most appropriate *unless* there is some good reason to adopt the conventions of typesetting. This means using the word processor as a peculiarly helpful typewriter, making use of the editorial facilities of the program but not the typographical ones.

The reason is twofold: firstly, that there is nothing worse than a botched piece of typography – far better to stick with competent typewriting style; secondly, that just as some people feel that typed communications are less personal than handwritten ones, many feel that a typographical text is less personal than a typed one.

Thus traditional typing conventions are best for ordinary business letters and reports. But much the same goes for manuscripts being prepared for submission to a publisher. In the case of manuscripts:

*   use A4 paper (to fit on standard copyholders, etc.);
*   leave good margins (to give space for comments and typographical instructions);
*   use double spacing (to give the editor space for corrections);
*   make paragraph openings full out;
*   insert an extra line space between paragraphs;
*   use a serif typeface;
*   use a double hyphen to indicate a dash;
*   write in tricky bits by hand: see MATHEMATICAL WRITING;
*   clip sections together (to minimise risk of pages getting out of order); and
*   number the pages (in case they escape from the clips).

If there is a chance that the keyboarding will be used as the basis for typesetting, there are ways in which the original keyboarding can help. However, these may depend on the conversion program being used, and you should seek instructions from the people who will be doing the conversion.

The two absolute rules are: (1) to be consistent (i.e. always achieve the same effect in the same way); and (2) to do as few clever things as possible (since it is easier to insert cleverness than to remove cleverness which is not needed).

(2) Copy preparation – typesetting style   If you seriously expect your keyboarding to look like professional typesetting, you must know the answers as well as the questions. If you imagine that printing on a typographical printer will suddenly turn a typed page into a typographical page, you are doomed to be disappointed. A typeset text will generally have:

- single spaces after punctuation marks;
- no line space between paragraphs;
- indented openings to paragraphs other than the first after a heading;
- italics for stress (rather than the traditional typewriter's under-lining);
- a distinction between hyphens, en-dashes and em-dashes (see DASH…);
- a distinction between opening and closing quotations marks ('true quotes');
- a distinction between hard and soft spaces, and between thin and thick spaces; and
- a range of accents, special sorts and ligatures (fi, fl, æ, etc.).

If the keyboarding is consistent, most of the conversion from typewriting conventions can be done programmatically.

However, even this will not be true of mathematical setting and tables. The chances are that these will all have to be rekeyed, and the best that the manuscript can show is the intended content and layout: see MATHEMATICAL WRITING (3).

kilometre   Some assorted points are worth noting:

(1) Pronunciation   Why there should be any doubt about the pronunciation of this word is a puzzle. The word was coined in 1791 by the revolutionary French, who sounded it something like /keelo-mettr'/. When Australia metricated its measures, the pronunciation which was officially adopted was /killa-meter/. This might have been the end of the matter had not /k'lommitter/ received the patronage of Gough Whitlam, otherwise a man of considerable wisdom and good taste. (I have heard, but never understood, his argument.) The ABC has recently accepted it as a legitimate variant.

ACOD$_1$ listed /kill-ommitter/ as a 'disputed usage' (which it defined elsewhere as one which, 'though widely found, is still the subject of adverse comment by a significant number of educated writers'), and this was probably a correct report. Mac$_1$ optimistically made no mention of it, presumably hoping that it would go away. But it didn't, and Mac₂ lists both.

RW specifically deplores it, and so do I; not because of the French connection, but because it destroys the symmetry of the set: we do not say /mill-immitter/, etc, and none of the other *kilo-* words has the stress on the *o*. For more about this argument, see -METRE....

(2) Spelling   While the pronunciation should not be a matter of argument but is, the spelling should be but isn't. *Chiliometre* would be an etymologically sounder form (see K) and the American *-meter* makes better sense than our Gallic *-metre*. But we can't change now.

(3) Usage   The use in Australian speech of the abbreviation *K* (i.e. /kay/) for *kilometre* and *kilometre per hour* is not understood in Britain or the USA; and see MILEAGE. For other usage rules, see SI UNITS.

kine-   See CINE-… and K.

knot   Towards the end of the sixteenth century, the British Admiralty equipped each of its ships with a rope and a sand-glass to measure its speed. The ropes had a sea anchor (known as a *log*) at the end and knots in them at regular intervals, and the speed was measured by paying out the rope over the stern and counting the number of knots which passed before the sand-glass ran out.

The Admiralty had worked out that, by having the knots at intervals of 47 feet 3 inches and a 28-second sand-glass, the device would give a value *almost* equal to the speed in nautical miles per hour, where a nautical mile was 6080 feet. This figure was the distance on the surface of the earth which represented a shift of one minute of latitude at the equator, rounded to the nearest ten feet. In days before there were pocket calculators, this speeded the process of plotting courses and positions.

The ropes and sand-glasses have long since disappeared, but the habit of expressing speeds of ships and ocean currents in this rather strange unit has stuck (see NAUTICAL FOLLIES); worse, it was adopted for aerial navigation, and provides the international standard.

The only unpardonable error is to talk about knots per hour. If it were knots per anything, it would be knots per 28 seconds. But it isn't. It is just knots. A speed of 1 knot (i.e. 47 feet 3 inches in 28 seconds) is the same as 1.852 km/h.

The word *log*, of course, moved from being the sea anchor itself (as in the phrase *heave the log*) to being the record of the ship's movements, and then into general language as a record book and as a verb meaning 'to record'.

Koori   We should approach this word with a bit of care. It is increasingly used as a synonym for *Aboriginal*.

AND shows sporadic citations over a very long period, and the word appeared as a colloquialism in the first edition of Mac (1982); but it achieved greater currency and stature after being the title of a book (*Koori*, by James Miller, published in 1985). In it he writes:

> The word Koori ... is a generic term that was used by my ancestors and other people of the central coast of New South Wales to identify themselves.

James Miller's main point was that all existing terms were created by and remained the currency of whites, and either were derogatory or were liable to become derogatory in circulation. The community therefore needed a name which was its own property, and *Koori* was a good candidate. Note that Miller was not asserting that *Koori* was ever used all over Australia, nor that it originally meant 'Aboriginal' as distinct from 'non-Aboriginal'.

However, *Koori* has been promoted by some Aboriginals as an appropriate generic for all Aboriginals, belonging as it does to the first people to suffer from the white invasion.

At the same time, it should be noted that other Aboriginals do not see themselves as Kooris. In Western Australia, the term *Koori* is perceived as the name of specific Aboriginals of the eastern States, and they are puzzled (and offended) to be called *Kooris* themselves. They accept it with good grace when visiting Sydney, but it is seen as a denial of their own identities, just as the Scots feel if they are called *English*.

South Australian Aboriginals have a collective name, but it is *Nungas*. Even in the eastern States, *Koori* is only used unequivocally by a handful of largely urban communities. Nevertheless, the ABC tends to use *Koori* as if it meant 'Aboriginal', and such is the power of radio that this may sooner or later become true.

In the meantime, non-Aboriginal writers and speakers are best advised not to use the word *Koori* unless quoting from Aboriginals or specifically invited by Aboriginals to use it.

A very large number of spellings have appeared over the years, ranging from *Curry* to *Koorie*, but *Koori* seems to be the best.

See also ABORIGINES..., BLACK..., KRIOL and PREJUDICE.

Kriol   Mac defines *Kriol* as 'the creole used by Aboriginal people living in an area from north-west Queensland across to the Kimberley Ranges of Western Australia'.

This definition cuts a number of knots. The debate is over a fairly fundamental question, namely, whether the language exists at all.

On the one side, its supporters say that Kriol is an emergent language spoken and understood by several thousand people, English-based but too far from English (and with too many non-English characteristics) to be called a dialect. By listening to Kriol speakers, they have been able to codify a grammar and compile word lists sufficient to produce books written in Kriol, which are found to be understood by people all over a wide region.

Others, however, explain the same facts differently. They point to the way in which two people who are learning French can communicate with one another successfully in a version of French because they both adapt French in the same way. Kriol, they say, is in essence 'Aboriginal English', a respectable modern equivalent of the stereotypical broken English put into the mouths of Aboriginals in nineteenth-century novels, many of whose features it shares. The argument for this view is that while the version of it spoken by any given group will contain many Aboriginal words and sound patterns, these elements will vary from community to community, while the elements which hold the versions together as a lingua franca are largely English.

Between these two extremes are those who identify not one Kriol but a great range of creole languages, varying from community to community, their content depending on the extent of the contact with English and local vernacular speech patterns. They note that these languages vary from one another not only in the local vernacular content, but also in the precise meaning which they give to English-derived words.

Meanwhile, the perception of the single lingua franca as a creole (which the name Kriol implies) seems to beg the question. A creole is generally defined as a pidgin which has become the first language of those who speak it (see PIDGIN…), and is therefore able to fulfil all normal language needs. These conditions do not seem to be fulfilled by Kriol as currently codified (though the individual local creoles come much closer to it).

Nevertheless, the fact that a single version has been written down may well have the effect of homogenising the variations and encouraging its development, so the claims of its promoters may prove self-fulfilling. Whether this would be a good thing for the communities involved is another question.

L

L Our labial consonants *L* and *R* are commonly confused by the Chinese and Japanese, but less often in exchanges within the European languages. An example is the Dutch word *frijbuiter*, pronounced (roughly) */fry-bouter/*,which was anglicised as *freebooter*. This was a bit of a mistake, as the Dutch was all about free booty, not free boots. However, worse was to come: the French made it *flibustier*, and the Spanish *filibustero*, which in turn was anglicised as *filibuster*. Both derivatives turn up in our Parliament, but are rarely confused.

laboratory Where should we put the stress? In Britain and Australia, the more common pronunciation is */l'borra-tri/*. Americans sometimes say */l'borra-tory/*, but more often say */labbra-tri/*. The latter is surprising, as the American tendency to enunciate all syllables would favour the former (see STRESS).

The question is happily solving itself, since the almost universal usage is the unequivocal *lab*.

laid See LAY….

language The word *language* can be used in at least four different ways. It would be helpful if we had four different words, but we do not.

(1) If we are asked what language we speak, we may say 'English'. We can also say 'I speak English, but I speak it very badly'. Here, language means a way of talking. Each language has a set of conventions, rather like the conditions for membership of an exclusive club, over which individual speakers have no control. We can break some of them some of the time, but if we break too many too often, we are no longer speaking English: we are out of the club.

In this sense of the word, there is no such thing as an Australian language; Australians speak English. If we want to be more precise, we can say that there are a large number of Australian languages (those of the indigenous people), while we speak Australian English, a dialect characterised (as are British and American English) by certain variations round a common core. We control the variations, but can only change the core by winning the unanimous support of the other users.

(2) Each one of us has a way of speaking which is his or her own *private language*, governed by rules which we ourselves make, and which we therefore speak perfectly – by definition. It does not matter whether it is English or Swahili or a mixture of the two; it is our own language, and we control it.

In this sense of the word, there is already an Australian language, whose content is those words and constructions most Australians understand and use. It has its own range of registers, its own educated and broad usage and its own set of accents. In short, we set its standards, just as we would if nobody else in the world spoke a language anything like it.

(3) There is a third usage, which occurs when, on the analogy of *scientific language*, we use the phrase *Australian language*. This is synonymous with *Australianisms*, and was the sense required in the title of Sidney Baker's book *The Australian Language*, a monumental assemblage of flora and fauna, Aboriginal words and slang expressions. But the insertion of *The* in the title implied something different: that we are speaking the Australian language when we use these words and expressions, but lapse into some other language when we say 'Good morning'. Since this mistake is easy to make, it is best never to use the phrase *Australian language* in this sense, but rather to say *Australianisms* or *Australian words and phrases*, as does *The Australian National Dictionary*. This topic is discussed further under AUSTRALIANISMS and DICTIONARY.

(4) There is a delightful usage in Aboriginal English: when they say 'I'll speak in language' or 'I'll talk language', they mean their Aboriginal language. It is as if they perceive the word *language* as connoting something personal, comfortable and friendly.

Latin(ate)   Latin, the language of *Latium* (the district of Italy where Rome stands), became the language of the Roman Empire, and for over a thousand years after the effective end of that empire it remained the European language of scholarship and the Roman Catholic church. In addition, its dialects provided the basis for a range of European languages from Romanian in the east to Portuguese in the west – the so-called *Romance languages*.

English, as a Romance/Germanic amalgam, shows its influence quite extensively.

The direct contribution is discussed under LATIN TAGS.

The indirect contribution has largely filtered through into English via Norman French. However, other bits have been filtered through the Germanic side, e.g. our word *street*, from the Latin *(via) strata*. In addition, there are word parts which reflect Latin even if incorporated into new formations. Thus *contra-indications* and *interstate* cannot be called Latin, though their components *contra*, *indicatio*, *inter* and *status* are all Latin words.

In this book, *Latinate* is used as a general term to refer to all the words which either are derived from Latin words, irrespective of the path by which they have reached us, or whose forms show signs of Latin inspiration.

The resultant patterns will be clear, and sometimes useful, to those who know some Latin. This may be a vanishingly small constituency, but the hope is that even those who cannot see the patterns will be reassured to know that some exist.

Latin plurals   See PLURAL DILEMMAS (3).

Latin tags   Anyone who thinks that there are not many Latin tags left in our common language should consider this list:

A.D. (anno Domini), *in the year of our Lord.*

a.m. (ante meridiem), *before noon.*

e.g. (exempli gratia), *for example.*

etc. (et cetera), *and the rest.*

i.e. (id est), *that is.*

n.b. (nota bene), *note well.*

p.m. (post meridiem), *after noon.*

Q.E.D. (quod erat demonstrandum), *which was to be demonstrated.*

R.I.P. (requiescat in pace), *Let him/her rest in peace.*

ab initio, *from the beginning*; rhymes with *fishy-oh.*

ad hoc, *to this (specific purpose)*; see AD HOC.

ad infinitum, *to infinity.*

ad lib(itum), *to (one's) pleasure.*

ad nauseam, *to (the point of) sickness.*

ad val(orem), (of tariffs) *according to value.*

alma mater, *a person's school or university* (literally *kind mother*); see below.

alter ego, *the other me, my second personality.*

bona fide, *in good faith,* say /*boner fidy*/; (bona fides = *good faith*).

curriculum vitae, *the course of one's life.*

de facto, *as a matter of fact*; see DE FACTO.

de jure, *according to law*; see DE FACTO.

ex gratia, *as a gesture of thanks*; say /*ex grahshia*/.

ex officio, *by virtue of office*; rhymes with *dishy-oh.*

in extremis, *on the point of death.*

infra dig(nitatem), *beneath one's dignity.*

in memoriam, *in memory.*

in situ, *in (its) original place.*

inter alia, *amongst other things*; rhymes with *failure.*

in toto, *entirely.*

ipso facto, *thereby.*

magnum opus, *great work.*

modus operandi, *way of working.*

modus vivendi, *way of living.*

nem(ine) con(tradicente), *with no one speaking in opposition.*

nihil obstat, *nothing stands in the way.*

non compos mentis, *not of sound mind.*

obiter dicta, *casual remarks* (*singular* obiter dictum); see PARENTHETIC(AL).

per annum, *per year.*

per capita, *per head*; see PER CAPITA.

per se, *by itself, essentially*; say /*per say*/ rathe than /*per see*/.

persona non grata, *an unacceptable person.*

prima facie, *at first sight* (of evidence = *immediately conclusive*); say /*primer fay-see-ay*/.

pro forma, *as a matter of form.*

pro rata, *in proportion.*

pro tem(pore), *for the time being.*

sine die, *indefinitely* (literally, *without a day*); see below.

sine qua non, *an essential condition* (literally, *without which not*); see below.

sub rosa, *under the rose, private.*

sui generis, *(the only one) of its kind*; say /*sue-ee jenneris*/.

terra incognita, *unexplored territory.*

terra nullius, *unclaimed territory*; see DISCOVERY....

verb. sap. (verbum sapienti sat est), *a hint is enough for the wise.*

vice versa, *the order having been reversed.*

For further examples, see BIBLIOGRAPHIES, LEGAL LATIN and LOGIC. In addition, bogus Latin abounds in biological nomenclature.

There are in addition many single words whose form is explicable only by reference to their Latin origin, but which are otherwise wholly assimilated (e.g. *affidavit, alias, alibi, exit, ignoramus, imprimatur, interest, interim, omnibus, placebo, stet*), and others again which bear evidence of their origins in their plural forms: e.g. *formula, bacterium, index*.

The pronunciation of these words and phrases has evolved over the years. Some, like *vice versa*, are totally anglicised. Others are very un-English: for instance, the word *sine* generally rhymes with *tinny* in the common-language tag *sine qua non* but with *shiny* in the more legal phrase *sine die*. The word *die* is either /*dye-ee*/ or /*dee-ay*/, depending on the judge. The pronunciation /*dee-ay*/ would seem to be better Latin, but we must remember that most of these terms stem from medieval legal Latin *as spoken in English courts*, at a time when respect for non-English pronunciation was at a low ebb. To 'restore' classical Latin pronunciation (even if we knew exactly what it was) would be totally inappropriate.

In the case of *alma mater*, we tend to say /*mahter*/, but the Americans (who use the phrase more frequently than we do) say /*mayter*/. However, they also say /*daym*/ where we would say /*dahm*/ in that notable alma mater of football, *Notre Dame*, and we certainly don't want to copy them on that one. In Australian courts, it is best to use the equally disturbing pronunciation used by the judges, since they are in charge and must be humoured.

In the list above, I therefore report acceptable pronunciations for the phrases which are most often in doubt. If they make Latinists wince, this is as it should be. In any case, those who are insecure about pronunciation are unlikely to use the words at all (nor should they), so there is in practice no major problem.

latter   See COMPARATIVE CHAOS (2).

launch   Until recently, *launch* existed as a noun only in the sense of 'a small motor boat'. The process of getting a ship into the water was a *launching*. Now, the metaphorical launching of many things, including political campaigns and new commercial products, is known as *a launch*. The odd thing is that the book publishing industry, which might be expected to be conservative in matters of language, leads the field.

laundry   The use of this word for a small room in a private house is a by-product of an old Australian domestic building regulation requiring that the washing of clothes be physically separated from the preparation of food. In Britain and America, the word *laundry* implies a large scale, generally commercial operation.

lay, laid, laying   When Bob Dylan sang

> *Lay, lady, lay*
> *On my big brass bed…*

all the purists shuddered. He should have sung *lie* (unless, that is, the lady was a hen, about to lay an egg). The approved set is

He $\begin{pmatrix} lies \\ will\ lie \\ was\ lying \\ lay \\ has\ lain \end{pmatrix}$ on the floor and $\begin{pmatrix} lays \\ will\ lay \\ was\ laying \\ laid \\ has\ laid \end{pmatrix}$ the table.

The problem has arisen because the verbs *to lie* and *to lay* share some forms. It is not that 'I lay on the floor' is wrong. It is correct for the past tense, wrong for the present. The approved remediation is an explanation that *lie* is intransitive, and *lay* is transitive, the difference in meaning being summarised in the sexist mnemonic:

> *He laid whatever could be laid:*
> *An egg, a table, and a maid.*

However, Dylan and his followers may not be confusing the two words at all: 'confusion' suggests two-way traffic, but all this traffic is from *lie/lain* to *lay/laid*. Maybe *lain* (the rarely used and slightly archaic-sounding past participle of *lie*) is on its way to becoming *laid*, with the rest changing in sympathy. Alternatively, Dylan may be remembering William Douglas's lines:

> *And for bonnie Annie Laurie*
> *I'd lay me doun and dee.*

Here, the transitive verb *to lay* is used reflexively to mean *lie*. It is a very small step indeed to turn such a usage into an intransitive one.

Time is on Dylan's side. In ordinary speech, the substitution of *laid* for *lain* and *lay* is already common; indeed, it is to my ear the majority usage. It is less common in writing, but much more so than it was (say) ten years ago. We may regret or even deplore this, but that's how language develops.

Rather than saying that it is an ignorant confusion between *lie* and *lay*, therefore, let us say something more polite: that the transitive use of the verb *to lay*, which until recently was an archaism preserved only in some nautical jargon, is re-establishing itself in colloquial speech and is gaining ground in formal speech.

That way, we have a gracious way out if we lose the battle – which we will. In the meantime, those of us who care will continue to *lie* on the beach.

lay-by   In Australia, a *lay-by* is a procedure for time payment in which the goods are held by the vendor until payment is complete: 'Put it on the lay-by'. In Britain, it is a parking bay beside a main road. Incomprehension is mutual

AWEG reports a variant without a hyphen: *layby*. This is a word which needs one.

lead(ing)   See FONT.

legal language   When we say that a document is in *legal language*, we generally mean *legalese*. This is not just a few jargon words set in a context of common language, as with *scientific language*, but a whole manner of writing bearing little relationship to the conventions of normal written English.

It is noted for: (1) using words which do not exist in common language; (2) using words which have a different meaning in common language; (3) bizarre conventions stemming from long-forgotten problems; (4) anonymity; (5) pleonasm; and (6) mindless repetition.

(1) There are no *codicils* in real life, still less *torts*. Such words cause few problems, however, because they are recognised as strangers. Some, indeed, are unavoidable, there being no term for them in common language. Lawyers are probably no worse than plumbers: it is just that we have greater need to understand the legal system than the plumbing system. Legal writers who hope to be understood by lay readers should avoid such terms where possible, and explain them when forced to use them.

(2) Far more dangerous are the words which can be misunderstood. For example, if we *discover* a document, we mean we found it in a bottom drawer. But the legal sense of discovery is like *disclosure*: lawyers may require you to *discover* a document, i.e. take the cover off it and show it to them. Writers should school themselves to identify these ambiguities and (if the words must be used) make their meaning clear, as with any other ambiguities.

(3) The habit of omitting punctuation from legal documents was once a protection against alteration, as was the habit of repeating spelt-out numbers in arabic numerals, e.g. *twelve (12)*. Happily, most modern legal documents are properly punctuated, the danger of alteration having been reduced by the invention of the typewriter. But people go on writing *twelve (12)*, believing, perhaps, that it makes their tawdry document look official.

(4) Many solicitors preserve the practice of remaining anonymous, i.e. signing letters illegibly over the name of the firm. This is a survival of an eighteenth century practice which other professions and trades have abandoned. Its purpose was to distinguish a letter written by a person in a private capacity from one written in an official capacity, given that both would be handwritten. The typewriter, and universal use of printed letterheads, has removed the reason for this practice.

(5) The long convoluted sentences with strings of synonyms, giving each paragraph the look of an extract from *Roget's Thesaurus*, are not inspired by the need to cover all eventualities. They date back to the eighteenth century, when lawyers were paid by the line, so they naturally tried to make every document as long as possible. By the time piecework rates ceased, this literary style had become entrenched, and people believed that a plain language document was in some way not right.

Many publishers' contracts are, regrettably, good examples.

(6) Those who draft legal documents tend to adapt an existing model rather than starting from scratch. The justification is that a pre-existing text can be assumed to have stood up to scrutiny, and there is truth in this; but it can lead to situations which are at best ludicrous and at worst disastrous.

(a) The models followed may not be the best. It is mindless copying which has caused an archaic and perverse style of writing to survive and become equated with legal propriety.

(b) Clauses covering new situations get added far quicker than irrelevant or obsolete clauses are removed, so that documents become longer and longer, and important clauses get lost in a porridge of trivia and irrelevance.

(c) The extra words, so far from 'covering all eventualities', are either worthless or restrict the document. Generic statements cover everything; lists imply boundaries. Very often, legal documents (including Acts of Parliament) are clarified simply by *removing* words.

(d) While the obscurity of the documents may neither help nor hinder those who are acting in good faith, it unquestionably helps those who wish to evade their responsibilities: the 'small print' syndrome. In the days of printed forms, it was easy to tell insertions and alterations from the standard verbiage, because the new matter was typed or handwritten in spaces left for the purpose. The word processor makes it possible to reproduce huge documents with minimal fuss, and to make subtle changes at any point without leaving any tell-tale footprints in the surrounding sand.

Happily, our better legal firms are aware of all these problems. A good 'standard' contract will have all variable and unusual elements in a distinctive type, and some firms are offering plain language documents. We should encourage the rest to follow suit.

legal Latin   The survival of Latin tags in our legal system is primarily designed to give mystery and majesty to otherwise ordinary mortals and their fallible proceedings, as is the case with wigs and robes. This is not the place to give an exhaustive listing of these terms, but here are a few which occasionally stray into common language:

corpus delicti, the essential facts about the offence. (The body of a murder victim is not itself the *corpus delicti*, but can be part of it.)

in absentia, in absence.

in camera, in private (literally 'in a private room').

in flagrante delicto, in (the act of) a flagrant offence.

in loco parentis, in the place of a parent.

nolle prosequi, not to wish to prosecute.

non liquet, it is not proved.

sine die, indefinitely (literally 'without a day').

sub judice, under (consideration by) a judge.

The following have specific application:

A *caveat* (= let him beware) is a condition under which a legal transaction takes place. The catch phrase *caveat emptor* means 'let the buyer beware'.

Habeas corpus is not so much a tag as a catch line, these being the first two words of the phrase *Habeas corpus ad subjiciendum* ('You should bring the body (= person) to trial'), which prefaced a law preventing imprisonment without trial.

Nisi (= unless) in the phrase *decree nisi* means that the decree will become *absolute* (= final) on a given date *unless* overtaken by subsequent events or proceedings.

An *affidavit* (= he has sworn) was originally the first word of the declaration by the clerk to whom the sworn statement was made; it now refers to the statement itself.

Many other phrases which had their origin in the courts are now in the streets, e.g. *de facto, alibi*. For a comment on these, and on pronunciation of Latin, see LATIN TAGS.

legend   See MYTH....

less   See FEW....

letter writing   Those who have no problems with business letter writing should not read what follows. They know what they want to say and how they want to say it, and delight in flouting convention. Others, however, seek guidance; and it is at least a good idea to know what the conventions are before deciding to abandon them.

The invention of the fax has had a profound effect on correspondence. Many people who would automatically follow all the old conventions in letters dispense with them in faxes, adopting a memo-like format with no frills. It is likely that this will hasten the end for many existing conventions, like addressing a total stranger as 'Dear —'. At the moment, however, the conventions are alive and well. There are even laborious rules covering the layout and punctuation of addresses. This article concerns itself only with literary content.

(1) The envelope

If your intention is to make a point, by all means address a committed *Mrs* as *Ms*, or vice versa. But if you want to get them on your side, you do not alienate them before they have even opened the envelope. It is a courtesy to name people in the way they like to be identified.

(a) *Names of men:* The current standard is *Mr Alan Smith* or *Mr A.B. Smith*. *Mr Alan B. Smith* sounds American and *Alan Smith, Esq*, is unequivocally British (and obsolescent British to boot).

The unadorned *Alan Smith* is sensible and, while still unusual, is rapidly gaining popularity, especially if you can start the letter *Dear Alan* (see **(2)** below).

If the given name and initials are not known, and *Mr Smith* looks too stark, a useful formula is *The Taxation Department, Attn. Mr Smith*.

(b) *Names of women:* The maritally ambiguous term *Ms* saves most of the heartache, and is used everywhere. The only surviving peril is an encounter with one of those who demand their *Mrs* or *Miss*. Sensible people note these preferences in address books, etc., so that at least they do not make the same mistake twice. Meanwhile, many women prefer to appear on envelopes unadorned, e.g. *Karen Smith*, and the popularity of this is encouraging the similarly unadorned version of male names.

The old convention was that *Mrs Alan Smith* was a married woman whereas *Mrs Karen Smith* was a widow or divorcee. This is obsolete. Women addressed as individuals should always be assigned their own given names.

(c) *Names of couples*: *Mr and Mrs Alan Smith* and *Mr and Mrs A.B. Smith* remain the styles used on business letters, but on personal letters, *Alan and Karen Smith* is very common.

If addressing two people whose surnames are different, write the two names as you would if addressing them individually, linked by *and* (i.e. *Messrs* and *Mesdames* are no longer used in such situations).

The term *Messrs* is sometimes added to the names of the partners in a professional group (e.g. *Messrs Snipcock and Tweed*), but this convention is dying. Its use on names of firms (e.g. *Messrs BHP Limited*) is dead.

(d) The simplest layout convention for addresses is to align the left-hand ends of the lines, and to omit all end punctuation.

(2) The letter

(a) Write your address at the top right of the page.

(b) Write the date under your address.

(c) Write the name and address of the addressee on the left, starting just below the level of the date, and using the same style as will be used on the envelope. (Since the recipients presumably know their own address, this is only required for your records. It is a convention which dates back only to the invention of carbon paper. In the days when clerks were employed to copy all the letters in a big round hand, the addressee's name appeared only on the copies.)

(d) The 'greeting' should be by name wherever possible. If the letter is addressed to a specific person, however unknown to you, the greeting should be in related form:

        Mr Alan Smith…   *Dear Mr Smith…*
but   *The Manager…*   *Dear Sir/Madam….*

If you are on familiar terms with the recipient, the greeting can be *Dear Alan*, but this may annoy a perfect stranger. (Whether it should annoy him is debatable; that it may do so is unquestionable. It annoys me, for a start.)

If you do not know the sex of the recipient, *Dear Sir /Madam* remains the safest formula, although it has an archaic ring to it, and is due for replacement if a replacement can be found. The greeting *Gentlemen!* is wrong on all counts: it is sexist and perceived as an Americanism.

(e) It is often helpful to preface the message with a headline saying what it is all about, and in particular quoting the reference number from any letter to which you are replying, e.g. *Transfer of title: your ref. SJO/JB 1038.*

(f) The normal sequence for the body of a letter is:
(1) Acknowledgements (e.g. formal thanks for letters, etc., received)
(2) Answers (to requests for information, etc.)
(3) News and general information
(4) Your own requests.

However, if the sole purpose of a letter is to request something, this should be the first *and last* item. No business letter should be longer than it needs to be.

If a letter has to be long, it is both courteous and practical to flag any point requiring immediate action. It might be argued that people, however busy, *should* read carefully every letter, however long, which is addressed to them, but the reality is that they do not and will not. An action flag (e.g. the word *Action* written in the margin beside the relevant paragraph) improves the chances not only of getting action, but of the whole letter being read.

(g) The valediction balances the greeting. A common relationship is:

      Dear Sir …   *Yours faithfully*
      Dear Mr Smith …   *Yours sincerely*

Write your name in block letters under the signature. If you feel strongly about *Mrs/Miss/Ms*, specify the one you like. If you do not, you cannot complain if the reply uses a standard form (probably *Ms*).

liable   *Liable* is a legal word, whose closest surviving relative is *lien*. It is correctly used in the sentence *I am liable for damage done by my dog.*

It is permissible to extend it to other forms of risk: *You are liable to be run over*; but it is best not used with an inanimate subject (*the car is liable to run you over*) as the car is *not* liable – unless you are suggesting the medieval practice of punishing inanimate objects which cause damage by destroying them.

liberal/Liberal   See POLITICS (2).

licence/license   The current convention is to spell the noun with a *c* and the verb with an *s*. This is sometimes justified by the analogy of *advice/advise*, but the analogy is weak: there, the difference in spelling reflects a difference in sound; in the case of *licence/license*, as with *practice/practise*, there is no such distinction. (See -ISE/-IZE/-ICE (2).)

It is not a convention with a particularly impressive pedigree. Until the eighteenth century, the distribution of *c* and *s* spellings was random, reflecting the fact that they were both derived from the same word. The Americans (led by Webster) decided to standardise the spelling. However, they settled on *license* in this case but *practice* as the common form for *practice/practise*.

The rational solution is to standardise on *c* in both cases – and all cases where we have an /s/ sound (as we and the Americans already do with *advance*, *dance* and many other cases) and to reserve the *s* for cases like *advise* in which a /z/ sound is to be used.

I do this myself, hoping to change the world. My scrupulous copy editors always correct it, whereupon I correct it back. Whoever sees the proofs last wins.

lie   See LAY....

ligature   Ligatures are typographical characters formed from two or more letters. They are used for two purposes, phonetic and practical.

(1) Phonetic ligatures   The ligatures æ and œ show that two vowels are to be sounded as one. They can be contrasted to *diereses* (e.g. *aë*, *oë*, etc.) which show that the two vowels are to be pronounced separately. For a discussion of the relationship between these words and the words *digraph* and *diphthong*, see DIGRAPH....

Ligatures appear to have been used first in certain French words containing strings of vowels whose value was ill-defined: *œil*, *œuf*, etc. These spellings were not attempts at phonetic renderings – French dictionaries explain to their readers that the words are pronounced 'euil' and 'euf'. Their object was more to retain a trace, albeit dim, of the etymological origins of the words (in this case the Latin *oculus* and *ovum*) and in particular to allow the words to retain their original place in alphabetical listings. Likewise, the French adopted the dieresis to show that two consecutive vowels were to be sounded separately: *Noël*, *naïf*.

At the end of the eighteenth century, an attempt was made in Britain to make some etymological distinctions by the use of these

same devices. Thus they wrote *æsthetic* but *aërobic*, to show that the
ae represented two quite different sets of characters in their Greek
originals, *αἰ* and *ἀη* respectively.

Use of the dieresis never got off the ground (though it can be seen
in some books of the period); but the ligature was more successful,
particularly in new words being coined from classical roots:
œsophagus, hæmoglobin (*æ* = Greek *αι*) and *mediæval* (*æ* = Latin *ae*). In
an attempt at consistency, there was an effort to apply the same
rules to words already established in the language in other spellings, so that some authors of the period wrote of *œconomics, Ætna*
and *sæcular*, but this was less successful in the market place. Meanwhile, they were not foolish enough to pursue consistency all the
way and write *poem* as *pœëm*. At least, I don't think anyone was that
silly.

The Americans were for a time very enthusiastic about the
dieresis, using it on words like *coöperate*, though this is now no
longer the case. They were never very interested in ligatures, partly
because in so many cases they had adopted simple *e* spellings
(*esophagus, hemoglobin, encyclopedia*).

In Australia, British usage was at first followed, but today our
dictionaries are unanimous in rejecting the use of ligatures and
diereses in English words. We should all follow their lead. However, we might follow ACOD (against the others) in retaining them
in French words and phrases (*hors d'œuvres*), if only to show that it
is not mere ignorance which makes us reject them elsewhere.

(2) Practical ligatures   The most common surviving ligatures are
the *fi* and *fl* ligatures available on most typographical computers,
and the *ffl* available on some. Their purpose is to enable the characters to fit more snugly together. In the days of manual typesetting,
however, many more were used, particularly of kerning characters
(see KERN). As kerns tend to get broken off in the handling of type,
kerning pairs were made as ligatures.

In addition, common pairs of characters were often produced as
ligatures, to speed the setting. They were used only for blended
pairs , i.e. pairs which could not be separated by hyphenation. These
ligatures are clearly identifiable in old books: ct st sk ck.

like   There is an ambiguity here which needs to be watched. Consider
the following sentences:

(1) *Marsupials like mammals suckle their young.*
(i.e. 'marsupials suckle their young just as mammals do').
(2) *Marsupials like wallabies and bandicoots suckle their young.*
(i.e. 'marsupials, e.g. wallabies and bandicoots, suckle...').
(3) *Marsupials like wallabies can escape bushfires by jumping through
them* (i.e. 'marsupials which are similar to wallabies can...').

The ambiguity here is similar to that discussed under OR, and is
closely related to the confusion of defining and non-defining rela-

tive clauses – see RELATIVE CLAUSES (1). The danger of misunder-standing can sometimes be reduced by punctuation but the best cure is amputation: use a different, unambiguous construction.

limited   The word means *having limits*, its antonym being *unlimited*. It does not mean small or low, though it is often so used, as in such phrases as *a person of limited intelligence* and *...of limited means*. It is sad that so precise and useful a word should be abused in this way.

In the names of companies and other incorporated bodies, the word means that the owners, while having every intention of holding on to the profits if all goes well, have only limited liability for its debts if it goes badly.

liquidity, solvency   These terms have quite distinct meanings: *liquidity* refers to ready cash, while *solvency* refers to net assets, i.e. total cash and property (*assets*) minus total debts (*liabilities*).

Thus people are *liquid* if they have access to enough ready cash to be able to conduct their day-to-day transactions. If they have not, they have a *cashflow* problem.

People are *solvent* if they either have no debts, or are able to pay them as they fall due. If they are unable to cover their debts, they are *insolvent* (even though, having cash in their pockets for the bus home, they are *liquid*).

lists   Compilers of lists face chronic problems is two areas: (1) punc-tuation and (2) logical structure.

(1) Punctuation   The normal way of introducing lists is with a COLON.

(a) If the list follows straight on, it is considered to be a grammatical continuation of the introductory sentence:

> *The flag is in three colours: red, white and blue.*
> *Which is it: knife, fork or spoon?*

Note that the question mark is delayed until the end.

The only question here is whether there should be an extra comma, before the *and/or*, as here:

> *The flag is in three colours: red, white, and blue.*

Some house styles (including that of the Oxford University Press) require the extra comma. I prefer to leave it out. We don't need it when there are only two items (*The flag is in two colours: white and blue*). It is only needed when there are items which are not separated by an *and*. (We often use a slight pause in speech for the same purpose.) Anyway, the editors at OUP are tolerant, and they let me do it my way, even pointing out if I have accidentally done it their way.

However, my way does lead to an inconsistency (which is prob-ably why they prefer theirs): in cases where the items are long, and particularly if they have commas as internal punctuation, semi-colons may be better as item-dividers, and the extra mark before the *and/or* is needed if it is to match the changed speech rhythm, as in the following:

> *There are three flags: the red cross of St George, the patron saint of England; the diagonal blue cross of St Andrew, for Scotland; and the diagonal red cross of St Patrick, for Ireland.*

In general, speech patterns are the best (though not infallible) basis for good punctuation.

If the items are numbered, the word *and* can be omitted (i.e. it is assumed to be *and* unless *or* is specified). Again, a semi-colon is the best punctuation, and it needs a full set:

> *The three colours are: (1) red; (2) white; (3) blue.*

(b) If writing such a list in a column, there are two approaches. The first is to regard it as a single sentence, a vertical layout of the style in (a) above. In this case, semi-colons are the best punctuation, whether or not there is an item number:

first item;	or	(1)	first item;
second item;		(2)	second item; or
third item.		(3)	third item.

Note that the items should not have initial capital letters, any more than they would when written in a line.

However, this can cause trouble if any items run to more than one sentence, as in *the following:*

(1) suppose that the text in a list item is long, so that the natural way to punctuate it would be to break it into two sentences separated by full stops; it may then look awkward with only commas and semi-colons;

(2) We change the rules. Although the capital letter and the closing full stop (as used in this item) are logically wrong, they are less disturbing than the artificial punctuation used in (1).

(3) We justify this by saying that the opening colon was a logical flag, indicating that a list was to follow, rather than a grammatical one indicating an open sentence.

(c) Lists attached to a question present a particular problem. In prose, we can write:

> *What is the answer: yes or no?*

If written in a column, the best solution is to repeat the question mark on each item, and in this case capitals, though strictly illogical, may look more natural:

What is the answer:	or	*What is the answer:*
(a) yes?		*(a) Yes?*
(b) no?		*(b) No?*

If there is a problem with this (which may happen if the introductory question is long and self-contained) it is best to make two sentences, abandoning the colon:

> *Is there any way in which we can solve the problem? Yes or no?*

(2) Logical structure The most common source of inelegance in lists is grammatical inconsistency. Here is an example:

The points to watch when buying a car are:
    (a) *price*
    (b) *is it comfortable?*
    (c) *the fuel economy is important.*

Ideally, all members of a list should have the same grammatical status, e.g. they should all be nouns, or all be statements, or all be questions, and this should be related to the grammatical structure of the preamble. In the above list, (c) is not only inconsistent with the others, but also inconsistent with the preamble. So we could write:

either   *(a) price;*   or   *(a) How much does it cost?*
           (b) comfort;   *(b) Is it comfortable?*
           (c) fuel economy.   *(c) Is it economical on fuel?*

literally There are not many words on which the purist should stand against all attack, but the word *literally* is one. It should *never* be used as a general intensifier. It should be used only to warn that an expression which is often used metaphorically is about to be used in its original sense. I should say *I literally turned the filing cabinet upside down searching for the missing letter* only if I actually rolled it over and stood it on its head.

logic A few of the technical terms of logic have strayed into common speech, and if we are going to use them we may as well use them correctly.

(1) A **deductive** or **a priori** (= from an earlier, say /*ah pry-awe-rye*/) argument takes a generalisation and applies it to a specific future case. From the generalisation *that all children like chocolate* we can deduce *that this child* (whom we have not yet asked) *will like chocolate*. A syllogism (see below) is the classic form for deductive argument.

(2) An **inductive** or **a posteriori** (= from a later, say /*ah poss-teery-awe-rye*/) argument works backwards from a string of specific observations to an underlying generalisation. If every child we observe likes chocolate, we can *induce* the generalisation *that all children like chocolate.*

    For an example, see INDUCTION....

(3) An **empirical** argument is one whose validity depends on the fact that it works, although it does not explain why it works. *Empirical evidence linked cholera with bad water long before microbiologists were able to identify the bacteria responsible.*

(4) A **scientific** argument is one which starts from a **hypothesis** which appears to explain existing empirical evidence and makes verifiable predictions about future events or observations. If it is shown to be successful both in explanation and prediction, the hypothesis is on its way to becoming a **theory**; see THEORY.

(5) An **a fortiori** (= from the stronger) argument says that, if you believe that ten dollars will cover the taxi home, then *a fortiori* twenty dollars is even more likely to cover it. There is an *a fortiori* argument hidden in the process of democracy, namely, that the greater the number of people who support a policy, the more likely it is to be right.

(6) A **semantic** argument is one that is based on the meaning of words.

(7) A **syllogism** is a specific form of deductive argument consisting of two **premises** and a **conclusion**:

	1	*All men are born equal.*	(the major premise)
	2	*These people are men.*	(the minor premise)
Therefore	3	*These people are born equal.*	(the conclusion)

Unfortunately, syllogisms rarely present themselves in this tidy way except, as here, in definitions of syllogisms. However, complex arguments are often found on analysis to be extended syllogisms. The classic false syllogism has an incorrectly formulated minor premise:

	1	*All men are born equal.*
	2	*These creatures are born equal.*
Therefore	3	*These creatures are men.*

Incidentally, I see no merit in the convention which spells logical *premisses* thus: see PREMISES.

(8) **Occam's razor** is the principle that we should not multiply 'entities': a word is not explained by inventing a new word to explain it, or a mystery by inventing a new mystery. This means that the more cases an explanation covers, the better it is; and the simpler an explanation, the better.

The ABC spells this *Ockham's razor*, since this is the modern spelling of the place in Surrey, England, from which the original wielder of the razor, William of Ockham, got his name. It is a more friendly spelling.

(9) **Reductio ad absurdum** disproves an argument or statement by showing that, if true, it would have absurd outcomes. Thus, we are told that if $x^a = x^b$, then $a = b$. However, since $0^5 = 0^7$, it follows that $5 = 7$. This is absurd, so the original statement cannot be the whole truth. (It is, of course, true for all values of x other than 0.)

(10) An **objective statement** is one which, if true, will be equally true for all speakers and observers: *chocolate is not made from green cheese*; a **subjective statement** is peculiar to the speaker: *chocolate is revolting*.

(11) The phrase **post hoc, ergo propter hoc**, literally *after this, therefore because of this*, is a tag for an argument which confuses sequence with consequence: *I ate this chocolate, and next thing the sun went down. Therefore, eating the chocolate made the sun go down.* It is a common cause of error in inductive arguments.

lookout   The use of this word as *a point from which one can see a good view* is Australian; elsewhere such a place is called a *viewpoint*, or less often a *lookout point*. All other senses of the word are international.

lost positives   The discovery of lost positives is a good party game. The following are chosen to illustrate some of the negative and negative-like prefixes which may yield lost positives: *(an)archic; (de)capitated; (dis)illusioned; (in)delible; (non)descript; (un)kempt*. Curiously, *non-* is a particularly rich source: *(non)chalant, (non)committal, (non)sensical.*

Lost positives are of three main types: those which, like *kempt* (= combed), once existed but do so no longer; those which, like *illusioned*, exist but in another sense; and *false lost positives*, where the prefix is not a negative one, as in *The Lord maketh the intrepid trepid, and the industrious dustrious, and the dishevelled hevelled.* (Actually, there is a positive of the last one, but only in French.)

lots of, a lot of   These phrases certainly have a place in formal writing, but with a special purpose: to supply the common touch without descending into slang.

Either can stand for *much* or *many*, and it is the number of what follows (singular of plural) that determines whether the verb is singular or plural:

> *Lots of* ⎫ ⎛ butter *is needed…*
> *A lot of* ⎭ ⎝ eggs *are needed…*

This is a very strange idiom, since one might expect *lots of* to demand a plural verb and *a lot of* to demand a singular one.

lower case   This is a term of typography to indicate the small letters, a b c d e…, as opposed to upper case (= capitals) A B C D E…; see FONT. It is annoying that, unlike *capitals*, we have no plain language word for them. See FONT.

lunch   See MEALS.

M

madam(e)   *Madam* as a term of address is considered by some to be both snobbish and sexist. However, no better alternative has been found as the female equivalent of 'Sir' in business correspondence and in matters of protocol. See LETTER WRITING.

The Queen is said to be addressed by the special variant *Ma'am*, to rhyme with *jam*. However, Ita Buttrose declares that she calls the Queen *Madam*, so let that be the Australian style.

The addition of a final *e* lends the word a touch of Gallic mystery, and *Madame* was adopted as a form of title among teachers and practitioners of song and dance in the nineteenth and early twentieth centuries (e.g. *Madame Melba*). It survives in the names of clairvoyants and Chinese ladies. In common language, however, the word survives only in the sense of *the manager of a brothel.*

Mahomet   See MUHAMMAD....

malapropism   The word comes from *Mrs Malaprop*, the social climber in Sheridan's play, *The Rivals*, who tries to impress by using posh words but mixes them up. If the purpose is to expose her as a poseur, it is perhaps a good joke. However, if it is just to make her look silly, it is cruel, and incidentally dangerous, as few of us always get our words right. I certainly don't.

The same thing goes for malapropisms in real life. Some are funny, e.g. the senior Melbourne bookseller who always referred to a particular anorectic customer as *emancipated*. Some are allegedly informative, e.g. *Freudian slips*. They often mark the poseur, and if this is the case, those who produce them deserve all the contempt they get. But the border between poseurs and people who are just making a valiant attempt to increase their word power is slim, and if we want people to broaden their vocabularies, a few malapropisms are the price we have to pay.

The problem is generally one of register. It is easier for us to move down, i.e. talk in a register with a more restricted vocabulary than our own, than to move up, using words, usages and constructions which are not part of our normal speech patterns.

The true malapropism confuses two totally separate but similar words, e.g. *gambit* for *gamut*, *hone in* for *home in*, *infer* for *imply*, *mitigate against* for *militate against*.

A second class of problem arises from a failure to recognise largely arbitrary distinctions which have been made within a single word family, e.g. *alternative* for *alternate* and vice versa, *definitive* for *definite*, *disinterested* for *uninterested*, *fortuitous* for *fortunate*, *substantive* for *substantial*, *simplistic* for *simple*.

The variety of such confusions is such that those who track them down have a lifelong occupation, but unless the same confusion occurs frequently, the list is likely to be a catalogue of human frailty rather than a contribution to clear expression. Most malapropisms are never repeated. Furthermore, today's common malapropism (like today's misspelling or mispronunciation) is likely to be the mutant of tomorrow and the received version of the day after.

male, masculine   *Male* is the sex, *masculine* the gender. If this statement is puzzling, read the entry under GENDER.

malformations   The best new words are those whose sense is immediately apparent to the reader or listener. If, therefore, everybody knows what a *laundromat* is, or what the wordsmiths of the Myer Emporium meant when they invented an *Outdorium* and a *Toyteria*, what objection can there be to these words? Or to a *weedathon* or an *ergonopedic* chair (neither of which, to the best of my knowledge, existed before its appearance on this page)?

The objection is solely that these formations are made up of bogus, deformed, or ill-matched word parts.

The string *-(a)thon* has strayed from the end of *Marathon* (a village in Greece) into being a suffix connoting *going on for a long time*, as in *telethon* and *readathon*. In trade names; the string *-(o)mat(ic)* has strayed from *automatic* in a sense which required the *auto-* (= self) part, and *-(o)pedic* from *orthopedic* where the *ortho-* (= straight) part would have been more appropriate. But they seem to work.

Winston Churchill's *triphibious* was listed in ACOD₁, perhaps because of respect for its coiner, though he is not named. It was coined to describe Lord Louis Mountbatten's position as supreme commander of air, sea and land forces in South Asia in the Second World War. Though falsely formed, the analogy with *amphibious* was immediately recognised. The word *tribious* would have been better etymologically but probably not understood as clearly. More recent examples include *breathalyser* and *Reaganomics*, where the second halves evoke *analyser* and *economics*, but omit the vital parts of these words. *Triphibious* died and *Reaganomics* is obsolete, but *breathalyser* lives on. Why? Not because it is a better formation, but because there is a greater need for it.

Examples of bad matching of parts abound. The word *garbologist* for garbage collector yokes a modern English stem to a classical Greek suffix, and is a joke, but so does *speedometer*, which is totally accepted. The word *garbologist* is a joke not because it is a malformation but because it is an OXYMORON, *-ologists* being solemn folk whereas *garbos* are jolly.

Time is the best judge. Words that are readily understood and useful are likely to survive, however grotesque their form. Words that are not needed will soon die, but may die a bit sooner if their forms are grotesque.

malign, malignant See BENIGN....

mall This word means *a former city street, which is closed to all but pedestrian traffic*, or a similar area within a new shopping centre. A near-synonym is *pedestrian* or *shopping precinct*.

The pronunciation of *mall* varies. Our dictionaries accurately report that both /mal/ and /mawl/ are heard in Australia. /Mal/ seems to be the dominant pronunciation in Victoria and South Australia, and /mawl/ elsewhere.

The word is traced to the French *paille-maille*, the mallet used in a game in which a wooden ball was hit through an iron ring suspended in mid air. The game was riotous enough to give us the adverb spelt (and pronounced) *pell mell* = headlong. It was played in alleys, and provided names for two London streets, *The Mall* and *Pall Mall*, where it is pronounced /mal/.

man, mankind See SEXIST LANGUAGE (2).

manuscript, presentation of See KEYBOARDING.

margarine The fierce battles which were once fought over the pronunciation of the *g* in this word are now all but forgotten, victory having gone to the philistines.

All the academic arguments supported the hard *g*: etymology, normal phonetic rules and original practice. However, practicalities favoured the soft *g*: firstly, the word was commonly used in the short form, *marge*, which influenced the pronunciation of the original word by a form of back pressure; secondly, this was the way everybody was pronouncing it by then, so it was too late to change. As usual, the last argument carried more weight than all the rest.

marginal Let us not reduce this word to being another synonym for *small*.

(1) Its original literal sense can be seen in the surviving phrase *marginal note*, which means 'a note written in the margin'.

(2) This sense, applied in the phrase *marginal land* (= 'the bits of land on the edge, close to fences') came to mean land which was on the borderline between being and not being economically cultivable. It was then applied in a similar sense in such phrases as *a marginal seat*. This usage is now well established and useful.

(3) Accountants define the *marginal cost* of something as the direct cost, without overheads. Thus the *marginal cost* of running a car for a day is the costs incurred on the day: fuel, parking, etc., without allowing for any share of the overhead costs – registration, insurance, maintenance, depreciation, etc.

This last sense has caused the problem. When we speak of benefits being *marginal*, we should be making a very precise statement; but because marginal benefits are generally *small*, the word is taken to *mean* 'small'. This would not matter if we had some other word(s) for *marginal* in its important and precise sense(s), but we have not. Until some come along, let us fight for *marginal*.

masculine   See GENDER.

mass, weight   In the language of science, these are two different quantities:

(1) *mass* is an amount of substance, measured in kilograms

(2) *weight* is the measure of gravitational force, measured in newtons.

Common language recognises only one quantity, weight, and only one unit, kilogram.

So what? There are many occasions when technical usage differs in significant ways from popular usage, and usually the two co-exist quite happily. In the present case, however, the two collide: our school syllabuses require the scientific usage, so that in the primary classes they talk of buying potatoes *by mass*. But when we go shopping in real life, we still buy them by *weight*.

The theory was that, by being introduced to the distinction early, children would avoid the difficulty in sorting out the two concepts in their later scientific work. The underlying assumption was that this would soon become general usage, i.e. that common language would be changed via the primary school.

The attempt to enforce change this way was doomed; before giving up, however, we should consider the arguments for it.

For centuries, the difference between mass and weight was largely academic: the amount of substance in a body was calculated by measuring the downward force it exerted on a balance, and the two quantities were reasonably regarded as interchangeable. It was only in extreme cases, of which ordinary folk were not aware, that the quantities were seen to be different.

All this changed with the advent of space travel, and with it awareness of the *weightlessness* experienced by an astronaut in orbit or in deep space. It was obvious that the astronaut had not lost any skin and bone; all that had happened was a loss of net gravitational force. We then needed a word to describe the quantity that had *not* been lost – the amount of skin and bone – and the word adopted for it was *mass*.

The scientists went through their vocabulary and adjusted it to match: atomic weights became *atomic masses*, and weight, being a force, was henceforth measured in newtons, not kilograms. Thus the new word, *mass*, was applied to the common concept (amount of substance), while the common word, *weight*, was switched to the uncommon concept (downward gravitational force). The only word which survived the change was *weightless*.

All would have been well had the experts decided to retain the word *weight* for amount of substance, while coining a new word, say *downforce*, for the force of gravitational attraction, and (say) *force-free* and *force-freedom* for *weightless* and *weightlessness*.

We can still recover from the mistake. Recovery requires no change to the common language – it merely legitimises what is still the case, so inertia, that most reliable ally, is on our side. The change would be to scientific language, which is more amenable to direction.

It is unlikely that this will happen, but in any case writers who are not involved in mathematics and physics will inevitably continue to buy their potatoes by *weight* in *kilograms*.

Meanwhile the ultimate absurdity (common in primary school textbooks) is to use *mass* in sentences like 'the bridge broke under the mass of the truck', where *weight* would not only br more idiomatic but also be scientifically correct.

material   Use of this word to mean *serious* (as in 'Of the issues, some are *material*, others *trifling*') seems innocuous enough, but it is worth noting the other possible antitheses: 'Spiritual issues outweigh *material* ones'; 'The business faced personnel rather than *material* problems'; 'The objection was formal rather than *material*'. All this adds up to a nest of potential ambiguity. There are so many words meaning *serious* that adding *material* to the pile seems unnecessary.

mathematical writing   Mathematical writing is generally restricted to mathematicians, and the array of specialist vocabulary and conventions involved are beyond the scope of this book. The following notes are designed for writers who make occasional use of maths in their texts.

(1) The language of maths   Non-mathematicians rarely make mathematical statements, so the language of mathematics (unlike the language of science) rarely gets abused. The only serious case is the bogus equations used by social scientists: see OBSCURANTISM (5).

However, words which are in fact metaphors drawn from mathematics abound: the phrases *to the nth degree* and *the lowest common denominator* have been abused for so long that they have become clichés, and can be used without concern for their literal meaning. The word *function*, however, should be respected, and not used in solemn statements like 'Car ownership is a *function* of gender' when the relationship is in fact mathematically vague, falling short of the precision of functionality. For further examples of words whose mathematical sense should be respected, see EXPONENTIAL and MEAN.

(2) Ambiguities   A common mathematical ambiguity is discussed under PERCENTAGES. Anyone using the term *percentage* is strongly recommended to read the article, whether their purpose is to learn how to lie or how to avoid lying.

Another type of ambiguity arises in conversion of units. We are told that a pound is 454 grams, so the recipe writers cross out *1 lb* and insert *454 g*. But *454 g* implies a much more stringently accurate measurement than was intended in *1 lb*. Conversions should never involve a higher order of accuracy than that of the original figures. (See below, and under HISTORICAL WRITING.)

A more subtle error can arise through the failure to distinguish the integral (counting) numbers from the continuous (measuring and calculating) numbers. If you ask how many fingers I have, the answer 'Ten' is exact. But if you asked me how long the longest one was, the answer 'Ten centimetres' would be an approximation, and would still be an approximation if I said '9.765 cm'.

However hard we try, there will be ambiguities. Thus if we see the number 454, it is likely to be an exact counting number *or* an approximation, correct to 3 significant figures (i.e. somewhere between 453.5 and 454.5). But if we see the number 500, it can be an exact counting number, an approximate counting number or a measurement, and the context may or may not help. The following illustrates the problem rather than the solution:

Phrase	*Mathematical status*	*Meaning*
A $500 fine	exact counting number	exactly 500
A 500-student school	approximate counting number	say 450 – 550
A 500 g lump of cheese	coarse measurement	say 495 – 505
A 500-metre race	fine measurement	say 499.95 – 500.05

As writers, we should make sure that we make our meaning plain; unless, that is, we are wanting to deceive.

(3) Presentation   For conventions about writing numbers (i.e. when to use arabic numerals and when to spell numbers out in full), see NUMBER PHRASES.

If there are equations in your MS (and such things are liable to occur in detective stories, to say nothing of popular scientific writing), note that it is pretty pointless to attempt to achieve correct alignments on a typewriter or ordinary word processor. It is far better to mark the alignments required on the print-out, or (in the case of complex equations) to write them in by hand, since you can then show the typesetter exactly what layout you want, including internal alignments and your preferences about the relative size of the elements.

Fractions were always a problem on typewriters, and are not much easier on most word-processing programs. If your keyboarding is to be used as the basis for typesetting, the simplest option is to use the slash, e.g. 2/3, but this is not satisfactory when used on mixed numbers: 4 2/3. The next option is to use superior and inferior numerals: $4\frac{2}{3}$. *Split fractions* (e.g. $\frac{2}{3}$) are best left to the typesetter: even if you have an easy facility for creating them, the typesetter may well have to re-key them using a different routine.

The same goes for diagrams, charts and graphs. The cleverness of some computer programs encourages writers to draw their own, and if you have confirmed that they will be of appropriate quality, this is fine; if not, a hand-drawn rough, with the key geometric instructions given in a distinctive colour, is a better basis for re-drawing than (for example) a graphic which is accurate but which does not give the data on which it was based.

One convention that can usefully be adopted when keyboarding for typesetting is to make all pronumerals, etc., italic (e.g. '$x + y = 2$' and 'The quickest way to get from A to B is by bike'). This conven-tion is designed to avoid ambiguity, and is best adopted in original keyboarding because such items cannot normally be identified and changed by automatic routines.

math(s)   Americans learn *math*; whereas we (and the British) learn *maths*. Both find the other's usage odd, but both usages are so deeply entrenched that neither is likely to be overrun. The origins of this difference are, however, worth a couple of comments.

Until the late nineteenth century, *mathematics* was a relatively rare academic word, with no received abbreviation. It was not until then that it became an accepted term in secondary schools, and acquired its abbreviations.

It was originally a plural noun, as in the sentence: *the Mathematics include Arithmetic and Euclid*. It then became singular: *mathematics includes arithmetic and geometry*. When the abbreviated form was developing, we still had a hazy memory that the word was plural, and hence added the *s* to the end of the contraction, as with other plurals (*kilos, labs*). The Americans treated it as a singular noun which happened to end with *s*.

Which is correct? The US is more logical, being consistent both with the grammatical status and with the way we treat similar other abbreviated ex-plurals, e.g. we say *gym* rather than *gyms* for *gymnas-tics*, so those who believe in undivided truth have to support the Americans. But so long as its local practitioners speak of *maths*, we will not be wrong to do the same.

matinee   Why should an afternoon show be called a *matinee* (= morn-ing)? The answer is related to the changing times of meals. In seventeenth century France, the aristocracy ate their main meal of the day, dinner (*dîner*), at midday, and a *matinée* was a theatrical performance which took place before it. Later, *dîner* became an evening meal, and the pre-dinner performance happened in the afternoon; but it retained the name *matinée*. Voilà!

The word does not need an accent in English.

may, might   This verb has only these two forms. It has no infinitive or participles. The two forms have variously been distinguished as present against past, and as indicative against subjunctive, but these distinctions do not help very much in explaining current usage.

(1) In main clauses:

(a) Expressing probability:

> *I may go to Gosford today.*　　　　(= will perhaps)
> *You may find the job difficult.*
> *They may be policemen.*

In this usage, both *may* and *might* are present tense: If we say *I might go…*, the meaning is essentially the same, but the probability is lower. The fact that *may* and *might* are here virtually interchangeable here is perhaps the source of the problem in (2).

(b) Expressing permission:

> *I may do as I please.*　　　　(= I am allowed to)
> *You may put your feet on the table.*
> *Observers may attend but not vote.*

This usage has a formal, old-fashioned ring to it. It is more idiomatic to say *I can…* and *You can…*, despite that fact that this implies *ability* rather than *permission*.

(c) In *inversions,* both *may* and *might* again sound rather formal. The 1st person normally requests permission, the inverse of (b):

> *May/Might I leave the room?* (= am I allowed to …?)

Speakers who say *May I point out that…?* or *Might I add that…?* are not, however, requesting permission; they are going to finish their sentences whether you like it or not.

In the 2nd person and 3rd person inversions *may* and *might* part company. *May* expresses wishful thinking. This is an obsolete usage surviving only prayers and formula phrases.

> *May you be happy…!*
> *May the best man win!*

Might is a simple probability question, the inverse of (a):

> *Might you/she be in Gosford tomorrow?*

(2) In dependent clauses:

(a) *May* and *might* were once used as the basic auxiliary verbs in adverbial clauses of purpose, *may* being present sequence and *might* being past sequence:

> *I bring you salt, that your life* may *not lack savour.*
> *I brought you salt, that your life* might *not lack savour.*

This construction is on its way out; see THAT (CONJUNCTION).

(b) A similar distinction is alive (just) in indirect speech:

Present sequence	Past sequence
He says that he may come.	*He said that he might come.*

and in indirect questions:

He asks if he may come.	*He asked if he might come.*

However, the distinction between *may* and *might* is increasingly one of probability rather than sequence of tenses.

(c) In IF... CLAUSES, *may* and *might* normally have the range of meaning as in (1(a)) above.

If the sentence is a straight conditional, *may* and *might* are again almost interchangeable, the only difference being the degree of probability:

If you like snails, you $\left(\begin{array}{c} may \\ might \end{array} \right)$ *also like yabbies à l'escargot.*

However, in hypotheticals, where the verbs in the if... clause are in the subjunctive mood, the form is *might*, irrespective of tense:

If I were you, I might accept the offer.
If the government had acted, the problem might not have arisen.

This usages is, however, are slipping. Thus we hear:

If the government had acted, the problem may not have arisen.

This usage is countenanced by the arbiters of Australian style, e.g. the ABC, no doubt because it is so common in everyday speech that resistance is futile; and they are probably sensible not to resist.

For my money, however, the usage still smacks of foggy intellect, and has no place in formal writing. Both *may* and *might* can be used for outcomes which are possible; but if the chance never existed or has passed us by, the only word is *might*.

meals   Breakfast presents few problems: the name and the timing are pretty standard the world over. But other meals are confusing within Australia, as well as being a problem for travellers to other English speaking countries.

The midday meal is generally called *lunch* (or, in pretentious restaurants, *luncheon*). However, in the days before gas and electric stoves and lights, most households had their main meal in the middle of the day, and it was often called *dinner*. After dinner they could let the fire go out. The naming survives in some households, especially for the midday meal on Sunday. This need not be ambiguous: 'Will you come to dinner on Sunday?' is generally an evening invitation; 'Will you come to Sunday dinner?' is probably an invitation for midday.

The main issue, however, is the name and timing of the evening meal. In most Australian households, it is eaten between 6.00 and 7.00, is called *tea*, and may be followed by *supper* (a snack) at around 10.00. Others eat *dinner* at around 8.00. In general, the higher up the social scale you go, the later you eat the main evening meal.

In hotel dining rooms and restaurants, the evening meal is *dinner*. In the bars of hotels, however, the evening version of a *counter lunch* is a *counter tea*, and country (and 'country-style') hotels call the evening meal *tea*, the name giving warning that the kitchen will be shut by 8.30.

The traveller finds much the same range of confusions round the world, the differences reflecting social and practical differences. Countries which have a siesta tend to eat very late in the evening, ten to midnight being common in Spain, for example. The most frequent problem for Australians in Britain is an invitation to *tea*, which may be an invitation to the main evening meal or to a light meal served at 4.30, once known to the French as *le five o'clock*. The French usage gives the clue: ignore the word *tea*, and listen for the time. Similarly, an invitation to *supper* in Britain is likely to mean a main evening meal, distinguished from dinner only in being more simple and informal.

mean It is worth noting that there are three separate words here, not three usages of the same word.
  (1) First we have the verb, *to mean* = 'to signify', whose origins are obscure, but it probably shares some common ancestors with *mind* and *mentality*.
  (2) Next we have one of Germanic origin, related to the modern German *gemein*, originally meaning 'held in common' but coming to signify *inferior* (as have the adjectives *common* and *vulgar*), then *miserly*, and ending up as a childish word for *unkind*.
  (3) The third comes from the Latin *medius* via the French *moyen*, meaning *middle*. The original sense is best preserved in the phrase *in the meantime*. It also gives us the noun *means* = 'the intermediary steps', as in *the end justifies the means*, or 'wherewithal', as in *we do not have the means to do it*. And it gives us *mean* = 'average', as in *mean annual rainfall*, and its related noun, as in *the arithmetic mean*.

The first one is so distinct as to cause no problems, but either of the others would make sense in St Paul's statement *I am a citizen of no mean city* (though King James and his friends probably had (2) in mind). The third causes special trouble: see MEAN, MEDIAN.

mean, median There are two mathematical *means*, of which the most important is the *arithmetic mean*, also known as the *average*. The other is the *geometric mean*. The *median* is different again.
  (1) Unless otherwise stated, a *mean* is always an *arithmetic mean*. Thus the phrase *Greenwich Mean Time* arises from the fact that rotation of the earth, which governs our time system, is very slightly irregular. Rather than make daily corrections, the astronomers have calculated all the irregularities and plotted an average path down the middle, so that *mean time* is sometimes slightly ahead of the sun and sometimes slightly behind it.
     The *arithmetic mean* or average of n numbers is found by adding them all together and dividing by n.
  (2) The *geometric mean* of n numbers is the nth root of their product. It is tremendously useful if you are building a pipe organ.

(3) The *median* is also a useful concept. It is the value of the item nearest to the middle of an ordered list. Thus the *median age* of people who are 1,2,3,4 and 90 years old is the age of the third in the list, i.e. 3, whereas their *average age* is 20. If you are looking for the most *typical* member of a set, the *median* is the best choice, since the *mean* could be distorted by the presence of one very exceptional number.

meaning Humpty Dumpty's famous dictum 'When I use a word, it means just what I choose it to mean—neither more nor less' is to some extent true of all of us. We generally know what a word means *to us*. But if we expect to be understood, it is not a bad idea to make sure that other people use it the same way. Aberrant use by ordinary folk is called a *mistake*. We have to be tall poppies if our aberrations are to be accepted as legitimate variants.

If we use an unusual word, or a common word in an unusual way, it makes very little difference whether we are inventing it or digging it up in the recesses of a large dictionary. Either way, the message is at risk. Sensible writers will not expect their readers to rush to the dictionary to find out what they are saying, or justify their usage by pointing out that it is in the dictionary For them, words are not toys, but are raw materials to be moulded into an artifact. This gives us a very effective definition of the meaning of a word or sentence, and this is *the message it conveys to the intended reader*.

This distresses some people, who believe that words have a *real* meaning which exists irrespective of current usage. Some worship at the shrine of etymology, and this makes some sense: it certainly explains what a word once meant, and may be used as an argument against some new usage. But what of new usages which have become established? Does a cupboard still *really* mean a board for cups, so that when we use it in its current sense we are in some way wrong? If so, how far do we take this? Does 'gentle' *really* mean well-born? Does an *album* have to be white?

Those who believe in *real* meanings are like those who seek the *real* meaning of life: they are embarking on a fascinating but ultimately self-indulgent journey. At best, they will discover what they believe to be an authoritative arbiter, a dictionary or prophet to whose wisdom they will defer; they are unlikely to encounter meaning itself.

Similarly, if we want to coin a word or usage, we can do so; we all have equal rights in the democracy of language creation. But we do not add to the language merely by inventing and using a word. Others have to respond. An example may illustrate the process.

The verb *to burble* was said by the first edition of OED to mean 'to speak murmurously', and to date from 1891. However, as the second edition noted, the origins of this particular word are well known – it made its first appearance in Lewis Carroll's poem, 'Jabberwocky', in 1871:

> And as in uffish thought he stood,
> The Jabberwock, with eyes of flame
> Came whiffling through the tulgey wood
> And burbled as it came.

Was the first edition wrong in dating it from 1891? Not necessarily. In 1871, it was no more a part of the language than *uffish*, *whiffling* and *tulgey*, which occur in the same stanza, and none of which is in the OED. *Burbled* acquired meaning only when it started to have meaning for readers. The 1891 writer used it in a way which showed confidence that it would be generally understood. Thus the word was certainly not part of the language before 1871, but by 1891 it certainly was.

mechanic(s/al)   We do not get in much trouble with these words, but they can be used as a peg on which to hang a few points about etymology.

We start with an ancient Greek noun, *mechané*, a machine, which was particularly applied to engines of war and to a crane by which gods were lowered to Earth in the theatres of the day. However, it had originally meant *a clever idea*, so that the epithet for Odysseus, *polymechanos*, is generally translated as *wily* rather than as 'having many machines'.

As with all nouns in inflected languages, the last syllable of *mechané* changed according to the *case* and *number* required by the sense, so that the unchanging part, often called the *stem*, was just *mechan-*.

A common way of forming adjectives from nouns was by adding *-icos* to the stem. This gave the Greeks the adjective *mechanicos*. But one way of producing the Greek name for an art or science was to use the neuter plural of the adjective. The ending giving this sense was *-a*, so *expertise with things mechanical* was called *mechanica*. (Our word *esoterica* can be regarded as a pure transliteration of a similar Greek formation: 'things esoteric'.)

All these words were adopted by the Latin-speaking people of the Roman Empire, who soon found themselves with two adjectives. The one was a straight transliteration of the Greek original, *mechanic(us)*, meaning 'related to machines'. The second was formed by adding a *Latin* adjectival ending, *-alis*, to the Greek name for the study, which produced *mechanicalis* meaning (originally) 'related to *the study* of machinery'.

This usage explains some of our -IC/-ICAL distinctions:

electric   'powered by electricity', as in *electric light, electric trains*

electrical 'related to the technology of electricity', as in *Electrical Trades Union, electrical engineering*, etc.

In the case of the *machine* family, however, this convention has been lost: *mechanic* is a noun meaning *a person with a spanner*, *mechanics* is also a noun and means *the study of machines*, and the only adjective is *mechanical*, which has to carry both adjectival meanings.

All of this illustrates two points: the first is that the problem discussed under -IC(AL) goes back to the Romans, so if we want to find somebody to blame, there they are waiting. The second is that the way in which the various noun and adjective meanings have been distributed over the various forms appears to be largely random, and there is little satisfaction to be had from trying to find some logical basis for it.

media   This word was popularised by the advertising industry, the usage being in the sentence *The same media are used for news and advertising.* Thus the press was one *medium* and TV was another. 'The media' then became a collective for the press, radio and TV, and today is widely perceived as a singular word.

People who feel righteous indignation when they hear *The media is...* should take care, as they almost certainly accept other similar changes (e.g. *agenda*). Conversely, however, those of us (for I am among them) who cannot bring ourselves to say *The media is...* are more to be pitied than censured.

Meanwhile, in the world of clairvoyance, the plural of *medium* remains *mediums*. See SINGULARITIES (a).

medical mist.   The *mist.* here is as in *mist. pect.*, an abbreviation of the Latin words *mistura pectoralis*, meaning 'mixture for the chest'. For many years, *mist. pect.* was in every medicine cabinet, and as the main active ingredient in the version given to children was *laudanum*, tincture of opium, it was equally suitable for treating broken legs.

The jargon of medicine is second only to the jargon of the sea (see NAUTICAL FOLLIES) for sheer perversity. However, whereas the jargon of the sea is preserved largely to enable nautical folk to identify and correct the uninitiated, medical jargon was designed to be obscure. It reflected the belief that it was best for patients not to know what the doctor had diagnosed or prescribed.

The fashion today is for greater frankness. There has, however, been little or no progress in demystifying medical vocabulary, so that the frank truth is still delivered in code. Even doctors who genuinely want to give a clear explanation are often unable to talk other than in jargon.

For specific medical terms which can cause misunderstanding, see ACUTE..., HYPER-... and TRAUMA, and for a logical problem with medical jargon see OBSCURANTISM (7).

meet (with)   There is a clear distinction between these two in Australian English: *I met the Chairman yesterday* suggests that we ran into one another and exchanged greetings; *I met with the Chairman* *yesterday*, however, suggests a formal meeting with an exchange of news or views. American usage is similar.

The British use *meet* without a preposition in both senses, and perceive *meet with* as an Americanism whose infiltration should be resisted. Some Australian speakers feel the same way about it. They should not; the distinction is useful and elegant.

The phrase *meet up with*, on the other hand, is an unnecessary circumlocution for *met*.

meiosis It is a sign of the times that whereas Fowler was concerned about public misunderstanding of *meiosis* in its literary sense (= 'understatement'), our concern today is about the relationship between *meiosis* and *mitosis*, these being to cell biology what *stalactites and stalagmites* are to speleology. Which is which?

Mitosis is the key process for the growth of living things. A single cell divides into two identical cells, its chromosomes being split longitudinally to produce two identical sets of chromosomes.

Meiosis is the key process in sexual reproduction. In stage one, male and female cells split so that each of the product cells carries half of the chromosomes of the original cell. In stage two, the resultant *special reproductive cells* pair up to form a new cell which derives half its chromosomes from each parent.

membership This word can have three significantly different meanings: the state of being a member (as in *I renewed my membership*); the number of members (*The club's membership stands at twenty-five*) and the members themselves (*We must consult the membership*). The last of these three is at best redundant and at worst ambiguous, and should therefore be avoided.

mental maps This useful term describes the picture of the world held in any given person's head. We can never know how much the course of history has been determined by the mental maps of those who shaped our destinies, but it might well explain some of their stranger decisions.

The British see the world as a Greenwich-centred Mercator projection, in which Canada looms vast and pink in the top left, and Australia largish and pink in the bottom right. The terms Middle, Near and Far East arose from this map, and it is quite clear to Britons that Britain stands at the natural crossroads of communication between East and West.

Mr R. G. Menzies, the last of the great Anglophiles, nevertheless noticed that the *Far East* was to us the *Near North*, and that the two ends of the world actually joined up round the back, so that Australians could communicate directly with the Americans without going through London. This process distressed the British at the time, and is still viewed with suspicion, as if the trans-Pacific route were a sort of secret passage, used when we have something to hide.

Americans draw America in the middle. Despite this, they follow the British perception that *West* ends with Alaska and *East* runs all the way to Japan.

Australians were puzzled and slightly embarrassed when we saw the first world maps with Australia on the centreline. Today's young Australians, however, naturally draw the world map this way, and many naturally describe China, etc., as countries of the *Near North*. Despite this, terms like *Middle East* and even *Far East* survive in our vocabulary. See ANTIPODES.

All mental maps seem to be subject to gravity, so that everybody talks of 'up north' and 'down south'. This has an effect on our historical thinking: the hordes of Tartars, Mongols, Goths, Picts and so on, who tore Europe apart in the Dark Ages, all did so from a position of advantage: starting from positions *up there* in the north, they *descended* on the defenceless Mediterranean civilisations; it was downhill all the way. This saved Europe from invaders from the south: the Moors and Ottomans never had a hope. But Australians are aware that we have nothing to descend on but Antarctica.

meridiem　What is the meaning of the phrases *12.00 a.m.* and *12.00 p.m.*? Since *a.m.* stands for *ante meridiem*, before noon, and *p.m.* stands for *post meridiem*, after noon, neither *a.m.* nor *p.m.* can mean *noon*, and both could mean *midnight*.

It is agreed practice that midday is called *12.00 noon*, and it is *desirable* that midnight be called *12.00 midnight*. The normal convention is that midnight is 12.00 p.m. (which is followed by 12.01 a.m.).

The 24-hour clock, which eliminates this and many other dangerous ambiguities, is making modest progress in the Australian consciousness, and this is one of very few matters in which (thanks to its adoption by British Rail, perhaps influenced more by the need to fit in with European conventions than by common sense) British usage is ahead of ours.

metaphor　Metaphor is a very common figure of speech. It is not just a device for adding colour: it is a process by which language is constantly refreshed. Nevertheless, it has some pitfalls. In the present article, we will discuss (1) the mechanism of metaphor; (2) the dangers of metaphor.

(1) The basic mechanism is simple enough. We start with a very precise phrase, full of connotations: somebody, hundreds of years ago, saw a bull staring at him in a baleful way; and then saw an archery target staring at him. He called the centre of it the *bull's eye*, creating a metaphor drawn from his experience of bulls. This phrase then became one word, *bullseye*, which then became available for further metaphorical use as *a stroke of genius*, so that we may say that we 'hit the bullseye' when we say something peculiarly perceptive, drawing the metaphor not from the anatomy of cattle but from target practice.

Often the original sense is wholly lost, as has happened with the phrase *taken aback*. Originally, this was a nautical term describing what happened to a square-rigged ship when the wind suddenly shifted. To those who had experienced it, this was a very dramatic event, and it was therefore a vivid way of describing the behaviour of a person who had received a sudden shock. Today, the original nautical sense is largely forgotten, but the phrase is widely used and universally understood even by those who do not know its origins: in short, it now *means* 'disconcerted' and is available for use metaphorically in some fresh context.

Every new experience brings a new set of metaphors. Thus, for example, the inventors of computers applied many existing words metaphorically to equivalent electronic phenomena: a computer does not have a *memory*, still less *intelligence*, in the human sense, and cannot *read*, but its operations are vividly described by talking of *reading*, *intelligence* and *memory*. (See NATURALISTIC FALLACY.)

(2) The biggest problem is with the lost metaphor which is not really lost. Should we regard *bottleneck* as just another word for obstruction, so that a *big* bottleneck causes more trouble than a *small* one? Should we remember that a *backlog* is a big log at the back of the fire which stays hot and helps us get the fire going again next day? Or should we accept that it is now an accumulation of work, an obstacle to progress which must be *overcome*.

More dangerous still are phrases like *in the light of*, as in *In the light of what you say*.... It seems innocent enough, but how far can we go before we reach absurdity? *In the light of this newspaper article...? In the light of the power strike...? In the light of the blackout...?*

This problem has no simple solution. It is obviously absurd to attempt to preserve original senses of words whose parentage is long since forgotten, but if a word or phrase is still used in its original sense, using it metaphorically can easily make us say something very silly.

A good example of this problem is the mixed metaphor, which generally happens because the writer or speaker forgets the original connotations of a word. The best examples of this disease are either contrived by the writers of books like this or found in the speeches of politicians who, as Churchill put it, 'want to speak strongly but are not sure what they are going to say.' In real life, we do not often run across such a gem as 'All the evidence must first be sifted with acid tests'. Instead, we get dull ones like 'The government has raised the target for the industry', where there is a mix of two sports: *raised* from the bar of the high jump and *target* from archery. (See TARGET.)

Finally, what about the phrase which makes perfectly good sense, but happens to be a misunderstanding. An example is the phrase *forlorn hope*. It sounds easy: we know what the two words mean, and it does not sound like a metaphor at all. However, we are told that it started with the Dutch phrase *verloren hoop,* where *verloren* means *lost* and *hoop* is a *band of men*. The *verloren hoop* was a group of men picked for a very dangerous mission, so that it was assumed that they would never return. So when we say *There is still hope, but a forlorn hope...* we are misusing the phrase. But are we? The reality is that we all use the phrase as if *hope* had its ordinary meaning. If that is what we all mean and understand by it, that is what it now means.

This happens all the time. When troops move to *check* an enemy advance, or when we *check* that the front door is locked, it is irrelevant that *check* was originally a metaphor from chess: it is now a common language word with several senses. If a word has more than one meaning, we should make sure that our use of it is not ambiguous, whether it is a lost metaphor or has simply acquired new meanings with the passage of time. But the idea that its *real* meaning is the one it started with, and that all others are somehow insubstantial, is dangerous. If I say *I wiped the humour off the windows,* and when asked what I mean dash to a dictionary and show that the original meaning of *humour* was *moisture,* it merely indicates that I am not very interested in being understood. (For more on this particular word and its shifts of meaning, see HUMOUR.)

metaphysics   A student once asked a noted professor of English (David Bradley, as it happens) why he had described Donne first as *an Elizabethan poet* and then as *a metaphysical poet*. Which, she asked, was correct?

It was not a totally silly question. *Elizabethan* is a cut-and-dried description, whereas *metaphysical* is a term whose meaning, if any, is hard to define other than by example, and Donne's work is often cited in such definitions.

The *meta-* in *metaphysics* meant 'after', and the word was coined in the first century A.D. as the name for an untitled work by Aristotle which came *after* his *Physics* in a library catalogue. This volume dealt with questions about the nature of existence and knowledge, so *metaphysics* came to be a word for the philosophy related to these questions.

Later, a new explanation of the term gained currency. *Meta-* was taken to mean 'after' in the logical sense: that physics will take you so far, *after which* you have to ascend to the level of metaphysics. This was a misunderstanding of the term, but was so plausible that it became the accepted definition, and remains so to this day.

This is how the word has come to be used by the promoters of intellectual junk, who believe that they can protect their propositions against rational analysis by labelling them 'metaphysical'. It is sad that the word should be debased in this way, and desirable that it should be applied only to the topics in the relevant volume of Aristotle, notably *ontology* and *epistemology,* the philosophies which discuss the natures of *existence* and *meaning*. These cover some of the most profound and fascinating questions faced by humankind, and the word then regains respectability.

metre, meter, -metre, -meter   We have here questions of (1) spelling and (2) pronunciation. For poetic metres, see FOOT.

(1) Spelling   Australians follow British usage:

metre for poetic rhythm and for the unit of length;

meter for the measuring instrument (e.g. *gas meter*);

-metre for the units of length (e.g. *centimetre*);

-meter for all others, including instruments (e.g. *thermometer*) and for the names of individual poetic metres (*pentameter*).

Americans use *meter* and *-meter* in all senses.

Until the late eighteenth century, the word on its own was always *metre* and the word part was always *-meter*.

When words from the metric system hit English (first recorded by OED in 1797) the British adopted the French spellings of the units, ignoring the model of the existing *-meter* formations, while the Americans kept *-meter* spellings. Shortly afterwards (OED says 1812), the British adopted *meter* as the spelling for a new invention, the gas meter.

Which is best? If we were starting from scratch, we would go the American way. But were are not starting from scratch, and the British convention has the merit of distinguishing a *micrometer* (the instrument) from a *micrometre* (the unit of length), as well as making the spelling difference mirror the difference in pronunciation (see MICROMETRE…).

(2) Pronunciation   With the pronunciation, all variants of English have adopted a French-inspired pattern for the units, while retaining English-style stress for the instruments: */centi-meeter/* but */thermommitter/*.

The exception is *kilometre*, where some speakers have adopted the pronunciation */k'lommitter/*. There is no merit in this pronunciation, but that is not going to make it go away. See KILOMETRE.

metric units and quantities   See SI UNITS.

micrometre, micron, um, micrometer   An astonishing word which has entered the language is an 'um', for a *micrometre*. This unit, one millionth of a metre, also known as a *micron*, is properly abbreviated μm; but in the absence of μ from keyboards, this is often written *um*; and this has given rise to the totally improper but useful spoken form. See SI UNITS.

The unabbreviated word should be pronounced */micro-metre/*, to distinguish it from a *micrometer*, pronounced */my-crommitter/*, meaning 'an instrument for measuring small objects'. See METRE….

midday, midnight   See MERIDIEM.

mileage   Does this word still exist now that we have abolished miles? There is no such word as *kilometrage* (for which, given the dispute over the pronunciation of *kilometre*, we can perhaps be grateful). *Yardsticks* and *inchworms* have survived as words based on defunct units, and it is hard to see why *mileage* should not do the same.

The car salesman who used to say 'low mileage' now says 'low kays'. It is generally written *low k's*, which worries some people, but low *ks* looks worse (see APOSTROPHE (4)).

militate, mitigate   There is no such phrase as *to mitigate against*. If somebody says (for example) 'the evidence mitigates *against* his guilt', there are two possible explanations: usually, the phrase is an error for 'the evidence *militates* against his guilt' meaning that the evidence suggests that he is not guilty; or that the speaker meant 'the evidence *mitigates* his guilt', i.e. that, though he is guilty, there are *mitigating circumstances* which make us let him off with a caution.

It is thus a rare example of an ambiguous malapropism.

mischievous   The habit of inserting an extra *i* sound, making this word rhyme with *devious*, sends you straight to the back of the class.

mitosis   See MEIOSIS.

modal auxiliaries   The English language has a very simple tense structure, or a very complex one, depending on which way you look at it. It is very simple in that most verbs have only two tenses of their own, present and past, the remainder of the tenses being formed by compounds using *auxiliary verbs* with the infinitive or participle. It is complex because the ability to choose the right compound is one of the marks of the native speaker.

(Grammarians use the term *periphrasis* (and its adjective *periphrastic*) rather than *compound*. It suits formal grammar, being very Greek and mysterious.)

The word *modal* means 'influencing the mood of the verb' (and for a note on the word *mood*, see VERB). The term *modal auxiliaries* is often limited to the auxiliaries which produce a subjunctive-like atmosphere, but the borderlines are so hazy in English that it is reasonable to say that, since the indicative is one of the moods, all auxiliaries are modal.

Present tenses   We have a true present tense, e.g. *I snore*, alongside which are two compounds: *I am snoring* (the *continuous present*: modal auxiliary *to be* + present participle) and *I do snore* (the *emphatic present*: modal auxiliary *to do* + infinitive).

Future tenses   We have no true future tense, but fill future-like meanings with *I will..., I shall..., I am going to..., I am about to ...*, etc., followed by the infinitive. The distinction between *will* and *shall* is subtle (and changing, see WILL/SHALL), but the choice between these

and the various compound forms is so subtle that not even Fowler
tried to analyse them. We even use the present with a future sense
when we say 'I leave for Cairns tomorrow'.

Past tenses　　We have an 'undefined' (*aorist*) past, e.g. *I snored*,
alongside which are a range of others: *I was snoring* (the *imperfect* or
continuous past), *I have snored* (the *past perfect*), *I did snore* (the
emphatic past), *I had snored* (the *pluperfect*), etc.

Modal auxiliaries in interrogatives　　In general, modal auxiliaries
are the only verbs which can be inverted to form questions (e.g. *Did
you snore?*) or negative statements (e.g. *I did not snore*). *Snored you?*
and *I snored not* sound archaic.

Modal auxiliaries as subjunctives　　The subjunctive conjugations
in English have been reduced to a few small and tattered flags, but
the thoughts they represent – statements which for one reason or
another fall short of certainty – are as common and essential as ever,
so that as fast as the subjunctive goes into decline, modal auxiliaries
arise to do the same job.

Examples can be seen under THAT (CONJUNCTION)(1), where the
compound forms use *may* and *might*; under IF… CLAUSES, where
there are in addition compounds using *would, should* and *could*; and
under QUESTIONS. All these are (or can be seen as) modal auxiliaries.

modern　　Words go in and out of fashion. The word *modern* was so
fashionable and widely used in the 1920s and 1930s that it became
associated with the period, and was adopted as the label for one of
the dominant architectural styles of the time, *Modern Style*, and for
a short time, in the 1950s and 1960s, it actually had an old-fashioned
ring about it. A new word therefore became fashionable – *contemporary*. This in turn became passé in the 1970s.

Since then, both *modern* and *contemporary* have lost these period
connotations, so both can be used neutrally. However, period flavour survives in certain specific usages. Thus the label *Contemporary
Music* may mean styles which were fashionable in the 1950s, and a
distinction is made between *modern architecture (= recent)* and *Modern architecture* (= 1930s). In typography, the word *Modern* (again
capitalised) has an even more antique ring, being a label for some
fonts which were introduced in the nineteenth century, characterised by vertical shading.

For a quite serious ambiguity in the use of such terms, see
CONTEMPORARY.

Mohammed　　See MUHAMMAD.

monostable　　See ASTABLE.

Mont de Piete　　See CREDIT FONCIER.

moral(e)　　We have no problems with distinguishing *moral* and *morale*,
but the negatives cause trouble:

(1) an *immoral* person is one who contravenes accepted moral standards;
(2) an *amoral* person is one who does not recognise accepted moral standards;
(3) a *demoralised* person is a person whose morale is shattered; *non-moral* describes an issue which is not a moral one.

Demoralised has no positive equivalent.

moral rights   When used in the context of authorship, this term is generally understood to cover two issues: the *right of integrity* (that is, that a quotation must be faithful to the original) and the *right of attribution* (that is, that authors have the right to have their names attached to their work whenever it appears).

These rights are not yet part of the law of copyright in Australia. However, courtesy demands that we should behave as if they were.

Perhaps the most widespread breach occurs in photocopying in schools, where pages of textbooks are often reproduced under statutory licence without proper reference to author or source.

However, moral rights can also be infringed accidentally if the authorship of a work is not known. An example of this was *The Ballad of '91*, a song recorded by the Bushwhackers in 1981. It was current on the folk scene at the time, and was described on the label as 'traditional'. In fact, the words had been written by Helen Palmer c. 1957. Another example is the song *Kookaburra sits on the old gumtree*, which appears as 'Anon.' or 'Trad.' in many school song books, but was actually written by Marion Sinclair in 1934.

The moral is, of course, that there is really no such thing as a folk work: the author's name may be forgotten, but that does not mean that there was no author. 'Author unknown' is a more appropriate attribution than 'Trad.' (which implies spontaneous generation) or 'Anon.' (which should be used only if the author deliberately chose to remain anonymous). I would add that this a personal plea, not a statement of the received wisdom: the attribution *Anonymous* is used in almost every poetry anthology and dictionary of quotations.

The practical implications of moral rights are further discussed under QUOTATION.

Morse   Although Mac says we should write *morse* thus, without a capital letter, the practice of remembering people who invent things by giving their names capitals is a good one. This does not go for names associated with trivia, like wellington boots, raglan sleeves and sandwiches, but I like to remember old Samuel Morse: except that I always forget, and write *morse*.

Moselle   It is possible to argue that the wines produced in the Mosel valley of Germany are marginally sweeter, on average, than those of the Rhine. It is on this basis that *Moselle* (the French form of the name of this river) became the Australian generic term for sweet white wines sold in German-style bottles.

Unlike hock, claret and most other generic terms used in Australia, this one can be used successfully in its country of origin, i.e. you can ask for a bottle of Mosel (/*moh-z'l*/) and get one. See WINE NAMES.

Moslem   See MUSLIM.

motoring terms   The motor industry has spawned a vast specialist vocabulary. The key word, CAR, has an entry all to itself.

Australian motorists largely follow British usage. Our cars drive on *petrol*, not *gas(oline)*, and have *boots, bonnets* and *(mud)guards* rather than *trunks, hoods* and *fenders*. But we have American *mufflers* rather than British *silencers*, and some of us have *windshields* rather than *windscreens*. Our only unique usage is to paint our cars with *duco* (strictly the proprietary name of a Dulux product). Under the bonnet, most of the technical terms (*carburettor*, etc.) are common to all variants of English.

Early cars were mostly open to the elements, or had more or less ineffective canopies which could be erected when it rained. The first fully-enclosed cars were therefore something special, and were given names: *sedan* in America; *saloon* in Britain. These two terms battled in Australia in the twenties and thirties, but *sedan* won. By the thirties, most new cars in Australia were sedans, often with a *chassis* (/*shassy*/, a French word) imported from America and a locally-made body. The body-building industry was largely killed off by the almost universal adoption in the passenger car industry of *monocoque* construction (another French coinage, meaning *having one shell*). However, building bodies on imported chassis (/*shassiz*/ – the French can give us the singular, but we forge our own plural) survives in the case of trucks and buses.

The French developed a style called the *coupé*, the name being drawn from a horse-drawn vehicle which had a fully enclosed compartment for the passengers, while the driver sat out in the fresh air at the front. The style crossed the Atlantic, but became democratically reversed in the process, the enclosed part being round the seats for the driver and partner, the open part, containing the *rumble seat*, being outside at the back. It was pronounced /*coop*/. The British retained the accent, called them /*coopays*/ and called the rumble seat a *dickie*. Australia followed Britain. Later, the dickies disappeared, and the term came to be applied to any closed car with only two doors and little or no room for back-seat passengers.

Another French innovation was the *limousine*, a development of the coupé in which the windows were replaced with one-way mirrors, giving the occupants extra privacy. (The name came from an all-enveloping peasant cloak under which unspeakable things could go on.) At first, this term was used in English merely as a generic for large luxury cars rather than a specific style, but it was then applied specifically to *stretched limousines*, cars with extended bodies to give extra room in the back, originally designed for use by hotels in ferrying guests to and from airports. Today, the word *limousine* is likely to imply *length* rather than *luxury* (though some are also luxurious).

The American/Australian *station wagon* or *station sedan* was first known in Britain as a *shooting brake*, and later (from the 1960s) as an *estate car*. The only Australian contribution to this vocabulary is the *ute* (*utility*), a term which is, however, now understood quite widely in Britain.

Today, the coupé style is reflected in the *fastback*, and the station sedan/wagon style miniaturised in the *hatchback*, both words being international.

The term *lorry* was common in Australia as a horse-drawn bulk carrier, but the motorised equivalent was known from the start as a *truck*. Small ones are *panel vans* (known simply as *vans* in Britain). The first articulated vehicles in Britain were made by the Mechanical Horse Company, and what we call the *prime mover* (a phrase with a majestic teleological ring to it) is still known in South Africa as a *horse*. The other half of the articulated vehicle was called a *semi-trailer*, and this term (often abbreviated to *semi*) is now generally applied to the whole *rig* (an American term).

Very large vehicles were rare on British roads until the Second World War, when aeroplanes were carried around the country on *Queen Marys*. This term is now forgotten, but when huge continental trucks started appearing on British roads following Britain's entry into the European Common Market, they were called *juggernauts*, and this term has stuck. They have no idea what a *semi* is.

The distinction between a coach and a bus is reasonably clear: *coaches* carry people long distances and are well-appointed vehicles, (though their *rest-rooms* are in every sense euphemistic). B*uses* are simpler vehicles providing local public transport. However, while the local version is never a *coach*, the long-distance version may (particularly in America) be called a *bus*.

The common American road sign NO MOBILE HOMES sounds odd to us, but they feel much the same about our equivalent sign, NO CARAVANS, which suggests to them the threat of strings of camels.

Mr, Mrs, Master, Miss, Ms   We are talking here about the way people are addressed in speech and general writing. For the use of the words in correspondence, see LETTER WRITING.

Thirty years ago, there were *Mr*, *Mrs*, *Master* and *Miss*, with *Messrs* and *Mesdames*, *Masters* and *Misses* as their plurals. The points of interest are: (1) How did the terms arise? (2) Why is their use declining? (3) How are they used now, and where are they headed?

(1) Until the sixteenth century our ancestors got on very well without them. It was only then that the members of the new middle class, anxious to distinguish themselves from the untitled lower orders and unqualified for noble titles, caused these Clayton's titles to come into being.

The word *master* had long been associated with the guilds and learned professions. It was attached to job designations (Master Mason, School Master, Master of Arts) or to surnames (Master Roberts). They often abbreviated it 'Mr', writing 'a Mr of Arts'. By Shakespeare's time the rudiments of the system were in place: in *The Merry Wives of Windsor*, for example, we find Master George Page and Mistress Page, with their daughter, Mistress Ann Page, the names marking their social superiority to Bardolph, Pistol and Nym, but inferiority to Robert Shallow, Esquire, just as he was inferior to Sir John Falstaff. Note that the unmarried daughter, like her mother, is termed Mistress.

In the eighteenth century the abbreviated versions of these terms, *Mr* and *Mrs*, were adopted as words in their own right, and pronunciations were invented for them: /mister/ and /missiz/. The old term *Master* was left to boys, while the girls got *Miss*, another abbreviation for Mistress which had earlier meant 'a whore', but became respectable first as 'a young girl' and then as 'an unmarried female person'.

Finally, in the 1960s, *Ms* was invented to avoid prejudice, particularly on the part of bank managers, who made no distinction between married and unmarried men but treated married and unmarried women differently; see SEXIST LANGUAGE.

(2) There are many reasons for the decline of these words, but they fall into two groups: (a) the decline in the use of *Mr Smith* to distinguish him from Smith; (b) the decline in the use of *Mr Smith* in favour of John Smith.

(a) The honorifics no longer carry any social significance. When Thomas Hardy's young lovers said, passionately:

'I am Mr Smith.'

'And I am Miss Swancourt.'

they were showing that they were a cut above those who were known as *Smith* and *Elsie*. But today this point would hardly be noticed in Britain, still less in Australia.

In Australia, *Smith* (as a term of address) is a convicted felon, and then only within the courts and prisons. For women and girls, it was never used in any other context, and for men and boys it has disappeared even from the boys' private schools and men's clubs where it found its last refuge. Even in Britain, only vestiges of this usage survive in the schools and clubs. There, *Smith* may also be an elderly male servant or retainer; but this usage, too, is dying with its users.

(b) The second reason for the decline of the words is a swing away to less formal terms of address.

The days when two married women would address each other as 'Mrs Smith' and 'Mrs Jones' regardless of the length of time of their friendship are long gone, and the same goes for men in social situations. We introduce people by *given name plus surname*, and thereafter use given names only. This is particularly so of children, for whom Master is obsolete and Miss obsolescent. The strongest surviving honorific is Mr for senior males.

The net result is that Mr, Mrs, Miss and Ms are heard much less than they once were and Master is not heard at all. Indeed, the move to Ms, which has had immense impact on letter writing, has limited impact on the spoken language, simply because the words it replaced are not heard.

(3) Today, Mr, Mrs, Miss and Ms are used largely on occasions when the given name is not known, and the alternative would be the unadorned surname.

Furthermore, if the person has a specific title (e.g. Dr, Professor, Senator) this is used in all but the most informal occasions. (The female of *Mr Justice* — is *Justice* —.)

This leads to a problem: while Dr John Smith will not mind being introduced as John Smith, he is likely to object to being introduced as Mr Smith. This is particularly so with medical practitioners, although most of them do not hold doctorates and are permitted to use the title only as a mark of esteem. (This is not so in America, where it is normal for a general practitioner to hold an MD.)

There is the further anomaly that male medics who actually hold doctorates are likely to be 'specialists' and to prefer the title *Mr* to distinguish themselves from the common herd of *doctors*. Despite this, when consorting with known medical practitioners, it is safest to call them all *Doctor*.

The trend toward informality extends to business. Working colleagues will get on first-name terms immediately, though traces of the old protocols survive in some businesses between junior and senior staff. Customers, however, are still generally given Mr, Mrs, Miss or Ms until a personal relationship is established; this is particularly so in hotels and other service businesses.

None of this is observed in telephone canvassing, where totally unknown juniors are liable to phone people and address them cheerily with the question 'How are you this evening, Sam?'. I am not sure that this is a good idea. It appears to be a confusion between friendliness and friendship. While we no longer have to be formal with people who are our friends, and can be friendly with business acquaintants, it does not mean that we should greet strangers as long-lost friends. This merely cheapens the conventions of friendship.

Muhammad, Mahomet, etc.   What is the preferred spelling? Fowler supported *Mahomet*, on the grounds that no one had ever heard of *Mohammed and the mountain*; Barry Jones, in *The Macmillan Dictionary of Biography*, gives a cross-reference from *Mahomet* to *Mohammed*, but then cross-refers from *Mohammed Ali* to *Mehemet Ali*; Cassius Clay called himself *Muhammad Ali*, and Larousse mysteriously defines *Mohammed* as 'nom Arabe de Mahomet'.

Coming down to more earthly reality, a count of surnames in the Melbourne Telephone Directory, 1992 edition, showed the following:

Mohamed	32
Mohammed	16
Mahomad	14
Mahomet	8
Mahomed	4
Mohammad	3

Mohamod, Mohamoud, Muhhamed, Muhammad, 1 each.

Why, then, is this entry under Muhammad? Not out of respect for Cassius Clay, but because this is the spelling preferred by most Australian Islamic communities, and no one can ask for a better authority.

For the same reason, the adjective *Muhammadan/Mahometan/Mohammedan* (again, various spellings are found) should not be used at all. Why? Because Muslims ask us not to use it, wanting to stress that Muhammad holds a quite different place in Islam from the one occupied by Christ in Christianity.

The faithful are, as in this paragraph, *Muslims*, the faith is *Islam*, and the adjective used in virtually all contexts is *Islamic*. See ISLAM(IC).

multicultural(ism)   See ETHNIC.

Muslim, Moslem, Musselman   The dictionaries agree that *Muslim* is the preferred spelling, and in this they are in tune with the Australian Islamic communities.

The word is a past participle from the verb *aslam*, 'to submit', and is thus an adjective meaning 'submitted'. Most often it appears as a noun, meaning 'one who has submitted', i.e. a follower of Islam.

For the usage, see ISLAM(IC).

mutant spellings   If writers are sufficiently distinguished, they never make spelling mistakes: they merely produce what are termed *mutant spellings*.

Mutant means changing. This implies that an active process is going on, which will terminate with the triumph of the new spelling. The word is borrowed from genetics, however, where it is applied to a rare variant, often a one-off freak, of which only one in a billion proves successful and initiates an evolutionary change.

In spelling, we can do better than this. There are of course cases where a writer deliberately uses an unusual spelling with the intention of getting it adopted as standard. Such spellings need to be distinguished, and the term *mutant* is as good as any. But the term should not be applied to one-off errors.

myth, legend Both these words refer to the stories of the past which lie on the borders between history and fiction.

Legends are generally understood to have their origins in some historical event, though the original facts have been embroidered and distorted by oral transmission. Legend is alive and well in our society, resolving the dilemmas of history and producing black-and-white heroes and villains fighting clearcut issues. Ned Kelly is our great legendary hero.

Myths are less historical, but often form part of a set of stories which tell how the world came to be the way it is: there are creation myths, myths about landforms, myths about natural phenomena. The Aboriginals have a wealth of home-grown myths, but the White myths are largely imported from overseas.

In the modern phrase *urban myth*, the word has a slightly different meaning, namely, a story about a contemporary event which is not only believed to be true but is often said to have happened in the next street, but which on investigation is found to have no basis in fact whatsoever.

For another modern term in the same general area, see FACTION.

N

naivety/naiveté   Fowler looked forward to the day when the anglicised spelling of this word would be accepted.

In Australia, that happy day seems to have dawned. *Naivety* is the only way Mac spells the word, and it is the preferred spelling in ACOD. RW is therefore eccentric (but not of course wrong) in preferring the more French spelling; we can be grateful that at least we are spared *naïveté*.

The best pronunciation is something like /*nye-eeva-ti*/.

nationalities   The question relates to the formation of nouns from adjectives.

(1) The following have both adjective and noun in the same form, and the nouns are inclusive (i.e. cover both males and females):

-an   This form covers over half the nationalities in the world, e.g. an *Australian* person is an *Australian*.

-ese   *Beninese, Burmese, Chinese, Congolese, Gabonese, Japanese, Lebanese, Maltese, Nepalese, Portuguese, Senegalese, Sudanese, Surinamese, Taiwanese, Togolese, Vietnamese.* The noun *Chinaman*, and the noun and adjective *Jap*, are generally derogatory and offensive.

-i   *Afghanistani, Bangladeshi, Bhutani, Iraqi, Israeli, Kuwaiti, Omani, Qatari, Pakistani, Saudi, Thai* (formerly *Siamese*), *Yemeni, Malagasi.*

Also, a *Greek* person is a *Greek*, a *Cypriot* person is a *Cypriot*, and see *Monaco* below.

(2) Adjectives ending in *-sh* and *-ch* cannot be used as nouns:
French, English, Welsh, Irish

Add *-man* for the male noun, but use adjective + noun for the female: *Frenchman, French woman.*

Swedish, Danish, Finnish, Turkish, Polish

Inclusive noun forms are *Swede, Dane, Finn, Turk, Pole.*

Spanish   *Spaniard* is inclusive.

Scottish   *Scot* is inclusive but there is also *Scotsman*, derived from an alternative adjective *Scots*. The adjective *Scotch* should be kept for whisky.

British   *Briton* is inclusive, but rarely used: see BRITISH(ISM).

Dutch   Although *Dutchman* exists, it is faintly derogatory, perhaps because of the phrase '…or I'm a Dutchman'. A *Dutch man/woman*, stressed to make two separate words, is the most common form. It would be good if we could school ourselves to call them *Netherlanders*, but this will take time. See HOLLAND….

264

(3) There are many special cases, all giving inclusive nouns:

-land   The name of the country is its own adjective (we say *The New Zealand economy*) except in the case of *Iceland*, which has the adjective *Icelandic*. The citizen is *-lander: New Zealander, Newfoundlander, Easter Islander, Icelander*, etc.

Luxemburg   Luxemburger.

Malaysian, Malay, Malayan

     These have all been used as both adjectives and nouns at one time or another. However, the current official name of the nationality is *Malaysian*; Malay is used only in distinguishing *ethnic Malays* from Malaysians who are ethnic Chinese, Indians, etc.; and *Malayan* is best not used at all.

Monaco   This is used as its own adjective in the phrase *Monaco Consulate*, but the citizen (both adjective and noun) is *Monegasque*.

Philippine   Filipino.

In a number of cases there is no agreed English form, e.g. for a citizen of *Hong Kong, Ivory Coast, Lesotho, Myanmar, Niger* and *Upper Volta*. In such cases (and any other in which the name is either not known or awkward) it is best to use the name of the country as an adjective.

Swiss is an awkward case. The word exists as a noun, but has no easy plural (we cannot say *I met two Swisses*). It is best used only as an adjective.

(4) Words relating to Australian States and Territories:

-an   the adjectives ending in *-an* (*Victorian, South Australian, Western Australian, (Northern) Territorian* and *Tasmanian*) are also inclusive nouns, the last having *Taswegian* as a jocular alternative (cf. *Glaswegian*).

-sh   The normal adjective for *New South Wales* is *New South Wales* (e.g. *the New South Wales Government*), with *New South Welsh* as a jocular alternative; but the male inhabitant is a *New South Welshman*, female *New South Welsh woman*.

-land   The *Queensland* (adjective) population is *Queenslanders*.

native   The term *native* means locally-born. In the early nineteenth century, when Australian usage was developing, this sense was well understood, and as a result the word acquired two quite distinct meanings:

(a) *Aboriginal*, as opposed to *white*;

(b) of whites, *born in Australia* as opposed to *having arrived by ship*.

As the century went by, however, and the majority of the white population were born in Australia, the term came to be used largely of the Aboriginals. This usage survived until the 1960s in some States in the name *Department of Native Affairs*, but is now obsolete.

Meanwhile, the term had been revived at the turn of the century to distinguish those who were in favour of the White Australia Policy. This usage survives in the name of the *Australian Natives Association*.

Today, the only common use of the term is in the popular names of indigenous flora and fauna. When applied to people, the phrase *native to…* is acceptable, but its use as in sense (a) above is taboo. See TABOO WORDS.

naturalistic fallacy   The only reason to discuss this term is that it is useful in describing a class of mistakes in expression which are otherwise easier to *sense* than to *discuss*.

When we read that Aristotle explained gravity by saying that stones, etc., *liked* falling, we sense that something is wrong. We can explain our disquiet by saying that the word *liked* can only be used of living creatures, and that this is an example of the *naturalistic fallacy*.

The most common form is *anthropomorphism*, which refers to our tendency to give human form to things we do not understand. The obvious case is nature worship, where responsibility for natural phenomena like rivers and mountains, storms and floods, is given to human-shaped gods and spirits. However, it goes further than this: we like our computerised robots to have parts we can identify as 'fingers' and 'eyes', and are worried if the 'eyes' are on the ends of the 'fingers'.

Even if parts cannot be identified, we like to use friendly words for *functions*. For example, we use the terms *intelligence* and *memory* to describe attributes of computers; see METAPHOR. This is fine so long as we remember that the 'intelligence' of computers is in no way analogous to human 'intelligence'.

In short, the words are the harmless symptoms of a disease which may be dangerous. There is no danger in saying 'nature abhors a vacuum' provided we are merely using it as a vivid way of saying that gas pressure acts to eliminate any region of lower pressure; but 'abhors a vacuum' suggests that Nature has a particular emotional objection to a region of zero pressure. This is not only a naturalistic fallacy but also untrue: she loves it, and has created more vacuum in the Universe than anything else.

nature strip   This phrase, meaning a strip of grass between the footpaths and the roadway in suburban streets, is not generally understood overseas. It is also known as a *verge*.

naught, nought   All the dictionaries agree that the word is spelt *nought* in its 'zero' sense (see ZERO) and in the name of the game, *noughts and crosses*.

ACOD identifies *naught* as an archaic spelling of *nought* used in certain phrases (e.g. *come to naught*), its meaning in these phrases being *nothing*. Mac has for some reason a separate entry for *naught*, and defines its meaning as 'destruction, ruin or complete failure'.

The 'nothing' meaning is still current in some northern British dialects, where the word is pronounced (and spelt) *nowt*. Similarly, they say *owt* for *aught* = 'anything', a word which is otherwise totally obsolete, but this never made it to Australia.

nautical follies   The moment one steps aboard a boat, the language changes. Technical jargons are common enough for this to be no surprise, but there is probably no place in which a failure to use the right words is so socially disastrous as on a boat. If you have called it a *boat* when it happens to be, in the mind of its *skipper*, a *ship*, you have already committed the first sin. (See SHIP.) If you then say you would be happier going *downstairs* and sitting on the *floor* in the *kitchen*, you have chalked up three more.

The language of the sea may be divided into three parts: the practical, the historical and the perverse.

To have unequivocal names for positions and directions is of great practical value in navigation. Thus *port, starboard, bows, stern, fore* and *aft* are all succinctly defined in the frame of reference of the ship, and less ambiguous than *left, right*, etc., unless the ship is a stationary double-ended ferry. Thus, *port* does not mean *left*. It means *the left side of the ship as you face the bows*. The captain may be *left-handed*, but not *port-handed*. *Leeward* and *windward* are two more admirably practical words, particularly for those suffering from sea-sickness.

Equally practical are many of the names for items and events which do not occur other than on boats: *rowlocks, scuppers, gaffs* and *booms, jibs* and *spinnakers, tack* and *jibe*; and for the types of boat: *schooner, yacht, yawl, dinghy*. The Dutch can take a great deal of the credit or blame for the forms of some of these words.

Less useful, but historically and sometimes etymologically intriguing, are terms for objects for which appropriate common language words exist: *thwart, gunwale, portholes, log*. There are also many medieval survivals starting with *a-*, where the *a-* is a prefix meaning *on* or *at*: *aboard, abaft, abeam, astern, amidships, aback, aloft*. *Larboard*, a synonym for port, is happily obsolete.

Purely perverse are *ay ay, Sir* for 'yes', *companion* (which has only the remotest connection with the common language word *companion*), *accommodation* in the phrase *accommodation ladder, galley, sheet*, and the verbs *go about* and *bend*. *Galley* and *sheet* are particularly perverse, since they have multiple meanings within nautical jargon: given the small number of items to be named and the prodigious range of combinations of letters to apply to them, this duplication smacks of conspiracy.

Also perverse are the pronunciations and resultant special spellings. It is bad enough to take the words *boatswain* and *forecastle* and corrupt their pronunciation; worse then to represent these as *bo'sun* and *fo'c'sle*. Nautical pedants insist that *leeward* should be pronounced to rhyme with *steward*, and *rowlocks* to rhyme with *bollocks*.

Many nautical expressions have strayed into common language: *taken aback* and *taken by and large* are two which have lost even the faintest whiff of salt air. *Taken aback* is discussed under METAPHOR.

navvy   This British word is short for *inland navigator*, having first been applied to the men who provided the manual labour for the building of the canal system. It carried connotations of massive muscles, short temper and drunkenness. The arrival of earth-moving machinery rendered the navvy obsolete, though the word is still sometimes heard. Its nearest modern Australian equivalent is the colourless word *labourer*.

Neanderthal   If used technically in the context of *Neanderthal Man*, this word (the name of a valley in Germany) is best pronounced */-tahl/*. In common language, as a word meaning uncouth, it is sometimes anglicised, */-thahl/* or */-thawl/*. This pronunciation is best avoided, not because there is anything wrong with anglicising such words, but because it sounds as if you are not a good listener.

nearby/near by   The first is an adjective, as in *I swam at a nearby beach*. In other usages it is better to keep the two words apart: *Two sharks were basking near by*.

near miss   Logic might suggest that we should say *a near hit* rather than *a near miss*, but our usage often defies logic.

negative dilemmas   There are two major problems and a raft of minor ones, some of which are discussed under SINGULARITIES (g).

(1) Double negatives, e.g. *I'm not going nowhere.*   The rule in Standard English is quite simple: two negatives make a positive. Most of us regard this as simple logic, and regard double negatives as uneducated. We are then disturbed to find that double negatives are used to reinforce one another in many languages and dialects, and in English by Shakespeare.

The trouble with our convention is that it is easy to lose count, and to forget the quasi-negatives. Fowler produced the superb example *The Opposition refused leave for the withdrawal of a motion to annul an order revoking the embargo on the importation of cut glass*. Such a sentence is very bad manners. Good writers use positive forms wherever possible.

A similar problem is the mix-up between
There is no suggestion that Mr Perot will not stand.
There is no question that Mr Perot will not stand.
There is no doubt that Mr Perot will not stand.
The idiom is that the first two mean that Mr Perot *will* stand, while the third means that he *won't*; but all three are now heard with the

opposite effect. Whether this is a new Australian idiom or just confused writing, the message is the same: avoid these negative circumlocutions.

The *not un-* syndrome (e.g. *The gathering was not unpleasant*) must have seemed astonishingly clever the first time it was used, but it is now threadbare, and used largely in parody of those languid individuals who do not like to respond positively to anything. However, in our boardrooms, the phrase *not illegal* is a euphemism for *immoral*, and even this pattern has its place: to say that a usage is *not incorrect* is significantly different from saying that it is *correct*.

For examples of double negatives which do not cancel one another out, see REPETITIONS ....

(2) Floating negatives   See AMBIGUITY (7).

The simple negative sentence *I don't like that* (and thousands of similar sentences) can carry four implications.

> *I don't like that* (but perhaps you do)
> *I* don't *like that* but *I* may like it later)
> *I don't* like *that* (but I am prepared to put up with it)
> *I don't like* that (but I do like this)

The ambiguity is resolved in speech by putting stress on relevant words. Unless a writer uses underlining and italics (which can get very tedious) the written sentence is potentially ambiguous.

With some usages, there are clear rules, e.g. to place the *not* immediately before the word or phrase it applies to:

> *I am not flying to Perth, but driving.*
> *I am flying not to Perth, but to Albany.*

As with all ambiguities, there is no way to ensure that you avoid negative-related ambiguities, as they exist as much in the mind of the reader as in the text; but writers and editors should be quietly suspicious when they see negatives in a sentence.

negative prefixes   The English language possesses a wealth of negative prefixes: *non-, un-, in-, de-, dis-, a(n)-* and sundry others (e.g. *mis-, ab-, anti-*) which have a negative sense in certain contexts.

In the simplest cases, they are prefixed to common words to produce antonyms (*nonsense, unjust, indefensible, decontaminate, disadvantage, asymmetrical, mistrust, abnormal, anticlimax*).

In other cases, their usage is different from that of their structural antonyms: *canny* refers to people, but *uncanny* to things; *ease* is rarely thought of as the opposite of *disease*; or they may have an apparently non-negative sense: *valuable, invaluable* (see VALUE); or their form and sense may be modified: *aptitude, ineptitude*.

Some of the questions about negative prefixes are discussed in LOST POSITIVES and -ABLE.... In this article, the problems will be discussed in the context of the choice from among these prefixes when coining new words:

a- (*an-* when joined to a word starting with a vowel) is so ambiguous that one wonders why it is still used in new formations. Yet it was beloved of scientists in the eighteenth and nineteenth centuries (*abiogenesis, acaudate, anaerobic*), and later joined the behavioural scientists (*amoral, apolitical*). It still rears its head occasionally (see ASTABLE), almost invariably causing trouble. *It should not be used in new coinage.*

de- started life as a Latin prefix whose main meaning was *down* or *from* (*demotion* = a downward motion). This is not a negative – the antonym of *demotion* is not *motion*, but *promotion*. However, it was but a short step to words with a virtually negative sense, such as *deform*. All this happened in antiquity, and the resultant words came into English fully fledged. If this were the end of the story, new formations would be as inappropriate as those using *a-* and *in-*. However, the prefix gained new currency in our century, starting, it would seem, with the military jargon of the First World War, when the troops were *detrained, decontaminated* and finally *demobilised*. It is best regarded as a new English prefix, implying *action to reverse or undo a process which has already taken place.*

It is often abused: *de-escalation* (coined in the Vietnam War) was as fatuous and redundant a euphemism as *escalate*, and *de-seat* (of a parliamentarian) means no more than the existing *unseat*. However, *debug* is a very clear description of what one does with a defective computer program, and *debriefing* is a sensible complement to *briefing*, even if we do not like these words.

In new coinage, *de-* should always be pronounced *dee*. This is to avoid common confusions such as that between *defuse* and *diffuse*.

dis-, like *de-*, is Latinate, and originally carried the connotation of separation (*dissociate, disrobe*). In music, the word *discord* (meaning, literally, a separation of hearts) is the antonym of *concord*, neither word having anything to do with *chord*; but today the word *concord* is effectively lost to music, so that *chord* and *discord* are used as an antonym pair. For a note on *disinterested*, see INTEREST.

In new coinage, *dis-* is synonymous with *de-*, the one chosen being the one which sounds best; in effect, *de-* before consonants, *dis-* before vowels. Most of the resultant words are horrible, like *disinvestment*.

in- is almost as ambiguous as *a-*, being confused with *in-* in its positional senses *into, on*, or *in*. This does not matter with common words, since the sense is well known even if the etymology is not. However, there are cases which are at best unhelpful: for example, it seems perverse that *flammable* and *inflammable* are effectively synonyms rather than antonyms. Thus *in-*, too, should be avoided in coining new words.

mis- implies error: *quotation, misquotation*. However, if the term so modified is absolute, the effect can be negative: *mistrust* and *distrust* are effectively synonymous. In new coinage, it should be used only with the implication of error.

no- is an odd one, existing only in some special (and recent) usages, mostly informal: *no-man's-land*, a *no-hoper*, a *no-go* area. It is not a true prefix: *no* is here an adjective qualifying the noun which follows it: a *no-entry sign*, a *no-ball*, a *no-claim bonus*.

non- though of Latinate origin, was not used as a general negative prefix in antiquity. Even in Shakespeare's English, it was almost entirely restricted to some legal jargon, e.g. *non-suit*. There is no *nonsense* in Shakespeare. While most of them are simple opposites of established words, some have no positive equivalent, e.g. *nondescript* (coined in 1683), and *nonchalant* (imported from France in 1734).

Non- is particularly useful in denoting the complement of a defined set. Thus, if some drinks are *alcoholic*, the rest are *non-alcoholic*. Such terms occasionally acquire independent meaning, e.g. *Nonconformist*; but generally they have meaning only because we can define what they are not, e.g. *non-metals* has meaning only because we can define *metals*. For a distinction between *non-* and other negative prefixes, see MORAL(E).

A more recent development has been the use of *non-* with nouns to connote failure (*non-arrival, non-starter, non-event*) or with verbs to produce adjectives connoting avoidance (*non-stop, non-skid*). Some of these are ill-defined (e.g. a *non-event* can be either an event which fails to live up to expectations or one which doesn't happen at all). There is therefore something woolly about many of these phrases; nonetheless, they are often handy, and the usage is likely to flourish.

un- is the workhorse of English negatives. It can be used in almost every case as an alternative to *a-* and *in-*, and often for *de-* and *dis-*. (The distinction between *uninterested* and *disinterested*, though important, is purely conventional.)

It presents few problems. With the exception of a few words starting *uni-* (*un-ionised/union-ised*), it is unambiguous, and can be added to almost any adjective unless there is another strongly established form. The Germanic languages, from which it was acquired, use it across the board without apparent difficulty, even on nouns. Thus the Germans have the word *Unglück*, literally unluck, as the opposite of luck (compare *lucky/unlucky*). We use it with nouns only if they are palpably derived from verbs or adjectives (*unworldliness, untruth*), the only common exception being *unrest*.

neither The pronunciation remains arbitrary, but /*nye-ther*/ had the approval of Fowler, and is heard more frequently than /*nee-ther*/. The same goes for /*eye-ther*/.

neither ... nor Special problems attend *neither ... nor*.

(1) In a sentence like *Neither you nor I* am/is/are *competent*, all three have good logical support, but all three conflict with one or other of the eternal truths discovered by various purists.

Neither you nor I am competent follows the 'rule' that verbs should agree with the nearest subject, but sounds the worst.

Neither you nor I is competent has a verb which agrees with neither subject, but sounds better, perhaps because we perceive the sentence as *neither of us is competent*.

Neither you nor I are competent seems the most comfortable, but it is hard to justify. Is it a 2nd person singular to agree with *you*? Or are we perceiving it as 1st person plural, i.e. *We are not competent*? Those who trust formal grammar will be pleased to know that this is the form Latin would use: *... neque ego neque tu fecimus* (Terentius).

This is one of the very few puzzles on which Fowler admitted defeat. He recommends us to go back to taws and say something else (though not in those words – see TAWS).

(2) In the sentences *I neither eat bacon nor eggs* and *I neither eat bacon nor cook it*, the question is of word order. Other things being equal, *neither* will apply to the word which immediately follows, so the first sentence should have been *I eat neither bacon nor eggs.*

As it happens, it rarely matters, as the sense is generally clear from the context. However, the word order 'rules' can help to identify and solve ambiguities.

Nor is sometimes use to refresh a negative in a long sentence. Thus we may write *I do not say that it is impossible to go by bicycle from Perth to Cairns, nor that it would be a masochistic act*. Here, the word *not* is attached to *say*, and therefore covers the whole sentence, so that logically the word *or* would be better; but *nor* (implying *nor do I say*) may well be clearer.

Conversely, *nor* is essential and *or* wrong when they follow on the word *neither*. We never write *neither ... or.*

Netherlands, The This is the only correct name for the country we tend to call Holland. See HOLLAND....

New Australian According to AND, this phrase was first used in 1893 for those who went to Paraguay to found 'New Australia'.

Its real currency, however, dates from 1949, when Arthur Calwell, as Minister for Immigration, proposed it as positive alternative to *Balts*, *Reffos* and the various other derogatory terms in use at the time for new immigrants. It caught on rapidly and was widely used for some twenty years, but in the absence of any change in the prevailing xenophobia, it too became perceived as derogatory.

It is now best regarded as a technical term to be used only in historical references to the immigrants of the 1945–1965 period.

nexus   This word, meaning 'connection', is more commonly used and understood in Australia than in other English-speaking countries, perhaps because of its use in reference to the *nexus* in the Australian parliament – the constitutional requirement that the number of members of the House of Representatives shall be as near as possible twice that of the number of Senators. Indeed, *the nexus* is often used *absolutely* in this sense.

Since this is a unique phenomenon, the plural is scarcely used; when it is, it is *nexuses*, not *nexi*.

nice   Firstly, let us all agree that it is sad that so many people use weak, non-specific words when a little thought will identify a strong, specific one. This is a good argument for not using *nice* to mean 'pleasant'.

Secondly, let us also agree that it is very nice to have some weak, non-specific words to use when we do not want to make the effort to think of strong, specific ones, which is why you and I both use *nice* for 'pleasant' from time to time.

Thirdly, let us agree that *nice* retains a strong sense in such phrases as *a nice point* (= subtle, precise), and that we do not wish to kill it off. But this sense has existed alongside the weak sense for at least two centuries, which suggests that it is not under threat.

Finally, we should note that the weak sense was popularised in Britain at the end of the eighteenth century, after the American Revolution, and that the word is much less common in American speech or writing than in British or Australian. Where we would say *That's nice of you* and *That's a nice car*, Americans are more likely to say *That's good of you* and *That's a fine/great car*. But they then spoil it by saying *Have a nice day*.

no, not   See NEGATIVE DILEMMAS.

noisome   It may help avoid problems with the spelling, pronunciation and meaning of this word if we remember that it has nothing to do with *noise*, and everything to do with an obsolete word *noy*, which also survives in our word *annoy*. It is pronounced *noy-some*, and means annoying or unpleasant, particularly of smells.

nonce words   A nonce word is a term used by lexicographers for a word coined *for the nonce*, that is, *for the moment*. The word *euripidaristophanise*, for example, has impeccable Greek etymology, but to the best of my knowledge has been used only once in English (apart from lexicographic mention), and that was by me, in a school magazine, in the dawn of remembered time. It means *to lampoon*. Churchill's *triphibious* is another, discussed under MALFORMATIONS. Nonce words are, for obvious reasons, rarely found in dictionaries.

Nonce usages are even more rarely remembered. An example occurred on 4 October 1957, when the world was enthralled to hear a faint bleep from space. Within twenty-four hours, the term *bleep* had shifted from meaning a sound to meaning the man-made device emitting it (*Bleep circles Earth in 80 minutes*). Then the Russians told us that it was called a *sputnik*, and the need for a word carrying this sense disappeared. *Bleep* returned to its use as a sound, its use as *an artificial satellite* having gone from scratch to universal use and back to oblivion in less than a fortnight. No dictionary records this brief moment of glory, referring only to mundanities like the noise made by electronic bleepers.

none *None is…* or *None are…*? See SINGULARITIES (g).

nonetheless, nevertheless I write both these as single words.

nor See NEITHER and NEGATIVE DILEMMAS (2).

noun See GRAMMAR (3(c)).

noun adjectives, noun verbs The habit of coining new verbs and adjectives from nouns is well established in all languages. It is, however, simplest in non-inflected languages like English, as they can make the move without much variation to the form. Thus, if we coin a new noun, like *fax*, we immediately have an adjective (as in *fax machine*) and verb (*to fax*). From here, the inflections (*faxes, faxing, faxed*) develop easily and naturally.

In inflected languages, there may at first be considerable debate about which of several models will be followed. The French are still arguing about whether the imported word *interview* is masculine (the view of the *Dictionnaire Général*) or feminine (the view of the Académie), and whether the verb should be *interviewer* or *interviouer*. They are bemused by our word *interviewee*, with its feminine-looking ending concealing an inclusive meaning.

There are, of course, variant models in English. Thus the prefix *en-* (as in *encode*) and the suffixes *-ify* (as in *beautify*) and *-ise* (as in *computerise*) are just three affixes which produce verbs from nouns. But whereas in most languages such prefixes and suffixes are almost always needed, many words in English can be developed without them, as we saw with *fax*.

Because it is so easy, we ought to be very careful about doing it. There are basically two dangers:

The first danger is that we may coin some redundant words. Why do we *trial* new ideas, when the noun *trial* was formed from the verb *to try (out)*? The verbs *to network* and *to workshop* are among a host of new ones which may only give a bogus lustre to some fairly commonplace processes.

The second danger applies particularly to adjectives. It is that the use of unadorned nouns as adjectives can result in indigestible sentences. *I am sitting for the Driving Instructors Training College Entrance Examination* contains six consecutive nouns, of which the first five are acting as adjectives. This kind of sentence is a new arrival in English. Using nouns as adjectives was always possible, but piling them up in this way was a habit we laughed at when we observed it in the Germans. Admittedly, the Germans made it seem worse by omitting the word breaks and producing rather overlong words, but Mark Twain's ribald essay *On the Awful German Language* would apply very well to modern English.

If this kind of syntax were impossible (as it would be in French, for example) the sentence would have to read *I am sitting for the Examination for Entrance to the College for the Training of Instructors of Driving*. This is still an appalling wodge of information, but the relationship of each of the words to the rest is clear, and the information arrives in a very much more logical order, first establishing the major facts and then adding the detail.

*n*th   Fowler had a curious objection to the phrase *To the nth degree*: that *n* merely means an unknown, not necessarily large, number. This is true of *x* but less so of *n*, which is used to write the generic form of a series, e.g. we write x^1, x^2, x^3, ... x^n. It thus means 'to as high a degree as you care to go' which is pretty close to its usual metaphorical sense.

nuclear free   The phrase *nuclear free*, used of local government districts, is grammatically dubious (*nuclear* being an adjective) and hard to achieve without turning off the sun, but the intended meaning is generally understood.

number phrases   The following comments address some of the many problems which can occur in ordinary writing when numbers become involved.

(1) There is a general rule that small numbers in prose texts should be spelt out while large numbers are written in arabic numerals. Thus we write 'She owns two cars' but 'He has 4562 books'.

This is sensible, but there is debate about the borderline between large and small. Some style manuals base the distinction on the size of the number, saying that all numbers up to nineteen (or some other arbitrary figure) should be spelt out. I think it more sensible to base it on the number of words involved: a one-word number, even if it is a million, should be spelt out, and in most contexts two-word numbers as well. Effectively, this means all stations to one hundred, then non-stop to a thousand and a million.

However, slavish following of this (or any other) rule results in unnecessary absurdities like *He had between ninety-nine and 105 pots of honey*. Matching pairs are best handled consistently – in this case, as arabics. There is no question of rightness and wrongness here, it is a matter of visual aesthetics and suitability to the theme.

Arabics can generally be used in conjunction with abbreviated units (i.e. write *25 cm* or *twenty-five centimetres*, but not a mix of the two). If there are a lot of numbers (as in a mathematical or scientific text) all numbers may be in arabics, though again common sense should be applied: a single number word embedded in a paragraph of straight prose may be best spelt out.

Decimal fractions have to be in arabics. Incidentally, despite the way the police write point-oh-five, it is best to put a zero before the decimal point: *0.05.*

(2) A *billion* is one thousand million (10^9); see BILLION. A *trillion* is a million million (10^{12}), and then we have *quadrillion* (10^{15}), *quintillion* (10^{18}), etc. See STANDARD FORM.

(3) We talk about *Seven and a quarter million*, not *Seven millions and a quarter*, despite Fowler's liking for the latter. We would understand it, but there is a risk of ambiguity, i.e. that 7,000,000 ¼ was intended.

(4) In scientific and mathematical writing, we omit the commas from long numbers, but to extend this convention to popular writing is unnecessary. The reason for it is purely to avoid confusion between the European and Anglo-Saxon conventions, which is not a concern other than in technical writing; see SI UNITS (2(l)).

(5) *Ten times more…* is a mathematically sound expression, but *Ten times less…* (which is commonly used by advertising copywriters) is questionable. Presumably the copywriters feel that the unambiguous phrase *One tenth as much…* (which is generally the intended meaning) is not as dramatic.

(6) *Up to 132 …* is sound, and *132 or more…* is sound, but *Up to 132 or more …* is plain silly.

(7) The convention of double entry of numerals (*Employees are entitled to a five (5) minute tea-break*) is today a piece of nonsense. Its origins are discussed under LEGAL LANGUAGE (3).

numerals, alignment of   Columns of homogeneous figures should normally be aligned so as to maintain the place value, thus:

Diameter in microns

fat person	123 456
wool fibre	30
spider's web	0.567 8

In the days of manual typewriters this was tedious, involving laborious counting and checking ahead. Happily, most word processors have decimal tabulation facilities which do it automatically.

There are no rules governing the alignment of a non-homogeneous set of numbers, and flush left generally looks more natural, just as with text:

Number of pages	320
Price	$45.50

For the alignment of roman numerals, see NUMERALS, ROMAN (3).

numerals, roman   There are four problems with roman numerals:

(1) Comprehension   Very few people regularly come across, and hence can read fluently, any numbers beyond twelve; so they should not be used in any sequence going further than this unless the intention is to give the information (if, say, required to do so by law) yet at the same time to conceal it, as happens with the dates on films.

(2) Space   The length of roman numerals gets out of hand very quickly. Thus we reach four characters with VIII (8), five with XVIII (18), six with XXVIII (28) and seven with XXXVIII (38). Anyone tempted to quote large numbers in roman numerals should not only ask whether they will be understood, but also whether there will be room for them.

(3) Alignment   Roman numerals do not follow a place value system, so there is no logical reason to print them flush right. If anything, their logic favours a flush left alignment, but this can be set aside if there are other considerations. Thus where a column includes both romans and arabics, as is the case in the contents list of many books, the best practice is to make them all flush right; but wherever practical the old convention of *centring* columns of roman numerals is recommended.

(4)   When writing type specifications, it is best to capitalise *Roman* to distinguish *roman* = not italic from *Roman* = not arabic.

numerical prefixes   There is a general rule that, in new coinage, the number sequences should be consistent. If you feel this way, you should remember the sequences:

	one-, two-,...		*first, second,...*		*single, double,...*
	GREEK	LATIN	GREEK	LATIN	LATIN
1	mono-	uni-	proto-	primary	simple(x)
2	di-	bi-	deutero-	secondary	duplex
3	tri-	tri-	trito-	tertiary	triple(x)
4	tetra-	quadri-		quaternary	quadruple(x)
5	penta-	quin(qu)i-		quinternary	quintuple(x)
6	hexa-	sexa-			sextuple(x)
7	hepta-	septa-			
8	octo-	octo-			
9	nona-	novem-			
10	deca-	deci-			
10^2	hecto-	centi-			
10^3	kilo-	milli-			
Many	poly-	multi-			multiple
					complex

For prefixes beyond this range, see SI UNITS.

Nunga   See KOORI.

O

O, oh   The spelling *O* is required when this word introduces a vocative: *O Lord, O Caesar*. This usage is, however, obsolete, being used
in new writing only in prayers and review sketches about the
Roman Empire.

The spelling *oh* is required when the word is an exclamation on
its own: *Oh! What a mess!*

Between these two are a whole range of usages in which the
sense is ill-defined and the spelling varies, so that we can find good
support in the songbooks for *Oh, Shenandoah, Oh Shenandoah* and *O
Shenandoah*. However, a practical rule which will keep writers out of
trouble is that the word is always *Oh* when followed by a punctuation mark of any sort, and otherwise *O*.

Both are best written with a capital letter even in the middle of a
sentence: *Return, return, O Shulamite ....*

oaths and profanities   The word *oath* and its equivalent verb *to swear*
are used in two almost contradictory contexts, the language of
solemn undertakings and the language of the coarsest invective, the
most sanctified of language and the most profane. It says a great
deal for our mental agility that this rarely causes confusion.

Given the clarity of Christ's message that his followers should
not take the Lord's name in vain, it is strange that most Christians
enthusiastically swear on the Bible in our Courts. If they prefer not
to, they can always *affirm*.

(1) Swearing   When, in *Eric, or Little by Little*, the hero said 'What
a surly devil that is', his friend Edwin was shocked. 'A surly —? Oh,
Eric, that's the first time I ever heard you swear'.

Times have changed. Today, few would be able to say exactly
what had shocked Edwin, still less be shocked themselves. However, why does Edwin call it 'swearing'?

It all started with swearing in the 'sanctified' sense. A person
who wished to stress the accuracy of a statement might call up the
name of a relevant deity as witness to it: *by Jove, by God, by Christ*. In
the right context, all these (like the invoking of the various saints)
were perfectly respectable; but if used casually they were *profanities*.

Alongside these developed the *exclamations* we see peppered
through the pages of Restoration comedy: *God's truth!* (→ *Struth!*)
God's wounds! (→ *Zounds!*) *God's blood!* (→ *Sblood!*). Of these, only
Struth! survived into our century.

The words used in these oaths were called *swear words*, and, by a
sort of back-formation, the use of them became known as *swearing*,
even if no oath was involved. To return to Eric: he used the name
devil; this name was used in oaths; therefore it was a swear word;
and therefore when Eric used it he was swearing.

(2) Profanities   The word *profane* originally meant 'outside the temple', i.e. not sacred, so that (in particular) books could be divided into 'sacred' and 'profane'. It has since become more or less synonymous with 'shocking'.

The most effective profanity is one which shows contempt for whatever the society holds most sacred. Thus a deeply religious society generates blasphemy, a prudish society generates obscenity, and a hygienic society generates talk of excrement: *hell, fuck* or *shit*.

All three can be seen in English from Chaucer to the present day: Chaucer's Madame Eglantine (*Amor Vincit Omnia*) is paralleled by Monty Python's Leaping Sisters; but our society believes in so little that it is very difficult to be shocking. However, there is one type of communication which gives us some inkling of the mixture of horror and thrill people used to get out of blasphemy, and that is sick jokes. Really sick jokes, that is. Maybe we are fundamentally decent after all.

Meanwhile, our only really strong belief is in money. This is shown by our indignation when extremists have demonstrated their contempt for it by showering city crowds with banknotes. But no one has yet worked out a compelling money-based profanity.

For further uses of oaths and profanities, see EXPLETIVE.

object (direct and indirect)   In formal grammar, we talk about direct and indirect objects. Thus, *I gave the dog a bone* is analysed as *I gave a bone [to] the dog*.

Note that when a sentence is made passive, either the direct or the indirect object can become the subject, but if the direct object becomes the subject, a preposition has to be added before the indirect object:

>   *The dog was given a bone.*
>   *A bone was given to the dog.*

This kind of analysis is occasionally helpful in untying knots in sentences. Thus

>   *Ask me a question.*
>   *I am asked a question.*
>   *A question is asked [of] me.*

i.e. the direct object is *a question*, and the indirect object is *me*.

See CASE (2).

oblivious   The most common usage of this word today is as in the sentence 'He went on with his speech, *oblivious to* the heckling coming from the back of the hall'.

Strictly, there are two mistakes here: firstly, we should say *oblivious of*, not *oblivious to*; secondly, *oblivious* is all about *forgetting* something, not about *being unaware* of it.

However, if everybody is making the same mistake, it is a mistake no longer.

oboe   This word is one of the very few in our language which have succumbed utterly to spelling reform. The French *hautbois*, high wood, was *hautboys* in Shakespearean times, pronounced /*oh-boys*/. However, some inglorious reformer in the eighteenth century popularised the spelling *oboe*, so the etymology of the word went down the plughole.

obscurantism   Most of us assume that people who write and talk do so to communicate. However, this is not necessarily true. There are many writers whose main purpose is not so much to communicate as to demonstrate. Nor is this new. Remember the schoolmaster in Oliver Goldsmith's *Deserted Village,* whose

> *words of wondrous length and sonorous sound*
> *amazed the gazing rustics ranged around.*

If all we are wanting to do is to add to our list of publications, we may need to make the bricks without straw. So we will need to make sure that the writing is not read or, if read, that it is not clear enough to disclose that it has nothing to say.

The following is a guide to some strategies to minimise communication:

(1) Avoid active verbs   You can achieve ambiguity as well as turgidity by replacing all active verbs with passives: *A sunburnt country is loved by Mackellar (1912).*

(2) Be impersonal   Any sentence which establishes you as a sentient being with a personality may conceivably make the text readable or even interesting. Thus Dorothea Mackellar should have written *A sunburnt country is loved by the present writer.*

(3) Include frequent citations of your own publications   The sentence *A sunburnt country is loved by Mackellar (1912)* would have been particularly boring had it been written by Dorothea Mackellar herself.

(4) Use abstract nouns   The use of abstract nouns, particularly as the subjects of sentences, minimises the risk of making a comprehensible statement. Thus *The incidence of positive gender-based interactions is inhibited by affective forces operating in a reverse sense* will leave readers too bemused or bored to argue, whereas saying *Girls don't like boys* is likely to be wake them up.

(5) Use mathematical models   The use of mathematical models is a great elegance.

> *The standard model of human behaviour is*
> $$B = f(P,E)$$
> *where B = behaviour, f = a functional relationship of dependency, P= some aspects of personality, and E = some aspects of the external environment.*

If the writer had said 'People's behaviour depends on the sort of people they are and how the world treats them', he would not have won the respect which this mathematical model earned him.

(6) Use graphic models Words and short sentences are placed randomly in boxes distributed over the page, and joined with dotted lines and arrows. Some of the boxes should be shaded, and the arrows should be double headed, to avoid any risk of there being a path through the system. Boxes of different shapes can add greatly to the mystery and the aesthetic effect.

(7) Use and invent jargon The phrase *discremental exogenisation* is a useful example of an all-purpose obscure phrase. Note that all the word parts are authentic and they are assembled in a plausible order; all that is lacking is sense.

(8) Use initials *Discremental exogenisation* is intrinsically meaningless, but its meaninglessness can be pressed home by reducing it to initials: *It is arguable that a monotypical technostructure is informed by DE.*

(9) Devise new derivatives There are few words which cannot be made more obscure by the addition of a few syllables to an ill-defined but authentic base word. Thus, whatever *attribution* means, *attributional* is its adjectival form. Whatever *attributional* means, *subattributional* means *falling short of complete attributionality* in some undefined way. The word can spawn an infinite range of further derivatives of indefinite length, through adding *post-*, *neo-*, etc., to the beginning, and *-ise, -ism, -istic*, etc., to the end.

(10) Use commonspeak This is the antithesis of (8), in which common language words are subtly transformed so as to strip them of dictionary-supported meaning. The words *off, useful* and *better* can give us *offness, unuseful* and *betterise*. These words not only give a disarmingly common touch to the work, but can also add a surprising amount of obscurity to its meaning.

Ocker There are three contexts in which this word is used: of behaviour, of attitudes and of speech. Ocker behaviour is depicted as crass, and Ocker attitudes as ignorant, sexist and racist. But Ocker speech is different: the perception is at worst neutral and generally positive.

There are broad Australian accents which many people find ugly, but Ocker, as spoken by, say, Paul Hogan, is not one of them – people round the globe listen with fascination and delight. The literary embodiment of the Ocker voice, C. J. Dennis's *The Sentimental Bloke*, depicts a person with virtually no Ocker characteristics apart from his voice. Even when he speaks of 'a Dago band', there is no suggestion of xenophobia.

The question is, how should writers indicate that their characters are Ocker speakers?

For C. J. Dennis, the answer was easy: by putting in a great many Ocker-slang phrases, and providing a lot of phonetic clues:

Fer, as the poit sez, me 'eart 'as got
The pip wiv yearnin' fer – I dunno wot.

Nine clues in sixteen words, at least two of which represent normal speech sounds, *sez* and *wot*, and most of us would say something very like *Fer....*

In doing this, he was following a strong tradition. Dickens's Sam Weller, J. J. Bell's Wee McGreegor and Joel Chandler Harris's Uncle Remus all have their speech patterns reproduced in great detail; too great, perhaps, for modern readers. Thanks to the films, radio and TV, we have a fair idea what caricature Cockney, Glasgow and Afro-American voices sound like, and the constant re-spelling of common words, so far from helping us with the voice, is simply an obstacle to comprehension.

Ray Lawler handled it very differently. In the script for the Ocker classic, *The Summer of the Seventeenth Doll*, his characters never drop an aitch, the flags used being *-in'* for *-ing* and the occasional *gunna* for *going to*. But no worthwhile actor (or reader, for that matter) fails to get the voices right.

Modern writers merely put in enough flags to indicate the intended voice, and leave it to the readers to add the rest – as accurately as their knowledge of the relevant accent allows. If they don't know it, all the flags in the world will not help.

octopus   The plural is *octopuses*, not *octopi*. See PLATYPUS.

of   For a discussion of the common error of writing *would of* for *would have*, see HAVE.

of course   This parenthetical phrase, along with *clearly*, is generally used to mean that the writer is very uncertain about the truth of what is being asserted, and does not wish to be cross-questioned about it. *Manifest* has the same sense in *manifest destiny*, as does *self-evident* in 'We hold these truths to be *self-evident'*, these words being associated with concepts which are neither *manifest* nor *self-evident*, however pleasant it would be if they were.

officialese   *Officialese* is the written form of PLODDERY.

We all recognise officialese when we see it, and we are all quick to mock it. But it is less easy to know what we can do about it. It still appears in letters from government departments and large corporations, presenting problems similar to those discussed under LEGAL LANGUAGE.

I say 'still' because many major producers of officialese have recently made a very real attempt to raise their game. The outcome is most obvious on our roads, where both the design and wording of signs has changed totally over the last twenty years. Formulae like *Elderly Pedestrians Cross Here* have given way to pictograms, and where words are needed they are simple and direct:

WRONG WAY
GO BACK

If there were literary awards for good official notices, the unac-knowledged author of this masterpiece of clarity would deserve one. Conversely, the one who wrote
CYCLISTS
GIVE WAY
might have made it more clear whether it was an instruction to cyclists or a warning to motorists.

Road signs are, however, an easy case to deal with. The need for brevity and clarity is obvious: the readers have only a second or two to take in the message. Furthermore, the range of messages is limited, and special care can be taken with each one. The same goes for census and tax forms, where layout as well as wording can be, and are, given detailed attention by people who are expert in the art of clear communication.

The surviving problem, then, is to achieve a similar clarity in one-off letters and documents, produced by people who neither are, nor have access to, professional communicators. The traditional approach has been to issue style guides with lists of common errors, the implication being that you avoid the various errors recorded in the book, or edit them out if they have crept in.

I suspect that this does not address the real problem. Most of us are capable of making simple, clear statements when talking to our friends about something we understand. None of us talks officialese in ordinary conversation. The gobbledygook arises because we have an uneasy feeling that simple language is not official enough (just as we feel that legal documents have to be couched in 'legal language'), and we move into 'official language' without realising that we have done so.

A more promising approach is to start with a simple statement of the subject of the letter, expressed just as we would if we were talking to a friend. This sets the register (see REGISTER) for the whole letter. Once the register is established, it is unlikely that we will slip back into officialese in later paragraphs.

I am not saying that this will necessarily solve the problem: it may not generate an appropriate register, or may generate one which is too informal. Letters to and from officialdom often have to be stern: they are often about laws and regulations, and these are no laughing matter. But if the first draft, prepared as outlined above, seems too lightweight, it can be stiffened. This is far more likely to produce a clear final version than writing the first draft in a stiff, formal language and then softening it.

off-sider   This word is so common and well-understood in Australia that we can forget that it is meaningless outside our sea-girt land. Indeed, it can be worse than meaningless to foreigners, being assumed to be some sort of reference to soccer, and hence to mean a person who is in the wrong place.

The word is an Australianism, and originally referred to the person who looked after the off-side of a bullock team while the boss looked after the near-side. It is a positive word, implying a companionable relationship between boss and employee, for which the closest equivalent is perhaps the American *sidekick*.

-(o)graphy/logy/nomy/metry   Strictly speaking, the suffixes are -graphy, -logy, etc. For an example of an occasion for remembering this, see GENEALOGY. But we talk about 'ologies', so *-oligies* it is.

These suffixes originally had distinct meanings: *writing about…, talking about…, rules of…, measurement of….* Today, the distinctions between the first three have disappeared under a cloud of convention, so that the difference between *geography* and *geology, astrology* and *astronomy, ecology* and *economy, biography* and *biology,* cannot be explained by reference to them. However, *-metry* retains its strong commitment to *measurement*.

OK   There are a number of good arguments for admitting this 'word' into semi-formal writing, if only because it is already there, and throwing it out would be tricky. Considering the obscurity of its birth and the competition from other established words, its survival and growth is surprising, and shows that it has something very special to offer. It can be a verb, an adjective or a complete sentence with a rich variety of applications. A word for all seasons, in fact.

There seems to be a good argument for writing it *OK* (rather than *O.K.* or *okay*). Mac prefers *okay* but admits *ok, OK, o.k.* and *O.K.*; ACOD prefers *OK* but admits *okay*; AWEG goes for *OK* and does not like *okay*.

For my money, *okay* has no merit unless it were shown that this was the original form, which seems very unlikely (though the 'Oll Korrect' story sounds very like a leg-pull). I go with AWEG.

oligo-   This prefix means *few*. For a long time it existed in only a few words, notably *oligarchy*, where it means rule by a privileged group in society, as opposed to a *monarchy* (rule by one person) and a *democracy* (rule by the people).

Oligarchy has recently been joined by *oligopoly*, a word defined by Mac as meaning a situation on the stock exchange when there are only a few sellers; but it has today a more important use as a near-monopoly, that is, a market dominated by very few suppliers, as in the case of the newspaper and television industries.

one   For the use of this word as an inclusive pronoun, see EACH… and SEXIST LANGUAGE. For its use as a euphemism for I, see IMPERSONAL.

ongoing   Why do we all accept *oncoming*, as in the *oncoming traffic*, and *incoming*, as in *incoming telephone calls*, but have difficulties with *ongoing*, as in *ongoing problems*, and *upcoming*, as in the *upcoming budget statement*?

One explanation is a general objection to new usage, particularly if it is believed to come from America. Another is that, as with *scenario*, it is not the words themselves but the company they keep. There is also a complex argument about the conventions for forming prefix-plus-verb combinations from compound verbs consisting of a verb plus a preposition-like adverb. These rules allow us to say that a telephone call which is *coming in* is an *incoming call*, but not that a person who is *getting in* is an *ingetting person*.

Whatever the reason, however, the words *ongoing* and *upcoming* are widely regarded as boorish, and should be avoided.

on to/onto   Fowler put the problem clearly: 'Writer and printers should make up their minds whether there is such a preposition as *onto* or not.'

The major arguments for it are that it is directly analogous to *into* (whose existence and legitimacy are not in question) and that it occurs in the writing of many competent practitioners.

The main argument against it is that, in many of the sentences in which it occurs, either *on* would be sufficient by itself or *on* and *to* make separate contributions and should thus be kept apart.

Those who wish to use it should take care not to do so when the words make separate contributions to the grammar or sense of the sentence, e.g. After the party, we went *on to* Nina's, ... and went *on to* have coffee.

or   The dangers with this word are logical, and arise because it is used to express three significantly different thoughts. For example, in the early days of flying between Melbourne and Sydney, passengers were asked 'Tea or coffee?' *twice*:

(1) The first time, the correct answer was 'Yes' (which got you the cup) or 'No'.

(2) The second time, the answer was 'Coffee' or 'Tea' (which got the cup filled).

(3) If you were then asked whether you wanted to visit the 'flight deck or cockpit' the answer was again *yes* or *no*, because no other choice was being offered: they were simply two terms for the same part of the aircraft.

We have here three totally different usages of the one word. Some languages have three separate words, one for each.

Confusion over the meaning of *or* is one of the most frequent causes of genuine and even dangerous ambiguity, and is particularly insidious as the writer may find it hard to imagine that there could be any confusion. The sensible writer will regard *or* as one of those risky words which must *always* be watched.

-or/-our   Is it an error to write 'honor'? Logic is entirely on the side of those who would standardise on *-or* forms. The existence and survival of *-our* forms is just bad luck.

The words are based on Latin roots which had no *u*. The *u* was inserted by the French, and the words entered English in this form. In French, they were for the most part modified into the form *-eur*, e.g. *honneur* (though toujours *amour*).

The *-our* forms survived in English until the eighteenth century. Then the *u* started to disappear, and successive dictionaries published during that century show more and more words with an *-or* spelling. The set was then frozen by the arrival of Sam Johnson's dictionary. However, the Americans then declared their independence, and Webster continued the cleaning up process on their side of the Atlantic.

Australian dictionaries offer both forms without expressing preference (though they generally have main entries under *-our*, with cross-reference under *-or*), and this is a fair reflection of the reality. The Melbourne *Age* is the flagship of the *-or* lobby, having used this form ever since its first issue in 1853. Thus, to call *-or* an Americanism is absurd. However, on a headcount today (particularly if book publishers are included) the *-our* fans would probably win.

However, if there is any change at all, it *must* be in the direction of *-or*. Not even the most enthusiastic *-our* supporter advocates reverting to *-our* in those cases where Johnson did not use it, e.g. *terrour, governour*, etc.

In the meantime, the spelling *Labor* is the only correct form in the context of the *Australian Labor Party*, this spelling having been adopted as their own declaration of independence in the campaign against conscription in the 1914–18 war.

For a discussion of the next stage in the argument , see -ER/-OR. For discussion of another intrusive *u*, see COUNCILLORS....

oral, aural   Considering the prodigious number of possible combinations of letters available to us, it is astonishing that we have so similar a pair for two words which have to be carefully distinguished. *Oral* means 'of the mouth' and *aural* means 'of the ears'. Thus an *aural–oral test* is one in which the subject *hears* the stimulus and *speaks* the response.

We cannot change the language. What we can do is to avoid using these words whenever the choice is up to us, using instead *listening* and *speaking* (or similar precise, clear terms); and, if we have to use the words *aural* and *oral* in a spoken discourse, to warn the audience to watch out for the potential confusion, and pronounce the words in an exaggerated way if there is the slightest fear of misunderstanding.

organic   In the language of nutrition, an *organic vegetable* is one which is grown without the use of artificial fertilisers or chemical pesticides, etc. This usage is slightly strange, since all vegetables are by definition organic, as are almost all fertilisers and pesticides. But when we see a sign saying 'For sale: organic horse poo', we feel we must be getting something really special.

organic chemistry   For the general rules applying to the naming of substances, see CHEMICAL NOMENCLATURE. The present article is about the problems which are peculiar to organic chemistry, and which are liable to reflect in non-technical writing.

(1) Organic chemistry used to be, as the word *organic* implies, *the chemistry of living matter*, but today it is generally defined as *the chemistry of carbon*. The two definitions are effectively very similar, but the latter stresses the inclusion of man-made carbon-based molecules, e.g. the synthetic fibres and resins which are so much a part of our world.

(2) More than half the known substances on Earth are carbon compounds, thanks to the carbon atoms' capacity to bond to one another and to other atoms. To sort these compounds out, sundry systems have been introduced over the years, all of them aiming to develop names which reflect the structures, i.e. if you know the name of the molecule you know its structure, and vice versa. One such system, devised by IUPAC (the International Union of Pure and Applied Chemistry), has been adopted for use by schools and (with rather less success) universities.

In most cases, the rule given in CHEMICAL NOMENCLATURE holds: use the systematic name whenever the context concerns the chemical composition, and the popular name if the context concerns the effect or use of the substance. Thus the solvent and anaesthetic *chloroform* becomes *trichloromethane* if we are using it as a reagent.

(3) Organic chemistry has contributed a disproportionate share of the latest crop of technical terms which have strayed from science into the common language:

(a) *Poly-* (= many). One characteristic of some organic molecules is that they can link together to form *polymers*: chains of indefinite length. These give synthetic fibres and resins their great strength. This process is called *polymerisation*, and the polymers take their name from the component molecules plus the prefix *poly-*. Polymers whose names have entered common language include *polyester, polystyrene, polyvinyl chloride (PVC)* and *polythene*.

(b) *Saturated/(mono-/poly-)unsaturated*. These words, popularised by the nutritionists, are not in fact about nutrition, but about the state of the bonds between the carbon atoms in chain molecules. The bonds can be single, double or triple. A *saturated* molecule is one in which every bond is single, *mono-unsaturated* indicates one multiple bond and *poly-unsaturated* indicates more than one multiple bond. The nutritional significance of the distinction is not as simple as the advertisements suggest, but it is good to see such long words in the supermarket.

(c) *CFCs* (*chloro-fluoro-carbons*). Had this book been written in the 1970s, the idea that this term would ever be in the common language would have seemed highly improbable. Many of them were widely used as refrigerants and as propellants in pressure pack sprays, and they were seen as miracles of harmlessness, being neither toxic nor inflammable. They are now recognised as a source of damage to the so-called ozone layer, a region of the upper atmosphere where ozone (O_3) absorbs gamma radiation arriving from space.

orient The word *orient* started life rather over 2000 years ago meaning 'rising', and was applied especially to the rising sun; hence it came to mean the east, and this led to the adjective, *oriental*. Its exact antonym, 'the setting', is *occident*, which is occasionally used to mean *west*, and form the adjective *occidental*.

We should object just as much to being told we are 'in the orient' as we object to being told that we are 'in the Far East', when we know we are plumb in the middle. (See ANTIPODES and MENTAL MAPS.)

The early Christian churches were all supposed to be aligned to face the east, which was known as being 'easted' or *oriented*. Hence the word came to mean 'to line up a church in the easterly direction'. Then the connection with *east* disappeared, as it did with its opposite, *disoriented*. Today, we can 'orient' ourselves in any direction, the direction being our *orientation*, which in turn has given us the quite unnecessary verb *to orientate*, which means the same as *to orient*.

The latest episode in the saga is the sport of *orienteering*, in which contestants race across rugged and trackless country with the help of a compass. ACOD tells us that the word is Swedish, which seems highly improbable, but maybe the Swedes were the last people to manhandle it.

orphans Many of our words have been separated from their parents. This is an innocent enough process. Words change their meanings all the time, and it would be very foolish to attempt to stop this process. For example, the words *doyen* and *dean* are etymologically identical, but today, though they rub shoulders in the world of diplomacy, they have distinct meanings , and it would be absurd as well as futile to assert that they 'really' mean the same.

However, many etymological points are widely, if not always consciously, understood. Most of us recognise, for example, that a *two-wheeler bicycle* is a tautology, and that a *three-wheeler bicycle* is a contradiction in terms. One day, perhaps, the significance of the prefix *bi-* may be lost, in which case it will be not only acceptable but necessary to specify the number of wheels. Today, however, most educated people understand that a bicycle has *by definition* two wheels.

Between *doyen* and *bicycle* lie thousands of words whose etymological significance is in the process of disappearing, and purists
have to decide at what point their argument changes from precision
to boring pedanticism. *Sauce* is rarely made in *saucepans* and never
served in *saucers*, and our *larders* contain a lot more than *lard*. Is there
anything wrong with having a *Mardi Gras* on a Thursday or an
Oktoberfest in April? If so, why do we allow a *journal* to appear
weekly (and a *weekly* to appear monthly)? If we say that *decimate*
must mean 'kill every tenth person', do we insist that December is
the tenth month? And, if we do, will we also say that atheists should
not take *holy-days*, that *spinsters* should spin, and that a *highway*
cannot run through a tunnel?

It is all very well for us to jump up and down about somebody
committing breaches of etymological purity, but by definition this
means that we have the information required to identify the error.
Yet none of us is fluent in all the languages from which English has
drawn words. There is no comment in this book (or *Modern English
Usage*, for that matter, or *Right Words*) on any etymological mistake
in our use of Hindi or Urdu words, or in fact of words from any
language except the few western European and classical Mediterranean ones which we regard as part of the essential intellectual
corpus. Yet the chances that all the Hindi and Urdu words entered
our language with their etymological purity intact are very small.

So much for the problem. For a general discussion of the answer,
see CORRECTNESS.

outsize(d)   This technical term of the rag trade, coined in the 1880s,
was an instant popular success, being applied immediately to
chicken coops and steam engines. It was originally a noun (meaning
'a size outside the normal range') but rapidly became an adjective.
It does not need a final *d*, as it is neither the past participle of a verb
nor a member of a small class of adjectives derived from nouns, e.g.
one-legged, where the *-ed* suffix implies *equipped with....*

overlook, oversee, overview   The various senses of these words rarely
cause trouble for native speakers of our language, but are a mine-
field for those who are not, a point which those writing for second-
language readers should bear in mind.

The biggest problem is that *oversight*, which should logically be
what *overseers* do, generally means what overlookers do: *Your
account remained unpaid through departmental oversight.* But it then
returns occasionally to its more logical meaning: *The minister has
oversight of all departmental decisions.* At least, I presume that this
means that he oversees them. Perhaps the ambiguity is deliberate.

For a similar problem arising from the two meanings of *overlook*,
see AMBIGUITY (2).

owing to   See PREPOSITIONAL PHRASE.

oxymoron   This is a figure of speech, in which two words or phrases which would normally have contradictory connotations are put together for special effect:

Let us *agree to differ* (a *harmonious discord*).

There was a *deafening silence*.

A cliché, which is by definition a familiar expression, can sometimes be turned into a form of oxymoron by making an unexpected change within it:

He suffers from *delusions of competence* (cliché into oxymoron).

But it more frequently happens that oxymorons become clichés:

Fred was *conspicuous by his absence* (oxymoron into cliché).

For discussion of the possibility that *garbologist* is a one-word oxymoron, see MALFORMATIONS.

P

paddock   In Britain, *paddock* refers to a small enclosure for horses, situated conveniently close to the house so that the horses are available for riding at short notice. In Australia, it retains something of the British sense at horse racetracks, where it is an area set aside for saddling and unsaddling horses, but in common language it is the generic term for any enclosed piece of ground, particularly on a pastoral property, and it can thus be very large.

Conversely, *field*, which is the generic term in Britain, is applied less widely in Australia, its implication being a relatively small fenced area used for some specific purpose, particularly agricultural rather than pastoral. The British *playing field* is a *sports ground*.

pair   *A pair of* can be singular or plural, depending on our perception.

Joined pairs are always singular: *scissors, pants, spectacles*. Thus we say *A pair of pliers is missing*, although the pronoun might be either singular or plural: *It is on the table* or *They are on the table* (meaning 'the pliers are on the table').

We also use a singular verb with matching pairs: thus we say 'A pair of gloves *was* found under the chair', and we even say 'a pair of jacks *beats* a pair of threes', though plural verbs would be less shocking in such sentences.

As we move into non-matching pairs, however, the demand for a plural verb becomes more pressing. In 'The happy pair *were* farewelled by the bridesmaids' the plural verb is more common than the singular, and ad hoc pairings, like *a pair of prison escapees*, are always plural: 'The pair *were* seen scaling the wall...'. In both cases, the pronoun has to be *they*.

For a false pair, see FORCEPS. For other singular/plural questions, see SINGULARITIES.

pants   Australian males follow the Americans in wearing their pants *over* their *underpants*, not *under* their *trousers*, as the British do.

Knickers (short for knickerbockers) is another word on which there is divergence. The term originated in New York, where it was associated with the New York Dutch community, and in particular their baggy breeches. *Knickerbockers* became highly fashionable in the 1920s, and in America the short form, *knickers*, remains associated with male outer garments, though the actual garments retired to golf courses and are now seen only in old movies. The same fashion was known in Australia and Britain, however, as *plus-fours*. This left *knickers* free to become a wholesome word for what are coyly called *undies* when hanging out on lines, and *panties* or *briefs* in our department stores.

paper Choice of *stock* (= paper) for books is a highly technical business, depending not only on the desired style, weight, bulk, colour
and opacity, but also on the process, the nature of the image and the
type of inks to be used. The following notes are designed to help
writers to ask sensible questions and to understand the answers.

(1) Paper types Papers used in books are of four types:

(a) *Arts* (art papers) are made with clay as a filler to give them a
smooth finish. This makes them particularly suitable for reproduction of photographs.

Gloss arts are heavily *calendared* (rolled) with very hot roll-
ers, which vitrify the clay to produce, in effect, a porcelain
finish. They give spectacular results with colour printing, their
main disadvantage being *flare*, the pools of reflected light on the
pages which make reading difficult. They are thus ideal for
books which are essentially looked at rather than read.

Matt arts lack the vitreous finish, and provide a compromise
of good photographic reproduction and absence of flare.

One-sided (1/s) arts have the gloss finish on one side only,
and are particularly useful for book jackets.

(b) *Coateds* are newsprints which are spray-coated with a clear
enamel to give them a glossy finish. They are used mainly for
cheap illustrated magazines, but are occasionally used for books
where the need is for bright colour at low cost.

(c) *Printings* are the normal book papers like the one on which this
book is likely to be printed. They vary immensely; see (3) below.

(d) *Newsprints* are used for newspapers and cheap paperback books.

(2) Specification Stock is specified by name and weight, e.g. '85
gsm Bookprint Matt', where *gsm* stands for grams per square metre.

(3) Choice The key points are colour, finish, bulk and opacity.

(a) *Colour.* The key classes are the ultra-whites, the whites and the
creams. Alongside a white, an ultra-white will look slightly
bluish. Ultra-whites are best for colour work, but are hard on the
eye for text.

(b) *Finish.* The words *wood* and *weave* are all about smoothness,
wood being random fluff and *weave* being a deliberate texture.
Absence of wood is generally a good thing, but weave is what
gives many papers their character.

(c) *Bulk* means thickness, and depends on the weight and style. A
typical paper will have a calliper (= thickness) of 100 µm (widely
known in the trade as *ums*; see MICROMETRE...), i.e. 10 sheets to
the millimetre, so a 200-page (= 100-sheet) book will have a
calliper of one centimetre. However, the weight which gives
this bulk varies: around 65 gsm for newsprints, 80 gsm for
printings and 100 gsm for arts.

(d) *Opacity* is of great importance if the material includes drawings
or photographs with a heavy black image. It is less important

when the book is simply text backing text, as the *show-through* is less disturbing. In general, arts have greater opacity than printings of similar weight, thanks to their clay content. Among printings, the most opaque are those which have the highest bulk/weight ratio, e.g. the high-bulk or *featherweight* classes.

For a book of straight text, I go for a stock with plenty of weave and a dash of cream, high bulk if the book is less than 200 pages, and good opacity.

(4) Paper sizes Old terms which survive in a some contexts include *folio, quarto, octavo* and *sedecimo*, which indicated that the sheet had been folded to produce respectively two, four, eight or sixteen leaves. The various sizes of sheet were given names, some of which survive: demy (say /*d'my*/), crown, royal, medium and foolscap. Together, these words indicate the trimmed size of the finished book: thus *demy octavo* is 213 × 137 mm.

(Confusingly, the word *folios* is also used by printers and publishers to mean *page numbers*, e.g. *The folios in this book are centred at the head of the page*.)

In the international paper sizes, e.g. A3, A4, B4, B5, the number indicates the number of times the A or B sheet is cut or folded in half to produce the size in question. The B sheet is slightly larger, so that the sequence of key sizes is: A4 – 297 × 210 mm; B5 – 250 × 176 mm; A5 – 210 × 148 mm. The sizes are chosen so that the proportionality between depth and width remains the same when the sheet is cut in half (i.e. depth = width × √2), which is very logical, but results in shapes which are not altogether satisfactory for books. Hence the old sizes survive.

The standard sizes for mass market paperbacks, called *A format* and *B format*, have nothing to do with the international A and B sheets. *A format* is 181 × 111 mm; *B format* is 198 × 129 mm

para- This old Greek prefix originally meant *alongside*, as in *parallel* (= alongside one another) or *against*, as in *paradox* (= against received opinion). It was for centuries little used for new coinage, though the French had the latter sense in mind when they coined *parachute* (= against a fall) on the analogy of the earlier coinages, *parapluie* (= against the rain) and *parasol* (= against the sun).

(1) Recently, the *alongside* sense was revived in the term *para-military*. There was a clear need for such a prefix, and it was immensely successful. We now also have *para-medics*: people in our hospitals who do a defined professional job *alongside* the medical staff – occupational therapists, ambulance crews, etc.

(2) Meanwhile, however, the *against* sense of the prefix *para-* was revived in the term *para-normal*, which covers phenomena which defy explanation in 'normal' scientific terms. This use is understood in the term *para-psychology*. A *para-psychologist* is therefore not (as sense (1) would suggest) a person working alongside a

psychologist, but a psychologist whose interest is in paranormal phenomena.

Given this ambiguity, new *para-* words should be coined with care.

paragraph There are two purposes for paragraphs, the one logical and the other practical. The logical purpose is to signal stages in a narrative or argument. The practical one is to relieve the forbidding gloom of a solid page of text.

The word was originally applied to neither of these things, being a mark in the margin, and was used particularly in playscripts to indicate a change in speaker. Curiously, early texts did not specify who the new speaker was, leaving this to the wit of the actors.

In modern prose, a paragraph generally represents a new thought. It will therefore open with a clear clue to its content; an important statement made in the middle of a paragraph with a trivial opening can be missed even by quite careful readers. For the same reason, a new paragraph should not have pronouns standing for words or names in the previous paragraph unless the reference is absolutely self-evident.

The visual purpose of a paragraph requires that a break should appear every 6-10 lines, so the length of a paragraph will in practice be determined by the width of the column of text. In newspapers, each sentence may make a fresh paragraph. At the other end of the scale, an academic book can get away with one paragraph break per page, but no book ever lost its flavour by presenting itself in bite-sized chunks.

For a discussion of practical aspects of paragraphing in books, see TYPOGRAPHY (4).

parentheses *Parentheses* are marks which show that a word or sentence is an aside, independent of the grammatical structure of the sentence in which it appears. The word *parentheses* is sometimes taken to refer only to brackets. It does not. It covers a variety of devices, all of which perform the same task, of which the most common is probably brackets, but with dashes and commas as alternatives. (See PUNCTUATION (9).)

For the conventional distinction between round brackets (), square brackets [] and chevrons ⟨⟩, see QUOTATIONS (1). Braces {} are used in mathematics to indicate sets.

Parenthetic(al) is a literary technical term for 'in parentheses' which has strayed into common usage, a *parenthetical remark* being one which, if written, would be in parentheses. A *passing remark* is a better phrase meaning much the same.

The Latin tag *obiter dictum* (= something said on the way) is another near-synonym, but thanks to its use in legal language to mean *an opinion given by a judge which is not relevant to the case being tried, and as a result not binding,* it is sometimes taken to mean the exact opposite: 'a succinct definitive statement'. The phrase is best left to the lawyers.

parse   This word means *to identify the grammatical status of the words in a sentence*. An example of parsing is given under PARTS OF SPEECH.

participle   For a discussion of the present participle, see -ING FORMS.

The past participle presents fewer perils, but has some points of interest. Let us first define what we are talking about. The past participle is the form of the verb shown in italics in the following patterns:

	Past perfect active	Past perfect passive	Verb adjective
Transitive	I have *locked* the car	The car has been *locked*	A *locked* car
Intransitive	I have *fallen* from grace		A *fallen* angel

The normal indicator of a past participle is the suffix *-d*, *-ed* or *-t*, as in *heard, passed* and *spelt*. Other indicators are *-n* or *-en* as in *known, forgotten*, and a variety of 'strong' forms such as *bought, struck*.

(1) Meaning   The table above illustrates the point that, when used as adjectives, the past participles of transitive verbs have passive meanings (*a locked car* means *a car which has* been *locked*) while past participles of intransitive verbs are active (*a fallen angel* is *an angel who has fallen* all on his own). If a verb can be both transitive and intransitive, the past participle can be either active or passive (e.g. *a changed situation* can be one that *has changed* or one that *has been changed*).

Some verbs have more than one past participle (see (2)), and usage may assign them different meanings. For example, *strike* has both *struck* and *stricken*, but we are normally *struck* by lightning, thoughts and blunt instruments, but *stricken* with doubts, disease and pangs of conscience.

The classic illustration of split connotation used to be *hanged/hung*, but things may be changing. So few people have been *hanged* lately in Australia that the word has virtually passed from the vocabulary. As a result, when the present generation uses it, they use the only past form they know, i.e. *hung*.

Stringed/strung takes this process a bit further. Once upon a time, we might have said 'I have stringed the lyre', but *stringed* is only used as an adjective meaning 'equipped with strings', as in *stringed instruments*, and in all other contexts the word is *strung*.

(2) Forms   There are three basic classes, *weak* forms ending in (a) *-ed* or some variation thereof and (b) *-en* or some variation, and (c) *strong* forms, which involve a vowel change, e.g. *slide → slid*.

(a) Weak forms with *-ed* and variants: *-d/-t*

The only real problem here is to decide between *-ed* and *-t* forms when you know that both of them exist, as with *spelled/spelt* and *learned/learnt.* The short answer is that if the pronunciation gives a clear direction, follow it; if not, use *-ed*.

This answer arises from considering how the question arose. The *-ed* endings were originally sounded as separate syllables, e.g. *pass-ed, bath-ed,* as still happens with *part-ed* and many others. By Shakespeare's time, it had become common to swallow the last syllable, and writers showed that a syllable was to be swallowed either by replacing the *e* with an apostrophe (*learn'd*) or by replacing the *-ed* with a *-t* (*learnt*), the choice depending on their perception of the sound. This was particularly important in poetry, where the metre might depend on the right syllables being swallowed.

By the end of the eighteenth century, the *-ed* was always swallowed unless it came after a *t* or *d* (*batted, padded*). At this point, the spelling parted company with the pronunciation, the ending being generally written *-ed* irrespective of pronunciation. The only exceptions were one or two which had established themselves very strongly, some (e.g. *heard*) as the only forms, others (e.g. *past* and *spilt*) as variants.

In the case of *past/passed,* the two spellings acquired separate bundles of meanings. In most cases, however, they are simply spelling variants: if there is a distinction in meaning between *spelt* and *spelled, spilt* and *spilled* or *learnt* and *learned,* etc., it is not one which readers could be relied on to recognise.

This meant that, for example, *learned* was assumed to represent a single syllable. If they wanted it to make two syllables, they added an accent, making *learnéd.* Today, we do not even bother about the accent on *learnéd,* leaving it up to the reader to select the right pronunciation. (For a comment on this sort of 'reform' see SIMPLIC- ITY.) Other examples include *raggéd, crookéd* and *blesséd.*

Our *-t* spellings are thus survivors of a phonetics-driven variation, designed to give readers a clue to the sounds which the writers had in mind. If we are in doubt about the spelling, we should decide what sound we have in mind. If this does not help, the *-ed* is preferred, because although the *-t* sound is often represented *-ed,* the *-ed* sound is never represented *-t.*

Very young children clearly perceive *-ed* as the dominant past suffix, producing forms like *He's eated my chocolate,* or even adding the suffix to a strong past form, as in *I've begunned my breakfast.*

(b) Forms with *-en* and *-n*

These are a small set of very common words. Most of them go right back to Anglo-Saxon, and are relics of a common Germanic form, e.g. *given, driven, taken, been, grown, sown.*

The only problems are with occasional alternative forms: in the case of *striven* versus *strived, strived* is better, as *striven* is an interloper, remodelled on the analogy of *drive* and *give.* In the case of *sewn* and *sewed, sewed* seems to be preferred for forming verbs and *sewn* for adjectives: *I have sewed … a sewn garment. Proven*, though described as 'US, scientific and literary' in ACOD, is similar: *He has proved a liar … a proven liar*. There is no good reason for these distinctions, but it does not seem worth fighting about.

There is also a small matter of pronunciation. Many Australian speakers make *known, sewn*, etc., into two-syllable words, rhyming with *Rowan*. These are pronunciations with the best possible antecedents, going well back into Anglo-Saxon, though they probably reached Australia via Ireland. However, they light up the station switchboards when they are heard on the radio, so they are probably best avoided.

(c) 'Strong' forms

These are typically forms in which the consonant shell of the verb remains unchanged but the vowels change inside it: *hang, hung; sing, sung; hold, held; begin, begun*. The pattern here is slightly different from the pattern of the *-ed* forms. The first line of the table below shows that, in the case of the *-ed* verbs, the forms of the past participle are the same whether used in the formation of past tenses or verb-adjectives, and are also the same as the past tense of the verb. In the case of *to sink*, all three are different:

	Past tense	———— *Past participle* ————	
		in past perfect verbs	as adjective
ed forms	*I painted the boat*	*I have painted the boat*	*a painted boat*
sink	*I sank the boat*	*I have sunk the boat*	*a sunken boat*

This may be the source of the most common problem: we often hear *I sunk the boat*, and may assume that the error is in the form of the past tense (i.e. the 'correct' form is *I sank the boat*). However, what we are more likely to be hearing is an elided form of the past perfect: *I('ve) sunk the boat*.

The verb *to get* commonly makes *got* in Britain and in written Australian, and *gotten* in America and in some spoken Australian. This only illustrates the waywardness of fashion: *gotten* was marked 'obsolete' in the 1864 edition of Webster; yet it survives. Furthermore, there may be separate meanings: *have you got a ticket?* implies possession; *have you gotten a ticket?* implies acquisition.

In the case of *forget* fashion has gone the other way, the *forgot* being the loser (*Should auld acquaintance be forgot…?*) and *forgotten* the current favourite, in all senses. The old strong form *gat* survives only in the biblical *begat*.

(3) Usage *Possessed of an unusual intelligence, Fred was born in Koowee-rup*. There is nothing wrong with the grammar of this sentence, but the excessive use of this construction should be avoided. Adjectival phrases and clauses normally follow the nouns on which they lean, and the inversion makes extra work for the readers. The construction is particularly tedious if, as in the present case, the phrase has no real relevance to the topic of the main sentence.

When the weatherperson says *There will be a lot of cloud. Having said this, the sun will break through in the afternoon* we have a construction which is generally regarded as wrong, since it suggests that the sun will speak first and then break through. This is called an *unrelated* or *hanging participle*. It is very easy to make this mistake, partly because it is so closely related to the *absolute construction* (see ABSOLUTE (4)), as in *This said, the sun will break through*, which is regarded as all right on the grounds that, since the participle is passive, there is no missing antecedent.

Use of the hanging participle is a very minor crime. The difference between a hanging participle and the absolute construction is not clear-cut in English. Both give the reader a bumpy ride, but it is the inversion which causes the bumps.

particle   *Particle* is a grammatical term for a class of word which does not exist in English. However, when somebody says *You like it, eh?*, the word *eh* is doing a similar job. The workings of the sentence could be explained by saying that *You like it* is a statement of fact, but it is turned into a question by the addition of the question-indicating particle *eh*.

In short, particles are very small words which have no identifiable meaning, but indicate the grammatical status of the words, phrases or sentences to which they are attached.

parts of speech   Formal grammar recognises eight *parts of speech*: adjectives, adverbs, nouns, pronouns, verbs, prepositions, conjunctions and interjections. These are discussed briefly under GRAMMAR (3), and then in more detail in separate entries on each. The present entry discusses the problems of the formal approach.

Formal grammar was based on a very precise description of an inflected language, Latin, and Latin got it from another inflected language, ancient Greek. Every word in these languages can be very precisely *parsed*, i.e. categorised under one of the eight headings, with a full description of number, gender, tense and so on, as appropriate. There are a few cases where the same string of letters can have minor ambiguity, e.g. two cases of a noun or adjective may have the same form, but the majority of words are unique. In the first line of Virgil's *Aeneid*, we can name them:

Arma	*virum-que*	*cano*	*Troiae*	*qui*	*primus*	*ab*	*oris*
noun,	noun,	verb,	noun,	relative	adjective,	pre-	noun,
plural,	singular,	singular,	singular,	pronoun,	singular,	pos-	plural,
objective	objective	1st person,	genitive	singular,	subjective	ition	ablative
case,	case, mas-	present	case,	subjective	case,		case,
neuter	culine, with	tense,	feminine	case,	masculine		feminine
	attached	indicative,		masculine			
	conjunction	active					
arms	*man-and*	*I sing*	*of Troy*	*who*	*first*	*from*	*shores*

i.e. *I sing of arms, and the man who first from the shores of Troy....*

In the Latin, almost all the information given above would be available even if the words were taken out of context: *number, case* and *gender* for nouns and adjectives, *number, person, tense, mood* and *voice* for verbs. In the English, the only words which could be parsed on their own are *I* (pronoun, singular, first person), *and* (conjunction) and *of* (preposition). In all other cases, we can parse them only because their position in the sentence gives a clue to the meaning, and the meaning gives a clue to the part of speech they represent.

In Latin, the word order was nearly irrelevant to sense and could thus be used for special effect. Even the preposition, which (as its name implies) was supposed to come before its noun, was transposed in Ausonius' glorious one-liner:

Prima <u>urbes inter</u>, divûm domus, aurea Roma.

First among cities, home of the gods, golden Rome.

Just as a plant can be eaten without anyone knowing the difference between a sepal and a petal, so people can talk without knowing a noun from an adjective. It was only when the enthusiasm for analysis and naming of parts arose, hitting biology and language almost simultaneously, that the parts were identified and named; and, just as the first ancient biologists looked at the life forms they knew, and not at platypuses, cacti and blue-green algae, so the parts of speech were identified in the languages they knew best, Greek and (later) Latin, which were sufficiently similar for the same approach to work.

This ancient analysis gave us the parts of speech of what we call formal grammar. They are not natural or inevitable classifications. They are no more than a way of looking at language. If we were inventing one based on an objective examination of English, it would have to be based on word order, not the form of the word. However, we are not. The parsing-and-analysis approach used in formal grammar, together with its terms, have become established, and it is more sensible to make the best of it than to try to wipe the slate clean and start again.

However, if the explanations of formal grammar sometimes seem far-fetched or artificial, it is not surprising.

passive (grammar)   See VERB (2(c)).

pedant, purist   Both of these words mean *a person who comments on linguistic niceties which others find boring*. The difference is that you are a pedant, whereas I am a purist. This is because my standards arise from my direct understanding of the eternal truths, whereas yours stem from memory of some fusty old schoolmarm who taught you parsing. Compare BOURGEOIS.

pejorative   A term is *pejorative* when it has or acquires nasty connotations. Some words are born pejorative: *evil* is a pejorative version of the neutral *bad* when it comes to morals. Other words achieve pejorativeness: see SAVAGE for the way in which any word we apply to the unknown seems to go this way. And some have pejorativeness thrust upon them (see the comment on *appeasement* under CONNOTATION…). For discussion of some further terms and the problems arising from them, see EMOTIVE LANGUAGE, ETHNIC and PREJUDICE.

per capita   Those who have a smattering of Latin are worried by the phrase *per capita income*, since *per capita* clearly means *per heads*, not *per head*, and hence implies that your income depends on the number of heads you have.

The argument has some merit. The phrase had its origins in a procedure for dividing an inheritance. If the deceased had two children, who in turn had one and two children respectively, the estate might be divided *per stirpes* (half to each of the two *stirpes*, or families) or *per capita* (five parts, two going to the family with two *capita* and three to the one with three).

This information is not given with the idea that we should change our usage of *per capita*, which is generally understood, but to settle the dispute which presumably caused the reader to look this entry up, since there is no other reason to be concerned with the matter.

RW suggests that we should not use the phrase at all, but that instead we should say *a head* (and likewise *a year* instead of *per year*, etc.). It is sensible to stop using *capita*, but it would be sad to lose *per*, which adds precision to many otherwise ambiguous phrases.

percentages   Percentages can be a menace to writers, both in their writing and in real life. At the simplest level, it puzzles some people that, if I have *twenty* per cent *less* money than you have, you have *twenty-five* per cent *more* money than I have. However, it is really quite simple:

You	Me	Comparison		
$100	$80	I have $80,	which is $20 less than $100,	20% less
$100	$80	You have $100,	which is $20 more than $80,	25% more

This illustrates a very simple trick which can be used by salesmen and governments to deceive the public, known as *the concealed base*.

Thus, for example, when the government talks of bounties, and says that a bounty will be 25%, you might think that goods currently costing $100 will cost 25% less, i.e. $75. This is wishful thinking. The government means that the goods will cost $80, but that a bounty of *25% of this new price*, i.e. $20.00, will be paid to the supplier to make good the difference.

Similarly, if you hear that a $100 item is available at a special discount of 50%, and with a further 10% discount for cash, you might expect a total discount of 60%. However, the discount for cash will be based on the *new* cash price, i.e. 10% of $50, so the total discount is 55%.

Some publishing and printing contracts contain clauses stating
that authors' corrections over 5% will be charged as extras. But is it
5% of the *characters*, or 5% of the *words*, or 5% of the *lines*? In fact, it
is probably none of these things, but 5% of the *cost*. Since correcting
an error, however simple, can cost as much as setting a paragraph,
the five per cent allowance covers roughly one author's correction
every two pages, say 1% of the lines, 0.1% of the words, or 0.02% of
the characters.

Honest writers and talkers are scrupulously careful to make the
basis of calculation clear whenever they quote percentages, and
wise readers and listeners will check that the base is clear whenever
percentages are quoted at them.

perfect   For a discussion of whether something can be *more perfect
than perfect*, see COMPARATIVE CHAOS (1). For *perfect* in grammar, see
VERB (2(b)).

Perfect binding is the optimistic name given to the way in which
cheap books are bound, which involves cutting the spines from the
printed sections so that all the pages are separate, and then embed-
ding them in a quick-drying glue which bonds them to one another
and to the cover. Burst binding is similar, but involves puncturing
the spines rather than cutting them off. Alternatives include *sewn
binding, stapling, spiral (wire) binding* and *comb binding. Stitching* is
likely to mean *stapling*, not sewing.

period   See PUNCTUATION (3), where it is called a *full stop*.

periphrasis, circumlocution   See MODAL AUXILIARIES.

per pro/p.p.   People who sign other people's letters for them use this
little formula to show that they have done so. The question is: if a
letter is signed *Tom p.p. Harry*, who did what?

The phrase means *per procurationem* (= through the agency [of])
and *Tom p.p. Harry* can only mean that Tom composed the letter and
Harry signed it for him. However, many business firms tell their
staff to do it the other way round, a usage supported by *The
Macquarie Office Manual*, which asserts that the phrase means 'on
behalf of'. It doesn't (or, at least, it didn't).

person   In grammar, the 1st person is *I* or *we*, the 2nd person is *you*,
and the 3rd person is *he, she, it* or *they*. See VERB (2(a)) and PRONOUN
(2).

personally   It is not that we should never say 'Personally, I...', but we
should not use it simply to add emphasis. Why? Because this spoils
it for its important use as a separate entity: 'As a loyal party member
I will vote against this bill, although *personally* I do not object to it'.

phenotype, phenomenon, phenomena   *Phenotype* preserves the original sense of *pheno-*, which is all about *appearances* as opposed to

realities: a *phenotype* is a term for the observable features of an organism, as opposed to *genotype*, its genetic constitution.

A *phenomenon* was originally a mysterious manifestation, like an optical illusion, the antonym of a *reality*, but as more *phenomena* (plural), e.g. thunder and lightning, were explained by science, it came to mean any sort of manifestation, mysterious or not.

Phenomenal went in the other direction, moving from 'apparent' as opposed to 'real' into 'remarkable' as opposed to 'normal'.

philistine   'One looked down upon as lacking in culture, aesthetic refinement, etc.' So says Mac, not mentioning (and why should it?) that this may be a gross libel on a gifted people.

It is applied more specifically within the world of art, where people promoting new art may describe as *philistine* the views of others, however sophisticated, who do not share their tastes.

Although the word is intended as highly derogatory, the contexts in which it is used ensure that nobody feels insulted by it. We all know what we like, and have plenty of pejoratives to sling back: *highbrow, egghead, arty-farty*, and (most damning of all) *academic*.

phrase   A phrase is a group of words which can be treated as a single grammatical unit. In the following example, the *single words* in the first line are the exact grammatical equivalents of *the phrases* in the second:

ADJECTIVE		NOUN	VERB	ADVERB
The	*great*	*event*	*happened*	*yesterday*
The	*never-to-be-forgotten*	*Christmas party*	*took place*	*on Friday*

The phrases in the second line can, of course, be further analysed, but if the intention is to show the main structure of the sentence, splitting it into phrases is often more helpful than a word-by-word analysis.

The essential difference between *phrases* and *clauses* is that phrases do not contain (though they can *be*) finite verbs. (At least, that is my preference: for a rival definition, see CLAUSE (2).)

The phrase *on Friday last* is clearly being used as an adverb, and hence is an adverbial phrase; but the same string of words could also be an adjectival phrase: *the dance* on Friday last *was a great success*. In both cases they tend to *follow* the words they apply to. This is normal for adverbs, but adjectives in English generally come first:

	ADJECTIVE	NOUN	ADJECTIVAL PHRASE
I saw a	*disabled*	*man*	
I saw a		*man*	*with a wooden leg*

In the sentence:

The echidna is a larger, *though less delicious*, animal

the phrase *though less delicious* is clearly being used as an adjective, but is generally explained as a truncated concessional clause, from which some verb has dropped out. This is far-fetched and unnecessary. If *though* is replaced by *and* or *but*, we would not be looking for a missing verb. If we want a description which is more precise than *adjectival phrase*, we might call it a *concessional phrase*; the only problem then being that traditional formal grammar has no such category, possibly because it was not recognised (though it existed) in Latin.

physic(s/al/ian/ist), physio-   The words all come from the Greek *physis* (= nature), but have split into two families. The one family concerns itself with medicine (the obsolete term *physic* and the surviving *physician*, *physiology* and *physiotherapy*). The other family concerns itself with natural science (*physics*, *physicist*). The two families overlap in the word *physical*.

Pidgin   The term arose from the term *Business English* applied to an English–Chinese lingua franca, the word *pidgin* representing an alleged Chinese pronunciation of *business*. Its importance to us today is that it flourishes in New Guinea and the former British-administered territories in Melanesia, where its correct name is *Tok Pisin* or *Pidgin*, not *Pidgin English*. Being a language, it has a capital letter.

There was an evident need for a lingua franca in New Guinea, a region with no common language, and Pidgin emerged as the successful contender. It consists essentially of a large number of nouns and a very limited number of high-frequency, multi-purpose verbs, adjectives and prepositions. For example, a key preposition is *bilong*, which means 'of or related to' and can be used to turn nouns into adjectives as well as supplying possessives.

All this results in a language which is highly personal. A new idea is expressed not by coining a word but by coining a phrase; different speakers will coin different phrases, their forms reflecting the speakers' differing ways of thinking. However, the component words are understood by all, so the phrases compete for survival, and only the fittest survive.

This is the basis of its outstanding success. English may be the language of arts and letters and *Police Motu* a rival lingua franca with fairly wide currency, but Tok Pisin is the most widely-used of the three for daily business, the Courts and Parliament. It is as near to being universally understood as any language is ever likely to be in a region so divided by race, creed, aspiration and geography.

A number of Tok Pisin words strayed into the English of resident expatriates and hence into Australian English. Of these, the most widely recognised is *kai-kai* (= food), related to the Chinese *cai*.

pidgin, dialect, creole   It is important not to confuse a *pidgin*, a contrived language which is (initially, at least) nobody's first language, with two other classes of variant, a *dialect* and a *creole*. These last are the products of evolution, and are the first languages of those who speak them.

A *pidgin* is a language of communication, typically between European traders and their non-European customers. It draws words and structures from the languages of both parties, but is not a dialect of either, and is not easily understandable by speakers of either source language unless its conventions have been learnt. However, these conventions are few and simple, so that learners can make very rapid progress. See PIDGIN (above).

A *dialect* is a regional or social variety of a language. Its form may reflect the influence of more than one language, but it draws overwhelmingly from a single language, and is largely comprehensible to other speakers of that language. With time, extreme dialects may become incomprehensible to one another, even while both remain in touch with the standard form. Ultimately they lose touch even with the standard form, and become separate languages.

A *creole* is, like a pidgin, the result of the merging of two languages, typically a European and a non-European, but unlike a pidgin it is the first language of those who speak it. Thus we have Afro-French and Afro-English creoles in some of the former colonial territories in the Caribbean. A creole will generally develop from a pidgin, the change in name occurring when it becomes a first language.

Some writers assert, in fact, that a creole is by definition a development of a pidgin, to distinguish creoles from merged languages which never had a defined pidgin stage (e.g. English, in which the grammatical structures remained largely Anglo-Saxon while the vocabulary became heavily loaded with Norman French). This distinction is not clear-cut: some creoles seem to have developed in precisely the way English did; but to call English a creole offends some English speakers. For an Australian example, see KRIOL.

Pin Yin This is the name of the current standard way of transcribing Chinese into English, and is based on a phonetic transliteration of Mandarin. It should be used in preference to earlier systems, e.g. *Post Office Chinese* and *Wade–Giles*, though well-known historical figures (e.g. *Confucius*) are best left in their traditional forms.

The main problem with transliterating Chinese is that it is a tonic language: the meaning of a word depends on the tone as well as the content. In English, a rising tone indicates a question, and a falling one an answer. In Chinese, a variation in tone can alter the meaning of a phoneme, often in quite confusing ways. Thus, for example, the word *tang* (pronounced roughly like *tahng*) means *sugar* or *soup* depending on whether the sound is rising or flat.

Pin Yin uses diacritical marks to indicate this difference. The acute accent / ´ / indicates a rising sound, the grave accent / ` /

indicates a falling sound, the macron /‾/ indicates a high plateau and the breve /˘/ indicates a down-and-up swoop. (The umlaut used in *ü* is not a tone indicator – see vowel sounds, below.)

What follows is not an attempt at a pronunciation guide for those learning Chinese, but a guide to pronouncing Pin Yin transliterations in English.

The values of the consonants are (roughly):

b, d, f, g, j, k, l, m, n, p, s, t, w, y as in English. The *g* is always hard.

c   *ts* as in *flats*

h   is slightly guttural

q   *ch* as in *chin*

r   a non-English sound, half way between *r* and the soft *j* sound in *leisure*

x   *sh* as in *sheep*

zh hard *j*

The values of the vowels are (even more roughly):

a   *ah* (and similarly in blends, *an, ang, ar*)
       ai to rhyme with *my*
       ao to rhyme with *cow*

e   as in the French *de*, but the median *e* (as in *deng*) is sometimes described as a short *u* sound, and terminal *e* is more strongly voiced than in the French *de*, i.e. more like the *ur* in the English *fur*, but without any hint of a final r.
       ei as the *ay* in *pay*

i   as the *ee* in *sheep* (and similarly in the blends *ian, iang, iao, ie, in, iong* and *iu*). A median *i* is unvoiced after *z, c* and *s*, and a shwa after *ch, r, sh* and *z*. A terminal *i* after *z, c* and *s* is like the English *-ur* sound, as described in *e* above.
       ing as in English

o   to rhyme with *saw* (but cut short)
       ong as in English
       ou to rhyme with *toe*

u   to rhyme with *boo*, but to rhyme with *due* after *j, k, y* and *x*, and the same after *l* and *n* if it carries an umlaut, *ü*. After *i* it has an *o* sound, so that *liu* is more like the English *leo*.
       ua, uai, uan, uang, ue, üe, uo   *u* as English *w*
       un as in English

Thus Pin Yin, though a modern artifact, is not phonetically regular, and the values it places on some letters (especially *c, q, x* and *zh, e* and *i*) appear to us perversely chosen as well as ambiguous. It apparently makes slightly better sense to the Chinese, however, for whom it is part of a campaign to make Mandarin the standard dialect for internal communication.

Each Chinese character represents a single syllable, but the characters are ungrouped, so that there is no visible difference between a group of characters representing a single 'word' and a string of separate monosyllabic words. However, in Pin Yin there is a tendency to group syllables which belong together much as we do. Most notably, personal names are commonly written as a single-syllable family name followed by a two-syllable given name, whereas the earlier systems made these three words of one syllable each: *Mao Zedong* rather than *Mao Tse Tung*. For purposes of valuing the letters, however, the syllables must be regarded as separate, so that the *e* in *Zedong* is terminal (*Ze-dong*).

There is no reliable way of predicting the Pin Yin form from the earlier (e.g. Wade–Giles) forms.

plagiarism This word means the passing off of other people's literary creations as your own. Plagiarism of copyright material is called *piracy* and is actionable at law; plagiarism of non-copyright material may lead to loss of reputation. The essential feature of plagiarism is not so much the absence of *permission* as the lack of *acknowledgement*.

platypus The only decently-dressed plural is *platypuses*. The *-pus* is the Greek *pous*, a foot, whose plural is *podes*, as in ANTIPODES (= opposite the feet). *Platypi* is thus a barbarism, made no more respectable by being reported in Mac. The same argument applies to *octopus*.

Barbarians can defend themselves, however, by pointing out that the barbarism is at least as old as the Romans, who made the plural *polypi* from *polypus* (= many footed).

pleonasm This useful technical term describes the disease of using more words than are necessary, also known as *prolixity* and *logorrhea*. As one who is frequently guilty of it, I am reluctant to damn it too fiercely; but here are some dangers to watch for:

(1) Circumlocution: *I am not unmindful of the fact that you told me that you were in agreement with the proposition* = *I remember that you said 'Yes'.*

(2) Tautology: *I got up at 5.00 a.m. in the morning* = *I got up at 5.00 a.m.*

(3) Redundancy: *In an office environment…* = *In an office…*

This is not to say that using circumlocutions, tautologies and redundant words is always a sin. If it were, rhetoric would be a thoroughly wicked practice. But if they are not part of a deliberate rhetorical plan, they almost always damage the credibility of the writer or speaker.

ploddery There is a curious idiolect which is associated, not entirely unfairly, with Mr Plod, the police witness in a court of law, and is hence called *ploddery*. It is noted for PLEONASM (see above), for self-conscious use of less common words (*commence* rather than *begin*, *ascertain* rather than *find out*, *domicile* rather than *home*), for malapropisms (e.g. *simplistic* for *simple*, *definitive* for *definite*) and for using everyday words and phrases in ways which, while they are in the dictionary, are not the ways these words are normally used, e.g. *to acquaint with* (= to tell), *to effect* (= to make), *to occasion* (= to cause), *particulars* (= facts).

Some of the phrases heard in Court originate in the phrasing of the law itself: thus the phrase *to occasion grievous bodily harm* is a quotation (of sorts) from the Crimes Act, so while not being good English, it cannot be blamed on Inspector Plod, the Police Prosecutor. However, there is little in the law that says that Constable Plod should *proceed* rather than *go*, or that he should *partake of beverages* rather than *have a drink*

The other characteristic of ploddery is to construct sentences of quite unnecessary complexity, often starting with adverbial clauses which hang about in the corners of the Court, waiting for a main verb. Some people can do this sort of thing and get away with it. There are radio interviewers whose control of immensely long and complex sentences never ceases to astonish me. Just as I am thinking that they must have lost the thread, the ends are joined up and out comes an immaculate finished garment. Mr Plod, on the other hand, just runs the sentence on and on.

While Mr Plod is unquestionably the master of ploddery, few of us are free from blame. It seems that we believe that a simple sentence in plain language is in some way improperly dressed for Court (or for talking to officialdom generally).

Compare LEGAL LANGUAGE and OFFICIALESE.

plural dilemmas   For a discussion of the problem of deciding whether a word is singular or plural, see SINGULARITIES. In this article, we will discuss the formation and usage of plurals.

We should start with two reassuring rules: if you are in doubt, you are probably in good company, i.e. the dictionaries will be, too; secondly, in such cases the rules are likely to be complicated or ambiguous, and the best procedure is to go straight to a speller.

Having said that, the following may help to identify the cases you should worry about.

(1) *Normal rules – plurals in* s.

(2) *Other Anglo-Saxon plurals.*

(3) *Foreign forms.*

(4) *Words ending in* -o.

(5) *Words ending in* -f.

(6) *Mothers-in-law, etc.*

(7) *Plurals which are the same as singulars.*

(8) *Collectives which behave as plurals.*

(9) *Plurals with no singulars.*

(1) The normal English plural is formed by adding an *s* to the singular form.

Words ending in a consonant followed by *y* form plurals by changing the *y* to *ies* (*fly, flies*).

Words ending in an *s*, *x*, *z*, *ch*, *sh* or *ss* add *-es* (*bus*, *buses*; *box*, *boxes*; *buzz*, *buzzes*; *witch*, *witches*; *brush*, *brushes*; *grass*, *grasses*).

Words ending in *-o* are discussed in (4) below, and those ending in *-f* in (5) below.

(2) Anglo-Saxon, like other Germanic languages, had many plurals in *-en*, and a few survive: *child*, *children*; *ox*, *oxen*.

Another way of forming plurals in Germanic languages is represented in English by *man*, *men*; *woman* (wife-man), *women*; *louse*, *lice*; *mouse*, *mice* (cf. modern German *maus*, *maüse*).

Die, *dice*, however, recalls the French *dé*, *dés*, and see 9(c) below.

(3) Some imports, including some which are of long standing in the language, retain alien plural forms:

	Singular	Plural	Example
French	-	-x	tableau, tableaux
Ancient Greek	-on	-a	criterion, criteria
	-a	-ata	stigma, stigmata
Hebrew	-	-im	cherub, cherubim
Italian	-o	-i	graffito, graffiti
Latin	-a	-ae	nebula, nebulae
	-us	-i	locus, loci
	-us	-era	genus, genera
	-um	-a	bacterium, bacteria
	-ex	-ices	index, indices
	-is	-es	basis, bases (/*bayseez*/)
	-es	no change	series, series

But it is not as simple as that:

(a) In some cases, English-style and foreign-style plurals exist alongside one another: *tableaus* and *tableaux*, *cherubs* and *cherubim*. In most cases these are interchangeable, but we have *indices* in mathematics and *indexes* in books, and *stigmas* in biology and general language, *stigmata* in theology.

(b) Whether a word retains its foreign plural or acquires an English one is a matter of luck. For example, we see that *criterion* makes *criteria*; but *lexicon*, which might make *lexica*, actually makes *lexicons*. (Other Greek words in *-on*, e.g. *demon*, belong to other families and do not have plurals in *-a* even in the home language; if in doubt, the English-style plural in *-s* should be used.)

(c) If a word is best known in its plural form, the determination of its singular is even more difficult. This is one reason why so many plurals are commonly treated as singulars (*media*, *graffiti*), and why such singulars are then used as a base for a new plural: *data* (plural of *datum*) becomes used as if it were singular, and acquires the new plural *datas*. Before we hoot this down too loudly, we should consider the case of *agenda*, discussed in SINGULARITIES (1(c)).

(d) The reassuring general rule is that it is better to create a new

English-style plural (e.g. *lacunas* for *lacunae*) than to produce a *wrong* foreign plural (e.g. *stati* for *statuses*).

The enthusiasm for preserving foreign plural endings is quite recent: most of the ones which concern us arrived in the eighteenth and nineteenth centuries when great advances in science, demanding new vocabulary, coincided with a revival of interest in classical languages. By contrast, there are virtually no words in French for which a non-French plural is preferred: they describe *aquaria* as 'a private fantasy which, happily, is rarely encountered', and even write of German *lieds* rather than *lieder*.

(4) The plurals of words ending in *-o* present a peculiar difficulty, in that the rules are at best complex and at worst non-existent, and the experts not only quarrel with one another but fail to produce internally consistent advice. However:

(a) If you are uncertain, it is more than likely that other people are, too, i.e. both forms will be found to be acceptable. For an example, check dictionary entries for *innuendo*. However, in such cases *-os* is more likely to be right.

(b) The words which insist on forming plurals in *-oes* are few in number and relatively common, e.g. *potatoes, tomatoes, noes*.

(c) The words which prefer *-os*, by contrast, are a longish list: proper names, very long words, foreign-looking words and words ending in *-io*: *Romeos, armadillos, ghettos, arpeggios*.

(5) Most words ending in *-f* make plurals in *-ves*: *calves, selves, loaves*. A few do not: *roofs, reefs*. Others can go either way: *dwarf, hoof, oaf, turf, wharf* and *handkerchief*. Words ending in *-ff* generally make *-ffs*: *cliffs, muffs*. *Staff* makes both *staffs* and *staves*; but *staves* is now seen as the plural of *stave* (originally a back-formation from it). Words ending in *-ife* make *-ives* (*knives, lives, wives*) with *fifes* as an exception. *Strife* has no real plural, but if it had, it would be *strifes*.

(6) Compound nouns and noun phrases present some special problems. In the phrase *mother-in-law*, we see the *-in-law* element as a trailer, and happily make the plural *mothers-in-law*; and we are almost as happy about *governors-general*, but we see a *lieutenant-general* as a special sort of general, making the plural *lieutenant-generals* (see GENERAL).

The theoretic rule is that the plural *s* should be added to the noun which is the core of the noun phrase. In practice, this does not always help. There are some noun phrases which do not contain a noun (*forget-me-not*), and others in which there is a noun, but it is not the core (*fly-by-night*). These must have the plural *s* at the end.

In sum, it is best to add the *s* to the last word of the phrase *unless* it clearly belongs earlier. No one will be crucified, even for talking about *mother-in-laws, court martials* and *poet laureates*.

(7) Next, there is a long list of nouns whose plurals are the same as their singulars. Many of them are killed for fun: *trout, salmon, deer,* *grouse, buffalo, bison,* though it is no fun killing *sheep.* Most large edible fish are the same, perhaps because they are seen as collectives (see SINGULARITIES (2(i)) for a discussion of the phrase *half the fish…*). We are attacked by *sharks,* but go fishing for *shark* (which becomes *flake* on our menus; similarly, *ray* becomes *skate*). Smaller fish are more likely to have normal plurals (*sardines, leatherjackets*), but the smallest are known by a collective plural (*whitebait,* compare *plankton* and *krill*) where we say *The whitebait are…* if they are swimming about and *The whitebait is…* if they are piled on the plate.

(8) There are collectives which must be plurals (*the cattle are lowing*) and others that can be (*the livestock is/are fed*). But we say *a hundred head of cattle,* not *a hundred cattle* or *a hundred heads of cattle.*

(9) Finally, there are those plural words which for one reason or another have no singular. These include:

(a) *Words that are treated as plural although they were originally singular.* An example is *riches,* which started life as the French singular word *richesse,* and seems to attract a plural verb merely because it sounds plural. *Wages* is similar, its original singularity being preserved in the phrase *The wages of sin is death.* (The singular *wage* exists, as in the sentence *I was paid a low wage,* but this is a recent back-formation.)

(b) *Words which have a plural form for both singular and plural.* An example is the cricket *innings,* which attracts a singular verb when it refers to one event (and has a singular, *inning,* in baseball). The double plural *inningses* is more often heard than read. Similarly, snakes-and-ladders players say *The dice is…*; the singular *die* sounds pedantic in this context.

(c) *Words whose form is plural but which prefer (but do not insist on) a singular verb*: physical problems (e.g. *mumps, measles*), and mental ones (e.g. *mathematics, physics, economics, politics*). It is perhaps worth mentioning that the last set are effectively translations of Greek neuter plurals, and these attracted singular verbs in Greek, too. However, it is not being suggested that this is why we treat them as singular.

(d) *Words which possess a singular form, but cannot be used as singulars in some senses*: e.g. *troops.* We can say 'a thousand troops are being landed', but if only one of them is being landed, he cannot be *a troop,* and even *two troops* is more comfortable meaning *two groups* than meaning *two soldiers.* It seems that *troops* must come in numbers which represent a feasible fighting force.

    The rather different case of *scissors* is discussed under PAIR and that of *premises* (in the real estate sense) under PREMISES.

    See also NUMBER PHRASES, SINGULARITIES (I).

plurality   The use of this word in the American sense (the largest vote in a contest with three or more candidates, none of whom polls a clear 50%) would be particularly useful in Australia, where, thanks to the preferential system, such outcomes are common. This was recommended by Fowler even for British use. We, however, persist in using *majority* for the largest vote, and *absolute majority* to indicate a vote in excess of 50%.

poetry, verse, prose   When asked for a definition of poetry, Ian Mair was forthright. 'Amateurs' he said, 'write poetry; pros write prose'. Let us consider some components.

To call something *verse* is to say something about its form but not its content. Essentially, *verse* is rows of words which end short of the edges of the column, whereas *prose*, like gas, fills the space available to it. If *thought* is added, verse may become *poetry*, but prose remains prose. All poetry is verse, but not all verse is poetry.

So much for the simple answers. They are not, however, true. When we read, for example, the *Song of Solomon*, we are aware that we are reading passionate lyric poetry, even if the words are typeset as prose. (In well-designed Bibles, of course, the prose and poetical passages are distinguished, as they would be in any other book.)

Nor is it true that all poetry is verse. The term *verse* is generally taken to mean a disciplined structure and form, generally with metre and (other than in *blank verse*) rhyme, which much modern poetry lacks. Today, this does not matter; but in earlier times it was the key to the importance of verse: to make the words memorable. It is far easier to remember verse than prose, because the metre (and rhyme) provide clues to jog the memory of the reciter.

In the days before books were cheap and plentiful, this was very important. People were able to carry huge chunks of verse in their heads, whereas prose texts became garbled and were forgotten. This is the reason why almost all the earliest surviving literature is verse. Whatever was most important was stored as poetry: tribal lore and mythology, instructions on farming, gardening, building, engineering, astronomy and navigation. Leaving aside the overtly didactic works – technical manuals rendered in verse – many myths and epics were composed as practical lessons in geography or survival techniques, designed to be chanted and thus recalled when the need arose. (Aboriginal myths appear to contain many examples of this.)

This tradition survives in our more humdrum society in mnemonics. Thus

On Old Olympus' Towering Tops
A Finn and German Picked Some Hops

helps us to remember the order of the nerves in the brain of the dogfish, if we wish to do so.

However, once people could store information in private bookshelves (and, later, on computer disks), they depended less on their personal memories, and bookshelves and computers could store prose just as easily as verse. Hence Ian Mair's somewhat dismissive epigram. But he might have considered that today's advertising writers (who are nothing if not professional) use verse in the old way and for the old reasons. Thus

An apple a day
Keeps the doctor away

is the survivor of an early fruit marketing campaign.

In one respect, however, Ian Mair had a point. Our poets are making few contributions to the larder of well-remembered poetry, and whether or not you call this a renunciation of the poet's professional privilege and responsibility, it does seem a bit amateurish to be satisfied with communicating so little to so few.

It may be an awareness of this which has stimulated some poets to produce poetry designed for recitation, which they call *performance poetry*. The term and the tactics are new: the strategy is as old as poetry itself.

See RHYME and FOOT.

polis The word originally meant *city*, and gave us our word *politics* (originally, the affairs of a city-state). It was a lost root word until revived in the phrase *multi-function polis*.

It is hard to conceive a *polis* which performs only one function, but the term is not a tautology. Its connotations give a clue to a definition. The first connotation is of high technology industry, as with the phrase *technology park*; but it has the additional connotation that people actually live there. Thus it represents a break with the concept of zoning which has dominated Australian town planning for the better part of a century, and which inhibited the integration of industrial, commercial and residential activities.

This might not be a controversial issue, given that the reasons for the separation of functions (largely that 'industry' was perceived as inevitably offensive to the nose, eyes and ears) no longer apply. However, the term has further connotations of foreign investment and possible loss of sovereignty, and this has made the issue divisive. To its supporters, the term is synonymous with progress and future prosperity; to its detractors, it represents a cargo-cult mentality. It is one of the few cases where a clear definition, distinguishing the essential features of the concept from the negotiable ones, would save a lot of heart-ache.

polite usage The word *polite* is one of the sadder victims of the permissive society. It originally meant 'polished', indicating good taste and care for the better things of life, so that *polite usage* and *polite society* indicated 'the best' in aesthetic rather than social terms. (Note that it never had anything to do with *politics* or the *polis*.)

It then moved from the process to the product, becoming associated with 'manners', the set of rules governing behaviour at social gatherings and respect for elders and betters. This killed it. (The antonym of polite was *rude*, which suffered the same way, moving from meaning 'simple' or 'unsophisticated' e.g. of mud huts, to describing behaviour which shocked maiden aunts.)

It would be pleasant if a *permissive* society, one which permits people to be themselves, could allow within it a *polite* society in its original sense. Regrettably, this does not seem to be the case.

politics   We are concerned with: (1) *left* and *right*; and (2) party labels.
(1) Left and Right   OED says that the first use of *left* as a political label in English occurred in 1837, referring to the fact that in European legislatures it was traditional for those with liberal or radical views to sit on the left, as viewed from the President's chair. However, the French believe that this convention was imported from England.

Unquestionably, however, the current political sense of the word really dates from 1789, when the supporters of the French Revolution occupied the seats on the left of the assembly while the Royalists occupied the ones on the right. From then on, the word was widely used not only to describe revolutionary politics, but also radical politics generally, especially the ideas of Karl Marx.

By the 1930s, there was a clear polarisation of left and right, the right being occupied by the Fascists and Nazis and the left by the Marxist Communists. The whole spectrum of democratic politics managed to fit between these two extremes. Today, however, it is much less easy to apply the labels. 'Right' is applied unequivocally to military dictatorships and racists, but also to moral conservatives and free-market economists, and 'Left' has (particularly since the collapse of the Soviet Union) reverted to its position of opposition to these various forces, without any specific ideological focus.

In Australian politics, the left–right distinction has generally been one of relative rather than absolute positions. 'Left' has been generally associated with the labour movement rather than radicalism, and the 'Right' has often (and better) been termed 'Non-Labor'. The extremes within mainstream politics are, however, the *Socialist Left* and the *New Right*. Otherwise, the terms are really applicable only to extremist groups outside the political mainstream.
(2) Party labels   The labelling of political parties is an almost arbitrary business. It would have been very hard to tell from its name what the *National Socialist German Workers Party*'s policies were, but *National Socialist* and *Nazi* soon became clear enough. (See FASCISM.) The *Republican* and *Democrat* parties in the United States both espouse republicanism and democracy. Conversely, the label *Liberal* connotes the centre right in Australian politics, the centre in Britain and centre left in the United States.

In Australia, it is the word *liberal* which causes the most trouble, to the point that we use the term 'small-l liberal' to distinguish it from the party label.

The Australian Labor Party must be spelt thus; see -OR..., and see FACTION for a discussion of the party's usage of this word. It also uses the word *caucus* for the parliamentary party, and particularly for its meetings. The verb *to caucus* means *to meet as a caucus*, e.g. *The party caucused on the question of land rights*.

The name *Australian Democrats* was one of several which were considered (along with *National*) by R. G. Menzies for what became the *Liberal Party*, the decision being electoral rather than ideological. It was later chosen by a party dedicated to membership participation. Meanwhile the *Country Party*, originally dedicated to rural interests, has adopted the name *National* to broaden its constituency.

pondage   See DAM.

pragmatic   This word originally meant practical, as opposed to theor–etical. Thus while two judgements might theoretically be equally sound, one was likely to be better *pragmatically*, i.e. have a better outcome in the real world. The word has acquired a special meaning in Australian politics, where it means *having greater appeal to the electorate*.

preferentially   Using this word for *preferably* is a ploddish malapropism. *Preferentially* is best used only in a sentence like *I was treated preferentially*, meaning *I got better treatment than others*.

prefix   A *prefix* is a word part attached to the front of a word which modifies its meaning.

(1) Classes of prefix

(a) *Numerical prefixes*   We have the English (e.g. *one*-sided), the Latinate (e.g. *uni*form) and the Greek (e.g. *mono*plane). English numerical prefixes, generally hyphenated, are preferred for new coinage in general language, but the classical ones are widely used in science, and are generally not hyphenated. This can cause trouble – see BI-, HYPHENATION (1) and NUMERICAL PREFIXES.

(b) *Negative prefixes*   We have the English *un-* (as in *un*titled), a range of Latin ones, notably *in-* (as in *in*active) and the Greek *a-* (as in *a*morphous). For a discussion of the range and choice, see NEGATIVE PREFIXES, and for the blending of *in-*, see (2) *Blending of prefixes* below.

(c) *Adverbial prefixes*   Again, we have English, Latinate and Greek prefixes existing side by side: for example, *over*spend, *super*rich and *hyper*inflation, all of which are about excess of one sort or another. In older words, the significance of the classical prefixes is often more or less lost, e.g. one has to go to an etymological dictionary to find the significance of the *super* in *super*stition or the *hyper* in *hyper*bola, and this is even more so with the prefixes with weaker meanings. For an example, see INCIDENT....

(2) Blending of prefixes ending with a consonant

The word *irrational* is made up of the prefix *in-* (meaning *not*) and *rational*, the *n* having changed to match the following *r* to make it easier to say. This process is called *assimilation*. The same term can be applied to the way in which (for example) *in-* becomes *im-* before a *p*, as in *in-* + *ply* = *imply*.

Any discussion of a prefix can be assumed to apply to all its assimilated forms, and it has occasional relevance to hyphenation.

The most important examples of assimilation are all with classical prefixes. Basic meanings are given in each case, though their significance to current meanings is often obscure.

ab- (= *away from*) as in *abrasive* becomes *abs-* before *c* and *t* (*abscond*, *abstract*). If we want hyphenation to follow etymology, therefore, these should be hyphenated *abs-cond* and *abs-tract*. The only merit of this is that it occasionally helps with meaning, e.g. *abs-tract* is related to *sub-tract* and *tractor*, the *tract* part being about *pulling*. *Abscissa* is different: the second word part is *sciss-* (as in *scissors*) so the hyphenation should be *ab-scissa*. But not many people worry about such things these days.

ad- (= *towards*) as in *adhere* becomes *ac-* before *c* and *q* (*accord*, *acquire*), *af-* before *f* (*affect*), *ag-* before *g* (*aggressive*), *al-* before *l* (*allegation*), *am-* before *m* (*ammunition*), *an-* before *n* (*announce*), *ap-* before *p* (*appear*), *ar-* before *r* (*arrest*), *as-* before *s* (*assist*) and *at-* before *t* (*attract*).

con- (= *together with*) as in *construct* becomes *com-* before *b*, *m* and *p* (*combine*, *commit*, *compound*), *col-* before *l* (*collide*) and *cor-* before *r* (*correct*). In addition, *co-* is generally used before vowels, *gn* and *h* (*cooperate*, *cognate*, *cohabit*). In new coinage, we use *co-* (implying some sort of partnership) irrespective of the following letter.

ex- (= *out*) as in *extract* becomes *ef-* before *f* (*effluent*) and *e-* before *j*, *l*, *m*, *n* and *v* (*eject*, *elide*, *emend*, *enunciate*, *evade*). In new coinage, it is attached to nouns and means *former*. See EX-.

in- as in *intrude* (where *in-* is about position) and *inept* (where *in-* means *not*) becomes *im-* before *m* and *p* (*immense*, *improve*), *r* before *r* (*irradiate*).

ob- (= *in the way*) as in *obstruct* becomes *oc-* before *c* (*occur*), *of-* before *f* (*offer*) and *-op* before *p* (*oppress*).

sub- (= *under*) as in *submerge* become *suc-* before *c* (*success*), *suf-* before *f* (*suffer*), *sug-* before *g* (*suggest*), and *sup-* or *sus-* before *p* (*support*, *suspect*), and sometimes becomes *sur-* before *r* (so that the terms *subrogation* and *surrogate* share a single etymology). Note, however, that most of our *sur-* words have come to us via French, where *sur-* is a corruption of the Latin *super* (as in *survive*), and that in new coinage (where *sub* means 'under') it is not assimilated (*subcontinent*, *subfamily*, *subgenus*, *subpoena*).

All the above are Latin. We also have the Greek:

syn- (= *together*) as in *synchronise* becomes *sym-* before *b* , *m* and *p* (*symbiotic, symmetry, sympathy*) and *syl-* before *l* (*syllable*).

(3) Blending of prefixes ending with a vowel

Prefixes which end with a vowel are generally blended by elision rather than assimilation.

(a) One-syllable prefixes are not elided: *pre-empt, react, dioxide*.

(b) Elision is most common in numerical prefixes: thus *mon(o)* + *atomic* makes *monatomic*.

   If hyphenation is to reflect structure this must be watched. Thus *pentagon* is *penta* + *gon*, while *pentathlon* is *pent(a)* + *athlon*, where the + marks the word-part break and hence the best position for the hyphen.

   Elision of adverbial prefixes ending in vowels is restricted largely to some survivors from classical Greek, and are of little importance except in showing the relationships between words. Thus:

para- (= *alongside*) as in *paragraph* elides in *parenthesis* (*para*+ *en* + *thesis*) and in *parallel* (*para* + *allel*).

apo- (= *away from*) as in *apology* elides before a following *h* in *aphelion*. This explains the relationship of the words about satellite orbits:

FAR POINT   NEAR POINT
apogee   perigee   (*orbits round* ge, *the earth*)
aphelion   perihelion (*orbits round* helion, *the sun*)

For the elision of *anti-* see ANTE-....

prejudice   In the avoidance of prejudice, goodwill is not enough. One can have all possible goodwill but be unaware of a phrase which is going to cause distress. There are, of course, those who actually wish to make prejudiced statements. They represent a more profound problem, beyond the scope of this book. I start from the assumption that anyone reading this book wants to avoid prejudice.

   Writers and editors have access to advice from many organisations, giving rules for the avoidance of racism, sexism, ageism and other areas in which prejudice can exist; but while the rules are all very sensible, they tend to be simplistic, glossing over the questions which cause real trouble.

(1) The author's problem   The first problem is that sensitivities change over time. It is hard enough to avoid treading on the sensitivities of all possible contemporary readers, but impossible to predict the sensitivities of all future readers.

   The second problem is to decide whose sensitivities are to be respected. To take a very practical example, if sovereignty over a piece of land is disputed by two communities, as Kashmir is between India and Pakistan, it is impossible to draw a map without upsetting one or the other, and marking it 'disputed' may distress both.

The third problem is that in avoiding breaking one rule we can all too easily break another. A classic example of this is conflict between points (3(c) and (d)) in the list below.

The fourth problem is that respect for the sensitivities of others may cause us to suppress our own moral views. This may in most cases be a good idea, but if we feel strongly about something, we should not be afraid to say so. It cannot be prejudice to speak out against iniquity, even if it is enshrined in somebody else's religion or culture.

The solution lies largely in awareness. If we train ourselves to be aware of the problem areas, we have a chance of getting it right. Most of the problem areas are fairly well defined, and some of the key points to watch are discussed below.

In some respects, however, it is much easier to identify what is wrong with the *existing* writings of *others* than to avoid it in one's own new writing. Accidental ambiguities and innuendos are always possible, and authors should seek and then respect the reactions of readers and editors.

(2) The editor's problem The editor's problem is to balance a number of conflicting claims. These include responsibility to the author, to the reader, to those who may suffer as a result of prejudiced attitudes,, and to his or her own conscience.

Not so long ago, our understanding of prejudice was primitive, and there was a need for editors to develop awareness of the issues. Today, most editors are well aware of the issues, so we can move to discussion of the way in which this awareness can be manifested.

The major responsibility of the editor is to ensure that the author's message reaches the reader in the best possible condition, clear and intact, and one way an author can muddy the pool is to say something which, however innocent the intention, causes offence. In some areas, notably racism and sexism, there are TABOO WORDS, and it may take more than common sense to know which ones they are. The editor therefore can and must warn the author if the text contains anything which could cause offence.

However, if the 'offence' is deliberate (as it may be, quite legitimately, in a book which is a contribution to a debate), the editor is faced with a real dilemma. On the one hand, changes should never be made against the author's wishes or (worse) without the author's knowledge, nor should an editor act as a censor, telling authors what ideas they are permitted to have and what words they can use to express them – these are the actions of a thought-police. On the other hand, assisting a morally offensive text into the world is unconscionable. Most editors would be glad that they were never called upon to edit *Mein Kampf*.

If faced with editing a text they feel to be offensive, editors must first be very sure of their ground. They must not mistake unpalatable facts for prejudiced opinions, nor mistake strong advocacy for bias. They must also learn to distinguish good and bad arguments irrespective of whether they agree with the conclusions – and, if anything, the biggest danger is to fail to notice flaws in arguments which support a position we hold.

Secondly, editors must maintain a sense of proportion, not dissipating their energies in trivialities while a major problem remains unresolved, and remembering that rules which are appropriately applied to a school text for 12-year-olds will not necessarily be appropriate for a research monograph. We are talking, after all, of the potential damage which prejudiced statements can do, and this depends as much on the nature the readership (its size, age and sophistication) as on the content of the statement itself.

Thirdly, editors must be very sure that all changes are accepted by the author, and as far as possible accepted with enthusiasm and thanks. If an editor needs to bring pressure on an author in order to get agreement to the removal of a prejudiced statement, something is wrong, and it may be more profound than this particular dispute. The matter should be referred back to the publisher: see the penultimate paragraph of EDITOR (1).

There is a particular responsibility for editors handling the work of dead authors. The recent practice of re-editing classic children's books to remove violence, sexism and racism is well-intentioned, but has led to absurdities which may well be seen in the near future as a denial of their authors' MORAL RIGHTS. Similarly, rewriting history is unacceptable, whether the rewriting is done by a fascist, a Marxist or a liberal humanitarian.

In the last resort, an editor may feel that a text is so offensive that he or she cannot in conscience respect the author's right to the integrity of the text. If this happens, the editor has no option but to decline to do the job.

(3) Points to watch The following is designed as a short checklist of possible problem areas:

(a) *Avoid negative generalisations.* If, for example, the collective characteristics of a group are portrayed at all, they should be positive. Better still (given that all generalisations tend to be nonsense) *avoid them altogether*, though this may be tricky if we are discussing cultural norms. But we do not offset the defamation that all Aboriginals are thieves by the equally nonsensical assertion that none of them are.

(b) *Avoid taboo material.* Taboo words are fairly well known and (other than in the area of sexism – see SEXIST LANGUAGE) easy to avoid. But it is easy to overlook less self-evident taboos, e.g. against reproducing photographs of dead people.

(c) *Avoid paternalism*. We are not respecting a group if we draw examples of their 'success' only from those who have succeeded in our own culture.

(d) *Avoid material likely to arouse feelings of superiority in readers*. The reader's reaction may be very different from the writer's intention. Religious rituals may appear ludicrous, and pictures of low living standards can evoke contempt rather than sympathy.

(e) *Respect the historical record*.

(f) For editors – *respect the moral rights of the author*.

The greatest problems are to reconcile (c) and (d), and to reconcile (e) and (f) with the rest.

Points (c) and (d) can conflict when one is searching for positive models, e.g. the cover photograph on a book for schools on Black Australians. Should it depict (say) a tribal elder or an Aboriginal barrister? The Aboriginal least likely to evoke a feeling of superiority in middle Australia will be someone who has succeeded in the white world, but this can be seen as disrespect for Aboriginal values.

The historical record (e) is, unfortunately, intrinsically prejudiced. We generally get the story from the winning side, or the side which kept the best records, and this is just as true of social history as it is of military and political history. We hear more about the rich and famous than we do about the poor and humble, because it is they who get written about. This is itself an important lesson of history. We can correct the record where we find it to be false, and point out its bias; but we should beware of rewriting it because we find it unpalatable.

Finally, for editors, a watching brief must be maintained without infringing (f), the authors' rights. In particular, there is the right of *integrity*: their work cannot be changed without their approval. It is the responsibility of editors to draw alleged prejudice to the attention of their authors; but if the authors dig their toes in, editors must retreat.

Further discussion of this and related topics will be found under ETHNIC, SEXIST LANGUAGE and TABOO WORDS.

premises 'The premises were kept under observation,' says Mr Plod, and how right he is: we have here a plural word for a singular concept.

The word *premise* started as a term of logic, meaning a proposition from which logical conclusions can be drawn, as in a syllogism, which has two premises, and a conclusion. It passed into law as (amongst other things) *the list of the property covered by a deed of sale or bequest*, and hence came to be a general term for the property itself, and in particular for commercial real estate. The word retains a strong legal flavour, being not so much a building as a domain which a person controls and is responsible for.

Logicians tend to spell the word with an extra *s*: *premiss, premisses*. This form is etymologically sound, and if we are worried about getting our logical terms mixed up with our real estate, we can now distinguish the spellings in this way. It seems rather pointless, however, as the two senses are rarely confused, and I do not recommend this distinction.

preposition For a discussion of the place of prepositions in the scheme of things, see GRAMMAR (3(f)).

The name implies that it is *positioned before* something, and this has given rise to the self-incriminating advice *never use a preposition to end a sentence with*. There are many sentences which benefit from this advice, like the classic *What did you choose that book to be read to out of for?* But the problem is clumsy thought, not just word order.

There are many other cases where correction is impossible. For example, we often suppress relative pronouns, as in Henry Lawson's *'Vote for Blazes and Protection and the land you're livin' in'.* We would have to supply a pronoun, *which*, and the sentence would then cease to be an accurate representation of the way we speak.

Even if there is a pronoun available, it is not always right to move the prepositions in front of it. When Winston Churchill said (if he did) *That is a proposition up with which I will not put*, the sentence was not merely ludicrous, it was wrong. The supposed prepositions are not prepositions at all. They are parts of a verb phrase, *put up with* = tolerate, and they cannot be separated from it without violating the sense. This can be seen most clearly in *Shut up! Get out! Carry on!.* These 'prepositions' are acting as adverbs, and can certainly occur at the end of the sentence; they have nowhere else to go.

The distinction between a preposition introducing an adverbial or adjectival phrase and an adverb forming part of a verb phrase is generally clear. Compare the two sentences:

I saw the loot *which the thieves got away with.*
I saw the robbery *which the thieves got away with.*

These are not pretty sentences, but only the first could have its word order changed:

I saw the loot *with which the thieves got away.*

In the second, *with* is an adverb, part of the verb phrase, and cannot be moved away. But who would want to change even the first? If the original version was not pretty, the revised one is worse.

In general, if there is a noun or pronoun on which the preposition can easily be hung, hang it. But if the result is a sentence which sounds stuffy, either leave it at the end or rephrase the sentence. For a particularly vexed example of this problem, see WHO(M).

prepositional phrase A prepositional phrase is a phrase which acts as a preposition. Examples include *preparatory to, according to, owing to, irrespective of, regardless of, on account of, contrary to.*

One vexed case is *due to*. In the entry under DUE TO, there is a discussion of two ways of 'explaining' how an adjective like *due* can appear in a sentence without a proper antecedent, as in

The crops failed due to the drought.

The problem arises because, said Fowler, an adjective cannot have as an antecedent 'a notion extracted from a sentence'.

He proposed two separate explanations:

(1) In the case of *according to, owing to, on account of* and *contrary to*, we have adjectival phrases which have become prepositional phrases. *Due to* is hovering on the verge.

(2) He suggested that the rest must therefore be adverbs; and he invented the term *quasi-adverbs* to describe them.

Now, the simple answer is that *due to* has long since moved off the verge, and is now a prepositional phrase like the others.

Meanwhile, we still hear people quoting Fowler's argument about the inadmissability of 'a notion extracted from a sentence' as the antecedent of a relative clause. It may have been true in Fowler's Britain, seventy years ago, but it is certainly not true here and now. A sentence like *He rode down the hill on a skateboard, which was a silly thing to do* does not worry us. But any explanation of its construction involves using 'a notion extracted from a sentence' as an antecedent for the relative pronoun *which*. When grammar parts company with usage, it is a good idea to get a new grammar.

principal, principle   The old joke about the collective noun for *principals* being a *lack* of principals confuses the issue mightily. I try to remember that a *principal* has a *principal principality,* but no *principles*. But I often forget. There is no logic to the distinction.

print specification   The following checklist introduces the key words and provides a basic checklist of points to be covered; but technology is changing so fast that the detail is out of date as I write:

Item		Example
Extent (number of pages)		224 (Note 1)
Trimmed size, in millimetres		213×137 mm (Note 2)
Stock:	text (weight, style)	95 gsm Bookprint Matt (Notes 1 and 3)
	endpapers (ditto)	85 gsm Bookprint Matt (Note 3)
	jacket (ditto)	110 gsm 1-s art (Note 3)
Binding:	sewing	section sewn as 16s, endpapered (Note 4)
	spine	rounded, head and tail bands (Note 5)
	case material	navy blue Wibalin over 2400 µm boards (Note 6)
	blocking	blocked platinum spine only (Note 7)

Printing:	text (no. of colours)	1×1, black, no bleeds (Note 8)
	endpaper (ditto)	2×0
	jacket (ditto)	4×0 and lamination (Note 9)
Copy:	text (how supplied)	One-piece unimposed reflection art, with keylines for 24 square-finish halftones supplied as 24 contones to 6 reductions (Note 10)
	endpapers (ditto)	Base art plus overlay for second colour, spot colour only (Note 11)
	jacket (ditto)	Base art with keylines, 4-colour process supplied from Ektachrome transparency

NOTES

(1) This specification is for a book with illustrations integrated into the text. If the illustrations are printed separately, either as a section or as wraps (i.e. wrapped round a section of text), this should be indicated, e.g. '320 pp text + 16 pp photo section as 2 × 8pp wraps'.

(2) The vertical dimension is given first. 213 × 137 is the size once known as *Demy octavo*. Such names are now rarely used.

(3) For further notes on paper, see PAPER.

(4) The main alternative to sewing is *perfect binding*: see PERFECT. *Sewn as 16s* indicates that the 224 pp book will be printed as fourteen 16 pp sections. Smaller (e.g. 8 pp) sections increase the amount (and hence cost) of sewing, but improve the strength and handling of the book. The cheapest binding is *saddle-stitching*, using two or more *stitches* (wire staples) through the spine.

(5) Casebound books can have round or square backs. Perfect bound books are always square backed. Head and tail bands used to be an integral part of the sewing, but today are just decorative, like a clip-on bow tie.

(6) There are good arguments for using book cloths and cloth substitutes which are dyed (i.e. the colour runs right through them) as these are less likely to show wear. However, this precludes an exact match of colours, and it is therefore common to print the case colour on white material.

The name Wibalin used here is the trade name of a popular cloth substitute – in reality, a tough, embossed paper.

The best board for cases is known as *millboard*, but *strawboard* is commonly used for commercial bindings.

(7) Common alternatives include blocking in other metallic or non-metallic foils (or none, i.e. blind stamping) and extending the blocking to the front or back of the case.

(8) 1×1 indicates one colour on each side of the sheet. Full colour both sides would be 4×4.

Bleeds (photographs running right out to the trim of the page) can cause difficulties if they happen to fall on the edge of the sheet, particularly the *gripper edge* (i.e. the edge by which the sheet is drawn through the press).

(9) An attractive extravagance is a *french fold*, in which the top and bottom of the jacket are folded in, so that it shows no raw edge.

(10) There are many alternatives here, and these will determine the cost of the pre-press work.

One-piece indicates that all the base material (text and key-lines) are on the same piece of paper of film.

Unimposed indicates that each page is delivered separately, the *imposition*, i.e. arrangement to make up a *section* of (say) 16 pages, *eight backing eight* (= *eight to a view*), being done by the printer.

Reflection art indicates a right-reading positive on paper. Common alternatives are to supply film, positive or negative, right-reading or wrong-reading.

Reflection art can be pasted up (assembled in the traditional way, with scissors and paste) or assembled electronically. Illustrations may be supplied in position (the usual procedure with line drawings), or supplied separately. If supplied separately, it may be as *contones* (= continuous tone photographs), transparencies, screened bromides or screened negatives (see HALF-TONE), and their positions on the artwork may be indicated by *keylines* (hairline rule boxes) or *windows* (black areas on reflection art or positive film, or clear windows on negative film).

(11) Spot colour indicates solid areas of colour. If one colour overlaps another, it is best supplied on an overlay (a second piece of art carrying only the image for the second colour, and with register marks to indicate its position in relation to the base art).

(12) *Process colour* indicates that the transparency must be *separated* (see HALFTONE) to produce the four halftone images, one for each of the *process colours* (usually yellow, magenta, cyan and black).

privilege   It is not often that etymology is useful in deciding what a word does or should mean, but it is interesting that *privilege* has drifted so far from its roots. It started as a technical term of Roman law, *privilegium*, meaning a law passed for (or, originally, against) a particular person. It was then extended to mean a law passed for the benefit of a specific group in society and against the rest, and its beneficiaries became known as *privileged*.

Thus the privileged classes are not simply those who have more than the rest. We have a word for that, and it is *rich*. The privileged are those who owe their continuing prosperity to laws which further their interests. If we remember this, we can identify the problem of the *underprivileged* as one of law rather than wealth; of equity rather redistribution of wealth. Poverty may be difficult to eradicate, but we can eradicate privilege, the device which keeps the rich rich and the poor poor.

pro-active   This word, which swept into our language in the late 1980s, caught on immediately.

Pro-active was coined as a contrast to *reactive*: pro-active behaviour involves initiatives, while reactive behaviour is restricted to response to stimuli. This distinction is sometimes self-evident: we have the antithesis of *action* to *reaction* in physics. However, *active* and *reactive* do not make this contrast, so the word *pro-active* makes a useful point.

As it is useful, it is likely to survive, provided that it is not used as a trendy synonym for *active*.

product(ivity)   In common usage, a *product* is something tangible: a pumpkin scone or a barrel of oil. Some unproductive industries, e.g. banks, have recently started using the term *product* for the services they offer, a usage which seems to be a euphemism.

Similarly, the word *productivity* has a meaning in economics which departs from common usage. In everyday speech, *productivity* means *rate of production*, so that we can say *My productivity is at its best in the morning*. To the economist, however, productivity is the ratio between the *value* of goods and services produced and the *cost* of producing them, so that productivity can be increased not only by improving the rate of output but also by raising prices or lowering wages.

program(me)   This is another case where the British usage has changed since America went its own way. There was no thought of putting an *-me* on the end of this word until well into the nineteenth century, when the idea of printed theatre programs arrived from France complete with French spelling.

The extra *-me* was not added to pre-existing terms, e.g. *anagram* and *cryptogram*. The metric unit was at one stage written *gramme*, but this is no longer the case.

Mac has *program* as its headword, with *programme* added at the end as an alternative spelling, but then has *programme music*, with no alternative spelling offered, as its next headword. ACOD reports that *programme* is the normal spelling, with *program* labelled as a US variant, used in Australia in computer language. This seems like a good description of current Australian usage, but there is no value in the distinction, and the best solution is to use *program* in all senses – including *program music*.

pronoun   For a listing of the various classes of pronoun, see GRAMMAR (3(d)).

The most common problems with pronouns are (1) ambiguity and (2) agreement.

(1) Ambiguity   In the sentence

The witness said that he saw the accused hit the deceased with his umbrella

the umbrella could have belonged to the attacker, the deceased or the witness.

Once one has embarked on a sentence like this, there is no way out but to repeat the antecedent:

The witness said that the accused hit the deceased with his (the witness's) umbrella.

However, if constructing such a sentence from scratch, there is the option of reshaping it to avoid the ambiguity. Considerate writers hear the alarm bells of ambiguity in their ears whenever they write third person pronouns.

(2) Agreement   A pronoun must *agree* with its ANTECEDENT, i.e. have the same number, gender and person:

1st pers. sing.		*I*	*am*	in *my*	house
plur.		*We*	*are*	in *our*	houses
2nd pers. sing. *or* plur.		*You*	*are*	in *your*	house(s)
3rd pers. sing.	masculine	*Fred*	*is*	in *his*	house
	feminine	*Ann*	*is*	in *her*	house
	neuter	*The dog*	*is*	in *its*	house
plur.		*Fred, Ann and the dog*	*are*	in *their*	houses

It is generally understood that, in case of conflict 1st person overrides 2nd, and both override 3rd:

You and I become *we*	*You and I*	*are*	in *our* houses
You and she become *you*:	*You and she*	*are*	in *your* houses

If it is one *or* the other, we are in diabolical strife:

You or I	?	in	?	house
She or you	?	in	?	house

All solutions are awkward. In practice we would say *Am I in my house or are you in yours?*

This should not distress us. The rules of agreement arise from a mixture of logic and familiarity, and simply cannot deal with patterns which are logically difficult and rare. Some of these patterns would be perfectly simple in other languages with different agreement protocols. Similarly, some patterns which are easy in English are impossible to translate directly into other languages. When faced with patterns which are difficult in English, we simply have to select different patterns. A particular problem is the inclusive *he*: see SEXIST LANGUAGE and EACH (ONE)....

pronunciation   *Pronunciation* is the way a particular word is pronounced. It is thus distinct from *accent*, which determines overall patterns of pronunciation. Both, however, are topics which are loaded with snobbery and prejudice (see ACCENT), and the borderline between them is not clearly defined.

If we ask whether the 'correct' pronunciation of *castle* is /kah-s'l/ or /kass'l/, we are really asking a question about accent. This word is an example of a large range on which the value of the vowels varies. In this case, both are used by Australian speakers, and while it is generally true that Melbourne favours /kass'l/ whereas Sydney favours /kahs'l/, both can be heard everywhere.There is no 'correct' Australian version. On a head count /kass'l/ would probably win.

The case of *tomato* is similar, but the regionalism is more cut and dried. Virtually all Australians say /t'mahtoe/, while all Americans say /t'maytoe/. If we are in an American supermarket, we will get some glassy stares if we ask for /t'mahtoe/. If we use /t'maytoe/ in Australia, we will be understood, but we will be assumed either to be Americans or poseurs.

Some people talk about the 'correct' pronunciation of such words, but their arguments tend to be facile or ignorant. This is not to say that such divergences have no significance – they may label the speaker in ways like those discussed under ACCENT. But the issue is one of communication, not of correctness.

Is there, then, such a thing as correct pronunciation? The answer is yes: it is the pronunciation used by the person whose speech we would like to emulate. (See CORRECTNESS.) Thus it may vary from moment to moment: if one is in a supermarket, it is not a bad idea to emulate the vocabulary and pronunciation of the check-out person. So the issue of correctness slides into one of REGISTER.

However, the fact that there are several correct forms of some words does not mean that pronunciation is open slather. There are words which are in the process of change, like CHIMERA, where Mac recognises a pronunciation not acknowledged by ACOD (or me), but this is a small category. Most of our words have a single pronunciation which, while it may carry dialect variations, is fundamentally uniform. When people make *mischievous* into *mischevious*, this is wrong in any dialect.

Most of us get such words right simply because we hear them used and mimic what we hear. People who can get such words wrong are either deaf or have some sort of insensitivity which stops them noticing the difference between what they hear and what they say. The problem here is not knowledge, but attitude, and people who are worried about their pronunciation should learn to become more careful listeners.

A second source of pronunciation error is an attempt to say words which we have read but which we have not heard. The wider our language experience, and the better our mentors, the more likely we are to know what the received pronunciation of a word is, but this cannot always help people who are speaking in unfamiliar registers, e.g. newreaders suddenly presented with stories about technical developments in obscure areas of science.

There are no fail-safe ways of getting round these problems, but if insecurity leads to a reluctance to use new words, something is seriously wrong. This, then, is a plea for tolerance. If we hear pronunciations which we know to be wrong, we should simply realise that it is largely good luck that has put us in a position to notice the mistake.

Pronunciation of proper nouns   The pronunciation of proper nouns is a very special case, as the people who own them (including local inhabitants in the case of place names) have to be respected, i.e. their preferences should be discovered and followed. For a further discussion of this, see PROPER NOUNS (3) and FOREIGN WORDS... (4).

proper   This word is profoundly ambiguous, but the ambiguity generally causes puzzlement rather than misunderstanding.

(1) The original sense was of ownership, which survives in the words *property* and *proprietary,* and in the grammatical term PROPER NOUNS. The antonym is *common*, as in *common land* and *common nouns.*

(2) Next, phrases like *keep us in our proper places* (the places which belong to us) led to the sense of correctness – the *proper* place for anything is the ap*prop*riate place for it. This remains the most common use, and is the usual sense of the adverbial form, *properly*. The antonym is *wrong*.

(3) This in turn led to a moral sense, as in *He is a very proper person*, a sense also reflected in the noun *propriety*. This is a relatively rare sense of *proper*, but the negative forms *improper* and *improperly* are generally used in this way.

Thus the most common use of *proper* is in sense (2), e.g. *Did you use the proper spanner?* to which the reply is *No, I used the wrong one.* It would be odd to say *No, I used an improper one*, because *improper* carries connotations of bar-room jokes, professional malpractice and marital infidelity. Use of *proper* other than in sense (2) or of *improper* other than in sense (3) is not worng, but is liable to cause puzzlement.

proper nouns   The word *proper* in this phrase is related to ownership (see PROPER (1)). The names *Kalgoorlie, Nelson Mandela, Aspro,* and *The White House* are proper nouns, whereas *town, man, hat* and *aspirin* are *common nouns*, held *in common* between members of a class.

The concept of property is particularly important in the case of the so-called proprietary names, e.g. *Aspro*. Such names are private property, protected by law; see TRADEMARKS.

(1) Capitalisation   Proper nouns are generally given initial capital letters: *Australia*. Words formed from them are also capitalised: *Australian, Australianise*. For further notes on this, see CAPITALS, USE OF and CAPITAL LOSSES.

(2) Stability Historically, proper nouns have tended to resist change to their spelling more steadfastly than did common nouns. The name of the city, *Roma*, has remained unchanged for well over two thousand years, as can be seen from ancient inscriptions. Indeed, it is inscriptions and other indelible records which account, in part at least, for the stability of proper nouns.

The stability of form means that proper nouns often contain evidence of old forms of language. For example, when surnames were invented, many people adopted the name of their trade and called themselves *Smith*, but the spelling varied according to dialect and whim: *Smith, Smyth, Smythe*. Long after all these variants had given way to a uniform spelling of the common noun, *smith*, the variants survived in the proper noun.

(3) Pronunciation Stability has had the further effect of separating the pronunciation from the spelling, and then, on the say-as-you-write principle, dragging the pronunciation back to the spelling. Thus the British had reduced *Launceston* to two syllables (/*Larnston*/), but Australians have restored it to three.

A further oddity is illustrated by the case of the French surname *St Jean*. On coming to Britain, two things happened. Its pronunciation was anglicised as /*Sinjon*/, and its spelling was independently anglicised to St John. Hundreds of years later, we still have a barbaric French pronunciation attached to this soundly-formed English name. Some members of the St John clan are now encouraging a rational pronunciation, while other are rationalising the spelling.

However, the rest of us must await their pleasure. The absolute rule with the pronunciation of proper nouns is that the owner's wishes must be respected. See FOREIGN WORDS… (2).

protagonist We are told we can only have one protagonist, as it is a term from Greek drama meaning 'first actor', the second actor being the *deuteragonist*. As with so many etymological purities, it is worth remembering but not worth fighting for. The confusion probably arose from the belief that the prefix was *pro-*, meaning 'in favour of', whereas it is an elided form of *proto-*, meaning 'first', and the deuteragonist was often known as the *antagonist* (the 'counter-actor') because he played villain to the protagonist's hero.

Strictly, there should likewise be only one *antagonist*, but this is rarely commented on, while the *tritagonist* and *tetragonist* are never discussed at all.

protest Can we, as the Americans do, *protest our government's actions*, or should we *protest against our government's actions*?

Etymology is on our side. *Protest* merely means *to speak out* or *declare in public*; if it has a direct object, it has to be what we are declaring, i.e. *The plaintiff protested her innocence*.

However, apart from this and a few other related phrases, *protest* always means *speak against*, and the sense of the American version cannot be in doubt; nor does their usage destroy a subtlety of meaning (as *agreed* for *agreed to* does: see AGREE). If it comes, therefore, we should not be too distressed. And for an example of a trend the other way, see MEET (with).

public school This term means what it says in America, means *private school* in Britain, and is dangerously ambiguous in Australia.

The bizarre British usage stems from the fact that the original distinction was between a *private school* (where a rich householder paid a tutor to teach the children of the household) and a *public school* (attended by children from more than one household, paying fees to attend the school). As the fees put them beyond the reach of the general public, these *public schools* became today's *private schools*.

Unfortunately, the term *public school* came out to Australia in the baggage of some settlers, and is often used to describe some non-government secondary schools for boys, e.g. the so-called *GPS* (= Greater Public Schools) of Sydney. (The girls' equivalents are generally called *private schools*.)

The term *Public School* is also used as the official title of government primary schools in New South Wales and sometimes as a term for government schools in general. Another is State School, used variously of government schools in general and government primary schools in particular.

Because of these ambiguities, the labels *Public School* and *State School* should be used with caution, and explained if the context does not make the sense clear. Given that the term *independent* is also ambiguous (see INDEPENDENT), an even better procedure is to forget the whole lot and write of *government schools* and *non-government schools*.

The term *preparatory school*, which in Britain means a private institution for 9–13 year-old boys, i.e. preparatory to 'public school', is in America a private secondary school, preparing students for *college* (i.e. university). In Australia, the term is restricted to a few junior schools feeding private secondary schools.

publish, publisher, publication The verb *to publish* means to make public, the *publisher* is the person who does it, and *publication* is the name of both the process and the product. The terms seem simple enough, but are widely misunderstood.

(1) Publish, print The most common error is to use *publish* as a synonym for *print*. Publishing is a process which starts when the printing process is complete. Printing can occur without publication, e.g. if an edition is suppressed, withdrawn, or was never intended for publication; and publication can occur without printing, e.g. if manuscript copies are distributed to third parties.

We can therefore say that *The book has been published in an edition of 10,000 copies*, but we cannot say *10,000 copies have been published* until they have all reached their destinations in the hands of the public, and this may depend on the public response.

The term *desktop publishing* is an even greater misnomer, since the process it describes is not publishing or even printing, but electronic typesetting and layout. However, the phrase is well established, and provided that we remember that it has nothing to do with publishing, all is well.

(2) Publisher, editor   The second confusion is between the terms *publisher* and *editor*. Indeed, in French, the word for publisher is *editeur*, but this is probably not the source of the confusion.

A *publisher* is a person or corporation able and willing to take financial and legal responsibility for a publication, and hence the prerogative of deciding which projects should go ahead.

An *editor* is one of several people responsible to the publisher for ensuring that the literary form of the publication is as the publisher intended. Others may include designers to look after its appearance, and promotional and sales people to look after its distribution.

In practice, there is a great deal of difference between the operation of these definitions in book publishing and that in periodical publishing:

(a) In *periodical publishing* (newspapers and magazines), the publisher's prerogatives are rarely exercised: they are limited to the initial decision to call the periodical into existence and the final one to cause it to cease publication. Between these two moments, a person with the title *Editor* is assigned broad authority over what is published in each issue, executing it with the help of departmental editors and sub-editors, with or without interference from the publisher.

(b) In *book publishing*, the publisher's prerogatives (to decide whether or not a given book shall be accepted for publication) may be exercised daily, so an absentee or corporate proprietor, while retaining the responsibilities (financial and legal) cannot exercise the prerogatives. This is so in many firms in Australia, and the title *Publisher* is often given to a salaried person empowered to make the publishing decisions on behalf of the proprietors.

This is the source of the main misunderstanding, since the result is that the *publisher* within a book publishing company has a status similar to the *editor* of a periodical, while *editors* in book publishing are comparable in status to the *sub-editors* of a periodical; see EDITOR (1).

There is also a potential legal confusion. In publishing contracts, the contracting party is invariably 'the Publisher', but this refers to the corporation, not to the salaried individual with the title of 'Publisher'. In the case of a few private firms, they may be one and the same, but not many people would take on the legal responsibilities without the protection of limited liability.

(3) Commercial/Non-commercial publishing A *commercial publisher* is one who recoups the investment from sales. A *non-commercial publisher* may have a different source of funds and a different motive, e.g. the dissemination of a message. Thus a commercial publication has succeeded if it is profitable, irrespective of how or why the profit was achieved; a non-commercial publication is successful only if it reaches the hands of, and has the desired effect on, those for whom it was intended.

Self-publishing is the term used to describe an author-financed enterprise whose purpose is normally the same as that of commercial publishing, i.e. to produce and sell an edition; see SELF-PUBLISHING.

The phrase *privately published* sounds like an oxymoron. However, it makes sense if the above definition is remembered. It implies that the decision to publish is taken by an individual who is not a professional publisher, or that it is published to a restricted 'public', or both.

Vanity publishing is the technical term for the production of a *vanity edition*, i.e. one produced at the author's expense when the prime purpose is to see the work in print. This term begs the question, since the work may never be published at all in any meaningful sense.

(4) Publication There are several popular and legal definitions of 'publication', which vary according to the purpose to which they are put.

In common language, the word means both the process and the product: we could (just to illustrate the point) say *Publication of the publication will occur next week*. However, this apparent ambiguity rarely causes problems. The troubles all arise from the variations in the legal definition of the word in the 'process' sense:

(a) For the purposes of the law of defamation, publication can occur when a defamatory statement is exposed to the public in any form, and to however small a 'public'. It is subject to such limitations as parliamentary and legal privilege and 'qualified privilege', some of which are privileged under statute, and others under common law; but in theory a defamation contained in a letter from one person to another can be a libel.

(b) For the purposes of copyright law, publication is normally taken to be a significant event: the occasion when a reasonable number of copies are made available in some way or another to the general public. If this were not so, the act of showing a manuscript to a publisher, agent or reader could be deemed to be 'publication' (as it would be under the law of libel). This would have absurd implications under the law of copyright.

(c) In the case of books first published overseas, a more specific (but still very vague) definition is applied to the term 'publication in Australia'. This is discussed under COPYRIGHT (1(d) and (j)).

publishing contracts   The following notes are about contracts with book publishers. A brief section at the end covers works destined for magazines and periodicals.

There is no single set of terms which can be described as fair. We are talking about a market place, in which the publisher is trying to buy cheap and the author or agent is trying to get the highest possible price. The bargaining power of each side will depend on the attractiveness of the work: the publisher cannot risk losing an important, potentially lucrative work to a rival by offering too little; conversely, the author cannot risk losing a sale through asking too much.

Like any other contract involving the transfer of property, the negotiation can start with an offer to sell or an offer to buy. In practice, the first contract is generally drafted by the publisher and offered to the author for acceptance. However, many agents (and some authors) submit manuscripts on the understanding that they will be drawing up the contracts. Theoretically, it should make no difference – all terms in draft contracts are negotiable – but in practice the party whose draft provides the agenda for such discussions starts a lap ahead.

The essential terms of a contract are:

(1) A *definition* of the property involved;
(2) A statement of the *consideration* (the financial arrangements);
(3) A statement of the *rights and responsibilities* of both sides
(4) A *termination* clause.

(1) Definitions

(a) *Description of work* If the work does not yet exist, the contract should spell out what is expected in some detail: e.g. the length, scope and anticipated readership of the proposed book.

(b) *Licence or assignment* The normal publisher's contract conveys an *exclusive licence* to volume publication rights. Authors should not normally *assign* their copyrights, and if asked to do so should be sure that they know what they are doing.

(c) *Duration* The normal phrase is 'for the duration of copyright': see COPYRIGHT (1(h)). Its actual duration will then depend on the publisher's capacity to fulfil his or her obligations.

(d) *Territory* The normal phrase is 'throughout the world'. The purpose here is to ensure that all territories are looked after, and if authors have reason to believe that they can sell the overseas rights more effectively than the publisher, the licence should cover only the publisher's immediate territory.

If the contract is with an overseas publisher, it is vital that special arrangements are made about Australian territorial rights, both to secure them – see COPYRIGHT (1(j)) – and to ensure that Australia is treated as a domestic market for purposes of royalties.

(e) *Subsidiary rights* These include film and television adaptation and performance rights, translation rights and serialisation, reprint and quotation rights. As in (d), authors can retain these if they are willing and able to look after them, but it may mean a lot of work for very little return.

(2) The consideration

The consideration will depend on the earning capacity of the work. If it is very attractive, there is a seller's market in which the rights may well be auctioned to the highest bidder. At the other end of the scale is the work whose commercial value is so doubtful that the publisher may want a subsidy or guarantee before proceeding. The following are the main components to be negotiated:

(a) The normal consideration is a royalty agreement, with a base rate of 10% of the retail price, or a rather larger percentage of publisher's net receipts. Royalty agreements replaced the earlier 'equal share of profits' arrangements, which fell into disrepute because unscrupulous publishers managed to prove that they had made no profits.

(b) The royalty rate may be on a *sliding scale* based either on total sales or on rate of sale, reflecting the greater profitability of reprints.

(c) An advance on royalties may be paid. The amount will depend on the publisher's enthusiasm to secure the property, not on the author's costs in writing it. As a rule-of-thumb, an advance will rarely be more than half the royalties to be expected from the first edition.

(d) The consideration for subsidiary rights is usually a percentage of the income derived from them. The percentage may vary from a fifty–fifty split of trivial items, where the cost of administration is relatively high, to an eighty–twenty split in the author's favour on any major items, e.g. film rights.

(3) Rights and responsibilities

(a) Authors should have the right to the integrity of the material, that is, a provision that no changes can be made without their agreement. This does not mean that authors should resist the publishers' editorial suggestions, which may be of great value. But if a dispute arises, the authors should win.

The author should have the responsibility to deliver the material in good order. Unless otherwise negotiated in advance, this will generally include responsibility for providing any illustrations which are integral to the text and for the copyright clearance and fees on quoted matter, though this will often be negotiable. Authors also undertake to revise the work if revision (e.g. for a new edition) is needed.

(b) The publisher should have the right to decide questions about the 'manner of publication': how the book is produced, promoted, sold and distributed. As with (a) above, this does not mean that the publisher should resist authors' suggestions, but if a dispute arises, the publisher should win.

The publisher should have the responsibility to publish the work with appropriate despatch, to keep the work in print and available to the public, and to maximise the return from overseas and subsidiary rights. Rights then revert to the author in the event of the publisher failing to perform any of these obligations by simple breach of contract.

If the contract is with an overseas publisher, the publisher must undertake to fulfil the conditions to secure Australian territorial copyright, e.g. to publish in Australia within thirty days of publication overseas.

(c) There is a curious clause in many contracts called *the warranty clause*, by which authors are expected to warrant not only that the work is original and is their own property (which is fair enough) but also that the work contains nothing obscene, blasphemous, seditious or defamatory.

The biggest risk is accidental libel, about which no responsible person could give a warranty (see DEFAMATION), and many blanket warranty clauses have been deemed to be unenforceable at law on account of being 'unduly onerous'. By contrast, a publisher can reasonably require an author to draw attention to any material which is known to be offensive, and it is better that the clause should be worded this way.

(d) Many contracts include an *option clause*, giving the publisher first refusal of the author's next comparable work. This clause, too, is virtually unenforceable, if only because there are so many ways round it; but the thinking behind it is reasonable: if a publisher has spent a great deal of money on promoting a new author, he or she should be able to benefit from this investment if the work proves successful.

(4) Termination

Either party should be able to terminate the contract in the event of the failure of the other to abide by it. The termination clause should specify the machinery for resolution of disputes, and this machinery should be as cheap and simple as possible.

The termination clause is perhaps the most important of the lot. If all goes well, the contract is never looked at again; if something does go wrong, it may well be because of a contingency for which there was no provision, and a clear agreement on the machinery for arbitration is vital.

Contracts with periodicals

While quite comprehensive contracts are customary in the world of book publishing, they are relatively rare in the world of periodical publishing. This is particularly so with literary magazines, which may be managed in a less-than-businesslike way. Often, an author will send in an article, story or poem and get back a cheque. This is a very unsatisfactory situation which can cause real trouble if the work subsequently becomes very valuable, e.g. if a short story becomes the basis for a feature film.

The general assumption of the law is that, unless otherwise agreed, the author has sold only first publication rights. To make this clear, authors should specify what rights they are offering in the covering letter accompanying the submission (e.g. 'I would like to offer you first publication rights to the attached manuscript').

Contracts and literary agents

The variety and complexity of the points discussed above is the principal reason why literary agents stay in business. Many professional writers feel that their time is better spent writing (which is their field of expertise) than haggling (which is not).

Despite this, some authors resist the appointment of an agent because the agent will take at least 10% of the action. A good agent may well double the action, making the percentage seem very worthwhile. Paradoxically, the less difficulty writers have in finding publishers for their work, the more worthwhile it may be to employ an agent to do it for them.

However, finding a good agent may not be easy. There are only a dozen or so good ones in Australia, feeding over a hundred publishers, and finding a good agent who is prepared to take on an unknown author's first book may be as difficult as it is to find a publisher. This is not surprising. Agents do not make their money out of peddling unsaleable manuscripts round the publishers; they only take on books they feel pretty confident they can sell.

This is the source of the myth that agents have some magical power to persuade publishers to accept books for publication. Publishers do indeed take submissions from agents more seriously than they do direct submissions. Indeed, some major American publishers refuse to consider direct submissions. But this is not because of any magical power; it is solely because they know that if a good agent has chosen to handle a book, it is at least worth looking at. Furthermore, a good agent will not send romantic novels to publishers of motor manuals.

Bad agents are somewhat easier to find.

punctuation   The sole purpose of punctuation is to help the reader to understand the sense and tone of a text. On this simple foundation has been erected over the years a vast edifice of rules and conventions, the delight of pedants and the bane of school children, but largely ignored by the great writers. The following notes start with the most straightforward examples.

(1)   The exclamation mark | ! |

The exclamation mark is used to indicate that what goes before it is an exclamation, and should be enunciated as such: *Good heavens! Stop! Order!* At the end of a sentence, it can have the force of a full stop and be followed by a capital letter; but if it is in dialogue, the sentence can run on without a capital letter: *'Stop!' said the policeman.*

An exclamation mark is obligatory at the end of sentences like *How the mob howled! What a fiasco!* Expressions like *How dare you!* are questions, and should demand a question mark, but being rhetorical (i.e. not expecting an answer) they can be treated as exclamations.

Using exclamation marks to add an appearance of drama to a turgid narrative is an amateurish device, but is allowed in accounts of chess games, e.g. *B × Kt!*

An exclamation mark in brackets (!) is used by some writers to indicate that what they have just said is remarkable. It has a similar force to *(sic)* = 'thus', used to flag misspellings and blunders in verbatim transcripts.

Mathematicians use the exclamation mark to indicate a *factorial*: $4! = 4 \times 3 \times 2 \times 1$. No hint of drama there.

(2) The question mark | ? |

The question mark indicates that what goes before it is a direct question. Since this will have bearing on the way the beginning of a sentence is sounded, it is sad that we did not adopt the sensible Spanish habit (which, I am told, the Spanish are abandoning) of putting a repeater at the beginning of the sentence: *¿Who is Sylvia?*

The rules about capitalisation of words following a question mark are as for the exclamation mark.

Indirect questions should not be given question marks: *He asked who Sylvia was.*

The only problem arises with quasi-quotations, as in the sentence *To be or not to be, that is the question.* If this was set as a punctuation exercise, the correct answer would be that *To be or not to be* was a direct question, so we would write: *To be or not to be? That is the question.* It should be a solace to those who disagree, or who find punctuation difficult, to see what the editors have made of this and its following lines:

> *To be or not to be: that is the question:*
> *Whether 'tis nobler in the mind to suffer*
> *The slings and arrows of outrageous fortune,*
> *Or to take arms against a sea of troubles,*
> *And by opposing end them?*

According to normal rules, all the marks in this passage are wrong. There is no question mark on the initial direct question, a question mark at the end which is attached to an indirect question, and two colons which do *not* introduce what follows.

However, the marks fulfil precisely the 'sole purpose of punctuation' as defined at the beginning of this article: the first clause is to be sounded flat, although it is almost a question; the second, although referring back to the first, has to be linked tonally to the third, which would otherwise have no main clause to lean on; and the third, although grammatically a dependent clause, is to be sounded as a question.

It should be added that we have some nameless editors to blame for this. Shakespeare was as erratic in punctuation as in spelling.

(3) The full stop | . |

The full stop is a terminator, marking a strong pause in the flow to reflect a change of thought. This is reflected in its alternative name, particularly common in America, *period*.

The rule generally taught in schools is that every sentence should end with a full stop if it does not end in an exclamation mark or question mark, but this is not obeyed in real life: newspaper headlines, street signs, entries in tables, many poems and the headwords in the present work are printed without a terminator, the reason being that the termination is clear from other clues.

In addition, note that, if a sentence of dialogue does not end in an exclamation mark or question mark, it can end with a comma: *'Let's fight till six, and then have dinner,' said Tweedle Dum.* Here the two commas have quite different status, the latter being a terminator to Tweedle Dum's utterance.

Finally, the full stop is also used after some ABBREVIATIONS, and has numerous applications in mathematics and science.

(4) The colon | : |

Despite the evidence given above that Shakespeare (or his editors) thought otherwise, the colon is best used only to indicate the concept 'as follows', in the prelude to a list or explanation: *red, white and blue*. For some notes on the punctuation of lists which follow after a colon, see LISTS.

(5) The semi-colon | ; |

The semi-colon is best regarded as a strengthened comma. It is very useful in lists where the items are long: thus, we might use commas in *red, white and blue*, but put semi-colons between the items in *Blight was old, bent and bitter; but he was also surprisingly coherent, with an invective which startled his neighbours.* Here, a divider stronger than a comma was needed because the comma is being used as a lower level divider elsewhere.

Alternatively, the semi-colon can be seen as a weak full stop, marking the frontier between two complete sentences which could be totally separated by full stops but whose sense demands that they are treated as a single entity. This is particularly common in the rhetorical device called *chiasmus*, where two sentences mirror one another's structure: *the rain came down; up went the umbrellas.*

Vocally, this use of the semi-colon demands a pause as long as that for a full stop, but without the full stop's finality; the pitch of the voice should indicate that the sentence has longer to run.

(6) The comma | , |

Whereas all the other punctuation marks represent speech patterns or act as flags to intonation, the comma doubles as a logical device; and thence spring the problems, because different people perceive the logic of sentences differently.

Some will, I suspect, always comma-off self-contained phraselets. I have done this with 'I suspect' at the beginning of this sentence, not so much because I believe that this is how it will or should be said, but because it ensures that the words in the phraselet do not get caught up with the main structure of the sentence. Commas used in this way must come in pairs, like brackets, unless the phraselet has some other end marker, e.g. if it appears at the beginning or end of a sentence.

Conversely, it is not always appropriate to insert a comma wherever a speaker might pause. For example, if commas were inserted wherever Winston Churchill paused in delivering his Battle of Britain speech, it would be written:

> *Never, in the field of human conflict, was so much owed, by so many, to so few.*

The official transcript, however, has no commas at all, since it is logically a single entity.

The *One, two and three* convention requires us to insert a comma between members of lists except where there is an *and*. Others follow the *One, two, and three* convention, inserting commas after all items. I prefer the former. See LISTS.

For the use of commas in punctuating dialogue, see the next section.

(7) Quotation marks | '...' |

Australians use this phrase, and its short form 'quotes', in preference to 'inverted commas', despite occasional howls of rage from those who believe that these are Americanisms. It is particularly sensible to use the short form when talking about *single quotes* (' ') and *double quotes* (" "). (Because the quotation marks in the Palatino typeface used in this text do not show the distinction between opening and closing quotation marks as clearly as they might, the quotation marks in this section are set in the typeface called Bookman.)

The questions to be answered relate to: (a) the choice between singles and doubles; (b) the relationship of quotation marks to other punctuation marks; (c) uses on titles and labels; and (d) use for certain special effects.

(a) Single v. double   The normal rule is to use one style for 'first level' and the other for 'second level' (i.e. quotes within quotes). The Americans (followed by most Australian newspapers and magazines) tend to use double quotes for first level and singles for second level, and the British (followed by most Australian book publishers) use single, then double.

The great merit of this convention is that it is mechanical. The typist or typesetter does not have to stop to think.

The demerit of the convention also stems from it being mechanical, and is illustrated in the following:

> *When asked whether he had read 'The Dunciad' recently, he said 'No, I haven't read "The Dunciad" for weeks'.*

Logically, the two references to *The Dunciad* ought to be rendered in the same way.

It has been suggested, e.g. in RW, that we should make a *logical* distinction between singles and doubles, double quotes being used for direct speech and singles for all other purposes, including quotes within quotes:

> *When asked whether he had read 'The Dunciad' recently, he said "No, I haven't read 'The Dunciad' for weeks".*

Desirable though this might be, we should recognise that it might involve a lot of extra proof correction. The distinction between dialogue and the title of a poem is clear enough, but a suburbful of half-way houses lurks between these two extremes.

Which should we use? Assuming that we are under no constraints (e.g. somebody else's house style) it is entirely a matter of personal choice, aesthetic and practical rather than logical. I like the 'single first' convention in books in which quotes are largely used for purposes other than dialogue, and 'double first' in books with a lot of dialogue.

(b) Combining quote marks with other punctuation

(1) If the quotation ends but the sentence carries on, the quotation is terminated with a comma, not a full stop:

> *'I don't like it,' said the judge.*

If the speech ends with an exclamation or question mark, the sentence runs on as if they were commas, i.e. no capital letter:

> *'Silence!' said the judge.*
> *'What did you say?' asked the defendant.*

Note, however, that if the punctuation relates to the structure of the main sentence and not to the matter in the quotation marks, it should be left outside:

> *The response must be 'yes', 'no' or 'don't know'; there is no other option.*

(2) Some writers put a comma before the opening quotes in dialogue, thus:

The judge said, 'No'.

This comma is optional. The opening quotation mark and the capital letter provide more than enough indication of the break.

(3) The final full stop can cause considerable anguish:

(a) If the entire sentence is within the quotation marks, the stop should be, too.

'What did you say?'
'Nothing.'

(b) If the quotations are only a part of the sentence, the normal convention is to close the sentence with a full stop after the last quotation mark:

The response must be 'yes', 'no' or 'don't know'.

In this specific example, the convention is appropriate, but it may not always be – see *(d)* below.

(c) If the quotation is only part of the sentence but requires its own punctuation, as in the case of a question or exclamation, we can write

A common response is 'Why do you ask?'

i.e. the question mark, while applying only to the quotation, is taken as closing the main sentence as well.

(d) Can we treat a full stop the same way? Rule *(c)* allows us to write:

He said 'The Mercedes is parked in the shed.'

where rule *(b)* would ask for:

He said 'The Mercedes is parked in the shed'.

The latter is logically better, but can cause a ragged look to a column of dialogue, with a mix of styles *(a)*, *(c)* and *(d)*. In such cases, I ignore rule *(b)* and place all punctuation marks within the final quote.

(e) If the main sentence is a question, it must be closed by a question mark:

Did he say 'The Mercedes is parked in the shed'?

If, then, the quotation is itself a question, we should have:

Did he say 'Is the Mercedes parked in the shed?'?

Most of us would agree that one of them has to go, and (despite Fowler's view) it should be the second one. Why? Firstly because it is consistent with the decision on item (d) above; secondly because it is markedly preferable in some special cases, e.g.

Have you read 'Who Killed Kennedy?'

Here, closing the quotes without the question mark would be a misquotation of the title. The only alternative is to leave both question marks in; and this is not as unthinkable as some authorities, including Fowler, seem to think. Pedantic perhaps, but not unthinkable.

(4) If a quotation runs for more than one paragraph, the opening quotation mark is normally repeated at the beginning of the following paragraphs. (If this seems excessive, it is perhaps worth noting that when the use of quotation marks first became popular in the eighteenth century, it was common to repeat the opening quote at the beginning of every *line*.)

(c) Quotation marks on titles and labels   In academic writing, the rules of bibliography should be followed (see BIBLIOGRAPHIES). These require titles of complete works in italics (or, if the text is in italics, in roman), and reserve quotation marks for titles of sections of works, including articles from books and poems from collections; thus:

>   *He used to sing 'Nessun dorma' from* Turandot *in the bath.*

In less formal writing, including novels, the typeset version can stick more closely to the manuscript form, and all titles may well be put in quote marks:

>   *He used to sing 'Nessun dorma' from 'Turandot' in the bath.*

The presence and position of quote marks may be crucial:

'She is the Queen of Australia'	is probably a statement about the monarch;
'She is the "Queen of Australia"'	is probably about a boat;
'She is "the Queen of Australia"'	is probably about a theatrical performer.

(d) Other uses of quotation marks   Quotation marks around a word or phrase can carry a number of meanings:

(1) They can introduce new coinage:

>   *He called the creatures 'animalcules'.*

(2) They can indicate that a common language word is being used in a new jargon sense:

>   *The boiler is refilled under pressure by an 'injector'.*

(3) They can indicate that a new jargon word is being introduced:

>   *The rate at which a device can transfer information is given by its 'baud rate'.*

(4) They can indicate sarcasm:

>   *I had a 'holiday' in the City yesterday.*

These can cause trouble when read aloud. The speaker should aim to indicate the presence of inverted commas by tone of voice, and should have no need to say *...quote holiday unquote.....* That, however, is better than saying *...quote-unquote holiday...*, while the worst of all is making V-signs with one's fingers in the vicinity of one's ears.

(5) Quotes are sometimes used to indicate that the author is vaguely uneasy about the choice of a word or phrase, either because it is slang, or because its meaning is not quite what is intended:

>   *The government is 'up in the air' about the proposal.*

This convention is not recommended. If a word or phrase is not precise, or is in the wrong register, wrapping it up in quotation marks will not make it any better. A slang expression may, indeed, be ideal, but if so it will need no apology – indeed, wrapping it in quotes would destroy the effect.

Furthermore, this convention is used by sloppy writers as a substitute for thought and discrimination. Such writers use quotes not only round imprecise or inappropriate expressions but also (often in combination with underlining, exclamation marks and capital letters) to add emphasis to an otherwise artless narrative. They should not be encouraged.

(8) Dash: en-dash |–|**, em-dash** |—|

Dashes can be used with greater precision in typography than in manuscript or typescript, thanks to the variation in length and precise spacing. This point is explored under DASH....

The main use of dashes is as parentheses, particularly in dialogue, where brackets seem inappropriate to the speech patterns being represented. While they normally appear in pairs, fore-and-aft, a parenthetical remark at the end of a sentence requires no closing dash (unlike brackets, which must have equal numbers of openers and closers).

Hyphens were once used after colons (:-) to introduce lists. This is no longer done, but a spaced en-dash is sometimes used instead of a colon to introduce a list, particularly in less formal writing, e.g. *There are two divisions – sales and service.*

From this modest start, the dash has developed as the lazy writer's friend, a universal punctuation mark to save the labour of deciding which to use. This style can work well in handwritten letters, but is less appealing when transmuted into typescript and looks awful in print.

(9) Brackets |(...)|

Brackets are the most common way of showing PARENTHESES. They present only two problems: (a) brackets within brackets, and (b) correct use in academic citations and quoted matter.

(a) Brackets within brackets can be used with impunity if the matter enclosed in the inner brackets is short. Thus, in this book we have references in the form '(see PUNCTUATION (9))'. Problems only arise if the matter in the inner bracket is so long that confusion arises between the inner and outer brackets. In such cases one or other of the parentheses should be represented by dashes or commas rather than brackets, or the sentence rewritten to avoid the problem.

(b) In academic citations and quotations, square brackets [ ] are used for editorial comment and chevron brackets ⟨ ⟩ for restorations of mutilated texts, leaving round brackets for normal text requirements. For further discussion, see QUOTATIONS (1).

(10) Solidus | / |

A solidus, also called an *oblique* or a *slash*, is not a true punctuation mark, but rather a logical symbol with a variety of meanings:

(a) It provides the simplest way of typesetting fractions: 1/2, 33/64, km/h. The variant ½, $^{33}/_{64}$ uses superior and inferior characters which are available in all typesetting systems with a minimum of extra fuss, and is again a one-line setting. All other formats involve some sort of special setting, and although the flexibility of computer setting makes these less laborious than they were in the days of hot metal, they may add to typesetting costs.

Authors should remember this if discussing typesetting conventions. Metrication has reduced the occurrence of fractions greatly, with decimals used in many contexts (e.g. measurement of length) in which fractions were once the norm, so that total avoidance of fractions is today a reasonable aim. Failing this, one of the one-line styles shown above is cheaper than *any* of the multi-line styles.

Having said this, the decision must be made on clarity and the conventions of the topic, and it would be quite absurd to attempt to avoid multi-line setting in a mathematics or physics book.

(b) The solidus provides a way of offering alternatives: *M/F, and/or*. The convention seems to have started life on questionnaire forms, where it was often associated with the phrase 'Delete where inapplicable', and there can be no objection to its use there.

Problems arise when the convention appears in prose. Fowler took the extreme view, objecting to the use even of *and/or* except in legal and commercial documents. However, the convention is so well established and understood today that it seems pointless to object to it. It is undeniably useful, and it is clear even when read out as *and or* (i.e. there is no need to say *and oblique or*).

We ought to be cautious, however, about extending its use to other pairings. If there is a well-established way of reproducing it in speech, it is not too bad. Thus we may read *is/is not* as *is or isn't*, but we must then ask ourselves why we did not write *is or isn't*.

(c) Use of the solidus in place of a dash in such phrases as *the French/German border* is not recommended, as it can lead to accidental ambiguity. *The French–German border* (using an unspaced en-dash) is unambiguous.

Q

quagmire   *Quagmire* follows the majority of *qua-* words in being pronounced with a short /o/ sound: /*kwogmire*/. The only *qua-* words which are sounded with a short *a* sound are *quack* and *quango*. However, while *aquatic* is generally pronounced /*a'kwottic*/ in Australia, it is generally /*a'kwattic*/ in Britain.

qualification   It is worth distinguishing *qualification* from *certification*. A *qualification* is prospective, covering the qualities (aptitudes, attitudes, skills, experience, etc.) which a person requires for some *future* activity. The phrases *qualifying examination* and *qualifying round* preserve this sense, being events which *qualify* a person to proceed to the next round.

Certification, by contrast, is retrospective, a statement of a person's past achievement, issued on completion of a course or test.

If you read the dictionaries, you might imagine that there was no confusion. In their entries on *qualification*, Mac say nothing about certificates, and the only reference to a 'paper qualification' in ACOD is illustrated by the case of a document attesting to a person's income. Neither dictionary mentions the current common use of qualification as a synonym for *certificate of performance. Tertiary qualifications* should strictly mean qualifications to *enter* a tertiary institution, not, as is generally the case, the certificates issued on leaving it.

The shading of this distinction arises because many professions and trades have adopted an exit certificate from a training course as their sole entrance prerequisite, so that a certificate on the wall is in a real sense the person's 'qualification' to practice. If the certificate covers the appropriate qualities, this doubling of purpose is reasonable: for example, a driving test measures directly some at least of the qualities which make a good driver. But most university degrees, for example, are not qualifications for anything; they are simply certificates of achievement, which may or may not represent necessary or sufficient qualifications for any subsequent activity.

Happily, no qualifications are required for most human activities. There are courses in parenthood, some of which doubtless issue certificates, but the sole *qualification* is fertility. More to the point in the present book, the same goes for writers: the sole qualification is ownership of writing materials.

We are not going to change the language simply by pointing out a shortcoming in it. However, the confusion between certification and qualification does cause false expectations among students and graduates, and if we can be careful not to add to them, so much the better.

question mark   See PUNCTUATION (2).

questions, direct and indirect   In written English, questions can be of two sorts, *direct* and *indirect*: (1) *'Where do you live?'* is termed a *direct question*, and quotes the actual words used; (2) *She asked me where I lived* contains an *indirect question*; it reports that the question was asked.

(1) The simplest way of forming a *direct question* is to invert the subject and verb:

Statement	Direct question
He has agreed →	*Has he agreed?*

This was a normal way of forming questions in Shakespeare's time (*Stands Scotland where it did?*) but simple inversion is today confined to a limited range of auxiliaries and quasi-auxiliaries: *will/shall, may/might, can, ought to, must, would/should*, and all forms and uses of the verb *to be*.

In all other cases, the direct question is normally formed by using an appropriate inflection of the verb *to do*. So we would say:

   Does Scotland stand where it did?

A virtually identical construction, using a relevant inflection of the verb *to do*, is used if an *interrogative pronoun* is present:

   How do you *cook melons?*
   Why do you *do chemistry?*
   Where and *when* did you *have breakfast?*

To have can also be inverted when it is an auxiliary, but when it is not an auxiliary, as in *Have you a match?*, we are often happier to treat it like any other main verb, and use *do*: *Do you have a match?*

An interesting case involves the phrase *used to*. Is it an auxiliary verb (so that the interrogative of *She used to...* is *Used she to...?*) or a main verb (so that the interrogative is *Did she use to...?*)? For a discussion of this, see USE.

(2) *Indirect questions* are best thought of as *noun clauses*, the direct objects of the verb *to ask* (or another verb with the same effect); see OBJECT....

Indirect questions are introduced by an interrogative pronoun:

Statement	Direct question	Indirect question
He lied	→ *Why did he lie?*	→ *I asked him why he lied*

If it would have no interrogative pronoun in its direct question form, one is supplied, e.g. *whether* or *if*.

He agreed	→ *Did he agree?*	→ *I asked him if he agreed*
She does chemistry	→ *Does she do chemistry?*	→ *Ask her whether she does chemistry*

Idiomatic English has complicated rules about the tenses of verbs in indirect questions, and this causes some problems, particularly in the choice between *may* and *might*. This issue is discussed under SEQUENCE OF TENSES.

quite   It is worth noting that this word can have almost contradictory meanings. *It was quite dark* can mean 'it was totally dark' or 'it was fairly dark'. In speech, this is indicated by tone, but we might debate which Oscar Wilde had in mind when he had Lady Bracknell say, of a recent widow, 'Her hair has turned quite gold from grief'.

The most common usage today is 'fairly', and using it as 'totally' may be misunderstood or sound quaint. The only exception to this is in the phrases *Quite so* and in the negative, e.g. *It was not quite dark*. Here it always means 'totally'. This leads to the further anomaly that *It was not quite dark* and *It was quite dark* both mean 'It was dusk'.

quotations   When we quote an author's work, we have three responsibilities: the first two relate to the original author's MORAL RIGHTS of *integrity* and *attribution,* and the third covers the author's legal rights under copyright law. In what follows, the term *author* means the author of the quotation, and *you* are the person using the quotation:

(1) The right of integrity requires that any quotation you use must be accurate and, as far as it goes, complete. Selective quotation (i.e. the trimming of a quotation so that it misrepresents the author's views) and quotation out of context are two examples of breach of this right.

It is recognised, however, that trimming of quotations is sometimes essential, and conventions have been adopted which ensure that readers know where trimming has occurred. Adherence to these conventions is essential in academic writing, and they provide good guidelines for non-academic writing.

(a) If words are omitted in the middle of a quotation, the omission should be marked with an ellipsis (…). An ellipsis is also used at the beginning and/or end of a quotation to indicate that part of a paragraph has been omitted. The ellipsis is treated as a word, i.e. with a space between it and an adjacent word but no space between it and a following punctuation mark (or a preceding inverted comma).

(b) Explanatory interpolations must be clearly marked. The convention is that square brackets are used for this purpose. Thus:

[Mr Sparkes] was kicked to death by a duck

indicates that the beginning of the paragraph contained some irrelevancies whose only important point was an indication that *Mr Sparkes* was the subject of the sentence quoted.

Mr Sparkes was kicked to death by a quacker [duck]

indicates that you are providing an explanation of the author's meaning. (If it had been in the author's original text, it would be in round brackets.)

Chevron brackets are used to mark a *lacuna*. Thus

Mr Sparkes was kicked to death by a d⟨uck⟩

indicates that the edge of a manuscript page was torn off or illegible, but that this is what you believe the author wrote.

Integrity of the text is best ensured by keeping (and supplying to the publisher) a photocopy of the quotation as it appears in the source used. Needless to say, you should satisfy yourself that the sources are themselves accurate versions of the original texts.

(2) The right of attribution simply means that authors have the right to have their name attached to quotations from their work.

Closely related to this is the question of *acknowledgement*, which covers the bibliographic information which is required for academic citations and for copyright clearance, as well as being relevant to the author's right of attribution. Compiling an acknowledgement list can be a fearful chore if you do not maintain a record of the sources of the quotations:

(a) Whenever a quotation is extracted from a work, the full bibliographical details should be entered alongside the quotation in your text (even if they will subsequently be deleted) or, in the case of photocopies, on the photocopy.

(b) If the source is itself secondary (e.g. an anthology or paperback reprint) quote the primary source acknowledged in the secondary source.

The job may take a few minutes; but this is nothing when compared with the time taken to check the source of quotations which appear in a text without any indication of source.

(3) Copyright clearance must be obtained if the quotation is of copyright work. For a discussion of the relevant aspect of copyright law, see COPYRIGHT (2). The present article discusses practical problems with clearing copyright, and for this purpose the audit trail described in (2) above becomes vital.

In general, application should be made to the original publisher of the work, and fulfilment of the terms laid down by that publisher can be taken to be sufficient to fulfil your obligations.

However, it sometimes happens that publishers, by mistake or otherwise, give permission when it is not theirs to give. This will rarely happen with major book or periodical publishers, who keep full records, but it can easily happen with semi-amateur publishers of, for example, poetry magazines, who may have no contractual agreement with their authors and may in fact have no rights other than those covering the original publication of the work.

In the event of dispute, the fact that you have sought and obtained 'permission' can be evidence that your intentions were not evil, but you may still be liable to pay the fees, etc., to the real holder of the rights. If both the publisher of (say) the magazine in which the work first appeared and the publisher of the first book to contain the work claim copyright, the safest course is to seek instructions direct from the author.

R

racism, racialism   These are two forms for the same word. The shorter one is the more commonly used today; likewise *racist* rather than *racialist*. For a general discussion of the topic, see PREJUDICE. For a particular reference to *racist language*, see TABOO WORDS.

racket/racquet   Our dictionaries agree that the spelling *racket* can be used in all senses, with *racquet* as an alternative for the device used in tennis. ACOD prefers *racket* in all senses (following the OED tradition). Mac reports *racquet* the preferred alternative in the context of tennis. Australian sports stores and style guides seem to support Mac.

AWEG has an unusual entry: '*Racquet*, usual spelling in Australia for tennis, etc. bat, but racket is correct.' Correctness is at best a dubious quality (see CORRECTNESS), but if a spelling is 'usual', not only according to democratic consensus but also according to our dictionaries, our style guides and the practice of our best writers, it seems odd to label some other usage 'correct'.

As it happens, Fowler was equally dogmatic, but again without saying why. The word came, we are told, from the Arabic *rahat* via the French *raquette*, and has been battling it out with *racket* for five hundred years, so an awful lot of writers have been incorrect for a very long time.

radiation   This word is a good example of an ambiguity which is unlikely to cause trouble: it is the name both of a process and its product (as is PUBLICATION). It is noticed only in very odd circumstances, like attempting to translate the French sentence *La radiation est l'action d'emettre un rayonnement*, literally, 'radiation is the action of emitting radiation'. But it is interesting as an illustration of the difference between the French and English attitudes to language

The French had turned the Latin *radius* into *rai* (which gave us our 'ray', see RADIO) and then *rayon*, and when they needed a general term for light-like emissions, they ignored the existing term *radiation* and coined the noun *rayonnement*.

Meanwhile, in English, the meaning of the term *radiation* had been extended to cover this newly-discovered phenomenon. When the English-language articles on the subject were translated into French, the translators tended to use the identically-spelt French word, and this usage caught on. As a result, for some seventy years there were two words in French with effectively identical meaning, *rayonnement* and *radiation*.

In 1965 the problem was elegantly solved: a sub-committee of the *Académie des Sciences* considered the matter, and decided that both words could be preserved by dividing up the usages, making

348

radiation the process (e.g. 'surplus energy is emitted BY *radiation*') and *rayonnement* for the product (e.g. 'surplus energy is emitted AS *rayonnement*'). It did not matter that the allocation of the senses had no historical, etymological or popular support. They said 'Soit'; and so it was.

If only we had an Académie, it could give us answers to all our similar curly questions, like how to pronounce *either*. But then, we wouldn't listen to the answers.

radio   This word is now so much associated with broadcasting that such terms as *radio-chemistry* have become puzzling. It is reasonable to blame the French (see RADIATION).

At the end of the nineteenth century, a term was needed for the light-like emissions from pitchblende. Because they were so like light, the terms *ray* and *radiation* were applied to them. The hitherto unknown element from which they *radiated* was given the name *radium*, and the phenomenon was described as *radio-activity*. Other mysterious emanations were called *X-rays*, and again the related vocabulary used the *radio-* prefix, i.e. *radiology* and *radiography*. We might have talked of *ray-activity*, *rayology* and *rayography*, but as it happens we didn't.

radio, wireless   Meanwhile, yet another form of ray was developed as a means of sending telegraph messages without wires, a process known at the time as wireless-telegraphy or radio-telegraphy. These terms were then shortened to *wireless* and *radio*, *wireless* capturing the British market and *radio* the American. Australian usage initially reflected this split, so that American-inspired commercial *radio* battled it out with the ABC, which thought of itself as *wireless*, singing innocently 'The wireless says the time has come for all the girls and boys …to come with a hop, a skip and a run…'.

However, *radio* was also a word associated with new technology. Thus the first air traffic communications stations, set up in 1934 in Melbourne, Launceston and Darwin, were called *air radio* (later *aeradio*), *not air wireless*. Similarly, the detection and ranging device was termed *radar*, not *widar*.

In the RAAF during the Second World War the two terms co-existed uneasily. The operators were termed *W/Ops*, and the planes had *wireless aerials*, but the sets were usually *radios*. One convention was to interpret RT as radio *telephony* and WT as wireless *telegraphy*, i.e. radio meant voices and wireless meant morse; but this does not appear to have been officially adopted. By 1945, however, the term *radio* emerged victorious when the RAAF School of Signals became the Radio School.

In the past forty years the word *wireless* has all but disappeared, so that today it exists only in a few names, notably the Wireless Institute of Australia and AWA, Amalgamated Wireless (Australasia) Ltd, and in the vocabulary of the elderly.

railways   The technical vocabulary of railways is vast, and there is significant regional variation in practical applications. Any writer wanting to get it right should consult someone who knows, i.e. an appropriate railway buff.

Considering the impact of railways on social life, warfare and trade, their contribution to common language has been surprisingly small. Unlike nautical slang, which has contributed a great many metaphors (see NAUTICAL FOLLIES), railway jargon has never been shared extensively with the public. Furthermore, that which has arrived has come almost exclusively from America. Thus we get *railroaded* and *side-tracked* or *off the track*; we have *one-track minds* and *make the grade*, to say nothing of *climbing aboard the gravy train* and making *a whistle-stop*. These metaphors are all American: the original phrases do not exist in British or Australian railway usage. The phrase *go off the rails*, by contrast, could have started anywhere.

One possible reason for the paucity of railway metaphor is perhaps that the vocabulary, though vast, is almost entirely of new meanings for existing words, or assemblages of existing words. The Americans boldly coined *smokestack* for what the British continued to call a *chimney*, and the British coined *bogie* for what the Americans called a *truck*. For the most part, however, both took existing words and gave them new meanings, some of which are mentioned below.

Australia generally followed British usage. In the following list, which contains some of the words likely to occur in non-technical contexts, the British term occurs first, followed by the American in brackets, with a note on Australian usage *where it differs from British*:

railway (railroad); station (depot, though major city depots are *stations*); engine driver (engineer); guard (conductor); line (track, but for Australian usage see TRACKS); platform (track); points (switches); shunting engine (switcher); siding (side-track); sleepers (ties); goods wagon (freight car; Australian: freight wagon); van (box car); carriage or coach (car or passenger car; Australian: as British, but *car* for purposes of numbering and ticketing); platelayer *or* ganger (Australian: fettler); brake van (caboose); coupling (coupler); incline *or* bank (grade); connecting rod (main rod); regulator (throttle).

Since the end of steam traction, the literary influence of railways has shrunk from little to nothing.

rapt/wrapped in thought   The word *rapt* is from the same family as *rapture*, and means *in a state of rapture*: *the audience was rapt throughout the performance*. If this is the sense, *rapt* is the spelling.

The word *wrapped*, as in *The audience was wrapped (up) in the performance*, has the connotation of finding it intellectually absorbing rather than being carried away by it.

Nevertheless, the phrase 'wrapped in thought' was first written down as 'rapt' some five hundred years ago. The confusion of the two idioms is now so complete that it is difficult to disentangle them, but the distinction between emotional *rapture* and intellectual *enwrapment* may help. Meanwhile a further complication was the recent arrival of *rap-up*, as in 'He gave the book a good rap-up', which looks like a mishearing of *wrap-up*, but seems to have led to a new word, *rap* = review (i.e. 'He gave the book a good rap').

For a general discussion of the way mishearings and confusions can become new usages, see TRANSCRIPTION…(3).

ratbag   There are many ratbags in Britain, yet the term was until recently unknown. It still has a distinctly Australian flavour in the export market.

rationalist   This is a damaged word. Until the 1970s, it was associated with the Age of Reason and the assertion that the greatest possession of man was his mind rather than his soul. Rationalists were people who were opposed to all dogma, sacred or profane.

This changed in the 1970s, when it was used in the term *economic rationalist*, where it is associated with a specific dogma. At one stage, it looked as if the term had been usurped, so that *rationalist* on its own would imply *economic rationalist*; much to the distress of members of the Rationalist Society. (The same had happened with CHAUVINIST, though there was no Chauvinist Society to get upset.)

However, the damage to the word has not proved fatal. Its parent word, *rational,* has remained unscathed, and 'rationalist' continues to carry its old connotations of logic and good sense except in the context of economics.

re-   The problems here are of (1) meaning, (2) pronunciation (short or long, stressed or unstressed) and (3) hyphenation.
(1) Meanings   The prefix originally meant *back again*, as in *return*, but with emphasis on *back*, as in *repel*, though often the *back again* implication is weak (*receive*). In other words (including all new coinage) it means *again*, without any thought of *back,* as in *rebuild.*
(2) Pronunciation   In the old words *re-* is a short syllable (/r'turn/) unless the root word starts with a vowel (*react*), and in a few cases where a noun which has the same form as a verb has the first syllable stressed, e.g. /r'ject/, /ree-ject/. We can see the same pairings in *compact, impact*, etc.

Stress is particularly important when the two meanings collide, as with words like *recount*, where /r'count/ means 'tell (a story)' and /ree-count/ means 'count again'. Such words are often best hyphenated (and sounded /ree/) when used in the 'again' sense; see (3) below.
(3) Hyphenation   Hyphenation can be used to resolve doubt about pronunciation and meaning.

The simplest case is words which look slightly odd, e.g. *reenter*. Such words are best hyphenated (*re-elect, re-educate*). We do not seem to be worried by *rearrange*, but *reread* may look better as *re-read* and *reword* as *re-word*. *The Age Style Guide* hyphenates *re-urge*, a word which most of us are rarely tempted to use.

The more serious problem arises when there is a possible ambiguity of sense, as in the case of *recount* discussed above. If there is any risk of confusion, a hyphen will indicate that the *re-* is to be stressed and means 'again'. Examples include *reform, resign, recover, recreation, rejoin*.

A hyphen can be used to distinguish two meanings even if the pronunciations are the same. Thus, *relay* is best hyphenated in the sense *re-lay the carpet* (as opposed to *relay the message*). (In this particular case, hyphenation is not needed in the past tense as the spellings part company: *I relaid the carpet and relayed the message*.)

-re, -er *Centre* or *center*? We have here one of the very few cases in which a contrived spelling reform has been generally adopted. Noah Webster, seeking ways to make his American Dictionary different from Sam Johnson's (and hence to make a distinction between *English*, the common language, and *British* and *American*, the regional variations) hit on the *-er* spellings as a field for reform. He was not reporting an American variation, he was inventing one.

The fact that it stuck suggests that it was a good choice. Should we follow suit?

The arguments are not conclusive. The Americans are more consistent than we are, which sounds like an argument for them; but our inconsistency allows us to make distinctions which they cannot, e.g. between *micrometre* (a millionth of a metre) and *micrometer* (a device for measuring very small distances); but then, the chances of running into a sentence where an *-re/-er* confusion causes an ambiguity are monstrous small, whereas the distinction unquestionably generates spelling 'errors'.

Again, we could argue that the Americans are not totally consistent, having had to retain *acre* and *lucre*, which would otherwise change pronunciation; but they are a lot more consistent than we are, which should please the consistency-seekers. However, the question is not likely to be settled on its merits. The *-er* spellings are seen as Americanisms, and this would arouse all manner of irrational prejudices which would prove fatal to any reform.

readable, readability Readability, like STYLE, is an ill-defined phenomenon. It has two separate meanings, first as in the sentence 'Agatha Christie is very readable' and second as in 'The text scores well for readability'.

The first is a statement about the capacity of a text to grab and hold the reader, and is measured by watching how readers react.

The second refers to the outcome of objective tests of the 'readability' of a text. These are based on counting things: the average length of words, the average number of syllables in each word, the average number of words in a sentence, the average number of clauses in a sentence, and so on.

Have the two anything in common?

The tests certainly have some validity: longer words and complex sentences are harder to read than short, easy ones, and for a discussion of one context in which this is particularly true, see RETARDED READERS; so *other things being equal*, the tests do predict 'readability'. However, other things are not generally equal. If the tests are applied to, say, a Roald Dahl novel and a primary textbook aimed at children of the same age, the textbook will emerge as more 'readable'; but the children will still be reading Dahl avidly when the textbook has been discarded.

This is not surprising. The biggest contribution to readability remains the payload: short words and sentences will not stop a boring text from being unreadably boring, and long words and sentences will not stop the reader nutting out the meaning of it if it appears to be important, interesting or funny. It is sad that, for many children, the first experience of reading is with books of little interest or literary merit. The *process* of reading is taught as an end in itself, detached from its *purpose* – the gaining of pleasure and information. We are shocked that our children do not regard reading as a rewarding experience, when we have ensured that their early experience of it is unrewarding.

For creative writers, the significant point is that readability ultimately depends on having something to say and saying it in a fresh and vivid way. If the author has done this, an editor can tidy up any unnecessary obscurities. What an editor cannot do is inject wit and wisdom into a piece of flat, dull prose, however well it scores for 'readability'.

For editors, the major danger lies in forgetting that readability tests work only because more readable writers tend to use shorter sentences and words. Short sentences and simple words are a symptom of readability, not the cause of it. A skilled writer could devise a totally captivating children's story which scored badly on the tests, or a totally unreadable one which scored well. Thus, shortening sentences and shortening words will improve the text's 'readability score' without necessarily affecting its readability in the Agatha Christie sense.

realise   Provided that we remember that it originally meant *make real*, we can put together the various apparently unrelated senses of this word.

> *The picture was valued at $12m, but* realised *only $2 million at auction.*
>
> *He* realised *his childhood ambition.*
>
> *He* realised *that his childhood ambition would never be achieved.*

redundant   This word means *superfluous*, but the connotations have changed recently. The citations in OED show it as a rare word, used by Milton of a luxuriant head of hair and by Macaulay of surplus capital available for investment. In all cases it was a very positive term: there was no implication that the surplus was unwanted.

In the 1950s, it was popularised in the context of employees and productive capacity. It was an abstract term related first to automation, then to computerisation: *automation will render sweat and toil redundant* (= no longer necessary – a good thing). When the threat materialised, 'redundant' was adopted as a euphemism for *sacked*: workers were 'declared redundant'.

Meanwhile, *redundant* had also been adopted as a technical term of semantics to denote information whose removal would not impair the message. Thus, for example, in the sentence 'Gv Jn th bk', the message is pretty unambiguous apart from *Jn*, so we can say 'In the sentence *Give Jean the book* all the vowels are redundant except those in *Jean*'.

reflexive   As a term of grammar, this word describes a verb which has to be followed by (or has a special meaning if followed by) *myself, yourself, itself*, etc. The nearest approach to reflexive verbs in English is in some idioms, e.g. *to kick oneself* (where no kicking is involved); but in many languages, such verbs are common: in French, for example, *se passer, s'appeller* and hundreds of others.

register   When we want to talk to people, it is helpful if we can speak their language. This is obvious if we are talking to a foreigner who does not speak any English, and only slightly less obvious in the case of adapting our speech to be understood by a foreigner with only basic English, or of a very young child, or of the speaker of a very different dialect from our own. However, we also change our language to suit the occasion: the language of an academic debate is different from that of buying a newspaper.

Register is a general term for the combination of vocabulary, grammar and pronunciation which distinguishes various levels of language: formal from informal, educated from uneducated, specialist from non-specialist.

(1) Mobility between registers   It is generally easier to move down than to move up. Thus a doctor should be able to explain diagnoses to patients in lay language, but a patient cannot be expected to explain symptoms in medical language. A speaker who is accustomed to formal language is likely also to be fluent in informal registers, while the converse may not be the case. Those whose natural register is very informal can have difficulties in job interviews and lose the chances of promotion. You can say that this shouldn't be the case, but it is dangerous to say that it isn't.

(2) The mechanism of register   Writers may have the opportunity to re-work their writing to make it suit their readers; talkers have no such luck. Our words flow out at great speed – three or four per second – and this rate means that they arise from a conditioned reflex rather than a considered and controlled action. We find ourselves committed to words and grammatical structures before we can think them through, and clichés and grammatical tangles are the outcome. What we call 'an unhappy choice of words' is generally 'an unhappy *absence* of choice of words'.

The only way to change this is to re-condition the reflexes, and this is easier said than done. It is only with very great effort that new words can be deliberately added to the working vocabulary, the *reflex* stock. Similarly, new grammatical structures can be added to the stock (and entrenched grammatical weaknesses removed) only by deliberate practice, and this seems artificial and pretentious. We like the idea that language is a natural process.

Nevertheless, those who wish to do it (e.g. tongue-tied politicians who wish to make fluent impromptu public statements) have to do it, just as do those who want to learn to speak a foreign language fluently. The alternative in both cases is that responses will remain incoherent, ploddish or both.

(3) Translation between registers   Despite what was just said, a register is not a language; it is a level of language. If it were a language, any thought could be expressed in any register, but this is not the case. To write a knitting pattern in common language would not only be very tedious, but effectively impossible, and this is so for almost any specialist communication, from Zen to motor bike maintenance. Philosophers may argue about the primacy of thought over language (that is, can we have a thought if we do not have the words for it?) and obviously somebody must have been the first to have the thoughts and invent the words for them. But, for *most* of us on *most* topics, the range of our thoughts (and certainly the precision with which we can communicate them to others) is measured by the extent of our vocabulary and our mastery of grammar.

Ideas must often therefore be simplified when presented for popular consumption. In the case of technical jargon, this is unavoidable: there is no way in which the general public can be taught the technical vocabulary of, say, economics in order to participate in the great debates on the subject, particularly when the economists themselves are in disarray. But register problems present a real threat to the basis of participatory democracy – an informed electorate. Many of the great debates of our time, on conservation, defence, tax reform, 'right to life' issues and so on, have been bedevilled by the fact that very complex questions have been translated into registers which do not contain the necessary vocabulary, and it is not then surprising that decisions are made on evocative slogans rather than rational arguments.

(4) Failure to translate between registers   Many words change their meaning from one register to another. This is particularly common when the move is between common language and a technical jargon. The insertion of a technical term into an otherwise general language sentence can happen through ignorance or thoughtlessness: it often happens when people are asked questions about their jobs, and they slip unconsciously into the language of the workplace. This is bad manners but excusable. It is inexcusable if it is done deliberately, either in the belief that it will impress or (worse) in order to conceal the truth.

relative clauses   This is a grammatical term for clauses which act as adjectives, usually introduced by the **relative pronouns** *who, whom, whose, which* and *that*; see CLAUSE (2).

(1) Defining and non-defining   Relative clauses are divided into two types, *defining* and *non-defining*. Defining clauses tell the reader which item is being discussed. Thus

The man who was wearing a green balaclava shot the archbishop

implies that there were several suspects, of whom only one fits this description. A non-defining relative clause adds some further descriptive information. Thus

The man, who was wearing a green balaclava, shot the archbishop

is a factual account of the incident, the relative clause adding to the information about the culprit.

Non-defining relative clauses are often enclosed in commas, as in this case.

The defining/non-defining distinction has been used as the basis of a solution to the *that/which* dilemma, but it is not a very good one: see THAT, WHICH.

(2) Omission of the pronoun   If the relative pronoun is the object of the verb in the relative clause, it can often be omitted:

The house [which] I live in is just round the corner.
The thief picked up the balaclava [which] he had dropped.

This omission is only possible, however, if the relative pronoun is *not* the subject of the relative clause. We cannot omit *which* from:

The house [which] was burnt down has since been rebuilt.

Furthermore, it is risky to omit the relative pronoun unless the relative clause is short and has its subject at the beginning:

The house [which] despite some misgivings I had bought was burnt down

fails on both counts. But we might just get away with leaving out the *which* in:

The house [which] I had bought, despite some misgivings, was burnt down.

(3) Relative clauses of time, place, cause and manner   A number of other types of clause, similar to equivalent adverbial clauses, can be used as relative clauses:

This is the house where I was born.

> *That was the year when I was born.*
> *That was the reason why I was born.*

Thus the words *where, when,* etc., are in these sentences *relative pronouns.*

Similarly, *as* normally introduces an adverbial clause of manner, but in some usages is better regarded as a relative pronoun. The sentence

> *The man shot the archbishop as he had been instructed to do*

would generally mean *...in the manner laid down in the contract.* However, the same sentence could be intended to mean *...which he had been instructed to do,* and in this case it is better to label it a relative clause with *as* acting as a relative pronoun, its ANTECEDENT being the whole initial statement.

In the languages for which these labels were originally devised, there would never be any doubt: relative clauses are a tight, easily identified group. The doubts arise from an attempt to label English structures with the same names. If we had not drawn our first vocabulary of grammar from Latin, we would explain and label them very differently.

relay   See RE-.

relevant, irrelevant   These useful words have been badly mauled by our educationists. They are logical terms indicating whether or not an argument has a bearing on the point being discussed. Thus an argument might be *true but irrelevant.* Not surprisingly, the words were picked up by the general public, who had similar needs.

In the hands of the educationists, however, the focus shifted. The change started innocently enough, when *a skill which is relevant to a child's future* was shortened to *a skill which is relevant to the child.* The next moment, however, 'relevant to the child' was being equated with 'interesting to the child'.

The concern here is not about educational theory, but about the meaning of the words. If we claim that something is *relevant,* the implication is that it is useful for some specified *purpose.* Knowledge of bus timetables is *relevant* to anyone who wants to catch a bus; but this does not make this knowledge *relevant* to people in general. At least, that is what all our dictionaries tell is *relevance* means; but maybe the sense used by our educationists has now taken over.

If so, I regret it.

religious   It is commonplace to Catholics, but sometimes puzzling to others, that such a sentence as 'The school's staff includes four *religious*' does not mean that the rest are irreligious, but that only four are members of religious orders, 'religious' being a noun, not an adjective. The singular and plural forms are the same.

remedial   See RETARDED READERS.

repetitions and refreshers   If St Paul had had a keen sense of economy and less sense of theatre, he might have written 'Charity… beareth, believeth, hopeth, and endureth all things'. However, he was repetitious: 'Charity… beareth all things, believeth all things, hopeth all things, endureth all things'.

When we hear that we should not use the same word over and over again (a very sound piece of advice) we should remember that there are odd occasions on which repetition is very desirable. The rhetorical device illustrated above is one of them. Like many rhetorical devices, it rings false and cheap if used badly, but can be immensely effective if used well. Its main effect is rhythmic rather than semantic.

A second use of repetition is the refresher. The term is borrowed from commerce, where it refers to the sums which have to be fed at regular intervals into time-based devices like parking meters and barristers. In rhetoric, it refers to the optional repetition of words, either to resolve ambiguities or to remind the hearer or reader of the construction. It is thus the opposite of ELLIPSIS.

The simplest examples are refreshers hitched to ambiguous pronouns by means of brackets:

He said that he (the defendant) had not bailed him (the witness) up or taken his (the judge's) watch.

This crude device may be the only one available if the text is a verbatim transcript, but a writer, faced with the same problem, will be able to remove the ambiguity more subtly. Thus:

The witness said that the defendant had not bailed him up or taken the judge's watch.

The following sentence describes a further use of a refresher and (in the italic phrase towards the end of it) gives an illustration of the refresher itself:

If the writer fears that the reader is liable to have lost track of the grammatical construction in a long and complex sentence, one which uses a large number of subordinate clauses each of which has its own structure, so that the initial structure will have been forgotten long before the end is reached, as is the case with the present sentence (and not many readers would at this point remember clearly that what we are waiting for is the *apodosis* of a conditional phrase, or even know what the apodosis of a conditional phrase is, though it is explained in the section on IF… CLAUSES in this book); *if, as I say, the writer fears this,* a refresher is a possible answer.

In general, a better solution to the problem described above is to chop the sentence into two or more simpler sentences; but there are occasions when chopping it up would destroy an important symmetry, and this is where the refresher is particularly useful.

In other cases, the refresher may be added early, to signal what is to follow. The word *both* in *both … and,* the word *either* in *either …*

or and the words *not only* in *not only … but also* are essentially refreshers, clarifying but not altering the meaning of the sentences. The old Spanish convention about question marks provides another example; see PUNCTUATION.

There are no rules about the provision of refreshers. We are often unaware that a phrase of ours could be misunderstood and needs clarification until we find that we have been misunderstood. Significantly, however, great orators use refreshers extensively, recognising that they add clarity as well as thunder to a speech.

re-read The use of this word as a synonym for *read*, as in 'I was rereading Kant the other evening…', is an academic convention which should be used with great care. It may not be believed.

research As the name of an outer Melbourne suburb, this word is pronounced */Ree-search/*. In common language, however, the preferred pronunciation is */r'search/*, the other being perceived as an Americanism, and given that the *re-* does not have a strong sense of repetition (see RE-) there seems to be no merit in it.

reservoir For a discussion of the meaning, see DAM.

Henry Handel Richardson, in the opening chapter of *The Getting of Wisdom*, got the broad Australian pronunciation right when she wrote 'Res'vor', and this is the pronunciation of the Melbourne suburb. In other contexts, the better pronunciation is */rezz'vwah/*.

resile This word means *to jump back*, as of elastic bands, and is related to the common term *resilient*. It was restricted to legal jargon (lawyers *resile from contracts*, etc.) until introduced into the Senate; but it seems to have fulfilled a need, since it won bicameral (and bipartisan) support, being used in the House of Representatives shortly afterwards. The usage is generally negative: I *do not resile from my earlier view…*.

Most of us have plenty of more-appropriate words to express the same thought: *retreat, withdraw*.

respect In utterances starting *Mr Chairman, with respect…* the phrase *with respect* is a conventional signal that what follows is a dissent from the Chairman's ruling. It is thus a hypocritical euphemism. Nevertheless, the convention which demands it is a good one, giving the Chairman the opportunity to retreat on a specific point while maintaining overall authority. It is an expression for which no sexless equivalent (e.g. using *Chairperson*) exists. We have to say 'Madam Chair…'

The phrase ***with respect to…*** uses a more literal meaning of the word *respect*: *a backward glance*.

respiration The prime meaning of the word is *breathing*, and non-biologists are sometimes surprised to hear it used in connection with the digestion of food. This happens because biologists have chosen it as a term for the opposite of *photosynthesis*. The following comment is designed to cover this and some related vocabulary items which are sometimes misunderstood or misused.

In photosynthesis, plants take carbon dioxide from the air and water from the soil to form carbohydrate tissue. The process is *endothermic* (i.e. it requires an outside source of energy). The energy comes from the sun and is stored as the bond energy of the carbohydrate molecules, while oxygen is released.

In respiration, animals take carbohydrate food and 'burn' it in oxygen, the process being *exothermic* (i.e. it releases energy). It produces carbon dioxide and water, which are excreted.

The essential chemistry of *respiration*, therefore, is the oxidation of carbohydrates, which requires the *inspiration* of oxygen and the *expiration* of carbon dioxide, i.e. breathing; which is where we came in.

restaura(n)teur   ACOD lists *restaurateur* and does not make any mention of *restauranteur*. Mac₁ listed *restauranteur* and did not mention *restaurateur*. ACOD is supported by etymology (the word is French and analogous to *amateur*) and by overseas English usage; Mac₁ gave *restauranteur* on the grounds that this was the most commonly heard version and must therefore be reported. However, in response to a counter attack by purists, Mac₂ for once ignored the evidence of its ears, and gave *restaurateur*.

retarded readers   This article will discuss (1) the meaning of the term 'retarded' and (2) some of the issues that arise in writing books for slow readers.

(1) Meaning   As a technical term of education, *retarded* describes a relatively simple situation, a *retarded child* being one who is running behind schedule, but able to catch up if given half a chance, e.g. given *remedial* treatment – an intensive course designed specifically to make up for the lost time.

This is quite unlike the situation of ESN (= Educationally Sub-Normal) children, who are defined as suffering from a condition which is likely to prevent them from ever performing at the level normal for their age, though their performance can be improved by special educational experiences.

Not surprisingly, however, the term *retarded* has been adopted as a euphemism for ESN, as was its predecessor *backward*, and likewise *remedial* is used for educational activities for the sub-normal even if they do not pretend to supply any sort of *remedy*. This does not matter – what's in a name? – provided that the needs of the two groups are clearly distinguished. The evidence is, regrettably, that this is not so, with the result that migrant children who have no problem except lack of English are given education materials designed for children who are intellectually handicapped.

(2) Issues   Many people are called upon at various times to write texts which must be accessible to *incompetent* readers. They include people who write questionnaires and mail-order forms, instruction booklets, direction signs and, of course, advertising, as well as those preparing educational materials for slow readers.

There is a very simple method of replicating the problems of an incompetent reader. This is to try reading a text in a mirror, aloud. It not only slows the process down, making the reading process extraordinarily boring; it also reduces access to many of the less obvious aids to comprehension like the subliminal scanning of a passage for punctuation marks and other clues to tone and structure. It is a revealing experience, generating a noise just like a slow reader, right down to transposition errors like *was* for *saw*.

(a) The principal lesson that comes out of it is the value of brevity. Like the slow reader, you have to decode every word as a separate task, and it is immensely tedious. Many writers imagine that a light, chatty style will be 'simple' for readers. If every word is an effort, the fewer of them the better. Thus 'Write your name here' takes four times as long to read as 'Name' and is unlikely to be any more effective in getting the message across. Slow readers are not necessarily stupid.

(b) Similarly, providing a second version paraphrasing or explaining the first only increases the reading task. Writers (being by definition competent readers) tend to assume that reading is a linear process, and repeat important or tricky points. Slow readers do not: they prefer to re-read a puzzling passage than to be offered a new one covering the same ground.

(c) The third lesson is the value of a clear logical structure, with separate stages in an argument distinguished, and with a layout which complements or reflects this logic.

Note that the list does not include 'use short, simple words'. The vocabulary should be as complex as the topic demands. There is no point in using a long word if a short one would be a more natural choice; but it is equally pointless to write *oven* rather that *microwave* on the grounds that its length, or low placing on word frequency charts, makes it 'difficult'. Indeed, if the context is established (for example, if there is a picture of a microwave on the same page), the reader may find the word *microwave* easier to 'read' than *oven*, simply because he or she was expecting a long word starting with *m*.

rhyme   Rhyme is an essential part of some verse forms – the sonnet and the limerick, to name two very different models. However, rhyme was not found in the earliest verse. It occurred first accidentally in Latin pentameters, where a noun and its adjective often appeared at the ends of two half lines and, thanks to the inflections of the language, tended to rhyme.

> *Protinus est oculis | | cognita nostra tuis.*

The effect was pleasing to simple minds, and was then deliberately produced in medieval Latin verse.

It was also found to assist metre in making the lines more memorable, an important consideration in the days when books were scarce and expensive. This remains true. Not much free verse gets remembered, whereas quite trivial jingles stick in the memory. (See POETRY....)

Rhyme was at first spelt *rime*, and seems to have acquired its more pretentious spelling through being mistakenly associated with *rhythm*.

riches   See PLURAL DILEMMAS (9(a)).

riesling   The word may be pronounced /*ree-sling*/ or, if a more Germanic sound is preferred, /*reez-ling*/, but /*rye-sling*/ is wrong both ways.

road   A range of words is used to describe the state and status of roads. Let us consider them in ascending order of magnificence:

An *unmade road* is a piece of ground showing evidence of the passage of traffic, but otherwise in a state of nature. The term was used in the nineteenth century, and resurrected in the 1945–65 period, when suburban subdivision was permitted in many Australian cities without the obligation on the subdivider to attend to the roads. A *made road* (in, say, advertisements for rural real estate) can mean more or less anything from *formed* to *sealed*.

A *bush road* was used in the nineteenth century as a synonym for *unmade road*, but today indicates location but not state, referring to any rural road other than a highway.

A *formed road* is a technical term, not in general use, for a road which has been shaped with a bulldozer and/or grader to create a driving surface and gutters. In many cases the road will be formed from the local subsoil, but if this is unsuitable gravel or crushed rock may be used. Once it has been formed, the road can be kept in shape by regular visits from a grader, and is then known as a *graded road* (a phrase with greater currency). On road signs, such a road is often called a *gravel road*. The colloquial equivalent is *dirt road*, a term covering all roads which are not sealed.

An *all-weather road* indicates any road whose surface is sufficiently durable and well-drained to be passable when it is raining. (It does not imply that there is no risk of flash flooding.)

A *sealed road* is one whose surface is covered with bitumen, asphalt or concrete, and will thus be *all-weather*. Its other main characteristic is the absence of dust.

These words are all about the physical condition of the road. Cutting across these categories are the words describing the status of roads, which is roughly the same as saying who is responsible for their upkeep. Thus we have interstate highways, looked after by

State authorities but with federal money; other highways and main roads which are the responsibility of the States; and local roads which are the responsibility of the local authorities.

The term *highway* does not in theory say anything about the physical conditions; we may say 'Sections of the Bonang Highway are just a dirt road'. Conversely, *highway* is often used as a generic term for a major road, so that we may say 'Take the dirt road and turn left when you hit the highway' even if the sealed major road we are talking about is not a designated highway. This usage is also found in America, but not in British English, where the term *highway* exists only in special legal and historical contexts, e.g. *the Queen's highway, the Highway Code, highwayman* and in such phrases as *highways and byways*.

The terms *main road* and *country road* not only have their natural meanings, but may also indicate the authority responsible. Thus the *Department of Main Roads* in New South Wales covered the same range of roads as the one-time *Country Roads Board* of Victoria (now the *Road Construction Authority*).

A *trunk road* is an official Australian term for a major long-distance road which has not been designated a highway, but the term is not often used outside official and technical publications. *Arterial road* was a very rare technical term in Australia until adopted in Victoria to mean *an urban freeway built by an authority which has undertaken not to build any more urban freeways*.

The generic term for a restricted access road has emerged as *freeway*, though some earlier (mostly urban) freeways were called *expressways*, and have retained this name. A *tollway* is a freeway on which tolls are charged. *Motorway* is a Britishism, but is also the generic term in New Zealand.

road/street Within urban areas, Australian usage is reasonably consistent in differentiating between *Roads*, which are arterial, and *Streets/Lanes/Courts/Crescents /Parades/Places/Avenues*, which are local. The British habit of using the word *Road* in this sense is rare in Australia. If the name of the road indicates its direction, it is often spoken of with a definite article: *the Parramatta Road, the Dandenong Road*.

roman numerals See NUMERALS, ROMAN. In type specifications, the word *Roman* should be capitalised to distinguish it from *roman* = non-italic.

run-on sentence For an example which shows the nature of the crime known as the *run-on sentence*, see HOWEVER.

S

sack   Fowler reported that *sack,* in the sense of dismissal from a job, had moved from being slang to being colloquial. In Australia at least, it has since gone a little further than this, the turning point being perhaps the events of 11 November 1975, when the verb *to sack* was used even in formal accounts of the dismissal of the Prime Minister, Gough Whitlam, by the Governor-General.

There seems, however, to be a distinction between the noun (as in the phrase *get the sack*), which remains a near-slang colloquialism, and the verb, *to sack,* which is almost formal.

Fire, which Fowler reported as an Americanism which was making headway in Britain at the expense of *sack,* has lost ground in Australia, surviving largely with the particular connotation of dismissal by *visiting firemen,* that is, representatives of overseas parent companies clearing out unwanted senior executives of Australian subsidiaries. There are many other phrases in popular speech: thus one can get *the boot* or *the chop;* but the received euphemism is to be *declared redundant* or *retrenched* when one's firm *undergoes destaffing.* The legal term is *dismissal,* as in *wrongful dismissal.*

sacrilege(-ious)   Even people who have no doubt about the spelling of *sacrilege* often get *sacrilegious* wrong, relating it to *religious* and hence spelling it *sacreligious.* The word is *sacri + lege,* sacred + law. If we reverted to the older pronunciations /*sacri-leej*/ and /*sacri-leejus*/, people would perhaps be less likely to misspell them. But if we campaigned for this we might get shut away.

said   Three minor points:

(1) The word *said* meaning *aforesaid* or *aforementioned,* as in the sentence *The defendant stole the* said *lion from the* said *zoo,* is legalese and has no more place in proper prose than the aforementioned *aforesaid.*

(2) The inversion of *said* and its subject, as in *'No soft soap from strangers,'* said *the Puddin', rudely,* is fine in dialogue (e.g. in novels) but has no place in newspaper reports, unless the intention is to be contemptuous.

(3) Beware of the phrase 'said to be'. It is best used only in the sense of popular rumour (*These dogs are said to be unreliable*) and not used to introduce a new or unusual term (*These dogs are said to be 'anthropophagous'*).

sake   Goodness, Pete, Auld Lang Syne, you and I have one thing in common; we all have *sakes.* Precisely what sakes *are* is less clear. If the etymologists are to be believed, they originated in law, where *sakes* were akin to those equally mysterious phenomena, *behalves,* i.e. 'for my sake' = 'on my behalf'. But all this had happened before the thirteenth century, since when they have meant almost exactly what they do now – whatever that is.

Happily, we all seem to recognise a sake when we come across one.

Write *Pete's sake, goodness' sake* and *old sake's sake.*

Salt 'Congress is expected to pass Salt during its next session.' This unlikely proposition is printed in the style adopted by most of our newspapers for strings of initials: in this case for the *Strategic Arms Limitation Treaty.* (See ACRONYMS for discussion of the general rules.)

It raises four questions, the answers to which have wide application to other strings of initials:

(1) Should we prefer 'pass *the* Salt' (i.e. include the definite article)?

(2) How about 'pass the Salt treaty'?

(3) How about 'pass SALT' (i.e. write the name in capitals)?

(4) Is there any way out?

(1) In theory, we should treat an abbreviation exactly as we would treat the full version, and as we would always say 'pass *the* Strategic Arms Limitation Treaty' we should say 'pass *the* Salt'. In practice, we tend to preserve the article in cases where the initials are read out as separate letters, but drop it if they have become an acronym. Thus we have *'the* ABC' and *'the* GST' but 'ASIO' and 'GATT'. But it is not quite as simple as this: see ARTICLE.

(2) Writing 'The Salt treaty' resolves one problem only by creating another: a tautology. If you talk about *the FBT tax*, you risk being accused of muddled thought or ignorance or both. However, others (e.g. *PIN number*) are now so well established that they often sound peculiar without the tautology: e.g. anyone who says 'I have forgotten my pin' runs the risk of not being understood.

(3) Writing 'pass SALT' (i.e. in capitals) contravenes the rules in many style books, which state that acronyms should be written in upper-and-lower case: *Nimby* but *ESP*; *Anzus* but *USA.*

Recognising that this could produce some ambiguities, some style books are more selective, and give lists of acronyms which can be written in upper and lower case. *The Age Style Book* does this, and goes on to say 'Please confine the upper-and-lower approach to the cases listed here'. The words it lists as remaining in capitals include *AIDS,* but *Salt* is on the upper-and-lower list.

If the only reason for avoiding the all-capital style is that capitals straggle across the page, we can use SMALL CAPITALS: '...pass SALT'.

(4) Our decision must be based on the demands of good communication, and if this means some inconsistency, so be it. If the context and readership are such that '...pass Salt' gives no pause, it can stand. But in the last resort a re-write may be necessary, e.g. '...pass the Salt legislation'.

sanction   There is no point in trying to put the clock back: the word *sanction* has been used since the 1930s to mean 'punishment', e.g. the *economic sanctions* imposed on recalcitrant nations. However, there are still contexts where it has its earlier meaning. Etymologically, it is related to *sanctify*, and meant 'blessing': *the marriage has the sanction of the Church*. It then strayed into law, which gave or withheld its sanction (i.e. approval or disapproval) of people's actions. It was then a small move to make the word encompass the means available to the law to make its decisions stick, i.e. rewards and punishments, and then (since the law finds punishment easier than reward) to have its present most common meaning: a punishment by withdrawal of privileges.

satire, satirical   The essential point about satire is that it is reformist: it takes a look at situations or personalities, political or social, and delivers a message about them in very incisive terms. Thus, a joke or sketch does not become satire merely by being about a politician or public figure. Satire must have a point.

If it makes us smile (which it generally will) it may be because it is funny, but it is more likely to be because it is clever. It may use *parody* or *allusion*, two common components of satire which make us smile through the pleasure of recognition. The version of events may be exaggerated or even surrealistic; but the underlying purpose must be serious: to give the audience the satirist's insights into the events.

Sauternes   In France, this term refers to all the varied wines produced in the region of Sauternes, in the Gironde. The best known of these, however, are sweet white wines, including *Château d'Yquem*. In Australia, it is a generic term, less used today than in the past, for sweet white wines. See WINE NAMES.

savage   This word is one of many whose use reflects our fundamental xenophobia. Others include *wild, barbarian, pagan* and even *native*. They all started life with, and to some extent retain, purely descriptive senses: *wild* as 'uncultivated', as in *wild flowers* and *wilderness*; *barbarian* as 'saying *bar bar* instead of speaking proper' (see BARBARIANS); *pagan* first as 'civilian' and then as 'non-Christian'; *native* as 'locally-born'; and *savage* as 'belonging to the woods'. However, strangeness seems to lead immediately to contempt and rapidly to fear, so that *wild* comes to mean 'uncontrollably violent', *barbarians* and *savages* are associated with deliberate violence, *pagan* is pejorative when applied to religion (as is *heathen*) and is often used to mean 'uncivilised', and even *native* is associated with non-whites rather than place of birth.

Saxonism   This is the name generally given to the nineteenth-century British attempt to purify English of alien influences, the assumption being that Anglo-Saxon words are the true tradition and that all others, including Norman French, are interlopers. The word is useful because we continue to hold this view, and it has some merits. There were and are many cases of synonym pairs in which the Anglo-Saxon is down to earth and the French is ploddish, e.g. *begin* rather than *commence*, *get* rather than *obtain*, *give* rather than *donate*.

If taken much further than this, however, Saxonism can easily become absurd and even dangerous. *Betterment* is no simpler than *improvement*, *happening* is more ploddish than *event*, *bodeful* is more quaint than *ominous* and *forebear* is more pretentious (and harder to spell, it would seem) than *ancestor*. These are just four words which were promoted, with varying success, by nineteenth-century Saxonists.

The French are great purifiers, but we find the French objection to Franglais rather comic, particularly as it is so patently unsuccessful.

We found Hitler's attempt to Aryanise German ludicrous (e.g. when it produced *Funk-apparat* for *radio*) or offensive (given that it was an aspect of a diabolical racist ideology).

If we have these attitudes to French and German (which are overwhelmingly single-source languages and hence could in theory be purified without major disruption), it is hard to see how we can take a different view of English, an amalgam which, though still overwhelmingly Germanic in structure and basic vocabulary, derives most of its intellectual and cultural terms from Romance languages.

Conclusion: prefer simpler words. If this means often preferring Anglo-Saxon words, fine, but it should be because they are simpler, not because they are Anglo-Saxon.

scenario   The success of this word suggests that its arrival filled a niche. It was imported from Italy (in the 1880s, if the OED citations are a guide) and meant the sketch of a plot. It became very popular in the film industry, and then strayed into popular usage, where it is used metaphorically, but in a sense very close to its original one: the outline of a situation, or of the likely outcomes of various courses of action.

For some reason it is a word which gets people's goats. I suspect that this is not an objection to the word itself, but to its friends. It surrounds itself with *ongoing situations at this moment in time*; it suffers guilt by association in the phrase *worst-case scenario*, and those who use it are often pretentious bores. Hence we forget that it is a very tightly defined and useful word for which there is no true synonym. There are many times when I would like to use it, but of course I daren't.

schnapper   See SNAPPER....

science   This Latin-based word originally meant *knowledge*, but was particularly associated from earliest times with knowledge of the natural world. Today, this association is complete. Historical knowledge, for example, is not regarded as part of science, though our knowledge of pre-historic times is. Indeed, *science* is currently restricted not merely by the subject matter but also by the approach, so that we talk of the *pre-scientific era* and *pre-science* when discussing the alchemists, for example. The distinctive features of *the scientific method* are discussed briefly under LOGIC (4).

In the phrases *social sciences* and *behavioural sciences*, the word is used in its broader sense, and the word *scientific* cannot normally be applied to their research procedures. The key differences are discussed under THEORY.

selection, selectors   The phrase *On our selection* is likely to be puzzling to non-Australians, who know neither Steele Rudd's book nor the relevant meaning of the term *selection*. Indeed, the meaning has changed slightly over time.

Initially, the term applied to the system under which settlers who had no capital were permitted to 'select' a small block, often as little as 80 acres, of virgin land. Although the 'selection' was effectively a freehold title (becoming one if the selector cleared and fenced the land and paid a token rent), the holding was too small to provide a decent living. Selectors were therefore at the bottom of the agricultural and pastoral hierarchy, below those who held *farm leases*, leasehold land being assumed to be cleared and productive, and a long way below *squatters*, who occupied, illegally, large tracts of good pastoral land (see SQUAT...).

As the supply of virgin land ran out, the meaning of *selection* changed slightly. In particular, it was applied to blocks of land cut out from existing leaseholds and assigned to servicemen returning from the First World War. The connotation, however, continued to be of a block too small to provide a decent living.

Today, as can be seen from the citations in AND, the term is purely historical. Compare COCKATOO.

self-publishing   Self-publishing is a perfectly respectable activity, provided the term is not used as a euphemism for *vanity publishing* (see PUBLISH...). To avoid such confusion, I define it as *a method of publishing whose aims are the same as those of commercial publishing, but in which the publisher is the author.*

I make this point because a number of books have been written which purport to be guides to self-publishing, but which are largely concerned with book design and production. These are fascinating topics, but are probably the parts of the process which the self-publisher can most easily leave to others. It has also encouraged the belief that the process of publishing is complete when the printed books are delivered. In fact, it is about to start.

The commercial publisher's prerogatives are to decide what to publish and then to (1) edit, (2) produce, (3) promote, (4) sell and (5) distribute the books, or employ others to do these jobs, and to recover the costs from sales. The self-publisher may attempt to do all these things, but is then likely to do a lot of them ineffectively.

For self-publishers, the decision about what to publish is by definition easy, so we can go ahead without more ado.

(1) Editing Few people can edit their own work. At the very least, it is a good idea to ask an experienced editor to read the manuscript and compile an editorial brief which will identify whether further work is necessary. This may include legal worries; see EDITOR (1).

(2) Production When asked about book production, publisher Anthony Blond is said to have replied 'It's easy. I give the manuscript to a printer and say "Make it look like a Jonathan Cape book".' This is what all publishers used to do, and it is very appropriate for today's self-publishers. If the self-publisher wishes to become involved in copy mark-up, typography and design, fine, but a good typesetter and printer is likely to respond well to an Anthony Blond-style message, and will prepare sample settings and production dummies for approval before the work goes ahead.

(3) Promotion If a book is designed largely for a defined market (as many self-published works are), the self-publisher may know all the people who are likely to be interested and hence be able to do all worthwhile promotion without help. However, the wider the anticipated market, the harder it becomes. Even the large commercial houses rarely try to handle overseas promotion from Australia, leaving this to local distributors or co-publishers.

There are handbooks containing details of people to whom promotional letters and copies can be sent, e.g. *Margaret Gee's Australian Media Guide*, published twice per year by Information Australia, which can be consulted at a public library.

If self-publishers feel that their time is too valuable, professional book promoters will do it for a fee, and may have promotional ideas which the self-publisher had never thought of. A good publicist may also take on the job of selling serialisation and extract rights, and the rights for book club and large print editions.

(4) Selling The promotional effort may be wasted if the books are not available when the demand arises. With specialist books, promoted largely by direct mail, the mailing piece can include an order form for return to the publisher, and in other cases coupon offers in magazines may work. But with a book designed for a general market, *availability* means availability in the shops. Hence pre-selling is essential. Shops are unlikely to order unless the book has been shown to the buyer. And it is unlikely that the self-publisher has the time and energy to do this unless the market is very compact.

Arrangements must therefore by made well in advance either with a wholesaler who will both sell and distribute (see (4) below) or with commission salespeople, who will collect orders and refer them back to the publisher for fulfilment.

(5) Distribution   This term covers warehousing the stock, invoicing orders, packing and despatching them, receiving and crediting returns and finally collecting the cash. If a book is unsuccessful, this can be quite a light task, the kind of thing that can be looked after in the evening when lights are low. But successful self-publishers will soon decide to appoint a distributor.

Booksellers prefer to buy from distributors. However, this is not an objection to self-published books; the objection is to opening a new account just for one book, with all the palaver this involves in these labour-saving days of computers and central buying. (Saving trouble by paying cash rarely occurs to booksellers). But the effect is the same: it is easier to make a sale if the title will simply be added to the bookseller's next routine order to a distributor.

In Australia, the specialist distribution house is virtually unknown. Instead, we have publishers who offer distribution services to third parties, and wholesalers who maintain their own sales representatives. There is much to be said for making a single agreement covering (4) and (5).

semantic(s)   *Semantics* is the name given to the study of *meaning*. It therefore sounds like a topic which should be of interest to writers. In practice it is not; it is one of the more sterile parts of the wasteland between linguistics and philosophy, and those who loiter there tend to finish up reluctant to admit that any word has any meaning at all (see CATCH 22). Writers, who may have starving children to support, have to believe otherwise.

In common language, the word exists only in the phrase *semantic quibble*, which is a dispute which arises over, or because of, an ill-defined word or words. For the practical solutions, see MEANING.

sentence   The word comes from the Latin *sententia*, meaning an *opinion*. Hence the 'sentence' delivered by a judge is close to the original meaning; the grammatical sentence is a metaphor.

'Write complete sentences,' says the teacher. It sounds simple: a sentence is a string of words containing a finite verb, or one containing a subject and predicate. However, if this is so, then clearly we often do not talk in sentences.

> *'A pair of scissors, please.'*
> *'Like these?'*
> *'No. Bigger.'*
> *'How about these?'*
> *'Yes. How much?'*
> *'Ten dollars fifty.'*
> *'Thanks.'*

There are two ways of explaining this. The first is that these are not sentences, which means that we must invent a new name for them. The second is that they are all sentences, which means that we must revise the definition accordingly.

It does seem to be stretching this a bit to call a sign saying ONE WAY STREET a sentence, and some linguists have identified what they call the *Lapidary Style*, the name deriving from its original application to the grammar of inscriptions carved on rocks. However, if we do this, we have to have a new set of rules for distinguishing items which are not even grammatically sound examples of the lapidary style, e.g. WAY STREET.

One way to broaden the definition of *sentence* is to include verbless utterances where we can identify an obvious ellipsis:

[I would like] a pair of scissors, [if you] please.
[Would you like a pair] like these?
[The answer is] no. [I want a] bigger [pair].

The definition of *sentence* emerges: it is a string of words which is grammatically independent of any surrounding words, and conveys a complete message to its intended audience or readership. It will contain either a main verb or an equivalent ellipsis on whose essential content the writer/speaker and reader/hearer would agree.

sequence of tenses   There is an ancient rule known as the *sequence of tenses*, which purports to govern the way in which the tense of the verb in a dependent clause is related to the tense of the verb in the main clause. The two sequences are known as the *present* (or *primary*) *sequence* and the *past* (or *secondary*) *sequence*. The terms *present* and *past* are simpler, but note that the past perfect is in the present sequence.

An example is the relationship of the tenses of the verbs in indirect questions. In the following sets, any of the dependent clauses within each set can be attached to any of the main clauses within the same set.

The basic tenses of the present sequence are:

	main clause		*dependent clause*	
Present	I ask him	⎞	if he	likes scones.
Present continuous	I am asking him	⎟⎟	when he	is leaving.
Future	I will ask him	⎟⎟	where he	will stay.
Past perfect	I have asked him	⎠	whether he	can come.

The basic tenses of the past sequence are:

Past aorist	I asked him	⎞	if he	liked scones.
Past continuous	I was asking him	⎟⎟	when he	was leaving.
Pluperfect	I had asked him	⎠	where he	would stay.
			whether he	could come.

This list is not complete, but should be sufficient to identify the sequence of the other tense formations in English, e.g.

The future perfect: I will have asked… (present sequence)

The concept of the sequence of tenses was borrowed, as were so many of the concepts of traditional English grammar, from Latin, in which it works well. It does not work quite as well in English, as there are times when we break it, especially in indirect speech. For example:

He said that he lived *in Tasmania*

could report the statement 'I *once* lived in Tasmania' or 'I *now* live in Tasmania'. If we want to stress that he said the latter, we can write:

He said that he lives *in Tasmania*.

Despite its shortcomings, however, there are cases where, if a sentence sounds wrong, some thought about the sequence of tenses can help to explain why. This is particularly true with subjunctives, which may be past sequence even if they refer entirely to the future. For example, if you sense that something is wrong with

If I had my way, you will get the job

the sequence of tenses tells you that *will* (present sequence) should have been *would* (past sequence). However, this 'mistake' is so common now that it may soon become accepted usage; see MAY....

serious, solemn, sincere   Natural disasters are *serious*; funerals are *solemn*; and the eulogy may or may not be *sincere*.

Solemnity is all about the trappings and appearances; *seriousness* is about the underlying realities. If people wear an apparently *serious* expression on their faces all the time, we can be assured that it is only skin deep; hence it should be called a *solemn* expression.

Sincere is an even more abused word. It originally meant 'free from deceit', but came to be applied particularly to belief in some moral or religious teaching. As with seriousness, sincerity (a state of mind) was then confused with solemnity (a state of face), and then transferred to the object of the solemnity, so that a *sincere* song became a song with particularly nonsensical lyrics.

sesquicentennial   Those who are puzzled by this word are in good company. It was coined in America in 1880, with application to the 150th anniversary of the foundation of Georgia, and becomes a visitor to the language of Australia whenever something is 150 years old, which gives it permanent resident status here.

The etymology rests on the obscure Latin prefix *sesqui-*, which meant one-and-a-half, which survives in our dictionaries in only one other word, *sesquipedelian,* meaning a foot and a half long, and applied to unnecessarily long words.

In chemistry, the prefix is used to describe molecules composed of two atoms in the proportions 2 : 3, e.g. *sesqui-terpenes*, a word we are not often tempted to use. By contrast, the word *sesquicule* is derived directly from a genuine Latin original and means *having buttocks which are one and a half times too big*, a word well worth remembering.

sexist language   One of the main objects of concern of the feminist movement since the 1960s has been sexist language. However, the direction taken by reformers has varied according to the nature of the language they speak. In the case of English, the move has been towards inclusive language. In other languages, the move has been to develop feminine versions of masculine generic terms.

The difference is not in intention: in both cases, the changes were designed to force attention on the irrelevance of sex to most aspects of life and work. The difference stemmed from the way *gender* operates in the various languages. (In this book *gender* is used in its original grammatical sense, i.e. a word is *masculine, feminine* or *neuter*, whereas *sex* divides sexual creatures into *male* and *female* and makes everything else *neither*. For more on this, see GENDER.)

In the first edition of *Modern English Usage*, Fowler said: 'with the coming extension of women's vocations, feminines for vocation words are a special need of the future.' This is how it had worked in the past. The classic example had been the word *suffragette,* coined c. 1905 by female suffragists to distinguish themselves from the male-dominate suffragist movement. The issue was then visibility. And had Fowler been predicting German usage, he would have been quite right – that is the way they went in the 1970s and 1980s.

However, the general thrust in English has been the other way, towards the elimination of sex-distinctive forms. In German, a language with a strong gender structure, such elimination would have been impractical. But although the thrust of the two campaigns was diametrically opposed, the purpose of both was the same: by achieving changes in language which confronted everybody every day, the campaigns promoted awareness of the issues.

The attack on sexist language in English has had spectacular success in some directions but not in others. Why is this so, and what changes are still to come?

(1) Successes   The most dramatic changes have occurred in areas where the change is convenient to writers and speakers. Thus:

(a) The term *Ms* gained rapid and widespread acceptance. It was promoted not only to arouse awareness, but also because the use of *Mrs* and *Miss* had become a source of unequal treatment, particularly for women seeking credit. But it was also convenient, eliminating a whole class of errors and problems.

   A few people, mostly older married women, prefer to be called *Mrs*, feeling about it something like veterinarians do about being called *Doctor*, and their wishes should be respected. However, it is likely that *Mrs* and *Miss* will disappear completely over the next decade.

(b) The same can be said of the general elimination of gratuitous sex-based suffixes (-*ess*, -*ette*, -*iste*, -*trix*). Words like *authoress, usherette, typiste* and *executrix* are now rarely used.

The few survivors are those where the roles of the male and female remain separate. Thus, although we can say *Noni Hazlehurst is a fine actor*, she still becomes an *actress* for the purposes of a 'best actress award'. There are also honorifics like *Dame* (to say nothing of *Princess* and *Queen*) and we still read about *society hostesses*. (The male equivalents exist, but we do not call them *society hosts*.) And, of course, the original *suffragettes* must under no circumstances have their own chosen name retrospectively changed; this would be rewriting history.

(c) One quiet achievement has been the desexing of nursing, so that the terms *matron*, *sister* and *male nurse* are obsolescent; see HOSPITAL.

(2) Continuing problems There has been mixed success in areas where the change demanded is more radical, the offending word more entrenched or the proposed alternative more troublesome:

(a) The avoidance of the suffixes *-man* and *-woman* has gone quite well, particularly in contexts where a pre-existing inclusive term will fit: *the police, the chair*. In other cases, the use of *-person* has made some headway (e.g. *spokesperson*) though RW describes this as 'ungainly'.

There has been less progress in cases where the occupation is overwhelmingly male (*rifleman, fireman*), and there is a tendency to retain *-man* for the male and use *-person* only for the female. There are really three separate problems here. Most writers would no longer write *She is an expert craftsman*. Almost as many would notice and avoid the implicit sexism in *The work requires an expert craftsman*. But many would deny any sexism in *The work showed evidence of superb craftsmanship*, on the grounds that *craftsmanship* is simply a word for a particular sort of skill. Hence success in eliminating the first two has been much greater than progress with the third, particularly with words for which no simple synonym exists, e.g. *seamanship*.

(b) There has also been mixed success in the replacement of *he* as an inclusive pronoun (the most overtly sexist of all the offensive usages). On the credit side, writers now rarely use it, which suggests success; but the price is paid by their readers, faced with prose which is sometimes imprecise and often inelegant. Technically, there are many solutions: we can re-write sentences in the plural; we can use *he or she*, *he/she* or *s/he*; we can use *their* as if it meant *his/her*. But they are all intrusive, and the only real solution is the establishment of a new gender-inclusive pronoun, the singular of *they*. This has not happened

(c) The replacement for *man* the species has also proved difficult. This, too, is highly sexist. Some people say that the distinction is clear, but if this were really true we would see nothing odd in *Man suckles his young*.

Again, many solutions have been recommended, but the price for success in abolishing *man* has been an avalanche of turgid and often ludicrous replacements. The old usage is so entrenched in our dictionaries of quotations that it seems unlikely that it will die out.

(3) The future   Inasmuch as the purpose of the campaign against sexist language was to increase awareness of sexism and the denial of equity, it must be judged extraordinarily successful. Everyone is now aware of the issues. If equity has not been achieved, it is not because of any failure in the campaign of awareness.

This might suggest that enthusiasm for the hunt for sexist usage might wane. However, campaigning against offensive language is an absorbing pursuit, with high visibility and endless scope for extension. It is now moving from being a means to an end into being an end in itself.

The original campaign survived the mockery of its attack on words like *manhole* largely because the essential thrust of the campaign was seen as good and necessary. But if the essential thrust loses support, the suspension of disbelief comes to an end.

The campaign is being pursued by (amongst others) a small but highly vocal group of academic feminists who have moved from the quest for equity into the promotion of a *gynocentric* world. (The word is not yet in our dictionaries, but will shortly be). Whatever the merit of their views, they do not command very wide support. The danger is that if they ask us to do enough fatuous things, we will sooner or later start asking why.

We are now being offered an astonishing array of references to *man* and *masculinity* which are apparently to be avoided, from *man-eating lions* to *no-man's land* and the verb *to master*. This has nothing to do with sexist language, and simply brings the whole campaign into disrepute, endangering progress with the unfinished business in the area of equity.

The above examples are not invented by me as targets for ridicule. They appear (alongside, and not differentiated from, some very good advice about genuinely sexist language) in the AGPS *Style Manual*. Writers and editors should simply ignore these recommendations. It would be a denial of common sense to follow them; but it would be even worse to use them as a justification for not heeding the more sensible parts of the article.

shall, should   This is an unusual defective verb, having only these two forms. The use of *shall* is discussed under WILL…, and *should* under WOULD…, IF… CLAUSES and SUBJUNCTIVE.

ship   When is a ship not a ship? RW reports that, in nautical parlance, a ship must have square sails on at least three masts, but this is just one of those silly definitions which are fun to invent but have no effect on common language. There were ships before there were three-masters and there are still ships now.

Whatever the definition, there will always be borderline cases. Rather than start from the word and define it, we must start from the vessels and sort them out.

(1) Any vessel with oars is a boat. Any vessel that is not normally ocean-going is a boat. Any vessel which is regularly carried aboard another vessel is a boat. Any motor vessel with an outboard motor is a boat. Lighters, tugs and barges are boats. Submarines and double-ended ferries are boats. Yachts are boats (but prefer to be called yachts).

(2) Floating docks, oil-drilling platforms, buoys and other vessels whose main purpose is not travel, together with hovercraft, hydrofoils and windsurfers, are neither boats nor ships.

(3) Sailing vessels carrying square sails on three or more masts are ships. Ocean-going vessels for the transport of people and goods are ships. Large single-ended ferries are ships, at least when at sea.

There is really only one safe procedure: ask the captain.

simplicity   It is often said, and rightly, that the best writers of all ages have aimed at simplicity. It is also said, and rightly, that the conventions of punctuation, capitalisation, hyphenation and so on are all very complex.

These two statements have been put together into the proposition that a text can be made 'simpler' by ignoring the conventions, and minimising the use of capitals, hyphens and punctuation. This represents a very dangerous confusion of two separate thoughts.

The simplicity which has been the aim of all the best writers is simplicity *for the reader*. Precise use of punctuation is one way in which a complex text can be made simpler for the reader; hyphenation is another, and capitalisation is a third. This is what they were invented for. The earliest written texts had none of them, and were hard on the reader; the conventions developed over the years – *entirely for the convenience of readers*.

Simplicity for the writer is something very different. It may indeed be simpler for the writer to ignore the conventions of grammar, punctuation and spelling, but this is a simplicity which can only make the reader's task harder.

The conventions of writing, when properly used, are unobtrusive. They are rules of shared experience: words have agreed meanings and are spelt in agreed ways, sentences are structured according to agreed patterns and punctuated with agreed marks. The whole assemblage is self-explanatory. But self-explanatory does not mean self-generating. The reader only notices when the conventions break down, but the writer has had to make decisions all the way.

Producing a really simple text is thus not easy. Anyone can write a turgid or incomprehensible text; good writers are those who take the trouble to ensure that their writing transmits their message correctly, unambiguously and vividly to the reader. Some writers can produce clear, flowing texts first time, every time. But most of us have to work at it.

simplistic   A *simplistic* solution is not the same as a *simple* one. A simple solution is one which is easy but works; a simplistic solution is one which oversimplifies the issues and may not work. This is a useful distinction, and the use of *simplistic* as a more impressive-sounding synonym for *simple* is not only PLODDERY (bad enough) but also an abuse of the word.

singularities   Try adding *is* or *are* to the following:

the media...	*the formula...*	*the agenda...*	*the dogma...*
the data...	*the stigmata...*		
none of us...	*the family...*	*half of the fish... the news...*	
two dollars...			

One (or perhaps two)...

The tooth fairy (and other similar phenomena)...

These examples cover the main classes of problem which arise in deciding whether a particular word or phrase is singular or plural.

The problem with the first six (all words ending in *-a*) to decide whether they were ever plurals, and, if so, whether they still are.

If you do not know whether a word was ever a plural, it is very hard to guess. You can check in a dictionary, though this does not help if you are in the middle of a sentence in conversation. Assuming you cannot look it up, the best course is to use another word, and the next best is to make them all singular: the tendency is for plurals to become singulars, and saying *the dogma are* loses you more points than saying *the data is*.

In any case, irrespective of their origins, which of them are still plurals? The best procedure is to ask what other forms exist.

(a) *Media* was plural, but current usage is moving towards making it singular (*the media is to blame for exacerbating the dispute*). Those who like fighting lost battles may find this a rewarding one to fight, for the singular, *medium*, not only exists but exists in this context (*TV is the best medium for mass advertising*). I cannot say *the media is*, but that's my problem.

Incidentally, the plural of *medium* in the sense of *a clairvoyant* is *mediums*.

(b) *Formula* was never anything but singular, and its usual plural is *formulae* (though there is nothing wrong with *formulas*).

(c) *Agenda* was plural (meaning *things needing to be done*). However, the singular *agendum* is obsolete (except, if *Yes Minister* is to be believed, in the British Civil Service). Its meaning is expressed as *an agenda item*. Furthermore, we say *At the meeting, the two factions produced rival agendas*. So *agenda* has become an ordinary singular, complete with an English-style plural, and now means *a list*, not the contents thereof. The only unpardonable sin would be to treat it as analogous to *formula* and produce the bogus plural, *agendae*. *Candelabra* is also generally treated as a singular.

(d) *Dogma* was never anything but singular, and its plural is *dogmas*. (The etymologically-supported plural *dogmata* now sounds absurd, but is worth remembering to explain the connection with *dogmatic*.)

(e) *Data* was plural, and to most people still is, despite the fact that it has no singular. (*Datum* exists, but it means *a starting point for measurement*, and has its own plural *datums*; it is never used to mean *a single item of data*.) Even those who say *the data is…* do not say *two datas*, suggesting that they see *data* as a collective rather than as an ordinary singular. It is best to treat it as plural, i.e. to use *are* in common expressions like *the data is/are inconsistent*.

(f) *Stigmata* is plural. The singular is *stigma*, which has another plural, *stigmas*, for use in botanical and common language senses. *Stigmata* is used only in the *wounds of Christ* sense. Those who use the word are likely to know this, and those who do not know it are unlikely to use the word.

The next five items on the list represent mathematical rather than grammatical problems. These are generally solved as follows:

(g) *None* is a contraction of *no one*, and it must therefore (we are told) be singular: *None of us is…*. This is fair enough, but it raises another question. Is *zero* singular or plural? The sentence *If no competitor completes the course, no prize is awarded* is fine, but if three prizes were on offer, we would feel justified in saying *If no competitors complete the course, no prizes are awarded*. In similar conditions, *none of us are…* must be acceptable.

(h) The word *family* appears to be a straightforward singular, and if the same fate is overcoming all the members of a family, this is how it is treated: *The family was wiped out by the plague*. If the members are showing independence, however, it is better treated as plural: *The family were arguing among themselves*. But purists may well object to both, saying that it is best to recast the sentence as *The members of the family were…*.

(i) *Half* is similar: singular if we are talking of a single entity (as in *half of the fish was hanging over the side of the plate*), but plural if we are talking about individuals (*half of the fish in the tank were actually tadpoles*).

(j) *The news* is an original plural which has become singular (unlike *riches*, an original singular which has become plural). Shakespeare wrote 'These news would cause him once more yield the ghost', but we would unequivocally write 'This news…'.

(k) *Two dollars* is a normal plural if they are separate dollars (*Two dollars were found down the back of the armchair*), but singular if we are talking about a quantity of money (*Two dollars was enough to buy the whole pig*). This is relevant to the *less/fewer* debate. If we say *There were fewer than two dollars down the back of the armchair* we mean one coin or none; but if we say *There was less than two dollars down the back of the armchair* we mean a sum of between zero and $1.99.

The problem in the last two cases can worry very experienced writers, and there is no cut-and-dried answer. If there were no brackets, the question would not arise: it would be 'One or perhaps two are…' and 'The tooth fairy and other similar phenomena are…'. However, there is a general convention that words in brackets should not influence the structure of the sentence in which they occur, and this convention justifies a singular verb in both cases.

The question can only be answered pragmatically. After the plural phrase in the brackets, a singular verb may come as a shock. The longer the bracketed phrase, the stronger the expectation of a plural verb, and this is particularly so in speech, where the bracket is indicated only by tone. If the writer feels that a plural verb would be less likely to come as a shock, there can be no objection to using one. If in doubt, the safest procedure is to reword the sentence.

The examples quoted above are merely samples of some of the most common classes of problem. See also EACH ONE…, IS/ARE, NEITHER, NUMBER PHRASES, PAIR and PRONOUN (2).

SI units Unlike the French, who have their *Académie* to give them rules for the correct use of their language, English speakers have never had much time for rules. However, there is an exception to this in the case of SI units. Their form is precisely laid down in *Australian Standard 1000–1979: The International System of Units (SI) and its application*. This is not the place for a full explanation of the standard, but the following should answer most practical questions arising in non-technical writing.

(1) The system The letters stand for *Système International [d'Unités]*, so that, for a start, talking about 'the SI system' is a tautology.

The system is founded on seven 'basic' quantities:

QUANTITY	SYMBOL	UNIT	SYMBOL
length	s	metre	m
mass	m	kilogram	kg
time	t	second	s
electric current	I	ampere	A
thermodynamic temperature	T	kelvin	K
amount of substance		mole	mol
luminous intensity		candela	cd

The choice was arbitrary, i.e. it would be perfectly possible to devise a system based on other quantities.

The definitions of the units are similarly arbitrary, and have changed from time to time as new methods of expressing standards became available.

For example, the metre was originally defined as *one ten millionth of the distance from the north pole to the equator*. This was replicated on a platinum rod held in the French standards laboratory in Sèvres, which then became the standard, remaining unchanged even when it was found that the earth was slightly bigger than had been thought. The metre is now defined in terms of the wavelength of a specific radiation of the krypton atom, the merit of this definition being that it can be replicated in any competent standards laboratory, so we no longer need to dash off to Sèvres to check our measuring sticks. (The original definition remains useful – it helps us remember that the circumference of the Earth is almost exactly 40 000 km.)

Beyond the base units are two 'supplementary units', the *radian* for plane angles and the *steradian* for solid angles. Next, there are seventeen other quantities which are defined in terms of the fundamental units but have special names, e.g.:

QUANTITY	SYMBOL	UNIT	SYMBOL	DEFINITION IN FUNDAMENTAL UNITS
energy	E	joule	J	$1 \text{ kg.m}^2.\text{s}^{-2}$
force	F	newton	N	1 kg.m.s^{-2}
power	P	watt	W	$1 \text{ kg.m}^2.\text{s}^{-3}$

Finally, there are hundreds of other quantities for which the derived units have no special unit names, e.g.:

velocity	v	m.s^{-1}
acceleration	a	m.s^{-2}

The original Metric System used special prefixes for multiples and fraction of units:

Greek for multiples (deca- $= \times 10$, hecto- $= \times 100$, kilo- $= \times 1000$)
Latin for fractions (deci- $= \div 10$, centi- $= \div 100$, milli- $= \div 1000$).

SI borrowed the idea of using prefixes and extended it both ways, but the added names do not reflect the Greek/Latin convention of the Metric System:

tera-, T, as in terajoule, TJ	10^{12}	$= \times 1\ 000\ 000\ 000\ 000$
giga-, G, as in gigawatt, GW	10^9	$= \times 1\ 000\ 000\ 000$
mega-, M, as in megahertz, MHz	10^6	$= \times 1\ 000\ 000$
kilo-, k, as in kilogram, kg	10^3	$= \times 1\ 000$
no prefix	10^0	$= \times 1$
milli-, m, as in millilitre, mL	10^{-3}	$= \div 1\ 000$
micro-, μ, as in microgram, μg	10^{-6}	$= \div 1\ 000\ 000$
pico-, p, as in picofarad, pF	10^{-9}	$= \div 1\ 000\ 000\ 000$
nano-, n, as in nanometre, nm	10^{-12}	$= \div 1\ 000\ 000\ 000\ 000$

There are in addition exa-, E (10^{18}) and peta-, P (10^{15}) at the top and femto-, f (10^{-15}) and atto-, a (10^{-18}) at the bottom.

Note that SI recommends use of prefixes only for every *third* power. The original Metric System had them as well for 10^2 (hecto-), 10^1 (deca-), 10^{-1} (deci-) and 10^{-2} (centi-). Some examples of the others survive in popular usage (e.g. centimetre), and *hecto-* survives in the unit of area, the hectare, 100 metres × 100 metres, where the base unit (never normally used in Australia) is the *are*, 10 metres × 10 metres. However, the hectare is called an *SI-compatible* unit, not an SI unit in the full sense, as is the degree Celsius.

(2) Writing units and quantities   The important points for non-technical writing are the rules governing the way the units and quantities are represented. These rules are obligatory for technical writing, and it makes good sense to get to know them. The rules cover capitalisation, whether they are italics or roman, how they form plurals and how numerals are written:

(a) The symbols for SI *quantities* should be in italics, while the symbols for SI *units* should be in roman characters:

   Quantities: E   (energy) *F*   (force)
   Units: J   (joule)   N   (newton)

(b) The forms of the symbols for units are mandatory. The most common errors are to write 'sec' for s, 'degrees kelvin' for kelvin and '°K' for K.

(c) The symbols for units are not given a plural *s*. When writing out in full, we can write 'two metre' or 'two metres', but *must* omit the s in writing '2 m'. ('2 ms' would mean 2 milliseconds.)

(d) When written out in full, no units should be capitalised (e.g. kelvin, not Kelvin).

(e) The symbols for the units which are named after people have capital letters (A for André-Marie Ampère, Hz for Heinrich Hertz), while Georg Ohm is remembered by the Greek omega, Ω, as our O was seen as dangerously ambiguous.

(f) The *litre* is a special case. It was originally prescribed as l, but this was too easily confused with I and 1, and L is now not only permitted but preferred. (The confusion, evident enough here, is worse in sans-serif type. This should be remembered when choosing the font for scientific setting.)

(g) The rest of the units are given lower case letters.

(h) The system prefers the use of negative indices rather than slashes in (for example) metres per second, i.e. $m.s^{-1}$ is preferred to m/s. However, the system considerately allows the use of the slash by children and the general public.

(i) The system prefers the use of a point rather than a thin space to separate the elements in multiple units: thus metre per second is $m.s^{-1}$ rather than $m\ s^{-1}$, while the unspaced ms^{-1} is wrong – it can only mean 'per millisecond'.

When SI was first introduced to Australia, the thin-spaced version was recommended, but this was confusing, particularly

in handwriting; it is still widely used, but the use of the point is
strongly recommended.

(j) SI quantities are by definition in SI units. If we say 'A body of
mass *m*', the mass is *by definition* in kilograms. If we wish to
stress that this is so, we can say 'a mass *m* (in kilograms)' but not
'a mass *m* kg'.

(k) The decimal point can be on the line (1.0) or centred (1·0), and
the European convention of the decimal comma (1,0) is also
accepted.

(l) SI uses a space rather than a mark to group the digits in long
numbers. The following shows both the problem and the official
SI solution:

> *English convention:*   12,345.6789
> *European convention:*   12.345,678.9
> *SI convention:*   12 345.678 9

The space is optional in 4-digit numbers, but should be used if
4-digit numbers are tabulated with longer numbers.

(3) Some problems   While the main problem for ordinary folk is
to remember what the rules are, the writer who knows all the rules
still runs into difficulties.

(a) How do you distinguish roman and italic in handwriting?
Answer: If your handwriting is not up to it, don't try. If marking
up the text for a typesetter, underline the italic matter *in a
different colour*. However, remember that the typesetter probably knows the practicalities of SI as well as you do, so the
general instruction 'Follow SI style' should be sufficient.

(b) How do you distinguish roman and italic if working with a
typewriter or printer which cannot reproduce italic? Answer: as
above. Underlining is fine in the run of text, but underlined
matter in mathematical equations can be very confusing.

(c) What do you do if a unit, which should be in roman letters,
appears in a sentence which is in italics? Answer: it stays in
roman. *The mass is* 10 kg.

(d) What do you do if a quantity, which should be in italics, appears
in an italic sentence? Answer: it stays in italic. *The mass, m, is* 10
kg.

(e) For a discussion of the mass/weight question, see MASS....

small capitals   When typesetters talk about small capitals, they do
not mean capitals which just happen to be small. They mean spe-
cially-designed letters which have the shape of capitals but are only
a little taller than the lower-case x-height:

> CAPITALS, SMALL CAPS and lower case

Small capitals were not available on the Linotype and Intertype
machines which were used in the newspaper industry for most of
this century. As a result, they devised other ways of getting round

the straggly look of strings of capitals, one of which was to write the initials as words, e.g. Unesco. (See ACRONYMS and SALT (3).)

Originally, they were not just reduced versions of the ordinary capitals; they were reduced in size, but the thickness of the lines matched that of the lower case letters. In today's electronic typesetters, small capitals are just scaled down versions of the full capital. They are therefore slightly lighter than the equivalent lower case characters.

Small capitals are used for a number of aesthetic and logical reasons. Running heads were traditionally done in small capitals, letter-spaced:

SMALL CAPS LETTER SPACED

Some designers like to print the first phrase of each chapter in small capitals. In this book, small capitals are used for cross-references.

snapper/schnapper   The word means 'something which snaps', a fairly obvious name to apply to a fish, and it was apparently applied to a number of species at various times and places. However, Australians are clear about it – it applies to the genus *Pagrosomus* (ACOD), or is it *Pagrus Unicolor* (SOED) or is it one of the *Sparidae*, *Chrysophrys auratus* (Mac), or, as Mac goes on to say, 'any of various other fishes, e.g. bluefish, *Pomatomus saltrans*'?

No matter – the present book is, mercifully, not concerned with taxonomy or gastronomy. The only relevant question is one of spelling: *snapper* or *schnapper*? *Snapper* is clearly the older form, the first reference to it in Australian waters being, it seems, in Dampier's Journal for 1697, reported by OED and AND.

The origin of the spelling *schnapper* is clearly Germanic, but its provenance is less clear. OED asserts that its derivation is 'after the equivalent German *schnapper*', but how? Did the German community, remembering that there was a fish in Germany called a *schnapper*, apply this name to the Australian fish which happened to be *snapper* in English? Or did they hear it called *snapper* and spell it a German way? Or did an anglophone hear a German mispronouncing *snapper* and assume that it was a German word? However it happened, the spelling caught on and survived.

Snapper is the better spelling.

social aspirations   The social significance of aitches is not new, nor is it confined to English. Classical Latin and Greek both had aitches, and misplacing them was, as it is in British (and, to a lesser extent, Australian) English, a class indicator. Thus Catullus chides Arrius for talking about the *Hionian Sea*. With the lapse of time, however, fashion changed, so that prelates of the Roman church drop all their aitches, not only when talking Italian but also when talking Latin.

In British English, the dropping of the aitch has had a mixed social career. The Anglo-Saxons did not drop their aitches, but their conquerors, the Normans, did. The dropping of the *h* thus entered the language as a mark of social superiority. It remained so into the seventeenth century, when the compilers of *The Book of Common Prayer* wrote of *an* horse, assuming that it would be pronounced *an 'orse*. Shakespeare, writing for a less respectable audience, wrote *My kingdom for a horse*.

Meanwhile, however, a combination of influences, including the rise of an Anglo-Saxon bourgeoisie at the expense of the Norman aristocracy and, much later, the arrival of Dutch, and later German, kings and their courtiers, all of whom sounded their aitches, changed the social indicators, so that the aitch re-established itself in polite usage. Meanwhile, it had never disappeared from the vernaculars of East Anglia, the north of England, Scotland or Ireland. Dropping the aitch became characteristic of the working-class accents of southern England and the industrial midlands, and hence became socially unacceptable.

As so often happens, the English of the colonies reflected and preserved the habits of the main body of settlers. Thus American English is in some respects a fossil of eighteenth-century bourgeois British English, and the dropping of aitches is virtually unknown, though curiously some Americans say *'erbs* for herbs.

There are individual words whose aitches are dropped in all dialects: *heir, honour, hour* and their relations, */forrid/* for *forehead*, and the elisions *I've* and *I'd*. Fifty years ago, it was also 'correct' to say *an 'otel* rather than *a hotel*, just as we might in the cases of *hors d'œuvres* and *an haut couture salon*, and it was common to do the same with *home* in the phrase *at 'ome*, and *humour* in the phrase *sense of 'umour*.

In Australia, some Broad and General speakers drop their aitches, but others, especially those of Irish descent, sound them with enthusiasm, even reviving the one on the word 'aitch'. We have adopted *hotel* as our own, always giving it an aitch (while deriding those who sound the aitch in *haut couture*); we also give an aitch to *home* and (generally) to *historian*.

Note that we can say *a historian* or *an 'istorian*, but not *an historian*. The belief that the word *historian* does not obey the general rules about *a* and *an* is a misapprehension. The same goes for *hilarious*. Drop the *h* if you will; but do not say *an* and then sound the *h*.

The lesson from this tangled web of anecdote is clear – that there is nothing intrinsically meritorious about sounding one's aitches or dropping them. Cultivated Frenchmen cannot make an aitch sound, while the Germans have never been tempted to drop them. Meanwhile English speakers have vacillated down the centuries, with the sounding of the aitch unquestionably on top at the moment.

Thus current advice is to sound all aitches *unless* the word is on the list given above (*heir, honour*, etc.) or is non-naturalised French;

in which case either pronounce it in a reasonably Gallic way (see
FOREIGN WORDS...(4)) or (better) use an English equivalent.

soluble/solvable *Soluble* (with its related *insoluble, dissoluble* and
indissoluble) and *solvable* (*unsolvable, dissolvable, undissolvable*) are in
theory synonymous, but in practice not so. The usage is well understood by native speakers, and is supplied merely to generate sympathy for foreigners:

FORM	CHEMICALS	CROSSWORD PUZZLES	MARRIAGES AND PARLIAMENTS
solve, (un)solvable	No	Yes	No
dissolve, (un)dissolvable	Yes	No	Yes
solution, (in)soluble	Yes	Yes	No
dissolution, (in)dissoluble	No	No	Yes

sorts   The term *sorts* is used in the jargon of typesetting to describe the
various special characters required for foreign and mathematical
setting. It is a useful heading under which to discuss the 'diacritical
marks' (as the linguists call them) used in English writing, of which
the largest single set is *accents*.
   acute accent, as in *résumé*. Its effect is to indicate that a vowel is not
      mute. In most cases (including *résumé*), the words are French,
      but it is sometimes used for the same purpose on English words,
      e.g. to distinguish *learnéd* from *learned*. The same mark is used in
      PIN-YIN to indicate a rising tone.
   breve, as in *brĕvity*, is a mark placed over a vowel to indicate that it
      has a short sound. In PIN-YIN, it indicates a tone which swoops
      down and up.
   cedilla, as in *façade*. Its effect in French is to soften a *c* which might
      otherwise be read as /k/. They are rarely necessary in angli–
      cisations, though the phrase *soupçon de je ne sais quoi* is still
      French and thus perhaps needs one.
   circumflex, as in *fête*. The original significance of the circumflex in
      French was that letters had dropped out, a spectacular example
      being *même = me (ipsissi)me*. *Fest, fiesta* and *feast* are all etymo-
      logical cousins of *fête*. Circumflexes are needed in English writ-
      ing only if the word is still being treated as French, e.g. the
      circumflex can be omitted from *fête*, but perhaps retained on *bête
      noire*.
   dieresis, as in *Noël*. Its effect is to indicate that the *vowel* is pro-
      nounced separately from the one before it. See DIERESIS, and
      compare *umlaut* below.
   grave accent, as in *compère*. Although in theory French accents are
      supposed to help with pronunciation, Dupré remarks sadly 'Il
      n'est pas rare que l'accentuation soit en désaccord avec la
      prononciation', and proceeds to list some of the astonishing
      disaccords. The grave has no place in English, and is only

retained on palpably French phrases like *crème de la crème*. It is used in PIN-YIN to indicate a falling tone.

macron, as in *vāgue*, is a mark placed over a vowel to indicate that it is long or stressed. In PIN-YIN, it indicates a high tone.

tilde, as in *señor*. This Spanish device recalls the dropping of an *i* (*senior*, *signor*, and *señor* are cousins). As it makes a real difference to pronunciation, it is best retained.

umlaut, as in *Müller*. In German this mark indicates the dropping of an *e* following an *a, o* or *u*. It is not retained in anglicisations, where such a mark indicates a DIERESIS (see above). Herr Müller may thus become Mr Muller, Mueller or Miller. It is also used in over *u* in PIN-YIN, where it indicates a sound something like the *ue* in *due*.

The above list covers the marks most likely to be encountered in English. There are, of course, many more. The German *ß* is generally transliterated as *ss*. The Scandinavian *å* and *ø* are sometimes retained in English (*Ångström, øre*), but the roman alphabet versions of Slav languages (Polish, Czech, etc.), which use diacritical marks to modify many consonant as well as vowel sounds, and of Vietnamese, where the marks are used to represent tonality, generally lose their marks in anglicisation.

See also DASH..., LIGATURE and PUNCTUATION for some other subtleties not available on typewriters.

speech, direct and indirect   In written English, speech can be represented in two ways, termed *direct* and *indirect*:

(1) *'I live here'* is called *direct speech*, and quotes the actual words used, enclosing them in quotation marks.

(2) *She says that she lives here* contains *indirect* or *reported speech*; it reports that the statement was made.

(1) Direct speech, as used for dialogue in novels, presents few problems. This is not to say that all writers write good dialogue, but the problem is of content rather than of any technical shortcomings. It is either so far from natural speech patterns that it is unconvincing or so close to them that it is boring.

The main question is the conventions about punctuating direct speech. This is discussed under PUNCTUATION (7).

(2) A piece of indirect speech is (in grammatical terms) best thought of as a *noun clause*, the object of the verb *to say* (or another verb with the same effect).

He said   his piece   (noun)

       that he was thirsty   (noun clause)

Questions arise over the habit of omitting the conjunction 'that':

He said he was thirsty.

This is a perfectly respectable idiom, and there is no suggestion that it should be avoided. However, it can cause problems for readers if 'that' is omitted from sentences in which the reported speech does not follow on immediately after the word 'said':

> *The Prime Minister said on some occasions the debate had gone on too long.*

There are two possible positions for the conjunction 'that', either before or after 'on some occasions', giving rise to two different meanings for the whole sentence, and it would have been helpful to the reader if the writer had shown where to put it.

Other problems are discussed in the entry on SEQUENCE OF TENSES.

spelling problems   We generally think that spelling problems arise largely from the inconsistency of English spelling. In practice, this is only one source, possibly the least common. This discussion is in five parts:

(1) Problems related to the writer (of which the most extreme is *dyslexia*).

(2) Problems stemming from ambiguities in the language.

(3) Problems stemming from ambiguities in the phonetic system.

(4) Spelling and the word processor.

(5) Does it matter?

(1) Spelling and the writer   In the end, good spellers are people who know when a word *looks* wrong and therefore should be checked in a dictionary or speller. They have thousands of visual images of words in their minds, and spell by choosing the appropriate image. They notice spelling mistakes because warning bells ring when they see a non-conforming pattern.

Many excellent books have been written on the way in which we acquire these visual patterns. Learning spelling as a separate skill, as happens in 'spelling lessons' using prepared lists, can be useful in establishing the basic rules and the resultant word attack skills, and in learning the spelling of specific problem words; but it seems that the patterns, like the melodies of music, imprint themselves best by use: the best way to learn to spell is by reading and writing.

If no spellings look any more wrong than others, you are in trouble. You cannot check every word, and do not know which ones to check. This is the situation of the true dyslectic. Reading in a mirror enables us to appreciate something of the dyslectic's problem (see RETARDED READERS). Writing in a mirror (so that it reads correctly in the mirror) is worse.

True dyslexia is, however, rare. What we are talking about is just bad spelling, which most often stems from a lack of awareness. Teachers may be doing children no service by failing to point out that their spelling is bad (see (5) below).

(2) Ambiguities in the oral language   Some of us have trouble with *their/there* confusions, or write *could of* where we meant *could've*. Again, the problem is lack of reading experience. We can be taught the difference between *weight* and *wait*, *hear* and *here*, *witch* and *which*; but there are thousands of similar sets, and ultimately we have to add them all to our subconscious stock of patterns if we are to choose the right one without immense labour.

This may sound like a non-answer to the problem, but in fact it is an answer which makes practical sense. Our stock of patterns is not just of sound/spelling relationship, but also sound/spelling/meaning relationships. We draw on this stock of knowledge all the time when we are writing, and most of the time get it right without being conscious of having made a decision. If we occasionally pick the wrong one, we should not fret; we should just remember to look out for it in future.

(3) Ambiguities in the phonetic rules   Despite the irregularities, most of our words follow the basic rules.

There are, of course, mnemonics to help us with classic problems: *I before E except after C* helps us with words like *piece*, and we then have to learn exceptions like *seize* by rote – unless our reading experience tells us that it looks wrong the other way.

We need, of course, to start from a mastery of the basic rules – the normal values of the consonants and vowels, and the ways in which these may change: for example, that a short vowel before a single consonant (e.g. the *at* in *mat*) is lengthened if there is a following *e* or *i* (as in *mate* and *mating*) so that we have to double the *t* to keep it short (as in *matted* and *matting*). We then have to remember that the Americans do not bother to do this if there is no ambiguity (*travelers* where we write *travellers*), and that we do the same in some cases (*paralleled* rather than *parallelled*).

Even here, however, the main value of the rules is to identify a problem area: to make us stop and check if we are not sure. Experienced readers spell most of the time by reference to a mental store of patterns, and only occasionally by a knowledge of rules.

Finally, there are numerous cases where the 'authorities' will differ: for an example, see JUDGEMENT…. There are plenty of wrong ways of spelling words, but there is often no one 'correct' way: see CORRECTNESS.

(4) Spelling and the word processor   The widespread use of word processors, with their capacity to check spellings and suggest corrections, is likely to improve our spelling greatly. So far from taking away the need to spell well, it will encourage us to spell better, because by pointing to our mistakes it identifies the words we need to watch.

The effectiveness of spellchecking systems varies greatly from program to program, and is one of the key points to watch in selection of a program. The best programs offer a range of spelling options, i.e. Australian, British or American, are very good at telling you what you had meant to write, and have a facility for the compilation of 'user dictionaries' separate from the main dictionary. (These are preferable to systems which allow the reader to add to the main dictionary itself, though the capacity to remove unwanted options from the main dictionary is very useful.)

We should remember, however, that a spellchecker will not warn us if we have written the wrong word (e.g. *there* for *their*). Newspapers, which use them extensively, have fewer straight misspellings than they did, but perhaps more cases of wrong choice of word.

Some spellcheckers will also warn us if we have written the same word twice, and if we have no capital letter after a full stop; grammar checkers are also available. But we must be aware that the more classes of error a program watches for, the more often it will query items which are perfectly correct, slowing down the process and ultimately encouraging us to turn the correction routines off.

(5) Does it matter? Why should we bother about spelling? If Shakespeare didn't worry about inconsistent spelling, why should we? Specifically, should we run the risk of obstructing the creative process in children by correcting their spelling?

Imagine for a moment the infant Mozart, climbing down from the piano stool clutching the manuscript of his first piano sonata. Would he have been pleased to have been patted on the head and told that he was a clever lad, when he knew that his notation was so peculiar that his intentions would not be understood by anyone else?

Certainly the creative process is vital and should not be interrupted, and there are some non-Mozarts who would probably appreciate the pat on the head rather than the warning. But most people, including young children, write in order to communicate, and are well aware if they are not communicating. They want to get it right. Spelling does matter, and we know it.

spelling reform It is widely believed that bad spelling is peculiar to English and to our own age, and that this is because English is the only language with irrational spellings. All these propositions are false. Spelling errors occur in all languages, both ancient (as we can see from inscriptions) and modern, and irrational spellings occur within all written systems.

It is, however, true that English spelling is, by international standards, peculiarly irrational. There are several reasons why this is so.

English started as an amalgam of two major languages which used different spelling conventions (see ENGLISH (1)), so English never had a spelling system giving a one-to-one relationship between sound and spelling. Thus *ch* can make at least four noises – as in *chain, loch, champagne* and *charisma* – and conversely the sound /k/ can be made in at least five ways – as in *kind, case, charisma* and the two in *quick*. It would have taken a very radical spelling reform to produce a single coherent system from this mess, and such a reform has never happened. Early attempts were related to the development of modern English (see ENGLISH (1)), when not only the spelling but the words themselves were in dispute.

The great enthusiasm for lexicography in the eighteeenth century also produced some ad hoc reforms, but since then English has become so widely dispersed that coherent reform is difficult. So long as writing is the preserve of a few educated people, uniform spelling is relatively unimportant and can be maintained without special effort (as it was for centuries with Latin). It is only when there is a serious attempt to spread literacy through a community that uniformity becomes important, but the same process makes it very difficult to achieve.

In the case of English, the problem is particularly difficult. Its writers split into two major spelling camps, British and American, with other smaller camps, including Australian, vacillating between the two or sometimes marching out on their own. In addition, it is the language of higher education in many other countries (e.g. Papua New Guinea) and the dominant second language all over the world. Under these circumstances, the chances of reaching universal agreement on modest reforms, as happened recently in Portuguese, are slim. Meanwhile the chances of major reform, as have happened in Italian, are non-existent.

However, there are also logical difficulties in achieving a truly universal and consistent phonetic system which apply even within languages like Italian. Written Italian is a reasonably faithful phonetic representation of the educated Italian of Rome, but not of the Italian of Sicily. This reflects the dominant status of Rome, and there is not much the Sicilians can do about it. But it does mean that, for many Italians, the system falls a long way short of consistency.

In English, however, even this limited success is improbable. There is no one dominant version, and it is overwhelmingly unlikely that the British would accept a phonetic system which depicted one of the American accents, or vice versa. In British (and Australian) English, the words *born* and *drawn* are perfect rhymes, and would thus end in the same three letters; in American, they are totally different sounds.

Such spelling reform as has occurred has tried to remove some of the more extreme inconsistencies. In the case of the *-our/-or* word endings, for example, British spelling had been frozen in the middle of a period of change, during which *governour* had lost his *u* but *flavour* had kept it. Webster, freezing American fifty years later, was more systematic on this one. But he had no grand design.

Happily, although English spelling is so illogical that no one ought to be able to master it, very many people do. The arguments of the spelling reformers would prove even more conclusively that no one could ever learn to write Chinese. Compared with Chinese, English spelling is rich in phonetic clues.

In sum: the possibility of total phonetic regularity exists only for a language which is both uniform and static in time and place. Minority languages can come nearer to this ideal than the major ones, but all are systems which have a phonetic base supporting a superstructure with varying degrees of irregularity depending on the number and distribution of its speakers, the pace of change in adopting new words, and the extent to which uniformity is regarded as valuable. English, being a language which is widespread, voracious of imported words and lacking any central authority, presents great practical obstacles to spelling reform.

This is not to say that spelling reform is pointless. This book supports a number of minor reforms, as noted, for example, in the entries on LICENCE… and -ISE/-IZE/-ICE, and the world is richer for the existence of the various spelling reform lobbies. But let us not imagine that the only thing standing in the way of reform is mindless conservatism, or that anyone, even George Bernard Shaw, has produced a practical program for radical reform which could be implemented if only we had the will to do so.

squat(-ter, -tage, -tocracy)   The verb *to squat*, in the sense *to occupy a building or land without the owner's consent*, is an American term dating from c. 1800, quickly adopted in Australia. Outside Australia, it remained a rare term until after the Second World War, when it was applied to a new phenomenon – the occupation of vacant buildings by (especially) the homeless young. In this application, the house where people squat is a *squat*.

In Australia, however, the word had enjoyed a great flowering. Initially, the term was applied to unauthorised occupation of land within areas which had been declared open for settlement; later, it also referred to the occupation of areas which had not been declared open for settlement. This was the case in Victoria, where the first squatters arrived in 1834, occupying land without any negotiation either with the Aboriginal inhabitants or the colonial authorities. Squatting thus had connotations of illegality. However, the squatters soon became so rich and powerful that the *squattages* were retrospectively legitimised either as freeholds or as *squatters' leases*. The descendants of the squatters became the *squattocracy*.

Thus, the squatter, mounted on his thoroughbred and accompanied by troopers one two three, was an illegal occupant of the land; not under arrest for trespass, but enjoying the protection of the law.

standard form   Standard form is a mathematical convention for representing large and small numbers. All values are represented as numbers between 0 and 10 multiplied by a power of ten. In translating from standard form to normal numbers, the decimal point is shifted one to the left for every positive power, one to the right for a negative power.

normal		standard form
250	=	2.5×10^2
2500	=	2.5×10^3
2.5	=	2.5×10^0
0.025	=	2.5×10^{-2}
7038.83	=	$7.038\ 83 \times 10^3$
0.00029	=	2.9×10^{-4}

The system has a number of advantages, the most obvious being that it helps to avoid 'order of magnitude' errors in calculations (i.e. getting the decimal point in the wrong place, or having the wrong number of noughts). The universal use of calculators has if anything increased the risk of such errors.

While this notation is rarely appropriate for literary writing, it is very useful in tabulations involving very large and very small numbers, particularly the latter, and the system is certainly well worth mastering if you ever make order-of-magnitude errors in your own calculations.

state Apart from its general senses, *state* has two quite distinct meanings in politics, as shown in the phrase *state enterprise*. We may be talking about a government enterprise, as distinct from a private enterprise, or an enterprise run by a *state* government, as distinct from one run by the federal government. This distinction is understood in America but not in Britain, where *the state* is always the central government.

To minimise the ambiguity illustrated above, my scheme is:

(1) To capitalise the word *State* whenever it refers to one of the Australian States, irrespective of context. Thus I write *Education is a State responsibility* (unless I forget to, of course).

(2) To avoid using the word *state* as a synonym for Commonwealth in such phrases as *the interest of the state*. Variations on *Commonwealth* and *Australia(n)* will cover most cases.

The suggestion about capitalisation is in conflict with the rules given in many style manuals, in which we are told not to capitalise *state* other than in formal references: *the State of Victoria*. If writing for newspapers or other publications which prescribe style, that style should be followed.

station The dominance of the military in the early history of white Australia left little mark on the language of Australians, but a spectacular exception is *station*. In the early days of the colony, the word was used to cover all places where the colonial administration was active, which meant every settlement. Thus from strictly military outposts, the term was extended to convict stations (established for the employment of convicts on road building, etc.), to

Aboriginal stations (the first Reserves) and finally to the stations of free settlers: cattle stations, sheep stations and so on.

Initially, the term was used both for the tract of land and for the dwelling, so that colonists could talk of a settler *taking up additional stations to sustain his herds*, but could also say that he was *building a station on his sheep-run*. With the passage of time, the term has settled on the tract of land, while the building has become the *homestead*.

The word is today largely restricted to pastoral properties. Agricultural properties are *farms*, and the generic term (as this sentence suggests) is *properties*. However, to call a *hobby farm* a *property* can sound slightly pretentious. (See CAPITALS, USE OF (4).)

stationary/stationery   *Stationery* is the paper, *stationary* is the standing still. Those who find the distinction between these two spellings perverse should take comfort: it *is* perverse. At a time when most traders were itinerant, one who took up a fixed *station*, known as a *stationer*, was exceptional. One trade which was particularly noted for staying in one spot was that of books and writing materials. Hence the term *stationer* became attached to them, and the word *stationery* (or *stationary*) was attached to their wares. The spelling distinction followed much later. The wheel of fortune could have stopped the other way round, but it didn't.

stereotype, stereotypical   Our dictionaries give little hint that the word *stereotype* is part of the currency. They all give the lion's share of the space to its original meaning in relief printing, a technology which survives only in museums and the wording of publishers' contracts.

Meanwhile the word lives on in a quite different sense. It is used of a set of generalisations which form a person's perception of some person or group of people, so that we can say *He fits perfectly the popular stereotype of a bank manager*.

In theory, any set of generalisations could form a stereotype, so that a 'popular stereotype' could be a positive one; in practice, it tends to be used only of negative images, so that if we talked about *a stereotypical pop star*, it would indicate that we didn't think much of pop stars or, perhaps, popular taste.

However, it tends to be even more specific than this: it is applied to sets of generalisations which are phrased in negative terms and which have socially destructive outcomes, dividing one section of the community from the rest: see PREJUDICE and SEXIST LANGUAGE.

still   We should be careful when using this word. If we write *It is* still *less appropriate…*, we may either mean *It is even less appropriate* or *it is, even today, less appropriate*, and a genuine ambiguity can arise.

stress   In his long and fascinating essay on the subject (which occurs in his entry on 'recessive accent') Fowler identified three forces at work in determining the placement of the stress in words:

(1) There is a tendency for only one syllable to be stressed (unlike French, which normally places equal stress on all syllables).
(2) This stress tends to come earlier rather than later.
(3) Operating against (1) and (2), we have a 'natural repugnance to a rapid succession of light syllables'.
We might add:
(4) If a word is very long, or if it is assembled from parts, each making a recognisable contribution to the sense (e.g. *under-rated, super-natural, centri-fugal*), the stress treats them as separate, so that such words have two or more stressed syllables. However, if the awareness of the origins becomes clouded (*superfluous, interstices, handkerchief*) the word is treated as a single whole.
(5) There is a general tendency, particularly with modern technical terms, to use a pronunciation which shows the relationship between words. Thus, we put a double stress on *centrifugal* to preserve the relationship with *centrifuge.*

It would be good to have a word for the last-syllable stress. Happily, there is one, *oxytone*, duly recorded in Mac (though its siblings, listed below, are not):

oxytone	accented on the last syllable	di-dum
paroxytone	accented on the last syllable but one	dum-di
proparoxytone	accented on the last syllable but two	dum-di-di

These words are used in what follows purely for economy, not with a view to popularising them.

(a) Words of one syllable
There is only one place for the stress, but this is a good moment to remember that stress can be affected by grammar and sense. We are talking here about the stress which attaches to the words in a neutral state, e.g. if read one by one from a word list. Many words, notably the articles *the* and *a/an*, but also many prepositions and auxiliary verbs, are commonly unstressed when incorporated into phrases and sentences. Sentences are given logical and grammatical shape by adding, shifting or removing the 'neutral' stress.

(b) Words of two syllables
Approximately 95% of these are paroxytone, dum-di. The rest are oxytone, di-dum, or double oxytone, dum-dum.

Generally, the oxytone words are those in which the first syllable is, or is perceived to be, a prefix (e.g. *enchant, deduct, become, aghast, maintain*). However, in words like *debug* and *defuse*, where the *de-* is effectively a separate semantic element, we get the double oxytone.

There are also many cases where stress is used to distinguish different parts of speech, e.g. the verb /c'ntract/ versus the noun /con-tract/, and others where the decision appears to be arbitrary, e.g. the various usages of /c'mpact/ and /com-pact/.

(c) Words of three syllables

Approximately 80% of these are proparoxytone, dum-di-di (e.g. *fugitive, currency*).

If a two-syllable oxytone word, e.g. *enchant*, is extended by adding a suffix, the stress stays on the same syllable. Thus *enchanted* is paroxytone, di-dum-di.

If the addition is at the beginning, e.g. *disenchant*, it stays oxytone, but the rhythm is dum-di-dum rather than di-di-dum. This can be regarded as a single pattern with double stress, but it is better to treat it as two separate stress patterns, either *dum* di-dum or dum-di *dum*.

The reason for treating it as two separate stress patterns is that this is clearly what happens in cases like *over-ride* and *under-take*, where the stress pattern of the components is preserved. Note that a word like *overhead* has the dum-di-dum stress in the sentence *The crane was overhead* but a normal paroxytone pattern in *an overhead crane*, the loss of the second stress showing that it is an adjective linked to the following noun. This also happens in *This is the ABC* (dum-di-di dum dum dum) and *This is the ABC News* (dum-di-di dum-di-di dum).

(d) Words of four or more syllables

If a long word has only one stressed point, it will generally be proparoxytone, i.e. on the third syllable from the end, as in *simplicity* and *Christianity*. It seems that we like dactyllic patterns (see FOOT) and are reluctant to have more than two unstressed syllables following one another. When faced with three or more, we have a number of solutions:

(1) In some cases (e.g. *alimony, alienate*) we live with the string of three unstressed syllables.

(2) In other cases, we move the stress back to preserve a paroxytone pattern, e.g. *human* makes *humanity*.

(3) In *sanitary* (and many other words with *-ary* and *-ory* endings) British and Australian speakers tend to avoid the triplet by swallowing the penultimate syllable, making /sanit'ri/, whereas American speakers (who tend to enunciate all syllables) break the word into two paroxytone patterns, making /sanny tairy/. Similarly, in comparable, we swallow the second syllable, i.e. /comp'rable/, while the Americans retain the earlier /c'm-parable/. For an odd exception, see LABORATORY.

(4) Our normal procedure with very long words is to break them into smaller chunks, each with its own stress pattern, as in the word which is generally quoted as being the longest in English, *antidisestablishmentarianism*, and in some chemical terms which are much longer, like *cyclopentanoperhydrophenanthrene*. Within each chunk, the rules are straightforward, so the only problem is breaking the word at the right points. In the case of the terms

organic chemistry, common sense is not enough, and while it is unlikely that this particular molecule will ever enter the general language, some hyphenation would be helpful if it did, e.g. *cyclo-pentano-perhydro-phen-anthrene*. There, isn't that better?

strong, weak   These terms have two important senses when talking about languages.

(1) Strong/weak tenses   There are basically two ways in which the past tenses of verbs are formed. The *-ed* forms are called *weak* and those which depend on other modifications, notably to the vowel sounds, are called *strong*. A few verbs have both:

> To strive   *weak past:*   strived
>   *strong past:*   strove

(2) Strong/weak senses of a word   A strong sense of a word is one which has a clear bundle of connotations; a weak sense is one where the meaning depends on context. Thus *wedding* has a very strong sense, with specific application, whereas *event* has a weak sense: it could cover a wide variety of phenomena.

Many words have both weak and strong meanings. Thus *case* (see CASE) has strong meanings in the language of law and luggage, but weak in phrases like *In case of fire, shout 'fire'* (a quotation reported to me by David Cunningham, who saw it in a hotel in Pakistan). In the sentence *What did you do?* the verb *to do* provides both the auxiliary verb *did* (with no meaning at all, but supplying the sense of time past) and the main verb *do*, which provides such active meaning as the sentence has.

style   There are two meanings of this word which must be distinguished:

(1) *Style* in the sense of *skill* or *panache*: *'Horne writes with style.'*
(2) *Style* in the sense of *manner*: *'The book is written in an informal style.'*

The distinction between the two senses may not seem very important, but it helps us to distinguish between two very different books which are sometimes confused, a book on style and a style manual.

(1) A book about style in sense (1) will be asking what it is that makes some writing flow swift and deep while other writing trickles from puddle to puddle. It will be analytic rather than prescriptive, and contain more questions than answers.

It will identify the elements which make up style, and give the reader the vocabulary for discussing them. It may also occasionally give advice; but it will be reluctant to say what is correct, for the very good reason that really stylish writers can get away with breaking almost every rule.

(2) A style manual is a different proposition. Typical of them is a guide to what is termed *house style*. A house style guide is concerned with style in sense (2): the set of rules which have been adopted by a particular printer or corporation. It can therefore cut the knots instead of untying them, and hence be brief and didactic (see HOUSE STYLE).

The Age Style Book is a model of the second kind of book. It is a set of answers, the assumption being that, other things being equal, those who write for *The Age* should follow its instructions, and freelance contributors cannot be surprised (though they can complain) if an *Age* sub-editor changes their texts to match this style. (The way in which the name of the newspaper is handled in that last sentence is based on their style: the definite article in the title is dropped if the name is used adjectivally.)

A style manual is thus an authority within its own parish. It is best to follow *The Age Style Book* if writing for *The Age*. It is even legitimate for independent writers to decide to adopt the *Age* style as their own. But it cannot be used to prove that some other style is wrong.

The *Style Manual for Authors, Editors and Printers*, published by the Australian Government Publishing Service, is another useful and largely sensible manual whose advice many authors, editors and printers choose to adopt, but as with *The Age* guide, it cannot be used to prove that some other style is wrong.

Inasmuch as it is either, the present work is a book on style, not a style manual: my aim is to help people make up their own minds rather than to give simple answers to complex questions. When I cut knots, I do so in the first person.

subheadings   A subheading (or *subhead*) is a phrase or short sentence which appears in the middle of a text, often in a different typeface and with extra space round it. Subheadings are sometimes called *cross-headings* (or *cross-heads*), and the normal abbreviation is *Xhd*.

The main purpose of subheadings is as logical flags: they indicate a change of topic, both closing off what has gone before and introducing what comes next. In this book, there is little need for them, as the entries are separated by a thin space and introduced by a headword in bold. This is sometimes called a *shoulder head*, and if it hangs out slightly from the rest (as here), a *hanging shoulder*.

In newspapers and magazines, subheadings are often used more for psychological or cosmetic reasons than logical ones: to break up the text into bite-sized chunks. Such headings are inserted according to the demands of layout, i.e. they are not integral to the text, and they are inserted at layout stage.

Subheadings can be distinguished by having extra space above them, by being larger than the text, by being in bold or italic type, or by being in a different font (e.g. a sans serif font). This will be up to the typographer.

Writers and editors are only concerned with the use of subheadings as a logical device. This only becomes a troublesome issue if two or more levels of subheading are used. The hierarchy should be clearly indicated (*A, B, C,* etc.), so that the typographer can choose an appropriate range of styles which make it clear.

The most common problem arises when there is a hierarchy of perhaps five levels of subhead, and the writer fails to keep track of it. It is all too easy to label a cross-heading '*B*', not noticing that the structure of the logic makes it inferior to an earlier '*C*' subheading.

The best procedure is to make a list of the headings, indenting it to show the logical hierarchy:

> *The Gorton administration*
>> *Economic policy*
>> *Foreign policy*
>>> *Overseas aid*
>>>> *Aid to Thailand*
>>> *Vietnam War*
> *The McMahon administration*   etc.

It may seem laborious to do this, but once done it provides an easy reference point for new insertions, as well as an aid to marking up. It will often identify logical problems before they cause real trouble.

subject   In grammar, a subject is 'the member of a proposition about which something is predicated' (ACOD). This works well in most simple sentences:

Subject	Predicate
Skating	
He	*is undignified*
Putting your head in a bucket	
What happens after that	

The examples show that the subject can be a noun, a pronoun, a noun phrase or a noun clause; that the rest of the sentence is called the *predicate*; that the subject is in the *nominative* (= *subjective*) case (see CASE); that the subject normally comes before the verb; and that the verb must agree with it. Inversion of the order produces a question – see QUESTIONS. Every finite verb needs a subject except in the imperative: *Go home!*

It **as a subject**   There are some special idioms involving *it* and *there*. In the sentence *It is raining,* the word *it* does not stand for anything in particular, i.e. there is no sensible answer to the question 'What is raining?'. We explain it by saying that *to rain* is here an *impersonal verb*, the word *it* supplying a non-specific subject just to get the show on the road.

A slightly different case is the use of *it* in the sentence:

> *It is no good kicking it.*

Here we have the *anticipatory* use of *it*, signalling an inversion of subject and verb. If we ask *What is no good?*, we can get an answer: *Kicking it is no good.*

The same applies to the following:

It follows that pigs cannot swim

the purpose being to allow an inversion of subject and verb which will get the emphasis in the right place.

The same purpose is achieved by the word *There* in the sentence

There comes a time when all must rest....

The inversion here becomes clear if the phrase following the verb *to be* is plural:

There are many ways to pluck a duck.

The verb agrees with what follows – a plural – a clear indication that the subject is the phrase *after* the verb, and the status of *there* can be seen by removing the inversion:

Many ways to pluck a duck are there.

In short, *there* is not a pronoun, but an all-purpose, essentially meaningless adverb.

subjunctive   Let us (1) see what we are talking about, and then (2) see why the problems arise.

(1) The richest source of subjunctive forms is the verb *to be*, which has three:

Be it ever so humble, I dream of home.   (Action in the present)
Were it up to me, I *would* chop it up.   (Action in the future)
Had I *been* told, I *could* have got rid of it. (Action in the past)

Thus the present subjunctive has the form of the infinitive (*to be*); the future subjunctive has the form of the past indicative plural (*were*); and the past subjunctive has the form of the pluperfect indicative (*had been*).

All these can be rephrased using an *if...* clause:

Even if it *be* humble, I dream of home.

If it *were* up to me, I would chop it up.

If I *had been* told, I could have got rid of it.

The sense of the subjunctive is perhaps best seen by comparing *I will if I can* (a straight conditional, with two indicative verbs) with *I would if I could* (a hypothetical, with two subjunctive verbs).

The subjunctive is also used in a special usage reserved for requests and proposals, and especially for motions put to meeting:

He has asked that he be allowed to stay.

I move that standing orders be suspended.

(2) The subjunctive is to many people a bewildering, even threatening phenomenon. There are several reasons for this:

(a) English subjunctive uses forms of the verb which exist as indicatives or infinitives, so we cannot identify the subjunctive *forms* as clearly as (say) the French and Germans do, and cannot agree about them when we do.

One extreme view, indeed, is that the subjunctive does not really exist in English: that the alleged subjunctive usages are best considered as aberrant uses of the indicative and infinitive forms. This is implausible – whether we say *If I were you* or *If I was you*, it is not a past tense: we are still talking about the present and future. So far from helping, this merely kills off the only explanation of this usage which we can muster.

Another view is that subjunctives are all dying. This is more like the truth. In particular, the present subjunctive is dead except in a few and cliché expressions (*Be that as it may…, If the truth be known…*). The reason for this is that we can no longer distinguish between the present hypothetical, *If the flag be flying*, and the straight conditional *If the flag is flying*. In other usages, the use of subjunctive forms of main verbs is almost dead, but we use MODAL AUXILIARIES (e.g. *would, should, could, may, might*) which do the same job.

(b) The name *subjunctive* is perhaps another contributor to the problem: it was sensible for Latin, where subjunctives were used in a wide variety of 'subjoined' clauses (roughly what we call *dependent* clauses); but our usage would be better described by some word suggesting a mood of uncertainty tinged with wishful thinking: *I would if I could*. (The term *optative* exists in formal grammar for a related mood which was deemed non-existent in English. This would perhaps have been better, with its hint of *optimism*.)

(c) The third main contributor to the problem is that the auxiliaries we commonly use to express the subjunctive are ambiguous (all of them can be used in indicative senses). This point is further discussed under WOULD… and MAY….

Anyway, whatever the source of the problems, the usages in question are not going to die off merely by changing the way we explain them.

Specific problems with the subjunctive are discussed under IF… CLAUSES.

substantial, substantive   The word *substantive* is used in only one context in real life, and that is the distinction between a *procedural* motion and a *substantive* motion in a parliament or committee. Perhaps because substantive motions are by definition more important than procedural ones, the word has become a parliamentary malapropism for *substantial*, and this trivial disease (an acne rather than a cancer on the body politic) is spreading through the community. It should be persuaded to stay in Canberra.

suburb   In British English (and, curiously Mac and ACOD) the word means a residential area remote from the centre of a city, and the adjective *suburban* is thus pejorative term, referring to those unfortunates who live beyond the reach of real society. Thus Epping is, but Kensington is not, a suburb of London. In Melbourne and Sydney, both of which have their Eppings and Kensingtons, all are

suburbs, the distinction being that our Kensingtons are *inner suburbs*. This phrase sounds like an oxymoron to British ears.

The pejorative sense prevails in Australia, however, in such
phrases as *suburban housewife*. Thus, although Vaucluse is a suburb
of Sydney, its homemakers are not *suburban housewives*. Australian
suburban housewives inhabit outer suburbs, as in London.

subway   This word is in very frequent use in America, where it means
an urban underground railway. It is less frequent in Britain, where it
means *a footpath in a tunnel under a railway* or (less often) *under a main
road*. In Australia, it is used in this sense, but can also mean *a cutting
allowing a road to pass under a railway or another road*.

sulfur, sulphur   The spelling *sulfur* was until recently an Americanism. It is now the official spelling for chemistry (if we are to regard
IUPAC, the International Union of Physics and Chemistry, as official arbiters) and is likely to become the ordinary Australian spelling in all contexts except pre-existing proper names, e.g. *Sulphur-
crested Cockatoo*. The same goes for its derivatives, *sulfurous*, etc.

No one should complain. So far from being an American invention, *sulfur* is the older form. Both were used in Latin, but *sulfur*
came first. Indeed, the source of the *ph* is obscure. It was not, as are
most occurrences of *ph*, a transcription of the Greek ϕ (phi). It seems
to have been introduced to give an air of Greek sophistication to a
simple Latin original, just as *lacrima* became the Greek-looking
lachryma.

supper   See MEALS.

synonym, antonym   *Synonyms* are words which have the same meaning; *antonyms* have opposite meaning. Thus the word *begin* has
synonyms which include *start* and *commence*, and its antonyms
include *finish* and *end*. Synonyms can be extremely useful in avoiding repetition of words, and no writer should be without *Roget's
Thesaurus* or some similar work, which is essentially a list of synonyms and antonyms.

Of course, vanishingly few words are true synonyms. Even
begin, start and *commence* have their separate bundles of connotation
and application. Thus races *start* and *finish*; books *begin* and *end*;
policepersons *commence*.

T

taboo topics   There are some topics we have to be very careful about if we are not to get into trouble. They include religion, death, race, sex, excretion and gender.

(1) Within each category, there may be taboo words – words which seem to enshrine objectionable attitudes, and which we are therefore not allowed to use. These are discussed under TABOO WORDS.

(2) Because we want to talk about them, we have in many cases adopted specialised vocabularies which avoid naming the topic too obviously, though we all know what the words mean. These are discussed under EUPHEMISM.

(3) Because they are forbidden topics, they are topics in which it is easy to be shocking; hence they provide the vocabulary for deliberately shocking language, which is discussed under OATHS… and EXPLETIVE.

(4) The topic of gender is a special case, because one problem concerns the meaning and use of the term *gender* (discussed under GENDER). The topic popularly associated with *gender* is discussed under SEXIST LANGUAGE.

taboo words   There are some words we are not allowed to use. They fall into two categories, which might be called (1) bad language and (2) offensive language.

(1) Bad language   We all get a thrill from using words which are shocking. The words we find most shocking vary from time to time and from person to person, but sex, religion and excrement are perennial shockers.

In the case of religion, it is not the words that are taboo, but their use in a secular context, i.e. blasphemy. In other areas, there are words which are (at any given time) absolutely taboo: there is no respectable use for them.

For example, the word *fuck* was for many years absolutely taboo. Its presence in a text was taken as *prima facie* evidence that the text obscene, and this was the main reason why D. H. Lawrence's *Lady Chatterley's Lover* was published in Britain for many years only in an expurgated edition. Why this particular word was deemed so shocking is less clear. The word *occupy* disappeared from English for two centuries from (roughly) 1550 to 1750 for a similar reason, i.e. the word had been 'ill-sorted' (as Shakespeare put it) by being applied to sexual intercourse, but it shocks no one today.

The sensitive writer avoids causing shock unless the intention is to shock. There are, however, times when causing shock is a legitimate purpose. Furthermore, it is hard to see how anyone except the reader is disturbed or disadvantaged by shocking words, and the reader has the option to stop reading.

If it can be shown that it is more than this – that the words can cause trouble which goes beyond the shock of reading them – we are talking about offensive language.

(2) Offensive language The most important example of offensive language is the language of racism. It can again be argued that the words themselves are neutral; that the problem is the attitudes they enshrine. However, it does seem that there are certain words which are not only offensive to the readers and to the people to whom they are applied, but which also promote offensive attitudes. In times of war, derogatory terms are deliberately promoted, with the intention of dehumanising the enemy. It seems to work.

Of course, if people are already hostile towards a group (as, for example, has happened in Australia towards almost every wave of new immigrants), whatever word is applied to them becomes offensive. Some of these are pejorative from the start: *reffos* was never anything but offensive. But they may start as neutral or even positive. For the classic case of this, see NEW AUSTRALIAN, promoted as an alternative to the offensive terms but in the end becoming one itself. Conversely, an offensive term can eventually become neutral or even affectionate if hostility dies down. For example, the term 'Balts' was second only to 'reffo' as the most offensive term in the Australia of 1945–50, but can now be used positively as a collective for the citizens of the independent Baltic states.

'Balts' and 'reffos' are two words which we can talk about today, because no one (we hope) is still using them pejoratively, or suffering from the xenophobic prejudice they enshrined. Indeed, the hostility towards these people is as incomprehensible today as today's xenophobias will be another forty years on. The rhetoric is always the same, scrawled on the walls and encouraged by academic apologists, whose usual assertion is that fear of strangers (which is what *xenophobia* means) is natural, the implication being that anyone who does not share their fears is somehow unnatural.

Too much is at stake to start arguing about the extent of the damage such words actually do. They certainly enshrine racist attitudes, and their use contributes to a climate within which, as in war, people can act inhumanely towards others. Conversely, avoidance of their use tacitly enshrines our opposition to these attitudes. It is the least we can do.

The same goes for the taboo words of sexist language. It is idle to point out that, for example, the term *sheila* was once widely used neutrally as the female equivalent of *bloke*. It was also used in an offensive way, enshrining a stereotyped attitude to women, and people who use it today cannot be surprised if they are assumed to be using it in this way and hence to be sexist. However, the campaign against sexist language does seem to have taken a peculiar twist: I still cannot see any sexism in phrases like *no-man's land*, but we are told there is; see SEXIST LANGUAGE.

In the case of the Aboriginal communities, there are of course offensive terms which should be absolutely avoided, but there are many other words which must be used with care. These are not always easy to predict. For example, the words *piccaninny*, *native* and *tribe* are taboo. That *piccaninny* is offensive is not at all surprising given its association with slavery. *Native*, used as a noun, has the problem that it evokes the paternalism of the missionaries; but it can still be used as an adjective in its literal sense, i.e. *indigenous*, as in the phrase *native plants* – see NATIVE. *Tribe* is another odd one. In many contexts, it has a trenchant quality, evoking the ancient divisions of Rome, Israel and the indigenous people of North America; but the adjective *tribal* (in such phrases as *tribal violence*) certainly has connotations of primitive irrationality, and Aboriginals associate it, too, with a patronising attitude, preferring the terms *language group* or *clan*. To me, the first of these is insipid and the second wildly inappropriate, evoking memory of the feuds of Clan McTavish; but it is not my corns which are being trodden on.

Likewise, some Aboriginals prefer *the dreaming* to *the dream-time*, partly because the latter evokes the old stereotypes and partly because it suggests a lost past, whereas the phenomenon is very much of the present. Others again distinguish the two, e.g. the Kukatja people, who have two words, *tjukurrta* and *tjukurrpa*, the first of which can be translated *the dream-time* and the other *the dreaming*. At least, so I am reliably informed: on matters like this, most of us can only listen and learn. In any case, we must remember that such terms are the product of whites, seeking words to translate concepts for which they had no equivalent.

The above examples are merely intended to illustrate the complexity of the problem, not to supply an answer. There is no way in which writers can avoid making mistakes, particularly when last year's normal usage can become this year's taboo word; but there is likewise no excuse for making the same mistake twice.

Conversely, those who are on the receiving end ought to be very careful about equating the use of a taboo language with hostility. 'The proper study of mankind is man' is now regarded as sexist; but this was not so when it was first uttered; if we assume that anyone who utters such a remark is ideologically unsound, we will develop an unduly pessimistic view of the world.

tall poppies

There was an anthropoidal ape, far smarter than the rest,
And everything that they could do he always did the best;
So they naturally disliked him, and they gave him shoulders cool,
And when they had to speak of him, they said he was a fool.

We have come a long way since then, of course, but some vestiges of this primeval attitude remain in our behaviour and our language. (Incidentally, if anyone knows who wrote the poem from which this verse is taken, I would be glad to hear, as I quote from memory, and cannot give it proper acknowledgement.)

Tall poppies are those whose names are household words other than for sporting or criminal activities, and in particular for intellectual achievement; but the term contains the threat of head-lopping, known as the *tall poppy syndrome*. It is not peculiarly Australian, being derived from a story in Livy's *History of Rome*, where a man who has been asked for advice about how to gain control of a town walks down his garden path lopping off the heads of the tallest poppies. However, if the democratisation of any society can be measured by its enthusiasm for cutting its tall poppies down to size, Australia is unusually democratic.

target A target is a fixed object at which you are supposed to aim. It is not designed to be *pursued* or *reached*, and those who *pass* their targets must be assumed to have missed them. Furthermore, those who set up targets are not necessarily making them harder to hit by raising them, and certainly not by making them bigger.

So much for logic. Do we therefore correct those who strive to *shatter* their *optimistic targets*? We should, because *target* still retains a clear meaning, both in its original and its metaphorical senses, which need not and should not be lost. If we want to *shatter* a cliché, it should be a *barrier*, and if we want an *optimistic* cliché, let it be a *forecast*.

Many people find *target* particularly offensive when used as a verb. If we started campaigning against nouns which have strayed over the border and become verbs, we would strip the language of many useful words, and the ways in which this one is used are generally faithful to the original sense. I suspect that, as with SCENARIO, the real trouble is not the usage itself but the company it keeps.

tautology A tautology is a word or phrase which merely repeats the sense of another word or phrase in the same sentence. It is much more common in speech than in writing.

The true tautology is illustrated by the sentence:

I got up at 3.00 a.m. in the morning.

These are rare. However, we have a similar phenomenon in phrases like *ISBN number*, *SI system* and *SEATO organisation,* which might be called lost tautologies, the speaker being perhaps unaware of (or having forgotten) what the initials stand for. It is not as easy as we may think to avoid these: see SALT.

Next come the intensifiers: *true facts*, *grateful thanks*, *usual habits*, *sick patients* and *free gifts*. They ought to be tautologies, and often are;

but we can have *false facts, insincere thanks, unusual habits, healthy patients* and *expensive gifts,* so perhaps they are not tautologies after all.

But we can hardly argue about *I myself personally, at this moment in time, now look back in retrospect at the final completion.*

taws The phrase *go back to taws,* meaning *go back to the beginning,* is Australian, and puzzles foreigners. A *taw* is most often a choice marble, but is also a marker in hopscotch, and this is the most plausible origin of the expression.

taxi, cab Until as recently as 1900, *cab* was the normal English word for a vehicle plying for hire, and London cabbies were still resisting the introduction of the *taximeter,* an 1890 German invention for recording the length of the cab's journey. However, cabs with the device, i.e. *taximeter cabs,* were very popular with the public, and by 1907 were known as *taxis,* the term *cab* coming to mean one of the rival vehicles without the device. With the victory of the taxis, use of the word *cab* declined, though London taxi drivers are still called *cabbies.*

Meanwhile in America the cabs quietly took the taximeters on board, and there was never any clear distinction between taximeter and non-taximeter cabs. Hence the vehicles remained *cabs,* driven by *cab-drivers.*

In Australia, the taximeters arrived with the first motorised cabs, and the word *taxi* became associated as much with *motor* as with the taximeter. The word *cab* stayed with the horsedrawn vehicles, the last of which were taken off the streets in the twenties. It appears that, for a short time in the late 1920s, the motor vehicles which plied for hire remained *cabs* while those which were hired by phone were *taxis,* but this distinction was shortlived. Either way, the main point is that *cab* is strictly an archaism, not an Americanism.

The word *cab* has always been commonly heard and universally understood in Australia. In particular, it appears in the phrase *first cab off the rank,* and in the name of the Yellow Cab Company, a US-based franchise operation which rose to success by supplying free vehicles to film companies, thereby ensuring that its name was constantly before the public. It also gains fresh currency from other corporate imports, like *Cabcharge.* Nevertheless, most of our commercial and legal references are to taxis, as are signs at airports and on *taxi*-ranks, and in the all-Australian word *taxi-truck.*

The verb *to taxi,* of aircraft, arose in the Second World War, when military aircraft awaiting take-off were ordered to taxi, i.e. to form a line at the end of the runway, as on a taxi rank. The meaning then transferred to the movement of aircraft towards the taxi area, and then extended to cover any movement on the ground other than actual take-off and landing runs. Today, all paths for aircraft movement other than runways are called *taxiways.*

taxonomy   The sorting of all the myriad forms of life into neat sets of *kingdoms, phylla, classes, orders, genera* and *species* is one of the great triumphs of nineteenth century science. As an exercise in the coining of new words, however, it was less happy. The word for the process should have been (and, briefly, was) *taxinomy*, being formed from *taxis* (= group) + *nomia* (arrangement). This was forgivable, but next moment they back-formed *taxon* as a bogus Greek word for a group, complete with a bogus Greek plural, *taxa*. The word is in all our dictionaries, so there is nothing we can do about it.

The first purpose of this entry was in its first sentence, which gives the hierarchy of sub-divisions in the standard taxonomic system.

The second purpose is to record that the system, known as the Linnean System in honour of its inventor, Carl Linné, identifies flora and fauna by quoting the last two stages in the classification: genus and species, in a Latin-like form. The convention is to write these in italics, with a capital letter on the genus but not on the species, thus: *Eucalyptus viminalis*. (If mentioned, earlier stages in the classification are in roman type.)

tea   See MEALS.

tense   There are only two tenses in English, *present* and *past*. The English way of constructing other tenses is discussed under MODAL AUXILIARIES.

than   The most common argument is about *different than*, which is discussed under DIFFERENT....

This apart, the problems arise from the use of *than* with comparatives.

The basic usage is seen by comparing *She likes you more than I*, and *She likes you more than me*. Both are sound constructions, but have different meanings. They involve ellipses (i.e. the omission of words), and you have to decide what is left out in order to decide whether it is *I* or *me*. The first means *She likes you more than I [do]*, and the second means *She likes you more than [she likes] me*.

The next group of problems arises if *than* is used following a word which has some of the sense of a comparative but is not actually one:

> *He had hardly set out than he was arrested.*
> *He preferred to go to gaol than to pay the fine.*

Both of these are very awkward. It is best to use *than* only after a true comparative, e.g.:

> *He had no sooner set out than he was arrested.*
> *He went to gaol rather than pay the fine.*

This last sentence is an example of a further problem. In general, whatever follows the word *than* must be coherent with something which goes before, but this sentence breaks the rule. Coherence would suggest that it should be *He went to gaol rather than paid his fine*. Formal grammar tells us that this is grammatically sound, but if it makes sense at all, it is not the intended sense. The issue is not whether *pay* is right; it is unquestionably a good idiom. The problem is to explain it.

The key point is that, whatever mood or tense we make the main verb, the phrase *rather than pay...* remains the same, e.g.:

He would have gone to gaol rather than pay the fine.

The best solution is to describe *rather than* as a prepositional phrase taking an infinitive verb. Just as we might say *... in preference to paying the fine* or *...in order to avoid the fine*, we say *...rather than [to] pay the fine*.

that, which   Are there really any 'rules' governing the choice between these two?

The cake which I baked choked him
The cake that I baked choked him

Fowler, introducing the topic, pointed out that grammarians have even less influence on what actually happens than the most modest of them realise. It really does not matter what his, or this, or any other book says; speech patterns move under the influence of forces far stronger than any we can muster.

Nevertheless, Fowler went on to make an intriguing proposal: that the word *that* should be used in defining relative clauses and *which* in non-defining ones. Thus we should say

The cake that I baked choked him

if we want to *define* which cake did the choking, and

The cake, which I baked, choked him

if we wanted to give some additional information about the cake. He also noted that the non-definitive ones are separated off by commas.

This is a splendid suggestion, resolving the dilemma in a sensible way. It is not surprising, therefore, that it has been grabbed by some style manual writers and turned from a suggestion into a rule. This implies that the translators of the Bible were wrong when they wrote

The stone which the builders rejected has become the head of the corner.

The reality is that the translators of the Bible were not wrong. We are talking here about an attempt to create a new convention, and while we can give it our best wishes, and attempt to follow it ourselves, and even impose it on others if we are in control of a publication with a house style, we should be careful about claiming that we are doing so *because it is correct*. Fowler, who invented it, made no such claim. It was never more than a useful proposal.

However, though useful, it doesn't always work. While we are happy about *The house that Jack built*, we are less happy about *The man that came to dinner.* In short, *that* works better as a stand-in for *which* than for *who.* It would be easier to apply if it worked across the board.

There is a more profound problem if the relative pronoun is attached to a preposition. In a sentence like:

This is the file in which the letter will be found

we would be required to write:

This is the file that the letter will be found in.

There is nothing immoral about ending a sentence with a preposition, but we don't want to make it compulsory.

For all these reasons, Fowler's idea is to be followed when other things are equal; but if other things are not equal, we should have no qualms about not following it.

Meanwhile, his point about using commas to distinguish non-defining from defining relative clauses holds.

that (conjunction)   The word *that* can introduce a variety of clauses, including noun clauses (see SPEECH...), adjectival clauses (see RELATIVE CLAUSES and THAT, WHICH), and under CLAUSE (2). This entry discusses the two main classes of adverbial clauses heralded by *that.*

(1) Final clauses   These are also known as *adverbial clauses of purpose.* The rules say that verbs within the final clause will have the subjunctive auxiliaries *may* or *might, may* if the main verb is present sequence and *might* if it is past sequence; see SEQUENCE OF TENSES:

He kept ten thousand servants, that the poor might not lack bread...

In practice, final clauses which display this basic form are very rare outside poetry (and books on grammar, of course). The conjunction is often reinforced by *so* or *in order*, and *might* is often replaced by *would* or *could*:

We turned off the TV so that he could have a good night's sleep.

If the subject of the final clause is the same as the subject of the main clause (e.g. *we* instead of *he* in the above example) we can use *in order to* or *so as to* or just *to* with an infinitive verb:

We turned off the TV [in order/so as] to have a good night's sleep.

This is a construction we are very happy with, so much so that we use it much more than the equivalent final clause. We have to make the two subjects the same, which we do by a number of devices, including idiomatic weak uses of the verb *to get*:

The bans will be lifted in order to get the work completed on time.

(2) Consecutive clauses   These are clauses showing *consequences* or outcomes. They are normally heralded by *such...* or *so....*

She had such a bad cold that she couldn't sing.

The dog is so old that it never plays tennis.

In general, we use *so...* before an adjective or adverb and *such [a] ...* before a noun. *So...* can also come before a verb (*God so loved the world that...*) but this sounds stilted in ordinary usage.

If the *so* comes immediately before the *that*, the *so* refers to everything that has gone before. In this usage, *so* can appear without *that*:

> *The grog ran out, so [that] they all went home.*

In this usage, we have effectively two main clauses linked by *so* rather than *and*. Similarly, *and* can be said to introduce a consecutive clause in *He was caught speeding and lost his licence.* Applying the labels of formal grammar to English structures requires us to look at thought patterns as well as word patterns.

(3) Distinguishing between final and consecutive clauses   The difference between these two in English is quite subtle. In the following pair, the difference is explained by the words in brackets:

> *I planted a lemon tree so (that) I would always have fresh juice.*
>
> > (*Getting juice* was the purpose of planting the tree, whatever the actual outcome was.)
>
> *I planted a lemon tree, so (that) I have always had fresh juice.*
>
> > (*Getting juice* was the outcome, whatever the original purpose.)

In other languages, the distinction between the two is so clear that it makes sense to give them different names, and this distinction has been imported into English.

A more sensible approach in English would be to say that we have here two types of *intention/outcome clause*.

(a) If the intention is clear but the outcome uncertain, we use a subjunctive-like verb for the outcome, just as we do in hypotheticals. (See IF… CLAUSES.)

(b) If there was a logical or cause-and-effect relationship between intention and outcome, we use an indicative verb.

the   The OED has over ten thousand words on the subject of *the*. It is very good on the ways in which *the* can be used, but doesn't always say why it is *not* used in many others.

(1) Why do we say 'I work for *the* ABC' but not 'I work for *the* ASIO'?

(2) Why do we say 'I fell in *the* Yarra' but not 'I climbed *the* Kosciusko'?

(3) Why do we say 'I've got *The Age* on the line' but not 'I've got a *The Age* reporter on the line'?

The answers are not as simple as the questions:

(1) Initials   It seems that when a string of initials becomes an acronym (i.e. is pronounced as a word) it is personified, and therefore needs no article, whereas so long as it remains a string of initials it is perceived as an amorphous mass, and needs the article. This explanation is supported by many examples: we say 'I work for Unesco' but '…*the* FAO', '…Nato' but '…*the* EEC', '…Westpac' but '…*the* ANZ' etc.

At least, that is one explanation. However, there are many exceptions. Some organisations have no articles even if their initials are spelled out, e.g. 'We watch *the* ABC' but 'We watch SBS'; conversely, we say 'I work for *the* RAAF' even if we are making it an acronym, i.e. /raff/.

The best explanation concerns itself with fashion. The modern corporate practice is to encourage the dropping of the definite article. Hence the more recently an organisation was founded (SBS), or renamed (Westpac) or had a corporate facelift (CSR), the more likely it is to have been promoted without a definite article, and the way the organisation talks about itself is likely to be decisive.

(2) Locations   English is unusual in giving definite articles only to a very few geographical locations, notably rivers, regions and seas (*the Murray, the Mallee, the Tasman*). Groups of mountains get them, e.g. *the Grampians*, but a single mountain rarely does (e.g. *The Pinnacle*). By contrast, the French give the definite article to countries, islands, mountains (unless their name includes the word *Mont*), lakes, capes, streets, railway stations – almost everything, in fact, except towns. The Germans do the same apart from countries and islands.

OED says that we put the article in if the name is a description, and quotes 'the Land's End' and 'the Matterhorn'. This sounds reasonable, but is not true. We no longer say *the Land's End*, and we say *the Matterhorn* not because we think it looks like the horn of a Matter, but in imitation of the German usage. Likewise, we are imitating the French usage when we say *the Rue de Rivoli*.

(3) Noun-adjectives   The dropping of the article from *The Age* in 'an *Age* reporter' (recommended in *The Age Style Book*) is best explained by saying that it is treated like any other noun, losing its article as it becomes an adjective, just as we say *a United States Embassy*. However, we are talking here about perceptions, not sense. Thus, if the definite article is not English, it survives (e.g. *The La Perouse Community Development Project*), and I have a feeling that most people would say ...*my The Who album* rather than ...*my Who album*.

their, they   Fowler says that these words are 'liable to misuse as common-sex singulars', but goes on to show that this abuse has been going on for years; that, in fact, the objection to it is modern.

This problem is discussed under SEXIST LANGUAGE (2) and EACH (ONE)....

theory   The term *theory* is used in at least four quite different ways, and confusion between these is a significant barrier to understanding.

(1) *A scientific theory* is a tested hypothesis, which has been found to explain all current observations and to make verifiable predic-

tions about future events. If any of its predictions then fail, the theory must be modified or abandoned.

(2) *Historians* use the word *theory* more loosely, requiring theories to offer an explanation of some past events but not to make verifiable predictions of future events (e.g. *the conspiracy theory*). Any number of historical theories can therefore be applied to the same events without excluding one another, and any given theory can survive the disproof of any or all of its specific applications.

(3) *Economists* also talk of *theories*, but they do not require them to explain the past or, in any verifiable sense, predict the future. As a result, economic theories are essentially speculative, and they tend to be *discredited* rather than *disproved*.

(4) *Common language* uses *theory* much as the economists do: that of an unsubstantiated and unverifiable assertion, e.g. *I have a theory that things would be better if we all stood on our heads.*

The relevance of this is that it results in statements like 'the Big Bang is only a theory', whose implication is that it is just an idle speculation. This is a confusion of sense (4) and sense (1). Similarly, the debate between evolution theory and creation theory is as much a debate about the definition of *theory* as it is about the facts of the case.

third party   The term *third party* is drawn from law, where the *first party* is the plaintiff, the *second party* is the defendant, and the *third party* is an innocent bystander caught up in the action.

In the case of *third party insurance*, the word continues to have the same connotations, though there may be no second party involved.

thither   See HITHER.

tire, tyre   Our dictionaries tell us that *tire* is an Americanism, while knowing that this is not the case. OED gives 1796 as the first date for *tyre* in the relevant (i.e. 'detachable rim') sense, but records *tire* in this sense in 1782. Thus the Americans preserve the older version, and *tyre* is a British regional variation which we have adopted. Despite this, we treat *tire* like a cousin with some shameful inherited disease.

This is not a knock-down argument for *tire* or against *tyre*. Tradition and precedent are only two of many criteria by which we can judge our language. But we should be cautious about saying that those who write *tire* are defiling the language.

tmesis   When John O'Grady writes '...up at Tumba-bloody-rumba shooting kanga-bloody-roos' he is employing an ancient device called *tmesis*, the cleaving of a word and the insertion of some other word in the cleavage.

toilet   See EUPHEMISM.

tooth comb   Despite the evidence of the dictionaries, there is no such thing as a *tooth-comb*. Teeth are brushed; it is hair that is combed. The error arose from a mis-reading of the phrase 'fine-tooth comb'. This achieved currency as a metaphor, e.g. 'The lawyer went through the document with a *fine-tooth comb*', and this was misrepresented as a *fine tooth-comb*. The pronunciation changed, with stress on *tooth* rather than *fine* and *comb*. Next thing, the *fine* disappeared and we were left with this mysterious device, a tooth-comb.

Of course, once the error had occurred, it was given retrospective sanction. Today, people do indeed go through documents with tooth-combs. Some even use the word *tooth-comb* for the gadgets to remove fleas from dogs, and if enough people make a mistake, it ceases to be a mistake and becomes a mutant usage. But I reckon this one remains a mistake.

tracks   Two disparate matters deserve comment:

(1) Track, trail, path   If public noise is anything to go by, Australians are very sensitive about *tracks*. There was a fearful hullabaloo when tourist authorities proposed a name containing the word *trail* for a cross-country walking track, and reasonably so: *trail* is the American word for what we call a *track*, and it would therefore have been an AMERICANISM. Despite this, the American phrase *nature trail* has been accepted, perhaps because it is seen as analogous to a *paper trail*, i.e. the trail is a series of events rather than the track through them. In addition, our horsefolk and motor cyclists ride *trails*.

In Britain, cross-country walkers follow *paths*. There, a *track* implies use for transport or communication rather than recreation. In Australia, *paths* are generally urban phenomena, either in a garden or beside a road (where they are more often *footpaths*). The latter are *pavements* in Britain. This can be dangerous for the British, as Americans drive their cars on the *pavement* and walk on the *sidewalk*. In Australia *pavement*, if used at all, means paving materials for garden terraces.

(2) Track/platform   When we go to the railway station, we go to *Platform 3*, not (as the Americans do) to *Track 3*, a usage reflecting the fact that platforms on American stations (other than the subway) are rudimentary.

However, whereas in Britain (which gave the world railway platforms) the train itself is on the *lines*, in Australia it is more likely, as in America, to be on the *tracks*, and our level crossings say '2 tracks'. (The word *track* exists in this context in Britain, but in technical rather than general usage.)

The railway *line* was originally short for 'a line of rails', and is generally used, even in America, when referring to destinations. Thus, although the Chattanooga Choo-Choo leaves from *Track 29*, it will then go down the *Chattanooga line*, just as we go to *Platform 3* for the *Dandenong line*.

trademarks   Our business firms employ an army of public relations folk whose job it is to persuade us that their brand names are synonymous with the product, losing their capital letters and becoming generic terms. Thus we may *hoover* our carpets with an *Electrolux*. (New Zealanders *lux* their carpets with a *Hoover*.)

However, if it can be shown that a trademark is in common usage as a generic term, it loses the protection of the law. Having succeeded in getting their words into the language, therefore, they then employ a second army, this time of lawyers, to get them out again.

Among the words which are in the language and which are or were trademarks are the following:

Biro	*say* ball point (pen)
Caterpillar (of tractors)	*say* tracklaying or crawler
Duco	*say* spray enamel or paint
Kleenex	*say* tissue
Sellotape/Scotch Tape	*say* sticky tape
Thermos	*say* vacuum flask
Xerox	*say* photocopy or photostat

Whether you choose to use them broadly and risk prosecution, or avoid using them except for the correct brands of product, is a decision which must rest with the individual writer. Dialogue in a novel, for example, would simply not be authentic if it had the truckie saying 'You've scratched me spray enamel', and 'You've scratched me duco™' is absurd. But in technical writing on cars or paints, use of the trade name as a generic would be totally improper.

trade union   The plural is *trade unions,* despite the British *Trades Union Congress.*

trailer words   There are words which seem unable to travel on their own, but have to hitch on to other words. Thus *fro* only exists in *to and fro, spick* (and *span* in this sense) only in *spick and span, hue* (in this sense) only in *hue and cry,* and *yon* only in *hither and yon.* Indeed, *hither* itself only really survives in this phrase and *hither and thither.* Perhaps they are not trailers at all, but permanently coupled pairs, like articulated buses.

On the other hand, *flotsam* and *jetsam,* which are invariably used together, have distinct meanings (*floating wreckage* and *jettisoned goods* respectively). However, they are generally used metaphorically (e.g. of derelict people) where they are two words with but a single thought. Likewise, the phrase *sound and fury* brings together two words which have separate senses, but which together have a third sense.

transcription, problems of   Written language is a transcription of spoken language. This is not the whole truth – some classes of words tend to be written before they are spoken (e.g. acronyms), and phrases like 'small-l liberal' are spoken representations of a convention of writing. However, it is unquestionably true that speech came before writing.

If there are problems with transcription, it is partly because written language is by its very nature conservative. Our spelling is fundamentally that of 1750, fossilised by Sam Johnson. But the other trouble is that it was not phonetic even then: it preserved distinctions which were no longer present in speech (write, right, rite) and of necessity does not reflect changes which have happened since.

(1) Ambiguities   When we read in a newspaper that a disgraced priest is 'only allowed to administer rights to the dying' we can be pretty sure that the archbishop who made the statement was thinking of 'rites'. In short, the spoken version is ambiguous but the written version is not, and the transcriber picked the wrong option.

This does not cause problems as often as one might expect. We are no more likely to get confused between (say) *there* and *their* in transcribing than we are in our own composition, and, if we do, it is not because we are unaware that the sound covers two words, but because we have forgotten which spelling goes with which word.

(2) Misunderstanding   The reporter who wrote 'rights' could have (a) understood the sense, but believed that the word for 'rituals' was spelt r-i-g-h-t-s, or (b) have thought that the archbishop was talking about 'rights', i.e. in the semi-legal sense. Our discrimination can never be more acute than our understanding of the language and its various usages, and 'administer rights to' is not an absurd expression.

This is an argument both for and against spelling reform. The reformer argues that it is all rite to rite all rites the same way, as we are merely replicating existing ambiguities which rarely cause trouble in speech and cannot cause more trouble in writing. The spelling conservationist says that it is a good thing that some at least of the distinctions which have been lost in speech are preserved in writing. I tend to favour conservation.

(3) Mishearings   The range of possible mishearings is so vast that there is no way that a comprehensive list could be compiled. No list could have predicted Monica Dickens's celebrated error at the book signing session, when she inscribed a copy to 'Emma Chizzit'.

There are many lessons to be learnt from all this. Firstly, it helps if draft transcriptions can be checked by the speaker. Secondly, speakers and transcribers should note carefully any errors which arise, speakers with a view to improving their enunciation (or even changing their vocabulary) if a word seems to be causing trouble, and transcribers with a view not only to correcting the draft but also to learning what to watch out for in future.

transitive   This is a term of grammar applied to verbs. A *transitive verb* is one which, like *to eat*, can have a direct object: e.g. I *ate* the canary. See VERB (1).

transparent, translucent, opaque   Clear glass is *transparent*, i.e. light rays pass through it with minimal distortion. Ground glass is *translucent*, i.e. light rays pass through it, but are so diffused that all that comes through is an even glow. Black glass is *opaque*, i.e. no light rays pass through.

It would be unusual to say that a wall was opaque. *Opaque* is generally used for an object or material which might be, or sometimes is, transparent or translucent.

A material which appears to be opaque when lit from the front but shows silhouetted shadows when lit from behind (e.g. a net curtain) is said to be *diaphanous*.

Clear water is known technically as *pellucid*, and murky as *turbid*. (This word originally meant *stirred up*, and I prefer *clear* and *murky*.)

Transparent is used in two diametrically opposed metaphorical usages. When we say 'His motives were transparent', we mean we could see them clearly. When a computer manual says 'The subroutine is transparent' it means that we are unaware of it.

trauma   Until the First World War, the word *trauma* was simply medical jargon for an externally-induced wound (as distinct from a *lesion*, the crater formed by an internal problem). It was a rare word, occupying only eight lines in the OED, which was about as short as an entry ever went.

Then the psychoanalysts started talking about *psychic traumas*, wounds to the soul. These proved, as our banks might say, a very successful product. *Trauma* entered the English language around 1910, and within a decade it was in the romantic novels. Now we all have traumatic experiences every day in the supermarket.

Meanwhile the doctors continued with their lesions and traumas, and when they wanted a new name to replace the ambiguous term *Casualty Department* in hospitals, they picked the ambiguous term *Road Trauma Department*.

truck   In Australia, a *truck* is unambiguously a road vehicle. In Britain and America, they have trucks on the railways (though in quite different senses):

	Australia	America	UK
Road	truck	truck	lorry
Rail	freight wagon	freight car	truck (properly a *wagon*)
Rail	bogie	truck	bogie

trunk   As items of baggage, trunks are now so rare that, if the word is used (as happens in auction sales of deceased estates), they are called *cabin trunks*.

The Americans, of course, have *trunks* rather than *boots* at the back of their cars. This usage, while still an AMERICANISM, is entering our language stealthily and, being a less ambiguous term than *boot*, deserves encouragement.

try and...   See AND.

turbid(ity)   See TRANSPARENT....

typography   *Typography* is a mixture of art and craft. For writers, the art of typography is something to be appreciated but not necessarily understood. But there is something to be said for understanding the vocabulary, plus perhaps some rudiments of the craft, if only to be able to have a sensible discussion with typographers.

The basic vocabulary is covered in the entry under FONT.

(1) Set   *Set* is the width of the type area. Ideally, it should allow not more than 65 characters to the line. *Reason:* more than this requires most readers to take three eye-fixes to the line, which slows the reading process and hence reduces comprehension. *Solution:* raise the type size *or* reduce the width.

Newspapers and many magazines are designed for one eye-fix per line, which makes reading them easier still.

(2) Typesize and leading   If (say) 11/13pt is making the text run too long, beware of solving the problem by reducing the *leading*, e.g. 11/12pt. *Reason:* the eye responds to the white, not the black. 11/12pt may be too dense for easy reading. *Solution:* try 10/13pt, and if that doesn't work, 10/12pt.

The number of characters on a line will vary from face to face:

> This is 9pt Palatino: abcdef ghijkl mnopqr stuvwxyz
>
> This is 9pt Times   abcdef ghijkl mnopqr stuvwxyz

A closer *optical equivalent* to 9pt Palatino is 10pt Times:

> This is 10pt Times: abcdef ghijkl mnopqr stuvwxyz

(3) Typefaces   Variations of size and the availability of bold, italic and bold italic versions mean that most books can be set entirely in one face. If there is to be a second face, use it for display (headings and subheadings) only. Be very cautious about using two or more different typefaces for the text. *Reason:* an experienced typographer can get away with it, but in the hands of an amateur the result is likely to look a mess.

Choose an ordinary-looking typeface for the body text. *Reason:* idiosyncratic typefaces are fine for titling, but if used for text can become a very tired joke after a few pages.

Be careful about using sans serif types in books where the confusion of the unit 1, capital I and lower case l could be confusing:

| Times | 1 I l | Helvetica | 1 I l |
| Futura | 1 I l | Bookman | 1 I l |

Type styles, alignments and ornaments used in title pages, chapter headings and subheadings should all be coherent with one another. *Reason:* typography should be like wallpaper: it should provide a unifying background for the variable elements.

(4) Justification   *Justification* is the name for the insertion of extra word spacing and letter spacing to make the lines the same length.

If in doubt, always justify printed text. *Reason:* the pattern of short lines at paragraph ends helps the reader to see the logical shape of the text. In particular, justification stresses the paragraph breaks.

The alternatives, known as *flush left* (= *ragged right*) and *flush right* (= *ragged left*) are useful for specific purposes: flush left settings can avoid 'wind' (very large spaces between words) or excessive hyphenation. (This is often seen in crossword clues, where the set of the lines is short.) But a long unjustified text can make very tiresome reading.

(5) Indentation   The first lines under chapter heads and subheads should be full out. *Reason:* the purpose of a paragraph indent is to show the break, and is not required if the break is shown in another way. See also (9) below.

(6) Paragraph numbering   When numbering paragraphs, make absolutely sure that there is no risk of confusing the paragraph number with the text. The present fashion for using numerals or letters without brackets or full stops may look very clean, but can be confusing to the reader. The problem is most often seen in the *answers* sections of mathematics books, where question numbers, pronumerals and numerical solutions run on without any punctuation.

Use of hierarchical paragraph numbers (e.g. *1.2.1*) to indicate their logical status is a very useful device, originally used in legal documents but now adopted in many technical and academic works. The typographical problem is to make them prominent enough to do the job without producing an aesthetic disaster. It is very difficult for a paragraph starting *10.5.1.4.1* to look gracious, but if such numbers are to be used, grace must give way to practicality. To make them small destroys their utility without necessarily improving appearances.

(7) Subheadings   The hierarchy of subheadings must be made visually clear. It is generally found that a centred heading outweighs any side heading; a bold heading outweighs any non-bold heading; and a heading in capitals or small capitals outweighs any heading in lower case. Thus a safe five-level hierarchy using the same face as the text would be: (1) bold capitals, centred; (2) bold capitals, flush left; (3) bold u&lc, flush left; (4) italic capitals, flush left; (5) italic u&lc, flush left.

(8) Running heads   The normal convention is to run the volume title on the left hand pages and the chapter title on the right hand pages. In reference works, more informative running heads may be desirable, e.g. the *taglines* in dictionaries. In this book, the tagline picks up the first new headword on the page if there is one, and otherwise the word to which the page is devoted.

No running head can be given on pages carrying *chapter drops* (= the style for displaying a chapter title). This is an argument (but rarely a very strong one) for using *running feet* rather than running heads.

(9) Folios *Folio* is the jargon word for page number. Folios are generally part of the running head, and the convention is to switch the folio to the foot on any page (e.g. chapter drops) where there is no running head.

(10) Quotations Quotations can be flagged by indenting one or both sides, dropping the point size, changing to italic and/or inserting space above and below.

If the quotes are long, dropping the size and indenting may be a mistake, as it can result in a whole page of forbiddingly small type. In such a book, a change to italic, in the same size as the body type, with a thin space above and below, is one possible option.

(11) Line spacing The use of leading and line spacing to show the logical shape of a text is one way in which helpful typography differs from typography which is merely pretty.

There is normally no extra line spacing or leading between paragraphs. (Typists, by contrast, use a full line space to show the paragraph breaks.) However, this convention presupposes that the paragraph breaks are clear from the indentation of their openings and the pattern of justified line endings. If this is not so, an extra thin space is useful. (It is used in this book.)

Spacing can be particularly useful to give shape to lists and tabular matter. For example, extra space can be inserted above and below lists and tables, giving them something of the appearance of illustrations. Similarly, space above and below a cross-heading will give it prominence even if the type is the same as the body text. A line space can also be used in place of a subheading to indicate a major logical break. In this book, an extra 3pt space is provided between headwords.

Reverse leading is often used on title lines. A reverse leaded line is one whose body height is less than the type height, e.g. 24/22pt. The idea is to hold the lines very tightly together.

tyrannise If Fowler is to be believed, the British are *tyrannised over* by their government. We are just *tyrannised* by ours.

tyre See TIRE....

U

um   See MICROMETRE… for a note on this bizarre new word.

underlie, underlay   The problem here is exactly the same as in *lie/lay*, except that in theory the verb *to underlay* does not exist at all except perhaps in the context of carpets, so there should be less reason for confusion. Despite this, *underlay* has taken as large a share of the *underlie* market as *lay* has of the *lie* market, supporting the view that the lie/lay issue is not so much one of confusion as of amalgamation: see LAY….

   As a noun, *underlay* is a totally respectable generic term for the the things which go under our carpets, our flatbed printing presses and mattresses.

underprivileged   This extraordinary euphemism for *poor* is now firmly entrenched, so it is idle to object to it. However, like so many euphemisms, it is often used to take the mind off the real problem. However, it could be put to good effect: see PRIVILEGE.

unheard of   This phrase does not generally mean what it says. It smacks of moral dereliction. When, however, the Victorian police spokesman said 'It is unheard of for a policeman on point duty to be run over by a tram', he presumably meant it literally: that he had never heard of it happening before.

uninterested, disinterested   See INTEREST.

unique   For a discussion of the possibility that one thing can be *more unique* than another, see COMPARATIVE CHAOS.

university   The colloquial usage is sufficiently important to be worth mentioning.

   Australians *go to Uni*, or *go to the Uni*. This abbreviation sounds very quaint to the British and Americans.

   The Americans will almost invariably name the specific establishment, even if it is Georgia Tech, but the normal generic is *college*. This applies even at the top of the social ladder, so that they have *the ivy league colleges*, not *the ivy league universities*. Meanwhile, the snob word is *school*, as in *Yale is a good school*. This sounds quaint in Britain and Australia, where *school* is applied at tertiary level only to a department within a university, e.g. the Law School, and a statement like *The ANU is a good school* sounds either mistaken or vaguely condescending.

   The British also *go to college*, except for those who go to the best-known foundations, who (like the Americans) name them, e.g. *I go to St Andrews*. If pressed, however, they would call them universities, not colleges, *college* being for them a term for one of the various institutions which make up the university.

Note that nobody *goes to the 'Varsity* other than in old American movies and in New Zealand. It is a term which was rarely used outside Cambridge except in some specific phrases, e.g. *the 'Varsity match.*

For further subtleties, see GRADUATE.

unless and until   See IF AND WHEN.

unmade   See ROAD.

upcoming   See ONGOING.

update   The objections to *upcoming* (see ONGOING) do not apply to *update,* this being a word which, although perhaps ugly, performs a very useful function which no other word does as well.

upward(s/ly)   The best rule is to use *upward* as the adjective, *upwards* as the adverb with verbs and *upwardly* as the adverb with adjectives:

> *The first beat was an upward flick of the baton.*
> *He pointed upwards and sent Marsh back to the pavilion.*
> *Do not despise the upwardly mobile.*

The phrase *upward of* (as in *upward of half a million*) seems an unnecessary synonym for *more than,* but some people seem to find it useful. It has the merit of being better than ...*upwards of....*

us, we   See CASE (2).

use   The senses of this word fall into two groups:

(1) Those which are all about *utility*:

> *He used the chisel as a screwdriver.*

(2) Those which are about *what is usual:*

> *He is used to eating fish.*

The two groups overlap in the word *usage,* which is about *use* of words in the employment sense, but is also taken to imply *that which is usual.* The pronunciations have parted company, /yoozed/ for the former and /yoost/ for the latter.

There is a third sense which appears at first sight to be completely separate, in which *used to* is generally described as an auxiliary verb supplying a past continuous tense:

> *He used to eat fish.*

But how did this usage arise? A good explanation is that it is a surviving relic of an idiom which is now lost. Until the seventeenth century, English speakers could say

> *He uses to eat fish*

meaning *He is accustomed,* to... i.e. exactly the same sense as the modern *He is used to....* The past tense of this idiom was *He used to eat fish;* and it was this usage which turned itself into an auxiliary.

The point is relevant to the question about inversion of this phrase. We generally say:

Used he to eat fish?

but we often hear, particularly from Americans:

Did he use to eat fish?

Most Australians feel that *Did you used to...?* sounds wrong; but it is an unusual mistake. We do not make it in any other similar pattern. So why would anyone make it here?

The 'mistake' is completely explained if it is a dimly transmitted memory of the time when 'use to' was not an auxiliary; when *Did you use to eat fish?* was as natural as *Did you use a knife?*

This does not make it good current usage. But it does make it slightly less disreputable – a dialect archaism rather than a mistake.

utilise   This is a ploddish word for *use*, and serves no good purpose.

V

value   An accountant, it is said, is one who knows the price of everything and the value of nothing. However, the wordsmiths of the supermarkets know what they mean when they write *Value $5.95 Our Price $3.95*, and so do we. But it is sad that we do. *Value* is a useful word which has nothing to do with recommended retail prices, and we will miss it when it has gone.

valuable, invaluable, valueless   *Invaluable*, so far from being the opposite of *valuable*, means that the item is of such high value that it is beyond price. The antonym of *valuable* is *valueless*.

van   The use of this word as a short form of *vanguard* has no currency in Australia, so Meredith's lines

> *Love meet they who do not shove*
> *Cravings in the van of love…*

will be understood by most people, if at all, to refer to a motor vehicle. But they will already have been bemused by the tortured form of the first line. It is a good example of how not to write poetry, in fact, and the usage of *van* is just another nail in the coffin of comprehension.

vandalism   Should we re-define *vandalism*, on the grounds that most of the Vandals were (at least as compared with the Goths, whom we associate with church architecture) very gentle folk?

The general question here is discussed under ALLUSION. The answer is that the word *vandalism* has totally detached itself from its origins. In any case, there are no Vandals around to complain.

van Gogh   There is no agreed anglicisation of this name. Should we say it after the manner of the Dutch, the Americans or the British?

His way is dangerous, as it contains too many un-Australian sounds for safety. The *van* is rather like */fun/*, but almost swallowed into */f'n/*; and *Gogh* consists of two guttural *h* sounds, rather like the noise of clearing one's throat, separated by a vowel whose sound hovers between the *aw* in *law* and the *ow* in *low*. If this isn't very clear, ask a Netherlander and stand back.

The Americans say */van goe/*, which is very easy but seems to be unnecessarily divergent. How they got the idea that the final *gh* was mute is a mystery; probably some plausible but unreliable authority set a pattern which they all seem to have followed. The British say */van goff/*, which is also easy, and less divergent.

Mac offers both these pronunciations, but does not mention the one most Australians use, namely, */van goch/*, to rhyme with the Scottish *loch*, which is the best of the lot. Let us continue to go our own way. One small gold star for Australia.

veranda(h)   RW says that there is no good reason to add the *h*, and it is true that, etymologically, the *h* makes no sense. The word certainly came here from India, and an *h* was added to many Hindi words on their way into English (e.g. *howdah*, *maharajah*); but the origins of *veranda(h)* are obscure. The general view is that it is a Hindi version of the Portuguese *varanda*, but it could have been the other way round.

AWEG says that the more common spelling in Australia is *verandah*; in the Melbourne Yellow Pages, *verandahs* outnumber *verandas* by fifteen to one, including a firm called *Trendy Carports and Verandahs*, who should know.

AND supports it, too, citing dozens of examples, the earliest of which spell it *viranda* and *varando*, after which it settled down to *verandah* except for a period from around 1910 to 1960 when, if the citations are an accurate representative cross-section, the *h* went on holiday.

Conclusion: the *h* gives the word a nice oriental touch. So be it.

verb   The discussion which follows is largely to introduce the vocabulary needed to talk about the problems with this most complicated of grammatical phenomena.

(1) Transitive and intransitive verbs

(a) Verbs which have direct objects are called *transitive verbs*:

  I *ate* the budgerigar.
  She *understood* what he was saying.

(b) Those which cannot or do not have direct objects are called *intransitive verbs*:

  They *chatted* for some time.
  One *flew* over the cuckoo's nest.

(c) Some verbs can be used both ways:

  The batsman *moved* ⎧ quickly   (*intransitive*)
                      ⎩ his feet   (*transitive*)

(2) Finite verbs

Finite means *finished*: a finite (= *main*) verb can make complete sense on its own. Finite verbs are *conjugated* (inflected to show person, number, tense, voice and mood):

(a) Number and person

	Singular		Plural	
First person	I	am going	We	are going
Second person	You	are going	You	are going
Third person	He/she/it	is going	They	are going

(b) Tense   English verbs have only two true tenses – present and past. The other tenses are produced by adding auxiliary verbs rather than by modifying the verb itself. The traditional names for the tenses really make little sense in English, but they are included for what they are worth:

	Imperfect (= *continuous*)	*Perfect* (= *finished*)	*Aorist* (= *undefined*)
Present	I am sitting	–	I sit, I do sit
Past	I was sitting	I have sat	I sat, I did sit
Future	I will be sitting	I will have sat	I will/shall sit

(1) The forms using *do* and *did* are emphatic. However, they supply the normal, unemphatic forms for questions and negatives:

> *Did you sit here? Yes, I sat* but *No, I didn't sit.*

(2) Other tenses include the *pluperfect* (*I had gone*). In addition, many of these tenses have a variety of subjunctive forms. These are discussed under IF… CLAUSES (2), and for more about the forms, see MODAL AUXILIARIES, WILL… and WOULD….

(3) In talking about other languages, including Latin and French, the terms *imperfect* and *aorist* are commonly used absolutely to mean the *past imperfect* and the *past aorist*.

(c) Voice   Verbs can exist in two voices, the *active* voice and the *passive* voice. The passive voice is made up from an inflection of the verb *to be* and the *participle*. Thus:

$$I \begin{Bmatrix} ate \\ am\ hiding \\ have\ sat\ on \end{Bmatrix} the\ buns. \quad The\ buns \begin{Bmatrix} were\ eaten \\ are\ being\ hidden \\ have\ been\ sat\ on \end{Bmatrix} by\ me.$$

Since the passive transformation involves making the *object* of the active sentence the *subject* of the passive one, intransitive verbs (e.g. *go, sneeze*) cannot be used in the passive voice.

(d) Mood

(1) The *indicative mood* is the normal form of direct speech. It indicates what is the case. All the illustrations so far have been of indicative verbs.

(2) The *subjunctive mood* is used in certain subordinate clauses and some idiomatic phrases. Subjunctive verbs have an air of uncertainty or wishful thinking about them:

> I *will* if I *can*.   (*indicative*)
> I *would* if I *could*.   (*subjunctive*)

See SUBJUNCTIVE and IF…CLAUSES.

(3) The *imperative* is used for commands (*Sit!*).

(3) Non-finite verbs

Non-finite forms of the verb are:

(a) Infinitive   The *infinitive* (e.g. *to sell*) is a form whose status is well defined in Latin but not in English. It is most often used as a verb-noun:

> *To err* is human
> I want *to go home*

The infinitive is interesting largely because we are told that we must not split it; see INFINITIVE.

(b) **Participles**   The *present participle* (e.g. *going*) and the *past participle* (e.g. *gone*) are often used as *verb-adjectives*, as in the phrases
the going price
a *foregone* conclusion
but they are also used in the formation of some tenses, e.g.
I *was crossing* the road when I *was knocked* down
where *was crossing* is a past imperfect active and *was knocked* is a past perfect passive. See -ING FORM and PARTICIPLE.

(c) **Gerund**   The gerund is another *verb-noun* which has the same *-ing* form as the present participle, e.g. *going*. It appears in such sentences as *The going was good*. See GERUND… and -ING FORMS.

Why do we have two names for the *-ing* form? The simple answer is 'because they were different in Latin'. However, the distinction is in this case useful. If the word *gerund* had not existed, we would have had to invent one.

viable   If used in its original specific sense, *capable of life*, e.g. of embryos, this is an excellent word. Nor need we complain if it is applied to, for example, schemes for a self-sustaining economy, where the original sense is thoroughly appropriate. It is a waste of a good word, however, to use it as yet another synonym for *feasible*, *practicable*, *workable*, etc.

Victorian   Just be careful about the ambiguity of this word: when we speak of 'Our Victorian legal system', we could be speaking of the State, the period or, all too often, both.

view   There are some idioms with the word *view* which, while rarely causing trouble, need to be watched:
in view of   There is a double ambiguity in the sentence:
He didn't take his clothes off in view of the neighbours; …
The sentence could go on:
… he took them off out of sight of the neighbours.
… he took them off because of the need to wash them.
… he kept them on when in sight of the neighbours.
… he kept them on because of their threats to call the police.
point of view   A *point of view* is the position from which something is viewed. It should not be confused with (a) the view itself or (b) the thing being viewed. Thus
(a) Rather than *You are expressing my point of view*, we should say *You are expressing my view(s)*.
(b) *From the point of view of income tax, the budget is a disaster* is odd, since the income tax has no point of view. The phrase should be applied only to sentient creatures.

vulgar   See COMMON….

W

W   This is the only letter in our alphabet which was not present at all in the Roman alphabet, and is an English invention dating back to the seventh century A.D. It was used to represent the /w/ sound, previously represented by the Latin V, which was then in process of change to a /v/ sound.

The Germans adopted the new letter, but used it to represent the /v/ sound.

It is still very rare in French, being restricted to recent imports from German and English, and is sounded as /v/. Thus, although we feel that *wagon-lit* is the French for a sleeping car, they regard it as a semi-naturalised foreigner. If they wish to represent the English sound /w/, they use *ou*, e.g. *ouest*.

The result of this extraordinary bit of phonetic chaos can be illustrated with the first consonant of the Latin word *vinum*, meaning *wine*.

In Latin, it was written	*V (vinum)*	and sounded	/w/
In French, it is written	*V (vin)*	and sounded	/v/
In German, it is written	*W (wein)*	and sounded	/v/
In English, it is written	*W (wine)*	and sounded	/w/

Walhalla   When talking about Wotan's headquarters, it is appropriate to sound the *W* as a *V*, and in this context it is often anglicised as *Valhalla*. However, the goldmining town in Victoria is spelt and pronounced with a *W*.

wave, waive   We *wave* flags but *waive* our rights.

we   For a discussion of the confusion of *we* and *us*, see CASE (GRAMMAR).

(1) The royal we   The royal *we* was a noted feature of Shakespeare's English. In the last scene of *Macbeth*, Malcolm is initially shown talking quite normally, but five lines later, having been shown the head of Macbeth and been hailed as King by his retainers, his first word is *We*. How different from our own dear Queen.

(2) The editorial *or* collective we   For most of us the risk of royalty is remote, but risk of the editorial or collective *we* somewhat greater. It is used by members of groups (newspaper editorial teams, committees and corporations) to indicate that they are at that moment speaking for the group. A member of a group who puts a private view under the group flag is guilty of misrepresentation, and groups which allow their members to use *we* cannot then distance themselves from what has been written.

(3) The authorial we   Most of us feel very insecure about writing *I* in formal writing. The pressure comes from three directions: (a) the instruction that certain classes of writing, especially scientific, should be impersonal; (b) the general injunction against egocentricity; (c) a natural desire to share the blame.

(a) For a discussion of impersonal writing, and how to personalise it, see IMPERSONAL.

(b) Self-effacement is a great virtue, but causes problems. Changing *I* to *one* or *we* is no defence against a charge of egocentricity; saying *the present writer* is worse; and worst of all is the habit, common for some reason among trade unionists, of referring to themselves by their own surnames.

Fowler said 'Modern writers are showing a disposition to be bolder than was formerly fashionable in the use of *I* and *me*, and the practice deserves encouragement.' Alas, his encouragement of the practice scarcely extended to doing it himself, other than in anecdotes. His opinions are generally uttered impersonally: 'It is desirable…'. I sympathise.

(c) The use of *we* to share the blame is not quite as wicked as it may seem.

It is certainly wrong to use *we* instead of *I* on a statement of personal experience or opinion, especially if the intention is to give it an appearance of greater weight and general approval. It is wrong because it is misleading.

However, it is all right to use *we* instead of *you* or *they* on statements about undesirable attitudes and practices, thereby accepting a share of the public guilt. One must be careful about this: if one admits to too many faults, readers sense insincerity and feel patronised. In any case, it is a lot easier to say what we *should* do than to do it.

A third use, which is also fine, occurs if I believe that my readers would like to join me in some assertion or plea. Thus, it would be at best silly, and at worst self-aggrandising, to say *I believe that…* followed by a statement of a widely-shared community attitude.

weak   For the two senses of *weak* in grammar, see STRONG…

weir   See DAM.

well   For some thoughts on *as well as*, see AS.

were (to), was (to)   These words can be past indicatives or present subjunctives.

I *was* at home yesterday.   *(past indicative)*
If I *were to* go home now, I might catch a burglar.
                (present subjunctive)

The use of *were* for *was* in the first (i.e. *I were at home yesterday*) is heard in certain British rustic dialects, but is otherwise an error occasionally heard on the lips of the very young.

The use of *was* for *were* in the second (i.e. *If I was to go home now…*) is increasingly common, to the point that it is now normal except in certain set phrases (e.g. *If I were you*).

The otherwise admirable *Oxford Guide to English Usage* suggests that when we say 'If I was to go home…' we are using a past indicative instead of a past subjunctive. This is a strange statement: it is neither past nor indicative. Fowler rightly described the tense as 'not past time, but utopia, the realm of non-fact or the imaginary'; it is either present or future, but cannot be past. Nor is it any less subjunctive in sense than *were*. In short, when discussing the sentence 'If I was to go home…', the issue is simply whether or not we accept that the form of the subjunctive has changed, so that it conjugates *like* a past indicative.

OGEU also makes a strange statement about a sentence quoted from Joyce Cary:

> *Her mother suddenly demanded to know if she* were *pregnant.*

OGEU justifies this usage on the grounds that 'there is doubt of the answer'. If this were the issue, all genuine questions would have subjunctive verbs. The question of doubt is relevant in conditional clauses, but the *if* here is not a conditional. We have here an indirect question, and the verb should be the past indicative, *was*.

when   Does the phrase *if and when* have any purpose? Yes: see IF AND WHEN.

whether or not   This is a very useful phrase to close off all options at the outset. 'Whether or not the debate is conducted in the manner the honourable member thinks it ought to be…' is simpler and more elegant than 'Whether the debate is conducted in the manner the honourable member thinks it ought to be or not…'.

The trouble is that it is so tidy that we tend to hitch 'or not' on to 'whether' as a sort of trailer, even if an alternative possibility is being described, so that we get absurdities like 'Whether or not you agree, or whether or not you take a different view…'.

We should school ourselves not to add the trailer unless it is needed.

whilst   Use *while* rather than *whilst*; see AGAIN….

white   When used to describe people, this word covers a variety of shades of pink. Horses which are actually white are called *grey*, and people who are actually white are called *dead*. See BLACK….

who(m)   The dilemma is best seen when *who* and *whom* are used as interrogative pronouns (*Who did it? Whom did the police arrest? To whom did the lawyer speak?* or *I asked him who did it, whom the police had arrested, and to whom the lawyer had spoken*).

Formal grammar tells us that *who* is the subjective case and *whom* is the objective case, and that the subjective case is used only for subjects of sentences, while the objective case is used for direct objects and after prepositions. So far, so good.

Observation, however, tells us that the word *whom* is obsolescent, surviving in formal written English, but becoming rare in normal speech. Many educated speakers will say *Who did the police arrest?* even though they would write *Whom….* In speech, *whom* survives strongly if it is attached to a preposition, as in the sentence *To whom did the lawyer speak?*; but in the variant *Whom did the lawyer speak to?* the *whom* is slipping, a common normal conversational version being *Who did the lawyer speak to?*

This makes things difficult for the grammatical fundamentalist. When all the shouting dies down, the only way we can identify grammatical errors is when they sound wrong. If an idiom doesn't sound wrong and gets itself used, it must sooner or later cease to be wrong.

We may regret the passing of the *who/whom* distinction, but realists will recognise that it is passing. We have learnt to live without *whither* and *whence*, and will doubtless survive without *whom*. Meanwhile *whose* is alive and well, acting as a gender-inclusive possessive case for the neuter *which* and the masculine/feminine *who*.

will, shall   Once upon a time there were strict (and complicated) rules for the use of *will* and *shall*, and those who believe that life was not meant to be easy can seize these rules and try to follow them.

There are two good reasons not to. The first is that Australians have never observed the rules, and there is no reason to start now. The second is that, despite the assertions of Fowler that those to the manner born understand and follow the rules, the evidence is otherwise. Either that, or there are now precious few who are to the manner born.

Nevertheless, Fowler was right in declaring that no self-respecting book on usage could fail to report the traditional rules, so we will report them.

The traditional rules are:

> Straight future:
> | | |
> |---|---|
> | *I/we* | *shall* … |
> | *you/he/she/it/they* | *will* … |
>
> Intention:
> | | | |
> |---|---|---|
> | *I/we* | *will* … | (= intend to…) |
> | *you/he/she/it/they* | *shall* … | (= are instructed to…) |

The argument in favour of these rules is that they allow us to express subtle shades of meaning: thus there is a difference between *I shall be home at six* and *I will be home at six*. However, although there may be a difference between these two statements, it would be rash to rely on Australian readers to notice, still less take the point. Or British readers, for that matter.

When used in questions, these senses are inverted:

Shall I… ?	*Am I instructed to… ?*
Shall you… ?	*Are you going to… ?*
Will I… ?	*Am I going to… ?*
Will you… ?	*Please…*

These rules are, as we will see, slightly less moribund.

In considering Australian usage, it is best to start from the assumption that *shall* does not exist and then check the cases where it does.

(a) The most common usage, in expressing both straight future and intention, is neither *I will* nor *I shall*, but *I am going to* … , etc. This is perhaps the main reason why the issue is not more pressing: for many people, it never arises.

(b) When *will/shall* is used, it appears most frequently as *I'll…*, etc., where it is not clear whether *will* or *shall* is intended.

(c) The traditional rules are still valid in the inversions. We say:

> *Shall I answer the phone?* (= would you like me to…?)
> *Will you have some more cake?* (= would you like…?)

For the use of *would* and *should* in such sentences, see WOULD….

(d) The traditional rules also survive in legal usage. For example, our constitution says

> *There shall be a Federal Executive Council…*

but this usage does not exist in normal spoken or written Australian.

wine names The vocabulary of Australian wine has been radically overhauled over the last twenty-five years. Before that, there were few widely-recognised classes of wine: *hock* (German-style dry white), *chablis* (French-style dry white), *moselle* (German-style sweet white), *sauternes* (French-style sweet white), *claret* (light red), *burgundy* (full-bodied red), *champagne*, *muscat*, *port* and *sherry*. The distinction between 'German style' and 'French style' was largely in the shape of the bottles. Notes on the Australian usage of some of these terms are found under HOCK, MOSELLE, etc.

These names reflected the classification used by British wine merchants. With the exception of *claret*, all the names originated from geographical locations. In adopting them, Australian winemakers were accepting the supremacy of the European industry, and the industries of America and Africa tended to do the same. There was even a wine called Spanish Sauternes.

Recently, there has been a general drift away from these names, for two reasons. Firstly, sundry protocols, e.g. the French *Appellation Controllée*, restrict the use of certain names. Although Australian law does not recognise these protocols, respect for them is growing, if only because Australian wines would otherwise be excluded from the EEC market.

Secondly, the Australian industry has moved from mimicry to creating its own styles, and copycat names are increasingly inappropriate. The more common procedure today is to use the names of grape varieties, e.g. *cabernet-sauvignon, chardonnay, frontignac, hermitage, pinot noir.*

withhold   Please give it both its aitches.

Wobblies   The full title of the Wobblies, the IWW, is *Industrial* (not *International*) *Workers of the World.* They survive in Australian folk history largely for their abortive attempt to set fire to Sydney during the First World War. They are little remembered elsewhere (even in their native USA), and allusion to them should therefore be made with care.

word order   Word order is crucial to sense in English. The grammatical status of words, their relationship to one another and hence the clarity of the whole sentence, are largely determined by word order; see GRAMMAR.

(1) The basic rules   In the sentence

> *The cat ate the canary*

we know which ate which by word order, i.e. the normal sequence of an English sentence is *subject–verb–object.*

Adverbs and adverbial phrases come as close as possible to the words to which they refer, with a preference for modifiers coming before and qualifiers after the verb. However, their placement varies according to taste as well as some complex conventions. See (3) below.

Adjectives and adjectival phrases generally come directly before the nouns they qualify. This means that if, for example, two nouns appear immediately following one another, the chances are that the first one is being used as an adjective. Hence in

> *The State Government Insurance Office*

we have three nouns, each acting as an adjective with respect to the next one. Adjectival clauses normally come after the noun; adjectival phrases are vagrants. See (4) below.

(2) Subject/verb inversions   The most common effect of inversion of subject and verb is to turn a statement into a question: *I was there* becomes *Was I there?*

However, further inversions can achieve special effects. *There I was* and *There was I* are quite different in sense from the original pair, but differ from one another only in tone and emphasis.

In verse, of course, inversion is common:

> *Then rested he 'neath the tum-tum tree*

and   *The pig it was who died*

but in modern English prose the only other *normal* inversions of subject and verb are:

(a) In dialogue, the 'say' verb and its subject are commonly inverted if they occur *after* a passage of direct speech:

'Off with his head!' quipped the Queen.

(b) Hypothetical or concessional clauses can be created without using 'if' or 'although' by inversion of a subjunctive auxiliary and its subject:

O had I the wings of a turtledove... (= If I had...)

Be it ever so humble, I dream of home. (= Although it be...)

The former remains quite common (e.g. *Had I known, I would have told you* and *Should you need more, let me know*) but is slightly pompous. The latter is largely poetical, but survives in the cliché *Be that as it may....*

(3) Adverb inversions The positioning of adverbs is very tricky. While there are clearly rules which generally apply (see ADVERB), they are often deliberately broken to achieve special effects:

(a) For emphasis:

The city lay below us → *Below us lay the city.*

In modern English, this inversion is only available with adverbs of position and time.

Away went the puddin'...

After the Great War came the Depression.

(b) In the idiomatic use of *there is...*, as in

There was movement at the station...

the word *there* is best seen as an adverb of place (as it would be in *There goes the baby...*). But it has lost its meaning, becoming no more than a signal warning of an inversion.

(c) Floating adverbs If we write

When we arrived, he was unfortunately playing the tuba

the sense is clear enough: the misfortune was ours. However, if we write

When we arrived, he was happily playing the tuba

the probability is that the happiness was his. Yet the grammatical patterns are identical. The clue to the meaning comes from common sense, not from grammatical rules.

We have here a conflict between the basic rules and the stylistic options. The rules tell us that *happily* is correctly placed in this slot and *unfortunately* is misplaced. But there may be no better place for it.

If the sense is clear, there is no problem. If there is a risk of ambiguity, it can sometimes be resolved by wrapping these *floating adverbs* in brackets or commas:

When we arrived, he was, unfortunately, playing the tuba.

However, in the last resort there may be no option but to reword the sentences so that there is no doubt about the point of reference of the adverb.

(4) Adjective inversions   The simple rule is that single-word adjectives come before, and adjectival phrases and clauses after, the noun or pronoun to which they belong. (See ADJECTIVE.)

(a) The rules for single-word adjectives are extended to adjectives with modifying adverbs attached to them, and to strings of single adjectives:

> I made a *very bad* mistake.
> You must wave a *green and yellow* flag.
> She drove a *battered grey early-model* Holden.

(b) An adverbial phrase used adjectivally can also be positioned before the noun:

> They did an *under-the-counter* deal.

(c) Floating adjectival phrases and clauses.

> *Standing on tiptoe, the bannisters were still above her head.*

Strictly speaking, there is nothing wrong with this: the phrase *standing on tiptoe* can be attached to any following noun, and the sense tells us that it is the pronoun *her*. However, it is generally good practice to use this inversion only when the noun to which the phrase belongs can come immediately after it in the sentence.

The second is the other way round:

> *The body of Clytemnestra lies on a platform covered with blood.*

What is covered with blood? Maybe it is all over everything, but that is not good enough. Miss Marple wants the precise details, and this report does not satisfy her.

work practices   See EUPHEMISM.

would, should   The problem here is similar to that desicrbed under WILL…, but with complications.

The basic rule is that *would* is related to *should* as *will* is to *shall*, and many writers attempt to make this distinction. However, as we saw in WILL…, the distinctions are not clear, and they are ignored by many of our best writers, so this does not get one very far.

The first complication is that *would* and *should* have both indicative usages and usages as modal auxiliaries. The second complication is that the usage in both cases is in process of change.

(1) Indicative usages   *Would* and *should* are the past tenses of *will* and *shall*.

> I hope that you will come   →   I hoped that you would come.
> I hope that I shall come   →   I hoped that I should come.

It has to be noted, however, that the distinction between *would* and *should* in these sentences is even more hazy than that between *will* and *shall*. Most Australian speakers use *would* in both cases, even in formal writing, while in speech the form would be *you'd* or *I'd*, which evades the question.

Should has a second indicative meaning, this time in the present tense, as in the sentence *I should go, but I won't*. Here, *should* is a synonym for *ought to*. Like *ought to*, it forms a past tense by adding *have* on the end: *I should have gone*. There is no question of its turning into *would* in the 2nd and 3rd persons – it is *should* in all three.

In inversions, there is a distinction similar to the one noted in WILL… (c), as in the sentences:

> *Would you answer the phone?* (implying 'please do so').
>
> *Should I answer the phone?* (implying 'ought I to?').

There are also sundry idiomatic indicative uses of *would*. The first is as a synonym for 'used to', as in the sentence:

> *All day long he would sit there, dreaming.*

In historical speculations, *would* is effectively a synonym for 'must', but with hypothetical connotations:

> *Kelly would have realised at that moment that he was a dead man.*

(2) Modal usages   The main use of *would* is as a modal auxiliary, especially in sentences involving *if…* clauses, e.g.

> *If I were you, I would eat it.*

Again, the alleged rule says that it ought to be *should* for the 1st person and *would* for the 2nd and 3rd persons, so this should have been

> *If I were you, I should eat it.*

However, once again this distinction is not often recognised in Australia, and would in most cases be elided out of existence: *If I were you, I'd eat it.*

Should occasionally occurs as a modal in the *if…* clause itself:

> *If I should die, think only this of me…*

Here the form is always *should*, not *would*. Its effect is to stress the uncertainty of the event occurring: *If you should run into him…* suggests that the event is slightly less likely than *If you run into him….* Note that in this case *should* is never elided, which confirms the suspicion that the elided forms are all perceived as *would*.

wrapped, wrapt   See RAPT….

X

xenophobia   See PREJUDICE.

-xive, -xion/-ctive, -ction   There seems to be no merit in writing *connexion, inflexion* and *reflexion*, as Fowler did. The spellings *connection* and *reflection* may be less pure etymologically, but they are well established.

In the case of *connective, inflexive* and *reflective* there is no debate: the forms *connexive* and *inflexive* being totally obsolete and *reflexive* surviving only as a term of grammar (where its pronunciation as well as form have parted company with the far more common word, *reflective*).

Y

Y *Y* is a consonant if it appears at the beginning of a syllable, and a vowel, similar in effect to *i*, elsewhere.

Exceptions to this are limited to sundry non-English proper nouns: the elements *ytterbium* and *yttrium*, from the Swedish town of Ytterby (in whose quarry they were first found), and *Yvonne*. The initial letter of the Belgian town of *Ypres* is also a vowel, and should be pronounced /*Eepr'*/, the attractive pronunciation /*Wipers*/ being restricted to the military.

Y has a curious history. It was used in Latin for transliterations of the Greek upsilon (whose sound was close to *i*), and its French name, *i grec*, recalls this fact. In English, its vowel use is indistinguishable from *i*, so that when spelling reformers suggest abolishing its use as a vowel one must have some simpathi. But it hasn't happened. But it was never a consonantal sound in Latin: no Latin words start with *Y*.

It appears that, during a rationalisation of the alphabet in the thirteenth century, they decided to abolish an old letter, called *yogh*, and the under-employed *Y* was chosen to replace it. Thus the vowel and consonant versions should be thought of as separate letters which happen to have the same form.

In French it is used as a consonant largely in words of non-French origin, e.g. *yaourt* and *Yankee*, plus the single indigenous common-language word *yeux*. In English, it is used to represent the Germanic *j* as in *jahr*, year (see J) and *g* as in *gelb*, yellow (the *g* being pronounced /*y*/ in many Low German dialects; see YARD...).

yard, garden In Australia, this pair of words provides a social indicator. Modest houses have *yards* at the back, in which the owner may or may not have *made a garden*. The corresponding area behind a more pretentious house is called a *garden*, even if it shows no signs of horticulture; and the yard, if there is one, will be a paved area surrounded by buildings, akin to a stableyard.

The former is similar to American usage, the latter British.

However, the term *backyard* as applied to small-scale commercial activity appears to have started in Australia, but is now widely understood. It can have a connotation of illegal activity, as in *backyard abortionists*, or of poor workmanship, and is generally contemptuous, unlike *cottage industry*, whose associations are with the wholesomeness of spinning wheels and clay.

The verb *to yard* is described by OED as 'colonial and US', which sums us all up pretty well. It is common in Australia, where the verb-noun *yarding* implies a saleyard, as in *There was a heavy yarding of cattle at Wagga yesterday*.

It is almost irrelevant to add that they are both derived from a common ancestor, the changing of *g* to *y* being a common metamorphosis in Germanic words; see Y.

ye   Old form of *you*; see YOUS.

Note that the *Ye* in *Ye Olde Tea-Shoppe* has nothing to do with this word. Here, the *y* is the typographical character used by early printers to represent an obsolete character, known as *thorn*, for the /th/ sound. Hence the word *Ye* is simply an archaic way of writing *The*, and is pronounced /ye/ only in ignorance or jest.

yet   If we want to say *I have not yet met him* there is a great deal to be said for saying just that, and not *I have yet to meet him* or *I am yet to meet him*, particularly if we are not sure which of these is right. Both of these are grammatically sound, but have different meanings, as can be seen by removing the word *yet*. The second is the equivalent of *I have not yet met him*.

you, your, you're   There are two problems here:

(1) No one confuses *we're* with *our* or *he's* with *his*, but because of the similarity of sound, confusion of *you're* (= you are) with *your* (= belonging to you) is common. It is, however, a product of carelessness rather than ignorance of the difference, so it is merely a point to be watched.

(2) The wrong decision between *you* and *your* (as in the sentence *I don't like* you/your *being left out*) is discussed under -ING FORMS.

yous   In the sentence *Are yous going shopping?* the word *yous* is today regarded as a barbarism. What is its future?

In today's standard English, *you* is the least inflected of the pronouns. The same word is used for singular and plural, and for subjective and objective cases.

This was not always so. The following table shows a larger set, as used in the Authorised Version of the Bible:

	Singular			*Plural*	
Subjective	*Objective*	*Possessive*	*Subjective*	*Objective*	*Possessive*
thou	thee	thy	ye	you	your

The pattern was never quite as simple as this suggests. In Shakespeare, virtually contemporary with the Bible, *thou* and *thee* occur as 'familiar' terms, as are *tu* in French and *du* in German. They also have a social significance: the lower orders address one another as *thou*, and the master addresses the servant as *thou*, but the servant addresses the master (and the masters address one another) as *you*.

By the time Captain Cook crashed into Australia, respectable people used *you* for all occasions: for singular and plural and for subjective and objective. *Ye* and *thou* were virtually obsolete, while *thee* and *thy* survived only in a few rural dialects and the bizarre Quaker 'plain speech' (which had *How thee?* for *How are you?*). The term *plain speech* is, however, significant; it implies a memory of a golden age of rustic simplicity when people said *thee*.

The lack of distinct singular and plural forms is often annoying, and it is nice to think that this was the original reason for the evolution of *yous*. There is a similar development in America, where *you all* (pronounced /y'ahl/) is common south of the Mason-Dixon Line.

The trouble is that both *yous* and *y'all* are already used indiscriminately for singular and plural, destroying the whole purpose of the exercise.

The word is sometimes spelt *youse*. This, too, destroys its purpose.

Z

Z Australians are quite likely to say /*A to Zee*/ when meaning 'from beginning to end', but when spelling out words the letter is /*zed*/. It is also /*zed*/ in the *M to Z telephone directory*. It seems, in fact, that /*A to Zee*/ is a special phrase, imported complete with pronunciation and then naturalised, but that if this pronunciation is used in any other context, it is an Americanism.

zero *Nil, nought, oh* and *zero* are all ways of saying *0*, the arabic *zifr*, the symbol for the empty wire on the abacus. Each has its supporters: footballers say *nil*, cricketers say *nought*, telephonists say *oh* and mathematicians and tax collectors say *zero*. Tennis players have their own private word, *love*, which is supposed to be a corruption of the French *l'oeuf* (= the egg), and bridge players talk of *voids*.

Outside the specialities, however, the telephonists win. We use *oh* not only in telephone numbers, but also in flight numbers, breathalyser readings and room numbers in hotels.